Literature of Nature

Literature of Nature

An International Sourcebook

Edited by

PATRICK D. MURPHY

Contributing Editors

TERRY GIFFORD

KATSUNORI YAMAZATO

FD

FITZROY DEARBORN PUBLISHERS

CHICAGO · LONDON

For information write to:

FITZROY DEARBORN PUBLISHERS
70 East Walton Street
Chicago, Illinois 60611
USA

or

310 Regent Street
London W1R 5AJ
England

Cataloging-in-Publication Data is available from the Library of Congress and the British Library

ISBN 1-57958-010-6

First published in the USA and UK 1998

Typeset and printed by Braun-Brumfield, Inc., Ann Arbor, Michigan
Cover designed by Peter Aristedes

Contents

❧

Section 4: Africa and the Arab World

Africa

The Arab World

❧

Section 5: Latin America and the Poles

Brazil

The Caribbean

Preface

In 1994, Gary Kuris, then senior editor for a publishing company that specialized in one-volume encyclopedias, approached the Association for the Study of Literature and Environment about the possibility of producing an "encyclopedia of literature and environment." A call went out to the membership, and various individuals expressed interest in that project. Eventually, the proposal that I developed for such an encyclopedia was approved by the publisher, and I began work on assembling its table of contents and a list of contributors. In a year's time it became increasingly clear that the subject matter was too large and diffuse to produce a comprehensive encyclopedia that would have entries on everything from classical Greek natural history treatises to green cultural studies. In dialogue with Gary, I revised the project, designing it as an international handbook rather than an encyclopedia, although it was clear to me from the start that it should not and could not be a formulaic handbook in which each chapter looked the same, with the same kinds of information and same format for every national literature treated. Rather, the diversity of the genres, modes, and orientations of literary representations of nature and of human interaction with the rest of the natural world had to be reproduced in the diversity of chapter formats. Many contributors had a clear idea of how to proceed with the material they wished to treat, but others were more tentative, and their chapters were shaped through our dialogue. Once the drafts began coming in, I realized that indeed they would have the formal variety that I sought to match the variety of their contents and that such variety itself would educate the reader in appreciating the cultural diversity that makes up a necessary part of human and all other biological diversity.

The process of obtaining an international mixture of contributors required extensive use of listservs and the Internet, and I am grateful, first of all, to the many hours that my research assistant in the early stages of this project, Joseph Register, devoted to posting the call to various listservs and fielding many initial queries. In addition, Terry Gifford agreed to invite, coordinate, and review the submissions for British and Irish literatures, and for that I am very grateful. Likewise, Katsunori Yamazato, through the Association for the Study of Literature and Environment—Japan, was instrumental in arranging for the Japan chapters and shepherding them through to completion. Even as work went forward, I continued to solicit contributions to cover neglected or omitted subjects, and, toward the end of the editing process, I also had to find eleventh-hour contributors to replace those who had promised to deliver an essential chapter but found themselves unable to do so. During the year in which the chapters were being submitted to me, Donelle Dreese served as my research assistant and proved invaluable in attending to the myriad details, complications, and unexpected problems that would arise in any editing project, especially one of this magnitude. At one point in the project, I remarked to a colleague, "working as an editor with other academics is like herding cats." Nevertheless, while some contributors took much longer than they expected—and I hoped—to deliver the final version of their chapters, I am extremely grateful for the fact that nearly everyone who made an initial commitment to the project followed through on it.

Unbeknown to those who had made an early commitment to this project and who delivered their essays in a timely manner, I encountered an unexpected complication that threatened the project only a few months before I had the entire manuscript completed. With more than 900 pages of the manuscript ready for production, and after Gary Kuris had resigned as senior editor, the publisher that had initially approached me about the encyclopedia project underwent an internal restructuring and informed me that my contract was canceled. Fortunately, and with great foresight, Fitzroy Dearborn Publishers came forward to purchase the contract and make a commitment to publish this volume.

Others, of course, have also been very helpful to me. Cathy Renwick, secretary of the Graduate Program in Literature and Criticism, handled an innumerable number of faxes and helped out with various other details. Malcolm Hayward, Director of the Graduate Program in Literature and Criticism, provided encouragement and financial assistance for photocopying and other related expenses, while Don McClure, Chair of the English Department, secured supplies for me at a point in the year when my printing activities threatened to bankrupt the department. I also wish to thank various individuals who expressed interest in hearing about this project and its preliminary results along the way: Charlotte Walker of State University of New York–Oneonta, who invited me to the Sharp Eyes II conference; Tony Hunt and Nandita Batra, who invited me to the Caribbean College English Association conference; Greg Garrard, who invited me to the University of Wales for the Literature and the Natural Environment conference; Al Rubiano and Mary Axtmann, who invited me to the University of Puerto Rico, Rio Pedras; and Paula Willoquet-Maricondi, who organized a set of panels on literature and the environment for the American Comparative Literature Association meeting in Puerto Vallarta, Mexico. And, I must also mention Bonnie Murphy, who engaged in many conversations with me about the project and shared both my moments of elation and my moments of frustration along the way.

PATRICK D. MURPHY

Editor's Note and Guide to Usage

Literature and nature have been intimately interlinked in the long history of literary production throughout the world, especially when oral as well as textual forms of literature are taken into account. For example, the ancient Sumerian *Epic of Gilgamesh* records the contradiction between the city and the wilderness and the conflicting values of their inhabitants. In addition, it builds its plot in part around the destruction of forests through the cutting and transporting of timber to meet urban needs. In China, an entire nature-oriented aesthetic movement, Mountains and Waters, developed and flourished for centuries—the ideograms of the words "mountains" and "waters" combined are the word for nature in Chinese—and Dōgen's thirteenth-century "Mountains and Waters" sutra influenced not only Japanese poetry in the ensuing centuries but also American poetry in the contemporary period.

While one might say that nature has always permeated literature, it has done so in varying degrees and has been critically received in vastly divergent ways. It has perhaps received no greater neglect in the Anglo-American intellectual tradition than in the early twentieth-century period of modernism and the early years of contemporary postmodernism. While many poets, novelists, and essayists continued to emphasize nature in their writing, the academic establishment tended to ignore such authors and such an emphasis. By the 1960s in the United States, this neglect was initially rectified in the classroom more than in published criticism with courses designed to reflect the rise of the contemporary conservation movement and growing public awareness of a proliferating array of environmental crises.

Through the teaching of courses variously labeled "Man and Nature," "Nature Writing," "Environmental Literature," and "American Pastoralism" as well as the conference presentations and publications that such teaching spawned, a nascent literary canon began to form.

Numerous nineteenth- and twentieth-century works that had gone out of print were brought back into print or published in paperback for the first time, while others were reissued in more affordable versions with introductions that placed these books in the context of a growing field of what has come to be called ecological literary criticism, or ecocriticism for short. While all three genres of poetry, fiction, and nonfiction were being taught, nonfiction—works generically, aesthetically, and thematically ignored in other literature courses—received the most attention. In particular, works arising from the Anglo-American tradition of natural history writing were markedly in the foreground of such courses and criticism.

While such works represent a vital and significant field of writing about nature, they proved too narrow a genre to define adequately the purview of the rapidly growing field of ecocriticism. Nature writing as a category was simply insufficient to account for the variety of the representations of nature to be found in all of the literary genres in the United States and Great Britain, much less in the rest of the world. Hence, it could not be the foundation for ecocriticism but perhaps at most a starting point, and ecocritics over the past two decades in particular have worked to broaden the scope and orientation of ecocritical reading. In the United States this development might be characterized as the movement from *The American Nature Writing Newsletter* to the journal *ISLE: Interdisciplinary Studies in Literature and Environment* and the formation of the Association for the Study of Literature and Environment. This development was spurred on by the degree to which newer scholars and many senior ones were utilizing the tools provided by structuralist and poststructuralist literary theory to rethink many of the critical preconceptions that had guided the critical movement in its early years. They also were challenging the canons of American and British literatures that had excluded or treated as secondary the literature that these critics found most worthy of study. Certainly this activity was aided and to some extent guided by developments in the fields of environmental ethics, environmental and regional history, and such new scientific fields as ecological genetics, the new physics, and conservation biology.

Nevertheless, at least in the United States, the United Kingdom, and Canada, critical attention tended to remain rather parochial, almost exclusively Anglo-American in focus, and still heavily biased toward nonfiction. For example, a review of the essays collected in *The Ecocriticism Reader: Landmarks in Literary Ecology* (1996), edited by Cheryll Glotfelty and Harold Fromm, published in 1996, reveals that the vast majority of literary examples in those essays comes from the ranks of nonfiction, while fiction is a distant second, and poetry hardly mentioned at all. Yet, it is quickly apparent to anyone reading outside of these national traditions, and even multiculturally within them, that the literary world is far wider than can be envisioned through a lens ground exclusively for the viewing of nonfiction. The evolution of ecocriticism requires the development of a truly international perspective on the field of literary representations of nature, even if that perspective were limited to emphasizing the past two centuries. *Literature of Nature: An International Sourcebook* is one of the first steps in that direction.

In a way, then, this volume is both the logical culmination of a process set in motion decades ago—the rise of an American ecocriticism—and I hope the inspirational impetus for the development of an international, cross-cultural, multifoundational ecocriticism, which does not yet exist. Before making a few remarks about the organization and contents of *Literature of Nature*, let me provide a brief critical perspective to explain my orientation as editor of this project.

Location, Location, Location

People know very well that almost anywhere they go on Earth, human beings have been there before, and likely live there now, and have told and written stories about that place. People are preceded at home and away by a storied residence of human inhabitation. They are also preceded by a storied transience of human disregard for the demands of inhabitory lifestyles and their recognition of reciprocity between the domestic and the wild, the human and the nonhuman. These two different stories delineate the difference between a planetary orientation and a global outlook, or what Gary Snyder has referred to as ecosystem culture and biosphere culture in "The Politics of Ethnopoetics" in *A Place in Space: Ethics, Aesthetics, and Watersheds* (1995). The ecosystem culture is attentive to local particularity and the benefits of heterogeneity, while the biosphere culture relentlessly attempts to homogenize the peoples of the world in the interests of transnational economics.

Many people involved with ecological criticism, with the study of nature in literature, and with finding ways of being in the wild are skeptical of postmodernism and poststructuralist theorizing, and rightly so. But one idea that this periodization of the contemporary age as postmodern and the intellectual discussions about this condition have produced is the dethronement of the idea that there is a single universal story to which all great literature aspires. As ecological criticism gains momentum as an international movement and establishes itself as an academic discipline, its practitioners need to be vigilant about avoiding the impetus toward canon formation. They ought to be wary of prescriptive critical formulations.

One way to maintain such vigilance is to pay careful attention to location, location, location. The first of these locations is the geographic one. The second of these locations is the historical one. And the third of these locations is the self-awareness of where actual readers and critics stand, of their own geopsyches, of their own subject constructions, of their own narratives and storied residence. For a while here, I would like to take a little walking tour through these three locations in the style of what John Burroughs and other naturalists might call a ramble.

Geographic Location

Anyone engaging with nature writing or any other kind of literature attentive to the natural environment as setting, character, or subject will invariably be aware of the specificities of location. And in order to sharpen this focus on geographic location, I will allude only to the literature of the past two centuries, the focus of this sourcebook. With this literature readers want to know: where does the action take place, how does the main character view it? Do they have here another London urbanite coming upon the Scottish moors for the first time and seeing them through a rosy filter well deployed by Sir

Walter Scott or Robert Louis Stevenson? Or do they have instead the images of a daily life in intimate, and therefore rarely romantic, contact with the soil and the land through labor, as in Patrick Kavanagh or Emily Lawless? Do they have the vision of the coast range, the ocean, the cypresses and the rocks and crags that almost guarantee a story of human tragedy etched across the face of an inhuman world, as in the long narrative poems of Robinson Jeffers? Or do they see a desert landscape deadly to many but enriching to those who fit their lives to its rhythms and patterns, as lovingly depicted by Mary Austin? Or, as a final pair of examples, do they have a meditative speaker, such as William Wordsworth, wandering through England's Lake District with the help of his sister, Dorothy, finding philosophical lessons for humanity in wild flowers and running streams, while his friend Samuel Taylor Coleridge conjures lurid allegorical images of the sea and the albatross?

Such descriptions are, or ought to be, familiar enough to anyone who has spent time with the major anthologies available to date of the literature of nature or of nature writing. Yet, they are exclusively Anglo-American, just as the current anthologies tend to be. That is all right as long as readers continuously remind themselves that such books contribute to the defining of traditions within just a few national literatures and omit a great deal even from these literatures along the way, particularly in terms of indigenous and other visibly ethnic writers. But these anthologies and my previous examples do not even adequately represent the diversity of depictions of nature and human interaction with the rest of nature in English-language literature.

When readers turn to the English-language literatures of the Caribbean, as well as Australia, India, and Africa, they will see again signal differences in emphases. In Jean Rhys's *Wide Sargasso Sea* (1966), the vitality and chaotic complexity of the jungle and the fecundity of the young female protagonist are set against the pallid Rochester and his visions of well manicured lawns and stately gardens. The desired domesticated nature of England set against the repelling wild vegetation of the Caribbean tells a story of not just sexist domination but also of colonial oppression and cultural destruction. Not surprisingly, much recent Caribbean literature focuses on the return from the metropolis as a process of recovering identity, and such recovery is dependent upon a return to a relationship with the land, its rhythms, cycles, and bounty.

While *Wide Sargasso Sea* focuses on the colonizer versus the colonized, the literature of some other English-speaking areas is even more complicated. Just as the United States began as a settler colony, so too did Australia and New Zealand. And in both cases one finds a complexity in defining the national literature, because there is the literature of the migrant populations who have become the dominant cultural, political, and economic force but have not clearly or successfully established themselves as inhabitants of those places. Originally suppressed but now avidly studied, readers also have the literatures of the indigenous peoples, who have taken up the colonizer's language as unavoidable or necessary for the dissemination of much of their own literatures and their own writing about nature to a wider audience. When readers look at Australia, the outback and the bush loom large and represent how vast the differences are in contemporary Aboriginal epic songs and novels from much of the natural history writing and the nonfiction, as well as the poetry and fiction of the white settlers. What one group called home was perceived on one side as a perilous wasteland and on the other as a deadly jungle, with climate another of its weapons against the encroachments of European civilization. The impact of colonization and settlement upon this region can perhaps best be understood in the title of the novel by Colin Johnson (Mudrooroo), *Doctor Wooreddy's Prescription for Enduring the Ending of the World* (1983).

Could there possibly be any other nation state as complex as India? And yet when confronted with this particular location, it is important for readers to admit the degree to which a colonizer's literature, much of which is not even written by settlers but by tourists, visitors, and military outposters, dominates our impressions of the land, its people, and its natural diversity. So that when readers come across the literature arising out of the Chipko movement—the women's movement to protect the northern forests from clear-cutting and destruction for the introduction of exportable cash crops and urbanization–they must step back for a moment. Nothing in the works of Rudyard Kipling or E. M. Forster prepares readers for a literature critical not only of the multinational corporations and their continuing postcolonial exploitation but also of the comprador bourgeoisie who have no understanding of the forest communities who resist the ecological destruction of their habitats. And when readers come to the writings of someone like the Bengali author Mahasweta Devi, they must be cognizant of the degree to which colonial and transnational exploitation are bound up with perceptions and representations of nature in contemporary postcolonial writing. Such a binding occurs not only in India and the Caribbean but also other areas as well.

For example, just in those areas of Africa in which the dominant literary language for literature is English, it quickly becomes apparent that for many contemporary African writers the environment cannot be treated without attention to violence, warfare, government corruption, and transnational corporate greed. From Chinua Achebe to Ayah Kwei Armah, Wole Soyinka to Alex Laguma, ecological destruction is depicted as part and parcel of postcolonial governmental corruption and the insanity of civil wars. It is impossible to treat even the study of animal behavior in Africa without recognizing the impact that war has on every aspect of human and nonhuman nature.

War and environment is, however, a far cry from the literature that emphasizes solitary individuals spending a long, slow, meditative day at the ocean watching the comings and goings of creatures all smaller than one's hand. Yet, in understanding the significance of geographic location in the practice of ecological criticism, in the practice of the study of literature and the natural environment, readers must figure out how to develop paradigms and critical orientations that enable them to encompass such a range of material, from Rachel Carson's *Silent Spring* (1962) to Ngugi wa Thiong'o's *Petals of Blood* (1977). Such paradigms must help one to realize the extent to which, when thinking of geographic location, such geography includes the human, the cultural, and the economic as well as, and as much as, it does geological formations, animal migratory behavior, and weather patterns. If indeed the International Panel on Climate Change's estimations about global sea level rise due to the greenhouse effect are borne out, the understanding of the impact of climate change on the high water marks along the river Thames in London will be due to a nature made more wild by the material effects of human cultural practices in specific geographic locations.

For many island cultures, whether those of the North Atlantic, the Caribbean, or the South Pacific, depictions of place are a combination of the land and the sea. And some of the smaller inhabited islands of the world today, such as the Marshall group in the western Pacific, face the threat of extinction if indeed the seas rise due to the greenhouse effect. And while the sea is therefore a direct threat to their existence, how rarely do we find it treated as such in the literature. Rather, it is very often the deepest source of human inspiration.

Attention to the location of literary production about the sea may very well offer to us very fruitful cross-cultural studies of perceptions and representations of human engagement with the majority of our world. The Earth is, after all, predominantly a water world rather than a land world, and island nature literatures can well remind us of that fact, even though the majority of literature studied today as nature writing largely hugs close to the shore or travels well into the interior. Perhaps a rare exception is that of the writing of Malta's national poet, the late Dun Karm, who has written as inspirationally about Malta's interior as he has about the sea around it. While island literatures provide the basis for that cross-cultural study of those people for whom home is water and soil simultaneously, as distinct from those who venture from land to sea, readers will also need to be attentive to cross-cultural studies of the diversity of island literatures, the Mediterranean, the Caribbean, the Indian Ocean, the Pacific, and those even larger islands of Iceland, New Zealand, Indonesia, and Japan.

Historical Location

Earlier I mentioned the example of the *Epic of Gilgamesh* to ask whether or not ecocritics frequently are looking far enough back in time for an understanding of the traditions, cultural influences, sociopolitical factors, and environmentally shaping effects on the formation and development of nature literature through the centuries. The American transcendentalists were heavily immersed in the texts of classical Greek as well as Roman pastoralism. They often came to natural history writing out of their own interest rather than through formal training. Alexander and Wilhelm von Humboldt and their German philosopher peers heavily influenced their idealist thinking, while Edgar Allan Poe's nature fantasy, *The Narrative of Arthur Gordon Pym* (1838), reflected the infatuation American authors had for the rapidly developing field of Egyptology. Egyptian hieroglyphics and their decipherment became part of the intertextuality of amateur efforts to "read Nature's book" in nineteenth-century New England.

Where do the Druids fit in today to the tradition of English nature writing? To what degree do readers need to take a look at the influence of various modern popularizations and fantasy inventions of medieval nature worship to understand some of the late twentieth-century American and British authors? Gary Snyder, for instance, was heavily influenced by the publication of Robert Graves' *The White Goddess* (1948) while he was in college, reading it alongside the anthropological recovery of ancient Native American myths through the work of Franz Boas, John Swanton, and others.

My point here is that many oral traditions have infiltrated, been revitalized by, and formatively influenced the perceptions of nature by many of our contemporary writers, even though those oral traditions have been rendered through anthropological transcriptions, folklore, and fictive revisions by their contemporaries and immediate precursors. And yet all too frequently, editors and others talk about nature writing as beginning in the eighteenth century with the English author Gilbert White. That is one historical tradition, the natural history, scientific classification tradition, but it is just one. And I find it unlikely that White arose *ex nihilo*. In rethinking the historical location of much of our modern writing, we need to ask in what ways the landscape of Broceliande in the Breton Lays or, closer to home and more proximate in time, the pastoral characteristics of J. R. R. Tolkien's Middle Earth have shaped the imaginations of our current ecological writers.

Readers will find some of the examples that I have used thus far in various chapters of this volume, but they will not find all of them. For one thing, I have ranged farther back in time than was possible for the contents of this volume to encompass. For another thing, when covering a particular period or national literature, a chapter author may have chosen to emphasize some different aspect of the pertinent literature. That is the difference between a sourcebook and an encyclopedia. As I indicated in the Preface, attempting to generate an encyclopedia of the literature of nature, covering all national literatures and all historical periods, is not yet feasible, nor is it likely to be enclosed within the covers of a single volume. To limit the scope of this volume in order to keep the work manageable, I limited my contributors to emphasizing the literature of the past two centuries. And rather than saying a little about everything, the chapters that follow go into greater depth and detail about selected topics and literatures, but

with the purpose and the achievement of providing the most comprehensive study of its kind ever undertaken.

The writing of the present day is my focus, and I tend to read the literature of earlier times through that particular lens, and no doubt that orientation influenced the emphasis of this volume. Such a focus works for me as well as the trifocals I am wearing do, but I recognize that it is a limited perspective. As Carolyn Merchant in *The Death of Nature: Women, Ecology, and the Scientific Revolution* (1980), and other writers in other works, have observed, Europe went through a series of human-induced ecological crises throughout the Middle Ages, into the Enlightenment, and continuing into the present day. The Greeks and Romans faced such ecological crises even earlier than northern Europe, which may have been coping more with weather-induced ecological change. Surely, then, the tendencies in literary history toward universalization and canon formation based on the alleged universality and timelessness of great works have suppressed literature that focused not on the more allegorical characteristics of the pastoral but on the warning signs of the nature-culture conflict. What kind of work is needed to recover a counterculture of literature that may have been Earth-oriented, as one finds in the ecological writings of that medieval abbess Hildegard von Bingen, for instance? Why was the work of seventeenth-century English poet Thomas Traherne buried for so long and even now relegated such a minor place in the anthologies? Perhaps he has appeared to be too much of a tree, sun, and flower hugger in his *Centuries of Meditation* to fit into the parameters of the metaphysical tradition.

Ecocritics have already been busily engaged in recovering and promoting neglected works through writing about them, getting them brought back into print, and teaching them to keep them in print. But there is a need to move beyond the enclosure and initiate or intensify efforts to rewrite the general canon, not only of various national literatures but also the general canons of western and world literatures.

As the work with travel writing has been showing in recent years, the recovery of neglected works must go hand in hand with rethinking the historical location of literature, its situatedness within ideologies of domination, oppression, and liberation. Colonial literature, for example, particularly needs to be rethought in terms of the environmental and natural philosophy of travel writing, science writing, anthropology, race relations, and missionary records.

Self-Situated Location

Just as with the Londoner who is suddenly transported to the Scottish moors, or an English gentleman lost in a Caribbean jungle, or an African student relocated to a college in an inhospitable climate beneath constellations he has never before seen, so too do readers and critics come upon literature that they have not previously encountered. And like those characters, readers scan these new horizons and look upon these strange locales from a perspective already well established, one that may have stood them in good stead on the safe and familiar terrain of the canon, of the officially "good" literature, but one that often does not suffice for determining their bearings.

In addition to geographic and historical location, there is also one's own personal location, or situatedness. Where was a person born? What was his or her relationship to the surrounding natural environment, and how much contact was there with that environment? Was a person a sickly child shut up with books as friends or out on the playing fields getting muddy? I grew up in a small town in the U.S. Midwest and spent time playing in barns, wading in creeks in summer, and skating along them in winter. I played army in the woods, built tree houses and underground forts, as well as castles in the snow and tunnels through ripe wheat fields. In high school I cut the corn out of the beans in the field behind my house and later strung barbed wire fence and buried dead cattle. Today I take care of about three acres on the edge of town and have observed as many as 10 white-tailed deer at a time, some of them fawns, in our yard. I am also constructed in my relationship to the rest of nature by genetics. I am color-blind and discern far fewer colors in the world than many of my peers and have had to cope with asthma resulting from environmental pollution that has precluded high-altitude hiking.

There is that kind of personal situatedness— one built up through individual contact with the natural environment often against the grain of the culture—that affects a reader's location in relation to the literature he or she studies and helps to explain why an individual enjoys certain kinds of literature more than others and different types at various times during his or her life.

There are also the myriad currents of cultural formations that have influenced, and at times determined, a person's initial reactions to insects, large mammals, the ocean, and the mountains. There are the religious and scientific values through which readers have been brought up to believe that they inhabit a fallen world or else a world perfectible through technology. Without time spent in reflection about individual self-location—a person's particular situatedness through nature, culture, and individual physiology—people are more likely to be determined by ideological formations that they might very well reject as a result of careful consideration than if they take the time for such understanding of the I-as-particular-reader, rather than as a general reader.

Gregory Cajete, a Tewa Pueblo Indian, has written about what he defines as the "geopsyche" in *Look to the Mountain: An Ecology of Indigenous Education* (1994). By this term he means the way that one's conscious and unconscious are shaped and influenced by place of birth and upbringing. He is not only referring to that phenomenon so many displaced people experience of arriving somewhere they have never been and feeling suddenly as if they had come home but also to the way that one's culture interacts with place and shapes the mind of each member of the culture. There are the direct contacts with the natural world in which one is raised. There is also the ways that one's culture, community, and family—at times in contradiction to each other—shape the preconditions and the interpretations of that direct contact, reinforcing certain impressions and reactions and rejecting or resisting others. The unconscious is not only affected by such overt cultural pressures but also by the rituals and rhythms of the community.

As discerning individuals, critical readers need to recognize the manifestations and representations of such psychic patterning in the literature that they choose to read. For instance, in the United States there are the two famous Johns, Muir and Burroughs. Muir often portrays himself as a heroic individualist who relishes the isolation and danger of the solo mountain climbing expedition and lavishes poetic language in his essays in appreciation and generation of the sublime. Burroughs largely repudiates the sublime, warning in one of his essays against building one's house in a location with the most scenic overlook because one risks becoming overstimulated. Likewise, people appear regularly in his essays, often as companions on fishing or hiking expeditions or as inhabitants of the land through which he travels. How does one account for this dichotomy among contemporaries? Their diverse reactions to Alaska on the Harriman expedition indicate quite clearly that it was not just a matter of the locale each traversed but rather some orientation toward nature deeply ingrained in them much earlier in their lives.

Likewise, how are readers to come to terms with the immense variety of cultural and geographical backgrounds of the international community of environmental writers encountered today? Readers must remind themselves repeatedly of where they are standing, and of what they look like—both how they imagine themselves to be and how they are likely to look to these writers—as they seek to understand and to evaluate their work.

Today across the United Kingdom as across the United States the definition of such terms as English Literature and American literature are becoming ever more complicated. Further, the literary and cultural traditions that inform that literature are becoming more diverse as the ethnic and religious minorities—whether recent immigrants or ancient inhabitants—remain unassimilated, if not in language then very much in cultural, religious, and family structure terms. In some ways, this diversity may prove to be even more pronounced when looking at contemporary literature treating nature and engaging environmental issues. While many contemporary ethnic writers may draw on the dominant written literary tradition for their style and aesthetic inspiration, they often draw on their ethnic cultural heritage, particularly the oral traditions, and their ancestral lands, religious beliefs, and healing practices for their intellectual, empathetic, and sensory engagement with the uncultured dimensions of the material world. While it is the case that the term nature and its various semiotic meanings are cultural constructs, human perception is sensory as well as cognitive. More to the point, there exists in the world very much that remains fundamentally and utterly uncultured, such as the monsoon season and monarch butterfly migrations. And often it is the ethnic writers, the postcolonial writers, the indigenous authors, who tap into historical cultural formations that give greater credence to other forms of human perception than the rationally conscious in their literary works, as demonstrated by much

of the literature discussed in various chapters of this volume.

The Contents of This Volume

In order not to colonize the literature of the world by means of a critical perspective derived from predominantly Anglo-American examples, I set out from the beginning to include as diverse a representation not only of national literatures but also of critical approaches to those literatures. The only overriding requirement was that any critical approach selected must be written in a style and language accessible to the sourcebook's readers. Even when queried, I declined to provide either a formulaic format for the chapters or foundational definitions of the terms "literature" and "nature" that would determine what would be included or excluded in the case of a specific literature. Rather, the authors of the 65 chapters have presented not only their interpretations of the representative examples for their subjects and the kind of breadth or depth suitable for their purposes but also explicitly and implicitly their critical criteria. Thus, different writers use different terms, such as nature and environment, and distinct criteria are established from one essay to the next. The only major restriction was the chronological one, which I have already discussed.

Through maintaining a multiplicitous approach to the examples selected and the critical orientation offered in each chapter, this volume provides a fairly comprehensive international overview without establishing a prescriptive canon or a master critical theory that reductively unifies the diversity and disparateness of the literature treated. Thus, this volume can remain what it is meant to be: an opening statement, and an invitation to further work in the developing dialogue between literary production and critical analysis of the way that the peoples of the world have responded and are responding in writing to significant changes in the relationship of humanity and world.

The 65 chapters of the *Literature of Nature: An International Sourcebook* are divided into six sections of unequal length. The literatures of the United States and Canada receive by far the most attention in this volume, 21 chapters. This emphasis in part results from the more developed state of ecocriticism in North America. It also represents an effort to be responsive to the anticipated interests of many of the volume's readers, which is to say that for an English-speaking audience, English language literatures and literatures readily available in translation have been afforded the most attention.

The second section, with 15 chapters, is devoted to Europe, with an emphasis on Great Britain. At the same time, significant attention is given to the literature of Russia. Obtaining contributors for this section of the sourcebook proved to be surprisingly difficult, particularly for the literatures of Eastern Europe. It is my impression that at this point in time there is tremendous activity in such countries as Poland, Hungary, Bulgaria, and others concerning environmental issues, but the attention is all occurring in regard to economics, politics, and policy studies, with virtually no consideration of the role of literature in the development of cultural attitudes toward nature or in reflecting changing environmental attitudes and actions. It is likely that these countries, as well as those states other than Russia that were once part of the Soviet Union, have a rich literary tradition, but with the exception of Russian criticism, little academic attention is being paid to it as of yet.

The third section covers Asia and the Pacific and consists of 11 chapters. As with Europe, the coverage here is selective, with strong attention to English-language literatures but also to China, India, and Japan. The fourth and fifth sections treat Africa and the Arab world and Latin America and the poles, respectively. In addition to national literatures, the latter section also contains chapters devoted to literature about the Arctic and Antarctica, where human inhabitation and visitation are pushed to the extremes. While the chapters in these sections are fewer in number than in the preceding ones, they tend to have a much greater breadth of coverage. Of these 10 chapters, seven of them go beyond the parameters of national literatures and treat the literatures of larger regions, while another chapter takes a single region, the Amazon, and looks at representations of it in various national literatures.

The sixth section breaks with the national and regional coverage of the rest of the volume to contain chapters on various topics. A review of the chapter titles in this section suggests the necessity for this arrangement where such topics as science fiction, green cultural studies, aesthetics, and women's travel literature are concerned. The subjects of these chapters in several instances provide a basis for rereading the material presented in the national literatures chapters

from additional perspectives beyond those pursued with any one of the national literatures treated.

Each of the 65 chapters in this volume ends with a list of Selected Works and Further Reading that will help to open wider the door to the topics. The book concludes with a Title Index, which lists references to works discussed in text, and a General Index.

Conclusion

While reiterating here that this volume is the most comprehensive attempt at mapping an international review of the modern literature of nature ever published in English, I also want to emphasize that it is not the final word but the opening, provocative word. Here I use "provocative" in a positive way, wanting to imply its role in stimulating further reading, further consideration, and further criticism. Such further reading should consist of rethinking and amending what has been written here, but it must not stop there. Such further reading should also lead to filling in this volume's gaps and omissions. It would be wonderful if a companion volume treating the national literatures here omitted and providing additional detail on the national literatures already included were warranted in a few years. It would be even more wonderful if a volume of this size were warranted for each of the national literatures contributing to an understanding of humanity's position within the rest of nature. I trust that if the readers will lead, the critics will follow in this regard. English-language readers may also lead not only in seeking critical writing about the literature of nature worldwide but also in clamoring for translations of the many literary works mentioned in these pages that have not yet been translated into English or that have been allowed to go out of print, perhaps without ever becoming readily available or known to what would have been an appreciative audience. Translations and anthologies are very much needed so that the readers of this sourcebook may not only read about Taiwanese environmental literature or Latin American ecological poetry but may also read it in translation when they are unable to read it in the original language. It is a big world out there, and many people are writing about it. I would like the readers of these words to think of *Literature of Nature: An International Sourcebook* as their letter of introduction to a vast number of those authors.

Selected Works and Further Reading

Cajete, Gregory, *Look to the Mountain: An Ecology of Indigenous Education,* Durango, Colorado: Kivakí, 1994

Carson, Rachel, *Silent Spring,* Boston: Houghton Mifflin, 1962; London: Hamilton, 1963

The Epic of Gilgamesh, translated by Nancy K. Sandars, Baltimore, Maryland, and Harmondsworth, England: Penguin, 1960

Glotfelty, Cheryll, and Harold Fromm, eds., *The Ecocriticism Reader: Landmarks in Literary Ecology,* Athens: University of Georgia Press, 1996

Graves, Robert, *The White Goddess: A Historical Grammar of Poetic Myth,* New York: Creative Age, 1948; London: Faber and Faber, 1948; amended and enlarged ed., New York: Farrar, Straus & Giroux, 1966

Johnson, Colin, *Doctor Wooreddy's Prescription for Enduring the Ending of the World,* Melbourne, Australia: Hyland House, 1983; New York: Ballantine, 1986

Merchant, Carolyn, *The Death of Nature: Women, Ecology, and the Scientific Revolution,* San Francisco: Harper & Row, 1980; London: Wildwood House, 1982

Ngugi wa Thiong'o, *Petals of Blood,* London: Heinemann, 1977; New York: E. P. Dutton, 1978

Poe, Edgar Allan, *The Narrative of Arthur Gordon Pym,* New York: Harper & Brothers, 1838; also published as *The Wonderful Adventures of A. Gordon Pym,* London: W. Kent, 1865

Rhys, Jean, *Wide Sargasso Sea,* New York: Norton, 1966; London: Deutsch, 1966

Snyder, Gary, *A Place in Space: Ethics, Aesthetics, and Watersheds: New and Selected Prose,* Washington, D.C.: Counterpoint, 1995

Traherne, Thomas, "Centuries of Meditations," in *Centuries, Poems, and Thanksgivings,* vol. 1, edited by H. M. Margoliouth, Oxford: Clarendon, 1965

Section 1:

The United States and Canada

Writing About Nature in Early America: From Discovery to 1850

Rochelle Johnson and Daniel Patterson

The history of writing about nature in early America is as varied and variegated as the amazing lands the writers attempted to represent with their words. Between 1493 and 1850, the reasons for writing about nature changed constantly. Over these three and a half centuries, changing cultural conditions led authors to reflect different motives for representing nature in various ways, and these motives and methods in turn reflect large developments in science and epistemology. Out of the early writings about nature finally emerges, in the late eighteenth century, what we today think of as nature writing–texts in which authors, in representing the natural world in language, deliberately bring together science and literature, and description and meditation, in order to effect some artful end. Before nature writing emerges, though, writing about nature serves various ends and takes different forms.

Generally, works that represent the New World in the sixteenth and seventeenth centuries are imbued with an unrestrained imperialistic ethic of domination. Plants, animals, and minerals existed to benefit humankind, according to these works, and the indigenous humans could be dismissed or eradicated as unworthy of God's bounty since they lacked the drive, knowledge, or technology to exploit and develop the land. By the late eighteenth century, while the ethic of colonization and domination had by no means disappeared, the ways that Europeans were living in the New World had changed. These changing conditions, along with developments in natural history and epistemology, provided the conditions for a new literary genre.

When the first European navigators and explorers began finding their way to the Americas, the attempt to represent these lands in words began. Since explorers such as Columbus and Cortés had personal careers to advance, they mainly described nature only to the extent that it offered gold, commodities, and promises of successful imperialism to their Spanish monarchs. For example, in writing about his first voyage, Columbus was willing to deliberately misrepresent what he saw in order to advance himself: he reports the harbors of Hispaniola as being "incredibly fine," and claims, "there are many great rivers with broad channels and *the majority contain gold*" (p. 117; emphasis added). Amid such distortions, however, early explorers did, on occasion, try to convey the actual splendor of the New World to their aristocratic readers. In these descriptions, these writers often relied on broad and vague generalities. Columbus wrote of Hispaniola in 1493:

> [E]verywhere I went the nightingale and many other birds were singing. There are palms of six or eight different kinds–a marvellous sight because of their great variety–and the other trees, fruit, and plants are equally marvellous. There are splendid pine woods.... There are many kinds of birds and varieties of fruit.... The mountains and hills, the plains and meadow lands are both fertile and beautiful. (pp. 116–117)

In this passage, Columbus perhaps unknowingly reveals the limits of his language and his inability to precisely describe what he sees to his readers. (The nightingale, for instance, was a European bird, and not the bird Columbus heard.) And so amid the representations of nature by Columbus and by other early explorers, we find both subtle and overt assertions of the difficulty of finding words for New World plants, animals, abundance, and experiences. Columbus was often so bound by what he wanted and needed to see that he could not see the New World's body in any context except his own. While some of this limitation resulted from incomplete knowledge, much of it resulted from the fact that detailed, precise, and accurate descriptions did not mesh with the need to gather information relevant to imperialist goals.

Núñez Cabeza de Vaca's narrative of his eight-year (1528–36) trek from the northern Gulf Coast to western Mexico, however, reflects a more detailed knowledge of the land. While his purpose is primarily to record his story and to convince the monarchs that the native peoples can be converted and colonized by peaceful, rather than violent, means, he also conveys much information about the plants, animals, climate and indigenous cultures of the region. Among the most noteworthy moments in his narrative are his brief natural history essays on the opossum and the buffalo, the first European accounts of both animals.

In 1562 Jean Ribaut, a Huguenot military captain, sailed up the East Coast from just south of the St. John's River in present-day northeast Florida to the Charleston harbor. His purpose was to find a suitable site for a Huguenot settlement, but also to benefit the French monarch and people by reporting "all the comodities that might be founde and seen in that lande" (p. 53). After narrating the easy and cordial alliance he established with a native group near the St. John's River, he allows himself space to express his enthusiasm for the bounty and variety of the place:

> [We] enterd and veued the cuntry therabowte, which is the fairest, frutefullest and plesantest of all the worlde, habonding in honney, veneson, wildfoule, forrestes, woodes of all sortes, palme trees, cipers, cedders, bayes, the hiest, greatest and fairest vynes in all the wourld with grapes accordingly, which naturally and withowt mans helpe and tryming growe to the top of okes and other trees. . . . And the sight of the faire medowes is a pleasure not able to be expressed with tonge, full of herons, corleux, bitters, mallardes, egertes, woodkockes, and of all other kinde of smale birdes, with hartes, hyndes, buckes, wild swyne, and sondery other wild beastes . . . and to be shorte it is a thinge inspeakable, the comodities that be sene there and shal be founde more and more in this incomperable lande, never as yet broken with plowe irons, bringing fourthe all thinges according to his first nature, wherof the eternall God endued yt. (pp. 72–73)

By representing this place as an original Paradise, Ribaut suggests a sense of freedom to possess this land in a timeless, original state of innocence. While acknowledging that his experience in that environment surpassed the capacity of language to communicate, he shows a self-consciousness about representing nature in language that remains rare until the sublime becomes a literary issue in the eighteenth century. Even when he pulls this passage away from his "pleasure" and toward somebody else's "comodities," he emphasizes the limits of language in order to evoke a natural bounty beyond imagining: "it is a thinge inspeakable."

Part of the challenge of promoting settlement was finding the words that would precisely shape a natural realm that Europeans would find so attractive that they would settle there. And so, while writers continued to commodify plants and animals, their audiences broadened. They emphasized the possible gains for an individual over the gains of a corporate imperialistic project. In 1588, to promote Ralegh's Virginia colony, Thomas Hariot, in his *A Briefe and True Report,* contained all of Virginia's plants, animals, and minerals into three types of commodities. This oversimplification focused readers' attention on direct profits and represented Virginia as a place that will "returne you profit and gaine" (p. 350). Hariot mentioned only 12 of the 28 mammals he had the names of, because only those 12 "be good meat" (p. 369).

In New England, John Smith moved beyond the standard promises of fertile land and abundant forests, and represented fish in 1616 as, literally, money: "And is it not pretty sport, to pull up two pence, six pence, and twelve pence, as fast as you can hale and veare a line?" (p. 347). He also transformed wild birds of prey into entertainment for aristocrats accustomed to falconry: "Gentlemen" can substitute "fowling and fishing, for hunting and hauking" since in New England "the wilde haukes" will give them "some pleasure, in seeing them stoope (six or seaven after one another) an houre or two together, at the skuls of fish in the faire harbours . . . and never trouble nor torment your selves, with watching, mewing, feeding, and attending them" (p. 347). Smith, like Hariot, gave his readers a natural world that beckoned them to settlement.

William Wood continued this emphasis on the personal pleasures of the New World in his less innocuous, but gleeful 1634 recommendation of another sport available in New England: "No ducking ponds can affoard more delight than a lame Cormorant, and two or three lusty Dogges" (p. 33). Such a violently anthropocentric ethic— while extreme—is consistent with the general attitude toward nature apparent in the writings of Wood, Thomas Morton, and John Josselyn. These "gentlemen" writers from abroad often put the land on the same confining and appropriating pedestal on which they put women. We read in their representations of nature what they needed nature to be for successful settlement: a woman yielding to the male aggression she had longed for through centuries of benign treatment by Native Americans. In Morton's verse prologue to *New English Canaan*, New England is "[l]ike a faire virgin, longing to be sped / And meete her lover in a Nuptiall bed . . . being most fortunate / When most enjoy'd" (p. 114). Characteristically, in his work Morton simply named a plant or animal and then cavalierly noted its usefulness as food, commodity or entertainment: "Turkies there are, which divers times in great flocks have sallied by our doores; and then a gunne, being commonly in a redinesse, salutes them with such a courtesie, as makes them take a turne in the Cooke roome. They daunce by the doore so well" (p. 192).

As with Wood and Morton, Josselyn's ethic of domination pervades his 1674 representation of New England life forms, but with Josselyn this ethic is so extreme that it becomes a contempt for anything that cannot be commodified or sensationalized. All but commodity is equally unworthy of knowing, unless the author finds it useful as sensationalism. So he creates a place with sea serpents, little pygmy mummies that children collect, turtles with three hearts, and weird sex that results in creatures that are half lion and half pig. Incongruously, however, Josselyn utters the principles of a kinder teleology: "There are certain transcendentia in every Crea-

ture, which are the indelible Characters of God, and which discover God; There's a prudential for you. . . ." (p. 64). Since he so consistently undermines any moments of a gentler ethic, it is difficult to read him as other than the embodiment of rabid exploitation. By commodifying and appropriating nature, Wood, Morton, and Josselyn might have avoided a close knowledge of the natural environment, but they all do account for the principle plants and animals of New England as a means of informing prospective settlers of the bounty of the New World.

As a permanent settler, and as a Pilgrim hoping to help establish a theocracy in New England, William Bradford represented nature somewhat differently because he wanted only those who shared his religious vision to settle there. In the first decades of the Plymouth plantation, Bradford pointed to one of the colony's chief problems as resulting from profit-minded ship owners who would transport anyone to New England, regardless of their reasons for going, so long as they could pay. This brought "many unworthy persons," who "pestered" the Pilgrims' new land (p. 357). Bradford's construction of the New England wilderness reflects his sense of the Pilgrims' mission of continuing the work of the Reformation in the New World. His wilderness served his propagandistic purpose of shaping his Pilgrim colleagues as self-sacrificing, suffering workers of God in a "desert" that, in its hostility to humans, was easily comparable to the Biblical desert, where Yahweh tested and finally rewarded his chosen people:

> they that know the winters of that country know them to be sharp and violent, and subject to cruel and fierce storms . . . what could they see but a hideous and desolate wilderness, full of wild beasts and wild men–and what multitudes there might be of them they knew not . . . the whole country, full of woods and thickets, represented a wild and savage hue. (p. 70)

Such an uninviting and even lethal wilderness is intended to discourage profit-minded settlers and to encourage only those driven by the Pilgrims' view of a sin-stained natural world.

Many of the accounts written by missionaries, explorers, travelers and military officers from the late seventeenth century to the American Revolution are largely silent about nature, focusing mainly on narratives of people (both

Native and Euro-American), politics, and religious work. Writings by Father Louis Hennepin, Samuel de Champlain, John Lawson, and Robert Rogers, for example, only incidentally describe the nonhuman environment; these works do, however, contribute to a greater knowledge of the land and climate among general readers and thereby help to create interest in American places and life forms. Hennepin, who accompanied LaSalle's exploratory party around the Great Lakes and in the Mississippi River Valley, offers the first description of Niagara Falls, an early account of an Indian buffalo hunt, as well as a brief natural history sketch of the opossum. Such texts presented readers with isolated bits of natural description and contributed to the rise of nature writing.

Nature writing was one of the various cultural phenomena (such as the novel, modern science, or the Reformation) that rose out of the epistemological shift toward empiricism that matured in Europe in the sixteenth and seventeenth centuries. Among the necessary conditions that gave rise to nature writing was the new emphasis and insistence on empiricism, and its corollary premise that events in nature have physical, perceivable causes and that these must be discovered so that human society can advance itself. Empiricism legitimated the individual's perception of the world and altered how individuals perceived their place in the natural world.

Francis Bacon provided a significant discussion of this epistemological development in the *Novum Organum*. Past ages, according to Bacon, were led astray by an adherence to Aristotelian thought, the chief flaw of which was a reliance on deductive methods; Aristotle "made his natural philosophy a mere bond servant to his logic, thereby rendering it contentious and well-nigh useless" (p. 54). While Aristotle made some use of experience, he did not draw conclusions strictly from it: "having first determined the question according to his will, he then resorts to experience, and bending her into conformity with his placets, leads her about like a captive in a procession" (p. 61).

Most of Bacon's contemporaries hindered the advancement of science by similarly subordinating experience to logic and to prescribed categories of thought. This limitation of thought had become institutionalized, argued Bacon, and "the studies of men . . . are confined and as it were imprisoned in the writings of certain authors, from whom if any man dissent he is straightway arraigned as a turbulent person and an innovator" (p. 89). The goal of Bacon's "Instauration," his program of radical cultural renovation, was to increase the human understanding of physical causes in the universe so that a "natural philosophy" could be derived from principles verifiable by experience and experimentation. This empirical approach to understanding nature would free human society from the deductive past and enable meaningful progress for civilization.

Empiricism brought a new legitimacy to individual perceptions of the natural realm. One important manifestation of this new scientific freedom was Carl von Linné's *Systema Naturæ*, which contained his system of nomenclature that propelled botany to the avant-garde of the new sciences. Linnaeus's binomial system of classification proved to be so useful and simple that "botany became a kind of game. Princes rearranged their gardens, professors reworked the national floras, and amateurs everywhere took up botany." This system became so influential and widespread because of its reliance largely on inductive methods–that is, on the individual's direct observations of plants–and it contributed to the development of nature writing by presuming "the validity of the world as man actually experienced it" (Larson, 32–33).

As widespread and as liberating as Linnaeus's nomenclature was, it still assumed the fixity and continuity of species and a hierarchy of life forms determined by God: it was still based firmly in a teleological worldview. Something like the Great Chain of Being still provided the controlling metaphor for organizing the facts of natural history. Between 1760 and 1790, however, botany and zoology led the way toward a "natural method" of classification, a method that rose out of the belief that the perceived order of nature–and its continuities of varied life forms–was the result not simply of the will of the Creator, but of discernible physical processes that occurred over periods of time (Larson, 28–60). Thus, a genus, as one example, was no longer conceived of as a divinely appointed and neatly bordered group of species; it became rather "a congeries of species connected at an imperceptible nexus but without strict limits" (Larson, 39). By the end of the eighteenth century, science was becoming more modest; naturalists set for themselves goals more attainable than the discovery and articulation of metaphysical truths. The life histories of the many species of flora and fauna became more important than the revelation of a hierarchy of life forms.

This general movement from teleology and toward what we now call ecology is one of the conditions that fosters nature writing. There are many other contributing factors, but among these are the depths of knowledge that Euro-Americans earned through several generations of experience with the land, and the vigorous new life of natural history as a popular subject, no longer reserved only for university-trained scholars. A sense of loss also occasionally looms into view. Having seen the forests cleared and certain animal populations depleted, some writers reflected a new cultural awareness of the life of their land.

J. Hector St. John de Crèvecoeur, just before and during the American Revolution, wrote essays from the perspective of an American farmer advocating an ideal balance between the urban and the wild. His model of American progress involves a first wave of barbaric hunters who precede the farmers into the wilderness. Because of their proximity to wilderness, these hunters are morally inferior; they "appear to be no better than carnivorous animals of a superior rank" (*Letters*, 72). They are nevertheless necessary to the advance of civilization because the hunters drive the predatory animals and indigenous peoples from the wilderness, leaving it ready to be cleared for agricultural development: "thus the path is opened for the arrival of a second and better class, the true American freeholders, the most respectable set of people in this part of the world" (*Letters*, 79). The ideal society is a rural one in which people cultivate the land and avoid the overcrowded, oppressive conditions of urban environments.

Crèvecoeur represents the American landscape as a determining force in the successive stages of the hoped-for progress of American civilization. In the largest sense, he shows a causal relationship between the availability of open space and the civil and religious liberties enjoyed in America. More specifically, however, he shows that the farmer's proximity to nature stimulates his thoughts and even leads him to an artistic sensibility. Crèvecoeur epitomizes this progress in a stroll Farmer James—his narrative persona—takes one evening. James is "astonished" by natural phenomena. He delights in this walk through his "low grounds" and in "the myriads of insects" he watches "dancing in the beams of the setting sun." Crèvecoeur develops this astonishment to specific curiosity about the

"wonderful change" that occurs in the development of an egg, which leads him finally to question how inferior the instinct of a chicken is to the reason or consciousness of a human (*Letters*, 55). Thus, the ideal progress from agriculture to scientific curiosity to the sensibility that informs Crèvecoeur's art is epitomized, and has its origin in the sensory stimulation of a rural environment.

Crèvecoeur's other literary uses of nature are broad and varied. They range from the ridiculous to the idealized, and from the ecological to the sublime. The snake can hear, and a hornets' nest in the house is an effective means to control flies. The outdoors always provide solace for the soul, food for the body, and a place for the family of man. The local extinction of quails is lamentable and reparable. The farmer sees the necessity of forests and loves the woods even while clearing the land. And the hiding place of a loyalist fugitive is a "Grotto" deep in a wild area, "the most Romantick I had ever seen" (*More Letters*, 294–295). Finally, however, all of Crèvecoeur's representations and uses of nature are intended to demonstrate that knowledge of natural history contributes to the progress of human civilization.

Thomas Jefferson, with formal training in natural history, reflected the greater cultural currency of natural history by using it for nationalistic purposes in his *Notes on the State of Virginia*. In addition to prosaic accounts of his state's geology, flora, and fauna, he used his preparation in natural history in an extensive refutation of a French naturalist's claim that animals in America have degenerated from European counterparts. The two best known passages in this work, however, are Jefferson's literary descriptions of the Natural Bridge, and of the confluence of the Shenandoah and Potomac Rivers. These two conscious attempts at rendering the geologic as sublime reflect the culture's readiness for natural history to become literary art.

To a significant extent, the design of William Bartram's ambitious project, his *Travels*, appears to take advantage of the new cultural value placed on natural history writing. Although he was trained as a field botanist, he made abundant use of literary techniques—most notably personification and the narrative strategies of travel writing—to bring his scientific studies into the realm of literary art and thereby enliven for general readers the scientific facts and processes of botany and other natural sciences. This design shows Bartram's awareness that readers' imaginations need to be trained to find the non-human world interesting and relevant. He noted this indirectly in the introduction to *Travels* where he told his readers that his own imagination can be "surprised" by objects "in the works of nature" when he leaves the "rich cultivated settlements" and enters the "high pine forests" or "dark and grassy savannas." The natural objects he sees in these places, however, "soon reconcile the surprised imagination to the change" (p. 13), and thus, he hopes, his readers' unprepared imaginations might also adjust.

Bartram's nature writing, then, is designed to train his readers to deepen their knowledge of their physical environment. His literary representation of the natural history of the sarracenia, or pitcher plant, for example, reflects this design. After describing the plant's ability to retain a surprising amount of water in its "funiculum," Bartram attempts to transform plant physiology into narrative:

> these waters which contribute to their supplies, are the rebounding drops or horizontal streams wafted by the winds, which adventitiously find their way into them, when a blast of wind shifts the lid; see these short stiff hairs, they all point downwards, which direct the condensed vapours down into the funiculum; these stiff hairs also prevent the varieties of insects, which are caught, from returning, being invited down to sip the mellifluous exuvia, from the interior surface of the tube, where they inevitably perish; what quantities there are of them! (pp. liii–liv)

By the use of narrative strategies, the sarracenia becomes a character with qualities and motives, an agent of actions. To the extent that Bartram was able to broaden readers' minds to accommodate more of the reality that science studies and presents (that is, "reconcile" readers' "surprised" imaginations), he was able to contribute to the gradual humbling of a long-standing ethic of domination.

In the first decades following the American Revolution, interest in the new nation's wild areas awakened and increased, and more and more, adventurous people of various motives made their way into regions unfamiliar to American citizens east of the Appalachians. As they wrote and published their observations and experiences, they participated in the larger project of writing the continent into the minds of Americans.

Between August 30, 1803, and September 26, 1806, Meriwether Lewis and William Clark wrote a million words about the continent they crossed with the "Corps of Discovery," the official exploratory party commissioned by President Jefferson. This tremendous collection of journal entries consists mainly of rough, firsthand observations and descriptions of the continent's native peoples, topography, weather conditions, animals, and plants, but also traceable through these million words is a sketchy, raw narrative of the men's experiences in the American wilderness.

Many of Lewis and Clark's pages are covered with rote details because they were gathering pure data. Many others, however, convey intriguing scientific description and analysis of flora, fauna, and geological formations. In a particularly significant passage, Lewis perseveres in his attempt to shape words into sentences that are precise enough to represent the colors of the black-billed magpie's feathers:

> the underside of the feathers is a pale black, the upper side is a dark blueish green which like the outer part of the wings is changable as it reflects different portions of light. Towards the the extremety of these feathers they become of an orrange green, then shaded pass to a redish indigo blue, and again at the extremity assume the predominant colour of changeable green. (3:84)

On rare occasions, Captain Lewis attempted to express his emotional responses to aesthetic experiences. On first viewing the Great Falls of the Missouri River in western Montana, for example, Lewis wrote a description of "this sublimely grand specticle" and then proceeded to critique his attempt (4:283). After noting the physical dimensions of the Falls, he went on to represent their dynamic action:

> a perfect white foam which assumes a thousand forms in a moment sometimes flying up in jets of sparkling foam to the hight of fifteen or twenty feet and are scarcely formed before large roling bodies of the same beaten and foaming water is thrown over and conceals them. In short the rocks seem to be most happily fixed to present a sheet of the whitest beaten froath for 200 yards in length and about 80 feet perpendicular. The water after

decending strikes against the butment before mentioned or that on which I stand and seems to reverberate and being met by the more impetuous courant they role and swell into half formed billows of great hight which rise and again disappear in an instant. (4:284)

His words, however, did not fully satisfy him: "[A]fter wrighting this imperfect discription I again viewed the falls and was so much disgusted with the imperfect idea which it conveyed of the scene that I determined to draw my pen across it and begin agin, but then reflected that I could not perhaps succeed better than penning the first impressions of the mind" (4:285).

No writing of nature in America is comparable in scope to the *Journals* of Lewis and Clark. This work collectively is so vast and so culturally significant that it has been discussed as the American epic. (See Furtwangler for the *Journals* as epic, as well as for treatments of the passages cited above.) In the history of writing about nature in America, Lewis and Clark's million words are rangy and gangling, touching on several categories rather than fitting neatly into any one, yet collectively they loom as a monumental achievement in America's literary history.

While Lewis and Clark would not have seen themselves as contributing to the literature of nature, several other writers—among them Thomas Nuttall, John D. Godman, and John James Audubon—consciously sought to devise new ways to give nature a literary form. As did his friend William Bartram, naturalist Thomas Nuttall relied on the travel narrative as the chief means of organizing and presenting his natural history to a general readership, but he emphatically explained that he in no way intended to appeal to the "taste" of typical travel literature readers, "a taste, which has no criterion but passing fashion, which spurns at every thing that possesses not the charm of novelty, and the luxury of embellishment." Writing natural history for him was a means of admiring "the wisdom and beauty of creation," and his purpose in publishing his observations was to communicate "the same amusement and gratification" (p. 7). Nuttall's reputation as an absent-minded botanist came from his own narrative accounts of being lost and in danger, but his reputation as a literary naturalist came from his success as the discoverer of "scores of new and unclassified plants, mineralogical specimens, fossil shells, fish, [and] insects" (Kastner, 270), and from the frank, compelling quality of his prose.

John James Audubon wrote five volumes of prose to accompany his paintings of American birds. The *Ornithological Biography* goes beyond simply providing text for his paintings; cumulatively it narrates Audubon's ornithological fieldwork and skillfully presents his natural history to a reading public. Audubon often invited his readers into his natural history by dramatizing and anthropomorphizing the behavior of birds and other animals. Typically, he also created a moral lesson to be learned from his representations of the natural world. For example, in his treatment of his "greatest favourite" of all the birds, the wood thrush, Audubon describes the bird's natural history, noting what it eats and its nesting behavior, but he also shows the artistic potential of ornithology:

> Seldom, indeed, have I heard the song of this Thrush, without feeling all that tranquillity of mind, to which the secluded situation in which it delights is so favourable. The thickest and darkest woods always appear to please it best. The borders of murmuring streamlets, overshadowed by the dense foliage of the lofty trees growing on the gentle declivities, amidst which the sunbeams seldom penetrate, are its favourite resorts. There it is, kind reader, that the musical powers of the hermit of the woods must be heard, to be fully appreciated and enjoyed. (Lyon, 133–134)

Following a violent but stimulating thunderstorm, Audubon reported that he was comforted by the voice of the thrush: "as if to console me . . . to cheer my depressed mind, and to make me feel . . . that never ought man to despair, whatever may be his situation, as he can never be certain that aid and deliverance are not at hand" (Lyon, 133). Audubon's achievement as a nature writer arguably rivals his achievement as a painter of birds; through five volumes of prose he represents the natural history of America's birds as literary art. The *Ornithological Biography* performs the cultural work of deepening Americans' knowledge of their physical environment.

John D. Godman's three-volume *American Natural History* performed a similar kind of cultural work. Godman combined his own observations of animals with observations culled from other natural history works. His project reflects his culture's growing interest in its natural history. His more narrative and contemplative work, *Rambles of a Naturalist*, reflects his belief that natural history has relevance to our imaginative and artistic sensibilities beyond its practical application. To this end he implies a call for a new literature that represents nature factually; "the beauty and excellence of poetry" can delude and provide "temporary gratification," but the new literature, because of its greater loyalty to the facts of nature, will bring a more enduring gratification and contribute to the intellectual and moral progress of the culture (*American*, 3:72).

While both Washington Irving and James Fenimore Cooper romanticized their representations of the American wilderness, as well as of specific flora and fauna, Susan Fenimore Cooper in her *Rural Hours*–the first book of nature writing by an American woman–became a voice for realism in natural representations. Like her contemporaries, Caroline Kirkland and Eliza Farnham, Cooper wrote to capture the daily life of her village; unlike them, however, she wrote to represent nature. She gave little space to stories about people in her book, focusing instead on the ecology of her Otsego Lake region, presenting her area's plant and animal life, as well as other aspects of her region: forests, rivers, weather patterns, and even agricultural practices. She also narrated the geologic and human history of the region.

Through both the form of the natural history essay and through narratives and descriptions of her walks and excursions, Cooper presented what ultimately emerges as her argument for a sustainable balance between human culture and its natural surroundings. In her recurring discussions of the forests, for example, Cooper praises the speed with which the wild land has been converted to cultivated farm land. On the other hand, she criticizes practices she deems unsustainable, particularly the rapid destruction of ancient forests for fuel and lumber: "One would think that by this time, when the forest has fallen in all the valleys—when the hills are becoming more bare every day—when timber and fuel are rising in prices, and new uses are found for even indifferent woods–some forethought and care in this respect would be natural in people laying claim to common sense" (pp. 213–214). She found no cause for restraint at all, however, in a report of 1,104 rattlesnakes having been killed in two days: "They are taken for their fat, which is sold at a good price" (p. 89).

A reader can often hear Cooper's reverence for the original, wild condition of her region. In the following passage, one also sees that Cooper valued the perspective gained by an understanding of the geologic history of her landscape:

The forest flowers, the gray stumps in our fields, and the heaving surface of our wild hill-sides, are not, however, the only way-marks to tell the brief course of cultivation about us. These speak of the fallen forest; but here, as elsewhere, the waters have also left their impression on the face of the earth, and in these new lands the marks of their passage is seen more clearly than in older countries. They are still, in many places, sharp and distinct, as though fresh from the workman's hand. Our valleys are filled with these traces of water-work; the most careless observer must often be struck with their peculiar features, and it appears remarkable that here, at an elevation so much above the great western lakes, upon this dividing ridge, at the very fountain head of a stream, running several hundred miles to the sea, these lines are as frequent and as boldly marked as though they lay in a low country subject to floods. Large mounds rise like islands from the fields, their banks still sharply cut; in other spots a depressed meadow is found below the level of the surrounding country, looking like a drained lake, enclosed within banks as plainly marked as the works of a fortification; a shrunken brook, perhaps, running to-day where a river flowed at some period of past time. (pp. 149–50)

Cooper's *Rural Hours* marked a new maturity in the genre of nature writing. Her model of nature was fully dynamic and evolving, never static–the works of creation are never complete. Cooper achieved her grace of style by joining so seamlessly the facts of natural history, her engaged social criticism, and her aesthetic response to the natural world. In the middle of the nineteenth century, American nature writing became a fully developed literary genre.

Selected Works and Further Reading

Audubon, John James, *Ornithological Biography, or An Account of the Habits of the Birds of the United States of America,* vol. 1, Philadelphia: J. Dobson, 1831; vol. 2, Boston: Hilliard, Gray, 1835; vols. 3–5, Edinburgh, Scotland: A. & C. Black, 1835–1839

Bacon, Francis, *Novum Organum,* London, 1620; also published as *The New Organon and Related Writings,* edited by Fulton H. Anderson, New York: Liberal Arts Press, 1960; London: Collier Macmillan, 1960

Bartram, William, *Travels Through North & South Carolina, Georgia, East & West Florida, the Cherokee Country, the Extensive Territories of the Muscogulges, or Creek Confederacy, and the Country of the Chactaws; Containing an Account of the Soil and Natural Productions of Those Regions, Together with Observations on the Manners of the Indians,* Philadelphia and London: James and Johnson, 1791; also published as *The Travels of William Bartram: Naturalist's Edition,* edited by Francis Harper, New Haven, Connecticut: Yale University Press, 1958

Bradford, William, *Of Plymouth Plantation, 1620–1647,* edited by Samuel Eliot Morison, New York: Knopf, 1952

Columbus, Christopher, *The Four Voyages of Columbus,* edited and translated by J. M. Cohen, Baltimore, Maryland: Penguin, 1969

Cooper, Susan Fenimore, *Rural Hours,* New York: George P. Putnam, 1850; London: R. Bentley, 1850

Crèvecoeur, J. Hector St. John de, *Letters from an American Farmer,* London: T. Davies, 1782; also published as *Letters from an American Farmer and Sketches of Eighteenth-Century America,* edited by Albert E. Stone, New York and Harmondsworth, England: Penguin, 1981

——, *More Letters from the American Farmer: An Edition of the Essays in English Left Unpublished by Crèvecoeur,* edited by Dennis D. Moore, Athens: University of Georgia Press, 1995

Furtwangler, Albert, *Acts of Discovery: Visions of America in the Lewis and Clark Journals,* Urbana: University of Illinois Press, 1993

Godman, John D., *American Natural History,* 3 vols., Philadelphia: H. C. Carey & I. Lea, 1826

——, *Rambles of a Naturalist,* Philadelphia: J. J. Ash, 1833

Hariot, Thomas, *A Briefe and True Report of the New Found Land of Virginia,* London, 1588; reprinted in *The Principal Navigations, Voyages, Traffiques & Discoveries of the English Nation,* edited by Richard Hakluyt, Glasgow, Scotland: James MacLehose and Sons, 1903

Hennepin, Louis, *A Description of Louisiana,* 1683; translated by John Gilmary Shea, New York: John G. Shea, 1880; reprinted, Ann Arbor, Michigan: University Microfilms, 1966

Jefferson, Thomas, *Notes on the State of Virginia,* Paris, 1784; London: John Stockdale, 1787; reprinted, Chapel Hill: University of North Carolina Press, 1954

Josselyn, John, *An Account of Two Voyages to New-England,* London: Giles Widdowes, 1674; also published as *John Josselyn, Colonial Traveler: A Critical Edition of 'Two Voyages to New-England',* edited by Paul J. Lindholdt, Hanover, New Hampshire: University Press of New England, 1988

Kastner, Joseph, *A Species of Eternity,* New York: Knopf, 1977

Larson, James, *Interpreting Nature: The Science of Living Form from Linnaeus to Kant,* Baltimore, Maryland: Johns Hopkins University Press, 1994

Lewis, Meriwether, and William Clark, *The Journals of the Lewis & Clark Expedition,* 8 vols., edited by Gary E. Moulton, Lincoln, Nebraska, and London: University of Nebraska Press, 1983–1993

Lyon, Thomas J., ed., *This Incomperable Lande: A Book of American Nature Writing,* Boston: Houghton Mifflin, 1989

Morton, Thomas, *New English Canaan or New Canaan,* Amsterdam, The Netherlands: J. F. Stam, 1637; also published as *The New English Canaan of Thomas Morton,* edited by Charles Francis Adams, Boston: Prince Society, 1883; reprinted, New York: Burt Franklin, 1967

Núñez Cabeza de Vaca, Alvar, *La relacion y comentarios del gouernador Alvar Núñez Cabeça de Vaca de lo acaescido en las dos jornadas que hizo a las Indias,* Valladolid, Spain, 1555; reprinted as *Castaways: The Narrative of Alvar Núñez Cabeza de Vaca,* edited by Enrique Pupo-Walker and translated by Frances M. López-Morillas, Berkeley: University of California Press, 1993

Nuttall, Thomas, *A Journal of Travels into the Arkansas Territory During the Year 1819,* Philadelphia: T. H. Palmer, 1821; reprinted, edited by Savoie Lottinville, Norman: University of Oklahoma Press, 1980

Ribaut, Jean, *The Whole & True Discouerye of Terra Florida,* London: Rouland Hall for Thomas Hacket, 1563; reprinted, De Land: Florida State Historical Society, 1927

Smith, John, *A Description of New England,* London: H. Lownes for Robert Clerke, 1616; reprinted in *The Complete Works of*

Captain John Smith (1580–1631), vol.
1, edited by Philip L. Barbour, Chapel
Hill: University of North Carolina Press,
1986

Wood, William, *New-England's Prospect,*
London, 1634; also published as *Wood's
New-England's Prospect,* Boston: Prince
Society, 1865; reprinted, New York: Burt
Franklin, 1967

Early American Natural Histories

Paul Lindholdt

Early American natural histories—accounts of nature in North America written between 1492 and 1800—are valuable in many ways. As literature, they delight us with their fresh views of a strange new world, with the undeniable priority of their power to document the emerging American culture. As flawed science, they show the ongoing contest between human fascination with rational order on the one hand and abiding mysteries on the other. As statements of interpretive ecology, these early natural histories introduce many of the sustainability issues—our ability to sustain natural resources—that perplex Americans today.

At a time when most literature was devotional or humanistic, early books about American flora and fauna offered alternate routes to the truth. They showed a healthy enlargement of concerns beyond one's God or oneself, which is not to say that vestiges of religion and humanism did not continue to complicate them. Religion remained in what we know as the "argument from design": that the marvels of creation offered evidence of an omniscient creator, making Him all the more worthy of our worship and awe. Humanism, the belief that human culture is the apex of creation, continued to flourish throughout early natural histories in what we now call utilitarianism: the belief that nature is valuable chiefly insofar as it can be used for human food, shelter, clothing, medicine or other profit.

In this 300-year period, the form of natural histories changed appreciably. The earliest travel accounts and promotion tracts usually included animal catalogs or reports of strange new species that possessed the power to threaten and amaze. Snippets of natural history inform accounts by Columbus, Verrazzano, Las Casas, Cabeza de Vaca, Hernando de Soto, Jean Ribaut, and Thomas Hariot. Some of these earliest nature reporters, ignoring the burden of proof

that falls on those who seek to persuade, resorted to verbal formulas (e.g., "It has been reported" or "A traveler held in high esteem has sworn") when trying to approximate the range of American rarities. By the eighteenth century, during the Age of Enlightenment, natural histories were being written in language that was more controlled in tone, plain in style, deliberate in its disregard of the author's personality, and skeptical in its point of view.

Histories showed nature was useful. In 1535 the French explorer Jacques Cartier, reaching landfall at Funk Island off Newfoundland, waited while his "men gathered two boatloads of great auk there, as Breton sailors relished their meat" (Morison, 392). That species, *Pinguinus impennis,* is now extinct. Robert Cavelier de LaSalle marveled at the herds of "wild cattle," or bison, whose populations he found to be "almost beyond belief" (Kastner, 9). Later writers, also mistakenly naming the American bison a "cattle" or "buffalo," showed how far they could presuppose the beasts' potential for domestication. As late as 1635, William Wood depicted moose as potentially useful oxlike beasts, so compliant that "the English have some thoughts of keeping them tame, and to accustom them to the yoake, which will be a great commoditie" (p. 21). Anyone who has seen blood in the eye of a huge cow moose bent on protecting her calf will appreciate the absurdity of this surmise. Wood also notes that cow moose are exceedingly "uberous," or full of milk, implying that these wild ungulates might consent to being milked each day as well as shackled to a plow (p. 21).

A reading of these early natural histories suggests that the American tall tale had its genesis in the seventeenth, not the nineteenth, century. Subtle showmen of printed words, the earliest writers exploited the land's extravagant fables and creatures to prompt colonial immigration. Christopher Levett, in his 1628 *A Voyage into*

New England, claimed to have "omitted many things in this discourse" that would diminish his credibility, such as fish "with manes, eares and heads" like horses' (n.p.). Levett's clever disclaimer that he would rather omit potentially incredible details than include them and raise suspicions is undercut by his tantalizing anatomical specificity. A century and a half later, in his *Travels*, William Bartram must have sounded even more exotic and extravagant when he issued this generally factual depiction of an alligator: "The waters like a cataract descend from his opening jaws. Clouds of smoke issue from his dilated nostrils. The earth trembles with his thunder" (p. 115). Readers relished fantastic tales, as they do today, and could claim to be improving themselves–learning about distant lands and creatures–while getting vicarious thrills.

Some writers of early natural histories wrote not only to attract potential colonists but to satisfy overseas patrons hungry for products to be traded on world markets, whether restoratives like "harts' horns" (deer antlers, still traded in Asia today) or rarities like the flying squirrels coveted by private collectors. Especially in the eighteenth century, specimen boxes routinely crossed the sea with their contents of live birds, plants, and animals for European scrutiny and propagation. Other naturalist-writers admired indigenous American creatures simply for the way they added to the storehouse of human scientific knowledge, an impetus that became greater once the Royal Society—founded in 1660—began to publish its *Transactions*. Prior to that, the gulf between fact and fiction was poorly lighted indeed, as in Captain John Smith's account of nocturnal cahow birds, an indeterminate but certainly remarkable species: "in the night if you but whoop and hollow, they will light upon you, that with your hands you may choose the fat and leave the leane" (2:342). Like those of many early travelers and promoters, Captain Smith's appeals to American natural history seem to have been chiefly gastronomic.

Even before the Royal Society was formed, and the Enlightenment ushered in greater critical discernment, some writers exhibited greater degrees of scientific disinterest than others. John Josselyn offered glimpses of genuine ecological insight in his two books, which are frequently interspersed with studies of *materia medica*— substances from nature used in medical remedies. Some of Josselyn's lore is medieval in origin, but other of his judgments are empirically

derived. He is remembered today not only through the Josselyn Botanical Society of Maine, the colony where he spent most of his time, but on account of his reputation as one who composed "the most complete natural history of New England in the seventeenth century" (Wharton, 847). Josselyn had the advantage of visiting the New World twice—from 1638 to 1639 and again from 1663 to 1671—thus witnessing changes in the ecology over a span of 33 years, as recorded in his book *Two Voyages*. He saw passenger pigeons in flocks five miles long during his first visit, but by his second voyage he noted discerningly of the birds, which are now extinct, that "they are much diminished, the English taking them with nets" (p. 71). Enthusiasm for the "New Science" of the eighteenth century has all but obscured the modest contributions of Josselyn, who could describe the New World phenomenon called the flying squirrel in his *Two Voyages* this accurately: "his skin being large and loose, he spreads it on both sides like wings when he passeth from one tree to another at great distance. I cannot call it flying nor leaping, for it is both" (p. 62).

Again, Josselyn's opbjectivity stands out when his work is compared with that of other pre-Enlightenment writers. William Wood, for instance, claimed that American Indians liked to leap astride swimming bears, the resulting contest yielding "more sportfull Bear bayting than Paris Garden can affoard" (p. 19). This appeal, tailored specifically to genteel European tastes for "recreation," anticipates the Davey Crockett legend. Wood also reported that bears survived the New England winters by "sucking their pawes, which keepeth them as fat as they are in Summer" (p. 20), a spurious explanation for hibernation that dates from the time of the Roman naturalist Pliny the Elder. The detail resurfaces in *A Week on the Concord and Merrimack Rivers*, where Thoreau employed it as a homely flourish of self-reliance: "The poet is he that hath fat enough, like bears and marmots, to suck his claws all winter. He hibernates in this world, and feeds on his own marrow" (p. 101). If Indians easily subdue bears in Wood's thin book, Josselyn cautions against overmuch complacency in the face of nature, warning that bears are unpredictable during mating season when "they walk the Country twenty, thirty, forty in a company, making a hideous noise with roaring, which you may hear a mile or two before they come so near to endanger the traveler" (*Rarities*, 13).

These examples illustrate a key difference between natural histories of the early colonial period and those of the late colonial and early national period. Very early naturalists relied more on imagination, speculation, and secondary reports than on empirical observation, data collection, and firsthand knowledge.

Natural history as scientifically defined today—sanitized of wonder, humor, and an honest sense of awe—emerged in America in the eighteenth century. Hyperbole and boosterism, however, still infected the sought-after objectivity believed to characterize sound science. Regardless of the storied tendencies of Enlightenment intellectuals to "number the streaks of the tulip," there is scant evidence in the Royal Society's *Transactions* of a scientific method that supposedly allows tentative truths to arise only from massive data (Wilson, 35). For many other reasons as well, early natural histories are little read today. The science they championed was often more incipient than actually practiced. They often indulged in high emotions, chiefly wonder and awe, an indulgence inconsistent with modern scientific standards of excellence. They eagerly exploited nature, which is distasteful to latter-day Romantic sensibilities. And they were routinely brash in their certitude that the rightful place of white Europeans is the top of the food chain. Early natural histories tend to inhabit a fertile but uncertain nether-realm that resides peculiarly between science and art.

Some would call that realm Romanticism. William Bartram, whose *Travels* has stood the test of time better than the work of most any of his peers, devoted himself to the place he was born. After a failed venture as a planter and four years of wandering to collect seeds and plants, he settled back home near Philadelphia and worked for 13 years on the manuscript of his only book, which was read and relished by Washington, Adams, and Jefferson and went through dozens of editions abroad, ultimately coming to influence Wordsworth and Coleridge. From its first paragraph, *Travels* privileges the awful and mysterious powers of nature: "the wide ocean, which, a few moments past, was gentle and placid, is now thrown into disorder, and heaped into mountains, whose white curling crests seem to sweep the skies!" (p. 29). His book is romantic to the core, and thus basically atypical of the natural histories of its era. In the years following his book's publication, Bartram declined offers to join the Lewis and Clark expedition, to attend a meeting of the American Philosophical Society to which he had been elected, even to become a professor of botany at the University of Pennsylvania.

Botany dominated the scope of early natural histories. Carolus Linnaeus of Sweden had issued his *Systema Naturae* in 1735, a book that revolutionized species identification and inspired a literary style and rhetoric (Regis, 15). Botanists Mark Catesby, Alexander Garden, John Bartram, and his son William all employed the Linnaean method and sent plants to patrons in England who brokered them to curators and scientists. Benjamin Franklin, promoter of both the American Philosophical Society and the Academy of Natural Sciences, as well as postmaster to the colonial capital of Philadelphia, gave American naturalists free postage when they sent specimens abroad. Alexander Garden of Charleston complained that his desire to "botanize" distracted him from his proper work as a physician. William Bartram's book, renowned among contemporaries for many reasons, not least of which was the quality of Bartram's drawings of plants, surpassed the work of all his peers except Jonathan Carver in its popularity, but Bartram saw few profits due to pirated editions overseas. Mark Catesby of Carolina, a talented illustrator, also worked in botany and is now known as "the colonial Audubon" for the quality of his drawings and for being the first to speculate that birds migrated to warmer climes instead of spending winters underwater or in caves. The formally uneducated John Bartram identified some 150 new botanical species, gained an international fame, and received a handsome salary upon being named King's Botanist. Mosses of the genus Bartramia, however, are the only plants that bear his name (Kastner, 65).

One of Bartram's allies and colleagues in natural history was President Thomas Jefferson, who earned himself a place in the annals of early science on the basis of his *Notes on the State of Virginia*, "an admirably researched and constructed monograph on the natural history, climate, resources, and geography of his native state, along with dissertations on its education and politics" (Kastner, 121). In a letter to William Bartram about some experiments he was conducting on flies for the American Philosophical Society, Jefferson confessed, "I long to be free for pursuits of this kind instead of the detestable ones in which I am now laboring" (Kastner, 120). Jefferson's choice of naturalist Meriwether Lewis to lead the exploring party with William Clark across the American frontier was an immense boon to the literature of early American natural history.

Engaging in one of the most hotly debated natural history issues of the century, Jefferson wrote his *Notes* to counter Buffon, de Pauw, and other French *philosophes* who asserted chauvinistically that New World animals were weak and degenerate relatives of more powerful European species. To refute the French on this matter, Jefferson quoted Catesby, Kalm, and his friend John Bartram of Philadelphia, America's first native-born naturalist of stature (Lyon, 36). Bartram, a Quaker by birth, found himself disowned by his fellows worshippers for denying the divinity of Christ and for voicing opinions like the following: "the creatures commonly called brutes possess higher qualifications, and more exalted ideas, than our traditional mystery-mongers are willing to allow them" (p. 36). A simple man, Bartram incurred the scorn of the many competitive virtuosi abroad.

From the standpoint of nature writing, the most compelling examples of early American natural histories are those like Bartram's that are "morally alive to the circumstances of the environmental moment" (Lyon, 23). Surpassing John Josselyn of Maine and John Lawson of Carolina (both transplanted Englishmen), Peter Kalm, the Swedish protege of Linnaeus, offered the most incisive commentaries on American natural resources and the ongoing impulse to exploit them unsustainably. Arrived from Europe where natural resources were being rapidly depleted, Kalm warned against the similar trends in America. He spent more than two years in the colonies, during which time he successfully spread the reputation of Linnaeus (Stearns, 530). It distressed Kalm to see colonists "bent only upon their present advantage, utterly regardless of posterity. By these means the swamps are already quite destitute of cedars" (p. 300). Such selfishly utilitarian attitudes toward the land by Euro-Americans can be contrasted with the legendary Native American belief in the need to consider the impacts of one's actions not only upon the present generation but upon seven generations hence. Not all of Peter Kalm's observations were critical of European expediency. He also "noted in passing that Catholic Canada was grateful to the Pope for classing the beaver as part fish so it could be eaten on fast days" (Kastner, 37).

Kalm often combined observations of nature with social commentary. Perceiving an early need for hunting laws, he declared sagely: "In spring the people will steal eggs, mothers and young indifferently, because no regulations are made to the contrary. And if any had been made, the spirit of freedom which prevails in the country would not suffer them to be obeyed" (p. 153). Such trends were most noticeable to foreign travelers and first-generation immigrants like Crevecoeur, who also lamented the detrimental effects of independent and anti-social behaviors.

Michel Guillaume Jean de Crèvecoeur, the "American farmer," as he became known after the publication of his *Letters from an American Farmer*, espoused a liberal agrarian philosophy akin to what we know today as bioregionalism. Also called the "colonial Thoreau," he was more interested in the pastoral dream of life within a decentralized society than in nature and ecology proper. In his *Letters* Crèvecoeur anticipated by many decades U.S. twentieth-century natural resource wars, when he noted that old-growth forests were not being logged sustainably: "Our ancient woods kept the earth moist and damp, and the sun could evaporate none of the waters contained within their shades. Who knows how far these effects may extend?" (Lyon, 35). Conservation biologists have set themselves the task of answering that question today. One effect of cutting the last of the nation's ancient forests, these biologists allege in trepidation, is to effect global warming and to hasten extinction rates.

Much of what we look for in nature writing today can be found aplenty in early American natural histories. Readers who are willing to take these antique writers on their own terms can discover fine and affective prose, modest scientific insights, and keen attention to issues of sustainability.

Selected Works and Further Reading

Bartram, William, *Travels Through North & South Carolina, Georgia, East & West Florida, the Cherokee Country, the Extensive Territories of the Muscogulges, or Creek Confederacy, and the Country of the Chactaws; Containing an Account of the Soil and Natural Productions of Those Regions, Together with Observations on the Manners of the Indians,* Philadelphia and London: James and Johnson, 1791; also published as *The Travels of William Bartram,* edited by Mark Van Doren, New York: Macy-Masius, 1928

Josselyn, John, *An Account of Two Voyages to New-England,* London: Giles Widdowes,

1674; also published as *John Josselyn, Colonial Traveler: A Critical Edition of 'Two Voyages to New-England'*, edited by Paul J. Lindholdt, Hanover, New Hampshire: University Press of New England, 1988

_____, *New-Englands Rarities Discovered,* London: Giles Widdowes, 1672; reprinted as *New-England's Rarities Discovered,* Chester, Connecticut: Applewood, 1991

Kalm, Peter, *Peter Kalm's Travels in North America: The English Version of 1770,* edited by Adolph B. Benson, New York: Dover, 1987

Kastner, Joseph, *A Species of Eternity,* New York: Knopf, 1977

Levett, Christopher, *A Voyage into New England Begun in 1623 and Ended in 1624,* London: William Iones, 1624; reprinted in *Maine in the Age of Discovery: Christopher Levett's Voyage, 1623–1624, and a Guide to Sources,* Portland: Maine Historical Society, 1988

Lyon, Thomas J., ed., *This Incomperable Lande: A Book of American Nature Writing,* Boston: Houghton Mifflin, 1989

Morison, Samuel Eliot, *The European Discovery of America: The Northern Voyages, A.D. 500–1600,* New York: Oxford University Press, 1971

Regis, Pamela, *Describing Early America: Bartram, Jefferson, Crèvecoeur, and the Rhetoric of Natural History,* DeKalb: Northern Illinois University Press, 1992

Smith, John, *The Complete Works of Captain John Smith (1580–1631),* 3 vols., edited by Philip L. Barbour, Chapel Hill: University of North Carolina Press, 1986

Stearns, Raymond Phineas, *Science in the British Colonies of America,* Urbana, Illinois, and London: University of Illinois Press, 1970

Thoreau, Henry David, *A Week on the Concord and Merrimack Rivers,* Boston: James Munroe, 1849; London: John Chapman, 1849

Wharton, Donald P., "John Josselyn (c. 1608–1675)," in *American Writers Before 1800: A Biographical and Critical Dictionary,* vol. G–P, edited by James Levernier and Douglas R. Wilmes, Westport, Connecticut, and London: Greenwood, 1983

Wilson, David Scofield, *In the Presence of Nature,* Amherst: University of Massachusetts Press, 1978

Wood, William, *New-England's Prospect,* London, 1634; also published as *Wood's New-England's Prospect,* Boston: Prince Society, 1865; reprinted, New York: Burt Franklin, 1967

Science and the Shaping of Nineteenth-Century American Nature Literature

Laura Dassow Walls

Nineteenth-century science both created and constrained the possibilities for nature literature, making their relationship an uneasy one throughout the century. This was the Age of Science, as intellectuals then and since have styled it, and the general fascination with the emerging and rapidly changing sciences of astronomy, geology, the "new" geography, biology, chemistry, physics, anthropology and psychology opened a space for those writers, whether scientific or popular, who could interpret science for a popular audience and explain what the dazzling advances meant for "modern" life. The dynamic and increasingly connective power of science seemed to promise that the whole of nature was at last coming under the grasp of the human mind, validating ancient intuitions of the holistic interconnections of the universe, and yet, much about science seemed alienating to those left behind by its increasingly esoteric character.

Romantic literary artists who were deeply engaged with science—Wordsworth, Coleridge, Carlyle, Ruskin; Emerson, Thoreau, Poe, Whitman–also found themselves registering fierce protests against it. William Wordsworth imagined the Poet and the Man of Science walking side by side, the Poet "carrying sensation into the midst of the objects of the Science itself" (pp. 606–607); yet in his poem "The Tables Turned," he famously objected that "Our meddling intellect/Mis-shapes the beauteous forms of things;/—We murder to dissect" (pp. 130–131). Henry David Thoreau found in science a way to love nature, yet lamented the "inhumanity of science" that "tempted" him to kill a rare snake to ascertain its species: "I feel that this is not the means of acquiring true knowledge" (*Journal*, VI:311). Walt Whitman wrote that the true use of poetry would be "to give ultimate

vivification" to science, and he stuffed his notebooks with science news—yet in a well-known poem he turned his back on the "charts and diagrams" of the "learned astronomer" to look up "in perfect silence at the stars" (pp. 564, 271).

Criticisms of science such as these have suggested to influential critics such as Alfred North Whitehead and M. H. Abrams that Romantic writers fundamentally rejected the mechanistic and soul-deadening rule of science in favor of the integrative power of organic nature, but this view tends to project twentieth-century divisions and fears onto the past. In fact, European and American Romantics drew on the power of the dynamic new sciences to correct and extend the philosophy of the Enlightenment. Among both educated and popular audiences, literary and scientific cultures interpenetrated each other well beyond midcentury, although disciplinary barriers arose between them as tensions mounted.

Indeed, it was the very hardening of the distinction between science and literature that gave rise to nature literature. For instance, William Bartram's *Travels* is read today both as a contribution to American science and as a landmark of early American nature writing. By midcentury, however, the professionalization of science was relegating the naturalist to amateur status, and increasing specialization was weakening the generalist's claim to scientific authority. In particular, the laboratory-based and reductionist biologist, intent on physiological processes rather than whole organisms, elbowed aside the field-based and holistic natural historian. In the United States, this contest was played out over the 15 years following the arrival in 1846 of the Swiss glaciologist and zoologist Louis Agassiz, who from his position at Harvard reorganized American science according to European professional standards. These were also, as it happened, Thoreau's most productive years. As opposed to Bartram, Thoreau has only recently begun to receive sustained attention as a contributor to American science.

The very withdrawal of the professional scientific specialist from the world of the educated lay reader opened a new space for writers like Thoreau and John Burroughs, who were willing to engage a broader audience through common experience of nature and to provide the wide-ranging philosophical syntheses that scientific precision discouraged. By century's end, journalism had largely taken over the task of translating science to a mass audience, but as late as the 1870s science writers were often themselves working scientists. Charles Lyell, Alexander von Humboldt, and Louis Agassiz all shared their vision with an educated public who attended their lectures, read their articles, and turned their books into scientific best sellers. And while amateur natural historians were screened out of the newly formed scientific societies, anyone from novice to professional could play a symbiotic role as field-collector and correspondent for the scientific centers. Louis Agassiz and Asa Gray at Harvard and Spencer F. Baird at the Smithsonian Institution all relied on an enormous network of specimen collectors who were often themselves competent local authorities in zoology and botany. Finally, a proliferation of textbooks and handbooks like those of Elmira Lincoln Phelps and Asa Gray encouraged the study of natural history, especially botany, as a genteel and healthful pursuit for young people and women. This trend may have "feminized" nature study, but it also granted women new access to fields traditionally reserved for men. By century's end, scientific amateurs had not disappeared at all, but rather, had formed their own local associations and networks, filling the social space opened, then abandoned, by science. In short, as science withdrew from common experience, both popular science and nature writing emerged to fill the gap between science and popular culture.

Throughout the nineteenth century, the scientific method was developed, regularized, instituted and coordinated through advanced university education (as at Harvard, Yale, and Johns Hopkins); through scientific societies like the American Association for the Advancement of Science (founded in 1847) and the National Academy of Sciences (established by an act of Congress in 1863); through aggressive government funding; and through ever-more-specialized science journals. The resulting methodological polarization resulted in a familiar distinction. Where stringent disciplinary training valued scientific distance and objectivity, the nature writer celebrated connections and sympathy with one's fellow creatures. Where the scientist presided over a sterile laboratory, the nature writer immersed himself in the raw experience of wild nature. Despite this dichotomy, tensions existed within science itself, and dilemmas shaped nineteenth-century nature literature in diverse and even conflicting ways.

Four interrelated issues suggest the mixed and complex legacy conferred by natural science to its popularizers and interpreters. First, was knowledge of nature best gained by a trained professional elite, or through democratic participation by all concerned? Second, was truth about nature best reached through a priori reasoning and tested under controlled laboratory conditions, or through lived experience in unpredictable wild nature? Third, was science a natural ally of religion, or did science need to distance itself from faith—and vice versa? Indeed, was nature really a morally meaningful and designed creation, or had natural systems somehow organized themselves in a contingent and alien universe? Finally, was "nature" separable from human purpose, making it available for spiritual aid and material exploitation? Or, were natural processes bound inextricably with human purpose, catching both in an ecological web that wove mind and nature together?

Each of these four issues takes up one facet of a single interrelated complex. Individual practitioners can seldom be neatly categorized. Consider for example the first question raised above: was science elitist or democratic? Louis Agassiz (who was lionized wherever he travelled) argued that scientific truth "must be woven into the common life of the world," and he attempted through his popular lectures, books, and articles to open his insights to the common reader. Yet he agonized that the steep "threshold" of scientific discipline cut science off from common understanding: "Nature does not open her sanctuary without exacting due penance from her votaries" (pp. 42, 297). Despite his ideals, his own science became a priesthood open only to the select few, those talented students, like Samuel H. Scudder and Nathaniel Shaler, who survived his strict training to mature into the next generation's scientific leaders. Thoreau was for a time one of Agassiz's specimen collectors, but he gained his own scientific training not in the scientific centers but through the informal networks that supported them: books and articles, lectures, personal contacts, and in Thoreau's case, association with the Boston Society of Natural History, which was then still an active research institution but would soon be converted to a museum and educational center. Thoreau attempted to weave science into common life by forging a natural science that would be participatory and radically democratic. In "The Succession of Forest Trees," Thoreau not only advanced a scientific theory but appealed directly to landowners, suggesting they learn scientific principles in order to better manage their forest land. Thoreau's experiment was cut off by his untimely death, but the direction he was taking can be seen in *Faith in a Seed,* which finally makes available some of his long-unpublished manuscripts.

Only two years after Thoreau's death, George Perkins Marsh independently offered a vision of participatory and democratic natural science quite similar to Thoreau's in his popular book *Man and Nature.* Yet Marsh did so not as a practicing scientist but as an avowed amateur, inviting his readers to become not mere observers of nature but activists who contributed to a common stock of knowledge. In contrast to Agassiz's "sanctuary," the study Marsh recommended "allows its votaries to occupy themselves with such broad and general views as are attainable by every person of culture," without years of special study. To wait for the "slow and sure progress of exact science," he argued, was to condemn the earth, "our dwelling," to certain destruction. Marsh urged his lay readers to contribute to an informed national policy of enlightened management of nature (pp. 17, 52). Of the three—Agassiz the professional scientist, Thoreau the passionate practitioner, Marsh the dedicated hobbyist—only Thoreau is typically called a "nature writer," yet all three saw themselves contributing both to the love and understanding of nature, and to the shared social and cultural enterprise of science. Despite his intentions, Agassiz's practice cut science off from the experience of the nature enthusiast, and Marsh's advocacy led not to literary contemplation but to government policy. It was Thoreau who tried to join all three.

Second, was scientific truth best reached through a priori reasoning or through experience in nature? For all his desire to bring science to the people, Agassiz also believed that knowledge was best reached through a priori reasoning and tested under highly controlled conditions. Part of his legacy was a pedagogy of intense observation of the isolated natural object with the goal of achieving the ultimate insight into the object's true nature, literally its "idea" in the mind of God—since to Agassiz, all objects in nature were thoughts of God materialized. This idea, associated with German *Naturphilosophie,* offered a powerfully integrative view that dominated pre-Darwinian biology. Emerson, for instance, had long been attracted to it through his reading in Goethe, Schelling, Oken, and others. Agassiz also brought to America certain European ideals: "Truth" was achieved through a strenuous discipline that demanded the student remove himself from the common confusions of daily life to that carefully prepared theater of knowledge, the scientific laboratory. Agassiz and his students were enormously influential in the development of institutionalized American science, which insists upon a rigorous and exclusive course of university-based training through which the student learns to see with the eye of the scientist.

What, then, of the observer who, by preference or circumstance, lacks access to such specialized and centralized training? Agassiz's own mentor, Alexander von Humboldt, promoted another model that was also tremendously influential in the United States. Living nature, like human history, said Humboldt, was too full of "accidental individualities" and "variations" for knowledge of it to be "based only on a rational foundation, that is to say, of being deduced from ideas alone" (*Cosmos,* I: 49–50). One must physically immerse oneself in wild nature, become an explorer who gathers observations, notes, and specimens from the widest possible field and who opens himself to all nature's influences. Only then, when drenched in lived experience, can one begin to speculate and connect what has been seen, smelled, and felt into the patterns that might indicate natural laws. Humboldt was a key figure in integrating the expanse of wild nature with the emerging cultural institutions of professional, middle-class, modern science. He helped organize the international networks of scientific societies, linking far-flung collectors with scientific centers, and his example served as a model for the exploring expeditions, such as those of John Charles Frémont and John Wesley Powell, that mapped the American West. Popular American culture saw him as the global explorer who connected a young American republic with the wider world, our "second Columbus" who had discovered America for science.

Humboldt's practice and writings advocated a proto-ecological view in which man and nature were fully integrated. In the preface to the first volume of *Cosmos,* Humboldt announced that the higher aim of his studies had been "to comprehend the phenomena of physical objects in their general connection, and to represent nature as one great whole, moved and animated by internal forces" (p. vii). Indeed, by century's end Humboldt's comprehensive science, dubbed the "new geography," had evolved into (and been wholly absorbed by) a new scientific specialty— "ecology." His own primary experience of wild nature had been gained during his five-year exploration of South and Central America, from 1799–1804, and translations of his popular books—*Personal Narrative, Views of Nature,* and *Cosmos*—captured the imaginations of Thoreau, John Muir, and the artist Frederic Church. They each read and idolized Humboldt, and each sought in his own way to recreate the Humboldtian venture in which the love of wild nature led first to the desire for knowledge, then to an ethic of freedom and an aesthetics of science expressed in literature and art.

Third, were science and religion allies or rivals? More than anyone else, Charles Darwin had absorbed and developed the rich scientific possibilities of Humboldt's theories. Ironically, Humboldt's optimistic view of natural forces in dynamic harmony was dismissed by the same generation that accepted Darwin, in a contest that at last definitively split science from religion. Darwin had inherited a tradition that saw nature as God's divine creation and science as the reasoned understanding of God's great design. This belief, "natural theology," which had animated Gilbert White's classic *Natural History of Selborne,* accounts for the young Darwin's otherwise puzzling decision to become a clergyman. Until the opportunity for global exploration turned him in a more secular direction, Darwin had planned to follow the honored Anglican tradition popularized by White. He would become the parson-naturalist whose explorations of parish nature showed forth the beauty and ingenuity of God's creation. Until well past midcentury, science was generally understood to be the ally, not the rival, of religion, particularly in America. In the decades before Darwin, most of America's scientists— Benjamin Silliman, Louis Agassiz, Asa Gray, Joseph Henry—were deeply religious men.

The certainty that nature is not only a carefully designed creation but also morally meaningful continues to underwrite the spiritual element in American nature writing; to the older Anglican tradition, American writers and intellectuals like Thomas Jefferson, the poet Philip Freneau, Ralph Waldo Emerson and Walt Whitman added the special conviction that America's Destiny was uniquely bound to the vast spiritual and material resources of the North American continent.

As the fate of Enlightenment deists like Tom Paine suggests, the post-Revolutionary United States had little use for European "materialists" who replaced God with Natural Law and excluded divine explanation from science. Although Humboldt's Enlightenment-based cosmic ecology had made no mention of God, his emphasis on natural harmony allowed his work to be taken up by natural theologians. Darwin's *Origin of Species* on the other hand gave tremendous authority to the suppressed view that natural systems had somehow organized themselves, and that human beings, instead of being embraced and reflected by a separate and morally correspondent universe, were the product of uncaring and amoral natural forces. The shock of Darwinian ideas finally succeeded in driving science and religion into separate spheres, with the result that science would govern natural knowledge and religion would guide spiritual belief. Here, too, in the gap opened by the hardening of barriers, nature writers like Muir and Burroughs would continue to insist on the continuities between humanity and nature, and on the regenerative possibilities of their differences. As Burroughs put it, "If Nature planned and invented as man does, she would attain to mere unity and simplicity. It is her blind, prodigal, haphazard methods that result in her endless diversity" (p. 99). Burroughs's new natural theology was both higher and wilder than the old:

This is the way of the Infinite—to multiply endlessly, to give a free rein to the physical forces and let them struggle with one another for the stable equilibrium to which they never, as a whole, attain; to give the same free rein to the organic forces and let their various forms struggle with one another for the unstable equilibrium which is the secret of their life. (p. 100)

Burroughs rides serenely above the turbulent waves of post-Darwinian science, mediating between scientific truth and human life by offering a spiritual interpretation of the Darwinian sublime.

Fourth, were man and nature separate, or bound together by the very process of perception? In *Nature,* a landmark for American nature literature as well as the popularization of science, Ralph Waldo Emerson erected a scale of uses for nature, from commodity to spirit, assuming in the traditional natural theological manner that nature was a separate creation of God intended for the use and service of Man. "Nature," wrote Emerson, "is thoroughly mediate. It is made to serve. . . . One after another, his victorious thought comes up with and reduces all things, until the world becomes, at last, only a realized will,—the double of the man" (p. 28). This vision of an ultimately humanized nature accords well with the nineteenth century's rapid technological development and widening scientific understanding: poetry, science, and technology were coordinate ways of accomplishing the Emersonian goal of taking nature into the mind. Yet Emerson resisted not only the utilitarian callousness of such a view, but the Cartesian divorce of mind and matter that underwrote it. The new science that so attracted Emerson celebrated not division and categorization but dynamic and organizing process, including the mysterious but powerful process of knowledge: "Nature is the incarnation of a thought, and turns to a thought again, as ice becomes water and gas. The world is mind precipitated, and the volatile essence is forever escaping again into the state of free thought" (p. 555). Nature as "fate" becomes the raw material of thought as "freedom," and the dynamic antagonism of these two poles generates the process of human life. Ultimately thought cannot be separated from material nature; the mind knows itself only as it penetrates matter, and fate and freedom slide into each other in what Emerson calls a "web of relation" in which the planet is not made, but "makes itself," and life is not directed from above, but is "self-directed" (pp. 961–962). Nineteenth-century science bore within it both fields of possibility: dualistic exploitation as well as ecological interrelation; deterministic law given from above as well as self-organizing freedom rising up from below.

Nature literature inherits both extremes and, as in Emerson, weaves contradictions together into a tangled complex not easily broken into neat analytical categories. And yet, it is possible to distinguish two complementary and internally coherent strategies for understanding nature, based on the preference given to rational or empirical modes of reasoning. Both modes believed in nature as one great, interconnected whole, although "rational" modes began by assuming, as did Coleridge, Emerson, and Agassiz, that the universe, as a designed whole, could be grasped through an a priori process of reason whereby the mind of man would mirror or follow the mind of God. Since such insight demanded either disciplinary training or intuitive genius, it was available only to a select few, and the truths those few disseminated to the many would show forth the harmony of the Creation with the purposes and laws of the Creator. Human beings were installed as rulers or stewards of a nature intended for human use— although as Marsh warned, our independent power over nature was a uniquely dangerous force, to be countered only by an increase in knowledge.

The "empirical" mode began by asserting, like Humboldt, Thoreau, and William James, that the universe was not designed but self-generating, hence infinite, open-ended and unpredictable. Such a universe could be known only through experience, not thought, hence detailed knowledge of nature in all its manifestations must be sought first-hand, and connected by the perceiving mind into patterns and hence into descriptive laws. All humankind participates in this on-going and all-inclusive endeavor, either by helping to gather and consolidate knowledge or by absorbing and applying knowledge for the advancement of humanity.

This is not to say that those who favor one mode cannot borrow from the other. A "rational holist" can, as Goethe and Agassiz did, work with delicately nuanced empirical details; an "empirical holist" can, as Asa Gray and John Muir did, be convinced that empirical details ultimately proclaim a divinely designed universe. From the two modes arise two quite different concepts of nature. From the "rational" mode arises the ideal of wilderness as a separate and primal domain from which all contaminating traces of humanity have been erased, an Edenic Garden preserving a pure, eternal, and harmonious Creation before the Fall, offering emotional and spiritual release from the confusion and pollution of human society. From the "empirical" mode arises the concept of ecology, wherein nature is not a bounded place but an ongoing creative process, not wilderness but Thoreau's regenerative "wildness"—a dynamic interaction of energy and matter that ultimately involves not only all the sciences but all the ways in which mind and nature interpenetrate and create each other. Both concepts are of tremendous importance to twentieth century thought. The wilderness ethic, which values "pristine and unspoiled" nature purified of human contamination, and an ecological ethic, which acknowledges the human as part of the living process of nature, both arose from longstanding but quite different scientific traditions that were contesting for dominance in the nineteenth century, and both derive emotional power from their redemptive aesthetics of nature.

It was the eruption of Darwin's ideas that shifted the balance. Natural scientists now tended to postulate not the loving, designed and morally significant universe of natural theology, but the indifferent, contingent and amoral universe of Darwinism. As the gap opened by scientific professionalization and specialization widened into an abyss, nature literature sought to heal the wound by reminding its readers of the many ways human beings are intimately connected with nature, a part of—not alienated from—the sublime whole. In a sense, the very success of nature writers such as John Muir, John Burroughs, and Ernest Thompson Seton marks the finality of the split between science and literature. Canonical literary artists, such as "naturalists" Stephen Crane, Frank Norris and Jack London, reiterated humanity's alienation from a harsh and indifferent nature. As Crane wrote in his autobiographical story, "The Open Boat":

When it occurs to a man that nature does not regard him as important, and that she feels she would not maim the universe by disposing of him, he at first wishes to throw bricks at the temple, and he hates deeply the fact that there are no bricks and no temples. . . . A high cold star on a winter's night is the word he feels that she says to him. Thereafter he knows the pathos of his situation. (pp. 84–85)

In contrast to Crane's existential dread, the unperturbed loyalty of the "naturalists" to the scientific viewpoint and to the older popular and didactic tradition still marks them as non-literary. At century's end, nature writers continued to provide links to and understandings with the sciences, but if this had seemed daring and innovative, even oppositional, in the age of Emerson and Thoreau, now in the twentieth century the nature writer's persistent attachment to natural science was dismissed as old-fashioned and nostalgic. Those who continued to believe in nature created a new and separate genre in effect, and only now is nature literature vying to be integrated, once again, into the literary canon.

Selected Works and Further Reading

Abrams, M. H., *The Mirror and the Lamp: Romantic Theory and the Critical Tradition,* New York: Oxford University Press, 1953; London: Oxford University Press, 1971

Agassiz, Louis, *Methods of Study in Natural History,* Boston: Ticknor and Fields, 1863

Bartram, William, *Travels Through North & South Carolina, Georgia, East & West Florida, the Cherokee Country, the Extensive Territories of the Muscogulges, or Creek Confederacy, and the Country of the Chactaws,* Philadelphia and London: James and Johnson, 1791; also published as *The Travels of William Bartram,* edited by Mark Van Doren, New York: Macy-Masius, 1928

Botting, Douglas, *Humboldt and the Cosmos,* New York: Harper & Row, 1973; London: Sphere, 1973

Bramwell, Anna, *Ecology in the 20th Century: A History,* New Haven, Connecticut: Yale University Press, 1989

Burroughs, John, *Accepting the Universe,* Boston: Houghton Mifflin, 1920; London: Constable, 1920

Coleridge, Samuel Taylor, *Hints Towards the Formation of a More Comprehensive Theory of Life,* London: John Churchill, 1848; also published in *Miscellanies, Aesthetic and Literary, to Which Is Added the Theory of Life,* edited by T. Ashe, London: George Bell, 1885

Crane, Stephen, *Tales of Adventure: The Works of Stephen Crane,* vol. 5, Charlottesville: University Press of Virginia, 1970

Daniels, George H., *Science in American Society: A Social History,* New York: Knopf, 1971

Darwin, Charles, *On the Origin of Species: A Facsimile of the First Edition,* edited by Ernst Mayr, Cambridge, Massachusetts: Harvard University Press, 1964

Emerson, Ralph Waldo, *The Early Lectures of Ralph Waldo Emerson,* vol. 1, edited by Stephen E. Whicher and Robert E. Spiller, Cambridge, Massachusetts: Harvard University Press, 1966

———, *Essays and Lectures,* New York: Library of America, 1983; Cambridge: Press Syndicate of the University of Cambridge, 1983

Frémont, John Charles, *Report of the Exploring*

Expedition to the Rocky Mountains in the Year 1842, and to Oregon and North California in the Years 1843–44, Washington, D.C.: Gales and Seaton, 1845; also published as *Narrative of the Exploring Expedition to the Rocky Mountains in the Year 1842, and to Oregon and North California in the Years 1843–44,* London: Wiley and Putnam, 1846

Goethe, Johann Wolfgang von, *Goethe's Botanical Writings,* translated by Bertha Mueller, Honolulu: University Press of Hawaii, 1952

Goldstein, Daniel, "'Yours for Science': The Smithsonian Institution's Correspondents and the Shape of Scientific Community in Nineteenth-Century America," *Isis* 85:4 (December 1994), pp. 572–599

Gray, Asa, *The Botanical Text-Book,* New York: Wiley & Putnam, 1842

Humboldt, Alexander von, *Aspects of Nature, in Different Lands and Different Climates; with Scientific Elucidations,* translated by Elizabeth Sabine, London: Longman, Brown, Green, and Longmans and J. Murray, 1849; reprinted, Philadelphia: Lea and Blanchard, 1983

————, *Cosmos, a Sketch of a Physical Description of the Universe,* 5 vols., translated by E. C. Otté et al., London: H. G. Bohn, 1848–1858; New York: Harper and Brothers, 1850–1870

————, *Personal Narrative of Travels to the Equinoctial Regions of the New Continent During the Years 1799–1804,* translated by Helen M. Williams, London: Longman, Hurst, Rees, Orme, & Brown, 1814; also published as *Personal Narrative,* translated by Jason Wilson, New York and London: Penguin, 1995

James, William, *A Pluralistic Universe,* New York: Longmans, Green, 1909; also published in *Writings 1902–1910,* New York: Literary Classics of the United States, 1987

Keeney, Elizabeth, *The Botanizers: Amateur Scientists in Nineteenth-Century America,* Chapel Hill: University of North Carolina Press, 1992

Lyell, Charles, *Principles of Geology,* London: J. Murray, 1830; reprinted, Chicago: University of Chicago Press, 1990

Marsh, George Perkins, *Man and Nature,* New York: Scribner's, 1864; reprinted, edited by David Lowenthal, Cambridge, Massachusetts: Belknap Press of Harvard University Press, 1965

Muir, John, *The Yosemite,* New York: Century, 1912; reprinted, Garden City, New York: Doubleday, 1962

Novak, Barbara, *Nature and Culture: American Landscape and Painting, 1825–1875,* New York: Oxford University Press, 1980; London: Thames and Hudson, 1980

Phelps, Elmira Lincoln, *Familiar Lectures on Botany,* New York: H. and F. J. Huntington, 1829

Powell, John Wesley, *The Exploration of the Colorado River and Its Canyons,* 1895; New York: Dover, 1961

Seton, Ernest Thompson, *The Arctic Prairies,* New York: Scribner's, 1911; London: Constable, 1912

Smith, Jonathan, *Fact and Feeling: Baconian Science and the Nineteenth-Century Literary Imagination,* Madison: University of Wisconsin Press, 1994

Thoreau, Henry David, *Faith in a Seed: The Dispersion of Seeds and Other Late Natural History Writings,* edited by Bradley P. Dean, Washington, D.C.: Island/Shearwater, 1993

————, *The Journal of Henry D. Thoreau,* 14 vols., edited by Bradford Torrey and Francis Allen, Boston: Houghton Mifflin, 1906; reprinted, 2 vols., New York: Dover, 1962

————, *The Natural History Essays,* edited by Robert Sattelmeyer, Salt Lake City, Utah: Peregrine Smith, 1980

Walls, Laura Dassow, *Seeing New Worlds: Henry David Thoreau and Nineteenth-Century Natural Science,* Madison: University of Wisconsin Press, 1995

————, "Textbooks and Texts from the Brooks: Inventing Scientific Authority in America," *American Quarterly* 49:1 (March 1997), pp. 1–25

White, Gilbert, *The Natural History of Selborne,* New York: Harper & Brothers, 1788; London: T. Bensley for B. White, 1789

Whitehead, Alfred North, *Science and the Modern World,* New York: New American Library, 1925; Cambridge: Cambridge University Press, 1926

Whitman, Walt, *Leaves of Grass: Comprehensive Reader's Edition,* edited by Harold W. Blodgett and Sculley Bradley, New York: New York University Press, 1965

Wordsworth, William, *William Wordsworth,* edited by Stephen Gill, New York and Oxford: Oxford University Press, 1984

Worster, Donald, *Nature's Economy,* San Francisco: Sierra Club, 1977; Cambridge: Cambridge University Press, 1985

Terror in the Heartland: Representations of the American Great Plains, 1930–1940

Brad Lookingbill

With dust-covered homesteads, barren countryside, dying livestock, and abject poverty, literary representations of the Great Plains unveiled terror in the heartland during the 1930s. Depression authors in the United States described an agrarian world turned upside down, or a spectacle of the environment that geographer Yi-Fu Tuan characterized in 1979 as a "landscape of fear." While actual climatic conditions generated reactions from various perspectives, fear of drought, famine, and cataclysm inspired a moment of environmental consciousness about the Great Plains.

Literature during the 1930s simulated an epic conflict with nature in the American Great Plains. Through literary interaction that offered a kind of mimesis, the dark imagery revealed a place not simply on the margins of space and time but at the core of a nation beset with crisis. If a previous generation of writings embellished an idealized frontier setting with formulaic offerings, then these Depression-era texts centered upon American dreams of progress with a modern sense of realism. The experiences portrayed by these texts reflected a time when Americans wherever they lived were experiencing a great deal of uncertainty. Within that context, a virtual desert in the Great Plains signified a landscape in desperate need of civilization to transform it, or so the literature of the 1930s claimed.

A variation upon this theme appeared in John Steinbeck's *The Grapes of Wrath*. The 1939 novel inspired the nation with its tale of a tenant-farm family, the Joads who, driven from their homes in Oklahoma, searched for a more promising land in California. With stark contrasts between the people and the land, the book accentuated human dignity and courage in struggle not only against nature—the droughts and the floods—but also against a mechanistic social

system of exploitation. The opening scene of the novel said that the land of the Great Plains was "crusted, a thin hard crust, and as the sky became pale, so the earth became pale, pink in the red country and white in the gray country." When the dust blew, the "dawn came, but no day," for in "the morning the dust hung like fog," and the "sun was as red as ripe new blood" (pp. 1–7). Civilization seemed to turn to dust, according to Steinbeck's metaphor about human alienation from nature, which left the land worthless and a people impoverished. The novel contrasted the desiccated heartland with epiphanies of oranges and grapes in California, and thus a chosen people began the exodus across the deserts toward their last best hope in the far West.

Frederick Manfred, while working as a reporter for the *Minneapolis Journal* in 1937, wrote the first draft of a novel entitled *The Golden Bowl*, which appeared in book form in 1944. The novel's setting in South Dakota revealed barns, silos, and the land itself "deserted," while a "gray dust films everything, even the moving things." Rotting bodies of dead animals laid facing empty water tanks, while skeletons of farms remained in "a dusty slumber." Whatever the accuracy of such graphic descriptions, Manfred's novel uncovered a spirited endeavor to achieve identity and put down roots when nature inflicted such punishing droughts and violent storms. The Thors, a resilient family who held stubbornly to the dying earth, refused to abandon their home. With "the great earth dying" while "the drouth wrinkles the skin of the old creature," wrote Manfred, "a desert drifts where once a home had been tucked away in a valley" (pp. 194–96). Into this apparent wasteland wanders Manfred's protagonist, Maury Grant, who embraces the redemption offered by the small homestead–the icon of American values–in order to transform the desert into a golden bowl.

Another novel written during the Great Depression underscored similar themes by placing the story of resistance within the context of the late nineteenth century. In 1936, John Ise published a semibiographical account of Kansas homesteaders, *Sod and Stubble*, that told a tale of the remarkable heroism of an immigrant family that battled for 20 years against drought, grasshoppers, prairie fires, dust storms, and depression. The imagery was familiar to Great Depression readers, especially when Ise described "roaring winds, swaying cottonwood trees, flying sand, rattling shutters and creaking doors and screens." While discouraged settlers trekked out of the drought-stricken country like the "retreat of the defeated legion," the homestead endured, "standing out on a treeless and fenceless expanse of waving grass—bare and lonely." The extreme environment of the past paralleled the one of the present; the pioneer encountered "a world rapidly shedding the wildness, the raw, savage loneliness of the uninhabited prairie, and taking on the habiliments of settled and orderly civilization" (pp. 2, 126, 258–259, 325). Even the courageous people of the old frontier faded from this landscape, but Ise limned an environment that empowered Americans not by the bounties but by the hardships of the place.

Lawrence Svobida, a western Kansas farmer turned author, doubted that the Great Plains environment offered any redeeming qualities in his published autobiography, *An Empire of Dust*. During the 1930s, according to Svobida, "the death knell of the Plains was sounded and the birth of the Great American Desert was inaugurated with the introduction and rapid improvement of power farming." Although Svobida's wheat farm failed to survive the dust storms and adverse climate, he resolved at first to save his land and business at all cost. The Great Plains farmer worked incessantly to gain a harvest, or to keep the land from blowing; but no effort proved effective while one was reaching "the depths of utter despair" (pp. 7–8, 80–81). Consider an encounter between a service station attendant and a tourist in Liberal, Kansas, which Svobida recalled:

The tourist stated with emphasis: "Why, this country is nothing but a desert!" The filling station attendant, resentful of this remark coming on the heels of the visitor's impressions of Death Valley, retorted: "You went through worse desert back there in California." "Yes, that is true enough," the tourist agreed with a smile, "but there aren't any fools out there trying to farm it!" (pp. 95–96)

While Svobida's autobiography underscored human frustration and failure, his first-hand account left the region as an empire of dust, that is, a land where the farmer resisted the fate of nature.

Poet Archibald MacLeish took a similar view in an extended essay in *Fortune* magazine in 1935 on what he called "the living and the dead land." The literary piece described the scene of "dead quarter sections with the hardpan clean as weathered lime and the four-room flimsy ranch houses two feet deep in sand." The grasslands of North America were dead, according to the poet, producing a place of human and environmental devastation with "stock tanks brimming full but not with water, trees dead and a raven's nest of fence wire in the branches—these the dust did." MacLeish opined no philosophic difference existed between "the fate of Antioch in Syria and the possible fate of Garden City in Kansas," since humankind has "learned, over the intervening years, to destroy his planet with an amazingly increased dispatch" (pp. 58–67, 190). Such lyrical details evoked the specter of a vast wasteland unable to support life in the Plains, a theme MacLeish expounded upon again in a pictorial poem, *Land of the Free*. For him, the dust storms and drought illustrated the nightmare of the Great Depression—the erosion of the American dream.

Conflating economic trauma and natural calamities, writer Sherwood Anderson offered a modern version of the nineteenth-century travel genre in a 1935 book, *Puzzled America*. Anderson set the scene with sand-and-dust drifts against the fences, trees killed by the drought, great patches of the trees' bark dropped off, and so on. In the midst of this fatal environment, "man's eternal struggle and so often tragic war with nature—his struggle to command and control—. . . is all there, to be seen, in the raw." Yet such a battle was not fought by individuals alone, since Anderson observed an assault by nature against the strength of entire communities. Indeed, the writer imagined the "worship, in the midst of the drought," of a "sun-burned people, men and women," who arrived from distant farmhouses, past their own fields "where the corn is shriveled away to nothingness, the fields their own hands have plowed, planted, and tended only to see the crops all burn away to a dry ash of dust." Anderson described boards of the church cracked from the dry heat, the paint on the boards fried in the hot winds, while the dust of the fields sifted in through the cracks. With a strategy to encourage empathy, the author lamented the suffering of undaunted people who prayed for rain but swallowed sand (pp. 203–217).

Walter Davenport's travel narratives in Collier's found famine, violence, futility, and insanity among the Plains men and women he encountered. In one 1937 account Davenport appraised the Great Plains to be "a desert in which nothing can survive." Observing the worst drought in the nation's history, he lamented "the wretched, naked desert the winds had left behind; the ghost villages, once the silvery ballyhoo of real estate racketeers; the abandoned farmhouses, buried to the eaves in eddying dust; the corroded tops of farm machinery, deserted in what had been fields and now buried in sand with only levers and rods protruding from their graves, like pitiful arms thrust upward, beckoning for help." Along the journey from Amarillo to Denver, the Great Plains environment was nothing if not the stage for drifted houses, abandoned farms, and government subsidy farmers (pp. 12–13, 73–77). Davenport's article received much criticism from the boosters of the Great Plains, and his sensational details crystallized the public anxieties about the decline and fall of American civilization.

With hyperbole, periodicals represented a place remote from the personal experience of urban readers as a symbol for national ills. During 1934, Meridel Le Sueur related in the monthly American Mercury a car drive "through the sizzling countryside." In the heart of the Great Plains, the daunted visitor discovered "something terrifying about this visible sign of disaster." Although the pall of dust "went into your nostrils" making it impossible to breathe, "the smell of hunger" that pervaded the heartland evoked terror. Most of all, said Le Sueur, the "whole country cracks and rumbles and cries out in its terrible leanness, stripped with exploitation and terror—and as sign and symbol, bones—bones showing naked and spiritless, showing decay and crisis and a terrific warning, bare and lean in Mid-America" (pp. 53–56). Why, asked the Mercury's H. L. Mencken, did those "unhappy herds of Ishmaelites flock into the desert," dragging across the Plains

their "helpless wives and children?" The Baltimore writer answered that the environment there "lay too far buried in primeval chaos for civilization ever to overtake it," and so the residents regressed "backward toward the stage of the first pioneers of desert nomads just come to the grasslands" (pp. 400–408). Indeed, Mencken warned that these farmers who homesteaded a wasteland appeared on their way back to the Stone Age.

Ernie Pyle, the most famous traveling reporter of the period, arrived in the Great Plains during the worst years of crisis. Pyle's serials, which appeared in various Washington, D.C., and national newspapers, described a regional calamity of unparalleled dimensions. In one dispatch he observed "the saddest land I have ever seen," which at the time seemed "a mild form of desert," or a "withering land of misery." As Pyle observed the environmental conditions from the Dakotas to Kansas, he, like others, lamented the social consequences of the drought scorching the Plains, which left behind nothing at all but "gray raw earth and a few farm houses and barns, sticking up from the dark gray sea like white cattle skeletons on the desert." With no end in sight, the desert threatened to overcome a people confronted with "the horror of a life started in emptiness, knowing only struggle, and ending in despair" (pp. 113–126). While these dispatches attempted to document a human story of hard luck, they offered a tragic scene that, in effect, cultivated a grim landscape.

Nevertheless, the tale of victimization by nature underscored an American triumph, or so certain writers proclaimed. In American Magazine during 1940, Don Eddy summarized no less than an epic struggle against "a savage enemy" in the "gaunt, gray wilderness," where farmers were "plowing new farms from the desert." The farmers of the Great Plains, whom Eddy called "men of God," possessed "a divine conviction of their ordination to subdue the wilderness." Eddy believed that the untamed environment provided the challenge that would allow the rediscovery of American strength "stirring deep in the dust of the Great Plains" (pp. 54–55, 89–92).

With a similar call to heroism, Harold Ward in Travel Magazine explored what "the maps once called 'The Great American Desert'" and found that federal government programs had begun "to transform another fragment of desert into a real homestead" (pp. 24–25, 48). With the fading of dust, drought, and depression, a sterile place in America's heartland yielded an oasis when transformed by the sturdy hands of an exceptional people.

In 1931, a few years before the impact of the winds of adversity became a national concern, Walter Prescott Webb published a benchmark description of the history of the people who settled the region. In his *The Great Plains,* Webb identified the distinguishing climatic characteristic of the physiographic environment—the source of regional exceptionalism—as "deficiency in the most essential climatic element—water." In these arid spaces, the Texas scholar explained, the flat, treeless landscape and sub-humid climate marked an institutional fault, where the "ways of travel, the weapons, the method of tilling the soil, the plows and other agricultural implements, and even the laws themselves were modified." Webb's historical narrative identified the Great Plains environment as a worthy antagonist of civilization, one that challenged national expansion and frontier settlement during the nineteenth century. Indeed, this land cultivated in people "a mysticism and a spiritual quality which have found expression in the lofty and simple teachings of Jesus and Mohammed," both of whom, Webb concluded, lived in "a region so like the Great Plains that the similarities have often been pointed out." Webb hoped that the terrain and its weather might contribute "much to a civilization that thus far is notorious for its devotion to material things" (pp. 140–225, 485–515). In other words, the text subscribed to the notion that physiographical aridity marked a land ultimately developing a superior civilization.

Paul Sears, who later became professor of conservation at Yale University, authored the most significant ecological literature of the decade. *Deserts on the March,* published in 1935, attempted to explain how mechanical invention and exuberant vitality challenged "the gentle grip wherein nature holds and controls the forces that serve when restrained, destroy when unleashed" (p. 12). Portions of the Great Plains, argued Sears, have become desert since the "girdle of green about the inland deserts has been forced to give way and the desert itself literally allowed to expand" (p. 112). Sears believed that natural equilibrium "must be restored and protected to an extent not yet dreamed of, not for reasons of sentiment," but because conservation offered "sources of certain return under all conditions" ("Floods," 9). Otherwise, America was "headed at full speed on a path that has brought destruction to others as well-meaning and as energetic as ourselves" in a region once known as the "Great American Desert" ("Death," 440). Indeed, the ecologist set the stage for conflict:

The plains are the classic ground for last stands. . . . Perhaps we shall understand this situation better if we look into another contest—agelong—which has been set in this theater . . . between grassland and desert. The scanty, irregular rainfall of the plains, the high, drying winds and the rapid fluctuation between blistering heat and paralyzing cold make this region the climatic borderland of the desert. Only by dint of countless centuries of effort is anything better than desert vegetation present. ("O, Bury Me Not," 7–10)

By employing the term desert as a warning about impending doom in the grasslands, ecologists such as Sears uncovered in their writing a powerful metaphor for civilization's mythical place outside of nature.

The popular economist Stuart Chase, who authored in 1936 the persuasive book, *Rich Land, Poor Land,* understood the foundations of civilization in economic terms. Since "dust is no respecter of property," Chase expounded, a single storm "will remove several inches of soil, first the loam and fine sand, then the coarse sand." Chase predicted that the wind in the Plains may take all the soil down to hardpan and "so create true desert conditions," which, of course, would undermine the sustainability of an agriculture base. The struggle against such a calamity, argued Chase, "must be collective, not individual" and would require a "new deal"—a phrase he coined (pp. 100–117). He believed that in order for the nation to progress and the poor lands to be transformed into rich ones, the restoration of the Great Plains must be linked to economic need.

That need inspired action when director of the Soil Conservation Service, Hugh Hammond Bennett, initiated a national crusade for soil-erosion control. Bennett, who earned the title "Messiah of the Soil," lamented the environmental waste in his magnum opus, *Soil Conservation.* According to Bennett, level plains country, which once supported lush stands of native short grasses, was now becoming a new kind of wilderness "with shifting sands left in the wake of dust storms." Whereas history represented "a record of man's efforts to wrest the land from nature," Bennett opined that "too frequently man's conquest has been disastrous."

His text recalled foreboding precedents: "Recent archeological evidence indicated that erosion doubtless played a large part in undermining and obliterating many ancient civilizations in Africa, in Near Asia, and in Central Asia" (pp.1–15, 727–731). Soil conservation offered salvation for civilization, however, and federal expansion of the Soil Conservation Service eliminated the potential deserts that overthrew regimes of the past.

Henry Wallace, secretary of agriculture under President Franklin D. Roosevelt, explained that Great Plains farmers, despite all of their virtues, remained incapable of solving such problems without national support. In *New Frontiers* Wallace called upon Americans to begin "putting our lands in order," a need that the chaos rampant across the Great Plains manifested. The nation produced a waste "even worse than the Chinese," and so "it will be necessary to get more and more of our people thinking seriously about the continuously balanced harmonious relationship which I call the Land of Tomorrow." Wallace compared this kind of transformation to a search for "the promised land," when an earlier people—"hardened by travels in the wilderness"—abandoned a vague, nomadic wandering and adapted themselves in some measure to the "commercial features of the Canaanite civilization" (pp. 239–248, 260–271). The crisis of the new frontier, at least according to the Secretary of Agriculture, included tribulation along the journey to a promised land.

Not surprisingly, publications for the New Deal accentuated triumph of the modern state over the irrationalities of nature, a theme particularly evident in *The Future of the Great Plains*. Authored by the Great Plains Committee, this widely read text feared that the current environmental calamity meant that "the steady progress which we have come to look for in American communities was beginning to reverse itself." In the Great Plains of the future (i.e., the one reconstructed with the aid of the federal government) the "land may bloom again if man once more makes his peace with Nature" and avoids the potential to "lapse into desert" (pp.1–3, 16). While suggesting a range of mechanisms for land-resource planning, the report summarized the clear and present danger in the Great Plains:

Today we see foothills shorn of timber, deeply gullied, useless or rapidly losing their fertile soil under unwise cultivation; the fertile earth itself drifts with the wind in sand hills and in dust clouds; where once grass was rank, cattle nibble it to the scorched roots; the water of streams and the ground waters too often irrigate poor land, leaving the richer thirsty; men struggle vainly for a living on too few acres; the plough ignores Nature's "Keep Off" signs; communities, for all the courage of their people, fall into decay, with poor schools, shabby houses, the sad cycle of tax sales, relief, aimless migrations. (p. 14)

If such dark imagery evoked a sense of chaos, then the power of the state promised to create order across the land.

During the 1930s, a wide range of literature illuminated the human fight against extreme temperatures, soil erosion, agricultural maladjustment, and howling winds in the nation's interior. While the environmental crisis exposed the nation to a range of anxieties, the emotive core recalled the assumption that a barren, uncivilized place—a landscape of fear—signified a challenge for American civilization. Literary descriptions of the climatic vicissitudes brought the wasteland into the experiences of readers outside of the Great Plains, thereby underscoring a modern sense about nature and, perhaps, an appreciation for good fortunes elsewhere. By mediating the catastrophe of a distant rural locale, these texts through the imagined forms and forces of nature produced a spectacle for an urban society confronting unemployment and insecurity.

Indeed, the representations of the American Great Plains placed a powerful landscape in national memory. Whatever the strategy of the individual author, depression literature abandoned a frontier countryside of open spaces, inviting vistas, or fertile gardens. Through the interplay of modern culture and the environment, the new iconography of a desert wilderness signified terror in the heartland, that place of tribulation encountered by a people and nation. The fictional and nonfictional worlds with chaotic black blizzards, devastated farmscapes, and great American heroism represented a point of departure beyond the tragedy of the Great Depression.

Selected Works and Further Reading

Anderson, Sherwood, *Puzzled America,* New York and London: Scribner's, 1935
Bennett, Hugh Hammond, *Soil Conservation,* New York and London: McGraw-Hill, 1939

Bonnifield, Mathew Paul, *The Dust Bowl: Men, Dirt, and Depression,* Albuquerque: University of New Mexico Press, 1979

Bowden, Martyn, "The Great American Desert in the American Mind," in *Geographies of the Mind,* edited by David Lowenthal and Martyn Bowden, New York: Oxford University Press, 1976

Chase, Stuart, "Disaster Rides the Plains," *American Magazine* 124 (September 1937), pp. 46 ff

———, *Rich Land, Poor Land,* New York: McGraw-Hill, 1936

———, "When the Crop Lands Go," *Harper's Magazine* 173 (August 1936), pp. 225–233

Davenport, Walter, "How Dry We Are," *Collier's* 87 (April 11, 1931), pp. 25 ff

———, "Land Where Our Children Die," *Collier's* 100 (September 18, 1937), pp. 12 ff

Eddy, Don, "Up from the Dust," *American Magazine* 129 (April 1940), pp. 54 ff

Hearn, Charles, *The American Dream in the Great Depression,* Westport, Connecticut: Greenwood, 1977

Hudson, Lois, *The Bones of Plenty,* Boston: Little, Brown, 1936

———, *Reapers of the Dust,* Boston: Little, Brown, 1957

Hurt, R. Douglas, *The Dust Bowl: An Agricultural and Social History,* Chicago: Nelson-Hall, 1981

Ise, John, *Sod and Stubble,* New York: Wilson-Erickson, 1936

Lange, Dorothea, and Paul Taylor, *An American Exodus: A Record of Human Erosion,* New York: Reynal and Hitchcock, 1939

Le Sueur, Meridel, "Cows and Horses are Hungry," *American Mercury* 33 (September 1934), pp. 53–56

Lookingbill, Brad, *Desert Myth: The Great Plains Environment and Depression America* (Ph.D. diss., University of Toledo), 1995

MacLeish, Archibald, "Grasslands," *Fortune* 12 (November 1935), pp. 58 ff

———, *Land of the Free,* New York: Harcourt, Brace, 1938; also published as *Land of the Free–U.S.A.,* London: Boriswood, 1938

Manfred, Frederick, *The Golden Bowl,* New York: Grosset & Dunlap, 1944; reprinted with an introduction by John R. Milton, Albuquerque: University of New Mexico Press, 1976

Mencken, H. L., "The Dole for Bogus Farmers," *American Mercury* 39 (December 1936), pp. 400–408

Pyle, Ernie, *Ernie's America: The Best of Ernie Pyle's 1930s Travel Dispatches,* edited by David Nichols, New York: Random House, 1989

———, *Home Country,* New York: William Sloane, 1940

Riney-Kehrberg, Pamela, *Rooted in Dust: Surviving Drought and Depression in Southwestern Kansas,* Lawrence: University Press of Kansas, 1994

Schama, Simon, *Landscape and Memory,* New York: Knopf, 1995; London: HarperCollins, 1995

Sears, Paul, "Death from the Soil," *American Mercury* 42 (December 1937), pp. 440–447

———, *Deserts on the March,* Norman: University of Oklahoma Press, 1935; London: Routledge & Kegan Paul, 1949

———, "Floods and Dust Storms," *Science* 83 (March 27, 1936), p. 9

———, "O, Bury Me Not; or, The Bison Avenged," *New Republic* 90 (May 12, 1937), pp. 7–10

Steinbeck, John, *The Grapes of Wrath,* New York: Viking, 1939; London: William Heinemann, 1939

Svobida, Lawrence, *An Empire of Dust,* Caldwell, Idaho: Caxton, 1940

Tuan, Yi-fu, *Landscapes of Fear,* New York: Pantheon, 1979; Oxford: Blackwell, 1980

United States Great Plains Committee (Morris L. Cooke, et al.), *The Future of the Great Plains,* Washington, D.C.: Government Printing Office, 1936

Wallace, Henry, *New Frontiers,* New York: Reynal and Hitchcock, 1934

Ward, Harold, "Conquering the Dust Bowl," *Travel Magazine* 74 (February 1940), pp. 24 ff

Webb, Walter P., *The Great Plains,* Boston: Ginn, 1931; reprinted, Lincoln: University of Nebraska Press, 1981

Worster, Donald, *Dust Bowl: The Southern Plains in the 1930s,* New York: Oxford University Press, 1979; Oxford: Oxford University Press, 1982

Wrobel, David, *The End of American Exceptionalism: Frontier Anxiety from the Old West to the New Deal,* Lawrence: University Press of Kansas, 1993

"The World Is the Greatest Thing in the World": The Objectivists' "Immanent" Pastoral[1]

Judith Schwartz

Pastoral poetry and Objectivist poetry might at first appear unrelated. While pastoral poetry has been traditionally defined as depicting idealized settings, Objectivist practice insists on the poet's "sincere" representation of the physical environment (Zukofsky, 20). And while pastoral poetry is notorious for its formulaic constructions, Objectivist poets experiment boldly with forms. Yet, Objectivist poetry displays surprising links with the classical pastoral of Theocritus and Virgil, while also engaging many other pastoral poems through quotation, parody and allusion. In addition, scholars have identified a number of complex issues in pastoral poetry, and Objectivist poetry explores many of these same issues.[2] The link between pastoral and Objectivist poetry is a fundamental one, and a study of that link may offer a valuable contribution to our understanding of the literary depiction of nature and the nature of poetics.[3] Our focus here will be on one issue related to Objectivist and pastoral poetry: that of contact between human artifice and nature as an issue of poetics as well as a poetic subject.[4]

Objectivist and pastoral poetry share a unique resistance to definition. Indeed, the term pastoral has become the subject of vigorous academic debate, with some critics seeking to define a pastoral essence, and others perceiving the term's multiplicity and choosing to highlight a particular pastoral issue. In the case of Objectivist poetry, a marked resistance to definition is built into the tradition—Objectivist poets rejected any attempt to describe a something called "Objectivism."[5] Defining these terms thus requires oversimplification, but is, I believe, necessary for an understanding of their relationship and their importance to ecocriticism.

Objectivist poets are linked by a grounding not only in modernist experimentation, but also in what Louis Zukofsky labeled "sincerity," "particularity," "musical" quality, and attempts to "think . . . with things as they exist" (*Prepositions,* 20). The Objectivists emphasize concrete details—the poem as object—rather than narrative or metaphor, and their work is notable for its brevity, serial presentation, remarkable use of sound, and metonymic juxtaposition. Zukofsky felt that poetry should "approach" music, and a fairly abstract, musical effect can be found in many Objectivist poems (*Prepositions,* 26).

Surprisingly, many critics have used similar language to describe the ancient Greek and Roman pastoral poetry. In the most recent edition of *The Princeton Encyclopedia of Poetry and Poetics,* C. John Herrington elaborates on Theocritus's *Idylls,* explaining the importance to Theocritus of "brevity," "musicality," and "precise detail" (p. 487). Pastoral theorist David Halperin, in explaining Frederic Schiller's classic notion of pastoral as "naive" poetry, suggests that "naiveté in art is the direct, spontaneous, and simple portrayal of nature *as it is,* without an intervening moral consciousness or elaborate aesthetic convention" (p. 43, my emphasis). And, in his classic book *The Green Cabinet,* Thomas Rosenmeyer compares pastoral form to "that of a suite or a similar musical form of successive units," declaring that "in Theocritus and Virgil the net effect of the structure . . . runs counter to Aristotle's recommendations" (p. 77).

Thus, in addition to exploration of issues surrounding the natural as opposed to the artificial, or human-made, Objectivist and pastoral poetry have in common a tendency toward serial construction, an emphasis on sound, and an investigation as well as manifestation of the commonplace. What emerges is an experimental tradition of poetic engagement with nature and culture as problematic, oppositional concepts. The Objectivists reconceive the pastoral—redefining and revising many pastoral elements—as part of a tradition of doing so.

Pastoral poetry and Objectivist poetry both explore the potentially destructive contact between human artifice and an idealized nature, but Objectivist work engages this issue within a syntactical vision of poetic contact. William Carlos Williams stressed that poetry should have "edges," or points of contact with the world. George Oppen defined poetry as "shipwrecks" or "site[s] where philosophical, ethical, political, and egocentric constructs . . . run upon the rocks of the actual" (Gadzinski, 1). Oppen thus proposes that poetry is fundamentally about a kind of destructive contact between human technology and nature. His image suggests that such destructive contact is necessary to engender creativity—there must be a collision of nature and human aptitude in order for there to be poetry.

When Oppen manifests his vision of a shipwreck metonymically in his poetry, a powerful reconception of the relationship between nature and culture emerges. In "Party on Shipboard," for example, an enormous ship "chips" an underwater rock as it docks in a harbor–an example of destructive contact between human technology and nature. Oppen juxtaposes this image with that of a tree, thus creating a scenario of contact between the two. The tree becomes "live wood," whose "fiber" moves through the "Branches and leaves / In the air" (p. 10). The phrase "live wood" signifies the tree's sap, whose upward movement suggests vigorous life. But the phrase is also oxymoronic in that "wood" is the name given to the tree as commodity. Oppen thus juxtaposes the technological, slightly destructive image of the ship with an ambiguous representation of a tree, embodying the ambivalence with which Western society perceives nature, and the uncertain status of trees and plants in a society that finds no inherent value in trees, but values a tree's potential only as lucrative commodity or beautiful object.

A number of Objectivist poems explore the ambivalent status of nonhuman nature in Western society. Lorine Niedecker's "Your Erudition" investigates the interaction of a kind of natural knowledge with "urbane," sophisticated ways of "knowing." In the poem, academic knowledge, weeds, and wild flowers become vital bedfellows, and the line between rural native and sophisticated student becomes blurred:

> Your erudition
> the elegant flower
> of which
>
> my blue chicory
> at scrub end
> of campus ditch
>
> illuminates (p. 180)

Niedecker juxtaposes sophisticated study—"the elegant flower" of "erudition"—with uncultivated nature, suggesting that the wild flowers in a ditch on a university campus enrich—"illuminate"—knowledge from books, and pitting natural folk experience against urban "booklearning." Niedecker also addresses another pastoral tradition: that of the university student lounging in the countryside. The speaker is not the traditional, urbane student extolling the virtues of idyllic nature, but one who is aligned with the flowers and the land, the modern equivalent of the pastoral shepherd. By insisting that the chicory "illuminates" academic study—with the word itself unpunctuated and thrown into relief by occupying its own line—Niedecker insists on the value of folk knowledge and on the inherent value of nature.

As Raymond Williams has revealed, pastoral poetry has long been concerned with a sharp, dichotomous comparison between the city and the country. Theocritus and Virgil both created images of simple life touched and corrupted by contact with urban society. Many of the their poems offer an image of contact in the form of an urban sophistication entering a simple rural setting, but a number of Objectivist poems manifest and reconceive this issue. In Charles Reznikoff's "Machine Age," for example, the poem's urban setting simultaneously engages and reverses the typical pastoral scenario. Here is the poem in its entirety:

> The girls outshout the machines
> and she strains for their words, blushing.
> Soon she, too, will speak their speech glibly.
> (p. 29)

Whereas traditional pastoral depicts an urban person's encounter with a pastoral space, Reznikoff's poem depicts a rural girl entering the coarse environment of an urban factory. Reznikoff juxtaposes the word "blushing," with its connotations of sexual innocence and traditional femininity, with his prediction of future corruption in the form of altered language. The girl then moves from a natural state—the physical response of blushing—to an unnatural linguistic form of communication involving shouting and straining, one that notably lacks the sophistication and artfulness of some urban language. It is clear that such a movement represents a form of corruption.

Many Objectivist poems explore pastoral themes in urban settings; most significant, for our purposes, is the engagement of these poems with the traditional pastoral *locus amoenus*, or ideal place. The concept of the *locus amoenus* is vital to pastoral, and also to ecocriticism, since it sheds light on traditional, Western literary perspectives on place. The pastoral *locus amoenus* is typically a rural or primitive locale, quite removed from the complexity, and much of the pain, of urban life. But Zukofsky's notions of "sincerity" and "thinking with things as they exist" engage this representation of idealized spaces, inspiring Objectivists' attempts to represent actual places without idealization, avoiding traditional pastoral's reification, and reconceiving the *locus amoenus*.

In section five of "History," for example, William Carlos Williams explores the possibility of a *locus amoenus* in the city. Notably, both the poem and the pastoral moment begin at "five o'clock," drawing a clear line between the mundane work day and the evening's festive activities. In what is probably an attempt at seduction (another pastoral motif), the speaker leads his partner to a city park, hoping to move beyond the humdrum reality of labor. The speaker describes the surroundings as an exotic pastoral oasis (with a "yellow and purple dusk," foreign inhabitants, and a glistening river) while simultaneously questioning its authenticity, asking "Will that do?" Williams renders it ironic and thus undermines his own, idealized constructions, calling attention not only to our desire for an idealized place, but also the imaginary nature of such an ideal.

A number of other Objectivist poems engage the pastoral *locus amoenus*. The second of Louis Zukofsky's *29 Poems* presents a glittering, urban space of neon, a "Bacchae / among electric lights" (*Complete*, 22). Clearly contrasting this urban space to a rural locale, Zukofsky describes a place where people stumble over "pavement" rather than "underbrush," and escape "not upon hills" but over subway

"stairs." The effect is one of exhilaration, but also uncertainty, for the people are running from the beautiful but crowded city square.

In "Red Hook: December," George Oppen creates a more bittersweet urban scene, a neighborhood street awash with multicolored Christmas lights. Here "one can be at peace" only briefly, and only "with wealth / the Shining wealth" (p. 124). Oppen acknowledges the appeal of this space when transformed at Christmas time, but his ambivalence dominates; this *locus amoenus* is not natural, and is possible only through human exploitation of nature and the subsequent creation of wealth.

Red Hook at Christmas is not unlike the Manhattan locale inhabited by the "grandchild of the shopping streets," in Oppen's "Pedestrian," which consists of a "mesh of wires" and huge buildings. In this poem, as in Reznikoff's "Machine Age," urban corruption appears in the form of a young female who lives permanently—to the dismay of her ancestors—among the lights of "wealth." Here the array of city lights is blinding and embittering, for the lights outshine anything natural or useful. Indeed, the girl is "surrounded" by "buyer's light, the store lights / Brighter than the lighthouses, brighter than moonrise" (p. 64).

Charles Altieri includes the Objectivists among those whom he calls "Immanentist," or poets in whose work "poetic creation is conceived more as the discovery and disclosure of numinous relationships within nature than as the creation of containing and structuring forms" (p. 16). According to Altieri, Immanentist poets seek meaning within and among the found objects of the world, attempting to avoid the imposition of prefabricated order. Altieri sheds light on the Objectivist practice's inherent rendering problematic of the dichotomy between nature and culture, for the Immanentists attempt to illuminate that which is already present in nature. In Objectivist practice, "writing occurs which is the detail, not the mirage, of seeing. . . . Shapes suggest themselves, and the mind senses and receives awareness" (Zukofsky, *Prepositions*, 20). The Objectivists attempt to minimize the artificial by interacting with, rather than dominating, nature's *materials*.

The thirty-seventh poem of Zukofsky's *Anew* engages this problem, offering a remarkable *scene* from nature, with careful emphasis on the role of the viewer in constructing that scene. Zukofsky presents a catalog of natural beauty without idealizing and with an emphasis on the human act of perceiving. Thus, while celebrating the scene's beauty, Zukofsky simultaneously establishes human perception as an important, if not the only, source for such beauty. Autumn's beauty—in the form of seeds and clouds—appears "where you look." The damp earth is described in terms of the way it "gives" beneath one's foot. Indeed, the poem ends with a vivid image of movement through rocks toward the ocean, where "You will see what soft blue is / . . . . Such eyes as you have" (*Prepositions*, 97). Recognizing the role of human perception in establishing nature's beauty, Zukofsky deconstructs his own pastoral image by locating its source in human sight.

In "An Objective," Zukofsky goes so far as to locate creativity in the body—in the "veins and capillaries," with "nature" as the "creator" of poetry (*Prepositions*, 23). By insisting on a physical source of creativity, Zukofsky blurs the line between humans and nature. If nature is the source of artifice, an artistic endeavor becomes a quite natural act, rather than a source of exploitation and human imposition on the world.

William Carlos Williams's "The Farmer" further demonstrates this point. According to pastoral theorist William Empson, the farmer is "in contact with nature"; he has "the wit of the unconscious, he can speak the truth because he has nothing to lose" (Alpers, 40–41). But Williams affords the farmer a different status. The farmer becomes an "artist figure," deep in thought, surveying his "blank fields," with his crops already in place "in his head." As in Zukofsky's poem above, Williams creates an image while simultaneously calling attention to its artificial nature (p. 186). In addition, Williams integrates artist and farmer, suggesting that the manipulation of nature for crops is not unlike the artist's act of manipulation, and that the artist's work is not, or should not be, an activity of the mind, wholly removed from the actual world.

These ideas also impact greatly upon the Objectivist representation of place, for this reconception of the artist's role with regard to nature coincides with a reconception of the positioning of humans and nature. In the autobiographical "Paean to Place," Lorine Niedecker constructs a metonymic list of her surroundings, referring to birds and fish, as well as "flood / Water lily mud / My life" (p. 215). In a clearly Objectivist move that is quite removed from the Romantic stance, which has the poet overlooking nature, Niedecker positions herself beneath the elements of the natural world, beneath even the "flood" and "mud." The poem reveals Niedecker's Objectivist tendency to question and diminish human dominance over nature, for she constructs an egalitarian relationship with nature.

Pastoral theorist Annabel Patterson points out that, because of its multiplicity, pastoral has had a "destabilizing" effect on the cultures that have read it closely (p. 9). The Objectivists recognize this multiplicity and present to us a revised pastoral. This multiple quality is of fundamental importance in negotiating the dualistic concept of nature and other in American culture; its recognition moves readers closer to a disabling of the nature-culture dichotomy, and closer, perhaps, to eliminating the human impulse to dominate nature.

Notes

1. The first quotation is George Oppen's, taken from a selection of Oppen's Daybook published in *The Iowa Review* (*see* Young). The term "immanent" is Charles Altieri's.

2. Among these issues are relationships between the rural and the urban, contrasts between sophisticated knowledge and rural sensibility, issues of private property, the messianic potential of the artist, the questioning of dualistic views of art and nature, and the tension between technological advancement and rustic simplicity. For further discussion of pastoral theory, *see* Alpers, Poggioli, Ettin, Haber, Halperin, Patterson, and Rosenmeyer.

3. A survey of Objectivist work reveals a number of environmental images. In 1920, Charles Reznikoff wrote, "They have built red factories along Lake Michigan, / and the purple refuse coils like congers in the green depths" (p. 29). In "Arizona," Louis Zukofsky remarks that the state's famous red "rocks" are "higher than the oil wells," but unable to negate them (*Collected*, 45). And in the 1960s, Lorine Niedecker wrote "Wintergreen Ridge," describing the activism of rural people who gathered, successfully, to block "bulldozers" (p. 184). Thus, although Niedecker is the only Objectivist who could correctly be labeled a nature poet, environmental awareness and concern for nature emerge throughout the movement, even among those who were immersed in cities.

4. The Objectivists include Lorine Niedecker, George Oppen, Charles Reznikoff, William Carlos Williams, Louis Zukofsky, Carl Rakosi and

the Englishman Basil Bunting. I have omitted discussion of a number of poems with clear references to ancient pastoral, such as Williams's pastorals and Oppen's "Eclogue," preferring to use the space here to explore less overt pastoral instances. In addition, I have opted against following a chronological discussion of the poems, choosing those with marked Objectivist elements, whether or not the poems were composed during a defined Objectivist period.

5. Louis Zukofsky eventually denied the validity of his founding definition of Objectivist practice, insisting that no poetic movement existed (Quartermain, 1).

Selected Works and Further Reading

Alpers, Paul, *The Singer of the 'Eclogues': A Study of Virgilian Pastoral,* Berkeley, California, and London: University of California Press, 1979

——, *What is Pastoral?,* Chicago: University of Chicago Press, 1996; London: University of Chicago Press, 1997

Altieri, Charles, *Enlarging the Temple: New Directions in American Poetry During the 1960s,* Lewisburg, Pennsylvania: Bucknell University Press, 1979; London: Associated University Presses, 1980

Buell, Lawrence, *The Environmental Imagination: Thoreau, Nature Writing, and the Formation of American Culture,* Cambridge, Massachusetts: Belknap Press of Harvard University Press, 1995

Ettin, Andrew, *Literature and the Pastoral,* New Haven, Connecticut: Yale University Press, 1984

Gadzinski, Eric, "Oppen: Open," Philadelphia: Temple University, Department of English, unpublished photocopy

Haber, Judith, *Pastoral and the Poetics of Self-Contradiction: Theocritus to Marvell,* New York and Cambridge: Cambridge University Press, 1994

Halperin, David, *Before Pastoral: Theocritus and the Ancient Tradition of Bucolic Poetry,* New Haven, Connecticut: Yale University Press, 1983

Herrington, C. John, "Greek Poetry," in *The New Princeton Encyclopedia of Poetry and Poetics,* edited by T. V. F. Brogan and Alex Preminger, Princeton, New Jersey: Princeton University Press, 1993

Love, Glen A., "*Et in Arcadia Ego*: Pastoral Theory Meets Ecocriticism," *Western American Literature* 27:3 (November 1992), pp. 195–207

Niedecker, Lorine, *From this Condensery: The Complete Writing of Lorine Niedecker,* edited by Robert J. Bertholf, Highlands, North Carolina: Jargon Society, 1985

Oppen, George, *The Collected Poems of George Oppen,* New York: New Directions, 1975

Patterson, Annabel, *Pastoral and Ideology: Virgil to Valéry,* Berkeley: University of California Press, 1987; Oxford: Clarendon, 1988

Poggioli, Renato, *The Oaten Flute: Essays on Pastoral Poetry and the Pastoral Ideal,* Cambridge, Massachusetts: Harvard University Press, 1975

Quartermain, Peter, *Disjunctive Poetics: From Gertrude Stein and Louis Zukofsky to Susan Howe,* New York and Cambridge: Cambridge University Press, 1992

Reznikoff, Charles, *The Complete Poems of Charles Reznikoff: Volume 1: Poems 1918–1936,* edited by Seamus Cooney, Santa Barbara, California: Black Sparrow, 1976

Rosenmeyer, Thomas G., *The Green Cabinet: Theocritus and the European Pastoral Lyric,* Berkeley: University of California Press, 1969

Williams, William Carlos, *The Collected Poems of William Carlos Williams: Volume 1, 1909–1939,* edited by A. Walton Litz and Christopher MacGowan, New York: New Directions, 1986; London: Paladin, 1991

Young, Dennis, ed., "Selections from George Oppen's Daybook," *The Iowa Review* 18:3 (Fall 1988), pp. 1–17

Zukofsky, Louis, *Complete Short Poetry,* Baltimore, Maryland: Johns Hopkins University Press, 1991

——, *Prepositions: The Collected Critical Essays of Louis Zukofsky,* Berkeley: University of California Press, 1967; London: Rapp and Carroll, 1967

Literary Environmentalists in the Generation Before Silent Spring, 1945–1960

Richard Harmond and G. A. Cevasco

The seemingly sudden appearance of a powerful environmental movement in the years just prior to 1970 is often traced to the publication of Rachel Carson's *Silent Spring* in 1962. Upon reflection, however, it would seem unlikely that one book by itself—as persuasive as its message certainly was—could have launched the modern environmental movement. Rather, it can be demonstrated that among the various factors behind the emergence of environmentalism were several generations of nature writers conveying information about, as well as affection and concern for, the natural world. As Wallace Stegner aptly remarked, "there was an environmental movement before Earth Day, a long, slow revolution in values of which contemporary environmentalism is a consequence and a continuation." This observation applies with particular force to the generation of literary environmentalists before *Silent Spring*, certain writers in the period 1945–60 who helped to recruit and to shape intellectually the environmental constituency that appeared after 1960.

Among the most noteworthy of these concerned writers are five authors who can be labelled "observers" and five who can be termed "critics." The former—Sally Carrighar, Louis J. Halle, Rachel Carson, Archie Carr and Edward Way Teale—were intent on informing their readers of the beauty and fascination of the natural world. The critics—William Vogt, Fairfield Osborn, Aldo Leopold, Joseph Wood Krutch and Marston Bates—went beyond the traditional, descriptive natural history essay to alert their audience to the threat posed by human activity to the natural world, and indeed to humanity itself.

The Observers

Sally Carrighar was a pianist, dancer, and a film production assistant before she found her true calling as a nature writer. After years of nature study, she developed her own rather unusual approach: portraying the lives of wild creatures from their point of view.

One Day at Teton Marsh is typical. Here she tells the stories of the insects, birds and mammals that inhabit the area in and around a marsh in Jackson Hole, Wyoming. At bottom, she depicts their lives as a stark struggle for survival. Thus, a mosquito having fed on the blood of a moose is in turn consumed by a dragonfly. A leech sucks the life out of a snail, only to be swallowed by a blue heron (which shortly before had narrowly missed making a meal of a frog). And while a trout manages to elude the talons of an osprey, a minx feeds greedily on a garter snake and a merganser. Carrighar also shows how many of the creatures of Teton Marsh depend for their survival on a pond that resulted from the instinctual dam-building of a family of beavers.

Occasionally, the hunted successfully ward off their attacker. Thus, in her book *Icebound Summer*, she deftly describes how a humpback whale, using his flippers and flukes as weapons, drives off a pack of killer whales intent on tearing him to pieces.

Although *One Day at Teton Marsh*, as well as *One Day at Beetle Rock* and *Icebound Summer,* contain a certain amount of anthropomorphism, Carrighar convincingly captures the experiences of the creatures she describes. As a *New York Times* reviewer observed, she "combines drama with the scientific precision that results from years of patient study and watching." It would be difficult to read her finely crafted, factually based books, and not have a clearer understanding of wild nature.

Like Sally Carrighar, Louis J. Halle did not set out to become an environmentalist. After his graduation from Harvard in 1932, he went to work for International Railways of Central America, El Salvador and Guatemala. Two years later he accepted an editorial position with Longmans, Green & Company in New York. In 1937, he returned to Harvard for graduate work, after which he joined the Department of State and served as a staff member for Inter-American Affairs.

During these early and formative professional years, Halle wrote *Transcaribbean, Birds Against Men,* and *Rivers of Ruin.* Of his three books, *Birds Against Men* gave special evidence of his keen interest in nature. Although Halle was not trained in ornithology, his work was so well-received that it was chosen for the John Burroughs Award in 1941. Having been so honored, it would seem that Halle would concentrate on nature writing, but instead in 1946 he accepted a position as Assistant Chief of Special Inter-American Affairs at the State Department. The following year he was appointed a Special Assistant for Pan-American Corporation Affairs. In 1950 he became an adviser in the Bureau of Inter-American Affairs and then shortly after a member of its policy planning staff. Despite all the time his positions demanded, he never abandoned his interest in birds and external nature.

In 1947, to follow up on the success of *Birds Against Men,* Halle wrote another ornithological study, *Spring in Washington.* This book contains detailed observations on the coming of spring in the nation's capital, on its bird life in particular, and on various manifestations of nature in the city, along its shores, creeks and marshes. With considerable delight, he expatiates on avian life, trees, the wind and weather, recording the natural emergence from the chill of winter through the beauty of spring into the splendor of summer.

In 1954, Halle was appointed to a research professorship in the Woodrow Wilson Department of Foreign Affairs at the University of Virginia, having earned such a position because of his many publications and expertise in international affairs. While at the University of Virginia, interest in world politics and the possibility of atomic destruction inclined him to write one of his most eloquent, enthusiastic, and provocative books, *Choice for Survival.* On one level, the work deals with the dangers of nuclear annihilation; on another, with what effect the vexing problem of advanced weaponry would have on the environment. Rebutting the prophets of doom, Halle argues in a calm fashion that humanity has a future.

Halle's reputation was such that he was invited to join the faculty of the Graduate Institute of International Studies, Geneva; he taught there between 1956 and 1977 and was then appointed professor emeritus. During the period of his tenure at the Institute, Halle wrote one of his most important books, *Dream and Reality: Aspects of American Foreign Policy,* a diplomatic history meant to illuminate the general nature of international relations and American foreign-policy problems.

A foremost expert in international affairs, Halle also serves as an excellent example of an individual not trained in the sciences whose avocation became nature and the environment. Most of his 16 books explore social and political themes, but his *Birds Against Men* and *Spring in Washington* encouraged his many readers to reflect upon the importance of ornithology. Just as coal miners used to send birds down into their mines to monitor the quality of the air, so, too, did Halle demonstrate that a concentration upon birdlife is one way to evaluate the environment.

What ornithology was to Louis Halle, ecology and marine biology were to Rachel Carson. Early in the 1930s, after graduating magna cum laude from Pennsylvania College for Women (later Chatham College) and earning a graduate scholarship at Johns Hopkins University, Carson accepted a teaching position in zoology at the University of Maryland. She also began writing feature articles for the *Baltimore Sunday Sun.* In 1936, she joined the U.S. Bureau of Fisheries, the first woman selected to fill a scientific position at the Bureau. She rose quickly in responsibility to staff biologist and editor of the agency's publications.

Although Carson conducted research at the Bureau in marine biology, her principal contributions were as a writer. At regular intervals her essays appeared in *Nature Magazine, Yale Review, New Yorker, Life,* and *Science Digest.* Her first book, *Under the Sea Wind,* received excellent reviews, but was not a publishing success. In 1951, her next book, *The Sea Around Us,* had an extraordinary reception. A consequence of her research and a study of geological evidence, the volume explores the processes that formed the earth, the moon, and the oceans; it also focuses on the part played by the sun, the rotation of the earth and the wind on the making of tides and their importance in regulating climate. That the book remained on the *New York Times* best seller list for 86 weeks, 39 of them in first place, is not surprising in the light of the rave reviews *The Sea Around Us* received. Hundreds of newspapers, periodicals, and journals printed panegyrics in its honor.

The Sea Around Us won the National Book Award for non-fiction and the John Burroughs Medal. In 1953, the book was made into a film that won an Oscar for the best full-length documentary. Honor after honor followed, and Carson became the recipient of more fame and glory than that bestowed upon any other nature writer, including medals from the National Audubon Society and the American Geographical Society. In 1980, she was awarded, posthumously, the Presidential Medal of Honor.

Carson, in short, was a talented, well-trained scientist who possessed the sensitivity and insights of a poet. She readily admitted to having an emotional response to nature. She said that the more she learned and wrote, the more she felt what she dubbed her "sense of wonder." With her literary skill she awoke the United States to the quality of life on our planet. All that she wrote, moreover, was eagerly received by countless readers who, because of her published works, were being alerted to environmental matters.

Carson's most celebrated work, *Silent Spring,* was a logical outcome of her dedication to nature study. The book had its origin in a question a woman put to her, a woman fearful the world would be made "lifeless" through the overuse of pesticides. *Silent Spring* was Carson's answer. Her best selling volume encouraged legislation regulating pesticides and intensified concerns for the environment.

While Archie Carr never achieved the fame of Rachel Carson, in his own way he was an important forerunner of contemporary environmentalism. Following completion of his doctorate in biology from the University of Florida in 1937, he was offered a six-year fellowship at Harvard's Museum of Comparative Zoology. Upon his return to Florida in 1943, he held a number of positions as educator and research biologist with a special interest in turtles. He taught at the University of Florida and the Escuela Agricola

Panamerica, Honduras. He also served as research adviser to the faculty at the University of Costa Rica, and technical director and executive vice president of the Caribbean Conservation Corporation.

In 1935, Carr published his monumental *Handbook of Turtles,* in which he not only classified some 79 species but also dispelled folklore and myths about the horny-plated reptiles. He then undertook numerous expeditions to Africa, Panama, Costa Rica, Trinidad, Brazil, Madagascar, and several other countries to continue his study of the breeding grounds, nutritional and migratory habits of turtles. About the same time, he played a leading role in establishment of the "Brotherhood of the Green Turtle," which later changed its name to the Caribbean Conservation Corporation. He also involved the Office of Naval Research in studying the navigatory prowess of turtles and was provided with the use of Military Air Transport for the relocation of certain breeds when this was thought necessary or advisable. His efforts in conservation were responsible for the stabilization and eventual increase in turtle population throughout the world.

In addition to his *Handbook of Turtles,* Carr wrote nine other books, the most significant of which are *High Jungles and Low, The Windward Road, Amphibians And Freshwater Fishes of Florida,* and *So Excellent a Fish: A Natural History of Sea Turtles.* Extensive research he undertook at Tortuguero and Ascension Island earned him the appellation "Turtle Man." The name also took into account the systematic and organized standards for research he conducted in various parts of the globe, as well as his efforts to educate students and anyone else he could interest in his specialized field of study.

Although Carr's efforts were rather narrowly circumscribed and somewhat emotionally limited, he was still acknowledged for his dedication and prolific writings. Among the dozens of awards bestowed upon him are Officer in the Netherlands Order of the Golden Ark, the David Girard Elliot Medal, and the Edward H. Browning Citation for outstanding achievements in conservation, a John Burroughs Medal for exemplary nature writing, a gold medal from the World Wildlife Fund, and special recognition from the New York Zoological Society. In 1979, the Florida State Museum established the Archie F. Carr Medal in his memory, and the University of Florida established an Archie F. Carr postdoctoral fellowship in 1983.

In addition to having a profound respect for the natural world, Sally Carrighar, Louis Halle, Rachel Carson, and Archie Carr were all excellent writers. Their many books, and the messages they carried, reached thousands upon thousands of readers. So, too, did the books of the naturalist and photographer Edwin Way Teale. In his very popular works, Teale's commentary and photographs seamlessly complement each other.

Teale had a happy childhood on his grandfather's farm in Indiana, where he early developed an interest in prairie insects and photography. When he was 12 he determined to become a well-known writer and famous photographer. Believing that he required a more distinguished name, he began to call himself Edwin *Way* Teale, rather than Edwin *Alfred* Teale. This early sense of gravitas increased as he grew older and is evident in the 30 books that were to follow through the years.

After graduation from Earlham College, he became an instructor in public speaking at Friends University, Wichita, Kansas. In 1925, he became an editorial assistant to Frank Crane. During the two years he worked with Crane, Teale developed a personal spirituality that demanded a reverence for all nature. In 1928, he accepted a position as a staff feature writer for *Popular Science Monthly*, which he held for the next 13 years. Not only did he produce numerous articles for *Popular Science Monthly*, but he also completed a book, *Grassroots Jungle*. Essentially, the work contains his keen observations of nature combined with his personal philosophical musings. In 1943, he published his autobiography, *Dune Boy: The Early Years of a Naturalist,* which is memorable for its details about how he taught himself to observe prairie insects and to master photography.

Blessed with a facile pen, Teale continued to turn out book after book to the satisfaction of his growing number of readers. Among his more successful titles are *The Lost Woods* and *Days Without Time*. He also edited Hudson's *Green Mansions*, Thoreau's *Walden, The Insect World of Henri Fabre,* and *The Wilderness of John Muir*. Through his own personal books and the editing of some of the greatest nature writers, Teale convinced Americans that they had a personal stake in the preservation of ecological zones. He continually emphasized that nature provides meaning for those perceptive enough to recognize its beauty, and he convinced his readers that it was to everyone's advantage to support national parks and the conservation movement.

Teale's work serves as a bridge between the more austere Thoreau and Muir, and the younger environmentally inclined naturalists who followed. To his credit, Teale was also the first to use the building of America's transcontinental road system and consequent access to national parks to convey to readers an amiable armchair view of our country's natural beauty. That he succeeded is obvious from the critical acclaim his work received. In 1966, for example, he was awarded a Pulitzer Prize for his *Wandering Through Winter*, the final volume in his "American Season" series for which he had already written *North With Spring, Autumn Across America,* and *Journey into Summer*.

Wandering Through Winter brought to a close a 15-year project and 100,000 mile trek from the Atlantic to the Pacific. In his "American Season" series Teale reflected on motor travel in an intentionally folksy, plain style of narration in an attempt to teach a whole generation how to experience and respond to nature.

The Critics

A century and a half after the publication of Thomas Malthus's famous *Essay on Population*, the debate on overpopulation, which subsided during World War II, was revived by William Vogt's *Road To Survival* and Fairfield Osborn's *Our Plundered Planet*.

William Vogt, a graduate of Bard College, a self-taught ornithologist, and former editor of the Audubon Society's Magazine *Bird-Lore*, had studied the population problem in Latin America during the 1940s. His reflections and conclusions on that problem were presented to the American public in his eloquent and informed *Road To Survival*. After surveying societies around the globe, Vogt observed that humanity had generally violated the laws governing its relationship with the environment by excessive breeding and abuse of the land, and suffered the consequences.

"The road to the survival of civilized life," Vogt emphasized, required that humankind reduce its waste of the earth's resources through such means as reforestation, controlled grazing and improved farming methods. He also believed that eventually there would have to be a curb to population growth. "Excessive breeding," he maintained, would result in an "ecological trap" for humankind (p. 284). He forcefully expounded such views in his last book, *People! Challenge To Survival,* which, like *Road To Survival,* is especially concerned with the worldwide population explosion and its consequences.

Like William Vogt, Fairfield Osborn was not a trained scientist, although he did grow up in a scientifically oriented household. His father, Henry Fairfield Osborn, founded the departments of biology at Columbia University and vertebrate paleontology at the American Museum of Natural History; and was a founder and first president of the Bronx Zoo and later served as president of the American Museum of Natural History. As a child Fairfield Osborn developed his own collection of animals and went with his father on museum expeditions for fossil vertebrates to the western United States and Egypt.

Despite this background, Osborn, after graduating from Princeton College, followed a business career. But in 1935 he quit the banking firm he had joined in order to pursue his passion for animals. He became secretary of the New York Zoological Society, and five years later in 1940 was named president of that organization. His interest in conservation led him to write an editorial in 1945 for the New York Zoological Society's Bulletin, *Animal Kingdom,* wherein he sounded the alarm about the depletion of forests, soils and water resources. He expanded his analysis in his book, *Our Plundered Planet.*

Our Plundered Planet is a soberly written book that warned that if humankind did not halt its assault on the land, modern civilization could not survive. "Another century like the last and civilization will be facing its final crisis," wrote Osborn (p. 37). Misuse of the land is an old story in human history, as Osborn explained, but the environmental assault had been greatly exacerbated in modern times by an expanding population. In countries overcrowded and underfed, like India and China, Osborn pointed out, the forests were cut down—leading to floods, soil erosion and polluted waterways— and the cleared land was overfarmed—ending in sharply reduced yields. The result was a grim cycle of increasing population, depleted land, famine and mass starvation.

Even in more favored lands, such as Australia, New Zealand, Argentina and the United States, Osborn found that all too often the forests had been razed, the land abused and wildlife destroyed. (Fourteen years before the publication of Rachel Carson's *Silent Spring,* Osborn expressed concern in his book about the possible long-term negative results on wildlife of using DDT.) Osborn concluded *Our Plundered Planet* not by offering specific remedies but with a starkly simple mandate: "Man must recognize the necessity of cooperating with nature" (p. 201).

William Vogt's *Road To Survival* and Fairfield Osborn's *Our Plundered Planet* were praised by most critics (while being damned by a few), and Vogt's book, a Book-of-the-Month-Club selection, was the best-selling book on conservation before *Silent Spring.* As Curt Meine has observed in *Aldo Leopold: His Life and Work,* both books "opened people's eyes." Still, it was Aldo Leopold's *A Sand County Almanac*—one of what Meine tellingly describes as "this triumvirate of premonitory postwar books" (p. 525)— that ultimately proved most influential.

Aldo Leopold, a professional forester, and from 1933 until his death in 1948 a professor of wildlife management at the University of Wisconsin, completed his most important written work, *A Sand County Almanac* a few months before he died. It was published in 1949.

A Sand County Almanac is divided into three sections. In the first, Leopold follows the changes that take place on his Wisconsin farm during the course of a year. Section II contains Leopold's personal experiences over a period of 40 years in various parts of the United States, and Manitoba. In this section he also reveals his life-long love of hunting that he traces to a "hereditary hunting instinct."

Sections I and II are engaging and informative, and show Leopold as an observant naturalist and a pleasing stylist, at once witty, modest and accessible. In Section III, though, Leopold gets down to the business at hand, and presents his concept of a "land ethic."

Behind Leopold's environmental perspective was his belief that land was not "a commodity belonging to us," but rather "a community to which we belong." And from this belief stemmed his "land ethic." Where traditional ethics had come to embrace all people, the "land ethic," in Leopold's words, "enlarges the boundaries of the community to include soils, waters, plants, and animals, or collectively the land." Under the constraints of such an ethic—which Leopold warned was an "ecological necessity"—questions about the use of the land would be judged, wrote Leopold, "in terms of what is ethically and aesthetically right, as well as what is economically expedient." And, he continued, a "thing is right when it tends to preserve the integrity, stability, and beauty of the biotic community," and "wrong when it tends otherwise" (pp. 239, 262).

A Sand County Almanac, which presented a new definition of conservation in the idea of a "land ethic," has been referred to as the bible of the environmental movement of the 1960s and 1970s. But it is well to recall that the book was critically acclaimed at the time of its publication, and its ideas soon filtered into the thought processes of other naturalists, among them Joseph Wood Krutch (who, in fact, reviewed the book for the *Nation* in December 1949).

From 1924 to 1951, Joseph Wood Krutch, was drama critic for *The Nation,* and a respected professor of dramatic literature at Columbia University. But a respiratory ailment prompted him to retire from *The Nation* as well as his teaching position at Columbia, and to move to Tuscon, Arizona. As he explained his exodus from New York, "I came [West] for three reasons: to get away from New York and its crowds, to get air I could breathe, and for the natural beauty of the desert and its wildlife" (*New York Times* May 23, 1970).

About the time of his arrival in Tuscon, Krutch's book, *The Desert Year,* was published. Based on vacation trips he had taken earlier to the Southwest, the book combines botanical and biological observations with philosophical ruminations. In part, Krutch wanted to learn how the desert flora and fauna were able to survive in a region of such scant rainfall. As he discovered, there were several strategies. Some plants, like the mesquite, sank very deep roots in the soil to locate the moisture they needed, while certain animals, especially rodents, survived without ever drinking water. *The Desert Year,* which won the prestigious John Burroughs Medal, also contains Krutch's reflections on what the desert had taught him about humankind. Among the lessons he learned—or relearned—wrote Krutch, was that "life is everywhere precarious, man everywhere small" (p. 270).

In his next volume, *The Voice of the Desert,* Krutch continued his observations and reflections on the Southwest. But toward the end of the book, Krutch the sensitive observer donned the robes of the concerned critic. In a chapter titled "Conservation Is Not Enough," Krutch argued that through waste, greed and self-centeredness, humankind had seriously upset the balance of nature, "and so endangered its own survival." Unless "we share this terrestrial globe with creatures other than ourselves," Krutch insisted, "we shall not be able to live on it for long" (p. 195).

Krutch had accomplished a rather unusual change from drama critic and English professor to environmentalist and amateur naturalist. And therein also was the source of much of his appeal. "His peculiar strength," as the botanist and ecologist Paul B. Sears of Yale pointed out, "lies in the fact that with his literary craftsmanship and great respect for scientific accuracy, he has been able to exert a wide influence over the country" (Stephen Fox, 232).

Krutch wrote in the tradition of Thoreau, John Muir and Leopold. Indeed, in *The Voice of the Desert* he acknowledged his substantial debt to Leopold. Marston Bates, too, drew on the work–among other authors–of Leopold, and of William Vogt and Fairfield Osborn.

Marston Bates, a biologist, was on the staff of the Rockefeller Foundation (1937–50), and professor of zoology at the University of Michigan (1952–70). His study of mosquito biology for the Rockefeller Foundation took him to Albania and Egypt and then to Colombia as director of a yellow-fever laboratory.

Due to the discovery by Walter Reed early in this century that the Aedes aegypte mosquito carried yellow fever, scientists grew confident that they could eliminate the virus. But yellow fever did not disappear, and there were serious outbreaks in Latin America during the 1930s. What Bates and his fellow scientists found in their research was that yellow fever was carried by different types of mosquitoes. This discovery opened the way to new efforts to control, if not eliminate, the virus. Bates elaborated on this finding in his important scientific study, *The Natural History of Mosquitoes,* published in 1949.

A few years later, Bates published an article urging his fellow scientists to write not solely to inform each other, but also to reach a larger readership. He followed his own advice in his book, *The Prevalence of People.* As the title suggests, the book is concerned with the "population problem." Bates affirmed his "considerate debt" to Vogt and Osborn, but his approach was his own. Perhaps not surprisingly for a biologist, he expounded on such subjects as human reproduction, longevity, infectious disease, and eugenics. In the end, however, Bates came to the same conclusion as Vogt and Osborn. Recalling how humans had sharply reduced the "hazards of existence," thus permitting the population to grow five-fold between 1750 and 1950, Bates stated simply that "if the human species is to survive there must also be a change in the birth rate" (p. 246).

Bates published his most influential and popular volume, *The Forest and the Sea*, in 1960. This book, a non-technical textbook in ecology, dealt with the broad sweep of living organisms–from plants and insects to animals and humans–and their environments. No careful reader of this lively and informed volume could avoid gaining a deeper sense of the complex inter-relationship among living things, and further, of humankind's impact on the environment. To protect that environment, Bates, citing Aldo Leopold, declared that "we need to develop an ecological conscience." "We remain important, you and I and all mankind," explained Bates, but "so is the butterfly—not because it is good for food or good for making medicine or bad because it eats our orange trees," but rather because it is "in itself as part of the economy of nature" (pp. 251–254). In a very real sense, *The Forest and the Sea* summed up much of the thinking of the previous generation of literary environmentalists.

Conclusion

The era from 1945 to 1960 is often seen as representing a low point in the history of the conservation movement. Such a view slights the work of literary environmentalists completed during this 15-year period. Among some of the most effective "observers" were the nature writers Sally Carrighar, Louis J. Halle, Rachel Carson, Archie Carr, and Edwin Way Teale. Through the sensitive and affectionate treatment of nature in their books, they helped to create a public opinion receptive to such measures as the Wilderness Act (1964) and the National Wildlife Refuge System Act (1966). Among the foremost "critics," William Vogt, Fairfield Osborn, and Marston Bates opened up the post–World War II debate on the population problem—a debate sustained in the 1960s and later by Paul Ehrlich and others. Aldo Leopold, Joseph Wood Krutch, and Bates contributed most significantly toward making the populace aware of the ecological perspective, that is, of the interrelatedness of all living things, including humankind. And, of course, Leopold's *A Sand County Almanac* provided an ethical underpinning for the modern environmental movement.

Selected Works and Further Reading

Bates, Marston, *The Forest and the Sea,* New York: Random House, 1960; London: Museum, 1961

——, *The Natural History of Mosquitoes,* New York: Macmillan, 1949

——, *The Prevalence of People,* New York: Scribner's, 1955

Brooks, Paul, *Speaking for Nature: How Literary Naturalists from Henry Thoreau to Rachel Carson Have Shaped America,* Boston: Houghton Mifflin, 1980

Carr, Archie Fairly, *Guide to the Reptiles, Amphibians, and Fresh-Water Fishes of Florida,* Gainesville: University of Florida Press, 1955

——, *Handbook of Turtles,* Ithaca, New York: Comstock, 1952

——, *High Jungles and Low,* Gainesville: University of Florida Press, 1953

——, *So Excellent a Fish: A Natural History of Sea Turtles,* Garden City, New York: Natural History, 1967

——, *The Windward Road; Adventures of a Naturalist on Remote Caribbean Shores,* New York: Knopf, 1955; London: Robert Hale, 1957

Carrighar, Sally, *Icebound Summer,* New York: Knopf, 1953; London: Travel Book Club, 1955

——, *One Day at Teton Marsh,* New York: Knopf, 1947; London: Michael Joseph, 1955

——, *One Day at Beetle Rock,* New York: Knopf, 1944

Carson, Rachel, *The Sea Around Us,* New York: Oxford University Press, 1951; London: Staples, 1951

——, *Silent Spring,* Boston: Houghton Mifflin, 1962; London: Hamilton, 1963

——, *Under the Sea-Wind: A Naturalist's Picture of Ocean Life,* New York: Simon & Schuster, 1941; London: Staples, 1952

Davis, R. G., review of *One Day at Teton Marsh, New York Times* (October 19, 1947)

Fox, Stephen, *John Muir and His Legacy: The American Conservation Movement,* Boston: Little, Brown, 1981

Gottlieb, Robert, *Forcing the Spring: The Transformation of the American Environmental Movement,* Washington, D.C.: Island, 1993

Halle, Louis J., *Birds Against Men,* New York: Viking, 1938

——, *Choice for Survival,* New York: Harper, 1958

——, *Dream and Reality: Aspects of American Foreign Policy,* New York: Harper & Brothers, 1959; also published as *American*

Foreign Policy: Theory and Reality, London: G. Allen & Unwin, 1960

——, *River of Ruins,* New York: Holt, 1941

——, *Spring in Washington,* New York: William Sloane, 1947

——, *Transcaribbean; A Travel Book of Guatemala, El Salvador, British Honduras,* New York: Longmans, Green, 1936

"Joseph Wood Krutch, Naturalist, Dies," *New York Times* (May 23, 1970)

Krutch, Joseph Wood, *The Desert Year,* New York: William Sloane, 1951; Harmondsworth, England: Penguin, 1977

——, *The Voice of the Desert: A Naturalist's Interpretation,* New York: William Sloane, 1955; London: Alvin Redman, 1955

Leopold, Aldo, *A Sand County Almanac: With Essays on Conservation from Round River,* New York: Sierra Club/Ballantine, 1966

Meine, Curt, *Aldo Leopold: His Life and Work,* Madison: University of Wisconsin Press, 1988

Osborn, Fairfield, *Our Plundered Planet,* Boston: Little, Brown, 1948; London: Faber and Faber, 1948

Stegner, Wallace, *Where the Bluebird Sings to the Lemonade Springs: Living and Writing in the West,* New York: Random House, 1992

Teale, Edwin Way, *Autumn Across America,* New York: Dodd, Mead, 1956

——, *Days Without Time,* New York: Dodd, Mead, 1948

——, *Dune Boy: The Early Years of a Naturalist,* New York: Dodd, Mead, 1943; London: R. Hale, 1949

——, *Grassroot Jungles,* New York: Dodd, Mead, 1937; London: Putnam's, 1937

——, *Journey into Summer,* New York: Dodd, Mead, 1960

——, *The Lost Woods: Adventures of a Naturalist,* New York: Dodd, Mead, 1945; London: R. Hale, 1952

——, *North with the Spring,* New York: Dodd, Mead, 1951; London: Eyre & Spottiswoode, 1954

——, *Wandering Through Winter,* New York: Dodd, Mead, 1965

Vogt, William, *People! Challenge to Survival,* New York: William Sloane, 1960; London: Victor Gollancz, 1961

——, *Road to Survival,* New York: William Sloane, 1948; London: Victor Gollancz, 1949

The World of the Beats and Others

Barry Silesky

The Beat Generation that rose to prominence in the 1950s remains the last group of truly popular poets in the English language. Their works have been translated into every tongue of the civilized world and spread throughout the globe. Audiences for Allen Ginsberg, Lawrence Ferlinghetti, and Gary Snyder filled halls while most poets (of which there are countless, due in no small part to the influence of the Beats) read to handfuls. Others associated with that group frequently draw full houses to readings also. And although the Beats continue to have more readers in the United States than any other literary group, their following in many other countries may even be larger.

Certainly their rise in the decade after World War II came in part as a reaction against a national atmosphere of self-celebration, fueled by wartime success and subsequent post-war prosperity. In such an atmosphere, there was little room for any commentary diverging from the ideology of success in which most participated. But many were, of course, left out of the prosperity celebration, or were simply put off by the pressure to conform to accepted ideas, and a few of the most articulate, touched by literature and its possibilities, came together in New York City, to form the nucleus of the Beat Generation at the end of the 1940s.

Although schools of writers and artists not so named by themselves (as the surrealists were by Breton), are largely media-critical inventions after the fact, and membership in the Beats is vigorously denied by most who have been associated with the label, there has been among them, as Gary Snyder pointed out in a 1974 interview, a common environmental concern and a certain "shared poetics." By "shared poetics," he goes on to explain, he means the use of colloquial language and visionary experience (Knight and Knight, 4).

The general championing of nature and the environment against what was perceived as the destructive forces of modern industrial urban society has also been generally shared, although articulated more specifically and expansively by some. In any case, common attitudes grew naturally out of the rebellion against the general praise of technological progress and the attendant despoiling of the environment that so often accompanies it.

If the Beats had a founder, it was probably Allen Ginsberg, although Jack Kerouac has almost as strong a claim. Ginsberg and Kerouac first heard the term from William Burroughs, who had picked it up from Times Square street hustler and petty criminal Herbert Huncke (Charters, *Portable*, xviii). The label went public through a 1948 conversation between Kerouac and John Clellon Holmes (Schumacher, 100–101), when Holmes went on to write "This is the Beat Generation" for *The New York Times* in 1952 (Silesky, 80). However the term originated (and there was much discussion about its true meaning among Kerouac and Ginsberg especially), Ginsberg was the one who did most to make it a national idea as the great amanuensis-enabler of the writers with whom he allied—first at Columbia University, where from 1943 to 1949 he was a student, poet, book reviewer, fiction writer, and editor of the student *Columbia Review* (Miles, 68); and certainly during the so-called San Francisco poetry renaissance of the 1950s, on which the media focused and so brought national attention to the Beats. It was in San Francisco in October 1955 that Ginsberg premiered his poem "Howl" at the Six Gallery reading he organized, which brought together Philip Lamantia, Michael McClure, Gary Snyder, Philip Whalen, and emcee Kenneth Rexroth. As much as any single work, that poem, with the attention Ginsberg drew to it, launched the movement.

His first published volume, *Howl and Other*

Poems, precipitated by the reading, and just the fourth of Lawrence Ferlinghetti's City Lights Books publications, is one of the landmark collections of the twentieth century. Its 11 poems bring together as well as any other book many of his central ideas. Nature is rarely a primary subject; but the core of all Ginsberg's work is an ongoing spiritual journey, and as a result, several of the poems speak clearly to this very urban poet's interests in nature and the environment. For aspects of nature, as in other poems urban industrial images and events, serve as agents of realization. At times they focus the poet's awareness of some transcendent moment; at others, they are at least an active part of the environment that leads to such experience.

"Howl" itself doesn't directly say anything about nature, but like others of his poems, it complains loudly about the forces of modern civilization that destroy nature and its people. Although the poem's habitat is urban to the bone, it is a world at least sporadically laced with elements of nature, whose presence announces the breadth of the experience. So the poem's "best minds" are seen in "backyard green tree cemetery dawns" and amid "sun and moon and tree vibrations in the roaring winter dusks of Brooklyn" (p. 10).

The most directly nature poem of that first collection is "Sunflower Sutra." It laments the alienation of the eponymous flower found in a railyard–alone and neglected, but still standing strong amid the debris of one of industrial civilization's most powerful symbols of speed, power and "progress." Ultimately, the flower is the unexpected occasion of the poem's discovery of inner beauty; that "We're not our skin of grime, we're not our dread bleak dusty imageless locomotive, we're all beautiful golden sunflowers inside . . ." (Ginsberg, *Howl*, 28).

This idea of natural elements that must be protected and fostered as essential parts of our spiritual connection to the world permeates much of Ginsberg's work, as it does much of the literature of the period. And as the Beat movement blended with the "counter-culture" of the 1960s, the emphasis on nature grew even more prominent. More than once, Ginsberg visited Ferlinghetti's rural cabin in Big Sur and wrote poems there depicting its lush environment, one of which in 1972 was made into a chapbook (Ginsberg, *Bixby Canyon*). But even in these, nature is never one thing; the ubiquitous elements of modern civilization are always part of

it: "rocky sandshore / Chevrolet writ / on radiatormouth . . ." (Ginsberg, *Collected*, 562).

As his career continued, the emphases of various poems and collections changed, but the elements comprising them remained essentially the same. At the risk of oversimplification, these essential concerns are the political, spiritual, and sexual realms, all in a primarily, although not at all exclusively, urban context. The elements of closely observed nature and industrial civilization, juxtaposed to create a sort of collage that is a portrait of Ginsberg's ongoing spiritual journey, continue throughout.

The graphic evocation of bodily functions is another persistent aspect in Ginsberg's work, and in his recent volume, *Cosmopolitan Greetings*, one of the last poems is a short one, placing him on the toilet, excreting (graphically, as usual) and reading *No Nature*, Gary Snyder's volume of new and selected poems. No doubt Ginsberg's locale seemed fitting to him for a poem about Snyder, as one significant thrust of Snyder's later works—not his poetry, but his essays, articles and talks—has been waste treatment and composting.

That interest is a natural outgrowth of Snyder's career; no other poet of his generation has devoted so much of both his writing and life to the exploration and preservation of the natural environment. His deep involvement in nature and the environment is an integral part of who he has always been, and his commitment, in both writing and life, has been one of the most powerful single influences in poetry in the second half of the century. As strong a statement of influence can be made regarding his devotion to Buddhism, which began when he was a student at Reed.

Born in 1930, Snyder grew up on a farm north of Seattle. By his own account he was taken early by the landscape around him and, as a first grader, found his own trail through the woods to school, while everyone else took the dirt road. At the age of 15 he had climbed to the top of Mount St. Helens (Timpanelli, 225–226); and by the time he was 19, he had topped a dozen summits in the Cascades. He went to Reed College in Oregon, where he roomed with Philip Whalen and Lew Welch, both, like Snyder, becoming significant poets connected to the Beat Generation in the 1950s and later, although Snyder's accomplishments far outpace them. He graduated with a degree in anthropology and linguistics in 1951, studied linguistics for one term at Indiana University, then came back West, and worked as a logger and a fire lookout in the Cascades. In 1954, he entered graduate school at the University of California, Berkeley, to study Asian languages and in 1956 left for Japan, where he spent most of the next 13 years studying Buddhism between a few journeys away—work as a seaman that took him to the Bay of Bengal, the Arabian Sea, and Samoa; to India, where he traveled and met up with Ginsberg; and back to the western United States.

He was always drawn back to the American West, he has said, by the landscape—the mountains and rivers of the west, and the natural world there (Snyder, *Mountains*, 153). His work throughout his career, of which his poetry has been a major part, has been devoted to furthering appreciation and preservation of what he has termed "wild nature," which includes those same forces within us.

Clearly affected by the examples of Pound and Williams, his poetry has been influential stylistically as well as in its content. Its focus is on direct image, with transitional elements and excess verbiage rigorously pared away. It's a style designed to imitate nature in the way objects are set together, seemingly casually, and without any extra coloration. One of the best examples remains his early poem, "Riprap," which is the word for a foundation wall made by fitting together irregularly shaped stones. As such, the term works well as a description of his verse style, as we see from the beginning of the poem: "Lay down these words / before your mind like rocks / placed solid, by hands . . ." (Snyder, *No Nature*, 21).

He has studied Chinese and other Eastern poetry, as well as Native American myth and stories, and these have been a major influence on the presentation of his subjects. "For me," he said in a 1973 interview, "it's the Chinese tradition and the tradition of Indian vernacular poetry, and also classical Sanskrit poetry of India, that I learned most from" (Torrance, 264). As a student he translated Chinese poet Han Shan's "Cold Mountain Poems" and wrote a biography of him, the poems later published in a 1957 *Evergreen Review*, then in later editions of his first book, *Riprap*, which was retitled *Riprap and Cold Mountain Poems*. His second book, *Myths & Texts*, utilizes traditional Native American elements, combining elements of the title into a series that makes a single long poem.

In late 1996, he completed *Mountains and Rivers Without End*, the book-length poem that he had begun some 40 years earlier. Deeply engaged with the natural world, as all his poetry, the title is that of a twelfth-century Chinese hand scroll, a reproduction of which he first saw as a student at Reed (Snyder, *Mountains*, 153). The new work that brought him to complete the poem is at least partly a result of his effort to "broaden the contexts of his thought and writing" beyond, as he said, "West Coast environmentalism and ecopoetics" (Torrance, 280).

According to Michael McClure, another participant in that Six Gallery reading, "Much of what the Beat Generation is about is nature—the landscape of nature in the case of Gary Snyder, the mind as nature in the case of Allen Ginsberg. Consciousness is a natural organic phenomenon. The Beats shared an interest in nature, mind and biology—areas that they expanded and held together with their radical political or antipolitical state" (Tonkinson, 313).

While most of these writers have looked at larger landscapes, McClure himself has focused more on the microcosm in his poetry—on the biology of self and nature. Like the other Beats, his interest, particularly in the late 1960s, has been in transcending ordinary consciousness. As he said in a 1970 statement, "In reading biology I hope to make the discoveries that will liberate man to exist in timelessness and a state of super-consciousness" (Charters, *Portable*, 264).

McClure was born in Kansas and came to San Francisco in 1954 to pursue a woman in which he was interested. He studied art and met poet Robert Duncan, becoming involved in the burgeoning San Francisco poetry world of the time. He has lived in San Francisco (and now Oakland) ever since. His poetry, always centered on the page, makes use of capital letters, spacing, and other typographical devices to draw attention to the visual along with cognitive content. Meantime, his interest in nature and biology, and humanity's role in it, has remained at center. We are, he says in a 1982 poem: "Linked part to part, toe to knee, eye to thumb / Motile, feral, a blockhouse of sweat . . ." (Tonkinson, 317).

Phillip Whalen, the Reed College roommate of Snyder and Lew Welch, is another important poet of that generation who also speaks frequently of nature and its preservation. Whalen became a Zen priest, and his concern with nature is an aspect of Zen focus, an interest also widely articulated by traditional Zen masters and poets. Even more, perhaps, than Ginsberg's or Snyder's, Whalen's poems are grounded in his lifelong spiritual practice. The images of nature in his poems are always an example of or means to insight and understanding.

Born in 1923, Whalen emerged from a Christian Science background, discovering oriental religions and Zen through local library books during high school in Portland, Oregon. After serving in the Army, he went to Reed, and also like Snyder, spent time in the Cascades and served as a fire lookout, occasioning at least one poem, "Sourdough Mountain Lookout," in which he announces his affection for "certain land and sea-scapes / the way light falls across them, diffusion of / Light through agate, light itself . . ." (p. 285).

After college, he also made his way to San Francisco and for some months shared an apartment with Snyder. When Snyder invited him to participate in the Six Gallery reading, he says that he didn't really think of himself as a poet, although he had long been interested in literature and writing.

Whalen's early poetry is often more fragmented than any of the others. His poems jump from image to image and event to event, usually without much in the way of transitional elements or narrative line. Like McClure's, they utilize various typographical features, employing all capitals in some places, all small letters in others, and other available variations, including spacing and organization. Although he has written less and less over the years, later poems have conformed more to the conventional style of the times, set up in regular stanzas against a justified left margin. Still, the voice remains resolutely colloquial, as has been a crucial aspect of both his style and that of the other poets with whom he has been associated, in poems that, also like theirs, emphasize visionary, immediate experience.

Gary Snyder's other Reed College roommate, Lew Welch, didn't reflect anything like the same level of interest in nature as the others, although images from nature do occur, and like that of many other poets of his generation, his work reflects the struggle to embrace the natural amid the cacophony of civilization. Born in Phoenix, Arizona in 1926, Welch's senior thesis at Reed on Gertrude Stein was praised by William Carlos Williams, whom Welch visited in New Jersey. After Reed, Welch went to graduate school at the University of Chicago, but he suffered a nervous breakdown there, wrote advertising for

a while (Allen, 445), then went back to San Francisco where he drove a taxi (Charters, *Portable*, 321), which occasioned a memorable "Taxi Suite" (pp. 21–24).

His struggle to integrate nature with the urban environment where he lived is perhaps seen most clearly in his poem, "The Image, as in a Hexagram" (p. 76), where he evokes a hermit alone in a cabin. Welch himself did spend some time at Ferlinghetti's cabin in Big Sur, once with Kerouac, but his constant struggle "to be a poet and at the same time support himself," as writer Aram Saroyan commented, eventually proved to be too much; in 1971, he took a 30–30 rifle into the mountains near Gary Snyder's rural California house and never returned (Charters, *Portable*, 312).

Phillip Lamantia, who also took part in the Six Gallery reading that opened the way to the Beat Generation, didn't read his own poetry there, but the poems of a deceased young visionary poet; and the choice clearly announced some of the commonality his work shares with the others who were there. Lamantia's poetry also emphasizes immediate, visionary experience, in a vernacular voice, although the syntax he drafts is much more difficult and complex than that of his contemporaries. He has been one of the only major American surrealist poets—so anointed at age 16 by Andre Breton when the surrealist founder published Lamantia's first poems in his surrealist magazine *VVV*—and his development as an authentic surrealist poet has continued. His major contribution has been the authentic rural American stamp he has put on the urban, European movement. Even the titles of his books and poems announce that context: *Meadowlark West* (his most recent volume), and "Wilderness, Sacred Wilderness," "Sweetbriar," "Shasta," "Redwood Highway," to name a few poems. His poems consistently employ imagery from the dramatic landscapes of the American West in poems that illustrate, as one critic put it, "the tension between 'the exaltation of reality and an omnipresent sense of the pain and terror inherent in life'" (Charters, *Portable*, 317–318).

Gregory Corso is the other major poet usually associated with Ginsberg and the Beats. Even more than Ginsberg and most of the others, he has been an urban poet, for whom nature is only an occasional image, usually treated in an ironic context. So in an early poem, "Old MacDonald wears clod-hoppers / in his walk through field of lilac and dandelion / A storm-trooper, like a Klee twittering machine, he stomps . . ." (Corso, 13).

The foundation of his work throughout his career has been the blend of classical mythology and popular culture, in a colloquial language flavored regularly with more traditional *poetic* diction. And always, the work has shown a robust sense of humor, which (surprisingly), except for Ginsberg's early work, has been largely absent from the poetry of most of his contemporaries.

Diane di Prima is the only woman poet associated with this almost exclusively male group. Born in New York City in 1934, she grew up there, and in the years after she dropped out of Swarthmore College, like Ginsberg and Snyder, she came to embrace Buddhism. She met Ferlinghetti, Ginsberg, and Corso shortly after they drew national recognition in the mid-1950s, and published her first book of poems, *This Kind of Bird Flies Backwards*, in 1958. Two years later her prose memoir, *Dinners and Nightmares*, drew substantial attention, and in the early 1960s she went on to work with Leroi Jones (Amiri Baraka) in publishing an influential mimeographed literary magazine, *The Floating Bear*.

Also like Ginsberg and Snyder, her use of nature has been rooted in her Buddhist orientation, which connects her with the natural world. Most notably, her *Loba* poems, written mainly in the late 1970s, use the wolf as a symbol of her own psyche, employing the animal's natural characteristics as it plies a multitude of landscapes. Her own travels—she taught extensively in that decade as a poet in prisons, schools and other venues in Wyoming, Montana, Minnesota, Arizona—certainly have been one of the influences informing her images and attitudes. Like the other Beats, she has employed an insistently vernacular voice, although later poems have increasingly abandoned narrative, finding instead a fragmented, modernist mode. At the same time, her engagement in Buddhism has focused her poems on the spiritual aspects of nature and its closely observed elements.

Lawrence Ferlinghetti is another who has insistently denied being a Beat poet, a denial whose appropriateness both his work and life confirm in several ways. But his participation in and contribution to the Beat movement of the 1950s and the youth counter-culture that grew from it in the next decade have irrevocably linked him to the group. Unlike the Beats, he has never been especially interested in the pursuit of spontaneity in his poetry, and his interest in Buddhism, which never became much more than a flirtation, only arose much later. Further, he wasn't really a part of the artistic and personal alliances that linked key figures Ginsberg, Kerouac, Corso, and Burroughs–at the time of their meetings in New York and emergence there and in San Francisco, Ferlinghetti was a doctoral student in Paris, then a married businessman in San Francisco.

But among qualities he has shared with the Beats is his insistently conversational and colloquial language, influenced in his case most obviously by French poet Jacques Prévert, which language is part of a style that is always inviting the reader into the experience of the poem and its point of view. Then, like Corso's, and Ginsberg's early work, there is a real sense of humor manifested in many of the poems—always, in Ferlinghetti's case, droll but inclusive of the audience. Perhaps most significant, however, is that from the beginning, his poems have been a consistent voice against mainstream, status-quo ideas, siding always with the less privileged and forgotten.

That sympathy seems a natural outgrowth of his own background as an orphan. Despite being raised partly by a wealthy and privileged family (the heirs of those who founded Sarah Lawrence College), Ferlinghetti was moved in adolescence to another family, and came of age essentially alone. After service in World War II, and completing his doctorate at the Sorbonne in Paris, he went by himself to San Francisco in 1951, where he met Peter Martin, son of the noted anarchist Carlo Tresca (Silesky, 56), and with him started City Lights, the first all-paperback literary bookstore in the United States. When Martin returned to New York a year after the founding, Ferlinghetti took over the store, and imitating models he had seen in Paris, began publishing inexpensive poetry books. The 1957 obscenity trial occasioned by the publication of *Howl and Other Poems* made it, Ginsberg, and Ferlinghetti nationally famous; and a natural audience for Ferlinghetti's own poems was created.

Although Ferlinghetti was, like the Beats, essentially urban in his background and tastes, his political sympathies, along with the popular culture movement in the 1960s, naturally drew him toward nature. In the mid-1950s he purchased a cabin in the Big Sur wilderness area south of San Francisco, and his work has regularly utilized aspects of nature, although not until the 1960s do poems praising nature and calling for its protection begin to appear regularly. He became more active in environmental politics in the 1970s, and those issues have been regular subjects of his poetry. Poems then and since have regularly spoken in his characteristic wry tone for environmental preservation and against its despoilment in the name of progress. At the same time, nature images have been a background for more meditative poems, with themes of art and social alienation that have been consistent throughout his career.

"A bunch of New York carpetbaggers," Ferlinghetti once termed the founders of the Beat Generation in a bemused aside, and as a central figure in their rise in the 1950s, he certainly would know. With important exceptions (Gary Snyder, Philip Whalen) their backgrounds, including Ferlinghetti's own, were urban, and their orientations remained so. But the cultural and political movements that they in no small way helped initiate drew them beyond the outskirts and to close relations with nature and the environment. There were exceptions (Bob Kaufman is perhaps the most notable, as a widely known, inventive San Francisco street poet in the 1960s and later), but none turned entirely away from the wild. It is a wild that was, and remains, a significant source for an entire generation.

Selected Works and Further Reading

Allen, Donald, ed., *The New American Poetry,* New York: Grove, 1960; London: Evergreen, 1960

Charters, Ann, ed., *Dictionary of Literary Biography: The Beats: Literary Bohemians in Postwar America,* vol. 16, Detroit, Michigan: Gale, 1983

——, ed., *The Portable Beat Reader,* New York: Viking, 1992; also published as *The Penguin Book of the Beats,* London: Penguin, 1993

Corso, Gregory, *Mindfield,* New York: Thunder's Mouth, 1989; London: Paladin, 1992

Di Prima, Diane, *Loba: Parts I–VIII,* Berkeley, California: Wingbow, 1973

——, *Pieces of a Song: Selected Poems,* San Francisco: City Lights, 1990

Ferlinghetti, Lawrence, *A Coney Island of the Mind: Poems,* New York: New Directions, 1958; London: Hutchinson, 1959

——, *Endless Life: Selected Poems,* New York: New Directions, 1981

——, *Her,* New York: New Directions, 1960

——, *Over All the Obscene Boundaries: European Poems and Transitions,* New York: New Directions, 1984

Ginsberg, Allen, *Bixby Canyon Ocean Path Word Breeze,* New York: Profile, 1972

——, *Collected Poems: 1947–1980,* New York: Harper & Row, 1984; London: Viking, 1985

——, *Cosmopolitan Greetings: Poems, 1986–1992,* New York: HarperCollins, 1994; London: Penguin, 1994

——, *Howl, and Other Poems,* San Francisco: City Lights, 1956

Kaufman, Bob, *Cranial Guitar,* Minneapolis, Minnesota: Coffee House, 1996

Knight, Arthur, and Kit Knight, eds., "Moving the World a Millionth of an Inch: Gary Snyder," in *The Beat Vision: A Primary Sourcebook,* New York: Paragon House, 1987

Lamantia, Philip, *Becoming Visible,* San Francisco: City Lights, 1981

——, *Meadowlark West,* San Francisco: City Lights, 1986

McClure, Michael, *Scratching the Beat Surface,* San Francisco: North Point, 1982

——, *Selected Poems,* New York: New Directions, 1986

Miles, Barry, *Ginsberg: A Biography,* New York: Simon & Schuster, 1989; London: Viking, 1989

Nicosia, Gerald, *Memory Babe: A Critical Biography of Jack Kerouac,* New York: Grove, 1983; Harmondsworth, England: Viking, 1985

Schumacher, Michael, *Dharma Lion: A Critical Biography of Allen Ginsberg,* New York: St. Martin's, 1992

Silesky, Barry, *Ferlinghetti: The Artist in His Time,* New York: Warner, 1990

Snyder, Gary, *Mountains and Rivers Without End,* Washington, D.C.: Counterpoint, 1996

——, *Myths and Texts,* New York: Totem, 1960

——, *No Nature: New and Selected Poems,* New York: Pantheon, 1992

——, *Riprap,* Ashland, Massachusetts: Origin, 1959

——, *Riprap and Cold Mountain Poems,* San Francisco: Grey Fox, 1965; reprinted, San Francisco: North Point, 1990

Timpanelli, Gioia, "Jumping over Bear Droppings," in *Gary Snyder: Dimensions of a Life,* edited by Jon Halper, San Francisco: Sierra Club, 1991

Tonkinson, Carole, ed., *Big Sky Mind: Buddhism and the Beat Generation,* New York: Riverhead, 1995; London: Thorsons, 1996

Torrance, Robert M., "Gary Snyder and the Western Poetic Tradition," in *Gary Snyder: Dimensions of a Life,* edited by Jon Halper, San Francisco: Sierra Club, 1991

Welch, Lew, *Ring of Bone: Collected Poems, 1950–71,* Bolinas, California: Grey Fox, 1973

Whalen, Philip, *Off the Wall: Interviews with Philip Whalen,* Bolinas, California: Four Seasons Foundation, 1978

_____, "Sourdough Mountain Lookout," in *The New American Poetry,* edited by Donald Allen, New York: Grove, 1960; London: Evergreen, 1960

Writers of the Adirondacks

Glenn Sandiford and John Cooley

This chapter treats the literature of a 6-million-acre state park in northern New York. Lying at the doorstep of the nation's greatest metropolitan complex, the Adirondack Park is the largest U.S. park outside Alaska, more expansive than Yellowstone, Yosemite, Olympic, Glacier, and Grand Canyon national parks combined. It is a land with chains of peaks soaring as much as a mile skyward, thousands of lonely lakes and ponds, and woods, woods, and more woods. A mantle of trees covers the entire region, from the High Peaks in the northeast quadrant of the park to the rolling country and broad plateaus of the south and west. To the untutored eye, these vast woods might seem unchanging, timeless, forever wild. Closer scrutiny reveals otherwise. The Adirondack woods are a patchwork of public wilderness lands and private working lands. A "forever wild" clause in the state constitution protects the wilderness, most of which is secondary growth thanks to destructive logging 100 years ago. The private lands—portions of which are threatened by development despite some of the most stringent backcountry zoning regulations in the nation—are mostly owned by timber companies and fish and game clubs, plus 150,000 year-round Adirondackers and another 250,000 seasonal residents. These people set apart the region from all other great wilderness areas. Many national parks and forests hide a few isolated souls, but only the Adirondack Park blends wilderness with a home for tens of thousands. And as Adirondack scholar Paul Jamieson notes, herein lies a clue to the question that has dominated the history of the region for 250 years. Just what is this land good for? Explorers, travel writers, poets, journalists, novelists, activists, and social critics have all grappled with this question.

In one sense, just about everything written about the Adirondacks can be classed as nature writing, since its woods, waters, and mountains are a fundamental element of Adirondack identity and life. This chapter will limit itself to authors for whom nature is a focus, rather than background. Moreover, although no Adirondack chronicle can ignore the stream of outsiders that have visited the region, primary attention will be given to writers who have lived there and whose work has been significantly influenced by this distinctive bioregion and its culture. Finally, readers seeking a broader view of Adirondack literature than is possible here should start with Paul Jamieson's superb anthology, *The Adirondack Reader*, which includes samples by dozens of writers. Dorothy Plum's bibliographies are even more exhaustive, although somewhat dated.

The Adirondack woods were once all wilderness. Indeed, when explorers first encountered the region in the late seventeenth century, the primeval forests covered one-quarter of New York State. But not until the 1830s—by which time Lewis and Clark had reached the Pacific— would the Adirondacks be explored in any detail, even though their southern boundary is only 200 miles north of Manhattan. A state geologist named Ebenezer Emmons conducted the first survey in 1837, during which he managed the first ascent of Mount Marcy, at 5344 feet the highest of the Adirondack peaks. Emmons's survey reports reveal a man to whom the Adirondacks meant much more than rocks and minerals. "It is not, however, by description that the scenery of this region can be made to pass before the eye of the imagination; it must be witnessed, the solitary summits in the distance, the cedars and firs which clothe the rocks and shores must be seen; the solitude must be felt. . . ." (quoted in Headley, ii).

Historian William Verner suggests Emmons' ascent and naming of Marcy placed the Adirondack wilderness in the minds of Americans for the first time. Moreover, Emmons's survey reports include mention of "a new field for relaxation from business—one which has peculiar advantages and many resources for restoring health and spirits, such as are unknown at the more fashionable watering places" (quoted in Jamieson, *Pilgrimage*, 1). But not even Emmons could have predicted how quickly this "new field" would catch on in the Adirondacks. Within a month of reading press reports of his Marcy climb, writers and adventurers were following his footsteps.

By now, and for the first time in their short history, Americans could live and even travel widely without encountering wild country. "From the vantage point of comfortable farms, libraries, and city streets," explains environmental historian Roderick Nash, wilderness became an "exciting, temporary alternative to civilization" (p. 57). Thus was born the era of the Romantics, an era greatly inspired by the Adirondacks. Among the literati of the major Eastern cities who journeyed north into the wilds was Charles Fenno Hoffman, editor of an arts weekly in New York City. Hoffman's childhood loss of a leg prevented him reaching the summit of Marcy—a "defeat" that caused him to break down and weep on Marcy's flanks—but he still managed to explore much of the wilderness with his guide. From those experiences came stories of bears and panthers, of precipitous gorges and great rock slides, of heroic and benevolent guides, which in 1843 appeared in Hoffman's two-volume book, *Wild Scenes in the Forest and Prairie*. It was the first mass audience book about travel and adventure in the Adirondacks, although it never threatened any sales records.

A more commercially successful writer was Joel Headley. An ex-minister and former reporter in New York City, Headley became one of the most widely read authors of the mid-nineteenth century, and in the process further opened the Adirondacks. Following two trips there, he published *The Adirondacks; or Life in the Woods*, in 1849. The book was a collection of stories written as letters to a friend in which Headley described the pleasures a cultivated vacationer might discover there. Intermingled with descriptions of the woods, theological observations, and social commentary are accounts of fishing trips and hunts, river drives, hikes, and mountain climbs. In particular, Headley's book was the first popular report of the Adirondacks' seemingly infinite stock of fish and game. Headley spoke of taking 50 trout in two hours, and of a friend who

in one hour of "great sport . . . , took a *hundred and twenty pounds* of trout" (p. 240, italics in original).

But already there were voices challenging this illusory abundance. Albany newspaper editor Samuel Hammond urged prophetically in his 1857 book *Wild Northern Scenes: or Sporting Adventures with the Rifle and Rod* that a circle of a 100-mile diameter be drawn around the Adirondacks and all the land within it be protected under the Constitution to remain forever a forest, there being sufficient room for civilization in other more suitable regions. Hammond's comments marked the first published advocacy for Constitutional protection of the Adirondack wilderness.

Other collections of Adirondack hunting and fishing tales followed in the next twenty years. Notable scribes included John Todd, Charles Lanman, and Alfred Billings Street. None of them earned fame or fortune, but it was through works such as theirs that a new American hero emerged—the Adirondack guide.

Although hardly the literary equal of Dante's Virgil, the Adirondack guide is still in a class of his own. The heritage began in the 1820s with James Fenimore Cooper's popular Leatherstocking tales, notably *The Last of the Mohicans*, in which Natty Bumppo, or Leatherstocking, is portrayed as the scout Hawkeye in the Lake George region. According to Jamieson, Leatherstocking was the fictional exemplar of the myth of the American as a new man, "innocent, unburdened by the sins of the past, and optimistic about his chances of making a new life in a new world" (*Pilgrimage*, 124). Leatherstocking took his place in American literature during the 1840s, at the same time the Adirondacks were opening to tourists. Writers flooded to the region, and found in their guides the embodiment of heroic Leatherstocking. If what was lacking in the reality was supplemented by the imagination, so be it. The Adirondack guides were still a remarkable breed. Senses sharpened by a lifetime of woodcraft, they were as attuned to the wilderness as the animals themselves, and equally resilient. But few people save the local villagers would have been aware of these extraordinary characters had it not been for the writers who lionized them before a national audience.

The Adirondacks continued to inspire literature during the Civil War period, especially among writers and readers seeking relief from the stresses of an increasingly urbanized society.

William Henry Harrison Murray was a Boston clergyman whose two summer trips to the Adirondacks became the basis for *Adventures in the Wilderness*. Published in the spring of 1869, Murray's book included a practical guide and manual for travel in the region, as well as 10 tales of adventure. Almost overnight, it became a bestseller—more than 60 printings would be issued—and the center of a storm of controversy as unprecedented crowds rushed for the Adirondacks that summer, a stampede known ever since as "Murray's Rush." Historian Warder Cadbury explains that Murray's images were so effective that "even the man in the street could easily understand and respond to what he had to say. In short, Murray quite literally popularized both wilderness and the Adirondacks" (p. 69)

But in doing so, Murray brought to light a dilemma that to this day remains unresolved in the Adirondacks and many other wild places. In the aftermath of his book, during the Gilded Years between 1870 and 1910 when the Adirondacks were the most fashionable summer resort in the country, the wilderness began to change. It became more "civilized," with hotels, roads, and other conveniences for the summer crowds. Thus the quandary raised—and in some sense created—by Murray was how to preserve wilderness while making the wilderness experience accessible to the masses.

One man who devoted much of his life to this dilemma was Verplank Colvin. Starting in 1872, Colvin spent almost three decades on a topographical survey of the Adirondacks that took him to every mountain, river, and lake in today's park. His annual reports to the state legislature for the years from 1873 to 1898, replete with tales of snarling panthers and terrifying night climbs, are described by former *Adirondack Life* editor Chris Shaw as "neglected masterpieces of the genre (of the literature of exploration), echoing accounts by Lewis and Clark, Henry Morton Stanley, John Wesley Powell, and Charles Darwin" (p. 279).

Colvin was also among the first to offer a vision combining utilitarian and moral values of wilderness. But his talk of a "mystery" in the Adirondack mountains, of a "oneness" in the region, underscores his essentially Romantic, nostalgic view of wilderness, like the writers and artists of an earlier generation. It is a view that continues to inspire subsequent generations too. In *Defending the Wilderness*, Adirondack crusader Paul Schaefer talks about wilderness renewing "our understanding of primitive things,

the sharpening of our sensibilities to the loveliness of rocks and sunsets and silence" (p. 212). Chris Shaw lauds wilderness with "*depth*, where crossing one range leads to a farther range, and beyond that to another . . . [a place] where there is nothing but the presence and the act" (p. 289). Scholar Philip Terrie yearns for eastern timber wolves and other extirpated large mammals, declaring in *Wildlife and Wilderness* that their reintroduction to the Adirondacks would be the true "hallmark of quality" and make the Forest Preserve whole again.

Less polemical, but equally nostalgic, is William Chapman White's 1954 classic, *Adirondack Country*. One of the most popular books ever written about the region, it is at once a history of the park, a portrayal of its people, and a tribute to its wilderness. It closes with a delightful month-by-month calendar of the Adirondack seasons that, although lacking the scientific and moral weight of Aldo Leopold's *A Sand County Almanac*, has the same poetic appeal. White writes in his entry for July that in the Adirondack woods, a man "can stand on a rock by the shore and be in a past he could not have known, in a future he will never see. He can be part of time that was and time yet to come" (p. 264).

Glenn Sandiford has an eye on past, present, and future in *Deepe in the Adirondacks*, his oral history of renowned Adirondack guide Tony Deepe. Born in 1908, Deepe is nearly as old as the Adirondack Park itself, allowing Sandiford to illuminate the history of the region with Deepe's often hilarious anecdotes. But Deepe is also a man who "has managed to retain his awareness of nature, an awareness of the context of his life. He sees himself as a strand in the web, not the spinner" (n.p.). Thus Sandiford's portrayal of Deepe is more than a biography—it is a field guide as to how humanity might once more live honestly and respectfully with nature.

Although Adirondack literature has been dominated by male writers and masculine viewpoints, women have been writing about the region since the mid-nineteenth century, and in recent decades their writing has achieved visibility and a diverse readership. Feminist scholar Kate Winter identifies some 50 books written by women who have lived in or made repeated visits to the Adirondacks. When women began to describe their experiences, it was on different terms than the traditional male aspirations to make wealth off the land while testing one's strength and endurance. As Kate Winter puts it, women have been inclined to see the Adirondacks as a place in which to "uncover and recover their latent talents and strengths." Their work tends to seek connection and partnership with wilderness, "by creating a larger web of care to include the earth" (p. 5).

Jeanne Robert Foster developed so close a relationship with her neighbor, Crane Mountain, that, as she embraced its rocky slabs she could feel "a strong force passing through" her. In her five volumes of poetry, including *Wild Apples* and *Adirondack Portraits*, Foster presents her personal encounters with wild country as well as the collective voices of her up-country neighbors and friends. The matter-of-fact directness of her conversational pastorals is reminiscent of the poetry of her regional neighbor and contemporary, Robert Frost, both of whom were skilled at capturing the colloquialisms and slow pace of country talk. In addition to representing vernacular materials and diction, Foster wished to say that wilderness people are specially strengthened, inspired and graced by the mountains that surround them.

Jean Rikhoff settled in the Lake George region where, impressed by its dramatic beauty and history, she depicted the early settlement decades in her historical novels *Buttes Landing* and *One of the Raymonds*. Like Rikhoff herself, the protagonist of her first novel moved to the Adirondacks from the Midwest. He fell in love with both the harsh landscape and Emily Gutherie, a tough and stubborn daughter of the north country. Much like Anne LaBastille, Rikhoff undercuts conventional assumptions that women merely tolerate frontier existence. Odder Buttes soon had to admit of his new wife that no matter how hard the task he set, she would set one harder for herself, always keeping up with him. In her two-novel saga Rikhoff chronicles 10 generations in the lives of two Adirondack families.

Many writers attest to the curative powers of the Adirondacks. Although these claims have at times been exaggerated, medical research has consistently verified the health benefits of mountain air and water. The young physician Edward Trudeau was seriously ill with tuberculosis when he came to the Adirondacks in the 1870s. As Trudeau narrates in *An Autobiography*, his health improved so dramatically after his arrival in the Saranac Lake area that he moved there permanently, and built a sanitorium in which to conduct research and assist others afflicted with the disease. Poet Adelaide Crapsey was among the many patients who came to Dr. Trudeau's

famous sanitorium. The balsam-scented mountain air and the sanitarium treatment extended her life, giving her the energy to perfect a cinquain verse form and to complete her collected poems.

Tuberculosis did not prevent popular outdoor writer George Washington Sears from canoeing several hundred miles through the central Adirondacks in the early 1880s. *The Adirondack Letters of George Washington Sears* is a reprint of Sears' travel accounts, which first appeared in *Field and Stream* magazine under the pen name of Nessmuk. More than a century later, Christine Jerome retraced Nessmuk's voyage in a nine-foot lightweight canoe of similar design to Sears' famous "Sairy Gamp." In *An Adirondack Passage*, which one critic described as coming closest to a nonfiction best-seller that the region had witnessed in years, Jerome pays tribute to Sears but also places a female perspective on writing about wilderness adventures.

Tuberculosis had left Martha Reben an invalid when in 1931 she read an advertisement by Fred Rice, a 55-year-old Adirondack mountain man who believed that total immersion in the remotest wilderness was the only real cure for tuberculosis and many other illnesses. Reben accompanied Rice to his camp at Weller Lake, and 10 years later was completely free of tuberculosis. Her daily journals became the basis for her three-book autobiography: *The Healing Woods*, *The Way of the Wilderness*, and *A Sharing of Joy*. In these works she claims that, unlike Thoreau's "voluntary simplicity," hers was necessitated by her illness. As she puts it, "the wilderness did more than heal my lungs . . . it taught me fortitude and self-reliance" (*Wilderness*, 10).

Anne LaBastille talks of the wilderness in similar terms. Arguably the best known among Adirondack women writers, LaBastille has contributed significantly to the region as a popular writer, wildlife biologist, and in advisory roles within the park. National acclaim greeted her first book, *Woodswoman*, in which she recounts her first tentative steps toward purchasing land, building a log cabin, and embarking on a life-long Thoreauvian experience. In *Beyond Black Bear Lake*, LaBastille describes the confidence and competence she has gained as a single woman living alone in a cabin surrounded by wilderness. With *Women and Wilderness* LaBastille enlarges her subject, presenting a history of women in frontier life, followed by interviews with a dozen women engaged in wilderness work.

Beyond Black Bear Lake also marks a shift in thinking, from illness and recovery in humans to health of the land. LaBastille graphically describes the destructive impact of acid rain and tourism on air and water quality and the overall health of the Adirondack ecosystem. Bill McKibben talks about similar issues, often on a global scale, only he extends the curative theme by emphasizing how the ancient relationship has been reversed; no longer nature's patient, humankind must become its physician. Thus for McKibben, a former writer for *The New Yorker* who has emerged as one of the country's most insightful nature writers, the Adirondack Park is as much idea as place, a great "experiment" about whether people can live in the same place as nature. McKibben is less interested in boundaries that separate people from nature than in finding ways that place one foot on either side of such boundaries—a middle ground where we must grow food and cut trees, while working out the meaning of being "a human animal." In his first bestseller, *The End of Nature*, McKibben uses simple acts like a walk beside a stream to illustrate how radically humans are altering the global environment. His second book, *The Age of Missing Information*, examines human inertia about these environmental changes by contrasting a day on an Adirondack mountaintop with a day in front of the television, and the information they each impart. The trilogy ends with *Hope, Human and Wild*, in which McKibben offers the Adirondacks and other parts of the world as places where humans are learning to set limits.

Conclusion

"Adirondack literature is an unparalleled mirror of the relations of Americans to the woods," according to Paul Jamieson (*Reader*, x). Through more than 250 years of writings, beginning with explorers like Ebenezer Emmons, through James Fenimore Cooper, "Adirondack" Murray, and other Romantics, and most recently Anne LaBastille and Bill McKibben, one can follow in Adirondack writings the transition from subjugation and exploitation of land to stewardship. At one point during the 1880s, the region so dominated the nation's literary landscape that, according to Roderick Nash, the Adirondack country has been written about more than any other U.S. wilderness region. Since then, many writers have succumbed to the grandeur of the West, but literary interest in the

Adirondacks has continued unabated, and in recent years has enjoyed a resurgence. Many of the region's writers—past and present—visited or moved to the Adirondacks in adulthood. But whether born there or newcomers, they all share a love of nature and a love of the region that Chris Shaw calls "one of the most singular geopolitical entities in North America."

Selected Works and Further Reading

Adirondack Mountain Club Bibliography Committee, *Adirondack Bibliography; A List of Books, Pamphlets and Periodical Articles Published Through the Year 1955*, Gabriels, New York: Adirondack Mountain Club, 1958

——, *Adirondack Bibliography Supplement, 1956–1965; A List of Books, Pamphlets and Periodical Articles*, Blue Mountain Lake, New York: Adirondack Museum, 1973

Burdick, Neal, ed., *A Century Wild, 1885–1985: Essays Commemorating the Centennial of the Adirondack Forest Preserve*, Saranac Lake, New York: Chauncy, 1985

Champlain, Samuel de, *The Voyages and Explorations of Samuel de Champlain (1604–1616)*, 2 vols., New York: A. S. Barnes, 1906

Colvin, Verplanck, *Report on a Topographical Survey of the Adirondack Wilderness of New York*, Albany, New York: Argus, 1873

Cooper, James Fenimore, *The Last of the Mohicans*, Philadelphia: H. C. Carey & I. Lea, 1826; London: John Miller, 1826

Crapsey, Adelaide, *The Complete Poems and Collected Letters of Adelaide Crapsey*, edited by Susan Sutton Smith, Albany: State University of New York Press, 1977

Emmons, Ebenezer, *Assembly Document No. 200, 1838*

——, *Geology of New York: Survey of the Second Geological District*, Albany, New York: W. & A. White and J. Visscher, 1842

Foster, Jeanne Robert, *Adirondack Portraits: A Piece of Time*, edited by Noel Riedinger-Johnson, Syracuse, New York: Syracuse University Press, 1986

——, *Wild Apples*, Boston: Sherman, French, 1916

Gilborn, Alice, *What Do You Do with a Kinkajou?*, Philadelphia: Lippincott, 1976

Hammond, Samuel H., *Hills, Lakes, and Forest Streams: or, A Tramp in the Chateaugay*

Woods, New York: J. C. Derby, 1854; also published as *Hunting Adventures in the Northern Wilds; or, A Tramp in the Chateaugay Woods, over Hills, Lakes, and Forest Streams,* New York: Derby and Jackson, 1854

_____, *Wild Northern Scenes,* New York: Derby and Jackson, 1857

Headley, Joel, *The Adirondacks; or, Life in the Woods,* New York: Baker and Scribner, 1849

Hoffman, Charles Fenno, *Wild Scenes in the Forest and Prairie,* 2 vols., London: R. Bentley, 1839; also published as *Wild Scenes in the Forest and Prairie with Sketches of American Life,* New York: W. H. Colyer, 1843

_____, "Wild Scenes near Home; or Hints for a Summer Tourist," *American Monthly Magazine* 8 (1836), pp. 469–478

Jamieson, Paul, *Adirondack Pilgrimage,* Glens Falls, New York: Adirondack Mountain Club, 1986

_____, ed., *The Adirondack Reader,* New York: Macmillan, 1964; 2nd ed., Glens Falls, New York: Adirondack Mountain Club, 1982

Jerome, Christine, *An Adirondack Passage: The Cruise of the Canoe Sairy Gamp,* New York: HarperCollins, 1994

Jogues, Isaac, Saint, *Narrative of a Captivity Among the Mohawk Indians, and a Description of New Netherland in 1642–3,* New York: Press of the Historical Society, 1856; reprinted as *Narrative of a Captivity Among the Mohawk Indians,* New York: Garland, 1977

LaBastille, Anne, *Beyond Black Bear Lake,* New York: Norton, 1987

_____, *Woodswoman,* New York: Dutton, 1976

_____, *Women and Wilderness,* San Francisco: Sierra Club, 1980

Longstreth, Thomas Morris, *The Adirondacks,* New York: Century, 1917

McKibben, Bill, "Adirondack Reprise," *Outside* (November 1991), pp. 124 ff

_____, *The Age of Missing Information,* New York: Random House, 1992

_____, *The End of Nature,* New York: Random House, 1989; London: Viking, 1990

_____, *Hope, Human and Wild: True Stories of Living Lightly on the Earth,* Boston: Little, Brown, 1995

Marshall, Robert, *The High Peaks of the Adirondacks,* Albany, New York: Adirondack Mountain Club, 1922

Murray, William, *Adventures in the Wilderness; or, Camp-Life in the Adirondacks,* Boston: Fields, Osgood, 1869; reprinted as *Adventures in the Wilderness,* Syracuse, New York: Syracuse University Press, 1970

Rebentisch, Martha, *The Healing Woods,* New York: Thomas Y. Crowell, 1952; published under the name Martha Reben, London: Hammond, 1954

_____, *The Way of the Wilderness,* New York: Thomas Y. Crowell, 1955; published under the name Martha Reben, London: Hammond, 1956

Rikhoff, Jean, *Buttes Landing,* New York: Dial, 1973

_____, *One of the Raymonds,* New York: Dial, 1974

Sandiford, Glenn, *Deepe in the Adirondacks,* Utica, New York: North Country, forthcoming, 1999

Schaefer, Paul, ed., *Adirondack Explorations: Nature Writings of Verplanck Colvin,* Syracuse, New York: Syracuse University Press, 1997

_____, *Defending the Wilderness: The Adirondack Writings of Paul Schaefer,* Syracuse, New York: Syracuse University Press, 1989

Sears, George Washington, *The Adirondack Letters of George Washington Sears, Whose Pen Name Was "Nessmuk",* Blue Mountain Lake, New York: Adirondack Museum, 1962

_____, *Woodcraft and Camping,* New York: Dover, 1963

Shaw, Christopher, "Empty at the Heart of the World," in *The Nature of Nature,* edited by William Shore, New York: Harcourt Brace, 1994

Street, Alfred, *The Indian Pass,* New York: Hurd and Houghton, 1869; reprinted, Harrison, New York: Harbor Hill, 1975

_____, *Woods and Waters; or, The Saranacs and Racket,* New York: M. Doolady, 1860; reprinted, Harrison, New York: Harbor Hill, 1976

Terrie, Philip, *Contested Terrain: A New History of Nature and People in the Adirondacks,* Syracuse, New York: Syracuse University Press, 1997

_____, *Forever Wild: Environmental Aesthetics and the Adirondack Forest Preserve,* Philadelphia: Temple University Press, 1985

_____, *Wildlife and Wilderness: A History of Adirondack Mammals,* Fleischmanns, New York: Purple Mountain, 1993

Todd, John, *Long Lake,* Pittsfield,
   Massachusetts: E. P. Little, 1845
Trudeau, Edward L., *An Autobiography,*
   Garden City, New York: Doubleday, Doran,
   1915
Warner, Charles Dudley, *In the Wilderness,*
   Boston: Houghton, Mifflin, 1878;
   London: Sampson Low, Marston, Searle
   & Rivington

White, William Chapman, *Adirondack
   Country,* New York: Duell, Sloan & Pearce,
   1954; reprinted, New York: Knopf, 1967
Winter, Kate, *The Woman in the Mountain:
   Reconstructions of Self and Land by
   Adirondack Women Writers,* Albany: State
   University of New York Press, 1989

Four Case Studies in Southern Nature Writing from Virginia's Blue Ridge Mountains and Shenandoah Valley

Michael P. Branch and Daniel J. Philippon

In their introduction to *The Norton Book of Nature Writing*, Robert Finch and John Elder comment that the Southeastern states appear "inexplicably under-represented" in the American literature of nature (pp. 27–28). Although Virginia's Blue Ridge Mountains and Shenandoah Valley encompass only a portion of one Southern state, the extent and diversity of nature writing that exist here suggest that the genre is alive and well in the Southeast and that its history in this region is as long and rich as in any other area of North America. Not only has this region inspired such classics of nature writing as William Byrd's *History of the Dividing Line*, Thomas Jefferson's *Notes on the State of Virginia*, and Annie Dillard's *Pilgrim at Tinker Creek*, but it has also been the subject of hundreds of literary meditations on nature by such well known writers as John Bartram, Andre Michaux, James Kirke Paulding, John James Audubon, William Gilmore Simms, David Hunter Strother, Walt Whitman, Bradford Torrey, Theodore Roosevelt, John Burroughs, Ellen Glasgow, Willa Cather, Donald Culross Peattie, Edwin Way Teale, Roger Tory Peterson, Christopher Camuto, and John Daniel, just to name a few. Indeed, so extensive is the literature of this region that we have chosen in this essay to limit our discussion to four texts by lesser-known authors who are particularly representative of the periods and genres in which they worked: Robert Fallam, Mark Catesby, Cornelia Peake McDonald, and Earl Hamner. In doing so, we hope not only to trace the development of natural representations in this region over time, but also to demonstrate the diversity of literary genres that merit designation as forms of environmental literature. Read-ers seeking a more detailed discussion of, and selection from, the nature writing of this region should consult our anthology, *The Height of Our Mountains: Nature Writing from Virginia's Blue Ridge Mountains and Shenandoah Valley*.

A Seventeenth-Century Explorer: Robert Fallam

Nearly a half century after the founding of Jamestown in 1607, a distinct class of frontiersmen began to emerge in Virginia, as a growing lineage of explorers pushed increasingly farther inland in search of precious metals, furs, and agricultural prospects. The second European to reach the Blue Ridge and document his discoveries after John Lederer in 1669, Robert Fallam was commissioned with Captain Thomas Batts to lead a party of explorers across the mountains in search of evidence of the South Sea, or Western Ocean. Although the colonists did not know the width of the continent, the South Sea was known to lie west of Virginia, and assuming that the waters of the western slope of the Blue Ridge flowed into the South Sea, Fallam sought to discover a tidal effect along a river or bay that would prove that the great ocean lay just beyond. Fallam's record of the month-long journey that took him beyond the Blue Ridge and into the Allegheny Mountains farther west was published in 1671 as *A Journal from Virginia*.

A Journal from Virginia has literary as well as historical value, due to Fallam's precise descriptions of the New World landscape and his ebullient optimism about the rich possibilities of the unexplored land west of the Appalachians. In the following passage, for example, he offers a pleasing description of the mountains, even as he wonders if he may actually be seeing the great Western Ocean: "[I]n a clear place at the top of a hill we saw lying south west a curious prospect of hills like waves raised by a gentle breese of wind rising one upon another. Mr. Batts supposed he saw sayles; but I rather think them to be white clifts" (pp. 189–190). *A Journal From Virginia* thus not only illustrates the way seventeenth-century Americans experienced, understood, and represented their environment, but also constitutes a document of genuine literary merit, given the freshness of Fallam's natural observations and the sensitivity of his linguistic descriptions.

Fallam's exploration narrative also prefigures later American nature writing in its braiding of close attention to the natural world with aesthetic sensitivity to the sublime beauty of the wilderness. Throughout his *Journal*, Fallam remarks upon the "stony, rocky ground" over which he travels, the impressive width and depth of the "great rivers" and "brave runs" he must ford, the "rich swamps" he is forced to circumambulate, and the "steep valleys" through which he ascends the mountains. "When we were got up to the Top of the mountain and set down very weary," he writes, "we saw very high mountains lying to the north and south as far as we could discern. . . . It was a pleasing tho' dreadful sight to see the mountains and Hills as if piled one upon another" (p. 188). Although current definitions of nature writing often fail to include such exploration narratives, *A Journal From Virginia* and other works like it constitute a rich body of early American environmental writing—particularly in the South—that deserves greater attention.

An Eighteenth-Century Naturalist: Mark Catesby

A particularly important eighteenth-century natural historian with strong ties to the region was Mark Catesby, the English botanist who lived in Virginia for seven years, from 1712 to 1719. Catesby was a gifted, self-taught artist, writer, and naturalist, whose life work, the monumental *Natural History of Carolina, Florida, and the Bahama Islands*, was so remarkably exhaustive that it stood as the authority on Southeastern flora and fauna for nearly a century after its publication. One of the earliest of the many ambitious itinerant naturalists to study American wilderness, Catesby made extensive walking tours during which he gathered specimens, made drawings, and took voluminous notes. Catesby

was innovative in his preference for drawing and describing live specimens; another innovation was his effort to categorize plant zones by dominant vegetation, an idea that Thomas J. Lyon has recognized as one of the earliest attempts to describe an ecotype by means of key species (p. 31). Catesby's contributions to American botany also prefigure and inform the plant studies of William Bartram; his volume on American birds became the foundation for the work of later ornithologists including Thomas Jefferson and Alexander Wilson; and his 220 meticulous plates of American flora and fauna pioneered the large format, illustrated natural history that would come to fruition in John James Audubon's mammoth, double elephant folio edition of *The Birds of America*.

Like most works of natural history from the period, Catesby's *Natural History* is devoted to cataloging and describing as many species of birds, fish, snakes, insects, and plants as possible. Although his writing is more formal than the narrative, essayistic mode of later eighteenth-century literary naturalists such as William Bartram, Catesby's work is distinguished by patient description and a sharp eye for detail. For example, where an early explorer such as Robert Fallam described the Virginia soil as "stony, rocky ground," Catesby the naturalist describes the geological diversity of that ground with unusual precision:

> The rocks of these mountains seem to engross one half the surface; they are most of a light gray color; some are of a coarse grained alabaster, others of a metallic luster, some pieces were in form of slate or brittle, others in lumps and hard; some appeared with spangles, others thick sprinkled with innumerable small shining specks like silver, which frequently appeared in stratums at the roots of trees when blown down. (Feduccia, 143)

And, although his work was primarily that of the naturalist in the field, Catesby's aesthetic appreciation for the southern landscape is often reflected in his literary celebration of the "delightful prospects" of the mountains, rivers, and "other beauties" of the Appalachian wilderness.

A Nineteenth-Century Diarist: Cornelia Peake McDonald

The work of Cornelia Peake McDonald offers an outstanding example of how we might view the war diary as environmental literature. At the request of her husband, who was away from home in support of the Confederate cause, McDonald faithfully kept her diary from March 1862 to August 1863, and she later reconstructed portions that were lost when the war forced the family to flee their Winchester home. The final work, a nearly 500-page holograph manuscript that McDonald copied out once for each of her eight remaining children, is replete with moving depictions of the Southern landscape as home, as a theater of war, and as a refuge from the trials of history.

In her diary, McDonald describes nature in ways that reveal the emotional suffering caused by war. "The autumn winds are whirling away the leaves from the trees, the sunshine looks cold and sad," she writes in October 1862. "Only a feeble chirp of a poor insect is heard now, of all the summer voices. Since last autumn, what a harvest Death has reaped!" (p. 84). McDonald resembles many nature writers in her enthusiasm for the wilderness and in her resolute sense that her journeys into the mountains result not only in relief, but also in a sort of purification of spirit that is ultimately impossible amid the tribulations of daily life. On one trip to the Blue Ridge, taken in November, 1862, she describes the "lightness of spirit, and exhilaration" she felt upon approaching the mountains:

First came the pale blue, faintly defined against the sky. Nearer and nearer as we came, they reared their rough, shaggy sides just before us; great mountains upon mountains. . . . The quiet and rest was so delightful to me that I felt as if I would be willing to leave the sweet home, much as I loved it (so changed it was, and so troubled was life within it) and live there in the peace and rest that I could find among those shades and nowhere else. (p. 86)

As a woman trying desperately to maintain her home and raise her children, McDonald finds in the natural world an invaluable refuge from the trials of war. Here, for example, is her reminiscence of the Shenandoah River:

[N]othing ever so fascinated me as it did, either afar when its glassy bosom mirrored the blue sky with its garments of white clouds, the fringe of thick trees on its brink, and the large wild birds sailing serenely over it, or when near enough to look down into

the clear green water. I used to spend hours gazing on it and fancying . . . that down there in those blue depths was a world of sweet repose, a blissful, fanciful world peopled with beings different from, and more delightful, than any I knew. (p. 88)

Just as distinguished nature essayists lead us into the natural world but guide us with their own perceptions, a diarist such as McDonald shows us the contours of the Virginia landscape but filters her descriptions through the sensibility of sorrow and loss that was the inevitable consequence of the Civil War. Like Dillard's *Pilgrim at Tinker Creek*, McDonald's diary is both a deeply personal response to her Shenandoah Valley home and a moving record of how emotional and physical landscapes intertwine in the imagination of the author.

A Twentieth-Century Novelist: Earl Hamner

Another writer whose work is centrally concerned with the imaginative richness of Virginia's natural environments is Earl Hamner, born in the hamlet of Schuyler, on the Rockfish River in Nelson County. A distinguished contemporary novelist, Hamner draws upon his deep, intergenerational connection with his native place in the foothills of the Blue Ridge Mountains, and his major work celebrates the traditional Southern virtues of family, community, Christian faith, and concern for the land. Hamner's romanticized portrait of rural Virginia is most effective in the novels *Spencer's Mountain* and *The Homecoming*, and in "The Waltons," the tremendously popular television series based largely upon these two books. For his readers and even for the many viewers of "The Waltons" unfamiliar with his novels, Hamner's idyllic vision of rural Southern landscape and character has proven remarkably compelling.

In *The Homecoming*, for example, Hamner's protagonist, Clay Boy (John Boy in the television series), has returned to his family's Virginia home for the holidays. While hiking alone in the snowy woods on Spencer's Mountain to cut a hemlock for the family's Christmas tree, the young man sees a female white-tailed deer (*Odocoileus virginianus*) feeding in a wild persimmon grove. When the doe, fleeing as she senses Clay Boy's presence, becomes inadvertently trapped in a deadfall of limbs and branches, Clay Boy's compassion for the struggling animal prompts him to help it escape. While he labors to free the doe, however, he has an unexpected encounter with a white buck of local legend, a powerful, ghostlike albino white-tail that promptly drives Clay Boy into the shelter of a nearby evergreen. As the enraged animal attacks him through the branches of the tree, driving at the young man with his antlers and slashing at him with his hooves, Clay Boy is forced to protect himself using an improvised pine knot torch, with which he eventually frightens the buck back into the forest. Successfully completing his efforts to emancipate the doe, Clay Boy then cuts a Christmas tree and returns with satisfaction to the family home and hearth at the foot of Spencer's Mountain.

As a premier example of regional environmental literature, Clay Boy's story is important for a number of reasons. Hamner's descriptions of the Appalachian "landscape of leafless trees, their dark, sleeping limbs starkly etched against the virgin snow" is detailed and precise, allowing his fictional narrative to invoke a powerful sense of place (p. 17). Moreover, Clay Boy's harrowing adventure with the two deer is not an initiatory but a reinitiatory experience: after a period of absence from his home landscape, he must undergo a symbolic, ritualized encounter with wild nature in preparation to descend the mountain and fully rejoin his family and community. By venturing into the wilderness alone, Clay Boy reconnects both with the landscape of his childhood and with the wisdom of his fathers: walking through a forest that "housed all those things mysterious" from his youth, and wielding his father's ax in order that he might retrieve a native tree to foster family unity and the connection of human culture with local environment, he recalls the fabulous tales of the white deer told him by his grandfather, a man who "spoke with authority, for he knew how to read the messages hidden in moon and cloud and wind" (pp. 16, 18).

In his admiration for the graceful beauty and the unfortunate plight of the entrapped doe, in his decision to free the animal rather than dispatching it as might befit the son of a hunter, Clay Boy asserts a powerful sense of connection with the nonhuman creatures who also inhabit the forest. His freeing of the deer dramatizes and enacts a respect for nature, a compassion for his fellow creatures that is vital to his membership in the larger, biotic community of Spencer's Mountain. And while the encounter with the legendary albino buck is a test of his resolution

and resourcefulness, it also serves as a salutary reminder of the "otherness" and inscrutable power of wildness. The forest would be impoverished without the presence of the legendary deer, the story seems to suggest, and Clay Boy's encounter provides him an invaluable, if unexpected, ritual of contact and communion with the uncontrollable life hidden within his ancestral wilderness. In its observation of nature, its sympathy for fellow creatures, its mythic resonance, and its exploration of the relationships between human culture and the natural world, Hamner's work suggests the value of fiction to our definition of nature writing and demonstrates the important role of landscape and place in the literature of the South.

Conclusion

By offering four case studies in Southern nature writing from Virginia's Blue Ridge Mountains and Shenandoah Valley, we have attempted to suggest the richness of literary natural history present not only in this region but also throughout the Southeastern United States. Robert Fallam, Mark Catesby, Cornelia Peake McDonald, and Earl Hamner together demonstrate both the vitality of nature as a subject for writers in this region and the wide range of genres through which these writers have addressed the natural world for nearly four centuries. If the Southeastern states appear under-represented in the American literature of nature, part of the reason for this discrepancy may be our tendency to overlook the tremendous wealth of writing about nature produced before the nineteenth century and in forms of literature other than the personal essay. As these representative texts demonstrate, however, by attending more closely to such genres as the exploration narrative, natural history, diary, and novel, and by examining works of these types in earlier periods, we soon realize how thoroughly Southern writers have been influenced by their respective places, and what important contributions these writers and these places have made to American environmental literature.

Selected Works and Further Reading

Audubon, John James, *The Birds of America,* London, 1827; reprinted, introduction by William Vogt, New York and London: Macmillan, 1937

Branch, Michael P., and Daniel J. Philippon, eds., *The Height of Our Mountains: Nature*

Writing from Virginia's Blue Ridge Mountains and Shenandoah Valley, Baltimore, Maryland: Johns Hopkins University Press, 1998

Byrd, William, *The History of the Dividing Line,* 1728; reprinted in *The Prose Works of William Byrd of Westover: Narratives of Colonial Virginia,* Cambridge, Massachusetts: Harvard University Press, 1966

Catesby, Mark, *The Natural History of Carolina, Florida, and the Bahama Islands,* 2 vols., London, 1731–43; reprinted, introduction by George Frick, Savannah, Georgia: Beehive, 1974

Dillard, Annie, *Pilgrim at Tinker Creek,* New York: Harper's Magazine, 1974; London: Cape, 1975

Fallam, Robert, *A Journal from Virginia,* 1671; reprinted in *The First Explorations of the Trans-Allegheny Region by the Virginians, 1650–1674,* edited by Clarence W. Alvord and Lee Bidgood, Cleveland, Ohio: Arthur H. Clark, 1912

Feduccia, Alan, ed., *Catesby's Birds of Colonial America,* Chapel Hill: University of North Carolina Press, 1985

Finch, Robert, and John Elder, eds., *The Norton Book of Nature Writing,* New York: Norton, 1990

Greene, Jack P., *Pursuits of Happiness: The Social Development of Early Modern British Colonies and the Formation of American Culture,* Chapel Hill: University of North Carolina Press, 1988

Hamner, Earl, *The Homecoming: A Novel About Spencer's Mountain,* New York: Random House, 1970

_____, *Spencer's Mountain,* New York: Dial, 1961; London: Corgi, 1978

Jefferson, Thomas, *Notes on the State of Virginia,* Paris, 1784; London: John Stockdale, 1787; reprinted, edited by William Peden, Chapel Hill: University of North Carolina Press, 1954

Lyon, Thomas J., ed., *This Incomperable Lande: A Book of American Nature Writing,* Boston: Houghton Mifflin, 1989

McDonald, Cornelia Peake, *A Woman's Civil War: A Diary, with Reminiscences of the War from March 1862,* edited by Minrose Gwin, Madison: University of Wisconsin Press, 1992

Garden Writing in the South

Karen Cole

The American South has often been imagined, by natives and outsiders, as a garden and its literary sensibility has frequently been called pastoral. Little attention, however, has been paid to its garden writing, to those works in which plots of land, whether called gardens or yards, have been planned, described and documented. The interplay between Southern horticultural writing and the region's more widely known fiction suggests that place and tradition have had a different meaning for garden writers.

The South's sense of place is notorious. Many have shown that one of the region's most formative myths is arcadian, a return to or preservation of the old times and simpler ways, marked by a working respect for nature and a practice of neighborliness. In *The Dispossessed Garden* Lewis Simpson argues that the Southern brand of the pastoral is essentially reactionary, an expression of the region's alienation from modernity. In *The Dream of Arcady: Place and Time in Southern Literature*, Lucinda Mac-Kethan characterizes the Southern pastoral as a literary device through which its writers might "expose or rebuke, escape or confront, the complexities of the actual time in which they have lived" (p. 3). Or as Eudora Welty, a lifelong Southern gardener herself, puts it in "Place in Fiction": "One place comprehended can make us understand other places better." A sense of place, she adds, is "essential to good and honest writing" (p. 128). In short, most agree with Richard Gray's recent assessment that this sense of place is "one of the structuring principles of Southern myth" (p. 173).

However fixed that mythic sense of place, the actual places change, especially gardens. In her earliest essay, garden writer Elizabeth Lawrence recognizes this impermanence: "When we begin a study of the gardens of the South, we too often find that while the houses connected with them are still standing, little is left of the original gar-

den, for gardens are more perishable than houses" (*Gardens*, 9). Works about the Southern garden, then, have been especially sensitive to the dynamics of landscape. Richard Westmacott has observed of the vernacular gardener in *African-American Gardens and Yards in the Rural South*: "Resourcefulness and adaptability are important to the self-image of the gardener who at the same time may be fiercely traditional . . . tradition and adaptation are not contradictory. Adaptation itself is a tradition" (p. 109).

For all who have tilled Southern soil, adaptability has been necessary. Albert Cowdrey's environmental history *This Land, This South* suggests that the region's soil and climate make it a difficult place to cultivate, whether Indian corn, King Cotton, or camellias. The weather is "melodramatic"; the climate, kind to humans, also nurtures pests and pestilence; the soil itself, leached by heavy rains for ages, has been reduced to a mixture of clay and the hydroxides of aluminum and iron. Despite the advertisements of an earthly paradise that prompted European settlement, the environment has resisted human cultivation and, in the process, demanded human respect: "An old, warm, and wet region largely covered with mediocre soils and a host to abounding life, the elemental South, since long before the first discovery by European man, has modified the health, wealth, and character of the societies that have occupied it" (p. 5).

If the South's gardening ways were from the first a matter of adaptation, the earliest writing about its horticulture encouraged exploitation as much as cultivation. For its first audience, the English aristocrats, garden fashion required rare and extensive collections from the New World. Through their work John Banister and Mark Catesby offered specimens and sketches of Virginia and the Carolinas. John Clayton's 1762 *Flora Virginica* provided the first Linnaean classification of the plants of the New World. And botanist John Bartram recorded his expedition to the newest possession of England in his *Description of East Florida* in 1765. But along with these more or less scientific descriptions were the accounts of promoters such as Robert Beverley, whose *The History of the Present State of Virginia* praises the new colony for its delights as both natural and improved garden. His description of the climate suggests a hothouse where plants "might be kept there green all the Winter, without the Charge of Housing or any other Care, than what is due the natural Plants of the Country, when transplanted into a Garden" (p. 123). His catalog of the various fruit- and nut-bearing trees, vegetables, and wild berries "growing upon wild Vines" (p. 133) sketches what Cowdrey calls a "realtor's Eden." Beverley, moreover, suggests that the Indians are, after all, fellow gardeners who "have growing near their Towns, Peaches, Strawberries, Cushawes, Melons, Pompions, Macocks, &c" (p. 181). Cultivation can only perfect this perfection: "A Garden is nowhere sooner made than there, either for Fruits, or Flowers" (p. 316). There are, in short, only three drawbacks: "Thunder, Heat, and troublesome Vermin" (p. 299). The promise is of a garden that can be had at the drop of a seed.

The *Garden Book* of Thomas Jefferson suggests otherwise. From 1766 to 1824, Jefferson recorded, with some regularity, new plantings, sowing times, transplanting methods and harvest dates, providing a yearly "Kalendar" of garden experiences at Monticello. Abundant and diverse, his garden of mostly fruits and vegetables suffered frequently from extremes of heat and cold; he reports of "a frost which destroyed almost everything"; the spring of 1804 he characterizes as "remarkably backward. We have had fires steadily thro' the whole month." And buried amid the crop yields (a 17-ounce quince or four stones of the Maddelena peach) is here and there a reminder of the human cost, rendered by the scientist's measure: "From a trial I made with the same two-wheeled barrow I found that a man would dig & carry to the distance of 50. yds 5. cubical yds of earth in a day of 12. hours length. Ford's Phill did it" (July 31, 1772). Monticello was then as now a symbol of the Enlightenment transplanted to the New World; its head gardener was methodic and experimental. Yet in its account the struggle to bring about a New World garden proves more difficult than Beverley's promise.

In the first decades of the nineteenth century, the Southern imagination seized upon the plantation garden as site and justification of its ways. John Pendleton Kennedy's *Swallow Barn: Or Life in the Old Dominion* depicts, among other things, the conflict between the institution of slavery and the pastoral image of the plantation. Swallow Barn is an "aristocratical old edifice" on the southern banks of the James River in a nook shaded by magnificent oaks, Lombardy poplars, a willow and a plum tree. In a late chapter entitled "A Negro Mother," Kennedy's narrator tells of old Lucy's cabin at a remove from the Quarter: "A garden occupied the little space in front of the habitation; and here, with some evidence of a taste for embellishment which I had not seen elsewhere in this negro hamlet, flowers were planted in order along the line of the inclosure and shot up with a gay luxuriance" (p. 384). The garden, now under the "thrifty care" of Lucy's daughter, comes to represent in the novel's terms the potential of Southern patriarchy to cultivate gallantry, heroism, and European values among the "humble slave of the Old Dominion" (p. 403). Simpson argues that the Southern literary imagination, as exemplified by Kennedy, resolves the antipastoral character of slavery by giving the chattel a pastoral relationship to the land. In *Swallow Barn* neither the slave garden nor the plantation itself requires much work; they are as much in harmony with one another as with their environment, static symbols of an old way already being scrutinized by debates in the Virginia legislature about suffrage and slave laws.

Those who planned and tilled the antebellum garden wrote more of its challenges than its symbolism. The years between 1820 and 1850 saw a shift of the Southern population from the Eastern seaboard to the Southwest. This migration spread what Cowdrey terms the "rowcrop empire"—a society of farmers, rich and poor, who shared a belief in their right to use the land and its dwellers as they saw fit and who, for the most part, accepted slavery as necessary (pp. 65–66). In the rural frontier, the vegetable patch was as much a necessity as the pleasure garden was a luxury, available to those few who had the extra hands or the extra energy at the end of a long day for its cultivation. Martha Turnbull, for example, provided nearly a half-century record (1837–95) of her gardening activities at Rosedown Plantation near St. Francisville, Louisiana. Her accounts of extensive box gardens, lists of varieties of camellias, orders for crape myrtles from New York all suggest the energy and resources that could be put into the plantation display. But her journal also records a pride in effort (she helped to prune the boxwoods, for instance) and the despair of losing individual plants, particularly during the Civil War. Here then is an intimate relationship with a working garden, not a static symbol.

In his narrative *Twelve Years a Slave*, Solomon Northup, from another perspective, details the hardships of carving out even the smallest plantation in central Louisiana. Born a freeman in New York, then kidnapped and sold into slavery in New Orleans, Northup tells of not only the emotional suffering of his bondage, but of the brutal toil of felling pines and clearing bayous for navigation, of long hours in cane brakes and cotton fields, of extreme heat, mosquito-ridden swamps, and bouts with malaria. In the center of his story is a brief account of a particularly kind plantation mistress and her garden, a "little paradise in the Great Pine Woods . . . the oasis in the desert" (p. 109). Some of the description is reminiscent of the early promotional literature, and probably bears the mark of Northup's editor, an attorney with literary inclinations: "The crimson and golden fruit hung half hidden amidst the younger and older blossoms of the peach, the orange, the plum, and the pomegranate; for, in that region of almost perpetual warmth, the leaves are falling and the bud bursting into bloom the whole year long." Yet the passage bespeaks first-hand knowledge of the diligence needed in "cleaning the walks, weeding the flower beds, and pulling up the rank grass beneath the jessamine vines" (p. 109). For both Martha Turnbull and Northup, the plantation garden is an accomplishment rather than an abstract notion of regional identity. Despite the sad irony that Northup pays tribute to the kindness of his mistress, his "protectress," the memory encompasses his contribution to a place "towards which [his] heart turned lovingly, during many years of bondage" (p. 109).

In the fiction of the postwar South, there was a parallel development of two conflicting trends, reflective of currents in the nation as a whole. C. Vann Woodward has characterized the mood: "Along with the glittering vision of a metropolitan and industrial South to come there developed a cult of archaism, a nostalgic vision of the past" (p. 154). Writing about the southern garden reflected both trends. *The Conjure Woman*, a collection of stories told by an old black gardener, is Charles Chesnutt's answer to the nos-

talgia, best represented in the works of Thomas Nelson Page and Joel Chandler Harris. The visions of these Southern apologists hearken back to an idealized Jeffersonian South—a gracious home, cultivated habits of aristocracy and agriculture, and the all but silent and efficient labor of slaves to keep it all going. As a black man, Chesnutt chose the standard features of this Arcadian dream to expose its hypocrisies.

The tales are complex, for they are filtered through the lens of a Northern agriculturist come South. "Mars Jeems's Nightmare," for example, depicts the patronizing view of both North and South: while it reveals the exploitation of Northern capital during Reconstruction, it also exposes the myth of the benevolent master-slave relationship. Taken on for his usefulness ("old Julius was familiar with the watercourse, knew the qualities of the various soils and what they would produce, and where the best hunting and fishing were to be had"), this former slave proves valuable for more than his understanding of the environment, which our Northern narrator explains as "doubtless due to the simplicity of a life that had kept him close to nature" (p. 64). The landowner celebrates the "peculiar personal attitude" Julius shows toward his land. Julius's cautionary tale is of slaveholder Jeems who, through conjuring, is transformed into a slave, found wandering the roads, and given to Jeems's brutal overseer to be tamed. Just before he is sold down river, the spell is removed; thereafter, Mars Jeems returns to his plantation to fire his overseer and begins to treat his slaves as human beings. The wisdom of Old Julius's tales is as much informed by his understanding of whites and their institutions as by his relationship to the land. In Chesnutt's fiction, we can recognize the transformation of the pastoral vision, although its site and central symbol, the plantation garden, remains much the same.

After the war, the conception of the garden itself had begun to change, and to change in ways driven by economic necessity. Women, faced with the need to earn a living, turned the acceptable leisure pursuits of painting, photographing, and writing about gardens into successful careers. May Brawley Hill's recent study *Grandmother's Garden: The Old-Fashioned American Garden 1865–1915* documents many such accounts of the Southern landscape turned tourist attraction. Watercolorist Alice Ravenel Huger Smith collaborated with her father, an amateur historian, on two preservationist works about their native Charleston: *Twenty Drawings of the Pringle House on King Street* and *The Dwelling Houses of Charleston*. Similarly Blondelle Malone, trained in New York and through a passing acquaintance with Monet at Giverny, returned to Charleston in 1908 to paint her family's and neighbors' gardens. These visions of the garden as art helped to preserve the region's gardening ways just as the work of other women recorded its hard times. The photographs of Frances Benjamin Johnson made picturesque old and untended sites throughout the impoverished South. Elizabeth Pringle offers an account of her struggles to maintain her own plantation in *A Woman Rice Planter*, a work that gives voice to the hardships faced by plantation mistresses and farm wives throughout the region.

The postwar South was far from being the romantic place of Harris's and Page's stories. Its rural population—still the majority through the first decades of the twentieth century—was especially poor, both white and black. This poverty was bred not only by an outdated and cruel economic and social order, but by the environmental facts of isolation and eroded soils. As Cowdrey puts it, "Poverty is no friend to natural resources" (p. 103). The *Progressive Farmer,* founded in 1886 by populist reformer Leonidas Polk, sought to bring news of agricultural affairs to otherwise isolated farmers and to foster acceptance of new, more science-based methods. One of the weekly magazine's first causes was to urge the state of North Carolina to found a state agency and to create a college of agriculture. Eventually to bolster its readership, the editors began to offer advice to farm wives, not only on the healthful benefits of a kitchen garden, but on the rudiments of domestic landscape design. An influential journal for almost a century, as Pierce Lewis demonstrates, the *Farmer* was renewed in the 1960s as *Southern Living.*

The shift from rural to urban can be traced in an interesting way in the garden writing of George Washington Cable. The final chapter of his 1914 *An Amateur Garden* recognizes in "The Midwinter Gardens of New Orleans" a gentility no longer possible in the restlessness of urban America. Conceding that the "formal" garden is available to the wealthy few, Cable claims that the "informal" or "free-hand, ungeometrical" garden is "for the great democracy" (p. 168). And the New Orleans garden—small, enclosed, and crammed with "the flowered robes and garlandries of nature's diplomacy and hospitality" (p. 175)–is precisely the plan to be adopted by

middle-class and particularly urban dwellers throughout the nation as a defense against the democratic tyrannies of haste, flat lawns, and joy in machinery. The tradition of gentility in the plantation South had been repackaged for urban America.

Perhaps the best known horticultural writer of the twentieth century is Elizabeth Lawrence, whose last and most passionate project was a history of Southern market bulletins. Subsidized by state agencies, beginning in the 1920s, these periodicals offered classified advertisements by farm men and women, who had livestock, equipment, plants, seeds, and bulbs to offer. The posthumous *Gardening for Love* is a glimpse of Lawrence's 20-year study (1959–78), which she hoped would reflect the "rich sense of social history of the rural Deep South" and would "speak of times and customs that are rapidly passing" (p. 24). Like Eudora Welty, who sent Lawrence her first market bulletin, she insisted on the garden as an experience rather than a symbol. In her influential *The Southern Garden*, for instance, Lawrence makes clear that all gardens are made possible through conversation, where the academic and the amateur have equal say. This common language, her works suggest, is socially and even politically important as a means to preservation.

Preservation itself takes on a different meaning for these two writers. Davyd Foard Hood's study of the histories of Southern garden clubs in the first two decades of the twentieth century makes clear their notion of garden history as a documentation of "the fragments that remain"; almost exclusively those fragments were of estate gardens. But in Eudora Welty's *Delta Wedding*, where the garden of matriarch Ellen Fairchild is preserved through the work of most of the Fairchild heirs as well as one of the black farm hands, the emphasis is on its plants: old roses, for instance, are carefully tended and called by name, and their cuttings offered as a wedding gift. In the Delta Eden, to borrow Louise Westling's term, of Welty's fiction, as in Lawrence's writing, the Southern garden is, among other things, a catalog of plant names. The final scene of the novel, three days after its culminating event, depicts Ellen renewing her yard by giving it a good soak with that most joyous of all modern technologies for the Southern gardener, the hose.

The introduction to Steve Bender's and Felder Rushing's *Passalong Plants* gives voice to this new conception of the Southern garden. After a

long list of the things it is not, the authors claim
what it is—a book about old plants and their
place in the region's past and future: "Old people. Young people. Memories. Shared experiences. Shared plants. Feelings, history, advice,
opinion." The garden is the place where the
flowers, trees, shrubs, vines, and bulbs are kept
as a kind of repository for past and present, a
site to hold the plants "Southerners grew up
with, fell in love with, can't forget, and unfortunately, have a devil of a time finding anymore in
garden centers" (p. 1). The book imagines gardening as friendly, both color- and class-blind:
"Luckily, to a gardener, all other gardeners *are*
friends." The plant swap advocated at the end of
the book, although reminiscent of Jefferson's
correspondents, is more inclusive: "Remember
to invite the general public, as well as garden
clubers, plant society members, local garden
writers, and extension agents" (p. 212). The
labor is to be supplied by family members and a
few yardless friends. The few hints about design
are decidedly "informal"—the whitewashed
tractor tire as divider or the bottle tree as deco-
ration. The Southern garden still embodies the
arcadian myth of a working respect for nature,
simpler ways, and neighborliness. But as a symbol, it has been transformed to represent neither
leisure, nor taste, nor the status of an old order.
At its most idealistic, it represents the hard work
and great pleasure of community, and a sense of
place and of past that is dynamic.

Selected Works and Further Reading

Bender, Steve, and Felder Rushing, *Passalong
Plants,* Chapel Hill: University of North
Carolina Press, 1993

Beverley, Robert, *The History and Present State
of Virginia,* London: R. Parker, 1705;
reprinted, edited by Louis B. Wright, Chapel
Hill: University of North Carolina Press,
1947

Cable, George Washington, *The Amateur
Garden,* New York: Scribner's, 1914

Chesnutt, Charles W., *The Conjure Woman,*
Boston: Houghton Mifflin, 1899; London:
Riverside, 1899

Cowdrey, Albert E., *This Land, This South: An
Environmental History,* Lexington:
University Press of Kentucky, 1983

Gray, Richard, *Writing the South: Ideas of an
American Region,* New York and
Cambridge: Cambridge University Press,
1986

Hill, May Brawley, *Grandmother's Garden:
The Old-Fashioned American Garden,
1865–1915,* New York: Harry N. Abrams,
1995

Hood, Davyd Foard, "'To Gather up the
Fragments That Remain': Southern Garden
Clubs and the Publication of Southern
Garden History," *Journal of Garden History,*
forthcoming

Jefferson, Thomas, *The Garden and Farm
Books of Thomas Jefferson,* edited by
Robert C. Baron, Golden, Colorado:
Fulcrum, 1987

Kennedy, John Pendleton, *Swallow Barn, or, A
Life in the Old Dominion,* Philadelphia:
Carey & Lea, 1832; reprinted, edited by Jay
B. Hubbell, New York: Harcourt, Brace,
1929

Lawrence, Elizabeth, *Gardening for Love: The
Market Bulletins,* edited by Allen Lacy,
Durham, North Carolina: Duke University
Press, 1987

———, *Gardens of the South,* Chapel Hill:
University of North Carolina Press, 1945

———, *A Southern Garden,* Chapel Hill:
University of North Carolina Press, 1942

Lewis, Pierce, "The Making of Vernacular
Taste: The Case of *Sunset* and *Southern
Living,*" in *Vernacular Garden: Papers of
the Dumbarton Oaks Symposium,*
Washington: Dumbarton Oaks, 1991

MacKethan, Lucinda Hardwick, *The Dream
of Arcady: Place and Time in Southern
Literature,* Baton Rouge: Louisiana State
University Press, 1980

Northup, Solomon, *Twelve Years a Slave,*
Auburn, New York: Derby and Miller,
1853; reprinted, edited by Sue Eakin and
Joseph Logsdon, Baton Rouge: Louisiana
State University Press, 1968

Pringle, Elizabeth W. Allston, *A Woman Rice
Planter,* New York: Macmillan, 1913

Simpson, Lewis P., *The Dispossessed Garden:
Pastoral and History in Southern Literature,*
Athens: University of Georgia Press, 1975;
London: Louisiana State University Press,
1984

Turnbull, Martha, *Rosedown Garden Diary,
1836–1895,* transcription by C. A. Haines,
Baton Rouge: Hill Memorial Library,
Louisiana State University, 1958

Welty, Eudora, *Delta Wedding,* New York:
Harcourt, Brace, 1946; London: Bodley
Head, 1947

———, "Place in Fiction," *The Archive* 67:4

(April 1955); also published in *The Eye of the Story: Selected Essays and Reviews,* New York: Random House, 1970; London: Virago, 1987

Westling, Louise, *Sacred Groves and Ravaged Gardens: The Fiction of Eudora Welty, Carson McCullers, and Flannery O'Connor,* Athens: University of Georgia Press, 1985; London: University of Georgia Press, 1987

Westmacott, Richard N., *African-American Gardens and Yards in the Rural South,* Knoxville: University of Tennessee Press, 1992

Literary Nonfiction Writing
of the American Desert

Andrea W. Herrmann

The term "literary nonfiction" was coined in 1980 by Ronald Weber in *The Literature of Fact* to describe writing of essentially factual content employing novelistic techniques. Authors writing in this manner, such as Truman Capote, Tom Wolfe, and Norman Mailer, were labeled New Journalists. Gradually, however, the label of literary nonfiction embraced a larger sphere of nonfiction writing—biographies, autobiographies, journals, memoirs, personal essays, nature writing, natural history, and other, less-established forms of writing, such as the prose poem. The determining factor is whether or not the writing is of sufficient caliber to qualify as literature.

Distinguishing between fiction and nonfiction is another issue. There is a growing awareness that most writing contains elements of both. Since much nonfiction writing consists of an author's recollection of past experiences filtered through his or her personal views of reality, to some extent the degree of nonfictionality is dependent upon the accuracy of the writer's recall and his or her faithfulness in rendering those memories into words. Generally, whether a piece of writing is "nonfiction" depends on whether the author, based on his or her sense of reality, has attempted to recreate the events and their meaning with a minimum of distortion for the reader. Of course we cannot know for certain the writer's intentions, but we can be sensitive to his or her faithfulness to a shared reality.

How can we account for the profusion of literary nonfiction written about America's deserts? It seems clear that both their fearsome austerity and sublime beauty have moved even those who did not think of themselves as writers to eloquence. As for prolific authors, such as Mary Austin and Mabel Dodge Luhan, their psychic connections to the desert have inspired them to produce their most acclaimed work. And it would appear that contemporary authors, worried that we are losing our last remaining wild places, write in an effort to preserve them.

I have placed the authors within one of four chronological time frames, each approximately 40 years in duration. They are the frontier era (to 1880), the turn-of-the-century era (1881–1920), the mid-twentieth-century era (1921–60), and the contemporary era (1961–97).

The Frontier Era (to 1880)

The frontier era acquaints us with the desert through the eyes of hardy travelers confronting an inhospitable land. Alvar Nuñez Cabeza de Vaca's *The Narrative* is the earliest account of literary nonfiction from an explorer of America's deserts. His impressive tale begins in the 1530s with a search for cities of gold in Florida. Hopelessly lost with three other companions and having to deal with hostile Indians, Cabeza de Vaca's band crossed the deserts of Texas, New Mexico, Arizona, and Mexico for eight years on foot, surviving by their wits and new-found abilities to cure the sick. This is an adventure story with psychological drama, riveting details, and anthropological and historical richness. Haniel Long's *Interlinear to Cabeza de Vaca* is a compelling version. Another intrepid, desert explorer from the frontier era is Eusebio Francisco Kino. His journals, *Kino's Historical Memoir of Pimeria Alta: A Contemporary Account of the Beginnings of California, Sonora, and Arizona,* let us see him in his many guises: as a pioneer, missionary, explorer, cartographer, rancher, and Italian Jesuit missionary. While promoting the expansion of Spain, Kino arrived in Baja California in 1681, traveled thousands of miles by horse-back, made the first maps of the Pimeria Alta (the Sonora border country), and founded numerous missions. A courageous explorer and a likable person possessed of incredible physical stamina and drive, Kino recounts his adventures in a highly readable memoir.

Many of the accounts of the early explorers' desert adventures are as thrilling as any Hollywood movie. Perhaps the best known is John Wesley Powell's dangerous expedition of the Colorado River. In 1869, with 10 men and four boats, Powell undertook his famous river voyage, which involved running hazardous rapids in 1,000 miles of mostly unexplored canyons. This desert area had consisted, according to Wallace Stegner, of "an empty, blistered, uninhabited, and unvisited wilderness" (Stegner, xii). Powell kept a sparsely worded journal that became the basis for *The Exploration of the Colorado River* five years later. David Teague sees Powell as an early example of desert transcendentalist, pointing out that Powell provides the reader with careful and detailed pictures of the landscape. While objections have been raised that parts were fictionalized, Wallace Stegner makes the case that Powell's narrative is meant to be an adventure story and that some tampering with details still leaves an essentially truthful record.

William Lewis Manly also recounted a page-turning adventure filled with amazing detail, particularly considering his book was written 40 years after the experience. Manly was a pioneer from Vermont who traveled across the West for what he termed "twelve long, weary months" (p. 498), which he vividly describes in his book, *Death Valley in '49*. His crossing saga, which takes place in a wagon train pulled by oxen, involves separations, wild rivers, encounters with Indians, and getting profoundly lost in Death Valley, where 13 comrades die. But Manly finds his way out and heroically returns to save several others in his party.

Unlike Manly, Raphael Pumpelly wrote about more places than the American desert in his books *Across America and Asia* and *My Reminiscences;* however, the American part of his adventures involved much action, including eyewitness accounts of Indian raids and bullet wounds. Pumpelly's travels from 1860 to 1862 also include his experiences as a mining engineer near Tucson, Arizona, and detailed descriptions of the plants and animals and poetic descriptions of the land.

Other works of literary nonfiction desert writing from the frontier era are John Charles Frémont's *A Report on the Exploring Expedition to Oregon and North California in the Years 1843–44* and Ignaz Pfefferkorn's *Sonora: A Description of the Province of Sonora.*

The Turn-of-the-Century Era (1881–1920)

In contrast to the adventures of the frontier era, the writers we encounter in the turn-of-the-century era have often lived close to the desert, studied it, and warmed to its subtle beauty. One of the most famous of these authors is Mary Austin. Her best-known literary nonfiction grew out of her spiritual connection to the desert. *The Land of Little Rain* is based on living close to the earth in the California desert, a country "forsaken of most things but beauty and madness and death and God" (p. 50). Thomas J. Lyon says, "Austin's particular genius was to see and record in process, the innumerable tiny adjustments of plants and animals, that taken together, make up arid biological communities" ("The Literary West," 719–720). Both landscape and community are important to Austin. Some critics believe *The Land of Journeys' Ending,* her other desert classic, is her best work, but both books are beautifully written.

Another woman who lived on the desert and wrote during this period is Idah Meacham Strobridge. Her *Sagebrush Trilogy: Idah Meacham Strobridge and her Works* contains *In Miner's Mirage Land, The Loom of the Desert,* and *The Land of Purple Shadows,* three books that teeter on the edge of the fiction/nonfiction divide. *In Miner's Mirage Land,* for example, Strobridge recounts lost-mine legends interspersed with essays about the desert. These books, written by an observant and introspective author, are rich in detail and description.

Of all the nonfiction writers known for appreciating the desert's beauty, John Charles Van Dyke, an Eastern art historian who ended up on the desert for health reasons, has influenced more desert writers than any other with *The Desert,* a perennial favorite. Peter Wild states that "Van Dyke was the first to look upon wastelands . . . as the fruitful apple of the spiritual eye. So much so that *The Desert* is the grafting stock of all other desert celebrations" (*The Desert Reader,* 111). Van Dyke expresses his views on the special value of deserts, rejecting, according to Wild, the pioneers' utilitarianism and replacing it with an airy estheticism, calling the desert "the most decorative landscape in the world" ("Sentimentalism," 127), and encouraging the public to see it on his terms. And we do. *The Desert* is a song involving natural history, philosophy, and a prescient understanding of the detrimental role humans play as destroyers of these fragile arid lands. By capturing its many colors and inhabitants in brush strokes of sparseness and simplicity, Van Dyke provides his view of the desert as art, making *The Desert* as relevant today as it was in 1901.

Following closely in Van Dyke's footsteps as an appreciator of the desert's beauty and of its value for the individual is George Wharton James. In *The Wonders of the Colorado Desert*, James describes the rivers, mountains, canyons, and springs, as well as the flora, fauna, and Indian culture of the Coachella and Imperial valleys. With an effusive style, he speaks of the desert's "sincerity" and believes that one cannot know the self in the "fictitious, unnatural" cities: "Oh, for the freedom of soul that comes from absolute openness, as freedom of the body comes in the desert!" (pp. 531–532).

Some authors of the turn-of-the-century era, while clearly appreciating the desert's unique beauty, come across more like early pioneers or adventurers. One example of a pioneer is William Temple Hornaday, who was a collecting zoologist, conservationist, and writer. Although the vicinity of Pinacate Peak had already been mapped for the Western world by Kino in the 1600s, it became *terra incognita* once again until Hornaday re-explored it. *Camp-Fires on Desert and Lava,* with its lunar-like lava flows and volcanic peaked landscape, garnered a wide readership in its day and is well worth reading today. And an example of an adventurer is Charles Fletcher Lummis (1859–1928), a newspaper editor in Ohio, who traversed an incredible 30 to 50 miles a day across the country, sending a weekly column during his trip in exchange for a job on the *Times* when he arrived in Los Angeles. These articles became *A Tramp Across the Continent.* This skillfully written book is full of lyrical descriptions of the land, characters speaking in dialects, and, although Lummis calls it a "truthful" account, narrow scrapes with death, some of which are probably exaggerations.

Other recommended literary nonfiction desert writing from the turn-of-the-century era are Clarence E. Dutton's *Tertiary History of the Grand Cañon District,* Carl Lumholtz's *New Trails in New Mexico,* and Martha Summerhayes's *Vanished Arizona: Recollections of My Army Life.*

The Mid-Twentieth Century Era (1921–60)

During the mid-twentieth century era authors frequently write not only of the land around them but also about the desert's human communities as well. For example, while running a trading post on the Navajo Reservation with her husband from 1914 to 1918, Hilda Faunce wrote a series of letters about their lives that became the basis of her book *Desert Wife*. In this perceptive portrayal of the intricate and respectful relationships that the author and her family established with the Navajos, Faunce crafts a beautiful narrative with complex characters. Another community-sensitive desert writer, much better known than Faunce, is Mabel Dodge Luhan. A wealthy, well-traveled New Yorker, Luhan wrote *Edge of Taos Desert* and *Winter in Taos*. Both nonfiction books proclaim her regeneration in, and love of, the Southwest. In *Edge of Taos Desert,* she sensitively portrays the beauty of the landscape around her and the white American, Mexican, and Pueblo communities in Taos, New Mexico, about 1917. In fact, Luhan becomes such a part of this diverse community, she ultimately separates from her husband to live with Tony Luhan, a Pueblo, whom she eventually marries, and remains in Taos until her death.

Another author with a concern for community in the arid West is Wallace Earle Stegner, an award-winning novelist, short story writer, essayist, historian, and professor of writing. He saw wilderness as "the geography of hope" and recognized its importance on character. In *Where the Bluebird Sings to the Lemonade Springs: Living and Writing in the West,* a collection of essays, Stegner laments the lack of community in the West, calling it "an overnight camp" and indicating that Westerners have space instead of place (p. 72). Stegner was concerned about the lack of water in the West and its allocation, and, he realized, this was intimately connected to Americans' desire to re-create their notions of beauty, instead of living on the land's terms. "You have to get over the color green; you have to quit associating beauty with gardens and lawns," Stegner tells us (p. 54). In *Beyond the Hundredth Meridian: John Wesley Powell and the Second Opening of the West,* Stegner shows us Powell's life as an explorer and, more importantly, his forward thinking as a government administrator and his (mostly failed) efforts to influence irrigation decisions and change land allocation policies in the West. Sensitive to the aesthetic value of our deserts, Stegner argues for the protection of the wilderness in the *Sound of Mountain Water* because it is "an intangible and spiritual resource" (p. 153).

One of the most highly regarded nature writers of the twentieth century is Joseph Wood Krutch. The author's two nonfiction classics, *The Desert Year* and *The Voice of the Desert: A Naturalist's Interpretation,* present lyrical portraits of the Sonoran Desert's flora and fauna. Krutch, a naturalist with a wise and witty voice, seasons his text with an occasional literary allusion and often personifies the animals he examines. According to Thomas J. Lyon, "his nature essays, particularly those built on the remarkable adaptations of life to desert conditions, have been some of the most influential of recent decades" (*This Incomperable Lande,* 296).

Other recommended literary nonfiction desert writing from the mid-twentieth century era are Edna Brush Perkins's *The White Heart of Mojave: An Adventure with the Outdoors of the Desert* and J. Frank Dobie's *The Voice of the Coyote.*

The Contemporary Era (1961–97)

During the contemporary era literary nonfiction has bloomed like desert flowers after a soaking rain. Many authors, such as Aldo Leopold, Edward Abbey, and Charles Bowden, although they sing the desert's praises, also sound alarms over the consequences of human encroachment. The first author of this period to bring attention to the emerging problems was Aldo Leopold. A forester, professor, and preservationist, Leopold became well known as a writer. His posthumously published collection of nature essays, *A Sand County Almanac,* which includes pieces about the desert, is a classic. This delightful book is written with a poet's sensitivity to language and a philosopher's sensitivity to nature. It helped earn him the title of father of wildlife conservation in the United States and still serves as a prototype for much contemporary nature writing. Robert Finch in his introduction to the collection points out that "Leopold calls for nothing less than a fundamental reform in our relationship with the land" (p. xxv).

Undoubtedly, the best known desert writer of the contemporary era, both as a fiction and nonfiction writer is Edward Abbey. A guru of the environmental movement, Abbey insisted he wrote personal history not natural history. *Desert Solitaire* is his most influential nonfiction work. Abbey believes "we cannot have freedom without wilderness," and his strong and eloquent stand against the encroachments of industrial society into the desert have made him a prophet and a visionary for many (Bishop, 13). But he is polemical, has a sardonic sense of humor, and his radical stances and negativity toward women have turned off others. A disciplined writer, he produced a large body of provocative and entertaining nonfiction, including: *The Journey Home, Abbey's Road, Beyond the Wall,* and *One Life at a Time, Please.* James Bishop Jr. has lauded him for his "graceful and musical prose" (p. 11).

Following in the footsteps of Abbey, but clearly with his own unique voice and message, is Charles Bowden. Bowden, a long-time resident of Tucson, Arizona, has written an impressive number of desert books, including *Blue Desert,* a collection of essays that reveals the paradoxes of the desert, the good and the bad of it, from his vantage as a newspaper reporter. In *Blue Desert* we meet a Bowden who has seen too much, who has drunk too much, and who shares it all in a heavily ironic, mystery-writer prose style. In *Desierto: Memories of the Future* we come in contact with a desert far different from the ones described by genteel nature writers. Instead, Bowden presents a desert usually hidden from the reader's view—the "bad part of town"—and makes us intimately aware of the conflict, turmoil, and violence out there, experiencing the sordidness and darkness within the deteriorated human psyche. Bowden, an irreverent but winsome raconteur, writes compellingly about disturbing topics in a provocative voice.

The ironies of contemporary desert life also come through in the works of other twentieth century writers, such as Bruce Berger and David Quammen. Bruce Berger's *The Telling Distance: Conversations with the American Desert,* which won the Western States Book Award in 1990, is a collection of 50 well-written essays and briefer pieces—some as short as a paragraph—reflecting Berger's personal, sometimes amused, often ironic reactions to the desert. David Quammen is a natural science writer, known for his natural history column in *Outside Magazine,* who also deals with social issues in the essays he has written about the Sanctuary movement. He is the author of *Flight of the Iguana: A Sidelong View of Science and Nature,* which contains three essays dealing with the Sonoran Desert.

Two well-known naturalists who write knowledgeably and well about the desert are Ann Zwinger and Terry Tempest Williams. Ann Zwinger, a natural history writer who most often writes about American deserts, illustrates her writing with wonderful drawings. Her *Wind in the Rock: The Canyonlands of Southeastern Utah* lets us experience with her "an exhilarating sense of immediacy" and the "heady taste of glory" she feels exploring the five canyons of the Grand Gulch Plateau in southeastern Utah (p. 7). Her *The Mysterious Lands* is a detailed exploration of the Chihuahuan, Sonoran, Mojave, and Great Basin deserts, which delineates and emphasizes the uniqueness of each. The nonfiction desert books of Terry Tempest Williams–a naturalist by training with a poet's ear and a writer's eye–include, among others, *Refuge*, in which Williams tells the story of her family's illness on the desert and "how we find refuge in change." *Desert Quartet*, a book with a small format, large type, and illustrations, could be mistaken at first glance for a children's book, but as soon as one reads, "Earth. Rock. Desert. I am walking barefoot on sandstone, flesh responding to flesh," one understands that this is an adult book, an evocative, erotic response to the desert that is beautifully written (p. 1).

Another evocative author is Leslie Marmon Silko, a member of the Laguna Pueblo and the author of numerous novels. In her essay, "Landscape, History, and the Pueblo Imagination," she shows the close relationship the ancient Pueblo people had with the land and how those beliefs continue today. They "could not conceive of themselves without a specific landscape" (p. 112). The barrenness of the Hopi land made them understand that there was little between them and the Earth. "Simply to survive is a great triumph ... every possible resource is needed, every possible ally" (p. 117). The Hopi view the Earth as the "Mother Creator," Silko tells us, something for humans to bond with, not conquer.

Other recommended works of literary nonfiction desert writing from the contemporary era are Reyner Banham's "The Man-Mauled Desert," Stephen Bodio's *Querencia*, Janice Emily Bowers's *The Mountains Next Door*, David Darlington's *The Mohave*, Alison Hawthorne Deming's *Temporary Homelands*, Diana Kappel-Smith's, *Desert Time*, Florence R. Krall's *Ecotone*, Gary Paul Nabhan's *Counting Sheep*, Reg Saner's, *The Four-Cornered Falcon*, and Rob Schultheis's *The Hidden West*.

This body of environmental writing reflects society's changing relationship with the American desert. The historical record we find in this environmental writing becomes all the more poignant as writers today articulate their deepest concerns about these, the country's last, wild, open places. This writing emphasizes the sense of urgency readers should feel about the threat to the deserts brought about by human development.

Selected Works and Further Reading

Abbey, Edward, *Desert Solitaire: A Season in the Wilderness,* New York: McGraw-Hill, 1968

Anderson, Chris, *Style as Argument: Contemporary American Nonfiction,* Carbondale: Southern Illinois University Press, 1987

Austin, Mary Hunter, *The Land of Journeys' Ending,* New York: Century, 1924; London: Allen & Unwin, 1924; reprinted, New York: AMS, 1969

———, *The Land of Little Rain,* Boston: Houghton Mifflin, 1903; London: Constable, 1996

Banham, Reyner, "The Man-Mauled Desert," in *Desert Cantos,* photos by Richard Misrach, Albuquerque: University of New Mexico Press, 1987

Berger, Bruce, *The Telling Distance: Conversations with the American Desert,* Portland, Oregon: Breitenbush, 1990

Bishop, James, Jr., *Epitaph for a Desert Anarchist: The Life and Legacy of Edward Abbey,* New York: Atheneum, 1994

Bodio, Stephen, *Querencia,* Livingston, Montana: Clark City, 1990

Bowden, Charles, *Blue Desert,* Tucson: University of Arizona Press, 1986

———, *Desierto: Memories of the Future,* New York: Norton, 1991

Bowers, Janice Emily, *The Mountains Next Door,* Tucson: University of Arizona Press, 1991

Darlington, David, *The Mojave: A Portrait of the Definitive American Desert,* New York: Henry Holt, 1996

Deming, Alison Hawthorne, *Temporary Homelands: Essays on Nature, Spirit, and Place,* New York: Picador USA, 1996

Dobie, J. Frank, *The Voice of the Coyote,* Lincoln: University of Nebraska Press, 1949; London: Hammond, 1950

Dutton, Clarence E., *Tertiary History of the*

Grand Cañon District, with Atlas, Washington, D.C.: Government Printing Office, 1882

Faunce, Hilda, *Desert Wife,* Boston: Little, Brown, 1934; reprinted, Lincoln: University of Nebraska Press, 1981

Frémont, John Charles, *Report of the Exploring Expedition to the Rocky Mountains in the Year 1842, and to Oregon and North California in the Years 1843–44,* Washington, D.C.: Gales and Seton, 1845; also published in *The Expeditions of John Charles Frémont,* vol. 1, edited by Donald Jackson and Mary Lee Spence, Urbana: University of Illinois Press, 1970

Hornaday, William Temple, *Camp-Fires on Desert and Lava,* New York: Scribner's, 1908; London: T. Werner Laurie, 1909; reprinted, Tucson: University of Arizona Press, 1983

Ingham, Zita, *Reading and Writing a Landscape: A Rhetoric of Southwest Desert Literature* (Ph.D. diss., University of Arizona), 1991

James, George Wharton, *The Wonders of the Colorado Desert,* 2 vols., Boston: Little, Brown, 1906

Kappel-Smith, Diana, *Desert Time : A Journey Through the American Southwest,* Boston: Little, Brown, 1992; London: University of Arizona Press, 1994

Kino, Eusebio Francisco, *Kino's Historical Memoir of Pimeria Alta: A Contemporary Account of the Beginnings of California, Sonora, and Arizona,* 2 vols., edited by Herbert Eugene Bolton, Cleveland, Ohio: Arthur H. Clark, 1919; reprinted, Berkeley: University of California Press, 1948

Krall, Florence R., *Ecotone: Wayfaring on the Margins,* Albany: State University of New York Press, 1994

Krutch, Joseph Wood, *The Desert Year,* New York: William Sloane, 1951; Harmondsworth, England: Penguin, 1977

———, *The Voice of the Desert: A Naturalist's Interpretation,* New York: Morrow, 1955

Leopold, Aldo, *A Sand County Almanac: With Essays on Conservation from Round River,* New York: Sierra Club/Ballantine, 1966

Long, Haniel, *Interlinear to Cabeza de Vaca: His Relation of the Journey from Florida to the Pacific, 1528–1536,* Santa Fe, New Mexico: Writers' Editions, 1936; reprinted, New York: Frontier, 1969; also published as

The Marvellous Adventure of Cabeza de Vaca, London: Souvenir, 1972

Luhan, Mabel Dodge, *Edge of Taos Desert: An Escape from Reality,* New York: Harcourt, Brace, 1937

———, *Winter in Taos,* New York: Harcourt, Brace, 1935; reprinted, Taos, New Mexico: Las Palomas, 1982

Lumholtz, Carl, *New Trails in Mexico,* New York: Scribner's, 1912; London: T. F. Unwin, 1912

Lummis, Charles Fletcher, *A Tramp Across the Continent,* New York: Scribner's, 1892; London: Sampson Low, 1892

Lyon, Thomas J., ed., *This Incomperable Lande: A Book of American Nature Writing,* Boston: Houghton Mifflin, 1989

———, "The Literary West," in *The Oxford History of the American West,* edited by Clyde A. Milner, Carol A. O'Connor, and Martha A. Sandweiss, New York: Oxford University Press, 1994

McClintock, James, *Nature's Kindred Spirits: Aldo Leopold, Joseph Wood Krutch, Edward Abbey, Annie Dillard, and Gary Snyder,* Madison: University of Wisconsin Press, 1994

Manly, William Lewis, *Death Valley in '49,* San José, California: Pacific Tree and Vine, 1894

Nabhan, Gary Paul, ed., *Counting Sheep: Twenty Ways of Seeing Desert Bighorn,* Tucson: University of Arizona Press, 1993

Núñez Cabeza de Vaca, Alvar, *The Narrative of Alvar Núñez Cabeça de Vaca,* translated by Buckingham Smith, Washington, D.C., 1851

Perkins, Edna Brush, *The White Heart of Mojave: An Adventure with the Outdoors of the Desert,* New York: Boni & Liveright, 1922; London: T. F. Unwin, 1923

Pfefferkorn, Ignaz, *Sonora: A Description of the Province,* 1795; translated and edited by Theodore E. Treutlein, Albuquerque: University of New Mexico Press, 1949

Powell, John Wesley, *Exploration of the Colorado River of the West and Its Tributaries,* Washington, D.C.: Government Printing Office, 1875; also published as *The Exploration of the Colorado River,* introduction by Wallace Stegner, Chicago: University of Chicago Press, 1957; London: University of Chicago Press, 1970

Powell, Lawrence Clark, *Southwest Classics: The Creative Literature of the Arid Lands: Essays on the Books and Their Writers,* Los Angeles: Ward Ritchie, 1974

Pumpelly, Raphael, *Across America and Asia: Notes of a Five Years' Journey Around the World and of Residence in Arizona, Japan, and China,* New York: Leypoldt & Holt, 1870; London: Sampson Low, Son and Marston, 1870

———, *My Reminiscences,* 2 vols., New York: Henry Holt, 1918

Quammen, David, *The Flight of the Iguana: A Sidelong View of Science and Nature,* New York: Delacorte, 1988

Saner, Reg, *The Four-Cornered Falcon: Essays on the Interior West and the Natural Scene,* Baltimore, Maryland: Johns Hopkins University Press, 1993

Schultheis, Rob, *The Hidden West: Journeys in the American Outback,* San Francisco: North Point, 1980

Sheldon, Charles, *The Wilderness of the Southwest: Charles Sheldon's Quest for Desert Bighorn Sheep and Adventures with the Havasupai and Seri Indians,* edited by Neil B. Carmony and David E. Brown, Salt Lake City: University of Utah Press, 1993

Silko, Leslie Marmon, "Landscape, History, and the Pueblo Imagination," in *Celebrating the Land: Women's Nature Writings, 1850–1991,* edited by Karen Knowles, Flagstaff, Arizona: Northland, 1992

Sims, Norman, ed., *Literary Journalism in the Twentieth Century,* New York: Oxford University Press, 1990

Stegner, Wallace, *Beyond the Hundredth Meridian: John Wesley Powell and the Second Opening of the West,* Boston: Houghton Mifflin, 1954

———, *The Sound of Mountain Water,* Garden City, New York: Doubleday, 1969

———, *Where the Bluebird Sings to the Lemonade Springs: Living and Writing in the West,* New York: Random House, 1992

Strobridge, Idah Meacham, *Sagebrush Trilogy: Idah Meacham Strobridge and Her Works,* edited by Richard A. Dwyer and Richard E. Lingenfelter, Reno: University of Nevada Press, 1990

Summerhayes, Martha, *Vanished Arizona: Recollections of My Army Life,* Philadelphia: Lippincott, 1908

Teague, David Warfield, *I Shall Give You Peace, and a Great Content: The Imaginative Conquest of the Southwestern United States* (Ph.D. diss., University of Virginia), 1994

Van Dyke, John Charles, *The Desert: Further Studies in Natural Appearances,* New York: Scribner's, 1901; London: Sampson Low, Marston, 1901

Wild, Peter, ed., *The Desert Reader: Descriptions of America's Arid Regions,* Salt Lake City: University of Utah Press, 1991

———, "Sentimentalism in the American Southwest: John C. Van Dyke, Mary Austin, and Edward Abbey," in *Reading the West: New Essays on the Literature of the American West,* edited by Michael Kowalewski, New York and Cambridge: Cambridge University Press, 1996

Williams, Terry Tempest, *Desert Quartet,* New York: Pantheon, 1995

———, *Refuge: An Unnatural History of Family and Place,* New York: Pantheon, 1991

Zwinger, Ann Haymond, *The Mysterious Lands: An Award-Winning Naturalist Explores the Four Great Deserts of the Southwest,* New York: Dutton, 1989

———, *Wind in the Rock,* New York: Harper & Row, 1978; London: University of Arizona Press/Eurospan, 1987

Women's Resistance in the Desert West

Susanne Bounds and Patti Capel Swartz

The stereotype of the desert: lifeless, desolate, barren, somewhere to get through to get to the other side. A final frontier in the United States, but only habitable or useful through much manipulation of nature: redirecting water, extracting mineral wealth, developing for malls and industry, using for bombing ranges.

Perhaps because of the manipulation to which women also are subjected in Western society to be "useful" or "habitable," women have been speaking eloquently for the land and life of the United States desert West to be left alone, to be allowed to be as it is and not subject to consumption and manipulation. Growing numbers of women have been writing in and of the desert West, "accepting a demanding and difficult landscape on its own terms and creating arts based on survival . . . [and finding that] . . . the vast and undominated scale of the land liberates woman from strictures of traditional femininity silencing her voice'" (Monk and Norwood, 42).

Kathryn Wilder, the editor of *Walking the Twilight* and *Walking the Twilight II*, discusses in her introductions the influence the environment has on women and their writing: "As the Southwest is shaped so visibly, tangibly, audibly even, by fire-rock, wind, and water, so are its people. . . . Emotional erosion takes place here" (*Twilight*, xv); the women are influenced by the land physically, emotionally, spiritually, and are writing fiercely to save that land that nourishes them most when it stays as it is. Environmental concerns manifest in their writings in a variety of ways: from using landscape as a character in fiction to considering the struggle over water rights in essays; from portraying the land as healer to constructing new ways to include the land in Western human mythologies. The Western desert woman writer is developing a genre of her own, one often not solely definable in terms of genre categorizations of poetry, prose, fiction, nonfiction or drama, and this essay and bibliography are designed to help begin to define what that genre may be and to provide a brief introduction to both established voices and new voices emerging.

Many new voices are heard in the anthology *Walking the Twilight*: Laraine Herring, Pam Houston, Lisa Chewning, Liz Besmehn, and Jo Ann Freed portray the desert as a place of healing, a place where everyday life falls to the side and what is basic, important to life, emerges. Luci Tapahonso gives a pile of rocks at the base of a mesa new meaning through a story of the death of an infant. Mary Hokanson tells the story of a child who leaves a calm life for a more chaotic one, and her descriptions of the land echo the emotions of the child. Della Frank addresses in poetic prose the sacredness of the land in Dine life through memories of her father, who was exploited along with the land in logging and mining industries in the Southwest. Ariana-Sophia M. Kartsonis depicts the desert lands as a woman's body, weaving the life and death of a relationship with the land. Teresa Jordan uses bone imagery to suggest the process of people becoming dried to their essences in the desert environment.

The forms and subjects of the writings in this anthology are rich. Pat Carr and Mary Sojourner build their stories around two environmental concerns of the desert West: Carr tells the story of a woman caught up in the stealing and vandalism of the black market artifact trade, also a theme of Anna Lee Walters's *Ghost Singer*, while in Sojourner's "Officer Magdalena, White Shell Woman, and Me," women are protesting uranium mining near the South Rim of the Grand Canyon. Her main character, Liz, states that those who protest "feel . . . the earth really is a woman, and She is being killed. I don't know if we're making that up, or if we're finally . . . remembering what we once knew" (p. 164).

Writers in *Walking the Twilight II* continue

many of the same themes, and again there are new voices along with established ones. Merion Morrigan Sharp, Karen Sbrockey, Liz Besmehn, and Sojourner use the land as healing places for their characters. Like Melinda Popham's novel *Skywater,* Sheila Goldburgh Johnson's "Tortoise Watch" revolves around an endangered species, while Cathryn Alpert's "Unnatural" reveals a mother's pain at losing her son because of his environmental activism. Pam Houston details the changes people undergo as they run a wild desert river, and in Anna Lee Walters's "Buffalo Wallow Woman" a woman confined to a mental hospital calls herself Buffalo Wallow Woman and uses the natural imagery associated with that name to offset the anguish of her everyday surroundings.

Debra Hughes-Blank and Patricia Clark Smith are two other local fiction writers for whom the desert land plays a role in shaping their stories and characters, as it does for Sojourner in her novel, *Sisters of the Dream,* which traces the experiences of a woman who has moved to Northern Arizona and begins to dream the life of an ancient Hopi woman. Through the dreams and the landscape of the area, she begins to heal from a difficult past, and Sojourner weaves in details of environmental issues that concern people of the area.

The environment also plays a large role in Leslie Marmon Silko's work. To her, landscape is inseparable from story, contributes to story, and often becomes a character in story. In "Landscape, History, and the Pueblo Imagination" Silko says, "So little lies between you and the sky. So little lies between you and the earth. One look and you know that simply to survive is a great triumph, that every possible resource is needed, every possible ally—even the most humble insect or reptile" (p. 94). In her collection of stories, photographs, and poems, *Storyteller,* and in her novels *Ceremony* and *Almanac of the Dead,* the landscape plays a major role, and she often refers to many of the environmental problems that plague people native to the Southwest: mining, ranching, development, loss of native plants and animals, loss of water due to diversion to other populated areas. The novels also deal with the connections between oppression of the land and native peoples. In *Sacred Water,* as in her *Storyteller,* Silko weaves text with photographs. She discusses the sacredness of water to the desert environment and the threats to that resource, including diversion to overpopulated areas and toxic nuclear waste runoff.

In *Taos Pueblo,* in which her text accompanies Ansel Adams photographs, Mary Austin, much earlier in the century, writes of water as "the wedding ring of the earth and the sky" (p. 8). Much of Austin's work focused on water rights and uses, but also on mineral rights, protesting appropriation of both in the name of progress and for capitalistic gain while ecosystems were being destroyed. Patricia Nelson Limerick describes the struggle to obtain water and the confusion about water rights and mineral rights in the West as well as the ecological destruction agriculture brought through farming, ranching, and grazing, themes that many writers resisting ecological destruction have explored.

María Amparo Ruiz de Burton, Sharman Apt Russell, and Austin were concerned with battles between ranchers and farmers over land use and public policy. In her 1906 *The Flock,* Austin examines shepherding in California, the dilemma of public lands. As Limerick indicates, the question of changes in ecosystems through conquest of the land for agricultural and mining purposes has never been resolved. Russell writes of the present-day controversies in New Mexico over the leasing of public land: conflicts between ranchers and wilderness groups that grazing leases create. Russell also explores the destruction of the inhabitants of natural environments and the civilizations that had previously existed on this land divining lessons to be learned by a population that needs to become "in love, at last, with their world" (p. 160).

These writers who recognize the importance of living with the earth rather than conquest of the earth and its people realize the contradictions that come with "progress" and attempts at "conquest." María Amparo Ruiz de Burton protested squatting and farming at the same time that she lauded the prosperity that railroads might bring to Southern California. Maxine Hong Kingston's *China Men* looks at attempts at conquest of land, the work accorded to Chinese immigrants, and attitudes toward the Chinese in the United States, weaving nature with racial and political issues.

The effects of colonization and appropriation of both land and resources are detailed in the works of a number of women writers, among them early writers or recorders from the 1930s Federal Writing Project contained in Tey Diana Rebolledo's and Eliana Rivero's *Infinite Divisions.* Colonial attitudes are also explored in the writing of Alma Luz Villanueva, the collected oral histories of Patricia Preciado Martin, the remembrances of Aurora Levins Morales and Rosario Morales in *Getting Home Alive*, and Sylvia Lopez-Medina's *Cantora*. Denise Chávez's *The Last of the Menu Girls* and Betty Louise Bell's *Faces in the Moon* examine growing up in the Southwest. Wakako Yamauchi's memoir, *Songs My Mother Taught Me,* describes agricultural life in California. Cherríe Moraga's *The Last Generation* looks at cultural losses as well as prejudice toward sexual difference. Paula Gunn Allen also looks at sexuality, gender roles, and nature together in her fiction and theory. Allen also edited the anthology *Spider Woman's Granddaughters*.

Mineral rights, oil rights, environmental contamination, misappropriation of monies and the lands of Native peoples, and murder is the topic of Linda Hogan's *Mean Spirit*. Hogan's writing is intertwined with her belief that balance in, and focus of, our lives depends on creating a world in which we are one part of nature. Hogan, like Joy Harjo, sings her belief in the unity of the natural and spirit worlds beautifully, and she, Harjo and Wendy Rose protest attempts to strip the world and its residents of unity and dignity.

Barbara Kingsolver's work examines pollution and the need for global commitment for humans in harmony with the earth. Ana Castillo's *So Far from God* looks at people dispossessed from the land they originally occupied. Set in a small community in New Mexico, Castillo's novel creates a world in which the natural, the supernatural, the supranatural, religion, human life, and the life of the earth intersect. As is Gloria Anzaldúa in essays and in her *Borderlands/La Frontera*, Castillo is concerned with dispossessed peoples who now work the land they once worked and enjoyed unimpeded by colonization and colonial attitudes. Both write of acceptance of people who will live in harmony in and with the world. As is Helena María Viramontes in her *Under the Feet of Jesus* and Lucha Corpi in *Cactus Blood*, Castillo is concerned with chemical contaminants and pesticides that affect the Chicano/a, Latina/o, and Native populations working with them. Castillo also creates a cooperative in which people can live simply, healthily, and in harmony with the land. Patricia Beatty's young adult book, *Lupita Manaña*, explores the separations of farm workers from families, as well as fieldwork in California.

Pat Mora's *Nepantla* explores life lived in the midst of nature, and her children's text *The Desert Is My Mother/El Desierto Es Mi Madre* is a lyrical exploration of the desert, beautifully illustrated. Bia Lowe's *Wild Ride* looks at nature and social organization in contemporary California through memoir. Teresa Jordan and James Hepworth's anthology of contemporary women writers points up the diversity of background of women writing about both the West and the Southwest while Francesca Lia Block's fantasy, *Ecstasia*, a book for young adults, examines contamination of culture and environment and portrays the desert as a place of escape and renewal.

Terry Tempest Williams is one of the most prolific women writers of the desert West, focusing her efforts on essays and stories centered around her home state of Utah. One of her early books, *Pieces of White Shell: A Journey to Navajoland,* details Navajo culture through nature, while in *Coyote's Canyon,* she tells stories to accompany dramatic photos by John Telford and creates a new mythology of the West, one in which we are not the conquerors, but only players in the drama of the land. In *Refuge: An Unnatural History of Family and Place*, Williams interweaves the story of her mother's death from breast cancer with the catastrophic flooding of the Bear River Migratory Bird Refuge by the Great Salt Lake. In the epilogue, "The Clan of One-Breasted Women," Williams tells the story of the women in her family, and of many women living in the West, acquiring breast cancer from fallout due to nuclear weapons testing in the 1950s and 1960s. In her most recent books, *An Unspoken Hunger: Stories from the Field* and *Desert Quartet: An Erotic Landscape*, she adds powerful statements about what nature means to us, what it should mean to us, and the perils we face if we do not realize the interconnections.

Also writing for the wildernesses of Utah and other areas of the desert West are Ellen Meloy in *Raven's Exile: A Season on the Green River* and Ann Haymond Zwinger in *Downcanyon: A Naturalist Explores the Colorado River Through the Grand Canyon* and *The Mysterious Lands: A Naturalist Explores the Four Great Deserts of the Southwest*. Meloy uses a season spent as a ranger in the Desolation Canyon stretch of the Green River to develop her ideas about what that stark landscape offers to us if left as it is and not subjected to the same devastation as Glen Canyon further downriver. Zwinger evokes the beauty of the Grand Canyon and Colorado River in *Downcanyon* and the Southwest deserts in *The Mysterious Lands*. In "Writers of the Purple Figwort," she discusses what she wishes to accomplish in her writing, and how that may be different from what she sees as more dogmatic environmental writing: through intimate description of the landscape, she hopes to entice readers into learning more about the land, which will then become part of their experience and therefore more valuable to them so that they will be more likely to want to preserve it.

Leslie Ryan lives in Montana, but writes of the desert in terms of bodily survival of women: her essay "The Other Side of Fire" is a tremendously powerful essay about sexual and physical molestation being healed by the challenges of desert survival, both for her and for young women she leads into the desert. "In order to survive there, I had to be fully present" (p. 364); demands of the desert landscape forced her to reunite her body and mind and soul, which had been torn asunder by early abuse.

Derrick Jensen in *Listening to the Land: Conversations About Nature, Culture, and Eros* talks with Linda Hogan, Starhawk, Dolores LaChapelle and Julien Puzey, and Susan Griffin. Hogan discusses language's power to influence our view of the world and the rule of money over the way we deal with the environment, while LaChapelle and Puzey discuss a complete change in our way of seeing the environment, from forming it to our needs, to us forming ourselves to it. Starhawk talks about developing spirituality and language to live differently on the earth and about her concerns about nuclear technology, so prevalent in the desert West, and Griffin connects pornography and environmental devastation, discussing sensuality and acceptance in both arenas.

Geographical representations of the environment of the Southwest, because actual land and conditions are not easily confined to the lines of a map or to the symbols on a printed page, are as likely to overlap and defy categorization as are the writers whose work considers the land and the environment. The Southwest has been, and often remains, contended and contentious. Writing of the Southwest is as diverse as the population. Women writing about nature create resistance to homogeneity and exploitation of the earth and its residents. As Luci Tapahonso writes: "This land that may seem arid and forlorn to the newcomer is full of stories which hold the spirits of the people, those who live here today, and those who lived centuries and other worlds ago" (*Women*, 6).

Selected Works and Further Reading

Adams, Ansel, and Mary Hunter Austin, *Taos Pueblo,* San Francisco, 1930; facsimile edition, Boston: New York Graphic Society, 1977

Allen, Paula Gunn, *Grandmothers of the Light: A Medicine Woman's Sourcebook,* Boston: Beacon, 1991

———, *The Sacred Hoop: Recovering the Feminine in American Indian Traditions,* Boston: Beacon, 1986

———, ed., *Spider Woman's Granddaughters: Traditional Tales and Contemporary Writing by Native American Women,* Boston: Beacon, 1989; London: Women's Press, 1990

———, *The Woman Who Owned the Shadows,* San Francisco: Spinsters, Ink, 1983

Anzaldúa, Gloria, *Borderlands/La Frontera,* San Francisco: Spinsters/Aunt Lute, 1987

———, ed., *Making Face, Making Soul/Haciendo Caras: Creative and Critical Perspectives by Feminists of Color,* San Francisco: Aunt Lute, 1990

Austin, Mary Hunter, *The American Rhythm: Studies and Reëxpressions of Amerindian Songs,* Boston: Houghton Mifflin, 1930

———, *The Arrow-Maker,* New York: Duffield, 1911; rev. ed., Boston: Houghton Mifflin, 1915

———, *The Basket Woman,* Boston: Houghton Mifflin, 1904

———, *Cactus Thorn: A Novella,* Reno: University of Nevada Press, 1988

———, *California: The Land of the Sun,* New York: Macmillan, 1914; London: A. & C. Black, 1914; rev. ed., *The Lands of the Sun,* Boston: Houghton Mifflin, 1927

———, *The Children Sing in the Far West,* Boston: Houghton Mifflin, 1928

———, *Earth Horizon: Autobiography,* Boston: Houghton Mifflin, 1932; reprinted, Albuquerque: University of New Mexico Press, 1991

———, *The Flock,* Boston: Houghton, Mifflin, 1906; London: Archibald Constable, 1906

———, *The Ford,* Boston: Houghton Mifflin, 1917; London: University of California Press, 1997

———, *The Land of Journeys' Ending,* New York: Century, 1924; London: Allen & Unwin, 1924

————, *The Land of Little Rain,* Boston: Houghton Mifflin, 1903; London: Constable, 1996

————, *Lost Borders,* New York and London: Harper & Brothers, 1909

————, *A Mary Austin Reader,* edited by Esther F. Lanigan, Tucson: University of Arizona Press, 1996

————, *Mother of Felipe, and Other Early Stories,* edited by Franklin Walker, San Francisco: Book Club of California, 1950

————, *One Hundred Miles on Horseback,* 1889; reprinted, Los Angeles: Dawson's Book Shop, 1963

————, "One Smoke Stories," *Yale Review* 22:3 (Spring 1933), pp. 525–532

————, *Santa Lucia, a Common Story,* New York and London: Harper & Brothers, 1908

————, *Starry Adventure,* Boston: Houghton Mifflin, 1931

————, *Stories from the Country of Lost Borders,* New Brunswick, New Jersey: Rutgers University Press, 1987

————, *The Trail Book,* Boston: Houghton Mifflin, 1918

————, *Western Trails: A Collection of Short Stories,* edited by Melody Graulich, Reno: University of Nevada Press, 1987

————, *Writing the Western Landscape,* edited and illustrated by Ann H. Zwinger, Boston: Beacon, 1994

Beatty, Patricia, *Lupita Mañana,* New York: Morrow, 1981

Bell, Betty Louise, *Faces in the Moon,* Norman, Oklahoma, and London: University of Oklahoma Press, 1994

Block, Francesca Lia, *Ecstasia,* New York: ROC, 1993

Castillo, Ana, *Massacre of the Dreamers: Essays on Xicanisma,* Albuquerque: University of New Mexico Press, 1994

————, *So Far from God: A Novel,* New York: Norton, 1993; London: Women's Press, 1994

Chávez, Denise, *The Last of the Menu Girls,* Houston, Texas: Arte Público, 1986

Corpi, Lucha, *Cactus Blood,* Houston, Texas: Arte Público, 1995

Harjo, Joy, *In Mad Love and War,* Middletown, Connecticut: Wesleyan University Press, 1990

————, *She Had Some Horses,* New York: Thunder's Mouth, 1983

————, *The Woman Who Fell from the Sky: Poems,* New York: Norton, 1994

Hogan, Linda, *The Book of Medicines: Poems,* Minneapolis, Minnesota: Coffee House, 1993

————, *Dwellings: A Spiritual History of the Living World,* New York and London: Norton, 1995

————, *Mean Spirit,* New York: Atheneum, 1990

————, *Red Clay: Poems and Stories,* Greenfield Center, New York: Greenfield Review, 1991

————, *Savings: Poems,* Minneapolis, Minnesota: Coffee House, 1988

————, *Seeing Through the Sun,* Amherst: University of Massachusetts Press, 1985

————, "Stories of Water," in *Northern Lights: A Selection of New Writing from the American West,* edited by Deborah Clow and Donald Snow, New York: Vintage, 1994

————, "The Voyagers," in *American Nature Writing, 1994,* edited by John A. Murray, San Francisco: Sierra Club, 1994

Hughes-Blanks, Debra, "Edna's Pie Town," in *Tierra: Contemporary Short Fiction of New Mexico,* edited by Rudolfo A. Anaya, El Paso, Texas: Cinco Puntos, 1989

Jensen, Derrick, *Listening to the Land: Conversations About Nature, Culture, and Eros,* San Francisco: Sierra Club, 1995

Jordan, Teresa, and James Hepworth, eds., *The Stories That Shape Us: Contemporary Women Write About the West: An Anthology,* New York: Norton, 1995

Kingsolver, Barbara, *Animal Dreams,* New York: HarperPerennial, 1991

————, *Another America/Otra América,* translated by Rebeca Cartes, Seattle, Washington: Seal, 1992

————, *The Bean Trees,* New York: HarperPerennial, 1989

————, *High Tide in Tucson: Essays from Now or Never,* New York: HarperCollins, 1995

————, *Holding the Line: Women in the Great Arizona Mine Strike of 1983,* Ithaca, New York: ILR, 1989

————, *Pigs in Heaven,* New York: HarperCollins, 1993; London: Faber and Faber, 1993

Kingston, Maxine Hong, *China Men,* New York: Ballantine, 1981; London: Pan, 1981

Lensink, Judy Nolte, ed., *Old Southwest/New Southwest: Essays on a Region and Its Literature,* Tucson, Arizona: Tucson Public Library, 1987

Limerick, Patricia Nelson, *The Legacy of Conquest: The Unbroken Past of the American West,* New York: Norton, 1987

López-Medina, Sylvia, *Cantora: A Novel,* Albuquerque: University of New Mexico Press, 1992

Lowe, Bia, *Wild Ride: Earthquakes, Sneezes, and Other Thrills,* New York: HarperCollins, 1995

Luchetti, Cathy, and Carol Olwell, eds., *Women of the West,* New York: Orion, 1982

Madison, D. Soyini, ed., *The Woman That I Am: The Literature and Culture of Contemporary Women of Color,* New York: St. Martin's, 1994

Martin, Patricia Preciado, *Songs My Mother Sang to Me: An Oral History of Mexican American Women,* Tucson: University of Arizona Press, 1992

Meloy, Ellen, *Raven's Exile: A Season on the Green River,* New York: Henry Holt, 1994

Monk, Janice, and Vera Norwood, "Angles of Vision: Enhancing Our Perspectives on the Southwest," in *Old Southwest/New Southwest: Essays on a Region and Its Literature,* edited by Judy Nolte Lensink, Tucson, Arizona: Tucson Public Library, 1987

Mora, Pat, *The Desert Is My Mother/El Desierto Es Mi Madre,* Houston, Texas: Piñata, 1994

———, *Nepantla: Essays from the Land in the Middle,* Albuquerque: University of New Mexico Press, 1993

Moraga, Cherríe, *The Last Generation,* Boston: South End, 1993

Moraga, Cherríe, and Gloria Anzaldúa, eds., *This Bridge Called My Back: Writings by Radical Women of Color,* Watertown, Massachusetts: Persephone, 1981

Morales, Aurora Levins, and Rosario Morales, *Getting Home Alive,* Ithaca, New York: Firebrand, 1986

Popham, Melinda Worth, *Skywater,* St. Paul, Minnesota: Graywolf, 1990

Rebolledo, Tey Diana, "Hispanic Women Writers of the Southwest: Tradition and Innovation," in *Old Southwest/New Southwest: Essays on a Region and Its Literature,* edited by Judy Nolte Lensink, Tucson, Arizona: Tucson Public Library, 1987

Rebolledo, Tey Diana, and Eliana S. Rivero, eds., *Infinite Divisions: An Anthology of Chicana Literature,* Tucson: University of Arizona Press, 1993

Rose, Wendy, *Bone Dance: New and Selected Poems, 1965–1993,* Tucson: University of Arizona Press, 1994

———, *The Halfbreed Chronicles and Other Poems,* Los Angeles: West End, 1985

Ruiz de Burton, María Amparo, *The Squatter and the Don: A Novel Descriptive of Contemporary Occurrences in California,* San Francisco: S. Carson, 1885; also published as *The Squatter and the Don,* edited by Rosaura Sánchez and Beatrice Pita, Houston, Texas: Arte Público, 1992

Russell, Sharman Apt, *Songs of the Fluteplayer: Seasons of Life in the Southwest,* Reading, Massachusetts: Addison-Wesley, 1991

Ryan, Leslie, "The Other Side of Fire," in *Northern Lights: A Selection of New Writing from the American West,* edited by Deborah Clow and Donald Snow, New York: Vintage, 1994

Silko, Leslie, *Almanac of the Dead: A Novel,* New York: Simon & Schuster, 1991

———, *Ceremony,* New York: Viking, 1977

———, "Landscape, History, and the Pueblo Imagination," *Antaeus* 57 (Autumn 1986), pp. 83–94

———, *Sacred Water,* Tucson, Arizona: Flood Plain, 1993

———, *Storyteller,* New York: Arcade, 1981

Smith, Patricia Clark, "Mother Ditch," in *Tierra: Contemporary Short Fiction of New Mexico,* edited by Rudolfo A. Anaya, El Paso, Texas: Cinco Puntos, 1989

Sojourner, Mary, *Sisters of the Dream,* Flagstaff, Arizona: Northland, 1989

Tapahonso, Luci, *Sáanii Dahataal: The Women Are Singing: Poems and Stories,* Tucson: University of Arizona Press, 1993

Villanueva, Alma, *Weeping Woman: La Llorona and Other Stories,* Tempe, Arizona: Bilingual, 1994

Viramontes, Helena María, *Under the Feet of Jesus,* New York: Dutton, 1995

Walters, Anna Lee, *Ghost Singer,* Flagstaff, Arizona: Northland, 1988

———, *The Sun Is Not Merciful,* Ithaca, New York: Firebrand, 1985

Wilder, Kathryn, ed., *Walking the Twilight: Women Writers of the Southwest,* Flagstaff, Arizona: Northland, 1994

———, *Walking the Twilight II: Women Writers of the Southwest,* Flagstaff, Arizona: Northland, 1996

Williams, Terry Tempest, *Coyote's Canyon,* photographs by John Telford, Salt Lake City, Utah: Peregrine Smith, 1989

———, *Desert Quartet,* New York: Pantheon, 1995

———, *Refuge: An Unnatural History of Family and Place,* New York: Pantheon, 1991

———, *Pieces of White Shell: A Journey to Navajoland,* New York: Scribner's, 1984

———, *An Unspoken Hunger: Stories from the Field,* New York: Pantheon, 1994

Yamauchi, Wakako, *Songs My Mother Taught Me: Stories, Plays, and Memoir,* New York: Feminist Press at the City University of New York, 1994

Zwinger, Ann Haymond, *Downcanyon: A Naturalist Explores the Colorado River Through the Grand Canyon,* Tucson: University of Arizona Press, 1995

———, *The Mysterious Lands: An Award-Winning Naturalist Explores the Four Great Deserts of the Southwest,* New York: Dutton, 1989

———, "Writers of the Purple Figwort," in *Old Southwest/New Southwest: Essays on a Region and Its Literature,* edited by Judy Nolte Lensink, Tucson, Arizona: Tucson Public Library, 1987

Conversions to Earth: Spiritual Transformations in American Nature Writers

F. Marina Schauffler

"The sickness of our time is not a political sickness," Wallace Stegner observed, "it's a soul sickness." Intractable social and environmental problems that appear to be external are rooted in the depths of our being. Technical and political measures may assuage outer symptoms, but only a change of inner ecology can restore environmental health.

Many writers, philosophers, and theologians have begun calling for such a spiritual and ethical transformation. Few, however, have a vision of how this change might be effected. With most research focused on external solutions to environmental concerns, little is known about the morphology of inner change—how such shifts in consciousness might occur (Bartky, 12).

The most compelling accounts of inner transformation may come from personal narratives. Numerous accounts of ecological awakenings are recorded in the essays, journals, letters and autobiographical reflections of American environmental literature. Entering into the patterns and rhythms of outer landscape, writers often come to redefine their inner terrain. Their concept of self expands, allowing greater empathy with what David Abram calls the more-than-human world. This profound reorientation can touch every level of being—intellectual, psychological, spiritual, ethical and practical.

In classical theology, such a change of heart and mind is called "metanoia," based on the Greek meaning "turning about." This turning, within the Christian tradition, implies a renunciation of old ways and adoption of new beliefs and practices. In ecological terms, metanoia represents nothing less than a conversion to earth, a commitment to re-envision one's place in the world and reform one's behavior accordingly. The turning is not to a particular doctrine but to a new mode of relation with the larger natural community.

Conversions to earth rarely occur as linear progressions marked by distinct or predictable phases. Metanoia represents a complex and evolving process in which accumulated insights gradually contribute to a profound shift in both consciousness and conscience.

While there is no "formula" for ecological metanoia, there are patterns that recur in many conversion narratives. Metanoia may be occasioned by periods of intense reflection, resulting from loss or illness. Often, the process is marked by visionary moments that serve as "ecological epiphanies." The resulting shifts in perception and practice typically prompt individuals to reassess their ecological worldview. Ecological awakenings can occur within any cultural context but are often most pronounced in writers rooted in Biblical faiths or scientific materialism (traditions that do not hold ecological interdependence as a central value).

Navigating New Terrain

More often than not, individuals do not seek out metanoia. It comes to them uninvited (and is not always warmly welcomed). An ecological conversion may be precipitated by a period of enforced introspection, brought on by illness or the loss of a loved one. The ardent preservationist and writer John Muir, for example, experienced a profound ecological awakening in the wake of a debilitating accident.

Gifted with a talent for mechanical innovation, Muir had—by young adulthood—invented several new machines and was working to improve the production capacity of a local factory. But, despite his mechanical aptitude, he was drawn to spend more time outdoors. Unresolved about what life course to pursue, he was "tormented with soul hunger" (Wolfe, 88).

At work one day in the factory, Muir lost hold of a sharp file that slipped and pierced the cornea of his right eye. The second eye soon became blind from nerve shock and sympathy, leaving him in total darkness for a month–unsure if he would ever see again. When his sight finally did return, he headed straight for the woods, committed now to following his passion for outdoor life. "This affliction has driven me to the sweet fields," he declared. "God has to nearly kill us sometimes to teach us lessons" (Wolfe, 105). Abandoning his job at the factory and the more domesticated landscape of his youth, he embarked on a decade-long "pilgrimage to the wild" (O'Grady).

Unforeseen losses can irrevocably change the contours of a person's life, eroding the bulwarks that once lent security and meaning. In her book *Refuge*, Terry Tempest Williams describes how the death of her mother and grandmother, and the flooding of a beloved wildlife sanctuary, reconstellate her inner world. As she moves through a landscape now void of familiar bearings, her life comes to pivot on the question: how do we find refuge in change?

> I am slowly, painfully discovering that my refuge is not found in my mother, my grandmother, or even the birds of Bear River. My refuge exists in my capacity to love. If I can learn to love death then I can begin to find refuge in change. (p. 178)

As Williams' experience demonstrates, metanoia does not transport one to a landscape of certainty. It demands that we embrace paradox—finding security in change, cherishing beauty in death and decay, joining fully in the wondrous and bittersweet dance of life. Like more conventional forms of conversion, ecological awakening is not a one-time event but an ongoing process of renewing and deepening our ties to the ecological whole. "We are not converted only once in our lives," Thomas Merton observed, "but many times" (Griffin, 177).

Ecological Epiphanies

The turning that characterizes ecological metanoia is gradual. Experiences may accumulate like compost in the dark layers beneath consciousness, with old perceptions slowly breaking down to nourish new growth (Tallmadge, 50). Or the transformation may involve a progressive shedding of old masks and habits, in a return to one's bedrock self.

These subterranean processes—slow and barely discernible—are occasionally illumined by a flash of mystical insight. "Crystalline moments," as Anne Morrow Lindbergh termed them (p. 109), cast one's life in a new light, irrevocably changing the contours of both inner and outer landscape.

Recounting her arrival in Wyoming, Lynne Bama captures the intense quality of such moments:

> I had climbed the ridge intently, concentrating on my footing. Only when I got to the top did I turn around and discover that the clouds on the other side of the valley had blown away. What had seemed to be a complete landscape had miraculously enlarged, and I found myself staring at an enormous volcanic rampart, its face streaked and marbled with veins of new-fallen snow.
>
> I sat down on a rock, stunned by this unexpected, looming presence, by the eerie combination of nearness and deep space and silence. In that moment the shape of my life changed. Two years later I moved to Wyoming and have since lived nowhere else. (pp. 50–51)

Epiphanic moments represent quantum leaps in perception, where one's vision is—as Bama suggests—"miraculously enlarged." The ordinary appears extraordinary and one catches a momentary glimpse into what Thomas Merton called "the hidden wholeness."

One of the best known examples of ecological epiphany occurs in Aldo Leopold's classic essay collection *A Sand County Almanac*. Recalling his early years as a forester when he was "full of trigger-itch," Leopold describes how he and colleagues responded to the sight of a mother wolf and cubs by "pumping lead into the pack . . . with more excitement than accuracy." The gunfire brought down the old wolf and Leopold reached her "in time to watch a fierce green fire dying in her eyes. I realized then," he reflects, "and have known ever since, that there was something new to me in those eyes—something known only to her and to the mountain" (p. 138).

That incident marked the beginning of a profound shift in Leopold's attitude toward the natural world, moving him from a utilitarian view of game management (in which all predators warrant extermination) to a life-centered ethic where the human is not "conqueror of the land community . . . [but] plain member and citizen of it" (p. 240).

Leopold's experience suggests that profound insights can break the surface of consciousness, sending ripples across the breadth of one's life. It may take years, even decades, to plumb the full depth of meaning held in a mountain's "deep space and silence" or in the "fierce green fire" of a dying wolf's eyes.

Returning after a quarter century to the mountain ridge where her epiphany occurred, Lynne Bama is struck by the gulf "between what I knew then and what I know now" (p. 52). That momentary flash of insight decades earlier sparked an ongoing quest to know the land in its entirety and learn from its stories. In this process, Bama moves—as Leopold did—from a vision of bountiful nature and unmarred beauty to a keen realization of how the surrounding ecosystem has been diminished by the loss of key predators, the overgrazing of livestock, and the introduction of non-native species. While this deeper awareness of place brings pain, it awakens an enduring sense of responsibility for the land.

Lives of Commitment

Metanoia calls for a depth of compassion and connection that is hard to sustain in a culture of rugged individualism and rational objectivity. Consequently, those who undergo ecological conversions often dwell on the margins of society, living "alone in a world of wounds" (Leopold, 197). With powers of perception and empathy focused by the experience of conversion, these writers perceive what others overlook or deny. Standing outside the mainstream, they strive to be fully conscious of "who, what and where [they] are, in defiance of those powerful forces in society—alcohol, drugs, television, shopping malls, motels—that aim to make us forget" (Norris, 23).

Their acute sense of ecological interconnection often inspires these writers to undertake visible "acts of commitment" (Noddings, 10). For some writers (e.g., Aldo Leopold, Wendell Berry, and Wes Jackson), this public demonstration of commitment involves restoration of degraded landscapes. Others enter the political realm, testifying to the loss of ecological integrity. Rachel Carson came to exemplify this role of ecological witness, describing the havoc wrought by rampant pesticide use in her best-selling book *Silent Spring*.

Like many converts to earth, Carson was a reluctant prophet, ill at ease with the public role into which she was cast. For years she resisted writing about pesticide use, trying to induce other writers to undertake the controversial and discouraging topic. (She invited E. B. White, among others, but he responded graciously that he thought her eminently qualified for the job.) Finally Carson could no longer muzzle her emerging ecological conscience:

The time had come when it must be written. We have already gone very far in our abuse of this planet. Some awareness of this problem has been in the air, but the ideas had to be crystallized, the facts had to be brought together in one place. If I had not written the book I am sure these ideas would have found another outlet. But knowing the facts as I did, I could not rest until I had brought them to public attention. (Brooks, 228)

As Carson's story illustrates, a profound shift in ecological sensibility often leads to a reassessment of old assumptions and the evolution of a new ecological ethic. Carson found that pesticide use raised profound moral questions about our responsibility as a species within the larger ecological whole. "There is all too little awareness," Carson observed, "that man is *part* of nature and that the price of conquest may well be the destruction of man himself" (Carson, 6).

Advocating for a philosophy akin to Albert Schweitzer's "reverence for life," Carson sought to balance technological progress with greater wisdom and humility. "Instead of always trying to impose our will on Nature," Carson asserted, "we should sometimes be quiet and listen to what she has to tell us" (p. 10).

Leopold came to a similar outlook in his later years, after failures in "game management" led him to form a "land ethic" honoring the intrinsic value of each ecological constituent. "The problem we face," he observed, "is the extension of the social conscience from people to land." That extension requires some form of metanoia. "No important change in ethics was ever accomplished," Leopold concluded, "without an internal change in our intellectual emphasis, loyalties, affections and convictions" (p. 246).

For Terry Tempest Williams, loss deepens her commitment to "question everything, even if it means losing my faith, even if it means becoming a member of a border tribe among my own people" (p. 286). Questions that begin at home, with speculation as to why so many friends and family are dying prematurely of cancer, lead to the recognition of abusive federal policies and a corrosive societal ethic that deems some people—and the earth itself—expendable. The only recourse, Williams concludes, is "to protest with the heart . . . [for] to deny one's genealogy with the earth [is] to commit treason against one's soul" (p. 288).

The testimony of writers like Williams, Leopold and Carson demonstrates both the challenge and potential of ecological transformation. Metanoia calls us to live with greater awareness and compassion, recognizing the intricate and infinite links between inner and outer ecology. These stories suggest that a cure for our "soul sickness" may lie in the cultivation of a new ecological sensibility.

Selected Works and Further Reading

Abram, David, *The Spell of the Sensuous: Perception and Language in a More-Than-Human World,* New York: Pantheon, 1996

Bama, Lynne, "The Unseen Mountain," in *The Earth at Our Doorstep: Contemporary Writers Celebrate the Landscapes of Home,* edited by Annie Stine, San Francisco: Sierra Club, 1996

Bartky, Sandra Lee, *Femininity and Domination: Studies in the Phenomenology of Oppression,* New York: Routledge, 1990; London: Routledge, Chapman & Hall, 1990

Brooks, Paul, *The House of Life: Rachel Carson at Work,* Boston: Houghton Mifflin, 1972; also published as *The House of Life: Rachel Carson at Work, with Selections from Her Writings Published and Unpublished,* London: Allen and Unwin, 1973

Carson, Rachel, "Of Man and the Stream of Time," Scripps College Bulletin 36:4 (1962), pp. 5–11

Griffin, Emilie, *Turning: Reflections on the Experience of Conversion,* Garden City, New York: Doubleday, 1980

Leopold, Aldo, *A Sand County Almanac and Sketches Here and There,* New York: Oxford University Press, 1949; London: Oxford University Press, 1968

Lindbergh, Anne Morrow, *Gift from the Sea,* New York: Signet, 1955; London: Chatto and Windus, 1955

Noddings, Nel, *Caring: A Feminine Approach to Ethics and Moral Education,* Berkeley: University of California Press, 1984

Norris, Kathleen, *Dakota: A Spiritual Geography,* New York: Ticknor and Fields, 1993

O'Grady, John P., *Pilgrims to the Wild: Everett Ruess, Henry David Thoreau, John Muir, Clarence King, Mary Austin,* Salt Lake City: University of Utah Press, 1993

Tallmadge, John, "Moving to Minnesota," *North Dakota Quarterly* 63:2 (1996), pp. 41–54

Williams, Terry Tempest, *Refuge: An Unnatural History of Family and Place,* New York: Pantheon, 1991

Wolfe, Linnie Marsh, *Son of the Wilderness: The Life of John Muir,* New York: Knopf, 1945

Knocking on Nature's Door: Religious Meaning in Twentieth-Century U.S. Poetry

Lex Runciman

Nature was the first literal fact of American experience. For Native Americans in 1620, nature was home. For William Bradford, Mayflower colonist and second governor at Plymouth, the countryside seemed a "hideous and desolate wilderness" (p. 62). For these early religious settlers, nature seemed not a place of beauty, not landscape or ecosystems to be protected by law or visited on vacation. Rather, this unknown and (to them) unsettled expanse was terrifying. It was unnamed, unmapped, unpredictable, and its rank, wild character reflected the human potential for temptation and unregulated evil.

Much of this view came directly from biblical sources, but it also followed a European literary tradition at least as old as Dante's *Divine Comedy*, where the protagonist finds himself lost in a "savage forest, dense and difficult, / which even in recall renews my fear" (p. 12). In Dante, it takes a journey through hell, purgatory, and heaven before that protagonist regains the path. Thus many of the earliest American writers saw nature as something fearful, uncivilized, and Godless. Only in work like Anne Bradstreet's "Contemplations" (published in 1678) can we see American landscape and nature looked at directly, freshly, as a place of beauty in itself, a place that might hold something holy.

By the nineteenth century, American writers had changed their view of the wildness of nature. Instead of terror and temptation, they saw landscape and nature as the unspoiled text of God–a source and setting both for transcendent experience and for the reaffirmation of what is essential in people. Thus Ralph Waldo Emerson's famous essay "Nature" says "In the woods, we return to reason and faith" (p. 10), and Henry David Thoreau in *Walden* calls nature "the poem of creation" (p. 390). The two great American poets of the nineteenth century, Emily Dickinson and Walt Whitman, both celebrate nature in their own ways, Whitman as the exuberant lover of the earth:

> Earth of the slumbering and liquid trees!
> Earth of departed sunset—earth
>   of the mountains misty-topt!
> Earth of the vitreous pour of the full moon
>   just tinged with blue! (p. 740)

and Dickinson, as the miniaturist who keeps her Sabbath at home and out of doors, "with a bobolink for a chorister / And an orchard for a dome" (p. 153). Both Whitman and Dickinson view nature as a source of imagery as well as the purest location for the indwelling beauty and mystery of all life. Their poetry becomes (in Dickinson more so than in Whitman) a record of their individual efforts to understand what nature might mean for human experience and what it might offer and mirror about God. This fundamental poetic effort to see clearly what may be at the transcendent heart of all things informs the work of the twentieth-century poets discussed here. And this ongoing poetic effort typically depends on two fundamental assumptions: nature itself is religiously charged with meaning, and nature provides the frame and setting that contains all human experience including all attempts to understand it. In short, nature is the doorway, and in their various ways the twentieth-century poets discussed below repeatedly try that door.

Frost, Jeffers, and Warren

Whatever their other concerns, twentieth-century writers have witnessed and lived astonishing cultural and technological changes. Robert Frost could easily enough have met Civil War veterans in his youth; by the time of his death in 1963, he had seen two world wars as well as the invention of the modern factory assembly line that further encouraged the migration of people from rural to urban living. In addition, the horse of his youth had given way to the automobile and to jet travel. Despite such changes, Frost's poems stay fundamentally faithful to the New England, rural, largely unmechanized countryside of his later childhood and early adulthood as a farmer in Derry, New Hampshire.

In the often-anthologized "Stopping By Woods on a Snowy Evening" (p. 207), for instance, the poem's speaker stops his horse-drawn sleigh on "the darkest evening of the year," a reference that carries clear emotional overtones even as it suggests December 21 (the shortest and therefore "darkest" day of the year). Why this speaker stops remains unanswered. It is snowing, he is presumably on his way somewhere, yet he stops by the woods of the title, remarks that he knows their owner, who lives "in the village," and he watches. Although the poem never makes clear exactly why, it is surely the woods themselves that hold this speaker's attention–they are "lovely, dark, and deep." And here in four simple words Frost unites the early religious tradition (nature as darkness) with the nineteenth century sense of wonder and mystery. For Frost's speaker, these woods seem to pose both a question and a promise–they are, after all, "lovely." In short, Frost's speaker quietly and anecdotally asks what nature and life itself might mean. The poem postpones any answer. The speaker simply continues on his journey.

In fact, the question of what nature means to tell people is never fully or finally answered in Frost's work. In "Storm Fear" (p. 19), a blizzard isolates the poem's speaker and his family— "Two and a child." The poem ends in the creeping cold and darkness, with the speaker worried about "Whether 'tis in us to arise with day / And save ourselves unaided." Yet only three poems later in "A Prayer in Spring" (p. 21), the speaker praises the flowering of the season and prays "keep us here / All simply in the springing of the year." Of course a prayer or request is not necessarily answered, and so even in "A Prayer in Spring," Frost manages to maintain what he sees as a truthful ambiguity: nature, even in spring, holds both life and death, flowers and blizzards.

In "Home Burial" (p. 55) the landscape holds only a reminder of death. A young mother whose child has recently died is confronted by her husband who has often seen her looking out a particular upstairs window. Looking out the same window, he sees the family graveyard with "the child's mound." Clearly their child's death is something they have not been able to discuss, and the poem records their efforts to try. Again this Frost poem ends without resolution, and although it is as much a poem about shared and unshared grief as it is anything else, "Home Burial" also insists on the mystery of death—something nature holds in itself and keeps from us, something about which words cannot be said. Thus Frost's poems (for other examples *see* "Lost in Heaven" or "Desert Places") often focus on the question of how to live in a landscape and within natural forces that embrace beauty and decay, transience and permanence, and an affinity for people as well as a complete disregard for us.

Still, some Frost poems record a remarkable if momentary union with natural processes. Knowing nature, in a poem like "Birches" (p. 117) for instance, means understanding some aspect of "Truth." And it means knowing that "Earth's the right place for love." Yet although Frost often looks for more (as he gazes at the woods in "Stopping by Woods . . . ," for instance) his understanding of landscape and nature remains almost uniformly uncertain, limited. One near exception may be the poem "For Once, Then, Something" (p. 208). The speaker here looks down into a well. He notes that normally the well water simply mirrors his own face "godlike / Looking out of a wreath of fern and cloud puffs." But this one time he sees past the surface, "Something more of the depths—and then I lost it." What did he see, however briefly? Only "something white, uncertain." The poem ends in radical uncertainty, the speaker sure only that something—he is not sure what—was seen that one time.

A near-contemporary of Frost, Robinson Jeffers lived his life on the opposite coast, on the then-wild Monterey peninsula, and Jeffers's poems of nature make Frost's look almost cozy. For Jeffers, nature is a supreme, remotely indifferent force evident in ocean, wind, rock, and the lives of predatory or scavenger birds—hawks and gulls; next to the tidal, pitiless grandeur and power of this nature, human beings often look vain and small. The great bulk of Jeffers's oeuvre is devoted to ambitious, lengthy narrative poems. But virtually all of Jeffers's books also contain briefer lyrics that at once point to and summarize his consistent interests.

In Jeffers's poem "Phenomena" (p. 165), for instance, nature is "the great frame" that accepts and hold everything from gulls to weather to airplanes and a lighthouse. Here, Jeffers's theme is beauty: "From the greatness of their element they all take beauty." But Jeffers can countenance twentieth-century humanity only in small doses. In "Shine, Perishing Republic" (p. 168), for example, he sees the century's history as one of corruption, rot, and decay, all of this a natural life-and-death process: "Out of the mother, and through the spring exultances, ripeness and decadence; and home to the mother." But like all the poets discussed here, Jeffers cannot simply observe this natural course; it fascinates him and is something to be interrogated. Or, to use Jeffers's own title, nature is "The Treasure."

In "The Treasure" (p. 169), Jeffers seeks to examine not human life, but that "Enormous repose after, enormous repose before." In this poem, the central religious transcendental essence cannot be said, cannot be spoken: "silence is the thing, this noise a found word for it." What nature is, the poem concludes, is unspeakable, a recognition that perhaps cannot help but challenge a writer, a person whose currency is language. And if the essence cannot be got at directly, Jeffers is often enough content to act as a critic and a stern celebrant of natural forces, what he calls in "Fawn's Foster-Mother" (p. 188), "the streaming arteries / The stir of the world, the music of the mountain." Such forces contain human activity and may be all we know of God, who, Jeffers concludes in "Triad" (p. 459) "is very beautiful, but hardly a friend of humanity."

Like the poems of Jeffers and Frost, those of Robert Penn Warren always work inside a moral framework that invokes landscape and nature as the source for and emblem of religious questions. At first glance, Warren's over-riding interests seem centered less on nature and landscape than on time and on the mystery of death. But these are intricately connected in the world of Warren's poems, and they lead to this character-

istically Warren-esque assertion in "Masts at Dawn" (p. 115): ". . . We must try / To love so well the world that we may believe, in the end, in God."

In fact, the speakers in Warren's poems often make the same sort of mental and emotional journey, going to nature (which, by definition, has no memory) in the effort to make sense of human experience, human memory. Thus "Reading Late at Night, Thermometer Falling" (p. 67) begins (as does Frost's "Storm Fear") with vivid descriptions of an ice-bound landscape that like the night itself is "windless, mindless, and long." The rest of the poem fills that mindlessness with the speaker's memory of his father's life, a father who says in this poem "It is terrible for a man to live and not know." Not know what? The poem does not explicitly say.

And at some fundamental level, Warren's poems assert nature is the teacher. Paying attention to nature may be, in fact, "A Way to Love God." For as the poem with that title suggests (p. 3), we can see only a reflection of the truth, just as "the line where the incoming swell from the sunset Pacific" can, to the watchful eye, reveal the ocean bottom below. Or, as that poem says later, "Everything seems an echo of something else."

In Warren's poems (as in Frost's and Jeffers's), nature is the great Other, the repository of knowledge that people can only imperfectly see, imperfectly hear or touch or read. For Warren, as he says in "Trying to Tell You Something" (p. 10), "All things lean at you, and some are / Trying to tell you something, though of some / The heart is too full for speech." In this poem, it is an ancient oak held together with cables and wires that is trying to speak, trying to tell us something. The poem is set in December and that great oak wants to tell us what it is like to be very old in a very cold time. For Warren's speaker, that oak contains in itself an elemental beauty and some bedrock truth, even if we are not quite sure what we are hearing or how we might act on it.

The poems of Frost, Jeffers, and Warren share a fundamental stance not too far from that of Emerson and Thoreau: namely that nature, human nature—and hence human action—are essentially connected even if we do not fully understand the complexities of that link. Almost never orthodox, and usually meditative rather than didactic, these writers use narrative and metaphorical language to pose (and occasionally begin to answer) essentially religious questions about life, death, and the idea of God.

Roethke, Oliver, Wright, and Berry

Especially in his long meditations, Theodore Roethke's poems stand alone in this discussion, for they reveal the consciousness of a mystic. Roethke's father owned a commercial greenhouse in Michigan, and his book *The Lost Son and Other Poems* celebrates that nearly pre-lapsarian greenhouse world of lush growth, the "urge, wrestle, resurrection of dry sticks / Cut stems struggling to put down feet." Even here in "Cuttings (later)" (p. 37), the second poem of that book, we can see the union of natural regrowth with religious imagery: "What saint strained so much," the poem asks. Yet in the several poems that form the first section of that book, the celebratory focus remains mostly a tribute to the mysteries of biology, to the "Root Cellar" and the "Forcing House" and the growth of "Orchids."

But with "The Lost Son," the lengthy title poem, Roethke moves into a rhetoric that is more than conventional meditation or narrative. In fact, in its five sections, "The Lost Son" uses language to at once paralyze a rational approach and also directly interrogate and invoke the mysterious center of both consciousness and nature itself. The poem performs a kind of psychic and religious journeying toward it knows not what. It records a descent out of logic and personality and into the rank chaos of elemental life until, in its fourth section, titled "The Return" (p. 57), the speaker emerges, a boy again, in his father's greenhouse. This location, however momentary, leads to some further understanding, some knowledge, however difficult to articulate, and the imagery Roethke uses is at once absolutely natural and clearly religious: "Was it light? / Was it light within? / Was it light within light?" The poem does not answer these questions, but it ends trusting that the experience may be repeatable.

In fact, again and again Roethke's longer poems enact a mystical effort at union with a natural wholeness that in Roethke's work is at once fully human consciousness and consciousness of God. Even merely the poems' titles reveal this effort: "I Need, I Need," "Bring the Day!" "Give Way, Ye Gates," "O Lull Me, Lull Me," "Praise to the End," "Unfold, Unfold" and so on. But perhaps Roethke's greatest and most ambitious effort of this sort is the sequence titled

"Meditations of an Old Woman." This 16-page poem consists of five meditations that cumulatively seek to say all Roethke knows of nature and the spirit and the quest for essential meaning. The speaker here, the old woman of the poem's title, admits she has "gone into the waste lonely places" (p. 159), wonders at some length about what it is we seek, and near the end admits "To try to become like God / Is far from becoming God" (p. 172). Always in this poem the speaker turns to nature and natural processes—to larks, worms, weeds, wind, seeds, and birds—as sources and participants in the understanding she seeks.

Often enough, Roethke's long sequences end in some calm participation with nature and all that is. As he says at the end of "Journey to the Interior," "when I breathe with the birds / The spirit of wrath becomes the spirit of blessing, / And the dead begin from their dark to sing in my sleep" (p. 195); and at the end of "The Far Field" he can say with certainty "All finite things reveal infinitude" (p. 201). Thus Roethke's poems claim a knowledge others lack; in doing so, he could sound (here in "The Rose") almost like Whitman: "Near this rose, in this grove of sun-parched, wind-warped madronas, / Among the half-dead trees, I came upon the true ease of myself, / As if another man appeared out of the depths of my being" (p. 205).

Although her rhetoric is less directly psychological and edgy, Mary Oliver's poetic aim is no less ambitious than that of Roethke's. As she says in the poem "Landscape" (p. 129), nature is the force and place (here a pond) she goes to daily to stay in touch, to keep the doors of her heart open, to keep something essential in the human spirit alive: "Every morning I walk like this around / the pond, thinking: if the doors of my heart / ever close, I am as good as dead." For Oliver, nature is the fundamental mystery, dependably present outside one's human experience and, with effort and devotion, dependably available in the observation of every leaf or snake or natural fact, an energy at once humbling and beautiful. Mary Oliver's sense of the bedrock dependability of nature contrasts markedly with the edgy uncertainty revealed in the work of Charles Wright. Exact contemporaries, speaking of these two writers together may serve to highlight both their similarities and differences.

For Oliver, nature is not simply trees, water, and weather, it is an ever-renewing and endlessly elemental present; as she says in "Humpbacks" (p. 168), "There is, all around us / this country / of original fire." Thus the speaker in Mary Oliver's poems very often seeks to locate herself and her consciousness entirely in that present, to (as the speaker says in "Entering the Kingdom") "learn something by being nothing / A little while but the rich / Lens of attention" (p. 190). For Oliver, the kingdom of nature is as necessary as eating, as present as air, breathed always yet often unconsidered or ignored. Apprehending that force means feeling and participating in "the perfection, the rising, the happiness" (p. 191).

Where Oliver trusts this natural force and often finds sympathy in its ever-present character, Wright almost always associates his remarkable natural landscapes with memory—either his own or the memory that is literature and art. Thus Wright is as apt to evoke the landscapes of Dante as he is those of his Tennessee childhood or his several years lived in Laguna Beach, California overlooking the Pacific. When he goes to nature divorced or separate from such human associations, he most often finds a great and unreadable emptiness, as here in "The Southern Cross": "Here is the truth. The wind rose, the sea / Shuffled its blue deck and dealt you a hand: / Blank, blank, blank, blank, blank" (*Thousand Things*, 45).

In fact, Wright's poems record a persistence of desire against a record of only occasional, partial attainment: "Not one word has ever melted in glory not one. / We keep on sending them up, however, / As the sun rains down" (*Thousand Things*, 111). Yet, like Oliver, Wright keeps paying a keen, fully human attention. He is often surprised he is sentiently alive, surprised at the fact of human company. And he can end a poem that has catalogued some of the mundane facts of January by noting how the days begin to get longer, how in time's hourglass "Single grain by single grain / Everything flows toward structure, last ache in the ache for God" (*Chickamauga*, 63). Wright aches for God, not as orthodoxy but as palpable presence. He knows in "December Journal" that "God is not offered to the senses" and yet he also asserts "The other world is here, just under our fingertips" (*Thousand Things*, 209, 211). As succinctly as any book or sequence in his career, Wright's *China Trace* records that deep desire, perhaps nowhere clearer than in the poem "Clear Night" (p. 61) whose speaker says "I want to be bruised by God." The poem ends with an unhearing natural world that can only answer "What?" while "the stars start out on their cold slide through

the dark." Mary Oliver and Charles Wright share a deep hunger for connection to nature. Oliver consistently finds it, although she rarely links it overtly to any discussion of God. Wright speaks of the idea of God that he seeks in nature but, more often than not, cannot dependably find.

And in contrast to all these poets, we have Wendell Berry, Kentucky farmer, essayist, and poet, whose work reveals the most traditionally faithful stance of any writer discussed here. Nowhere is Berry's natural and religious orientation clearer than in his book of Sunday contemplative poems titled *Sabbaths*, a book remarkable for its level of quiet; *Sabbaths* is not a book of avid or uncertain aspiration, it is, rather, a numbered sequence of affirmations. Thus Berry can say that the rot of dead leaves and the dance of live leaves "are gathered in a single dance," and "These passings resurrect / a joy without defect" (p. 12). Quietly, Wendell Berry is a Christian; he believes in resurrection, that "What stood will stand, though all be fallen / The good return that time has stolen" (p. 14). Berry's poetic decisions are consistent with his themes. His stanzas reveal careful attention to meter and, often enough, to rhyme, which Berry invokes as emblematic of the relationship between nature and God—one sounds the Other (p. 16).

In fact, the poems of *Sabbaths* take us almost full circle: in their insistence on a non-technological, non-pop-culture world separate from "the internal combustion of America" (p. 86), they suggest the world of Robert Frost. In common with Frost's rural New England, Berry's poems speak of rivers and fields, raincrows, harvest, leaf shadows, "The high leaves falling in their turns / Spiraling through the air made gold / By their slow fall" (p. 78). And one of the poems in *Sabbaths* seems almost a direct response to Frost's "Stopping By Woods on a Snowy Evening." While the speaker in Frost's poem only stops and looks at the woods, the speaker in Berry's poem crosses into them, arriving finally at relief and union—"the ease of sight, the brotherhood of eye and leaf" (p. 89).

In this comparison, Berry's poem neatly contrasts with Frosts, showing at once the two poems' similarities and differences. Both use the woods as a metaphor for nature itself, and both view nature as the source of one's knowledge of God. Frost stops—he does not know why—and he looks, but he goes on because he "has promises to keep" (p. 207). Wendell Berry crosses the field; he is at once confident and humble and more than willing to enter those woods. Alone among the poets here, Wendell Berry does not just knock on nature's door. He is familiar with the gate and knows "you cannot pass beyond it burdened" (p. 89). For Berry, natural landscape is not just the text of God, it is also the active scene of religious affirmation rooted in the Bible's Christian faith.

From the very first, nature and religion have been linked in the American mind. In twentieth-century U.S. poetry, nature (however reduced or distinct from technology or the daily news) has been present as a constant link to something larger that people are but a part of, and this linkage has been more widespread than this discussion can do more than suggest. In poets as diverse as T. S. Eliot, Gary Snyder, Pattiann Rogers, and Wallace Stevens, nature becomes an important avenue to approach the largest questions of human life.

Selected Works and Further Reading

Alighieri, Dante, *The Divine Comedy of Dante Alighieri: A Verse Translation,* translated by Allen Mandelbaum, Berkeley, California, and London: University of California Press, 1980

Berry, Wendell, *Sabbaths,* San Francisco: North Point, 1987

Bradford, William, *Of Plymouth Plantation, 1620–1647,* edited by Samuel Eliot Morison, New York: Knopf, 1952

Dickinson, Emily, *The Complete Poems of Emily Dickinson,* edited by Thomas H. Johnson, Boston: Back Bay, 1960; London: Faber, 1970

Emerson, Ralph Waldo, *Essays & Lectures,* New York: Library of America, 1983; Cambridge: Press Syndicate of the University of Cambridge, 1983

Frost, Robert, *Collected Poems, Prose & Plays,* New York: Library of America, 1995

Jeffers, Robinson, *The Selected Poetry of Robinson Jeffers,* New York: Random House, 1938

Oliver, Mary, *New and Selected Poems,* Boston: Beacon, 1992

Roethke, Theodore, *The Collected Poems of Theodore Roethke,* Garden City, New York: Doubleday, 1966; London: Faber, 1968

Thoreau, Henry David, *A Week on the Concord and Merrimack Rivers; Walden, or, Life in the Woods; The Maine Woods; Cape Cod,* New York: Literary Classics of the United States, 1985; Cambridge: Cambridge University Press, 1985

Warren, Robert Penn, *Selected Poems 1923–1975,* New York: Random House, 1976; London: Secker & Warburg, 1976

Whitman, Walt, *Leaves of Grass,* Garden City, New York: Doubleday, 1855; London: David Bogue, 1881

Wright, Charles, *Chickamauga,* New York: Farrar, Straus, and Giroux, 1995

——, *China Trace,* Middletown, Connecticut: Wesleyan University Press, 1977

——, *The World of the Ten Thousand Things: Poems 1980–1990,* New York: Farrar, Straus, and Giroux, 1990

American Ecobiography

Cecilia Konchar Farr

I have felt the pain that arises from a recognition of beauty, pain we hold when we remember what we are connected to and the delicacy of our relations. It is this tenderness born out of a connection to place that fuels my writing. —Terry Tempest Williams

Nature writing and life writing move toward each other, then away, returning for an insight or observation, again separating into distinct genres in the American literary tradition. This dance begins with the earliest oral narratives, repeats itself in travel writing and journals, and is elaborated in the burgeoning nineteenth-century literary movements of the newly united states. The American Self, the American Landscape: these were the preoccupations of the early literature of what was to become the United States. How are we different from Europe, from Africa, from Asia? What makes us unique? An easy answer to these questions was found in towering, impenetrable forests, vast mountain ranges and uncharted rivers and lakes. According to Lawrence Buell, landscape made America uniquely American, so much of our mainstream literary tradition became a pastoral one. The "essential America" has been for writers and critics, "exurban, green, pastoral, even wild" (p. 32). In our literature, nature was Americanized and idealized, and heroes were created to inhabit it.

Some of these heroes created themselves, calling on nature as a referent for their autobiographical self-definition. Sometimes the relationship between nature and narrator was harmonious, as in Thoreau's *Walden*, or in the poetry of William Cullen Bryant; sometimes it was confrontational, as in parts of Mary Hallock Foote's autobiography, *A Victorian Gentlewoman in the Far West,* or in early Puritan narratives. But always, in this genre of American "ecobiography," nature becomes an identifying canvas on which to write a self.

Robert F. Sayre, writing about the autobiographical tradition in American literature, states that "autobiography may be the preeminent kind of American expression" (p. 147). He theorizes that, for writers of autobiographies, America is not really a land but, rather, an idea (p. 149). "The autobiographical hero is the representative of the ideas that he has lived by and seen succeed or, in some cases, fail. The autobiographer is not only a 'who,' he is also a 'what'—what he lived for, what he believed in and worked for," writes Sayre (p. 150). This may be true of many autobiographies in the American tradition—those of Benjamin Franklin, Frederick Douglas, Olaudah Equiano, Henry Adams, or Harriet Jacobs. But for a significant number of autobiographers America is, most definitely, land. Constructed and idealized although it may be, the land that locates these writers begins as nature, as solid ground, as well as theoretical concept. Using Sayre's terms, the ecobiographer is also a where, clearly located in an American landscape.

Many critics have studied the separate traditions of American autobiography and American nature writing. From Bradford's *Of Plymouth Plantation* to Whitman's *Leaves of Grass*, from Walden Pond to the wild, wild West, these traditions have made use of shared texts. This article focuses on the space where the two traditions meet, in nonfiction autobiographical narratives centered on place—ecobiographies. Although we can trace this connection through many early texts, contemporary ecocriticism has provided the tools to bring these two genres together, by exploring more fully the ways we construct and interact with nature.

As with American nature writing, ecobiographical study would cite *Walden* as an exemplary early work. Thoreau's "simple and sincere account" of a man who has "travelled a good deal in Concord" (p. 46) is certainly an autobiography of place. Thoreau sought the woods because he wished "to live deliberately, to front only the essential facts of life, and see if [he] could not learn what it had to teach" (p. 135). For the purpose of this study, however, I will make a distinction between this earlier work, where nature serves as a backdrop for more central human endeavors, and later ecobiographical works, where nature and human endeavors are less easily separated. In the late twentieth century, with the rise of environmental consciousness and postmodern thinking, the borders between nature and self blur; indeed, both nature and self become contested territories. In ecobiographies, nature becomes us, and we begin to question who is constructing whom. As a colleague and I wrote, "the narrative 'I's . . . are as much constructed *by* Nature as they are constructing *of* Nature. . . . it is impossible to tell where the Self ends and Nature begins or where Nature ends and the Self begins: ego and eco are inextricably intertwined" (p. 203). To examine this relationship between eco and ego more closely, I will focus on two texts: Edward Abbey's *Desert Solitaire* and Terry Tempest Williams's *Refuge*.

I begin with Abbey's *Desert Solitaire* because it signals an important shift in nature writing, away from the careful chronicling and tone of acute observation that characterizes earlier works by John Muir, John Burroughs, Mary Austin, John James Audubon and others to a more self-centered text. Abbey claims in his introduction to "have tried to create a world of words in which the desert figures more as medium than as material. Not imitation but evocation has been the goal" (p. x). He writes:

This is not primarily a book about the desert. In recording my impressions of the natural scene I have striven above all for accuracy, since I believe that there is a kind of poetry, even a kind of truth, in simple fact. But the desert is a vast world, an oceanic world, as deep in its way and complex and various as the sea. Language makes a mighty loose net with which to go fishing for simple facts, when facts are infinite. If a man knew enough he could write a book about the juniper tree.

Not juniper trees in general but that one particular juniper tree which grows from a ledge of naked sandstone near the old entrance to Arches National Monument. (p. x)

This lone juniper, and other solitary trees and animals, appear throughout Abbey's memoir of "A Season in the Wilderness" as stand-ins for his own isolated state. It quickly becomes evident that this is autobiography, an invention of a narrative "I," as much as it is a study of the desert. By focusing on his "impressions of the natural scene" and acknowledging both the slipperiness of language and the inaccessibility of facts, Abbey gives himself permission to place himself in the center of this text. Nature is inimitable, not reproducible whole and entire. What Abbey promises to give us here is his desert, his solitude, his (carefully constructed) self.

Like Thoreau, Abbey lays claim to what Buell calls "an aesthetics of relinquishment" (pp. 143–144 passim), a sloughing off a civilization ("the clamor and filth and confusion of the cultural apparatus," Abbey writes) and a motivation to "confront, immediately and directly if it's possible, the bare bones of existence, the elemental and fundamental, the bedrock which sustains us" (p. 6). But Abbey does not take lessons from nature as much as he attempts to make a spiritual connection with it. Confronting "his" juniper tree, he muses, "Two living things on the same earth, respiring in a common medium, we contact one another but without direct communication. Intuition, sympathy, empathy, all fail to guide me into the heart of this being—if it has a heart" (p. 31). Abbey's narrative wrestlings with the metaphysical, sometimes jarringly self-conscious, are autobiographical struggles—struggles to be born, to know himself. The red-rock desert and its inhabitants are figured not simply as background to this struggle, but as fellow travellers. In "The First Morning" he describes a sunrise in these terms: "We greet each other, sun and I, across the black void of ninety-three million miles. The snow glitters between us, acres of diamonds almost painful to look at. . . . I am not alone after all" (p. 7).

But the desert is also cruel and the sun, at times, relentless. Abbey moves between depictions of an idealized, mythic landscape, a picaresque canvas peopled with strange characters, and nature writer's recitation of "simple facts." In a twist that makes this sub-genre of autobiography unique, Abbey the autobiographer constructs the desert to serve his self-construction, then Abbey the nature writer delights in the desert's disinterest in him. He writes, "The finest quality of this stone, these plants and animals, this desert landscape is the indifference manifest to our presence, our absence, our coming, our staying or our going. Whether we live or die is a matter of absolutely no concern whatsoever to the desert" (p. 301). Much of the narrative is taken up with Abbey's insistence, in the tradition of the environmental jeremiad, that the desert must be allowed to remain wild, indifferent, isolated, unpaved: closed to tourists, although he himself hopes to return to it. The final words of his text are first for the desert then for his autobiographical project: "The desert will still be here in the spring. And then comes another thought. When I return, will it be the same? Will I be the same? Will anything ever be quite the same again? If I return" (p. 303).

The significance of this ecobiography in the traditions of nature writing and autobiography are summed up here, where Abbey acts as environmentalist and life writer. Here Abbey's fate and the desert's are intertwined, as highways encroach on secluded sandstone monuments and the writer returns to the subways and taxi drivers of New York City. Nature becomes him; eco and ego are inseparable—and neither is immune to change.

Terry Tempest Williams inherits this tradition of ecobiography from Abbey and further defines it in her *Refuge: An Unnatural History of Family and Place*, an example of unabashedly autobiographical nature writing. I choose Williams's text as exemplary of this genre because of its connection to Abbey's and because of its similarity to other contemporary ecobiographies cited throughout this sourcebook, especially Kathleen Norris's *Dakota* and Annie Dillard's *Pilgrim at Tinker Creek*. These and other similar texts represent the successful hybrid of memoir and nature writing that is unique to, and characteristic of, the late twentieth century.

Williams's *Refuge* is a chronicle not of separation or relinquishment, but of deep involvement—with the Bear River Migratory Bird Refuge, with her dying mother and with the activist politics of the environmental movement. This involvement could, perhaps, be traced to other contemporary environmental writers, such as Wendell Berry, Rachel Carson or Gretel Ehrlich, who insist on their readers' engagement in the work for change. It could also be understood in the context of current feminist theories of autobiography. Among the earlier essays from

this school is Mary Mason's 1980 essay "The Other Voice." Central to her understanding of a distinct women's tradition in autobiography is the idea that "the self-discovery of female identity seems to acknowledge the real presence and recognition of another consciousness, and the disclosure of female self is linked to the identification of some 'other'" (p. 210). Whereas the tradition of autobiographies by women is made up of texts in which the narrator constructs a significant human other (the alterego of Stein's *The Autobiography of Alice B. Toklas*, for example) as an inspiration to self development, Williams provides us with both a human and a nonhuman other in her mother and the Great Salt Lake. More broadly speaking, nature serves, often, as an absent mother figure in *Refuge*.

Williams, like Abbey, seeks for a deeper connection to her landscape and the plants and animals that inhabit it. The birds of the wildlife refuge, who lend their names to the chapters of the text, are especially significant. She writes, "The Bird Refuge has remained a constant. It is a landscape so familiar to me, there have been times I have felt a species long before I saw it. . . . The birds and I share a natural history. It is a matter of rootedness, of living inside a place for so long that the mind and imagination fuse" (p. 21).

At one point, just before her mother's death, the narrator finds a dead swan along the shore of the lake, "its body . . . contorted on the beach like an abandoned lover" (p. 121). Williams prepares the swan for death, washing its bill and feet with her own saliva. Then she lies down next to it: "I imagined the great heart that propelled the bird forward day after day, night after night. Imagined the deep breaths taken as it lifted from the arctic tundra, the camaraderie within the flock. . . . And I imagined the shimmering Great Salt Lake calling the swans down like a mother. . . ." Finally, at dusk, she leaves "the swan like a crucifix in the sand" (pp. 121–122). She echoes this scene at her mother's deathbed, where she sits next to her mother and breathes with her. "Mother and I became one," she writes. "One breathing organism." And later, "I just closed my eyes and merged with her" (pp. 230–231). In Williams's ecobiography, nature is alive and spiritual as it is for Abbey, but not so much a disinterested other as it is a maternal one.

Williams uses this maternal connection to the land as motivation for environmental activism, for protests of both the government's nuclear testing that, she believes, poisoned her mother and other Utah "downwinders," and of the Mormon church's patriarchal authority that demanded a blind obedience to the leaders who tolerated the testing. She figures herself, "a Mormon woman of the fifth generation of Latter-day Saints" as "a member of a border tribe among my own people." She imagines this border tribe as a group of "women from all over the world" circling "a blazing fire in the desert" (pp. 286–287). These women dance and drum and sing of "walking gently" on the earth as they plan to "reclaim the desert for the sake of their children, for the sake of the land" (p. 287). Their silent protest is tied to their own maternity and the maternity of the earth:

> The women couldn't bear it any longer. They were mothers. They had suffered labor pains but always under the promise of birth. The red hot pains beneath the desert promised death only, as each bomb became a stillborn. A contract had been made and broken between human beings and the land. A new contract was being drawn by the women, who understood the fate of the earth as their own. (p. 288)

Williams then describes her own "act of civil disobedience," as she crosses the line at the Nevada test site in a community of women "soul-centered and strong, women who recognized the sweet smell of sage as fuel for our spirits" (p. 290).

Williams's *Refuge* is centered solidly in two traditions—both autobiography and nature writing. She finishes her moving, self-revelatory text with a call to environmental activism, a call tied inextricably to her concept of selfhood, as a woman connected to the desert by heritage and "soul-centeredness." Her narrative "I" is both ego-centric and eco-centric, a narrator setting up directional cairns for those who follow in this significant and popular genre of ecobiography.

Selected Works and Further Reading

Abbey, Edward, *Desert Solitaire: A Season in the Wilderness,* New York: Ballantine, 1968

Buell, Lawrence, *The Environmental Imagination: Thoreau, Nature Writing, and the Formation of American Culture,* Cambridge, Massachusetts: Belknap Press of Harvard University Press, 1995

Farr, Cecilia Konchar, and Phillip A. Snyder, "From Walden Pond to the Great Salt Lake: Ecobiography and Engendered Species Acts in *Walden* and *Refuge,*" in *Tending the Garden: Essays on Mormon Literature,* edited by Eugene England and Lavina Fielding Anderson, Salt Lake City, Utah: Signature, 1996

Mason, Mary G., "The Other Voice: Autobiographies of Women Writers," in *Autobiography: Essays Theoretical and Critical,* edited by James Olney, Princeton, New Jersey, and Guildford, England: Princeton University Press, 1980

Sayre, Robert F., "Autobiography and the Making of America," in *Autobiography: Essays Theoretical and Critical,* edited by James Olney, Princeton, New Jersey, and Guildford, England: Princeton University Press, 1980

Thoreau, Henry David, *Walden and Civil Disobedience,* Boston: Houghton Mifflin, 1960

Williams, Terry Tempest, *Refuge: An Unnatural History of Family and Place,* New York: Pantheon, 1991

North Woods Writers

Don Scheese and Claude Brew

A chapter on North Woods writers is an ideal project in which to engage the fundamental issues of ecocriticism. Ecocritics acknowledge both the primacy of the physical nonhuman environment in the creation of culture as well as the importance of human perception in verbally representing biogeography and cultural artifacts. Thus we address the following questions: What exactly is the North Woods? What geographical area (restricting our attention to North America) has it entailed over centuries of human occupation? What kinds of literature has it produced? What has been the relationship between the physical environment and the literature that has attempted to represent it? Finally, has there been a literature of another bioregion in which the physical environment has assumed a more dominant role?

A major problem in defining "the North Woods" is that the term is colloquial, not scientific. Dictionaries are of little help; one of the few that does include the term, *A Dictionary of American English* (1942), defines it simply as "Any one of several heavily timbered regions in the northern part of the United States or in Canada." This definition is useful, however, in its indication of the internationality of "North Woods" as a bioregion; the forest predates by millennia subsequent arbitrary political boundaries drawn on maps. Yet ecologists themselves disagree over the definition and geography of the northern forest. *The Sierra Club Naturalist's Guide to the North Woods*, for example, focuses on only the northern portions of Minnesota, Wisconsin, and Michigan (Daniel, Sullivan). But Robert Bailey in *Descriptions of the Ecoregions of the United States*, identifying a "Laurentian Mixed Forest Province," includes as well parts of Pennsylvania, New York, Vermont, New Hampshire, and Maine (pp. 20–22). The dominant tree species of this province are numerous, in part because they are part of an ecotone, a broad transition zone between coniferous forests farther north and deciduous forests to the south. In the *Historical Atlas of Canada* maps and accompanying description attest to the extensiveness of the boreal and mixed forests, from Labrador west to Saskatchewan and north to the Northwest Territories (Harris, 17–17A); clearly, "North Woods" from an ecological perspective is largely Canadian. Essential to the mythos of the North Woods is the existence of large, impenetrable tracts of forest. Disorientation, as we shall see, is a prevalent theme in North Woods writing.

Also essential to the definition of the North Woods, and also contributing to its imposing sense of disorientation, is the predominance of water and low topographical relief: a maze of lakes and rivers separated by forested hills and connected by portage trails worn into existence over thousands of years by Natives, voyagers, and modern recreationists. Over the lakes, formed by glaciers, and through the forests, growing from soil deposited by the ice sheets, evolved the dominant forms of transportation before modern times: the birch bark canoe in summer, the snowshoe in winter. Long harsh winters are a significant climatological factor in the North Woods, as integral to its conception as the fearsome insects, a product of all the water and warm, if short, summers.

Nature is dynamic, not static, and the North Woods illustrates this fact as well as any bioregion. Fire, through both lightning and human agency, played the most powerful role in shaping the forest before Euramerican settlement; and the extractive industries of trapping, logging, and mining have significantly reshaped the landscape since the 1600s. Of these three activities it is the fur trade that has assumed the foremost iconographic influence in the literature, to the extent that some writers (e.g., Knauth) define the boundaries of the North Woods largely in terms of the period and region of greatest production of furs: from Grand Portage in northeastern Minnesota to Fort Chipewyan in northeastern Alberta via a 2,000-mile-long waterway, during the heyday of the Hudson's Bay Company and other competing firms in the eighteenth and nineteenth centuries.

Native subsistence on and Euramerican over-exploitation of the physical resources produced numerous forms of literary expression, as did the conservation of what remained and the attempt to capture in words the awe, terror, and inspiration felt by inhabitants and visitors. We periodize and classify the literature of the North Woods in this way: pre-contact oral traditions of Native cultures; exploration and fur trade-related writings, 1500–1900; settlement and rediscovery narratives, 1800–1900; twentieth- century conservation and nature writing; fiction and poetry from the 1800s to the present. We construe the term "literature" broadly, as any form of oral or written expression that attempts to describe an experience in imaginative and/or historical fashion. In taking on the formidable task of reading and defining North Woods literature, one discovers—with a sense of awe not unlike Jacques Cartier as he explored the St. Lawrence River in 1535—that the literature of the region is as vast as the environment that inspired it.

Native American Oral Traditions

Much of the North Woods region, from Labrador to the Northwest Territories, was inhabited by Algonquian-speaking peoples, from the Montagnais in the east to the Cree in the West, in culture areas defined by modern anthropologists as "Northeast" and "Subarctic" (Trigger; Helm). These indigenous peoples were primarily a hunter-gatherer culture, necessarily mobile in order to capitalize on the periodicity of food supplies. Among the many tribes living in these culture areas was the Ojibwe, or Anishinabe, who by the late eighteenth century came to dominate the Lake Superior watershed (Helen Tanner, 17–18). Here we discuss the oral tradition of the Ojibwe, in its most venerable form: the creation myth.

"The native voice in American literature is indispensable," argues N. Scott Momaday. "There is no true literary history of the United States without it" (p. 6). Or of Canada, one should add, whose government has rightfully acknowledged its indigenous peoples as "First Nations." Momaday accounts for the long ne-glect of Native voices by literary historians over the years in various ways: the overwhelming amplitude of the many tribes' oral expressions in the forms of songs, prayers, spells, charms, omens, riddles, and stories; the incredible diversity and complexity of Native languages; the difficulty of recapturing the oral tradition in written form after centuries of discrimination, dispossession, and neglect. Still, Momaday maintains, "American literature begins with the first human perception of the American landscape expressed and preserved in language" (p. 6).

One of the functions of the creation story is to explain how the world came to be. Every culture, every society, has its own origin myth. Among Algonquian tribes the Earth-Diver motif has enjoyed its widest circulation (Wiget, 8). The Anishinabe version, passed down through generations of its own people as well as through Jesuit missionaries and nineteenth-century ethnologists, such as Henry Rowe Schoolcraft, goes like this: Some time following the creation of the world by Kitche Manido, the Great Spirit, a Great Flood occurred inundating much of the earth. Although many animals, some very powerful like the moose and eagle, tried to retrieve some land, only the humble muskrat succeeded, returning with mud between its paws. From this bit of dirt the Earth was re-created (Helen Tanner, 1–2). Aside from accounting for the world's origin, the tale also testifies to the power and presence of water in the North Woods landscape, and to the important role that all animals play in Native culture and the ecosystem.

Exploration and Fur Trade Writings, 1500–1900

The muskrat was among the fur-bearing mammals that Northeastern and Subarctic tribes trapped and traded. Inter-tribal exchanges occurred, of course, long before the French and English colonized Canada in the sixteenth century, but there is no question that it was the fur trade with Europeans that proved to be the greatest transformative force in North Woods Native cultures.

The fur trade also largely accounts for the early North Woods European literature—or the exploration history (Warkentin xiii). Literature in this instance consists of historical reports of European discoverers and explorers to authorities in the Old World to explain their findings and often justify or plead for further expeditions and outlays of expenditures. While generally considered factual reporting, the writings of these explorers, so strongly filtered through European preconceptions and prejudices, often distorted reality to such a degree that they assumed imaginative, if not fictional, qualities—and hence qualify as literature. European discovery of America thus amounts to a "long chronicle of blunted awareness, of slow recognition, of crucial facts never adequately understood. What often is most interesting is what American travelers did not see, either because they did not want to see it or because they were unable to do so" (Franklin, 17). The same can be said of the writings of Jesuit missionaries, although their accounts were as meticulous and accurate as those of any European observer (Hopwood, 21). Another, and unique, form of writing that came out of the encounter between the worlds of the Native and European was the captivity narrative, the transgressive qualities of which make for a fascinating study of the clash and mix of cultures resulting from the contact era. In this section we examine briefly North Woods writing by three different categories of writers: the discoverer-explorer, the missionary, and the captive, all a cause or consequence of that great colonialist enterprise, the fur trade.

Although Wayne Franklin in his study of early American literature distinguishes between the discoverer and explorer, he readily acknowledges that the distinctions are fine and to a large extent idealized. What is most characteristic of their reports is a sense of wonder before the spectacle of the New World, followed quickly by a calculating scrutiny of the utility of America's resources. In this regard Samuel de Champlain stands as the exemplary discoverer-explorer. Traveling and living in New France from 1603 to 1635, Champlain is generally acclaimed as the greatest writer of the period. In his reports there persists that fascinating tension present in virtually all exploration literature: the conflict between what one wants to believe about the country—the Arcadian or Edenic preconception of the New World—and the realities of its rigors and challenges, nonhuman and human. For example, as a result of his 1604–05 exploration of the Maine interior, Champlain comes to the profound conclusion that "it would be very difficult to ascertain the character of this region without spending a winter in it; for, on arriving here in summer, every thing is very agreeable, in consequence of the woods, fine country, and the many varieties of good fish which are found

there. There are six months of winter in this country" (p. 55). Although initially, like Columbus, in search of a Northwest Passage to the riches of the Orient, Champlain helped to transform "Kanata" (a Huron-Iroquois word for town or village) from obstacle into empire with reports of an abundance of forests, fertile soil, fish, and fur-bearing animals.

If Champlain provided a materialist take on the early colonialist perspective of the North Woods, then the Jesuits emphasized a spiritual reading, both positive and negative. Rendered over the years through the historian Francis Parkman, the novelist Brian Moore, the film director Bruce Beresford, the heroic, if misguided, actions and words of the missionaries become both pathetic and profound. Parkman better than any other writer captures the dedication and ordeals of the "black robes":

The Algonquin hordes were never long at rest; and, summer and winter, the priest must follow them by lake, forest, and stream; in summer plying the paddle all day, or toiling through pathless thickets. Bending under the weight of a birch canoe or a load of baggage,—at night, his bed the rugged earth, or some bare rock, lashed by the restless waves of Lake Huron; while famine, the snowstorms, the cold, the treacherous ice of the Great Lakes, smoke, filth, and, not rarely, threats and persecution, were the lot of his winter wanderings. (p. 369)

Northrup Frye identifies "a tone of deep terror in regard to nature" as an inherent quality of Canadian literature. Nowhere is it better visualized than the scene in the film *Black Robe* when Father LaForgue becomes lost in the forest. "It is not a terror of the dangers or discomforts or even the mysteries of nature," Frye writes, "but a terror of the soul at something that these things manifest" (p. 830). Why this abomination of the deep woods by so many Euramericans? Robert Pogue Harrison submits that since ancient times Western culture has been "a civilization of sky-worshippers, children of a celestial father. *Where divinity has been identified with the sky, or with the eternal geometry of the stars, or with cosmic infinity, or with 'heaven,' the forests have become monstrous, for they hide the prospect of god*" (p. 6; original italics). Black Robe believed that the forests were inhabited by the devil; many Natives regarded the missionaries themselves as demons.

Other great accounts of North Woods exploration—e.g., by Alexander Henry the Elder, Samuel Hearne, Alexander Mackenzie, David Thompson, J. B. Tyrell—cannot be examined here for want of space. But a few words need to be said of the largely mute subordinates of the explorers as well as of the independent trappers and traders. For it is a fact of the literary history of the North Woods that "the majority of French fur traders left indifferent narratives or none at all. The *coureurs de bois*, often illiterate, and frequently operating illegally, had seldom the ability or the desire to record their wanderings and transactions" (Hopwood, 22). This peripheralization of the *Canadien voyageur,* who was "fated to be canonized as a native Canadian 'type' at the same time as he was forgotten as a historical reality" (Warkentin, x), is compensated for in part by the songs of the voyageurs passed down to us through writers such as Grace Lee Nute and the wonderfully romantic images of the painter Francis Hopkins (Fowke, 166–173).

Yet a representative, if more complicated, example of the life of the *coureurs de bois* does exist, in writing, in English: *The Falcon: A Narrative of the Captivity and Adventures of John Tanner . . . During Thirty Years Residence Among the Indians in the Interior of North America.* First published in 1830, it tells of the author's incredible experience (told to an Army doctor) as a nine-year-old boy of white parents taken captive by a Shawnee raiding party in Ohio in 1789, and eventually sold to the Ojibwe, with whom he lived and traveled for the next three decades, from Lake Michigan to Lake Winnipeg. Tanner provides an enormously complex perspective on Native life, the fur trade, and the geography and natural resources of the North Woods. He tells of the powerful role played by Native women in their culture; of the dramatic impact of the fur trade, especially with its escalation resulting from increased competition between the Hudson's Bay Company and its rivals, on both Indians and whites; the frequent "starving times" he and his captors endured; and the process of "Indianization" he experienced. Indeed, as Louise Erdrich explains, Tanner's narrative is "probably one of the very few in the captivity genre that appeals strongly to Native Americans. But then John Tanner was culturally an Ojibwa, and as such he is claimed by many to this day, for he lived as an Ojibwa, married an Ojibwa woman, cared devotedly for his mixed-blood children, and was never able to

accommodate himself to a non-Indian life" (p. xi). When Tanner was in his 40s he returned to Anglo-American civilization but felt estranged from his original culture. He then simply disappeared in the forest, and his ghost (Erdrich claims) haunts the woods still.

Settlement and Rediscovery Narratives, 1800–1900

Just as Tanner's travels were (at least initially) a forced march, a life lived against one's will, so too was the experience of Susanna Moodie. Moodie and her husband emigrated to Canada in 1832, the decision to leave the homeland largely his, of course, reflecting the typical family dynamic involved in nineteenth-century emigration. By 1839 they had established a farmstead north of Lake Ontario. Drawn to Canada largely by promotional literature advertising the bush as productive farmland, the Moodies quickly discovered the realities of settling the North Woods. The lament for her former home in England, the capriciousness of the weather, the oppressive isolation suffered by the housewife: all become refrains in *Roughing It in the Bush*. That women's experience on the frontier is significantly different, and much less enjoyable, than that of men is affirmed by Annette Kolodny in *The Land Before Her: Fantasy and Experience of the American Frontiers, 1630–1860*: "Massive exploitation and alteration of the continent do not seem to have been a part of women's fantasies. They dreamed, more modestly, of locating a home and a familial human community within a cultivated garden" (p. xiii). *Roughing It in the Bush* has recently been reprinted, with a new introduction by Margaret Atwood, who has also written a book of poems in which she imaginatively recreates Moodie's experiences on the eastern Canadian frontier: "When I first reached this country / I hated it / and I hated it more each year" (p. 111).

Only after discovery and exploration, only after settlement, only after the process of colonialist exploitation of indigenous cultures and natural resources is well under way, can rediscovery of the land take place. A rediscovery narrative seeks to recapture the sense of awe felt by the original discoverers and explorers; it reveals discoveries psychological as well as physical; and its appeal is to audiences hoping to derive a vicariously felt wonder. The appearance of the rediscoverer coincides with the emergence of nature writing, defined as a first-person nonfictional account in a predominantly nonhuman environment combining the genres of natural history, travel writing, and spiritual autobiography (Scheese, 6).

The Maine Woods by Henry David Thoreau is a quintessential example of a North Woods rediscovery narrative. Based on three journeys to Maine in 1846, 1853, and 1857, the work describes Thoreau's experiences in what was proving to be the last frontier of the northeastern United States. Although by the mid-nineteenth century, much of the Maine territory had already been logged for its white pine and the Native Penobscots largely assimilated into Anglo-American culture, Thoreau manages to artfully combine a fear of the deep woods with its mythopoeic potential for inspiration. At the end of "Ktaadn," he celebrates the hinterland of Maine in one of the greatest paeans to the North Woods ever written: "the country is virtually unmapped and unexplored, and there still waves the virgin forest of the New World" (p. 83). Characteristically, Thoreau could make this claim even as he earlier lamented the inroads of the logging companies, a threat that compelled him in "Chesuncook" (the second of the three essays that comprise the book) to make one of the earliest calls for government preservation of and democratic recreation in wilderness areas: "Why should not we, who have renounced the king's authority, have our national preserves, where no villages need be destroyed, in which the bear and panther, and some even of the hunter race, may still exist, and not be 'civilized off the face of the earth'. . . ?" (p. 156). It was the diminishing North Woods in Eastern America, then, that helped to spur on the conservation movement in the nineteenth and twentieth centuries.

Twentieth-Century Conservation and Nature Writing

In *The Grand Portage Story*, Carolyn Gilman uses the Laurentian Divide just west of the Great Carrying Place of the fur trade as a way of distinguishing between two divergent responses to the North Woods that continue to characterize much literature of this region in the twentieth century. On the eastern side of the divide were the merchants of the fur trade, based in Montreal but traveling frequently to Grand Portage for annual meetings of the North West Company, who saw the wilderness primarily as a source of

profit. On the western side of the divide were Native American and other, largely French-Canadian, laborers who sustained the trade and, among Europeans, a number of "winterers," many of whom perceived the woods as something more than a resource to be exploited. Admittedly, these clerks and agents were often daunted if not horrified by their first encounter with the vast northern wilderness and its people; many, however, who "went in for the money, fully expecting to return, became absorbed by a culture whose slow rhythms and nonmaterial values took over their minds and hearts" (Gilman, 60). This division, between those who respond to the North Woods by wanting to exploit it, who remain "outside" what they experience, and those who identify with and seek to become one with the attitudes and values they find there, plays itself out repeatedly in the literature of the North Woods—most especially in the conservation and nature writing of the twentieth century.

The history of efforts at wilderness conservation, or even the contribution of the literature of the North Woods to this effort, is beyond our scope, but attention to two figures and their role in preserving the Quetico-Superior wilderness of Ontario and Minnesota will illustrate both. Ernest Oberholtzer and Sigurd Olson were very different writers, but each played a crucial role over a period of 70 years in the still-incomplete effort to preserve this central portion of the North Woods.

Carl Ernest Oberholtzer was born in Iowa in 1884, and later studied landscape architecture under Frederick Law Olmsted at Harvard. By 1906, he began to spend summers exploring the lakes along the border of Minnesota and Canada. In 1909 President Theodore Roosevelt took the first great step in preserving this area by establishing the Superior National Forest, and in the same year Ontario created across the border a million-plus acre Quetico Forest Preserve. In 1912, Oberholtzer and an Ojibwe known as Billy Magee, who became lifelong friends, carried out an epic six-month canoe journey of 2,000 miles through Manitoba and the Northwest Territories. Here is where the significant difference between Oberholtzer and Sigurd Olson becomes apparent: whereas Olson would publish nine books and innumerable articles about his travels and experiences in the North Woods, Oberholtzer never wrote a book, and the stories and articles he published were limited to journals and magazines of relatively small circulation.

Although he kept a journal of his 1912 journey, a full rediscovery narrative was not published until 1986, by R. H. Cockburn in *The Beaver*. Thus, while Sigurd Olson became one of the most well-known and popular North Woods nature writers, Oberholtzer remained almost unknown beyond a circle of conservationists concerned with the Quetico-Superior controversy.

Nevertheless, it is difficult to overestimate Oberholtzer's contribution to the long struggle for preservation. As a member of the Quetico-Superior Committee established by Franklin Roosevelt in 1934, and as president of the Quetico-Superior Council from 1927 to 1964, Oberholtzer lobbied tirelessly at preserving the North Woods, writing editorials and articles, issuing proposals and reports in behalf of an international peace park combining the Quetico Reserve and the Superior National Forest. In the autumn of 1929, for instance, he published articles in three successive issues of *American Forests and Forest Life* describing the Quetico-Superior, the efforts to exploit it, and his proposal for its protection. During this same time he lobbied for the Shipstead-Nolan Act, passed in 1930, "the first statute in which Congress explicitly ordered federal land to be retained in its wilderness state" (Searle, 89). Oberholtzer continued to be a central figure in the preservation debate until the passage of the Wilderness Act in 1964 and the eventual creation in 1978 of the Boundary Waters Canoe Area, a year after his death.

When Sigurd Olson first became involved in the struggle for preservation, writing to Oberholtzer in 1930 to ask how he could help, he had been exploring the border lakes for several years. Born in a Chicago suburb in 1899, he grew up in northwestern Wisconsin. After studying at the Universities of Wisconsin and Illinois, he moved to Ely, in Minnesota's Arrowhead, where he taught biology at its junior college. His first book, *The Singing Wilderness*, published in 1956, almost instantly established his reputation as a nature writer, but he had been active in the cause of North Woods preservation for nearly 25 years. It was during the post-war controversy over aviation in the Boundary Waters Canoe Area that Olson came into prominence among North Woods conservationists. As a result of his efforts, President Truman in 1949 issued an executive order "reserving the airspace above the [BWCA] roadless area to an altitude of four thousand feet" (Searle, 176), an act upheld in future court cases. Once established as a promi-

nent spokesperson for the cause of wilderness preservation, Olson, like Oberholtzer, continued to work for the cause until his death in 1982.

"There is magic in the feel of a paddle and the movement of a canoe," writes Olson in *The Singing Wilderness* (p. 82), and from the earliest encounters of European explorers with Native Americans in bark canoes, North Woods writers have been taken by this indigenous mode of travel. So many writers have couched their narratives about the North Woods in the form of a canoe journey that this may be said to constitute a distinct genre of North Woods literature. One of the most compelling of twentieth-century canoe narratives is Dillon Wallace's *The Lure of the Labrador Wild*, a tragic account of a journey up the Swan River from Hamilton Inlet on the coast of Labrador to Lake Michikamau and back during the summer and autumn of 1903. Young and inexperienced, Hubbard and Wallace set off for the interior of Labrador with no maps, a guide unfamiliar with the region, and only a vague idea of how their journey would proceed. While most canoe-journey adventure narratives relate excitement and danger, they normally end successfully—as does Olson's classic in the genre, *The Lonely Land*, describing a journey of six men in three canoes from Ile à La Crosse in central Saskatchewan down the Churchill and Sturgeon Weir rivers to Cumberland House. Olson concludes his narrative with a strong sense of accomplishment, of friendships affirmed, and of the desire to return to this lonely land. In contrast, Wallace's story ends with the death by starvation of his friend, Leonidas Hubbard, and near-death of their guide George Elson, a mixed-blood Cree, and Wallace himself, who survives only because Elson makes it out and sends back help.

Other canoe-journey narratives relate adventures as dangerous yet safe and successful. Olson's *The Lonely Land*, or the equally powerful *Dangerous River* by Canadian R. M. Patterson (set along the fabled Nahanni River in the Northwest Territories in the late 1920s), creates a feeling of the vastness and majesty of the great North Woods, invoking a twentieth-century version of the Romantic sublime. Three later accounts are also noteworthy: Paul Brooks' *Roadless Area*—Ontario, Constance Helmericks' *Down the Wild River North*—Northwest Territories, and John McPhee's *The Survival of the Bark Canoe*. The last describes the author's contentious and comical trip with Henri Vaillancourt, a legendary builder of traditional

Native American bark canoes. Retracing Thoreau's excursions on the Penobscot River, McPhee learns that Vaillancourt's virtues as a companion are fewer than those as a canoe builder. Others before McPhee noticed the stresses that a canoe journey can put on human relations; most such narratives, however, affirm the cementing of fast friendships.

If the North Woods' vast and pervasive waterways elicit narratives of canoe adventures, its great natural beauty and varied ecology also encourage many to stay, to live in place and observe closely. The chronicle of life in the North Woods, often arranged on the almanac pattern of *Walden*, has been a favorite form of North Woods writers in the twentieth century. While some deny it, most who go to the woods go, as Thoreau did, searching for a pastoral alternative to the distractions and enervating demands of modern culture. Few of these writers, however, are born in the North Woods; most come from somewhere else, usually somewhere south and urban.

It is difficult to find a work in which living in place in the North Woods is better represented than in Sigurd Olson's second book, *Listening Point*. No writer better embodies the experience of the "winterer" who travels to the North Woods, stays, and adopts the attitudes and values inherent in the wilderness. In *Listening Point* Olson writes of finding a place that represents the center of his existence:

> From this one place I would explore the entire north and all life, including my own. I could look to the stars and feel that here was a focal point of great celestial triangles, a point as important as any one on the planet. For me it would be a listening-post from which I might even hear the music of the spheres. (Olson, *Listening Point*, 7)

Olson describes how he found the site, built a cabin, and returned to this wilderness retreat for decades. He introduces his readers to its creatures and plants, its geology, its people. He also reveals the ways in which modern society intrudes. In "The Breaking" he admits to his horror when he hires a bulldozer to build a road to his cabin: "I was unprepared for this, the noise and violence, and I looked at the huge orange monster with apprehension and dismay" (p. 27).

But Olson is not a radical or purist with respect to wilderness preservation (Fritzell,

292–293). Later in the same chapter he contrasts the destruction wrought by the bulldozer with the breaking of ground by a team of plowhorses, and he valorizes the farmers' "fierce pride at giving something of value to the race, soil that for untold centuries had accumulated richness toward the time when they might take it for their own" (p. 30). Still later, he returns to the new scar of the bulldozer road and reflects that "in a year or so ferns and shrubs would crowd in from the edges and it would not seem as wide as now" (p. 31). Elsewhere Olson describes the heroic efforts of the fur traders, loggers, and miners. He is not oblivious to the destructive effects of these extractive industries; rather, he recognizes the need to reconcile the values of the winterer with those of the descendants of the Montreal merchants.

The spirit of these merchants remains very much alive in the North Woods. Peter Leschak, after leaving his native Iron Range for a brief encounter with urban America, returns to the life of a neo-pioneer in the North Woods of northern Minnesota, not far from Olson's haunts. *Letters from Side Lake: A Chronicle of Life in the North Woods*, is a curious mixture of wilderness appreciation and the exploitive attitudes pervasive among many Euramericans living and working in the North Woods. In "Battleground," Leschak helps a friend clear trees for a new electrical line. Near the end of the job, they encounter "a majestic, perfectly formed spruce—three feet in diameter at the butt and about sixty-five feet high." He notes that, unlike the Ojibwe, "we made no apologies to the doomed trunks. Except [this] one" (p. 27). In a ceremonious mood, he goes and buys a new ax so that the tree would not be "finished off with a mean and vulgar chain saw." Nevertheless, fortified with beer and presumably mindful that cutting down a three-foot diameter tree with an ax would involve a lot of work, he chainsaws through all but the final part of the tree. Several friends gather for the party to topple the tree with the ax. Leschak observes that "guilt, like many other things, is better shared," and that "instead of spruce boughs, the birds have wires to perch on. A dubious achievement" (Leschak, 28).

Despite the efforts of Leschak to make the North Woods say "spuds" and the admiration expressed by Olson for the farmer and his plowhorses, efforts to farm the North Woods have met with scant success, often resulting in failed farms and ruined farmers across the North Woods of Canada and the United States. Robert Treuer's *The Tree Farm* tells of the efforts of a family to reclaim such a failed farm and turn it to a use more suited to the soil and climate of northern Minnesota. More common among chroniclers of life in the North Woods are the settlers who move there, often from a large urban center, and live in retirement or on the proceeds of writing or some other activity that does not over-exploit local resources. A number of accounts in this category are excerpted in *North Writers: A Strong Woods Collection,* edited by John Henricksson. Among the more well-known nonfiction North Woods writers are Helen and Ade Hoover, who moved from Chicago to the Gunflint Trail in northeastern Minnesota. A writer of children's books, Hoover and her illustrator husband produced several charming reports of North Woods life, including *The Long-Shadowed Forest* and *The Gift of the Deer.* The latter describes successive generations of a family of white-tailed deer who visit the Hoovers' isolated cabin over several years, while the earlier book presents in succession from one spring to the next minutely detailed accounts of the local flora and fauna, from the largest mammals—moose, caribou, deer, bear—to the smallest insects and lichens. Few chroniclers of this country have observed more carefully or described in greater detail the ways and habits of the creatures of the North Woods. And most recently Jim Dale Vickery in *Open Spaces* has taken up the mantle of Sigurd Olson with narratives of his year-round explorations of the North Woods of Minnesota and Ontario based out of his cabin on the edge of the Boundary Waters Canoe Area.

Fiction and Poetry from the 1800s to the Present

A recurring theme in the literature of the North Woods is its overwhelming vastness. Perhaps its immensity contributed to the creation of larger-than-life, legendary characters. When Henry Rowe Schoolcraft arrived in Sault Ste. Marie in 1822 to fill the newly created position of Indian agent for the Upper Great Lakes, he was "quite ignorant of Indian culture" (Massie, 14). By 1856, however, when he published *The Hiawatha Legends,* he was an acknowledged authority on Native American—especially Ojibwe—oral "lodge stories." Schoolcraft's efforts to popularize "the thought and invention of the aboriginal mind" were less successful initially than was Henry Wadsworth Longfellow's *The Song of Hiawatha*, an epic poem based largely on Schoolcraft's earlier work.

Longfellow's *Song* enjoyed immense popularity in the later nineteenth century and was a staple in schools well into the later twentieth century. For many Euramericans, this poem was their introduction to the land and people of the North Woods, and did much to fix its mythology in their minds. When, for example, the young Eric Sevareid and Walter Port canoed down the Red River into Canada in 1930 en route to Hudson Bay (recounted in *Canoeing with the Cree*), Sevareid took with him the following preconceptions about Indians: "these [Natives] in the midst of civilization were the handsomest of all. Tall and straight, with long black hair and fine facial features, they were the characters of *Hiawatha* come to life" (p. 55). While Longfellow's direct experience with Native Americans was limited, and while he freely adapted to the service of his Ojibwe hero stories and legends that Schoolcraft had ascribed to various tribes, his descriptions of Native American beliefs and practices were taken as accurate—so much so that *The Song of Hiawatha* was used as a source for teaching Indian history to young Ojibwe children packed off to boarding schools in the early part of this century, when official government policy was to "eradicate the cultural boundaries that separated Indians and whites" (Gilman, 123).

While both Schoolcraft and Longfellow saw the North Woods and its inhabitants through the eyes of myth and legend, these were nevertheless sympathetic eyes. Just prior to his departure, Hiawatha relates to his people a vision of the arrival of Europeans in their "canoe with wings," and although he urges them to greet these strangers with "the heart's right hand of friendship," his vision also shows "our nation scattered" (Longfellow, 214–216). Longfellow seemed able to foresee only too well how Native Americans would be dealt with by their new neighbors.

The next effort to create legends out of the experience of the North Woods came from a group that changed the physical face of this country more drastically than any other—the loggers. Beginning in the New England forests of Maine in the 1830s, then spreading west across Canada and the northern tier of states from New York to Minnesota by the 1920s, the logging frontier all but eliminated the old growth pine forests of the North Woods. Like the fur traders before them, the men who carried out this enterprise created stories and legends to memorialize their exploits and heroes. By 1895–1907 stories of Paul Bunyan were circulating among lumberjacks, and by 1910 some of these were published in newspapers or in lumber company promotional tracts (Hoffman, 1–5). While many of these stories seem to have arisen as oral folk tales and legends, eventually they were composed and published by writers who were decidedly not loggers. Carl Sandburg's "Who Made Paul Bunyan" and Robert Frost's "Paul's Wife," first published in 1921, are among a large number of such tales collected in Harold W. Felton's *Legends of Paul Bunyan.*

While these tales focus on the heroic efforts of loggers, with little concern for the timber industry's wasteful legacy, North Woods writers for a century have lamented the devastation of the great forests. In "The Last Good Country," written in the 1950s, Ernest Hemingway's youthful hero Nick Adams leads his little sister through a swamp and tangle of slashings into a grove of virgin timber on the upper peninsula of Michigan, an island of forest inexplicably left by the loggers:

> They came from the hot sun of the slashings into the shade of the great trees. The slashings had run up to the top of a ridge and over and then the forest began. They were walking on the brown forest floor now and it was springy and cool under their feet. There was no underbrush and the trunks of the trees rose sixty feet high before there were any branches. It was cool in the shade of the trees and high up in them Nick could hear the breeze that was rising.

Later, Nick tells his sister, "they build cathedrals to be like this" (Hemingway, 516–517).

A recurring theme among North Woods writers is the power of the wilderness to transform those who enter. In Margaret Atwood's *Surfacing,* her narrator drives north toward a huge, unnamed lake in central Canada to investigate the apparent disappearance of her father from her childhood island home. Accompanied by three friends from the city, the narrator is at first as alienated from the north land as they. When the motorboat that ferries them to the island departs, "the space is quiet, the wind has gone down and the lake is flat, silver-white, it's the first time all day (and for a long time, for years) we have been out of the reach of motors. My

ears and body tingle, aftermath of the vibration, like feet taken out of roller skates" (p. 36). What follows is certainly a "journey into the solitary world of the psyche." For Atwood's heroine "the lake was the entrance," and "the island in the Canadian lake constitutes a green world of childhood remembered and a locus of transformation or rebirth" (Pratt, 139, 143, 151). Only when the woman has entered the depths of the wilderness, has dived into the lake to find the body of her dead father—or a vision of it—can she re-emerge to contemplate joining her lover, Joe, and to "reenter [her] own time." As she pauses before taking the first step, "the lake is quiet, the trees surround me, asking and giving nothing" (Atwood, 222, 224).

The North Woods has indeed produced a distinctive body of literature dominated by water and trees. While various civilizations over the years have certainly transformed the land, the physical environment continues to dictate the actions of humans. As Tim O'Brien writes in *In the Lake of the Woods,* a novel in which key characters simply disappear in the maze of woods and water, "The wilderness was massive. It was a place . . . where lost was a rule of thumb. The water here was the water there. Nothing in particular, all in general. Forests folded into forests, sky swallowed sky. The solitude bent back on itself. Everywhere was nowhere" (p. 239).

Selected Works and Further Reading

Atwood, Margaret, *Surfacing,* New York: Simon & Schuster, 1972; London: Andre Deutsch, 1972

——, "Thoughts from Underground," in *Selected Poems,* New York: Simon & Schuster, 1976

Bailey, Robert G., *Description of the Ecoregions of the United States,* 2nd ed., Washington, D.C.: U.S. Department of Agriculture, Forest Service, 1995

Beresford, Bruce, director, *Black Robe,* Samuel Goldwyn, 1991

Brooks, Paul, *Roadless Area,* New York: Knopf, 1964; London: Ballantine, 1971

Champlain, Samuel de, *Voyages of Samuel de Champlain, 1604–1618,* edited by William Lawson Grant, New York: Barnes & Noble, 1907

Cockburn, R. H., "Voyage to Nutheltin," *The Beaver* (January/February 1986), pp. 4–27

Daniel, Glenda, and Jerry Sullivan, *A Sierra Club Naturalist's Guide to the North Woods of Michigan, Wisconsin, Minnesota, and Southern Ontario,* San Francisco: Sierra Club, 1981

Felton, Harold W., ed., *Legends of Paul Bunyan,* New York: Knopf, 1947

Fowke, Edith, "Folktales and Folk Songs," in *Literary History of Canada: Canadian Literature in English,* edited by Carl F. Klinck, Toronto, Ontario: University of Toronto Press, 1965

Franklin, Wayne, *Discoverers, Explorers, Settlers: The Diligent Writers of Early America,* Chicago: University of Chicago Press, 1979

Fritzell, Peter, "Changing Conceptions of the Great Lakes Forest: Jacques Cartier to Sigurd Olson," in *The Great Lakes Forest: An Environmental and Social History,* edited by Susan Flader, Minneapolis: University of Minnesota Press, 1983

Frye, Northrup, "Conclusion," in *Literary History of Canada: Canadian Literature in English,* edited by Carl F. Klinck, Toronto, Ontario: University of Toronto Press, 1965

Gilman, Carolyn, *The Grand Portage Story,* St. Paul: Minnesota Historical Society, 1992

Harris, R. Cole, ed., *Historical Atlas of Canada: Volume I: From the Beginning to 1800,* Toronto, Ontario, and Buffalo, New York: University of Toronto Press, 1987

Harrison, Robert Pogue, *Forests: The Shadow of Civilization,* Chicago: University of Chicago Press, 1992

Hearne, Samuel, *A Journey from Prince of Wales's Fort in Hudson's Bay to the Northern Ocean,* London: A. Strahan and T. Cadell, 1795; reprinted, New York: Da Capo, 1968

Helm, June, ed., *Handbook of North American Indians: Volume 6: Subarctic,* Washington, D.C.: Smithsonian Institution, 1981

Helmericks, Constance, *Down the Wild River North,* Boston: Little, Brown, 1968; London: Leslie Frewin, 1969

Hemingway, Ernest, "The Last Good Country," in *The Complete Short Stories of Ernest Hemingway,* New York: Scribner's, 1987

Henricksson, John, ed., *North Writers: A Strong Woods Collection,* Minneapolis: University of Minnesota Press, 1991

Henry, Alexander, *Travels and Adventures in Canada and the Indian Territories Between the Years 1760 and 1776,* New York: I. Riley, 1809; new edition, edited by James Bain, Boston: Little, Brown, 1901

Hoffman, Daniel, *Paul Bunyan: Last of the Frontier Demigods,* Philadelphia: University of Pennsylvania Press for Temple University Publications, 1952; London: University of Nebraska Press, 1983

Hoover, Helen, *The Gift of the Deer,* New York: Knopf, 1966; London: Heinemann, 1967

——, *The Long-Shadowed Forest,* New York: Thomas Y. Crowell, 1963; London: Souvenir, 1965

Hopwood, Victor G., "Explorers by Land," in *Literary History of Canada: Canadian Literature in English,* edited by Carl F. Klinck, Toronto, Ontario: University of Toronto Press, 1965

Kenton, Edna, ed., *The Jesuit Relations and Allied Documents; Travels and Explorations of the Jesuit Missionaries in North America (1610–1791),* New York: Vanguard, 1925; London: Brentano's, 1986

Klinck, Carl F., ed., *Literary History of Canada: Canadian Literature in English,* Toronto, Ontario: University of Toronto Press, 1965

Knauth, Percy, *The North Woods,* New York: Time-Life, 1972

Kolodny, Annette, *The Land Before Her: Fantasy and Experience of the American Frontiers, 1630–1860,* Chapel Hill: University of North Carolina Press, 1984

Leschak, Peter, *Letters from Side Lake: A Chronicle of Life in the North Woods,* New York: Perennial, 1987

Longfellow, Henry Wadsworth, *The Song of Hiawatha,* New York: Ticknor and Fields, 1855; London: David Bogue, 1855

Mackenzie, Alexander, *Exploring the Northwest Territory: Sir Alexander Mackenzie's Journal of a Voyage by Bark Canoe from Lake Athabasca to the Pacific Ocean in the Summer of 1789,* edited by Ted Hayden McDonald, Norman: University of Oklahoma Press, 1966

McPhee, John, *The Survival of the Bark Canoe,* New York: Farrar, Straus, and Giroux, 1975

Momaday, N. Scott, "The Native Voice," in *Columbia Literary History of the United States,* edited by Emory Elliott, New York: Columbia University Press, 1988

Moodie, Susanna, *Roughing It in the Bush; or, Life in Canada,* New York: Putnam's, 1852; London: R. Bentley, 1852

Moore, Brian, *Black Robe,* New York: Dutton, 1985; London: Jonathan Cape, 1985

Nute, Grace Lee, *The Voyageur,* New York and London: D. Appleton, 1931; reprinted, St. Paul: Minnesota Historical Society, 1955

Oberholtzer, Ernest, "The Lakes of Verendrye: A University of the Wilderness," *American Forests and Forest Life* (September, October, & November 1929)

O'Brien, Tim, *In the Lake of the Woods,* Boston: Houghton Mifflin/Seymour Lawrence, 1994; London: Flamingo, 1995

Olson, Sigurd, *Listening Point,* New York: Knopf, 1958

———, *The Lonely Land,* New York: Knopf, 1961

———, *The Singing Wilderness,* New York: Knopf, 1956

Parkman, Francis, *France and England in North America: Volume 2: The Jesuits in North America in the Seventeenth Century,* Boston: Little, Brown, 1867

Patterson, R. M., *Dangerous River,* New York: William Sloane, 1954; London: Allen and Unwin, 1954

Pratt, Annis, "*Surfacing* and the Rebirth Journey," in *The Art of Margaret Atwood: Essays in Criticism,* edited by Arnold E. Davidson and Cathy N. Davidson, Toronto, Ontario: Anansi, 1981

Scheese, Don, *Nature Writing: The Pastoral Impulse in America,* New York: Twayne, 1996; London: Prentice Hall International, 1996

Schoolcraft, Henry Rowe, *The Myth of Hiawatha and Other Oral Legends, Mythologic and Allegoric, of the North American Indians,* Philadelphia: Lippincott, 1856; reprinted, New York: Kraus Reprint, 1971

Sevareid, Eric, *Canoeing with the Cree,* New York: Macmillan, 1935; reprinted, St. Paul: Minnesota Historical Society, 1968

Tanner, Helen Hornbeck, *The Ojibwa,* New York: Chelsea House, 1992

Tanner, John, *A Narrative of the Captivity and Adventures of John Tanner (U.S. Interpreter at the Saut de Ste. Marie) During Thirty Years Residence Among the Indians in the Interior of North America,* New York: G. & C. & H. Carvill, 1830; London: Ballwin & Cradock, 1830; also published as *The Falcon: A Narrative of the Captivity and Adventures of John Tanner,* introduction by Louise Erdrich, New York: Penguin, 1994

Thompson, David, *David Thompson's Narrative, 1784–1812,* edited by Richard Glover, Toronto, Ontario: Champlain Society, 1962

Thoreau, Henry David, *The Maine Woods,* New York: Houghton Mifflin, 1864; Cambridge: Riverside, 1864

Treuer, Robert, *The Tree Farm,* Boston: Little, Brown, 1977

Trigger, Bruce, *Handbook of North American Indians: Volume 15: Northeast,* Washington, D.C.: Smithsonian Institution, 1978

Tyrrell, James W., *Across the Sub-Arctics of Canada,* Toronto, Ontario: William Briggs, 1897; New York: Dodd, 1898; London: T. F. Unwin, 1898

Vickery, Jim Dale, *Open Spaces,* Minocqua, Wisconsin: NorthWord, 1991

Wallace, Dillon, *The Lure of the Labrador Wild,* New York: F. Revell, 1905; London: Hodder & Stoughton, 1905

Warkentin, Germaine, ed., *Canadian Exploration Literature: An Anthology: 1660–1860,* Toronto, Ontario: Oxford University Press, 1993

Wiget, Andrew, *Native American Literature,* Boston: Twayne, 1985

The Realistic Wild Animal Story*

Ralph H. Lutts

The late nineteenth century witnessed the development of a new and very popular kind of nature writing, the realistic wild animal story. Called a distinctly Canadian form of literature, it also became an important part of popular culture in the United States, especially at the beginning of the twentieth century. The wild animal story combined elements of nature writing and animal fiction.

Earlier forms of animal stories tended to be fictional accounts in which the animals were little more than humans in furry or feathery coats; sometimes they literally dressed in human clothing. English animal stories like Rudyard Kipling's *The Jungle Books* and Kenneth Grahame's *The Wind in the Willows* present animals as, essentially, English folks pursuing their roles in a social hierarchy (Polk, 52). The realistic wild animal story, however, emphasized the perspective of the animal itself. As Charles G. D. Roberts, one of the creators of the genre, put it, "the interest centres about the personality, individuality, mentality, of an animal, as well as its purely physical characteristics ("The Animal Story," 28). Furthermore, the animals "live for their own ends," rather than for human ends (Magee, 157). Although presented in story form and employing fictional devices, the authors assert that their accounts are factual and represent accurate natural history.

Over the years, these stories were largely neglected by scholars, perhaps because they were thought of as minor works written for children. Even Roberts' stories were not considered worthy of serious examination until the 1960s, despite the fact that he has been called the "father" of Canadian poetry and of Canadian literature as a result of his other writings, and

was knighted for his literary work. Ernest Thompson Seton,[1] another founder of the genre, was also overlooked by scholars, although his wild animal stories are the only ones to remain continually in print through the twentieth century. Since the 1960s, however, scholars have studied the genre. Most of their publications have focused on the work of its founders, Roberts and Seton. But many other authors wrote wild animal stories, including William J. Long (a contemporary of Roberts and Seton), Rachel Carson, Sally Carrighar, Fred Bodsworth and Farley Mowat.

There were many precursors to the wild animal story, but two books in particular paved the way and helped to create a market for the genre. The first was English writer Anna Sewell's novel about the life of a horse, *Black Beauty*. Although Black Beauty thought and spoke like a four-legged human, his message was an appeal for the humane treatment of animals. Its popularity marked the growing public interest in animal welfare. The second book was Rudyard Kipling's *Jungle Book*. Its enormous success both demonstrated the appeal of stories about wild animals, fabrications though they were, and further stimulated that market.

The realistic wild animal story burst upon the scene and achieved wide public attention with the publication of Ernest Thompson Seton's *Wild Animals I Have Known*, which went through sixteen printings in its first fours years alone. It was not, however, the earliest publication in this genre. American author Charles Dudley Warner was perhaps the first North American writer to describe events from the point of view of a wild animal. His story "A-Hunting of the Deer" depicted the hunt as the

*An extended version of this essay appears in Ralph H. Lutts, ed., *The Wild Animal Story,* Philadelphia: Temple University Press, 1998.

deer experienced it. Seton, a Canadian, first began to experiment with the genre with "The Drummer on Snowshoes," published in 1887 and brought it to fruition in his now classic tale of Lobo the wolf, "The King of the Currumpaw: A Wolf Story," first published in 1894. Charles G. D. Roberts, another Canadian, wrote poetry, novels of the Canadian wilderness and "hook & bullet" stories that, ironically, emphasized the viciousness of animals before developing his own realistic wild animal stories. His first venture into the genre was his classic, "Do Seek Their Meat From God." This and other wild animal stories were included in his book *Earth's Enigmas* (Poirier; Wadland, 166).[2]

Margaret Atwood proposed in her influential book *Survival* that a central theme in Canadian literature is that of survival, be it in the face of a hostile wilderness or threats to its culture. (By contrast, she proposes that a central theme in American literature is the frontier as a symbol of hope and new opportunities.) Associated with the survival theme is that of being a victim, which may in part be a response to the nation's colonial history. She also argued that closely associated with the theme of survival is "the will *not* to survive." "Certainly," she wrote, "Canadian authors spend a disproportionate amount of time making sure that their heroes die or fail. Much Canadian writing suggests that failure is required because it is felt—consciously or unconsciously—to be the only 'right' ending, the only thing that will support the characters' (or their authors') view of the universe" (p. 34). This argument stimulated a good deal of discussion, including contrary arguments (Altmeyer; Pritchard; M. MacDonald). Nevertheless, as she wrote, "Like any theory it won't explain everything, but it may give you some points of departure" (p. 35).[3]

The stories by Roberts and Seton seem to support this argument. Roberts "Do Seek Their Meat From God," for example, tells of a woodsman finding his child being stalked by mountain lions. He kills the cats, thus saving his child. But Roberts goes on to add an ironic twist: the lions' kittens are later found dead from starvation; the life of the woodsman's son was purchased at the expense of the mountain lions'. The woodsman and the lions were engaged in a common struggle to insure the survival of their young; they operated on the same moral ground. In another tale, one of Roberts' characters explained the nature of life in the wild by saying, "Oftentimes it's seemed to me all life was jest

like a few butterflies flitterin' over a graveyard" (*Heart*, 243). Trappers finally managed to lure Seton's extraordinary wolf Lobo to his death with the scent of his beloved mate, Blanca, who had been killed earlier. When his readers complained about the deaths of so many of his animal heroes, Seton explained, "The fact that these stories are true is the reason why all are tragic. The life of a wild animal *always has a tragic end*" (*Wild Animals I Have Known*, 12, emphasis in original).

Despite their commonalities, Robert's and Seton's animals are quite different from each other. Roberts' animals are immersed in the Darwinian struggle for survival and their deaths reflect this struggle. Yet, despite their universal deaths, life continues. As Joseph Gold observes of Roberts' stories, "In the long run death itself has no sting and is ironically defeated by the uses nature makes of its processes. All things conspire to sustain life and the stories create a very strong sense of rhythmic pattern and cycle of the seasons" (p. 25). In addition, by including humans in this common struggle Roberts demonstrated the kinship between humans and wild animals. This insightful contribution to literature provided a theme to which Roberts returned again and again. Seton's animals, on the other hand, were virtuous creatures. As Seton wrote, he "tried to emphasize our kinship with the animals by showing that in them we can find the virtues most admired in Man" (*Lives of the Hunted*, 9). He even argued that "The Ten Commandments are not *arbitrary laws given to man*, but are *fundamental laws of all highly developed animals*" (*Ten Commandments*, 4, emphasis in original).

If, as Atwood and others have argued, Canadian literature reflects a struggle for survival in a fearful wilderness, why do wild animal stories not depict wilderness animals as monsters? She answers this question by arguing that the animals are all victims, they are all killed, and Canadians identify with them as victims (Atwood, 75 ff.). This becomes another bond of kinship between animals and people (in this case, Canadians).

In domestic animal stories, the animals adjust to and serve the needs of their human masters. In Fred Gibson's novel *Old Yeller*, for example, the dog becomes a hero by defending a girl who had found a bear cub from the cub's mother. (In a wild animal story, the mother bear would have been the hero for trying to save her cub from the human.) (Oswald, 136) This emphasis on the human's interest over the animal's is characteristic of most American literature, in which animals tend to accommodate themselves to humans,[4] or serve as symbols or the goal of human action, as in Melville's *Moby-Dick* or Faulkner's "The Bear." "Indeed," writes James Polk, "the patterns in American writing about animals seem almost inverted in Canadian counterparts, where the emphasis is not on man at all, but on the animal" (pp. 52–53; Atwood, 74.)

Many authors in the United States did, though, produce their own body of realistic wild animals stories that emphasized the animals' perspective. However, these often presented a more romantic vision of nature and animals. The American William J. Long,[5] for example, denied that there was a Darwinian struggle for survival in nature based on his belief that wild animals have no awareness of such a struggle. He believed that life in nature is a "gladsome" life and that death comes swiftly and without trauma. He also argued that wild animals can reason and teach their young in much the same way as do humans, a central premise of his book *School of the Woods.* In his story "Wayeeses the Strong One" he even claimed as factual a story of a wolf leading a pair of lost Indian children to their home (*Northern Trails*). This upbeat vision of nature was particularly appealing to his American readers. Although Long had been largely forgotten, his books were quite popular and widely used in school classrooms during the first decades of the twentieth century.

Long may have been among the most romantic and anthropomorphizing of American nature writers, but he was not the only American writer to idealize animals. In James Oliver Curwood's *The Grizzly King,* for example, a grizzly bear confronts an unarmed hunter who had once shot him. The bear rears on his hind legs, ready to kill the hunter, but then decides to leave the frightened man alone and walks off.[6] The animal is represented as morally superior to the man—a theme often encountered in wild animal stories.

Stories about domestic animals tended to subsume the animals' interests to those of their human owners. However, some dog stories bridged the genres of the realistic wild animal and realistic domestic animal stories. Most notable of these is Jack London's *Call of the Wild.* This novel begins as a traditional dog story, telling of Buck's luxurious life on an estate, how he was kidnapped and sold to become a sled dog in Gold Rush Yukon and how he finally found kindness with a beloved master. But the novel ends as a wild animal story as Buck becomes aware of an inner urge to independence and the realization of his primitive nature as a wild creature. He eventually throws off the bonds of civilized domestication, runs off into the wilderness and becomes the leader of a wolf pack.

London's companion novel, *White Fang,* reversed the process; a wolf-dog born in the wilderness is found by humans and, after going through a series of owners, is tamed and becomes a family pet on an estate. Although it ends as a traditional domestic animal story, *White Fang* begins as a wild animal story and the portions describing White Fang's puppyhood are an outstanding example of the genre. London made a great effort to tell these stories from White Fang's and Buck's perspectives, without making them think entirely as humans do (*see* London, "The Other Animals"). In this respect, he was employing the tools of the wild animal story.

The Darwinian Revolution was a long and difficult process of intellectual and cultural change. As a cultural phenomenon, it required the public to learn and accept a new set of ideas regarding the nature of history, organic change and our place in the world. In a sense, this revolution is still in progress (Mayr). The realistic wild animal story was a response to Darwinism that presented readers with ways to accommodate to the notion of natural selection and the amorality of nature. Robert MacDonald, for example, sees the genre as a "revolt against instinct" and Darwinian amorality. In these stories animals do have their instincts, he contends, but they are also rational and ethical; they rise above instinct. "The works of Seton and Roberts are thus celebrations of rational, ethical animals, who as they rise above instinct, reach toward the spiritual" (p. 18). This is certainly true of the work of Long, who argued that animals reason, have souls and may even have an afterlife (*Brier-Patch Philosophy*). Spiritual matters aside, by the end of the nineteenth century many people recognized that instinct alone is not a sufficient explanation for much of animal behavior. However, the psychology of the day offered only the options of instinct or reason to explain behavior, which encouraged some people to opt in favor of animal reasoning.

Thomas Dunlap has argued that wild animal stories helped readers not to reject Darwinism, but to assimilate it. Roberts' stories, for example, often showed that humans and wild animals shared the common tasks of protecting, feeding and raising their young. If one prevailed over the other, they nevertheless shared the same moral ground and similar emotional and mental lives.

At the same time, humans also stood outside of nature by virtue of their ability to make and use tools, and to reshape and distort nature. Seton presented a similar view of nature, although he softened the Darwinian image of nature as a stage for carnage and placed a greater emphasis on humans as senseless killers.

Although wild animal stories employed narrative devices of fiction to engage their readers and tell their stories, they were marketed as natural history and their authors repeatedly attested to their faithfulness to nature. They frequently claimed that their stories were based on field observations and that the stories' events actually happened. Nevertheless, in 1903 the dean of American nature writing, John Burroughs, launched a blistering attack on what he called "sham naturalists." He argued that many popular writers, including Seton, Roberts, Long and London were frauds who overly dramatized animal life in order to sell their books to an eager but gullible public. This began the often humorous, but no less serious, Nature Fakers controversy (Lutts). Most of the writers kept their heads down, did not defend themselves publicly and escaped relatively unscathed. Long, however, aggressively defended himself in magazines and newspapers, which led to his becoming the focus of the battle. The controversy continued for four years until Theodore Roosevelt publicly supported Burroughs's position and condemned Long. The president expressed special anger at the publishers whose classroom editions of wild animal stories introduced shoddy and even bogus natural history into the public schools.

This battle was fought over three closely related issues. The first was the necessity of accuracy in nature writing, including wild animal stories. The controversy helped to establish at least informal standards of accuracy in nature literature. As Clarence Hawks, a minor practitioner of the wild animal story, wrote, "I now realized that if I ever make a bad break in regards to my natural history statements that I was doomed" (p. 118). The second issue was the question of what is the nature of animal mentality; to what extent are they governed by instincts or reason? This issue continued to be a topic of lively debate throughout the century. At its root, though, the controversy was about establishing a balance between emotion and science as means to understand and appreciate nature—the literary expression of a debate that was going on throughout the nature study movement at that time.

Although wild animal stories were an important expression of cultural responses to Darwinism, they were more overtly linked to the animal welfare movement. They presented animals as individual, sentient creatures capable of feeling mental and physical pain. They often appealed to, and promoted, humanitarianism by showing their readers, through the animals' own eyes, the impact of hunting and trapping. Seton, Roberts, Long and others presented predators in a more positive light than did most nature writing of their time. They often depicted wolves, for example, as sociable creatures who avoid humans, rather than bloodthirsty monsters eager to drag off children. Their visions of wolf behavior often turned out to be more accurate than were those of Theodore Roosevelt and most professional naturalists of their time.

The wild animal story seemed to die out in the early twentieth century. Alec Lucas suggests a number of contributing factors: "Perhaps people tired of learning that animals and men are alike and learned from two world wars that they are too much alike. Perhaps urban people, now removed three or four generations from their country forebears, have lost touch with nature almost completely. Unquestionably the biological sciences have been replaced in public imagination by the physical. What might once have been a nature story is now science fiction" (p. 388). William Magee argued that wild animal story writers faced a problem in making animals who lived for themselves interesting to human readers. They simply ran out of plots and ways to introduce variety into their stories (p. 164). Nevertheless, the wild animal story did not completely disappear.

Few women wrote wild animal stories during the first part of the twentieth century and none of their works have endured. It was two American women, however, who were responsible for the transformation and rebirth of the genre in the 1940s: Rachel Carson and Sally Carrighar. Most of the early writers of wild animal stories were interested in the lives of individual animals and their stories often promoted the humane treatment of individual animals. Carson and Carrighar, however, wrote stories that presented animals not so much as heroes and individual personalities, but as representatives of their species living within an ecological community of animals (Norwood, 238). Both based their stories on a careful reading of scientific literature, as well as observations in the field. Their stories, especially Carson's, grew more out of an ecological worldview than the humanitarian and animal rights perspectives emerging at the beginning of their century.

Under the Sea-Wind, Carson's first book and her only major excursion into the wild animal story, follows the activities and life cycles of marine animals and the ways their lives intertwine. It became a bestseller following publication of Carson's next book, *The Sea Around Us*. *Under the Sea-Wind* reflected the influence that Henry Williamson, English author of *Tarka the Otter* and *Salar the Salmon*, had upon Carson's writing (Brooks, 5–6), but its combination of lyrical prose, ecological vision and careful science was uniquely Carson's.

Sally Carrighar's first book, *One Day on Beetle Rock*, follows a day in the lives of a number of animals in Sequoia National Park. Each chapter tells the story of a single animal, much as in a traditional wild animal story. However, the animals featured in each chapter also appear in the other chapters, creating an interwoven tapestry depicting the animal community of Beetle Rock. Carrighar wrote that she had no model for the kind of writing she wanted to do, although Gale Lawrence has suggested that she may have been influenced by the work of Williamson and Carson. Both Carson and Carrighar allowed their readers to experience animal lives through the animals' own eyes. They were, though, very careful in their choice of language to avoid humanizing their animal characters. Theirs was a more behavioristic representation of wild animals, in contrast to earlier writers who presented animals as individual personalities, although Carrighar was later criticized for anthropomorphism.

Canadian writers made the next innovation in the wild animal story, which reflected growing public concern about environmental destruction and the extinction of species; the themes of survival and victimization carried to an extreme (Atwood, 76; Dunlap, "The Old Kinship," 116.). However, these were not the first writers to pursue this theme. Seton, for example, wrote in 1901 that, "I do not intend primarily to denounce certain field sports, or even cruelty to animals. My chief motive, my most earnest underlying wish, has been to stop the extermination of harmless wild animals" (*Lives of the Hunted*, 12). In addition, Grey Owl (Archie Stansfeld Belaney, an English emigrant to Canada who adopted the persona of an Indian) used his writing to help protect and restore the declining populations of beaver. Their stories, however, did not embody the ecological perspective

and environmental angst of more recent writers. In these new stories, individual animals became representatives of their vanishing species. The curlews whose lives Fred Bodsworth followed in his *The Last of the Curlews* were quite literally the last of their species. The destruction of the wolves in Farley Mowat's *Never Cry Wolf* were representative of the threat to all wolves in North America. Americans also adopted this approach. Sally Carrighar, for example, followed the life of a Blue Whale in her last book *The Twilight Seas*.

The realistic wild animal story is likely to remain a viable part of nature literature. Over the decades it has changed in response to the issues and concerns of the times, and it will continue to do so in the future.

Notes

1. Seton published under several variations of his name, including Ernest Seton Thompson, Ernest Seton-Thompson, and Ernest Thompson Seton. He settled on the latter. For his explanation of this, *see* his autobiography *Trails of an Artist Naturalist* (pp. 391–393).

2. Seton's story of Lobo of the Currumpaw was reprinted in his *Wild Animals I Have Known*. For Roberts's hook & bullet stories, *see* his *Around the Camp-Fire*.

3. Northrop Frye found Canadian poetry to reflect "a deep terror" in response to nature (p. 822). James Polk also argued that Canadian literature reflects a survival theme and a "jittery fear of wilderness" (pp. 52–53). For differing views, *see* Altmeyer, Mary Lu MacDonald, Pritchard (1982), and Pritchard (1984). On Canadian nature writing, *see* Raglon and Lucas.

4. *See* Johnson for a content analysis of 48 children's books in the realistic animal (not necessarily wild animal) story genre. The books were all published in the twentieth century. She does not distinguish between Canadian and U.S. authors or between wild and domestic animal stories. The vast majority of the stories, though, involve domestic animals.

5. Little is known about Long. The most detailed biographical treatment is in Lutts.

6. The novel may have some basis in truth; *see* Eldridge, 3–8.

Selected Works and Further Reading

Altmeyer, George, "Three Ideas of Nature in Canada, 1893–1914," *Journal of Canadian Studies* 11:3 (August 1976), pp. 21–36

Atwood, Margaret, *Survival: A Thematic Guide to Canadian Literature,* Toronto, Ontario: Anansi, 1972

Bodsworth, Fred, *The Last of the Curlews,* New York: Dodd, Mead, 1955; London: Museum: 1956

Brooks, Paul, *The House of Life: Rachel Carson at Work,* Boston: Houghton Mifflin, 1972; also published as *The House of Life: Rachel Carson at Work, with Selections from Her Writings Published and Unpublished,* London: Allen and Unwin, 1973

Carrighar, Sally, *One Day on Beetle Rock,* New York: Ballantine, 1944

——, *The Twilight Seas,* New York: Weybright and Talley, 1975; also published as *Blue Whale,* London: Gollancz, 1978

Carson, Rachel, *The Sea Around Us,* New York: Oxford University Press, 1951; London: Staples, 1951

——, *Under the Sea-Wind: A Naturalist's Picture of Ocean Life,* New York: Simon & Schuster, 1941

Curwood, James Oliver, *The Grizzly King: A Romance of the Wild,* Garden City, New York: Doubleday, Page, 1916

Dunlap, Thomas R., "'The Old Kinship of Earth': Science, Man and Nature in the Animal Stories of Charles G. D. Roberts," *Journal of Canadian Studies* 22:1 (Spring 1987), pp. 104–120

——, "The Realistic Animal Story: Ernest Thompson Seton, Charles Roberts, and Darwinism," *Forest & Conservation History* 36 (April 1992), pp. 56–62

Eldridge, Judith A., *James Oliver Curwood: God's Country and the Man,* Bowling Green, Ohio: Bowling Green State University Popular Press, 1993

Frye, Northrop, "Conclusion," in *Literary History of Canada,* edited by Carl F. Klinck, Toronto, Ontario: University of Toronto Press, 1965

Gold, Joseph, "The Precious Speck of Life," *Canadian Literature* 26 (Autumn 1965), p. 25

Grey Owl, *Pilgrims of the Wild,* London: L. Dickson, 1934; New York: Scribner's, 1935

Hawks, Clarence, *The Light That Did Not Fall,* Boston: Chapman & Grimes, 1925

Johnson, Kathleen R., "The Ambiguous Terrain of Petkeeping in Children's Realistic Animal Stories," *Society and Animals* 4 (1996), pp. 1–17

Kipling, Rudyard, *The Jungle Book,* New York: Century, 1894; London: Macmillan, 1894

——, *The Second Jungle Book,* New York: Century, 1895; London: Macmillan, 1895

Lawrence, Gale, "Sally Carrighar," in *American Nature Writers,* vol. 1, edited by John Elder, New York: Scribner's, 1996

London, Jack, *Call of the Wild,* New York and London: Macmillan, 1903

——, "The Other Animals," *Collier's* 41:24 (September 5, 1908), pp. 10 ff

——, *White Fang,* New York and London: T. Nelson, 1900

Long, William J., *Brier-Patch Philosophy,* Boston and London: Ginn, 1906

——, *Northern Trails: Some Studies of Animal Life in the Far North,* Boston: Ginn, 1905

——, *School of the Woods,* Boston and London: Ginn, 1902

Lucas, Alec, "Nature Writers and the Animal Story," in *Literary History of Canada: Canadian Literature in English,* edited by Carl F. Klinck, Toronto, Ontario: University of Toronto Press, 1965

Lutts, Ralph H., *The Nature Fakers: Wildlife, Science & Sentiment,* Golden, Colorado: Fulcrum, 1990

MacDonald, Mary Lu, "The Natural World in Early Nineteenth-Century Canadian Writing," *Canadian Literature* 111 (Winter 1986), pp. 48–65

MacDonald, Robert H., "The Revolt Against Instinct: The Animal Stories of Seton and Roberts," *Canadian Literature* 84 (Spring 1980), pp. 18–29

Magee, William, "The Animal Story: A Challenge in Technique," *Dalhousie Review* 44 (Summer 1964), pp. 156–164

Mayr, Ernst, "The Nature of the Darwinian Revolution," *Science* 176 (1972), pp. 981–989

Mowat, Farley, *Never Cry Wolf,* Boston: Little, Brown, 1963; London: Secker & Warburg, 1964

Norwood, Vera, *Made from this Earth: American Women and Nature,* Chapel Hill: University of North Carolina Press, 1993

Oswald, Lori Jo, "Heroes and Victims: The Stereotyping of Animal Characters in Children's Realistic Animal Fiction," *Children's Literature in Education* 26:2 (1995), pp. 135–149

Poirier, Michel, "The Animal Story in Canadian Literature," *Queen's Quarterly,* part I

(January–March 1927), pp. 298–312; part II (April–June 1927), pp. 398–419

Polk, James, "Lives of the Hunted," *Canadian Literature* 53 (Summer 1972), pp. 51–59

Pritchard, Allan, "West of the Great Divide: A View of the Literature of British Columbia," *Canadian Literature* 94 (Autumn 1982), pp. 96–112

————, "West of the Great Divide: Man and Nature in the Literature of British Columbia," *Canadian Studies* 102 (Autumn 1984), pp. 36–53

Raglon, Rebecca, "Canadian Nature Writing in English," *American Nature Writers,* vol. 2, edited by John Elder, New York: Scribner's, 1996

Roberts, Charles G. D., "The Animal Story," in *The Kindred of the Wild: A Book of Animal Life,* Boston: L. C. Page, 1902; London: Duckworth, 1903

————, *Around the Camp-Fire,* Boston: Thomas Y. Crowell, 1896

————, "Do Seek Their Meat from God," *Harper's Magazine* 86 (December 1892), pp. 120–123

————, *Earth's Enigmas,* Boston: Lamson, Wolffe, 1896

————, *The Heart of the Ancient Wood,* New York: Silver, Burdett, 1900; London: Methuen, 1902

Seton, Ernest Thompson, "The Drummer on Snowshoes," *St. Nicholas* 14 (April 1887), pp. 414–417

————, "The King of Currumpaw: A Wolf Story," *Scribner's Monthly* 16 (November 1894), pp. 618–628

————, *Lives of the Hunted,* New York: Scribner's, 1901; London: David Nutt, 1901

————, *The Ten Commandments in the Animal World,* Garden City, New York: Doubleday, Page, 1907

————, *Trail of an Artist-Naturalist,* New York: Scribner's, 1940; London: Hodder and Stoughton, 1951

————, *Wild Animals I Have Known,* New York: Scribner's, 1898; London: Hodder and Stoughton, 1898

Sewell, Anna, *Black Beauty: His Grooms and Companions,* London: Jarrold and Sons, 1877; Boston: American Humane Education Society, 1890

Wadland, John Henry, *Ernest Thompson Seton: Man in Nature and the Progressive Era, 1880–1915,* New York: Arno, 1978

Warner, Charles Dudley, "A-Hunting of the Deer," *Atlantic Monthly* (April 1887), pp. 522–529

Williamson, Henry, *Salar the Salmon,* London: Faber and Faber, 1935; Boston: Little, Brown, 1936

————, *Tarka the Otter: His Joyful Water-Life and Death in the Country of the Two Rivers,* New York and London: Putnam's, 1927

"A path toward nature":
Haiku's Aesthetics of Awareness

Tom Lynch

Learn about a pine tree from a pine tree, and about a
bamboo plant from a bamboo plant.
—Matsuo Bashô

At the end of an article exploring the relationship between haiku and nature, Bob Jones concludes that "haiku is less a style of poetry than a path toward nature, along which a certain kind of poetry tends to be written" (p. 23). The evolution of haiku philosophy and aesthetics in Japan and North America reinforces Jones's observation. Haiku is, by definition, a literary form concerned with cultivating an awareness of and finding modes of representation for the natural world. While one can find numerous exceptions to this norm in poems of psychological or erotic content, even these variations are usually justified by the suggestion that erotic or psychological events are also "natural." What one encounters in such cases, then, is a definitional dispute regarding the parameters of nature, not of haiku.

Traditionally, haiku is defined as a poem consisting of the Japanese equivalent of 17 syllables arranged in three lines of 5–7–5 syllables respectively, although often arranged as one line of three units in Japanese. In content, a traditional haiku portrays nature and usually contains a *kigo* or "season-word," a conventional shorthand indication of the season in which the poem is set.

Each of these traits, however, is problematic in English-language haiku. A Japanese word typically contains more syllables per unit of meaning than an equivalent English word, hence a 17-syllable poem in English is much "longer" than a 17-syllable poem in Japanese. To compensate, English-language haiku evolved toward shorter poems, usually of 12–14 syllables variously arranged in three lines.

Like the syllable count, the season-word tradition does not translate well into English. In Japanese haiku, various aspects of nature have come to represent various seasons. Some of these connections are obvious, such as snow and winter. But others are, or at least seem to be, arbitrary, such as the connection of the moon with autumn. In Canada and the United States, the wider variability of bioregions and climate and the absence of a season-word tradition make establishing a shared seasonal vocabulary more difficult. Nevertheless, reference to seasonal characteristics, whether by a season-word or some other method, remains common in North American haiku. A minimal definition of haiku in English, then, would be a short, imagistic poem expressing a moment keenly perceived linking nature, often in a seasonal context, with human nature.

Haiku evolved from *renga*—a form of linked verse in which stanzas are composed collectively and sequentially by a group. *Renga* was one of the dominant genres throughout the Heian (794–1185), Kamakura (1185–1333), and Muromachi (1333–1600) eras. In linked verse no logical or chronological sequence is followed. Every stanza but the first is written as a response to—and only to—the preceding stanza. The first poet, having no previous stanza to respond to, responds to the immediate natural circumstances surrounding the composing session. The time of day and season of year, suggested by a compelling natural image, usually form the basis of this opening stanza, referred to as a *hokku*.

Renga was exclusively a poetry of the aristocracy, and elaborate rules maintained elegance and decorum, but a more relaxed form evolved, termed *haikai no renga,* which was structurally similar but freer in diction and content. It was this genre that Matsuo Bashô raised to a high art in the late seventeenth century. (The term haiku is a conflation of the term *hokku* with *haikai no renga.*)

One of the frequent techniques Bashô used in his haiku was to bring together the small and transient elements of nature with nature's vast aspects:

On a bare branch
A crow alights–
Autumn evening.

The relative smallness of the crow on the branch is juxtaposed against the immensity of the darkening autumn sky into a harmonious image. At the same time, the dark crow settling onto the withered branch mirrors in microcosm the dark evening settling over the withered autumn landscape.

Shortly after composing "crow," Bashô began serious study under Zen Master Bucchô. During this period he wrote his most famous haiku:

The old pond;
A frog jumps in–
The sound of water.
  (translated in Blyth)

Western readers, especially when aware of the prestige of this poem, might be prone to search it for "deep" symbolic significance. But Zen long ago deconstructed the polarity between deep and surface level meanings. While one can certainly give the poem a symbolic, especially Buddhist, reading—the frog's splash is the world of phenomenon manifesting itself in the realm of non-being, for example—such a reading falsifies the spirit of the poem: a pond is a pond and a frog is a frog. To recognize the frogness of a frog, is, according to Zen, a more valid and difficult realization than to unravel abstruse symbology.

Among the aesthetic principles informing Bashô's work, two deserve special attention for the manner in which they lead the haiku poet toward nature. Loosely stated, one principle, *sabi,* suggests the poet's relation to nature as macrocosm, and the other principle, *hosomi,* to nature as microcosm. Makoto Ueda defines *sabi* as "the concept that one attains perfect spiritual serenity by immersing oneself in the ego-less,

impersonal life of nature. The complete absorption of one's petty ego into the vast, powerful, magnificent universe" (*Matsuo Bashô,* 30). *Sabi* is often translated as "sadness," "loneliness," or "melancholy." Its root is the verb *sabiru,* meaning "to rust," and implies the incessant decay wrought by the passage of time, which can be obliquely signalled by the season-word. In poems expressive of *sabi,* such as Bashô's "crow," nature is often shown as vast and overpowering.

Contrary to *sabi,* the aesthetics of *hosomi,* meaning "slenderness," focus on the poet's connection to the smallest aspects of nature. In such poems the poet "buries himself in an external object with delicate sensitivity" (Ueda, "Bashô and the Poetics of Haiku," 426). Makoto Ueda provides the following poem as an example of *hosomi:*

A salted sea-bream,
Showing its teeth, lies chilly
At the fish shop.

While Bashô established in haiku an austerity congruent with his philosophy, the next haiku poet of note, Yosa Buson, diversified the aesthetic palette. Buson was far better known in his own day as a painter than as a poet, and many of his poems reveal a profound sensitivity to subtle shades of color or to brilliantly tinted scenes. Likewise, he has a painter's awareness of perspective; the center of interest in his poems often resides in the interplay between close and distant events, or between large and small objects. Buson's haiku, however, are not just visual, they are richly sensuous.

Fireworks in the distance–
someone
lights a fire on the boat

The mountain darkens–
the maple tree's crimson
is taken away

Summer river–
how delightful to cross
with sandals in hand

evening breeze–
water laps against
the legs of the blue heron

The next haiku poet of importance after Buson, Kobayashi Issa, increased the subjectivity of haiku. His mother died when he was three, and this tragedy had a profound effect on his life and poetry, leading to an inward, psychological focus. Many of his poems express his childlike identification with the small, defenseless creatures of the world, reminiscent perhaps, of Bashô's poems of *hosomi*, but usually more subjective.

> Lean frog
> don't give up the fight!
> Issa is here!
> (translated in Henderson)

> Come with me,
> Let's play together, swallow
> Without a mother.

> Hey! don't swat him!
> The fly rubs his hands, rubs his feet
> Begging for mercy.
> (translated in Keene)

A beloved poet, some critics question whether, due to their excessive sentimentality, his poems expressing solidarity with the outcasts of nature ought to be called haiku.

Masaoka Shiki is the poet generally credited with bringing haiku into the modern era. He argued that due to his aesthetic sense, Buson, not Bashô, provided a model for modern haiku. Shiki saw haiku as an essentially aesthetic rather than spiritual endeavor. For his aesthetic theory, rooted in objective experience, he developed the term *shasei*, or "sketch from life." Poets, however, could not simply sketch anything; they had to be selective. At the same time, Shiki emphasized the importance of the imagination. Indeed Shiki's aesthetic principles seem contradictory—variously emphasizing either objective presentations of reality or subjective creations of the imagination. Such oscillation between objectivity and subjectivity recurs in the history of haiku and suggest the efforts of poets to balance inner and outer reality. Haiku are about nature, hence the need for "objectivity," but they are creations of human poets, hence the inevitability of the "subjective" experience. The effort to attain a refined balance of subjectivity and objectivity constitutes a major impetus to evolving haiku aesthetics.

> After the snake flees,
> how quiet the forest is!
> A lily flower.

> Shadows of the trees:
> my shadow wavers with them
> in the winter moonlight.
> (translated in Ueda)

Kawahigashi Hekigodô, a follower of Shiki, extended Shiki's experiments with modern haiku and rejected many of the norms of the genre, such as syllable count, but he still maintained the importance of the season-word as essential to haiku's attention to nature. Hekigodô eventually preferred to call his haiku simply "short poems."

> Fallen off the eaves,
> a pile of snow blocks the street
> in a slum area.
> After the riot
> an incomparably beautiful
> moonlit night.
> (translated in Ueda)

Another of Shiki's disciples, Ogiwara Seisensui, differed with Hekigodô about the proper subject matter of haiku. While still maintaining the genre's focus on nature, he endorsed a greater degree of subjectivity and stressed the role of the imagination in the creation of symbolically resonant haiku:

> The Milky Way too
> has become intense
> we said and parted
> (translated in Higginson)

Seisensui also rejected the necessity of the season-word. Although believing that haiku was concerned with nature, he did not think that nature need be restricted to those aspects traditionally associated with various seasons.

Responding to arguments that such innovative poetry was not haiku, Seisensui delineated the bounds between free-style haiku and free-verse poetry in a formulation crucial for our understanding of the genre. Free-verse poetry, Seisensui believed, could treat any subject, but haiku must address nature, expressing "a special relationship with nature that developed in the course of the verse form's history." Likewise, free verse traced the course of a poet's mental experience whereas haiku focused on "an instantaneous, intuitive perception" (Ueda, *Modern Japanese Poets*, 290). Additionally, Seisensui felt that his poems expressed a spiritual attitude toward nature very similar to Bashô's, so he wanted his poetry to be a part of the same tradition. Like Bashô, he saw haiku as a form of momentary enlightenment in which the poet experiences an ontological union with nature. "We want to contemplate nature from within," he proclaimed. "Instead of interpreting it by knowledge or appreciating it by aesthetic taste, we want to feel it instinctively with our entire being" ("Poetry of Enlightenment," quoted in Ueda, *Modern Japanese Poets*, 295).

A morning
of babies crying,
of roosters crowing,
with all their might.

The load taken down,
a chilly horse!
It rains.

a truck
loaded with steel:
trees along the street
about to bud.
　　(translated in Ueda)

In spite of experiments in haiku aesthetics by Western poets such as Pound, Williams, Lowell, and Stevens, a rigorous and informed attention to the genre did not arise until the end of the Second World War. The first volume of R. H. Blyth's influential four-volume *Haiku* appeared in 1949. Kenneth Yasuda's *A Pepper Pod* was published in 1947 and his *The Japanese Haiku* in 1957. Harold Henderson's *Introduction to Haiku* appeared in 1958. These works all emphasized the classical traditions of haiku, largely ignoring or, in Blyth's case, openly disdaining the modern free-verse form of the genre.

Blyth's work in particular emphasized Zen. Additionally, D. T. Suzuki and Alan Watts were publishing books on Zen that included discussions of haiku as a Zen art form. The poets of the 1950s, therefore, were aware of the spiritual context of the genre. Many of the Beat poets dabbled with the form, although the most successful haiku poet of this group, Kerouac, was attracted to haiku less as a form of nature poetry than because of its Buddhist philosophy and expressions of *sabi*. His "Blues and Haikus" collection successfully blends the melancholy of *sabi* with the world-weariness of the blues tradition.

In my medicine cabinet,
the winter fly
has died of old age.

Useless, useless,
the heavy rain
Driving into the sea.

Beginning in the early 1960s, a group of poets emerged in the United States and Canada whose literary output consisted primarily of haiku and who paid a sustained and learned attention to the form. Over the next few decades, furthered by a proliferation of journals such as *American Haiku* (1963), *Haiku Highlights* (later *Dragon-fly*, 1965), *Haiku West* (1967), *Haiku* (1967), *Modern Haiku* (1969), and *Cicada* (1977), as well as the formation of the Haiku Society of America (1968), Western World Haiku Society (1974), and the Haiku Society of Canada (1977), these poets adapted the aesthetics and philosophy of haiku to their own language and culture. The editors and writers for these journals strove to establish a North American version of haiku, struggling with questions of form (5–7–5 *vs.* free verse), content (nature *vs.* human), and approach (subjective *vs.* objective). In what follows I will consider the work of American poets O. Southard, Robert Spiess, Nicholas Virgilio, Raymond Roseliep, John Wills, Cor van den Heuvel, Gary Hotham, Anita Virgil, Alexis Rotella, Alan Pizzarelli, and Bob Boldman, and Canadian poets Eric Amann, George Swede, and Rod Willmot.

Important writers in the early period include Southard [also known as Mabelsson Norway], Spiess, and Virgilio. Southard's collection *Marsh-grasses* appeared in 1967. His poems are typical of some of the better examples of the genre at that time: They are 5–7–5 in form, they juxtapose two non-metaphorically related images across a caesura, and they are exclusively concerned with nature. His poetic diction and occasional inverted syntax suggest a lingering influence of the Western Romantic tradition:

The old rooster crows . . .
　　out of the mist come the rocks
　　and the twisted pine.

Robert Spiess, longtime editor of *Modern Haiku*, writes in a style formally similar to Southard's, although his diction is usually less poetic, more plain spoken. Many of his collected poems (*The Heron's Legs*, *The Turtles Ears*, *The Shape of the Water*) recount canoeing excursions on the rivers of Wisconsin, providing a stern-seat glimpse of river life.

Muttering thunder . . .
　　the bottom of the river
　　scattered with clams

Blue jays in the pines;
　　the northern river's ledges
　　cased with melting ice

In 1962 Nicholas Virgilio published an extremely influential poem that redirected the efforts of many other poets.

Lily:
out of the water . . .
out of itself.

This poem's minimalism and mystical suggestiveness appealed to many poets struggling with haiku at the time. Although most of Virgilio's poems were written in the 5–7–5 form, "Lily's" free verse also pointed North American haiku away from strictly classical Japanese models. Many of Virgilio's haiku emphasized his New Jersey urban landscape. Following the death of his brother in Vietnam, his poems took a decidedly somber turn.

into the blinding sun . . .
the funeral procession's
glaring headlights

autumn twilight:
the wreath on the door
lifts in the wind

Scott Slovic has proposed that the chief preoccupation of American nature writers is "with the psychological phenomenon of 'awareness'" (p. 3). If so, then by adapting the haiku tradition's emphasis on a related psychology of awareness, North American haiku poets have concerned themselves with some of the same key aesthetic and philosophic issues that have recurred in American nature writing. As haiku are nearly always about direct experience, the cultivation of "awareness" is an essential precondition. Ideally, this condition is achieved through openness to experience rather than through active seeking, in a manner reminiscent of the "Adamic" tradition of American literature according to which the writer attempts to view the world, perhaps impossibly, with an innocent eye, without conceptions or preconceptions. Cultivation of such a "beginner's mind" is the foundation of Zen practice and an important aspect of haiku's aesthetics of awareness.

Once the haiku poet experiences a perception suitable for a haiku, the aesthetics of the genre determine how to convey that experience. The two approaches can loosely be arranged around the poles of a "wordless" style and a "langauge-centered" style. Canadian critic and poet Eric Amann, borrowing from Alan Watts, has applied the term "wordless" to haiku that eschew the vast array of aesthetic and stylistic devices employed by Western poets in favor of a direct naming. Amann argued that Western haiku should be less concerned with the form of haiku, such as syllable counting, and more concerned with the essence, which he saw as a Zen-inspired awareness of the natural world. He revived in a more rigorous manner the Beat approach to haiku: simple, intuitive, spontaneous. Although some of his positions are open to dispute, his influence helped assure that Western haiku could develop beyond superficial imitation of Japanese models.

Wordless haiku appears, although of course is not, effortless; a reader notices not the skill, ingenuity, or wit of the poet, but solely the presence of the thing witnessed, ontologically regenerated (if not directly mirrored) by the experience of reading the poem. The goal of such haiku is for the poet's awareness of nature to awaken a comparable awareness in the reader.

Poets of the language-centered school, most notably Raymond Roseliep, have sought to bring traditional English-language tropes into haiku. Roseliep felt free to use rhyme, personification, hyperbole, metaphor, symbolism, conceptualization, and didactic comment in his haiku:

on the mink's footprint
an asterisk of daisy
shadow and substance

unlocking dawn
and dream:
what a key a bird is

A plausible, and to my mind decisive, objection to the language-centered school suggests that, if English-language haiku employs the literary devices of the English language tradition, it will become just a very short Western-style poem and lose whatever claim to distinction it might have. This issue is also important in considering haiku as a form of nature poetry. If what we notice in the poem is the brilliance of the poet's language, may the words not divert our attention from the natural objects named in the poem; the subject of the poem ceases to be nature and becomes our response to language. Furthermore, many tropes of the Western tradition such as symbolism and simile are designed precisely to lead us away from a natural phenomenon toward an understanding of what that phenonenon can be made to stand for or point toward, usually an abstraction.

On the other hand, proponents of language-centered haiku can counter that the muted style of wordless haiku, especially in an urbanized, sophisticated, jaded culture, may not sufficiently jolt the reader's perceptions to an awareness of nature, hence the need for the tools of language-centered haiku. Whether wordless or language-centered, however, the goal remains the same, the cultivation of an aesthetics of awareness.

The wordless approach to haiku can be found in the work of many contemporary North American haiku poets. For example, in the haiku of John Wills's objectivity and wordlessness are apparent not only in the lack of tropes in his haiku but also in the almost total absence of didactic statement, emotional terms, or symbolism. "Nothing's hidden," he says. Using Zen terminology, he describes his haiku as a sort of "open barrier": "Not a new kind of logic or belief but a way of awareness, or seeing, wakefulness" ("Conversation," 7).

> boulders
> just beneath the boat
> it's dawn

> beyond the porch
> the summer night leaning out
> a moment

> hermit thrush
> at twilight pebbles
> in the stream

For Wills, the best haiku are those in which, through the intensity of the emotions, a poet is utterly, if momentarily, absorbed in the natural world.

Cor van den Heuvel, with a similar conception of haiku, looks for the moment "when words become the things they describe" (Letter). This faith in the communicative efficacy of words is a prerequisite for his use of the "wordless" technique.

> dawn
> among rocks
> lights water

> the geese have gone—
> in the chilly twilight
> empty milkweed pods

> the sun goes down
> my shovel strikes a spark
> from the dark earth

A poet who has perfected the understated portrayal of nature is Gary Hotham. Profoundly subtle, he denies any Zen influence, but the aesthetics of Zen-oriented haiku, if not the philosophy, seem clear in his work. Hotham's understated haiku risk the reader's indifference, but he trusts that some readers will put in the effort to envision and appreciate his perceptions.

> distant thunder
> the dog's toenails click
> against the linoleum

> rest stop—
> in the darkness
> the grass stiff with frost

> no place
> to hide my hands—
> the rain begins

Anita Virgil's haiku also employ the wordless style, but they tend more toward symbolism. Perhaps because of her art training, she, like Buson before her, is very conscious of the visual aspects of haiku, and often emphasizes light and color. Advocating a very objective haiku, she nevertheless seeks to write poems that contain symbolic or "surplus meaning" (Letter).

> a phoebe's cry . . .
> the blue shadows
> on the dinner plates

> the swan's head
> turns away from sunset
> to his dark side

> the breeze
> off the Mississippi
> fills my skirt

Alexis Rotella has increased the psychological content of American haiku. Influenced by Roseliep, she is not averse to employing literary tropes. Disdaining objective nature sketches, she emphasizes human relationships in the context of nature, often blending nature images with human relationships to reveal some emotional circumstance of the human subject that harmonizes with nature:

> Family reunion:
> Grandma takes the hailstone
> from the freezer

> With wine glasses
> we stand and talk
> into the rhododendrons

Late August
I bring him the garden
in my skirt

Alan Pizzarelli's poems often skim the margins between haiku and senryu, a related genre that emphasizes humorous depictions of human nature.

the fat lady
bends over the tomatoes
a full moon

Others of his, however, reveal in the most urbanized of landscapes the same vision of natural processes that have occurred throughout the haiku tradition.

in the stream
a shopping cart
fills with leaves

twilight
staples rust
in the telephone pole

This last poem is as profound and literal an evocation of sabi, the incessant rusting of existence wrought by time, as exists in Western haiku.

Eric Amann, Rod Willmot, and George Swede have all been significant forces in English-language Canadian haiku. Amann, founder of the Haiku Society of Canada, was an early proponent of Zen aesthetics, and his career as a medical doctor has provided some haiku of arresting insights. He has also experimented with minimalist haiku:

The names of the dead
sinking deeper and deeper
into red leaves

Snow falling
on the empty parking-lot:
Christmas Eve . . .

scalpel blade thunderclap

Cold Christmas morning:
the hospital chaplain comes
to baptize the stillborn

While Rod Willmot has written many poems of traditional content, he, like Rotella, has also championed haiku focusing on human psychology and eroticism, a trend that seems especially popular in Canada. In 1983 he edited a collec-

tion titled *Erotic Haiku* in which he suggested that in "true eroticism . . . awareness and involvement coexist in exquisite tension, a tension that is really the essence of haiku" (n.p.). He finds it odd that haiku, a poetry of sensation, should have traditionally avoided those moments when our senses are most charged.

sudden rain
as we run, our beer-bottles
foam up over our hands

she wrings out her blouse
oat-field steaming
after rain

almost there her buttocks ripple in my hands

George Swede takes a similar approach, blending human relationships with nature and seeking psychologically charged moments. With Amann, he has also explored the possibilities of minimalism:

Divorce proceedings over
wet leaves stick
to my shoes

Almost unseen
among the tangled driftwood
naked lovers

Panties on the clothesline lingering mist

Although some of these haiku seem far from the ideals of Bashô, a plausible case can be made that they are simply extensions of haiku's aesthetics of awareness into broader realms of experience. The content of such poems, if not typically "nature," point toward a complication, and perhaps an effacement, of the simple boundary between the human and the natural, a goal of the haiku tradition for the past 300 years.

A poet who extends this tendency to, perhaps beyond, its logical conclusion is American Bob Boldman. Zen-inspired and koan-like, his work challenges our understanding of poetry, haiku, and the parameters of the nature/human duality, seeking to eliminate any distinction between himself and the external world of phenomena. Combining aspects of both the wordless and language-centered approaches, he renders an interior insight bordering surrealism.

Boldman believes that in order to write haiku the poet must dissolve the barrier between the ego self and the natural world. In a poetic meditation he muses, "write / haiku like your edges are disappearing" (p. 33). And his most characteristic haiku recreate moments in which the poet's ego boundary seems suffused with nature:

walking with the river
   the water does my thinking

the plants in the yard
   tonight i find them
entering my dreams

In other haiku this process is carried further, and Boldman seems to look out from within nature itself:

    in the moonlight
  the sea
rolling under my eyelids

Finally, we find some poems in which the poet express his literal transformation into nature:

   my hand
becoming
    crocus blossoms

Boldman's work points us down a path toward nature, at the end of which we dissolve.

Selected Works and Further Reading

Aitken, Robert, *A Zen Wave: Basho's Haiku and Zen,* New York: Weatherhill, 1978

Amann, Eric, *The Wordless Poem: A Study of Zen in Haiku,* 1969; reprinted, Toronto, Ontario: Haiku Society of Canada, 1978

Bashô Matsuo, *Back Roads to Far Towns: Basho's Travel Journal,* translated by Cid Corman and Kamaike Susumu, Fredonia, New York: White Pine, 1986

——, *On Love and Barley: Haiku of Basho,* translated by Lucien Stryk, Honolulu: University of Hawaii Press, 1985; Harmondsworth, England: Penguin, 1985

Beichman, Janine, *Masaoka Shiki,* Boston: Twayne, 1982

Blyth, Reginald Horace, *Haiku,* 4 vols., Tokyo: Hokuseido, 1949–52; San Francisco: Heian International, 1982

Boldman, Bob, *Eating a Melon: 88 Zen Haiku,* Glen Burnie, Maryland: Wind Chimes, 1981

——, *Heart and Bones,* Minibook 11, Glen Burnie, Maryland: Wind Chimes, 1985

——, *My Lord's Necklace,* Kettering: Portals, 1980

——, "A Page from Bob Boldman's *Journal,*" *Modern Haiku* 12:1 (1981), pp. 32–33

——, *Walking with the River,* Chapbook 8, Battle Ground, Indiana: High/Coo, 1980

——, *Wind in the Chimes,* Haiku and Short Poem Series 15, La Crosse, Wisconsin: Juniper, 1983

Buson Yosa, *Haiku Master Buson,* compiled and translated by Yuki Sawa and Edith Shiffert, San Francisco: Heian, 1978

Haiku Society of America, *A Haiku Path: The Haiku Society of America, 1968–1988,* New York: Haiku Society of America, 1994

Henderson, Harold G., *An Introduction to Haiku: An Anthology of Poems and Poets from Basho to Shiki,* Garden City, New York: Doubleday, 1958

Higginson, William J., *The Haiku Seasons: Poetry of the Natural World,* London and Tokyo: Kodansha International, 1996

Hotham, Gary, *Against the Linoleum: The Haiku Handbook,* Laurel, Maryland: Yigralo, 1979

——, *As Far as the Light Goes,* Chickadee Series 1, No. 1, La Crosse, Wisconsin: Juniper, 1990

——, *The Fern's Underside,* Juniper Series 2, La Crosse, Wisconsin: Juniper, 1977

——, *Off and on Rain,* Mini-Chapbook 3, West Lafayette, Indiana: High/Coo, 1978

——, *Pulling out the Bent Nail,* Minibook 16, Glen Burnie, Maryland: Wind Chimes, 1988

——, *This Space Blank,* Juniper Series 16, La Crosse, Wisconsin: Juniper, 1984

——, *Without the Mountains: Haiku and Senryu,* Laurel, Maryland: Yigralo, 1976

Howard, Dorothy, and André Duhaime, eds., *Haïku: Anthologie Canadienne/Canadian Anthology,* Hull, Quebec: Asticou, 1985

Ippekirô Nakatsuka, *Cape Jasmine and Pomegranates,* translated by Soichi Furuta, New York: Grossman, 1974

Issa Kobayashi, *The Autumn Wind: A Selection from the Poems of Issa,* translated by Lewis Mackenzie, New York: Paragon, 1957; London: John Murray, 1957; reprinted, New York and Tokyo: Kodansha International, 1984

Jones, Bob, "The Creative Process: Nature and Haiku Composition," *Modern Haiku* 23:3 (1992), pp. 13–25

Miner, Earl, *Japanese Linked Poetry: An Account with Translations of Renga and Haikai Sequences,* Princeton, New Jersey: Princeton University Press, 1979

Pizzarelli, Alan, *The Flea Circus,* Bloomfield: Islet, 1989

Roseliep, Raymond, *Firefly in My Eyecup,* Mini-Chapbook 5, West Lafayette, Indiana: High/Coo, 1979

———, *Flute over Walden: Thoreauhaiku,* West Lafayette, Indiana: Sparrow, 1976

———, *Listen to Light: Haiku,* Ithaca, New York: Alembic, 1980

———, *Rabbit in the Moon: Haiku,* Plainfield, Indiana: Alembic, 1983

———, *Sailing Bones: Haiku,* Ruffsdale, Pennsylvania: Rook, 1978

———, *Sky in My Legs,* La Crosse, Wisconsin: Juniper, 1979

———, *The Still Point,* Menomonie, Wisconsin: Uzzano, 1980

———, *Sun in His Belly,* West Lafayette, Indiana: High/Coo, 1977

———, *Swish of Cow Tail,* Amherst, Massachusetts: Swamp, 1982

Ross, Bruce, *Haiku Moment: An Anthology of Contemporary North American Haiku,* Boston: Charles E. Tuttle, 1993

Rotella, Alexis, *After an Affair,* Westfield, New Jersey: Merging Media, 1984

———, *Antiphony of Bells,* Mountain Lakes, New Jersey: Jade Mountain, 1989

———, *Closing the Circle,* Passaic, New Jersey: Muse Pie, 1985

———, *Clouds in My Teacup,* Glen Burnie, Maryland: Wind Chimes, 1982

———, *Harvesting Stars: Sequences on Li Po and Ch'in Kuan,* Morristown, New Jersey: Jade Mountain, 1983

———, *Middle City: Longer Poems and Haiku,* Mountain Lakes, New Jersey: Muse Pie, 1987

———, *Musical Chairs: A Haiku Journey Through Childhood,* Los Gatos, California: Jade Mountain, 1994

———, *On a White Bud,* Mountain Lakes, New Jersey: Merging Media, 1985

———, *Rearranging Light,* Passaic, New Jersey: Muse Pie, 1985

———, *Tuning the Lily,* Battle Ground, Indiana: High/Coo, 1983

Sato Hiroaki, *One Hundred Frogs: From Renga to Haiku to English,* New York: Weatherhill, 1983

Slovic, Scott, *Seeking Awareness in American Nature Writing: Henry Thoreau, Annie Dillard, Edward Abbey, Wendell Berry, Barry Lopez,* Salt Lake City: University of Utah Press, 1992

Southard, O., *Marsh-Grasses and Other Verses,* Platteville, Wisconsin: American Haiku, 1967

Spiess, Robert, *The Bold Silverfish and Tall River Junction,* Madison, Wisconsin: Modern Haiku, 1986

———, *Five Caribbean Haibun,* Madison, Wisconsin: Wells, 1972

———, *The Heron's Legs,* Platteville, Wisconsin: American Haiku, 1966

———, *The Shape of Water,* Madison, Wisconsin: Modern Haiku, 1982

———, *The Turtle's Ears,* Madison, Wisconsin: Wells, 1971

Stryk, Lucien, *Cage of Fireflies: Modern Japanese Haiku,* Athens: Ohio University Press, 1993

Swede, George, *All of Her Shadows,* Mini-Chapbook 15, Battle Ground, Indiana: High/Coo, 1982

———, *Endless Jigsaw,* Toronto, Ontario: Three Trees, 1978

———, *Eye to Eye with a Frog,* Haiku-Short Poem Series 11, La Crosse, Wisconsin: Juniper, 1981

———, *Flaking Paint,* Toronto, Ontario: Underwhich, 1983

———, *Frozen Breaths,* Minibook 6, Glen Burnie, Maryland: Wind Chimes, 1983

———, *The Modern English Haiku,* Toronto, Ontario: Columbine, 1981

———, *A Snowman, Headless,* Fiddlehead Poetry Book 262, Fredericton, New Brunswick: Fiddlehead, 1979

———, *This Morning's Mockingbird,* Mini-Chapbook 10, Battle Ground, Indiana: High/Coo, 1980

———, *Wingbeats,* La Crosse, Wisconsin: Juniper, 1979

Swede, George, Erica Amann, and LeRoy Gorman, *The Space Between: Binary Haiku,* Minibook 12, Glen Burnie, Maryland: Wind Chimes, 1986

Ueda Makoto, *Basho and His Interpreters: Selected Hokku with Commentary,* Stanford, California: Stanford University Press, 1991

———, "Basho and the Poetics of 'Haiku'," *Journal of Aesthetics and Art Criticism* 21 (1962), pp. 423–431

———, *Matsuo Basho,* New York: Twayne, 1970; reprinted, New York: Kodansha International, 1982

———, comp. and trans., *Modern Japanese Haiku: An Anthology,* Buffalo, New York, and Toronto, Ontario: University of Toronto Press, 1976

——, *Modern Japanese Poets and the Nature of Literature,* Stanford, California: Stanford University Press, 1983

Van den Heuvel, Cor, *A Bag of Marbles; 3 Jazz Chants,* New York: Chant, 1962

——, *Bang! You're Dead,* New York: Chant, 1982

——, *Dark,* New York: Chant, 1982

——, *EO7: or (Christ Should Have Carried a Pearl-Handled Revolver),* New York: Chant, 1964

——, comp., *The Haiku Anthology,* Garden City, New York: Anchor, 1974; rev. ed., New York: Simon & Schuster, 1986

——, Letter to Anita Virgil (April 21, 1972)

——, *Puddles,* New York: Chant, 1990

——, *Sun in Skull,* New York: Chant, 1961

——, *Water in a Stone Depression,* New York: Chant, 1969

——, *The Window-Washer's Pail,* New York: Chant, 1963

Virgil, Anita, *A 2nd Flake,* Montclair, New Jersey: privately printed, 1974

——, Letter to the author (March 10, 1990)

——, *One Potato, Two Potato Etc.,* Forest, Virginia: Peaks, 1991

Virgilio, Nicholas, *Selected Haiku,* Sherbrooke, Quebec: Burnt Lake, 1985; 2nd ed., introduction by Rod Willmot, Sherbrooke, Quebec: Burnt Lake, 1988

Willmot, Rod, ed., *Erotic Haiku,* Windsor, Ontario: Black Moss, 1983

——, *The Ribs of Dragonfly,* Windsor, Ontario: Black Moss, 1984

——, *Sayings for the Invisible: Haiku and Haiku Sequences (1977–87),* Windsor, Ontario: Black Moss, 1988

Wills, John, and Michael McClintock, "A Conversation with John Wills," *Modern Haiku* 7:2 (1976), pp. 6–8

——, *Reed Shadows,* Windsor, Ontario: Black Moss, 1987

North American Women in the Wilderness

JoAnn Myer Valenti

The existence of an organization called "Great Old Broads for Wilderness" with several thousand members across the United States comes as no surprise to those familiar with the bountiful literature produced by women about their experiences in, and love of, the natural environment, particularly as natives or newcomers in the western regions of the country. Women have a rich relationship with wilderness. This chapter introduces only a sampling of authors and titles.

Women's domain, rather than domestic, embraces nature and the wild. Some of the more familiar names associated with wilderness, the environment and related science issues include Rachel Carson, Margaret Mead, Marjorie Stoneman Douglas, and Jane Goodall. Some lists may well also include Pocahontas and Annie Oakley. Reading the work and about the lives of these women must surely have contributed to the extensive presence today of women in international environmental policy and leadership. Norway's first female Prime Minister Gro Harlem Brundtland is a prominent environmentalist. Anna Lindh serves as Swedish Environment Minister. Elisabeth Dowdswell heads up the United Nation's Environment Program (UNEP), and Carol Browner is administrator of the U.S. Environmental Protection Agency. Until she succumbed to cancer in 1996, Mollie Beattie served as the first woman to direct the U.S. Fish and Wildlife Service, and until 1997 Hazel O'Leary headed the U.S. Department of Energy.

Contemporary scholars have suggested an advantage for women in environmental communications. "Women (possibly have learned to) look at communication as a means to develop and maintain relationships" (Valenti, 42). The process by which an environmental agenda is set and acted on begins with a recognition of the need to transfer information effectively, sometimes in spite of barriers; women do this well.

Despite the evidence that women and men are more similar than different, women's experiences have frequently been marginalized in the past. Fortunately, a rediscovery and profusion of new non-fiction titles by women authors about the woman/wilderness experience, easily found now in libraries and on bookstore shelves, reveals women's long-term affair with the environment. This literature does not necessarily exclude the male experience since women tend to be more inclusive in relating personal stories and observations about their surroundings. As the authors provide a record from the gendered vantage point of more than half the population, nature serves an organizing role. Attention to these neglected narratives and the success of contemporary writers not only better balances the history of the human and nature encounter, but improves our understanding of the whole experience.

Anne Wilson Schaef, author of *Native Wisdoms for White Minds* and several titles addressing women's issues, describes American Indian women's reliance on story telling, more often oral and in congruent settings than in written form. "Even after we left the 'land of our roots,' my mother always insisted on going back every year and reconnecting with 'our land,'" she notes in "Return of a Native Daughter" (p. 73). The author, who was born close to the Arkansas-Oklahoma border, discovered her own Cherokee heritage after decades of living and working among Native elders around the world. Whether in search of personal histories (or "herstories" as some feminists prefer), or collecting community myths and legends, women have written to remember what would otherwise surely be lost even though intensely felt.

This literature captures memoirs, reflective narratives, and historical biographies, more so of whole families or community experiences than self-absorbed retrospects. Some autobiographical sounding titles such as *I, Mary* are immediately shadowed by subtitles (*The Biography of Mary Austin*) refocusing for the softer hues of ethnography or genealogy. Carolyn G. Heilbrun, who studies the way women write and talk about their lives, notes a deflection away from personal accomplishments and more passive self portrayals. Current women writers continue a sense of humility within their surroundings, but are more inclusive of themselves than deferential to all others.

Cowgirls: Women of the American West and *Riding the White Horse Home: A Western Family Album,* both by rancher/writer Teresa Jordan, offer intimate insight and personal disclosure. This literature chronicles lives connected to wild places and women who are physically tested, enduring all manner of tough things. Women in wilderness are often pioneers, the daughters and wives of ranchers, always independent and strong. Stories tell of great-grandmothers and grandmothers who at 80-plus years of age hike steep hills in places called Chugwater Creek or The Bowl, sometimes in long dresses hardly suited for the rugged terrain. But they know and describe in detail the geologic past and present. Their life stories evolve with the land in backdrops of mountains and what most people would consider harsh weather. Wind gusts come at 40 to 50 miles per hour. Snow does not melt, "it just wears out" (Jordan, *Riding*, 8).

These women writers do not just look at a landscape, they see the land, feel the wild deeply, and make love to a spiritual place. Legends and reality merge. Women and land connect. There is much walking, hiking, moving, and always a sense of impending loss. Others' lives may influence and make these women write, often finding themselves in the process, but an unrequited intensity makes it clear that not writing would be unthinkable.

Women write of rugged splendors, delights in the desert and hiking unexplored canyons, not in search of the ultimate wild flower, but the wild within every woman. Wilderness is not only an ecological entity or a conservation area, but a way of being and feeling whole. The stories may occur primarily out of doors, but these tales of free roaming and living routine lives in wild lands are about internal bonds with wildlife and natural vegetation. In *Letters of a Woman Homesteader,* Elinore Pruitt Stewart provides a record of a nineteenth-century Denver "wash woman" determined to conquer ranch life in Wyoming with twentieth-century spirit. A number of writers such as Maureen Beecher with *Eliza and Her Sisters* have relied on journals and diaries to bring pioneer stories to life. Kay Graber's *Sister to the Sioux: The Memories of Elain Goodal Eastman,* Isabella Bird's *A Lady's Life in the Rocky Mountains,* and Dottie Fox's *Below the Rim: One Woman's Adventures in the Grand Canyon* offer very personal, first hand accounts of women's encounters with wilderness. But women are rarely alone in nature.

Margaret E. Murie's *Two in the Far North* and, later, *Wapiti Wilderness,* co-authored with her husband Olaus, typify a near sub-genre of books written about married life in wilderness areas by spouses, generally the man presumed more renowned. Osa Johnson's *I Married Adventure* and Grace Murphy's *There's Always Adventure: The Story of a Naturalist's Wife* published in the 1940s stand as the Cinderella prototype for women longing for nature and eagerly accepting a companion ticket to a wild place. As the century ends, some recent titles offer reminders of the lesser attention traditionally paid to women's roles in the environment, for example *My Double Life: Memoirs of a Naturalist* by Frances Hamerstrom. Women as strong, individual, more self-confident or less self-deprecating can be found, not as one might presume from Jane Lawick-Goodall's title, *The Shadow of Man,* but in Audrey Sutherland's *Paddling My Own Canoe,* Peggy Wayburn's *Adventuring in Alaska,* and almost any title by Utah writer Terry Tempest Williams.

Williams's *Refuge: An Unnatural History of Family and Place* won instant literary acclaim and established her place as a twentieth-century visionary guided by an intimate relationship with her natural surroundings. In *An Unspoken Hunger: Stories from the Field,* and, more recently, *Desert Quartet: An Erotic Landscape,* this Western-based writer brings climax to women's literature in adulation of wilderness. Although well schooled in natural history, Williams demonstrates women's need to bypass the intellect and write from inner passions. "I fear it [canyon country] because it promises to be spontaneous, out of my control, unnamed, beyond my reasonable self," she writes in *Desert*

Quartet. "I desire it because passion has color, like the landscape before me," she continues. "It feels good . . . to inhabit my animal body" (p. 5).

Much more than personal memoirs, these women writers explore how wilderness sustains them. Kim Barnes offers a tortuous but reassuring chronology of adolescence in Idaho's logging camps. *In the Wilderness: Coming of Age in Unknown Country* portrays one young woman's retreat from a family of grifters and imposed religious restrictions, into the isolation and absolutism of the woods. Stars, dust, sunshine, snow, and wind help regain what has been lost, what is missed.

"The land and sky of the West often fill what Thoreau termed our 'need to witness our limits transgressed,'" writes Kathleen Norris on the first page of *Dakota: A Spiritual Geography.* In chapters interspersed with weather reports, Norris repeats the mantra for most women who write about wilderness: understand where we came from, cherish a sense of place, herald the essential of how we feel about who we are or can become. And only when our place is fixed in nature are we whole.

Companion contributions to these personal narratives about life in what Murie refers to as "emptier places," are collections of short stories and what might almost be viewed as how-to titles. Ann and Susan Zwingers' *Women in Wilderness,* Ellen Fagg's edited *The Way We Live: Stories by Utah Women,* May Swenson's *May Out West,* and Loraine Anderson's edited *Sisters of the Earth* offer prose, poetry, photographs, and psychological landscapes rich with descriptions of nature from desert air to snow-capped mountain wilderness. Maggie Nichols' *Wild, Wild Women* not so subtly provides a guide to enjoying the outdoors. Gretel Ehrlich's *The Solace of Open Spaces* tempts with the compelling lure of city life left behind for "luxurious lunar desolation." She writes, "Space has a spiritual equivalent and can heal what is divided and burdensome in us" (p. 14).

Susan Griffin's *Woman and Nature: The Roaring Inside Her* describes women's burden in an angry journal/collage of visions of men changing, harnessing, domesticating, and otherwise violating nature. Her rage transforms into control and stimulates the awakening of power in women's dialogue with the earth. *Wilderness Therapy for Women: The Power of Adventure,* edited by a group of academics, Ellen Cole, Eve Erdman, and Esther Rothblum, reminds us of the danger in isolating women from nature and of women's tenacity in writing with unbounded respect for the natural places they love.

Current literature in this genre promotes wilderness-like experiences in modern urban settings. Wayburn's *Adventuring in the San Francisco Bay Area,* first published in 1987 and revised in 1995, entices walking, hiking or kayaking through the natural history of this historic American West Coast city. A series of Sierra Club books profiles national, state, and local parks and provides tips from personal experiences in acres of unspoiled terrain and recreational shoreline. For example, profiles of 15 women living and working in the wilderness and an analysis of a study conducted by author Anne LaBastille was published by Sierra Club Books as *Women and Wilderness* in 1980.

LaBastille distinguishes between women who are wilderness professionals and those who use the wilderness for backpacking, climbing, skiing, and other recreational activities. She quotes former University of Michigan School of Natural Resources Dean Stephen Spurr as defining wilderness as "simply an ecosystem in which man is a relatively unimportant factor" (p. 288). Preservationists will likely find fault with Spurr's uncomplicated definition. Humans may be unimportant to the essence of wild bioregions, but, clearly the reverse, an extremely important and relevant role of wilderness in women's lives has been recorded in literature.

Selected Works and Further Reading

Anderson, Loraine, ed., *Sisters of the Earth: Women's Prose and Poetry About Nature,* New York: Vintage, 1991

Barnes, Kim, *In the Wilderness: Coming of Age in Unknown Country,* New York: Doubleday, 1996

Bateson, Mary Catherine, *With a Daughter's Eye: A Memoir of Margaret Mead and Gregory Bateson,* New York: W. Morrow, 1984

Beecher, Maureen Ursenbach, *Eliza and Her Sisters,* Salt Lake City, Utah: Aspen, 1991

Bird, Isabella L., *A Lady's Life in the Rocky Mountains,* New York: Putnam's, 1879; London: John Murray, 1879

Carson, Rachel, *The Sense of Wonder,* New York: Harper & Row, 1965

———, *Silent Spring,* Boston: Houghton Mifflin, 1962; London: Hamilton, 1963

Cole, Ellen, Eve Erdman, and Esther D. Rothblum, eds., *Wilderness Therapy for*

Women: The Power of Adventure, New York: Haworth, 1994

Douglas, Marjory Stoneman, *The Everglades: River of Grass,* New York: Rinehart, 1947; rev. ed., Coconut Grove, Florida: Hurricane, 1978

Ehrlich, Gretel, *The Solace of Open Places,* New York: Viking, 1985

Fagg, Ellen, ed., *The Way We Live: Stories by Utah Women,* Salt Lake City, Utah: Signature, 1994

Fink, Augusta, *I, Mary: A Biography of Mary Austin,* Tucson: University of Arizona Press, 1983

Fox, Dottie, *Below the Rim: One Woman's Adventures in the Grand Canyon,* Old Snowmass, 1986

Freeman, Martha, ed., *Always, Rachel: The Letters of Rachel Carson and Dorothy Freeman, 1952–1964,* Boston: Beacon, 1994

Goodall, Jane, *In the Shadow of Man,* New York: Dell, 1971; London: Collins, 1971

Graber, Kay, ed., *Sister to the Sioux: The Memoirs of Elaine Goodale Eastman, 1885–91,* Lincoln: University of Nebraska Press, 1978

Griffin, Susan, *Woman and Nature: The Roaring Inside Her,* New York: Harper & Row, 1978; London: Women's Press, 1984

Hamerstrom, Frances, *My Double Life: Memoirs of a Naturalist,* Madison: University of Wisconsin Press, 1994

Heilbrun, Carolyn G., *Writing a Woman's Life,* New York: Ballantine, 1989

Johnson, Osa, *I Married Adventure: The Lives and Adventures of Martin and Osa Johnson,* New York: Lippincott, 1940

Jordan, Teresa, *Cowgirls: Women of the American West,* Garden City, New York: Anchor, 1982; 2nd ed., Lincoln, Nebraska, and London: University of Nebraska Press, 1992

——, *Riding the White Horse Home: A Western Family Album,* New York: Pantheon, 1993

LaBastille, Anne, *Women and Wilderness,* San Francisco: Sierra Club, 1980

Mead, Margaret, *Coming of Age in Samoa,* New York: Blue Ribbon, 1928; London: Cape, 1929

——, *Margaret Mead, Some Personal Views,* New York: Walker, 1979; London: Angus and Robertson, 1979

Murie, Margaret E., *Island Between,* Fairbanks: University of Alaska Press, 1977

——, *Two in the Far North,* New York: Knopf, 1962

Murie, Margaret E., and Olaus Murie, *Wapiti Wilderness,* New York: Knopf, 1966

Murphy, Grace B., *There's Always Adventure: The Story of a Naturalist's Wife,* New York: Harper, 1951; London: Allen and Unwin, 1952

Nichols, Maggie, *Wild, Wild Woman: A Complete Woman's Guide to Enjoying the Great Outdoors,* New York: Berkley, 1978

Norris, Kathleen, *Dakota: A Spiritual Geography,* Boston: Houghton Mifflin, 1993

Schaef, Anne Wilson, *Native Wisdom for White Minds: Daily Reflections Inspired by the Native Peoples of the World,* New York: Ballantine, 1995

——, "Return of a Native Daughter," in *Women Transforming Communications: Global Intersections,* edited by Donna Allen, Ramona R. Rush, and Susan J. Kaufman, Thousand Oaks, California: Sage, 1996

Stewart, Elinore P., *Letters of a Woman Homesteader,* Boston: Houghton Mifflin, 1914; reprinted, Lincoln: University of Nebraska Press, 1961; London: University of Nebraska Press, 1993

Sutherland, Audrey, *Paddling My Own Canoe,* Honolulu: University Press of Hawaii, 1978

Swenson, May, *May Out West: Poems of May Swenson,* Logan: Utah State University Press, 1996

Valenti, JoAnn M., "Environmental Communication: A Female-Friendly Process," in *Women Transforming Communications: Global Intersections,* edited by Donna Allen, Ramona R. Rush, and Susan J. Kaufman, Thousand Oaks, California: Sage, 1996

Wayburn, Peggy, *Adventuring in Alaska,* San Francisco: Sierra Club, 1982

——, *Adventuring in the San Francisco Bay Area,* San Francisco: Sierra Club, 1987; rev. ed., San Francisco: Sierra Club, 1995

——, *Edge of Life,* San Francisco: Sierra Club, 1972

Williams, Terry Tempest, *Desert Quartet,* New York: Pantheon, 1995

——, *Pieces of White Shell: A Journey to Navajoland,* New York: Scribner's, 1984

——, *Refuge: An Unnatural History of Family and Place,* New York: Pantheon, 1991

Zwinger, Ann, and Susan Zwinger, *Women in Wilderness: Writings and Photographs,* San Diego, California: Harcourt Brace, 1995

Canadian Environmental Writing

Rebecca Raglon and Marion Scholtmeijer

> It's an immense night out there, wheeling and windy. The lights on the street and in the houses are helpless against the black wetness, little unilluminating glints that might be painted on it. The town seems huddled together, cowering on a high, tiny perch, afraid to move lest it topple into the wind.   —(Ross, 5)

This picture of a little prairie town, huddled against the vastness of the night sky, is one that eloquently summarizes much of the literary response to the Canadian landscape. Nor is Sinclair Ross's portrait of a little town and the Depression-era prairie surrounding it in his novel *As For Me and My House* an isolated one: over and over again writers of both fiction and nonfiction have juxtaposed the sheer immensity of the Canadian landscape with the tentativeness of the human presence upon it. It is an experience that tends to dwarf human pretensions, and further, one that has made a virtue of survival. Dealing with this landscape has been the prime artistic challenge for Canadian writers, something Hugh MacLennan notes in his nonfiction book *Seven Rivers of Canada*:

> How to use space in design, how to communicate its fullness, how to proportion human beings to it, how to reveal the effects of immense land horizons on the descendants of people whose traditions stem from little cities in Greece and neat countries like Italy, France, Holland and England—the artistic necessity here has been much more difficult than European critics ever seem to realize. (p. vii)

Canada is the second largest country in the world, with 10 million square kilometers of territory, varying from northern tundra, to boreal forest, seashore, mountains, lakes, and grasslands. Canada's coastline, bordering along the Atlantic, Pacific, and Arctic Oceans, is the word's longest. In close to 90 percent of this territory, no permanent settlements have been established. It has one of the world's coldest and harshest climates, and has developed a specialized vocabulary to describe its weather effects. Canada's tundra is the summer breeding ground for many species of birds and animals, and in many parts of the country predators such as wolves, grizzly bears, and cougar are still to be found. The sheer size of the country, its vast distances and space, is further emphasized by the relatively small population of 27 million people, 80 percent of whom live in urban areas close to the United States border (*Canada 125th*).

It is from this base that Canada's environmental literature is forged. The first to write about the land, and its inhabitants, were European explorers and in their accounts the desire to promote mercantile interests (particularly fur trading) jostled with descriptions of hardships endured. Thus Sir Humphrey Gilbert's 1583 delight with the abundant fish and wildlife in Newfoundland contrasts sharply with Jacques Cartier's 1534 description of the Gaspé area as "the land God gave to Cain" (Cook, 10). Early explorations of New France were conducted for The Company of New France (1627) and The Hudson's Bay Company (1670), and by the Jesuits who recorded their travels in *The Jesuit Relations and Allied Documents*. Exploration accounts in English rise to true artistry in Samuel Hearne's underrated *Coppermine Journey*, which tells of a 1,000-mile search for a fabulous copper mine, through Arctic and sub-Arctic territory. It is filled with careful, precise observations concerning the plants, animals, people, and natural features of the Arctic:

> I do not remember having met with any travelers into the high northern latitudes who said they had heard the northern lights make any noise. However, I can positively affirm that in still nights I have frequently heard them making a crackling noise like the waving of a large flag in a fresh gale of wind. (p. 114)

Two hundred years before Grey Owl, Hearne wrote of domesticating beavers, who came when they were called by name, and who "were as much pleased at being fondled as any animal I ever saw" (p. 119).

The most influential record of exploration in terms of Canadian environmental writing, however, is Sir John Franklin's *Narrative of a Journey to the Shores of the Polar Sea in the Years 1819, 20, 21 and 22*. What was most intriguing about Franklin has less to do with his record of exploration than with his disappearance after his ships became fixed in an icepack in 1847. As many as 30 search expeditions were dispatched, and his disappearance continues to exert a powerful influence even on recent Canadian works, including Rudy Wiebe's *Playing Dead*, a story of the expedition from the point of view of the natives and voyagers who died on the journey, and Mordecai Richler's *Solomon Gursky Was Here*, which adds a Jewish surgeon to the legend. Margaret Atwood's short story "The Age of Lead" in *Wilderness Tips* also uses the fate of the Franklin expedition to comment on contemporary ecological problems. "Maple groves dying of acid rain, hormones in the beef, mercury in the fish, pesticides in the vegetables" seem to be the cause of a variety of mysterious physical and spiritual ills, much in the way that the lead in the cans provisioning the Franklin expedition are speculated to have poisoned the men on the journey. "The whole expedition got lead-poisoning. Nobody knew it. Nobody could taste it. It invaded their bones, their lungs, their brains, weakening them and confusing their thinking, so that at the end those that had not yet died in the ships set out in an idiotic trek across the stony, icy ground, pulling a lifeboat laden down with toothbrushes, soap, handkerchiefs, and slippers, useless pieces of junk" (p. 168).

Settlement of Canada by Europeans occurred more slowly than in the United States, primarily because much of the northern part of the continent was administered by fur trading companies that saw settlement as antithetical to their economic interests. The intensive extraction of resources in Canada, which depended on good relations with the native population, internecine fighting between French and English, and a dearth of arable land, precluded the intensive type of European settlement that occurred in other parts of North America. As a result, although early exploration accounts are filled with descriptions of the lives of native inhabitants, much of the interior of Canada during the seventeenth and eighteenth centuries was depicted, in Germaine Warkentin's words, as a kind of "permanent resource base beyond the periphery of civilized society" (p. xv). Rupert's Land (the land area draining into Hudson's Bay) is thus both a place and a state of mind, an enigma that "provides a metaphor for Canadian discourse" (p. xiii).

Even in areas such as the Maritimes, which were among the first to be settled, there were frequently expressed doubts as to the fitness of the enterprise. Sir George Head notes in *Forest Scenes and Incidents in the Wilds of North America* that

> The soil in the neighborhood of Halifax is poor and rocky; and the black granite rocks and scrubby trees, which shed their tops through the snow, looked desolate in the extreme. Land notwithstanding, in the neighborhood, sells high; for people, so soon as they scrape together a little money by farming, flock to the seaports, and reverse the usual order of life by finishing with commerce, instead of retirement. (p. 20)

John Howison, touring parts of Quebec and Ontario, found the fields of crops cared for in an indifferent manner, and noted that homesteads seldom had a tree near them. "There is no difficulty in explaining the cause of the aversion with which the Canadians regard trees. Their earliest labour is that of chopping them down—they present on every side an obstacle to the improvement of their farms—and, even after the land is cultivated, the roots and stumps impede polishing and other field occupations" (p. 13).

Over and over again in nineteenth-century accounts one finds reference to stumps and the ugliness of the raw homesteads hacked out of the bush, contrasted with descriptions of sublime nature. Niagara falls is a favorite nine-teenth-century literary subject. Anna Jameson traveling through Ontario in the late 1830s described Toronto as "mean and melancholy" (p. 17), but found that the falls had a "wild and wonderful magnificence" (p. 45). Jameson, too, confronts Canadian space ("a boundless sea of forest"), on a summit of a hill near Lake Erie, and it is a moment that results in an unusual hesitation concerning the God-given destiny awaiting that landscape:

> When these forests with all their solemn depth of shade and multitudinous life have fallen beneath the axe—when the wolf and the bear are driven from their native coverts and all this infinitude of animal and vegetable being has made way for restless, erring, suffering humanity, will it then be better? *Better–I* know not. . . . (p. 146)

Settlement of New France and Acadia had begun in the seventeenth century. Land distribution in Quebec was based on the seigneurial system, which granted large tracts of land to upper-class individuals, in return for certain obligations, inducing the administration of justice and maintaining a priest. Most seigneuries were built along Quebec rivers, with habitant (tenants') homes clustered nearby. It was a system that established close-knit communities, and an almost mystical attachment to the land (well expressed in novels like Louis Hémon's *Maria Chapdelaine* or Ringuet's *Thirty Acres*). At the time France yielded Canada to Britain in the Treaty of Paris (1763) a mere 65,000 people clustered around 125 seigneurs. Isolated from France, these habitants nevertheless forged a strong will to survive. The rural novel of the nineteenth century gives testimony to the importance the land played in this struggle, and includes Patrice Lacombe's *La Terre paternelle* and *Jean Rivard* by Antoine Gérin-Lajoie. Poetry of the soil was also important, reaching its ultimate expression in the work of Alfred Desrochers' *L'Ombre de l'Orford* and poems such as "Hymne au vent du nord" (Smith). Napoléon Bourassa recounted the story of the forced 1755 deportation of Acadians from Nova Scotia to Louisiana in *Jacques et Marie*.

Following the conquest of New France by the British in 1763, settlement in Upper Canada (Ontario), Nova Scotia and New Brunswick intensified, particularly during the American Revolutionary War when the loyalists left the United States for Canada. British soldiers were entitled to land under new, liberalized land grant policies established in the nineteenth century. Two sisters, married to ex-soldiers who moved to Upper Canada during the 1830s, both wrote about their experiences as immigrants to Canada. Susanna Moodie and Catherine Parr Traill, however, told very different stories about the land in Ontario they were to call home. While Moodie's initial impressions of Canada in *Roughing It in the Bush* included her sense that the natural features possessed a "solemn grandeur" (p. 17), when faced with human settlement and its inevitable charred and blackened stumps, she concluded that "there was very little beauty to be found in the backwoods" (p. 293). Her sister, Catherine Parr Traill, by contrast, wrote about the natural world with both affection and knowledge; in her work, nature, particularly plant life, was portrayed with the kind of detail characteristic of the best naturalists.

The Backwoods of Canada, her account of her early years in Canada, best displays Traill's strengths as a nature writer. The book deals with birds, plants, flowers, animals, humans, insects, weather, crops, and crop diseases, as well as scenic wonders. In spite of the hardships faced, Traill's inclination is to accept her new home with a certain stoical cheerfulness. Rather than to pine for "home" as many of the women around her did, Traill advises her readers to make the best of their new situation, for there are many rewards for those who are alert to the beauties of the new land. One night, for example, returning home from a neighbor's house, she saw a pillar of green light rising up out of the pine forest:

> It was not quite pyramidical, though much broader at the base than at its highest point; it gradually faded, till a faint white glimmering light alone marked where its place had been, and even that disappeared after some half-hours time. It was so fair and lovely a vision I was grieved when it vanished into thin air, and could have cheated fancy into the belief that it was the robe of some bright visitor from another and better world. (p. 252)

During her long life, Traill also wrote fiction for young adults, a housekeeping manual for new immigrants, poetry, and several works of natural history including *Canadian Wild Flower, Studies of Plant Life in Canada*, and *Pearls and Pebbles; or, Notes of an Old Naturalist*.

As in the east, exploration preceded settlement in the Prairie Provinces. *Ocean to Ocean* by Rev. George M. Grant vividly recounts Sandford Fleming's 1872 expedition through Canada. Fleming was a civil engineer looking for a route for a railroad to the west. Writers, even writers of Traill's sensitivity, often complained of the "dreariness" or "gloominess" of the eastern forests, and relief was to be found on the prairies. Grant, who accompanied Fleming's expedition, writes of Saskatchewan that "The country was of varied beauty; rich in soil, grasses, flowers, wood and water; infinitely diversified in colour and outline. From elevated points, far and wide reaches could be seen. Here was no dreary monotonous prairie such as fancy had sometimes painted, but a land to live in and enjoy life" (p. 164). This is the voice of the cheerful imperialist, urging the new Dominion to open up prairie lands, as its neighbor to the south did, so that Canada, too, could become a great nation.

Grant's boosterism is not an isolated nineteenth-century phenomenon, and as the century went on the "rural myth" took hold. The historian W. L. Morton describes this myth as the "idea that the basis of welfare and virtue was the land and its cultivation. To British Canadians the myth was a blend of Arthur Young, William Cobbett, and Thomas Jefferson; to French Canadians it was an equally odd mixture of rural clericalism and Jean-Jacques Rousseau. Its great strength was that however traditional its origins, it was justified throughout the era because clearing and breaking land were the occupations of most Canadians" (p. 312).

The rural myth is the flip side of the garrison mentality that the literary critic Northrop Frye shrewdly saw as being a fundamental expression of the best Canadian literature. In *The Bush Garden* he speculates that one of the themes of Canadian literature is the way nature resists humanization: "One wonders if any other national consciousness has had so large an amount of the unknown, the unrealized, the humanly undigested, so built into it" (p. 220). What is important, according to Frye, is the position of the frontier. In the United States, humans could move out to the frontier, or retreat from it. In Canada, by contrast, even on the Atlantic seaboard, "the frontier was all

around one, a part and condition of one's whole imaginative being" (p. 220). A sense of vulnerability gives Canadian writing an affinity with the tragic, and, according to Frye, with the tragic comes a "sense of discontinuity, the feeling for sudden descent or catastrophe, that seems to me to have an unusual emphasis in Canada" (*Divisions on a Ground*, 80).

The novelist Margaret Atwood developed some of these ideas further in *Survival: A Thematic Guide to Canadian Literature*. Atwood believes that a central symbol to be found in Canadian writing is the idea of survival, or *la survivance*. Survival, furthermore, is multi-leveled: it can mean the survival of the individual in the face of natural disasters, or the survival of the French language in a sea of English, or the survival of a small country positioned rather perilously next to a far more powerful one:

> Our stories are likely to be tales not of those who made it but of those who made it back, from the awful experience—the North, the snowstorm, the sinking ship—that killed everyone else. The survivor has no triumph or victory but the fact of his survival; he has little after his ordeal that he did not have before, except gratitude for having escaped with his life. (p. 33)

Twentieth-century writers who grappled with life on the land certainly seem to provide evidence for these more somber interpretations of Canadian literature dealing with the environment. It is as if Canada's best writers are willing to go only so far in terms of portraying their country as the civilized garden. Most of the more thoughtful ones, as Jameson did, hesitate at least long enough to ask themselves if indeed what they have wrought is better. Some, particularly prairie writers, go considerably further in their critique of the rural myth. In Frederick Philip Grove's prairie novels, *Settlers of the Marsh* and *Fruits of the Earth*, the dominant impression created is of nature's indifference to human endeavor. The prairie works by its own vast laws, and human aspiration rarely succeeds against them. For the characters in Grove's novels this means struggle and tragedy. "The moment a work of man was finished, nature set to work to take it down again," Grove writes in *Fruits of the Earth* (p. 134). But there is more to Grove's vision than despair: in showing the defeat of humankind, this author pays tribute to the prairie itself, something he also did in his nonfiction works, *Over Prairie Trails* and *Turn of the Year*.

The effect of the prairie upon the human spirit was the concern of Sinclair Ross and Martha Ostenso, as well. A character in Martha Ostenso's most successful novel, *Wild Geese*, observes that "the austerity of nature reduces the outward expression of life simply, I think, because there is not such an abundance of natural objects for the spirit to react to. We are, after all, only the mirror of our environment. . . . [The people in this small community] are intensified figures of life with no outward expression—no releasing gesture" (p. 78). Sinclair Ross was a master at integrating human psychology with effect in the natural world. In the earlier-mentioned novel, *As For Me and My House*, nature reflects and answers the human state in the small prairie town of Horizon. Ross tells the story of the Bentleys' marriage as he moves symbolically through heat and cold and storm, cycling with the seasons. Nevertheless, Ross, like Grove, invokes the typical response of the prairie writer. Mrs. Bentley observes the hills surrounding Horizon and finds in their stillness and solitude a hostile presence, aligned against them, "for we dare not admit an indifferent wilderness, where we may have no meaning at all" (p. 100).

Canadian writing is deeply regional, and each region has produced writers with a nuanced sense of place. Still, there are echoes of both the garrison mentality and survival in the way nature is portrayed. Ernest Buckler writes from the Annapolis Valley in the maritime region. *The Mountain and the Valley* begins and ends with the "stillness" of the main Character, David Canaan. The stillness is preliminary to a grand revelation David has on the mountainside in which the "infinite" voices of nature are joined in unison with all the details of his life. He becomes "one" with nature, however, only by obliterating himself. The voices of nature "sounded and rushed in his head until it seemed as if he must go out into these things. He must be a tree and a stone and a shadow and a crystal of snow and a thread of moss and the veining of a leaf" (p. 292).

For the most part, Ontario writers seem to have felt themselves to be the keepers of the urban spirit in Canada. A few Ontario writers, however, have responded to the land in a way that makes their writing environmental. In *They Shall Inherit the Earth*, Morley Callaghan follows the Romantic pattern of an urban person's journey into the natural world. Michael Aikenhead's experience, however, is anything but Romantic. Out in the woods on a wolf-hunt, Michael says, "'If I stayed here, I'd just function like the deer or a fox or a wolf. I'd just be an organism, part of the living things around here; there'd be nothing distinctive about me'" (p. 188). Later, observing the carcass of a deer killed by wolves, he realizes that "justice" in nature is simply a pattern; nature sweeps on, "the stars would come out in the heavens and shine impartially on the agitated and the turbulent and complaining living souls" (p. 197).

Perhaps this sense of antihuman nature explains why the Ontario poet Al Purdy describes "The Country North of Belleville" as "the country of our defeat," "where the farms have gone back / To forest." Purdy's poetry draws upon natural scenes from all across Canada and often expresses the futility of human endeavor, including that of his own poetry. Dwarf trees on Baffin Island, for example, make him realize that he has "been stupid in a poem" ("Trees in the Arctic Circle"), stupid to express scorn at these seemingly diminished trees that are, in fact, untouched by any human opinion (*The Collected Poems of Al Purdy*).

Taking Margaret Atwood's *Surfacing* as a measure, Ontario writers appear to be struck by the utter impossibility of accord between humans and nature. In *Surfacing* Atwood divests her protagonist of all contact with human beings, preparatory to a return to the wild. Psychologically unbalanced to begin with, the woman who has this experience, however, goes bush-mad. The destruction of her sense of humanity represents the essence of the Canadian projection of what would happen in true contact with nature. "I am an animal or a tree," the woman thinks. "I am the thing in which the animals and trees move and grow, I am a place" (p. 181). The value of this experience lies in confronting the terror of a loss of social identity and "individuality."

Gabrielle Roy is a French-Canadian writer from Manitoba who writes about rural prairie life in *Where Nests the Water Hen*. Also, in *The Cashier* (*Alexandre Chenevert* in the original French), Roy's protagonist Alexandre, a troubled man, goes to a cabin in the woods where he finds that "in all his life nothing had ever made him feel so alone as this landscape so deeply at peace and foreign, to his cares as a human being" (p. 119). Marie-Claire Blais and Roch Carrier work more symbolically with the landscape. Central to Blaise's *Mad Shadows* is Patrice, a beautiful but mentally deficient lad. Water fascinates Patrice and in fact enters his being, and takes him over. When he has convulsions, his head is "plunged in fiery waters" and when he is desolate, he would "hold his arms toward an empty lake" (p. 117). Carrier chooses the forest for his symbolism. A key episode in *Floralie, Where Are You?* finds Floralie lost in the forest: "The silence in the forest was no longer a terrestrial silence, where you can still feel the heartbeat of life. Hellfire touched her heart; it burned. To keep her from getting away, needles from the underbrush clung to her dress, and their thousand claws held her back" (p. 31). Once again, the land is pictured threatening the human spirit, and human sanity.

Emily Carr's paintings of the forests in British Columbia are better known than her writings, but she provides finely honed observations of nature in several of her books. In *Klee Wyck*, Carr records her trip by canoe and boat to small First Nations villages along the coast of British Columbia. The people she finds in these villages have learned to live with the elements. She describes a totem pole of D'Sonoqua, the fierce, powerful "wild woman" of the woods. Carved out of a great red cedar, "she seemed to be part of the tree itself, as if she had grown there at its heart, and the carver had only chipped away the outer wood so that you could see her" (p. 33). Nature is mediated for Carr by the traditions of the First Nations people she encounters.

Malcolm Lowry resided in Dollarton, British Columbia, and left a remarkable record of his time spent there in his story "A Forest Path to the Spring." In one scene describing a winter storm, Lowry writes of an "elemental despair" (p. 255) and yet is able to provide a sense of relief at the end of his story when a stream making its way through the woods, "haggard and chill and tragic," is transformed on its last lap to the sea into "a happy joyous little stream" (p. 287). Lowry's human lives in this story are woven through and through with the lives of all around them, and are ultimately shaped by the same forces that shape the natural world. Earl Birney is a British Columbian writer whose poems describe places he has visited worldwide. However, he focuses on a mountainous region of British Columbia in one of his most widely read poems, "David" (*The Poems of Earl Birney*). The narrator of the poem and David are mountain climbers who find that the glory of the landscape turns to horror when David falls. The "gurgling world of crystal and cold blue chasms" metamorphoses into a hostile world of "sun-cankered snowbridge(s)" and "gaping greenthroated crevasses." Although it is unusual within Canadian responses to the environment to show nature changing with the human perspective, Birney's poem nevertheless arrives at a typical sense of threat.

Themes of survival, the garrison mentality, and fears of being extinguished by an indifferent environment promote one kind of environmental understanding. At its root is a wisdom that suggests that ultimately nature can not be trivialized or controlled. In its more shallow manifestations, though, such portrayals run the risk of forever pitting human culture against a hostile natural world. It would be unfair to suggest, however, that these are the only ways that Canadians have written about the environment. First Nations people have their own rich heritage of oral stories, most of which are legends about mythic figures who aid or obstruct people's efforts to live in nature. Pauline Johnson, a First Nations writer, achieved wide renown in the first decades of the twentieth century. Her poems, collected in *Flint and Feather*, express outrage at the treatment of First Nations people by colonists as she strives to reveal the life of her people to an unenlightened public. Many of her poems offer views of the natural world from the vantage point of a canoe, as in "The Song My Paddle Sings." In "Shadow River," Johnson writes that "The beauty, strength, and power of the land / Will never stir or bend at my command." Johnson is also the author of *Legends of Vancouver*, a collection of traditional tales that deal with familiar natural landmarks around Vancouver, British Columbia.

Nature writers provide another dissenting voice to the garrison mentality as Wayne Grady points out in his introduction to *Treasures of the Place: Three Centuries of Nature Writing in Canada*. In the twentieth century, nature writers such as Farley Mowat have campaigned tirelessly to change attitudes toward the natural world. *Never Cry Wolf* is Mowat's account of time spent watching a wolf family over several months in the Barrens of the North. In it, he satirizes the kind of scientific rigidity that claimed that wolves were indiscriminant killers, responsible for the decline of the caribou herds. Humor changed to intense anger with *A Whale for the Killing*, in which he uses the plight of a Fin Whale trapped in a Newfoundland inlet to reveal the pointless cruelty of the local residents to this individual animal and to speak out against the hunting of whales worldwide.

Lionel Stevenson first described the realistic animal story as a "wholly new 'genre' which Canadian authors have contributed to the world's literature" (p. 163). Margaret Atwood further points out that the realistic animal story, developed by Sir Charles G. D. Roberts and Ernest Thompson Seton, far from being a literary curiosity, is a genre that provides the key to the Canadian understanding of their position in the world, in that these authors "tell their stories from the point of view of the animal" (*Survival*, 74). Read symbolically, this means that Canadians, in theory at least, tend to identify more with "victims" than with "winners." Atwood speculates that Canadian identification with animal victims is "the expression of a deep-seated cultural fear." Just like their animal counterparts, Canadians, too, hold that "survival is the main aim in life, failure as an individual is inevitable, and extinction as a species is a distinct possibility" (p. 79). Ironies multiply upon ironies, however, when Canada becomes a hunting ground for the rest of the world, or finds itself exporting animals, such as wolves, to areas in the United States where they have been exterminated. (*See the chapter devoted to this subject for a more detailed discussion-Ed.*)

In the second half of the twentieth century, many writers have begun to react to a growing sense of threat, not from, but to, the natural world. Wayland Drew is one of the few good Canadian writers to speak about the thrill of killing animals in the wild. In *The Wabeno Feast* he describes the experience of an ex-hunter who once thought that the moment of shooting a grizzly bear was the finest in his life. The man has a change of heart, however, when he sees his actions as if on film, and, moreover, sees himself as a "Chaplin clown" repeating the same actions over and over again. Now when he sees hunters, he thinks, "Must they kill and kill every small, free thing until nothing remained that was not as trapped as they?" Drew's novel is an ecological fable, which draws parallels between Canada's fur trading past, and a contemporary, technological society nearing environmental apocalypse.

M. T. Kelly in the harsh, angry *A Dream Like Mine* juxtaposes a trendy fascination for First Nations' traditions against the reality of a people suffering from mercury poisoning. During a few nightmarish days the protagonist, who earlier has participated in a sweat lodge, suddenly

finds himself involved with Arthur, a psychotically angry man, a type of modern day trickster, who kidnaps the manager of Spruce Lands Paper in an effort to stop the pollution of his people's water. In one of the final scenes of the book Arthur snarls, a sound "so full of malice, so full of human sexuality and hatred as to seem supernatural" (p. 132). Perhaps, Kelly seems to be suggesting, hatred this intense is the only response there is to the kinds of insanity that has turned wild land, a land filled with life and spirit, into clear cuts and "cabin country."

Marian Engel's *Bear* also represents a departure from conventional approaches to nature. This novella describes the erotic attachment of a woman to a captive bear during a stay in the backwoods of Ontario. This bear would be a mere Jungian symbol, were it not for the fact that he is truly dangerous. One swipe from his claws leaves the woman fully aware of his animal nature. Timothy Findley takes Canadian sensibilities onto the world stage in *Not Wanted on the Voyage*. He presents his own version of the tale of Noah and the ark, critiquing patriarchy and showing how humankind "lost" nature. Animals speak to sympathetic human beings for most of the novel. At its end, however, the animals utter nothing but sounds unintelligible to even the most receptive human ear.

In his epic novel *Green Grass, Running Water*, Thomas King uses First Nations myth and humor to challenge Eurocentric perspectives on many things, including the natural world. A thread in the narrative concerns the damming of a river and the lone First Nations man's refusal to allow the hydroelectric work of the dam to begin. By the trickery of the four ancient and magical First Nations men, who have escaped from an asylum, three cars, a Nissan, a Pinto, and a Kharmann Ghia (King's love of wordplay here focuses on the names of Columbus's ships) first float toward, and then are hurled against, the side of the dam, breaking it wide open.

The word *Canada* is believed to derive from *kanata*, a Huron-Iroquois word for *village* or *community* (Lower, 1). Unlike what is found in American environmental writing, it is the relationship between the human community, and the land around it, that underlies Canadian environmental understanding. From early in the nineteenth century until late in the twentieth, in fiction, nonfiction, and poetry, there has been a constantly expressed anxiety about the survival of the Canadian community. Michael Poole, journeying by canoe through the inside passage, describes in *Ragged Islands* a deserted camping spot he is forced to use one night. All along the coast he has found former sites where people once lived—Indian villages, logging camps, fishing ports—deserted, and being reclaimed by nature. Poole finds something ominous in this disappearance of settled human life (there is no lack of yachtsmen cruising up and down, filling their freezers full of illegally caught shrimp).

> At high tide I had to retreat to the woods to find room to sleep. There was neither water nor driftwood for a fire. Yet none of these things could account for the dark malevolence that seemed to hover about the place, especially in the forest above the beach, where a populous village once stood. The site had once been open to sun and wind; but now closely grown cedars shut out the sky and most of the light. Dead limbs cascaded like lianas down the trunks and snaked over a forest floor so deep in needles that nothing green could grow. (p. 115)

In this place he feels that he is being watched by something, an experience that leaves him feeling that he "is an intruder on alien ground" (p. 115).

Canadians have rather reluctantly indulged in creating national myths for themselves because of an ongoing crisis concerning their identity and political survival. There are deep regional divides in the country, and yet, as Wayne Grady points out in his collection, *From the Country*, "Canadians are vitally interested in and aware of the geographical complexities involved in just being Canadian" (p. 10). It is the shared interest in the "geographical complexity" of Canada, its huge space and distances, which continues to underlie the best Canadian environmental writing.

Selected Works and Further Reading

Atwood, Margaret, *Surfacing,* New York: Simon & Schuster, 1972; London: Andre Deutsch, 1972

————, *Survival: A Thematic Guide to Canadian Literature,* Toronto, Ontario: Anansi, 1972

————, *Wilderness Tips,* New York: Doubleday, 1991; Toronto, Ontario: McClelland and Stewart, 1991; London: Bloomsbury Classics, 1995

Birney, Earle, *The Poems of Earle Birney,* Toronto, Ontario: McClelland and Stewart, 1969

Blais, Marie-Claire, *La belle bête,* Quebec: Institut Littéraire du Québec, 1959; also published as *Mad Shadows,* translated by Merloyd Lawrence, Boston: Little, Brown, 1960; London: Jonathan Cape, 1960

Bourassa, Napoléon, *Jacques et Marie: Souvenir d'un peuple disperse,* Montreal, Quebec: E. Senécal, 1866

Buckler, Ernest, *The Mountain and the Valley,* New York: Holt, 1952

Callaghan, Morley, *They Shall Inherit the Earth,* New York: Random House, 1935

Canada 125th Anniversary Year Book 1992, Ottawa, Ontario: Statistics Canada, 1991

Carr, Emily, *Klee Wyck,* New York and London: Oxford University Press, 1941

Carrier, Roch, *Floralie, Where Are You?,* translated by Sheila Fischman, Toronto, Ontario: Anansi, 1971

Cartier, Jacques, *The Voyages of Jacques Cartier,* edited by Ramsay Cook, Toronto, Ontario: University of Toronto Press, 1993

DesRochers, Alfred, *À L'Ombre de L'Orford,* Sherbrooke, Quebec: A. DesRochers, 1929; reprinted, edited by Richard Giguère, Montreal, Quebec: Presses de l'Université de Montréal, 1993

Drew, Wayland, *The Wabeno Feast,* Toronto, Ontario: Anansi, 1973

Engel, Marian, *Bear,* New York: Atheneum, 1976; Toronto, Ontario: McClelland and Stewart, 1976; London: Routledge & K. Paul, 1977

Findley, Timothy, *Not Wanted on the Voyage,* New York: Delacorte, 1984; London: Macmillan, 1985

Franklin, Sir John, *Narrative of a Journey to the Shores of the Polar Sea, in the Years 1819, 20, 21, and 22,* London: J. Murray, 1823; New York: Dutton, 1824

Frye, Northrop, *The Bush Garden: Essays on the Canadian Imagination,* Toronto, Ontario: Anansi, 1971

————, *Divisions on a Ground: Essays on Canadian Culture,* Toronto, Ontario: Anansi, 1982

Gérin-Lajoie, Antoine, *Jean Rivard,* 1862; translated by Vida Bruce, Toronto, Ontario: McClelland and Stewart, 1977

Grady, Wayne, ed., *From the Country: Writings About Rural Canada: A Harrowsmith Anthology,* Canada: Camden House, 1991

———, ed., *Treasures of the Place: Three Centuries of Nature Writing in Canada*, Vancouver, British Columbia: Douglas and McIntyre, 1992

Grant, George, *Ocean to Ocean: Sandford Fleming's Expedition Through Canada in 1872*, London: S. Low, Marston, Low & Searle, 1873

Grove, Frederick Philip, *Fruits of the Earth*, London: J. M. Dent, 1933

———, *Over Prairie Trails*, Toronto, Ontario: McClelland and Stewart, 1922

———, *Settlers of the Marsh*, New York: George H. Doran, 1925; reprinted, Toronto, Ontario: McClelland and Stewart, 1966

———, *Turn of the Year*, Toronto, Ontario: McClelland and Stewart, 1923

Head, George, *Forest Scenes and Incidents in the Wilds of North America*, London: J. Murray, 1829; reprinted, Toronto, Ontario: Coles, 1970

Hearne, Samuel, *Coppermine Journey: An Account of a Great Adventure*, 1795; edition edited by Farley Mowat, Boston: Little, Brown, 1958; Toronto, Ontario: McClelland and Stewart, 1958

Hémon, Louis, *Maria Chapdelaine*, Paris: C. Delagrave, 1916; translated by W. H. Blake, New York: Macmillan, 1922

Howison, John, *Sketches of Upper Canada*, London: G. & W. B. Wittaker, 1821; reprinted, New York: Johnson Reprint, 1965; Toronto, Ontario: Coles, 1970

Jameson, Anna, *Winter Studies and Summer Rambles in Canada*, London: Saunders and Otley, 1838; New York: Wiley and Putnam, 1839; reprinted, Toronto, Ontario: McClelland and Stewart, 1923

Johnson, E. Pauline, *Flint and Feather: Collected Verse*, Toronto, Ontario: Musson, 1912; rev. ed., New York and London: Hodder and Stoughton, 1913

———, *Legends of Vancouver*, Vancouver, British Columbia: McClelland, Goodchild and Stewart, 1911

King, Thomas, *Green Grass, Running Water*, Boston: Houghton Mifflin, 1993; Toronto, Ontario: HarperCollins, 1993

Lacombe, Patrice, *La Terre paternelle*, 1846; Montreal, Quebec: Beauchemin & Valois, 1871

Lower, J. Arthur, *Canada: An Outline History*, Toronto, Ontario: Ryerson, 1966; rev. ed., New York: McGraw-Hill Ryerson, 1973

Lowry, Malcolm, *Hear Us O Lord from Heaven Thy Dwelling Place and Lunar Caustic*, Philadelphia: Lippincott, 1961; reprinted, New York and Harmondsworth, England: Penguin, 1979

MacLennan, Hugh, *Seven Rivers of Canada: The Mackenzie, the St. Lawrence, the Ottawa, the Red, the Saskatchewan, the Fraser, the St. John*, Toronto, Ontario: Macmillan, 1961

Moodie, Susanna, *Roughing It in the Bush; or, Life in Canada*, New York: Putnam's, 1852; London: R. Bentley, 1852

Morton, W. L., *The Shield of Achilles: Aspects of Canada in the Victorian Age/Le Bouclier D'Achille: Regards sur le Canada de l'ére Victorienne*, Toronto, Ontario: McClelland & Stewart, 1968

Mowat, Farley, *Never Cry Wolf*, Boston: Little, Brown, 1963; London: Secker & Warburg, 1964

———, *A Whale for the Killing*, Boston: Little, Brown, 1972; Toronto, Ontario: McClelland and Stewart, 1972; London: Heinemann, 1973

Ostenso, Martha, *Wild Geese*, New York: Dodd, Mead, 1925; Toronto, Ontario: McClelland and Stewart, 1925

Poole, Michael, *Ragged Islands*, Vancouver, British Columbia: Douglas & McIntyre, 1991

Purdy, Al, *The Collected Poems of Al Purdy*, Toronto, Ontario: McClelland and Stewart, 1986

Richler, Mordecai, *Solomon Gursky Was Here*, New York and Markham, Ontario: Viking, 1989; London: Chatto & Windus, 1990

Ringuet (Philippe Panneton), *Trente Arpents*, Montreal, Quebec: Fides, 1938; published as *Thirty Acres*, translated by Felix and Dorothea Walter, New York and Toronto, Ontario: Macmillan, 1960

Ross, Sinclair, *As for Me and My House*, New York: Reynal & Hitchcock, 1941; Toronto, Ontario: McClelland and Stewart, 1941

Roy, Gabrielle, *Alexandre Chenevert*, Montreal, Quebec: Beauchemin, 1954; published as *The Cashier*, translated by Harry Binsee, New York: Harcourt, 1955; Toronto, Ontario: McClelland and Stewart, 1955; London: Heinemann, 1956

———, *Where Nests the Water Hen,* translated by Harry Binsee, New York: Harcourt, Brace, 1951; London: Heinemann, 1952

Smith, A. J. M., ed., *Modern Canadian Verse in English and French,* Toronto, Ontario: Oxford University Press, 1967

Stevenson, Lionel, "Nature in Canadian Prose," in *Appraisals of Canadian Literature,* Toronto, Ontario: Macmillan of Canada, 1926

Thwaites, Reuben Gold, ed., *The Jesuit Relations and Allied Documents: Travels and Explorations of the Jesuit Missionaries in New France, 1610–1791,* Cleveland, Ohio: Burrows Brothers, 1896; London: Brentano's, 1900

Traill, Catherine Parr Strickland, *The Backwoods of Canada,* London: C. Knight, 1836

———, *Canadian Wild Flowers,* Montreal, Quebec: J. Lovell, 1868

———, *Pearls and Pebbles; or, Notes of an Old Naturalist,* Toronto, Ontario: Briggs, 1894; London: S. Low, Marston, 1894

———, *Studies of Plant Life in Canada,* Ottawa, Ontario: A. S. Woodburn, 1885

Warkentin, Germaine, ed., *Canadian Exploration Literature: An Anthology: 1660–1860,* Toronto, Ontario: Oxford University Press, 1993

Wiebe, Rudy, *Playing Dead: A Contemplation Concerning the Arctic,* Edmonton, Alberta: NeWest, 1989

The Land Writes Back:
Notes on Four Western Canadian Writers

Pamela Banting

Debate about "eco-pornography" on the e-mail network operated by the Association for the Study of Literature and the Environment in 1997 prompted Richard Kerridge to address the following questions to the membership:

If, to be non-pornographic, representation must be intersubjective, how can ANY representation of nature be this? Many ecocritical debates converge on this question: how, in looking at nature, can any of us avoid the position of oppressive Subject? How can "nature," or any of its non-human parts, have a voice to be listened to, or a power of reciprocal representation? I guess that the Terry Tempest Williams text discussed here is taking one approach to this question, addressing nature as a lover in the rhetorical hope of getting some sort of answer, and turning up the erotic pressure as a way of hammering more and more frantically on that closed door. I agree with the readers who find this problematical. (p. 1)

Kerridge rightly notes that the problematics of representation make a reply from nature difficult to conceive. While I am not entirely certain that nature's reply in the manner sketched above is wholly desirable, neither am I assured of the impossibility of some kind of exchange between nature and the human subject. Nor, despite the lyric tradition, am I convinced that addresses to nature produce the subject only as aroused yet spurned lover. Critical work that has been done on nature writing and writing about place (on literature and the arts in general) proceeds out of representationalist aesthetics—simply put, the idea that landscape has a profound formative or informative influence on the writer, which s/he then re-presents or expresses in words. Often in our literary critical practices, as in our religions, which have been geared toward getting to the heart and soul of the matter, getting at the symbolic meanings of things, we have forgotten what Linda Hogan calls "the value of matter, the very thing that soul inhabits" ("Creations," 99). Such critical practices are biophobic, reflecting "the culturally acquired urge to affiliate with technology, human artifacts, and solely with human interests regarding the natural world" (Orr, 131).

However, many contemporary western Canadian writers who write about nature and sense of place are working to develop a means of speaking intelligibly and specifically about the ways landscape imprints itself upon us and the ways that imprinting is transferred from our sensory experiences, bodily motions, emotions, and visceral impressions onto the written page and into the spoken and chanted air. Writers such as Thomas Wharton, Sharon Butala, Don Gayton, and Sid Marty—to select just four—are working toward a rhetoric of ecological relationship that is not wholly reliant upon representation and Cartesian notions of the subject and of the body, and we need to develop a critical methodology for discussing these important aspects of their work.

Just as postcolonial writers in former colonies like Canada have been engaged in a long-term project of resistance and "writing back" to the Empire, so too, nature "writes back" to human subjects in languages that can be read and deciphered, provided we make the effort to learn new vocabularies and grammars. In Tempest Williams's words, "We call to the land—and the land calls back" (p. 87). Thomas Wharton, for example, structures his novel *Icefields* as a series of narrative fragments that he correlates with glacial moraine. In a radio interview, Wharton talks about the genesis of the structure of his book:

> Before I had much content, I knew the form that I wanted and I knew the style. I wanted a very fragmented book. I had an idea of how I would want it to sound; I wanted a very sparse book, and I guess in a way I was trying to do something analogous to the actual landscape,[1] the barren landscape and the fragmented rocks of the moraine. . . . The landscape is kind of the main character, the centre; the characters are almost what one could call fields of force, or objects within a field, interacting. . . . I didn't want too much psychological motivation in the story at first; I wanted to see if I could write a very *cold* book.

Tellingly, we have no lack of critical theory upon which we can draw to discuss the fragmented narrative of this or any other text as mimetic of the postmodern condition or of the deconstructed poststructuralist subject. We also have a large body of scholarship on the relationship between fiction and history. What we are missing, however, is a vocabulary, rhetoric and theory of how to speak about the relationship between fiction and geography or geology, between, for instance, textual fragments and glacial till. We do not know how to conceptualize landscape as fictive agent or character. Although, as I have argued elsewhere, postmodernist and poststructuralist theories can and ought to be productively channeled toward a reconsideration of the relationship between the subject and nature,[2] nevertheless their roots in and emphasis upon cosmopolitan culture has so far resulted in a tendency on the part of many such critics and theorists[3] to dismiss the very word "nature" as essentialist, to overlook nature and its significations and/or to use the idea of nature merely as backdrop (or scenery) against which to juxtapose their deconstructions of popular (media, that is, not vernacular) culture.

In addition to a crucial recognition by critics and theorists that the world is not always already entirely urban, what is needed is revision of the poststructuralist subject.[4] This subject is conceived of as constituted by and attentive only to humans' linguistic acts, not to what David Abram calls "the more-than-human world." In poststructuralist thought, "place" usually refers to the positionality of speaker and listener: race, class, gender, ethnicity, and/or sexual preference are duly noted and factored into the construction of the subject but geographical, geological, geopolitical, even simple material locations are not. For the majority of cosmopolitan poststructuralist theorists place is the library, the archive, the study, or the Internet, not the terrain or the soil where signature, events and context take place.

Alternatively, as Jim Cheney argues, to recuperate mythic images and narratives that garner knowledge of place and community, we must look to "the *mind*scape/*land*scape which emerges from our narrative and mythical embedment in some particular place. This begins with the inscribing of the nervous system in the landscape; the body is the instrument of our knowledge of the world" (p. 130). In *Icefields*, Wharton takes the notion of the biblical "Fall" as one of his fictional premises. The biblical story represents a Fall from a state of oneness with nature into a knowledge of good and evil or, if you prefer, into binary oppositions. What Wharton does is to subject his main character, Irish physician and botany enthusiast Dr. Byrne, to a literal and reversed fall. The novel opens with the following sentence: "At a quarter past three in the afternoon, on August 17, 1898, Doctor Edward Byrne slipped on the ice of Arcturus glacier in the Canadian Rockies and slid into a crevasse" (p. 1). Rather than falling out of a state of grace in nature, instead Byrne slips and falls headfirst out of the binaries of his European consciousness and into nature where, 60 feet down a glacial crevasse, wedged upside down thanks to his bulky knapsack, he begins his instruction in the language of ice. The novel explores the consequences of this Canadian version of "the Fall" and of what Byrne sees when he regains consciousness upside down in the glacier:

> There was something in the ice, a shape, its outline sharpening as the light grew. A fused mass of trapped air bubbles, or a vein of snow, had formed a chance design, a white form embedded within the darker ice and revealed by the light of the sun. A pale human figure, with wings. The white figure lay on its side, the head turned away from him. Its huge wings were spread wide, one of them cracked obliquely near the tip, the broken pinions slighted detached. (p. 11)

By virtue of Byrne's fortunate fall, both he and the reader of *Icefields* have their nervous systems embedded in the landscape of the Rocky Mountains.

But how does the land inscribe itself upon the flesh of our bodies? How are these inscriptions on our senses, muscles, viscera, and memories translated into writing? How do we develop a critical vocabulary for describing this manner of inscription? Sharon Butala has published a trilogy of novels and two collections of short stories about rural people and their physical, emotional and spiritual connections with the land. In her first nonfiction book, *The Perfection of the Morning: An Apprenticeship in Nature*, she describes how when she married and left both academia and the city environment to move to the shortgrass prairie of the Butala ranch near Eastend, Saskatchewan, a completely other landscape for her, memories of her childhood and of her mother began to surface. But contrary to what some critics have suggested, Butala does not draw an essentialist equation between earth and mother. Indeed, initially, when she and her husband-to-be are getting to know one another, it is because the material conditions of life on the ranch (outdoor toilet, wood cookstove) replicate those of her preschool years that they conjure early memories such as her mother's practice of placing lights in the windows so that bears, should they look in, would not see themselves reflected in the glass and try to get into the house. What Butala began to remember about the natural world of her early childhood

> was a combination of smells, the feel of the air, a sense of the presence of Nature as a living entity all around me. All of that had been imprinted in me, but more in the blood and bone and muscles–an instinctive memory– than a precise memory of events or people. I remembered it with my body, or maybe I remembered it with another sense for which we have no name but is no less real for that. As I returned to the ranch and hay farm to visit, the sense of this memory grew; I found myself inexorably drawn to it although I did not understand this at the time, preferring to accept the obvious romantic scenario of marrying and living happily ever after. (p. 9)

Upon later reflection, Butala configures her relationship with her new husband as not just romance but an attraction that also encompassed the natural world of the open prairie of the Cypress Hills region. At this important juncture in her life, nature exerts its call, and *The Perfection of the Morning*, a retrospective and introspective analysis of Butala's sensual engagement with the climate, vegetation, wild and domestic animals, history, and culture of her new home, is Butala's reply.

Because in European-derived postcolonial cultures land has come to signify livelihood, property, privacy, backdrop to human emotion and aesthetic response (the sublime or the picturesque), recreation, and tourism, we have not been able to understand the crucial role that landscape plays in story, literature or mythology. When we speak of the debilitating effects on native peoples of the loss of their land, we file this with our understandings of property and economy and seldom think of the place of land and landscape in native (or any) culture in other than merely sentimental terms. We dismiss reverence or even regard for rivers, lakes and trees as supernatural nonsense (tree-hugging), and so we view relationships to land in much the same way that many of our non-native ancestors viewed native culture upon contact—as childlike, simple, primitive, backward, underdeveloped, even embarrassing. We have forgotten or repressed the fact that culture and nature are capable of interrelation, and even of translation between one and the other. Instead we prefer to translate land into dollars and cents, real estate, jobs, outdoor sports and recreation, and a refuge from the stresses of our culture. However, like agriculture, culture too emerges from the land.

Like Butala, some researchers in the sciences of agriculture, biology and ecology are beginning to overcome these cultural biases and embarrassment[5] in order to investigate the relationship between nature and our bodies. In his first book of essays, *The Wheatgrass Mechanism: Science and Imagination in the Western Canadian Landscape*, range ecologist and writer Don Gayton describes a laboratory experiment in which subjects were instructed to try to influence a simple electronic random number generator:

> After several thousand tries, sure enough, the trend line of the influenced trials begins to deviate from normal random expectations, and the deviations pass the test of statistical significance. The Princeton scientists who did this work call the effect "anomalous information transfer from an agent (the subject) to a percipient (the random number generator) who are separated geographically and not connected by any normal information channels." . . . Perhaps more important is the possibility of subtle information transfer from the perceived back to the perceiver, laying the

foundation for our need for landscape. Rocks and grasses and mountains may have influence, something aboriginal cultures acknowledge and we have long suspected. (pp. 56–57)

Gayton comments provocatively that "Buffalo memory persists in the grasses, and they have not yet fully assimilated the cow and the fence" (p. 8).

In both of his two books Gayton attempts to restore the linguistic habitat of the word "landscape." He describes his project as undertaking to "free the concept of landscape from bureaucracies, from developers, and from its painterly, English countryside connotations, and give the word the boundless, Western Interior potential it deserved" (*Landscapes,* 21). In his second book, *Landscapes of the Interior: Re-Explorations of Nature and the Human Spirit,* he continues to interweave the poetic and the scientific, realizing that he cannot venture into the geography, geology and biology of "the Interior" of western Canada and the United States without taking into account his own subjectivity and even his flesh. So he deliberately places his body, and not merely his perceiving and recording consciousness, repeatedly on the line. In his essay "Primal," like Butala he too explores the notion of landscape imprinting itself upon us as small children, the romance and eroticism we sometimes experience in relation to landscapes that recall that primal one and, by contrast, the spiritual and psychological distress—claustrophobia, disgust, even madness—which can result from moving to a landscape very dissimilar from our natal one. In "Cowboy Fiction" Gayton writes about his childhood interest in cowboy writer and painter Will James, who was born Ernest Dufault in Quebec, and who, by the age of 15, was so consumed with the desire to be a cowboy that he moved to western Canada for four years, learned cowboy skills, changed his name to Will James and his language from French to English, before moving to the U.S. What fascinates Gayton is how James's "overwhelming fascination with a certain kind of landscape . . . caused him to bury one identity and create another" (p. 52). As Gayton notes, "Most of us allow fiction to penetrate only as far as our bookshelves, stopping it far short of personal identity. Will James did not" (p. 51). An extraordinarily adventurous border-crosser, not to mention reader, James crossed over into the textual landscape of the Western dime novels he had read, and went on throughout his life to create himself "as the main

character in his own novels." Perhaps we as readers and literary critics need to emulate James and seek to translate our reading not only into critical fictions but also into actions and changes in our lifestyles as well. As James's metamorphosis attests, both books and landscapes have the power to shape and transform our identities as subjects.

If Butala's *The Perfection of the Morning* deals with one woman's physical, emotional and spiritual connections with the land, Sid Marty's work emerges from this man's bodily engagement with the four elements, his community, and his families of origin and the family he has created together with his wife Myrna. In 1995 Marty—poet, singer-songwriter, and former park ranger whose first work of non-fiction, *Men for the Mountains,* has remained continuously in print since its publication in 1978—published a new work of non-fiction about the montane foothills of the Rocky Mountains, *Leaning on the Wind: Under the Spell of the Great Chinook.* This book is rich in historical, meteorological, anecdotal, and legendary detail about the Chinook and the ways in which it has affected the soil, vegetation, animals, native peoples and white settlers (or "seizers," as the Peigans called the first whites who came west seeking their fortunes) of Chinook country. As full of the weather as it is, this work of creative non-fiction owes a debt to the genre of the farmers' almanac, although the compendium of detail in *Leaning on the Wind* never impedes the narrative flow. The book contains information about the Chinook arch, alpenglow and moonbows; the tenacity and longevity of the bullpine; the semiotics of scalping and body mutilation of the Sioux, Cheyenne, Blackfoot, and Europeans; what it is like to go up in a glider plane; how the severe migraines that some people experience during a Chinook may be linked to a significant increase in positive ions; and how during the terrible winter of 1906 freezing and starving cattle wandered into towns "where they followed people into their houses in their desperation to find forage" (p. 77).

But detail is not the driving force of *Leaning on the Wind.* Marty doesn't lean only on the wind: he leans hard on language, forcing it to yield its full complement of wit, humor, insight, irony, history, political commentary, and mystery. For example, following an analysis of the English habit of simply ignoring one's local surroundings and acting as if one were still living in the Old Country, Marty comments wryly: "This

Raj on the Range was short-lived" (p. 78). After Sid and Myrna experience problems raising chickens and attempt to splint a chicken's apparently broken leg with a popsicle stick, they find out that one must control "the postmodern chicken environment" and feed quantity in a more scientific manner. One day during a particularly difficult financial period Myrna asks her husband what he would do if he won the lottery. He adapts an old farming joke and replies "Just keep on writing poems until it was all used up" (p. 159).

Marty was born and raised in Medicine Hat and after studying English at a university worked for a number of years as a park warden in "Banff National Car Park," as he calls it, and to his credit he allows his written language to reflect his small town heritage, work history and literary education. That is, Marty does not merely record the folksy sayings of his rural neighbors: he himself thinks in the vernacular and relishes and explores its nuances. He combines down-to-earth colloquial expressions and vernacular turns of phrase with more traditionally poetic language, and it is the confluence between these divergent streams that forms the river of his prose. The following passage about summer days when he was growing up illustrates both the way in which the oral, storytelling tradition and rhythmic, poetic prose meld in his writing and one of the many ways in which the prairie inscribed itself onto his body:

> Prairie kids back then ran through the summer half-naked, Coyote's children, brown as the wide South Saskatchewan River, in the days before the ozone hole, when the sun was the god of childhood. The big river held me in a fearful fascination. My father claimed that my Uncle Sid once caught a sturgeon there so large he had to winch it ashore with his jeep. Such a fish might inhale a small boy by accident, or so I reasoned. I stuck to the pragmatic shallows and the sandy bottoms, hunting for basking "suckers" and freshwater clams. Sometimes my bare foot slipped into quicksand, but I was light and quick myself, and swam clear. The river washed me clean and the prairie wind was my towel. (p. 83)

This passage combines skin memory, oral storytelling, possibly a tall tale, and, in the giant sturgeon, the ingredients of myth. Although Marty in a sense brackets the opportunity for mythmaking, putting his childhood fear of the sturgeon down to "reason," one could nevertheless opt to understand that word in terms of what Linda Hogan outlines as "sacred reason," a kind of mind "different from ordinary reason, that is linked to forces of nature" (*Dwellings*, 19). Like Wharton, Butala and Gayton, Marty approaches nature physically as well as intellectually.

So what, if anything, can critics do, for example, with the cognate relationship between glacial flow and narrative flow in Wharton's *Icefields*? Can we do more than note the metaphorical similarity and then pass on? Can we begin to understand metaphor differently—not only as a rhetorical device comparing likenesses between two things but also as "multiplicity simply there," as writer Daphne Marlatt once reconfigured metaphor. Furthermore, is there any point in elaborating an ecocriticism that posits a sort of biophilia between humans and nature, and between texts and natural processes? Can a book be "cold" in a sense other than an emotional one? Or are such relationships to be dismissed as essentialist? What might be the strategic ecocritical value in comparing Wharton's narrative technique with specific geophysical processes, as he himself does (each of the five main sections of *Icefields* takes the name of a geophysical feature associated with glaciers—névé, moraine, nunatak, ablation zone, terminus), instead of only with techniques of so-called international postmodernist fiction? Would readings of texts in relation to regional geographies contribute to the development of a more ecologically responsible criticism? Would such criticism develop readers' abilities to recognize their own surroundings in literature and to mobilize themselves politically, especially in cultures where the colonial cringe still dictates patterns of reader reception? Would teaching students to read both text and scree accomplish any worthwhile goals? Would such investigations provide a productive critique of and addendum to representation?

While the metaphor of nature as book is, as Gary Snyder rightly insists, both inaccurate and pernicious (p. 69), an acknowledgment that signification can be found in utterance, breath, books, scratches on vellum or paper, pixels on a screen, animal tracks and vocalizations, tufts of fur, geological strata, and even the chemical processes involved in plant life[6] may inform us with new knowledges—"tawny grammars," as Snyder calls them—about our environment. In other words, the work of these four western Canadian writers—as well as that of others, such as David Arnason, Dennis Cooley, Thomas King, Robert Kroetsch, Margaret Laurence, Daphne Marlatt, Fred Stenson, Guy Vanderhaege, Rudy Wiebe, and the writers included in my anthology, *Writing the Land*—demonstrate that an intertextual understanding of fictional and non-fictional narrative technique may be drawn from the geograph as well as from the historiograph, the autograph and the literary and theoretical canons.

Notes

1. The novel is set in and around Jasper, Alberta, and the Columbia Icefields in the Rocky Mountains.

2. *See* my book *Body, Inc.: A Theory of Translation Poetics*, for example.

3. *See* Eric Zencey's article "The Rootless Professors."

4. Because postmodern work employs poststructuralist theory, from this point forward I shall use the single term poststructuralist rather than repeat both.

5. Gayton writes: "Socially we denigrate strong attachment to natural landscape as an essentially feminine trait, unless it is coupled with an equally strong desire to extract natural resources from it. Landscape bonds are often kept private, like embarrassing birthmarks" (*Landscapes*, 75).

6. In *The Wheatgrass Mechanism,* Don Gayton writes about the "semiochemicals" that convey signals and messages between a given plant and a particular strain of bacteria that "capture atmospheric nitrogen, convert it to nitrate, and feed it to the host plant in exchange for a tiny dribble of carbohydrate" (p. 95).

Selected Works and Further Reading

Abram, David, *The Spell of the Sensuous: Perception and Language in a More-Than-Human World,* New York: Pantheon, 1996

Arnason, David, *The Dragon and the Dry Goods Princess: Stories,* Winnipeg, Manitoba: Turnstone, 1994

——, *If Pigs Could Fly: Stories,* Winnipeg, Manitoba: Turnstone, 1995

Banting, Pamela, *Body, Inc.: A Theory of Translation Poetics,* Winnipeg, Manitoba: Turnstone, 1995

——, ed., *Writing the Land,* Vancouver, British Columbia: Polestar, 1998

Butala, Sharon, *The Perfection of the Morning: An Apprenticeship in Nature,* Toronto, Ontario: HarperCollins, 1994; San Francisco: HarperSanFrancisco, 1995

Cheney, Jim, "Postmodern Environmental Ethics: Ethics as Bioregional Narrative," *Environmental Ethics* 11:2 (Summer 1989), pp. 117–134

Cooley, Dennis, *This Only Home: Poems,* Winnipeg, Manitoba: Turnstone, 1992

——, *The Vernacular Muse: The Eye and Ear in Contemporary Literature,* Winnipeg, Manitoba: Turnstone, 1987

Gayton, Don, *Landscapes of the Interior: Re-Explorations of Nature and the Human Spirit,* Gabriola Island, British Columbia: New Society, 1996

——, *The Wheatgrass Mechanism: Science and Imagination in the Western Canadian Landscape,* Saskatoon, Saskatchewan: Fifth House, 1990

Hogan, Linda, "Creations," in *Heart of the Land: Essays on the Last Great Places,* edited by Joseph Barbato and Lisa Weinerman, New York: Pantheon, 1994

——, *Dwellings: A Spiritual History of the Living World,* New York: Norton, 1995

King, Thomas, *Green Grass, Running Water,* Boston: Houghton Mifflin, 1993; Toronto, Ontario: HarperCollins, 1993

——, *One Good Story, That One,* Toronto, Ontario: HarperCollins, 1993

Kroetsch, Robert, *A Likely Story: The Writing Life,* Red Deer, Alberta: Red Deer College Press, 1995

——, *What the Crow Said,* Don Mills, Ontario: General, 1978

Laurence, Margaret, *The Diviners,* New York: Knopf, 1974; London: Macmillan, 1974; Toronto, Ontario: McClelland and Stewart, 1974

Marlatt, Daphne, *Ana Historic,* Toronto, Ontario: Coach House, 1988

Marty, Sid, *Leaning on the Wind: Under the Spell of the Great Chinook,* San Francisco: HaperCollins West, 1995; Toronto, Ontario: HarperCollins, 1995

——, *Men for the Mountains,* Toronto, Ontario: McClelland and Stewart, 1978; New York: Vanguard, 1979

Orr, David, *Earth in Mind: On Education, Environment, and the Human Prospect,* Washington, D.C.: Island, 1994

Snyder, Gary, *The Practice of the Wild,* San Francisco: North Point, 1990

Stenson, Fred, *Last One Home,* Edmonton, Alberta: NeWest, 1988

Vanderhaeghe, Guy, *The Englishman's Boy,* Toronto, Ontario: McClelland and Stewart, 1996; New York: Picador, 1997

Van Herk, Aritha, "Interview with Thomas Wharton," CKUA Radio, Edmonton, Alberta, February 1995

Wharton, Thomas, *Icefields,* New York: Washington Square, 1995; Edmonton, Alberta: NeWest, 1995; London: J. Cape, 1997

Wiebe, Rudy, *A Discovery of Strangers,* Toronto, Ontario: Knopf, 1994

———, *Playing Dead: A Contemplation Concerning the Arctic,* Edmonton, Alberta: NeWest, 1989

———, *The Temptations of Big Bear,* Toronto, Ontario: McClelland and Stewart, 1973

Williams, Terry Tempest, *An Unspoken Hunger: Stories from the Field,* New York: Pantheon, 1994

Zencey, Eric, "The Rootless Professors," in *Rooted in the Land: Essays on Community and Place,* edited by William Vitek and Wes Jackson, New Haven, Connecticut, and London: Yale University Press, 1996

Section 2:

Europe

Nature in the English Novel

Richard Kerridge

There is a tension between nature writing and the narrative drive of novels: between the stillness required of the observer of nature, and the movement of plot. In pausing to notice the natural world, a character becomes less an actor and more a watcher, mediator or proxy reader, even a narrator. Awareness of nature in novels often comes at moments of solitary relief or consolation, in which the character is able to forget the immediate pressures of plot and find the calmness of detached observation, in what feels like an escape from self. But plot and self have a delayed presence in these moments. What the natural world shows can be interpreted as symbolic or metaphorical enactment providing an emotional cue, as with the horses encountered by Ursula at the end of D. H. Lawrence's *The Rainbow*. Decisions crystallize for characters at such moments.

Nature comes into the English novel from direct observation and from numerous traditions. Some of these are: Virgilian and Ovidian pastoral, elegy, neo-classical landscape, prospect poetry, romantic encounters with nature-as-infinity, American transcendentalism, amateur natural history and Darwinian evolutionary biology. And ubiquitously, in English fiction, social class is projected onto nature.

The tension is between the roles of character and narrator, between being inside the plot and being outside. Cartesian dualism positions nature as object to the human subject, object of the human gaze, and "other" to self-conscious, rational human subjectivity. Accordingly, the observer of nature typically stands outside, looking in, like Darwin gazing rhetorically down at his "tangled bank" at the close of *The Origin of Species* (p. 459). Yet Darwin, as observer, is describing an evolutionary process that includes himself. Against dualism, there is the Spinozan tradition of monism, feeding into romantic perceptions of the world as one substance, with the human subject poised heroically at the edge of a sweeping infinity, drawn to both absorption and separateness. The position of the narrator changes with the pull of these rival attractions.

This problem of positioning the narrator, not too close nor too distant, neither too involved nor wholly untouched, is not specific to any concern with nature; it is the familiar terrain of novel criticism. Is the narrator external (a moralist, a scientist, a bird watcher in a hide) and omniscient, striving to hold a disinterested perspective that, in Matthew Arnold's terms, transcends the "ordinary self" (Arnold, 94–95)? Or does the narrative voice belong to a character, involved in the action and therefore taking a self-interested, unreliable view? Or again, is the narrator somewhere in between, a character physically present at the scene but passive and marginal? Alternatively, narrative may be the work of a multiplicity of voices, in Bakhtinian exchange with each other, the dialogue emphasizing the partiality of each. When Donna Haraway demanded recently that scientific natural history writing should acknowledge its own "situatedness" (Haraway, 183–201), she was asking it to become more novelistic: asking scientists to take up positions inside the plot, as characters and narrators. The history of the realist novel can be plotted by looking at shifts in narrative position, and so can the history of nature writing.

Romantic treatments of landscape were a transforming influence on novels. In Wordsworth's poetry, to encounter scenes in nature is to come upon unexpected depths of feeling. The traveller in the mountains experiences moments of intense emotion, prompted by dramatic natural scenes, and is drawn to perceive his self as continuous with the world rather than separate from it. The paradox is that this recognition is a moment of pausing and self-consciousness that disengages this individual from process and movement. The watcher is held at the edge of the natural landscape, unable to re-enter it, and resume his walk, without relinquishing the self constituted by the act of watching.

From the mid-nineteenth century onward, there is a tradition of fiction, realistic or melodramatic, in which this version of the romantic sublime—this pause at the verge of sublimity—is thoroughly integrated with plot. Wordsworthian intimations deepened the established convention that landscapes in novels both influenced and signified the moods of characters. After romanticism, these landscapes became an expression of the unexpected, unconscious, or inarticulate potential of characters, often in plots building up to explosive and tragic climaxes. Place (usually mountain, moorland or craggy coast, the only plausibly wild terrain remaining in England, but sometimes fenland or woodland) came to dominate some novels, as a way of representing the complex relations between the external world and the unconscious forces at work in the characters. Setting, in this tradition, is both commentary and extended metaphor. A defining example is Emily Brontë's *Wuthering Heights*. In Thomas Hardy's Wessex novels, especially *The Return of the Native* and *The Woodlanders*, landscape becomes environment, constantly developing and seen from a complex mixture of perspectives. Hardy adds to the romantic experience of nature a Darwinian perception of ecological interdependency and destructive evolution.

Among mid-Victorian amateurs, there was a fashion for natural history, especially for pursuits that gave the enthusiast the position of a god gazing into a little world: rockpool dipping, insect collecting, fern cabinets, fossil hunting. This vogue was clearly associated with Darwinism, and before that with the new science of geology popularized by Charles Lyell, with its disturbing proposition that the earth was millions of years old. After Lyell, recorded human history, let alone the hopes and fears of individuals, seemed small against the immensity of time. After Darwin, individuals faced the possibility that their strongest desires and efforts were helpless and insignificant against the large-scale processes of evolutionary history, even that their emotions and aspirations were reflexes inherited from earlier evolutionary phases.

The liberal realist novel was extremely influential in this period, as the literary form most identified with systematic attempts to find secular moral seriousness after loss of faith. George Eliot is the writer who most defines this tradition. She and her lover, G. H. Lewes, were enthusiastic amateur biologists; Lewes wrote popular science as well as fiction and philosophy. George Eliot's narrator speaks from a vantage point outside the action: that of the cosmopolitan intellectual with a wide range of historical, scientific and philosophical perspectives, selecting a set of provincial, ordinary characters, as specimens. This makes the writing sound arrogant, but the variety of approaches taken is so rich, the narrator is so acutely aware of the danger of condescension, and the characters are allowed such power to confound expectations and rise out of character, that the result is an exceptionally varied set of exchanges between internal and external positions. Readers are asked to enter sympathetically into characters' viewpoints, while remaining aware of their own externality; successively they are drawn in and shut out. This complexity is the substance of the novels, their liberalism and their generosity. Its limitation (in political terms a serious one) shows when a viewpoint is approached that has too little shared vocabulary with the narrator for the exchange to begin. Such characters, who could not be imagined reading the novel, remain impenetrable and other.

George Eliot's work shows a similarly complex ambivalence toward nature, which both attracts and threatens her narrative persona. Rationality and moral self-restraint are opposed to the heedlessness and egotism to be found in nature; yet nature is also seen as vitality and flowing, impulsive sympathy, in contrast to the narrowness and callousness of social normality. Sympathy, the keynote for George Eliot, is often represented as instinctive and sudden, a natural feeling that wells up through the surface of convention and ego. Nature signifies, at different times in her novels, lost harmony, repressed passion, childish egotism and destructive ignorance. In these novels that contain both Arnoldian and Darwinian elements, animal instinct, especially sexual instinct, can be dangerously anarchic and in need of civilization, or, once released, it can be the source of unselfconscious happiness and health desired in the romantic tradition. In *The Mill on the Floss*, rivers and floods are used to show both possibilities.

In much of her work there is a powerful drive to escape the physical and intellectual confines of provincial rural places. The provincial in her work is often an Arnoldian provincial, narrow and intolerant, showing a lack of vision identified with animal insensibility. But, having fled, the rational, liberal, cosmopolitan sensibility turns its attention back to the place it has left, both in nostalgic desire for reabsorption and in idealistic search for an all-inclusive imaginative sympathy. The local world will have all that any world can show. In *Middlemarch*, Lydgate, the doctor, attempts to complete this circle. He is provincial in that he works in a provincial town, but cosmopolitan in his aspiration to make scientific discoveries out of his work with his patients there. By seeing them as specimens, he sees them as universal. Lydgate's work parallels that of Farebrother, a local vicar who is a passionate entomologist, and also that of the novelist herself. All three are collecting particular specimens from which to derive general principles. It is when Lydgate believes too much in his own detachment that he becomes an ordinary self, a character rather than a scientist or narrator. He then succumbs to a natural force, sexual attraction, which he does not after all stand above, and makes his mistake.

Charles Kingsley, a founder of Christian Socialism, wrote *Glaucus*, a handbook of marine biology that provided much of the material for *The Water-Babies*. Despite the muscular Christianity of this novel, its use of freshwater and marine biology to provide the cast for an evangelical allegory places it in the same vogue as fictions more persuaded by Darwinism.

It is in the novels of Thomas Hardy that many of these attitudes to nature find their most intense configuration. Hardy is a key figure for ecocritical readers now: an immensely powerful novelist of sexual and social relationships, passionately responsive to the natural world. Enduringly, Hardy shows the importance of novelistic elements in nature writing. His narrative techniques can provide an elaboration of Donna Haraway's ecocritical requirement that natural history writers should "situate" themselves and their knowledges rather than appearing to be objective and external.

The Woodlanders opens with a description of what would be seen by an unspecified "rambler" arriving in the place where the novel is set (pp. 41–49). Out of this guidebook introduction to the region and its landscape, the particular neighborhood of Little Hintock slowly comes into focus. After several pages, the "rambler," who until this point might be anyone and functions as a generalized reader, is identified as a particular character, Barber Percombe. Abruptly he is distant in social class from the implied reader. Ceasing to be the reader's proxy, as he was at the outset, he becomes a character in the scene, an object of the reader's gaze. This change is emphatic, but the new position is not stabilized. Hardy frequently shifts the position of the implied reader and of various proxy readers, who are at different times observers and active characters. His observers are never disembodied. They move continually between the positions of subject and object, never resting for long as either. Readers are thus shown a series of intermediate positions. Nature, similarly, is always shifting and alternating, appearing as a knot of emotional significances and as an object of scientific observation. Hardy's narrative perspective sometimes draws back, to take in a wide sweep of landscape, and sometimes zooms in close, so that a newt rustling in the woodland leaves as it prepares for hibernation is suddenly audible to the heightened senses of the anxious Grace Winterborne (p. 377). In this way, sometimes to the point of narrative rupture, Hardy raises questions about the legitimacy of the reader's external, voyeuristic gaze. He makes the reader long for, or fantasize, the possibility of intervention, and thus emphasizes the exclusion that is the price of the reader's leisure and safety. This technique also reveals the dependency of nature on those who observe and construct it.

In *The Return of the Native* and *The Woodlanders*, in particular, numerous responses to nature are interspersed. Nature is the unselfconscious, instinctual drive to pleasure, or it is a Darwinian economy of insensible, competitive struggle, or, drawing on both of these, it is a place of temporary refuge gained only through a deliberate relinquishing of the selfconsciousness and wide perception that novelistic narrative cannot forsake for long. When Clym Yeobright, in *The Return of the Native*, discovers that his eyesight is weak, and has to abandon his studies to be a schoolteacher, he takes work instead as a furze-cutter on the heath. Here he discovers an awareness of the small creatures that surround him on the heath, the bees, butterflies, grasshoppers, snakes and rabbits, forgotten since his childhood. This is his "return":

> His daily life was of a curious microscopic sort, his whole world being limited to a circuit of a few feet from his person. His familiars were creeping and winged things, and they seemed to enroll him in their band . . . The strange amber-coloured butterflies which Egdon produced, and which were never seen elsewhere, quivered in the breath of his lips . . . Litters of young rabbits came out from their forms to sun themselves upon hillocks, the hot beams blazing through the delicate tissue of each thin-fleshed ear, and firing it to a blood-red transparency in which the veins could be seen. None of them feared him. (p. 312)

Nature here is a paradise temporarily regained. In relinquishing his claims to higher vision (and in descending the social order), Yeobright rediscovers an unselfconsciousness that enables him to be happy. He has, with a striking literalness, come closer to nature. The "knowledge" he has cast off is tacitly compared to the "knowledge" Adam and Eve got from the forbidden fruit, which caused them to feel shame, and to be expelled from Paradise. But Hardy is insistent about the cost of this return. This closeness to nature means loss of larger perspectives—loss, for example, of the scientific perspective that might enable us to foresee and prevent ecological disaster. Yeobright becomes as vulnerable as the animals and insects that cannot see what surrounds their lives.

Psychological landscapes appear in less realistic genres also: in the detective and adventure stories of Arthur Conan Doyle, and in romantic mysteries such as Daphne Du Maurier's *Rebecca*, or today's "Mills and Boon" popular romantic love stories. Green and wild places function in romantic novels both as metaphorical representations of longed-for, passionate emotion and as real places of escape, where characters can meet dangerous lovers and make dashes for freedom. Alternatively, in the action or adventure genres, nature becomes an active character, because the human characters are not watchers but engaged, usually in struggle with it. Colonial adventure stories of exploration and hunting,

such as Rider Haggard's *She* and R. M. Ballantyne's *The Coral Island* and *The Gorilla Hunters*, which feature lurid descriptions of nature, are of this type. Joseph Conrad makes a powerful combination of the romantic and adventure traditions. In *Lord Jim* and *Typhoon*, the oceans and storms provide ordeals to test the characters, while functioning also as models of the unselfconscious singularity of purpose required of a ship's crew. In Conrad, the ship sailing on a deep tropical sea represents the conscious self steering itself precariously, carried by the much larger forces of unconscious drives and evolutionary history. In *Heart of Darkness*, equatorial African jungle plays the same part, so that colonialists can venture into the interior in search of the mythical "heart," unfaceable and already known.

In E. M. Forster's *The Longest Journey*, the woods and fields are places where characters, only dimly realizing that they want to, find escape from oppressive convention. At the climax of *Maurice* (completed 1914; published 1970), a lover reaches out to Maurice, rescuing him from the isolation and inhibition society has forced on him because of his homosexuality. This rescuer is Alec Scudder, a gamekeeper who, like that other fictional gamekeeper, Mellors, in D. H. Lawrence's *Lady Chatterley's Lover*, signifies closeness to nature and the uninhibited naturalness attributed to the working classes. Alec comes to Maurice's window from the woods, at night. Nature provides a safe place for the male lovers to meet, enabling Forster to claim for homosexuality a discourse of naturalness. In Forster's *A Passage To India*, the Indian environment, in woods, in caves or as an immensity either side of a thin strip of road, is a disturbing surround for the British colonialists. Nature here is a representation of the uncertainties and repressed sexuality that surround the imperial stronghold, and an actual site for the dangerous release of repressed desire. Features of classical pastoral are reproduced, sometimes overtly, in these novels. Nature is used as a powerful other to society and convention, at times as a refuge and at times as a place of adventure and self-discovery. Return to normality and urban space is necessary but painful. This is a pastoral cycle, of flight or adventure followed by return.

In these novels, as elsewhere, representations of nature have the same features as patriarchal representations of women, colonial representations of colonized peoples, and middle-class representations of working-class people. Aggressively defined as subordinate, the oppressed group is then identified with desires and emotions in the oppressor that have also been imprisoned and subordinated. Oppressed people become identified with nature against civilization, and body against mind. Relations with these people become, for the oppressor, an encounter with the forbidden, the enticingly but threateningly free and formless.

One instance is Kipling's *The Jungle Book*. In this fable, as in many colonial adventure stories, nature has a clean nobility against which the indigenous peoples are represented as venial, cowardly and in need of colonial rule. A routinely racist example of such legitimating fiction (which persists in some television wildlife documentaries even now) is Percy Fitzpatrick's *Jock of the Bushveld*. The Empire seemed to give British middle-class colonial administrators the opportunity to become the aristocracy of a society modelled upon the social structure of home. Kipling offered them a myth of a renewed, primal aristocracy, drawing its energy and legitimacy from nature's hierarchies rather than from the exhausted feudalism that had lorded over them in Britain.

Mowgli, rescued and nurtured by wolves after a tiger has chased him from his parents, grows up as a noble savage, apparently with far more prowess and generosity than if he had remained with his people. After his defeat of the old ruling class, represented by the renegade, dishonourable and cruel aristocrat, the tiger Shere Khan, he assumes a role that represents Kipling's vision of a revitalized, natural aristocracy. Mowgli offers the colonialist an idealized picture of colonial rule. Leading the animals, he lives with them in their territory, is initiated into their culture and is willing to learn their skills, but he is always superior in his abilities. Always, finally, they drop their eyes in submission to him. In contrast to the village, where authority has degenerated, the jungle is represented as a chivalric society with a strict code of honor. Although some animals prey on others, they all share a brotherhood. A common greeting guarantees safety. The wolves are known as "the Free People," as if they were a utopian community (their names and rituals were subsequently adopted by Baden Powell's Boy Scout movement). Kipling is attempting to show the idealized form he wanted the British Empire to have, but, as it is the Empire, he is unable to exclude a feudal hierarchy or caste system. Some animals, such as jackals and dholes, are seen as unfit for membership of the brotherhood. Most despised of all are the monkeys, the "Bandar-Log," who kidnap Mowgli early in the story. Insistently, Kipling represents them as the masses, the unruly mob. Repeated emphasis is placed upon their fickleness and feeble powers of concentration. They are vain, slovenly and lazy, but dangerous because of their huge numbers and the way they can be seized with collective fury. In everyday life, the other animals disdain to notice the monkeys' presence in the treetops. The monkeys' real crime is that they are counterfeit men, a lower order that threatens to obliterate hierarchy (Fitzgerald is troubled by this, too, when he writes about baboons). While Mowgli offers aristocratic patronage, the monkeys threaten revolution, and Kipling is both afraid and contemptuous of this.

At much the same time as Kipling, H. G. Wells also problematized the boundaries between human and animal, and then recoiled in disgust, in *The Island of Doctor Moreau*. Wells expresses fears about a technological and democratic future. Anxiety about the erasure of hierarchies in an emerging modern society focuses on the capacity of technology to change nature. Dr. Moreau, on his sinister, colonized island, has performed vivisection on a collection of captive animals, turning them into half-human creatures. It proves impossible, however, to endow them with the docile, liberal consciences appropriate to their new status. They begin to degenerate, their animal behavior returning in destructive, distorted forms. In a bitter effort to control them, Moreau resorts to a brutally authoritarian regime, which confuses and shames their human feelings while failing to subdue their animal impulses. The novel warns that modern totalitarianism may come about because modern society has separated people from their instinctive nature, which will return in malignant forms. The novel is pessimistic about attempts to civilize the masses, who will become confused and vindictive once taken out of their natural place.

A fin de siècle yearning for a lost, feudal nature as an alternative to modernity expresses itself in the novels of Richard Jefferies and W. H. Hudson. Not all forms taken by these misgivings about industrial capitalist modernity were conservative. The Pre-Raphaelite utopian pastoral of William Morris's *News from Nowhere* became a source of pastoral elements in British socialism before late twentieth-century environmentalism took shape. This socialist tradition of nature drew upon Marxist constructions of the natural state as both pre-capitalist paradise and post-capitalist utopia. Socialist conceptions of the countryside as common property developed with the new popularity among the urban working classes of cycling and rambling. In the 1930s, this interest in nature produced challenges to land ownership in the mass-trespass protests, demanding access for leisure.

After Hardy, D. H. Lawrence took nature writing further still from the liberal-romantic tradition of mediating, self-conscious contemplation. Roger Ebbatson says that "the keynote of Nature in Lawrence is energy and movement" (p. 28). For Lawrence, the stance of self-conscious observation, the transfixed yearning for absorption, is a sickness, a distortion brought about by industrial modernity.

As a working-class writer hostile both to nostalgic, gentlemanly nature writing and industrial modernity, Lawrence is intensely ambivalent toward industrial capitalism. He hates it for its enslaving and dehumanizing effects, but loves and eroticizes its ruthless, unreflective power. He aligns nature strongly with the instinctual and healthy, but is fascinated by the brutality of this instinctiveness when thwarted or malformed. While Ursula Brangwen finds a powerful breaking of her locked emotions when she encounters and outfaces horses at the end of *The Rainbow*, Gudrun Brangwen shows symptoms of dangerous frustration when she maddens cattle by dancing amongst them in *Women in Love*, as does Gerald Crich violently forcing his horse to stand close to a passing train in the same novel (pp. 167–170, 110–113). Lawrence returns repeatedly to this outfacing, and imposing of will, that he sees as a way of starting movement and breaking the deadlock imposed by liberal self-consciousness.

A similar ambivalence, looking to different solutions, reveals itself in the modernism of Wyndham Lewis. His 1917 story "Cantleman's Spring Mate," depicts a humanity caught between two equally mocking and nullifying forces, nature and the machine (of which World War I is a logical expression). No respite is to be found from either. Cantleman, the protagonist, is at an army training camp waiting to be sent to the front line. Menaced by the interchangeability of the natural and the mechanical, he makes himself callous and sardonically mechanical in response, but as Paul Edwards has commented (pp. 30–32), this affords him no victory, since both nature and the war are insensible of his gesture and merely absorb him into their processes. Another Modernist approach to nature is Vir-

ginia Woolf's, particularly in *To the Lighthouse* and *The Waves*, where it is the motion of nature, its capacity to dissolve and remake forms, that both liberates and threatens.

Strongly associated with reaction to World War I was the emergence of the anti-urban, anti-modern 1930s ruralists, and their involvement with fascism. Nature writing in Britain has often since been associated, disastrously, with this period; that is one reason for the mistrust of nature writing shown by many recent writers and critics. The key figure in this association is Henry Williamson, with his novel-sequence *A Chronicle of Ancient Sunlight*, and his animal stories for children, such as the famous *Tarka the Otter*. Williamson saw World War I as a symptom of industrial modernity with its cataclysmic disruption of small, cohesive communities. As a result, he constructed nature as healing refuge, and defined his interest in nature in terms of local rootedness and opposition to cosmopolitan modernity. Williamson appeals to mythical pre-capitalist values, involving attachment to place, local dialect, historical continuity, mistrust of outsiders and stability of social hierarchies and bonds of loyalty. He does not have Lawrence's ambivalent, sometimes Freudian interest in the energies released by complex confrontations between nature and modernity: or, if occasionally he does, this interest registers only to be disowned in angry foreclosure (as sometimes happens in Lawrence, also).

Williamson's animal heroes, Tarka, Salar the salmon, Brock the badger, and others, possess an unconscious vitality, courage and unhesitating predatoriness that legitimates the remorseless way in which they, in turn, are hunted by men. These are violent hunting stories, bringing the North American tradition of Jack London and Roderick Haig-Brown to the more domestic English countryside. Otter hunting with hounds, celebrated and popularized by *Tarka the Otter*, only became widespread in Britain in the inter-war years, as part of a self-conscious ruralist vogue of resistance to suburban culture. Although Mary Webb's romantic novels, with their dialect and archaisms, were also taken up by rural revivalists in the 1920s, they offer a radically opposite picture to Williamson's. A bull about to be baited is described in *Precious Bane* as if it were a human baby (pp. 143–151): a clearer riposte to Williamson's mystique of toughness is hard to imagine. *Gone to Earth* makes a melodramatic critique of fox hunting. A different critique of ruralism, both Webb's and

Lawrence's, comes in Stella Gibbons's glorious parody of the solemnities of nature writing in *Cold Comfort Farm.*

Williamson was a prominent supporter of Oswald Mosley's British Union of Fascists, and this interwar period gave literary nature writing a set of political associations that had to be disowned. This was one reason why influential representations of nature, in post-war British culture, were predominantly found in television documentaries, novels for children and handbooks for naturalists, rather than in literary novels. Environmentalism now calls for a new alignment.

Socialist interest in nature continued in the twentieth century with George Orwell and Raymond Williams. George Orwell's *Nineteen Eighty-Four* sets out a vision of a future totalitarian state in which the ruling party attempts to extend its control into every corner of life. Rebellion comes from anything natural and uncontrollable. Winston Smith's resistance finds its first expression in his love affair with Julia, which is consummated in woodland, outside the city and beyond the reach of the all-intrusive telescreens: "Not merely the love of one person, but the animal instinct, the simple undifferentiated desire: that was the force that would tear the Party to pieces. He pressed her down upon the grass, among the fallen bluebells" (p. 132). Later it seems that at this moment they probably were, after all, under surveillance. The extent of the party's reach into natural territory shows, for Orwell, what is most terrifyingly new about modern totalitarianism. Winston places what hope he has in the "proles," the working-class masses of *Nineteen Eighty-Four*, because they apparently retain an instinctive, animal life that party ideology cannot penetrate. Orwell reverses the Marxist drive toward working-class consciousness; it is precisely the unconsciousness of the proles, their naturalness, that protects them from being possessed by the party. It is also this unconsciousness that will prevent them from rising in revolution. In Orwell, the Wordsworthian ambivalence toward unconscious Nature, the need to hold that position of poised externality, becomes the ambivalence of a middle-class radical toward working-class people. His desire to be one with them is countered by an equal need to be clearly apart from them.

From the interwar years onward, the tradition of landscape-dominated psychological novels was continued by such writers as John Cowper Powys, William Golding and John Fowles. In recent writing, a good example of this sort of involvement with nature is Graham Swift's *Waterland*, where the process of artificial drainage and silting that produces the ecology of the East Anglian Fens provides a physical environment, a history, and a complex metaphor. Jenny Diski's *Rainforest* and William Boyd's *Brazzaville Beach* both approach environmentalist field biology from the viewpoint of an interest in obsession. J. G. Ballard began his career writing apocalyptic ecological science fictions, such as *The Drought* and *The Crystal World*, and later produced a powerful realization of the eroticism of technology in *Crash*. More recently he has returned to attack environmentalism with crude hostility, in *Rushing to Paradise*. Ian McEwan's *The Child in Time* looks to nature, childhood and non-linear time for values capable of surviving and countering the Thatcherite period. Julian Barnes's *A History of the World in 10½ Chapters* repeatedly traps its reader in the undecidability of fears about environmental crisis. A. S. Byatt, in *Angels and Insects*, revisits Victorian nature writing in order to uncover the repressions associated with it, and explore the different economies of masculine and feminine versions of nature. In *Babel Tower*, she takes a similar approach to early studies, in the 1960s, of genetic coding, in snails. All these novels approach nature and environmentalism obliquely, with their main concern being to contextualize it, or explore its psychology. An environmentalist novel, approaching other areas of experience from an ecological sensibility, is still to come.

Selected Works and Further Reading

Arnold, Matthew, *Culture and Anarchy,* London: Smith, Elder, 1869; New York: Macmillan, 1875

Ballantyne, Robert Michael, *The Coral Island,* New York and London: T. Nelson, 1858

———, *The Gorilla Hunters,* New York and London: T. Nelson, 1861

Ballard, James Graham, *Crash,* New York: Farrar, Straus & Giroux, 1973; London: Jonathan Cape, 1973

———, *The Crystal World,* New York: Farrar, Straus & Giroux, 1966; London: Jonathan Cape, 1966

———, *The Drought,* London: Jonathan Cape, 1965; Boston: Gregg, 1976

———, *Rushing to Paradise,* London: Flamingo, 1994; New York: Picador, 1995

Barnes, Julian, *A History of the World in 10½ Chapters,* New York: Knopf, 1989; London: Jonathan Cape, 1989

Boyd, William, *Brazzaville Beach,* New York: William Morrow, 1990; London: Sinclair-Stevenson, 1990

Brontë, Emily, *Wuthering Heights,* London: Thomas Cautley Newby, 1847

Byatt, Antonia Susan, *Angels and Insects,* New York: Random House, 1992; London: Chatto and Windus, 1992

———, *Babel Tower,* New York: Random House, 1996; London: Chatto and Windus, 1996

Conrad, Joseph, *Heart of Darkness,* Edinburgh, Scotland: W. Blackwood, 1899

———, *Lord Jim,* New York: Franklin Watts, 1900; London: W. Blackwood, 1900

———, *Typhoon and Other Tales,* London: Heinemann, 1903

Darwin, Charles, *The Origin of Species,* New York: Modern Library, 1859; London: John Murray, 1859

Diski, Jenny, *Rainforest,* London: Methuen, 1987

Doyle, Arthur Conan, *The Lost World,* London: John Murray, 1912

———, *Tales of Terror and Mystery,* London: John Murray, 1922

———, *When the World Screamed and Other Stories,* London: John Murray, 1968

Du Maurier, Daphne, *Rebecca,* New York: Doubleday, Doran, 1938; London: Victor Gollancz, 1938

Ebbatson, Roger, *Lawrence and the Nature Tradition,* Atlantic Highlands, New Jersey: Humanities, 1980; Brighton, England: Harvester, 1980

Edwards, Paul, *Wyndham Lewis: Art and War,* London: Lund Humphries, in association with the Wyndham Lewis Memorial Trust, 1992

Eliot, George, *Middlemarch,* Philadelphia: Lippincott, 1872; London: Virtue, 1872

———, *The Mill on the Floss,* New York: Lovell, Coryell, 1860; London: Virtue, 1860

Fitzpatrick, Percy, *Jock of the Bushveld,* New York and London: Longmans, Green, 1907

Forster, Edward Morgan, *The Longest Journey,* London: E. Arnold, 1907

———, *Maurice,* New York: Norton, 1971; London: E. Arnold, 1971

———, *A Passage to India,* New York: Harcourt, Brace, 1924; London: E. Arnold, 1924

Gibbons, Stella, *Cold Comfort Farm,* New York and London: Longmans, Green, 1932

Haggard, Henry Rider, *She,* New York: F. F. Lovell, 1887; London: Longmans, Green, 1887

Haraway, Donna J., *Simians, Cyborgs and Women: The Reinvention of Nature,* New York: Routledge, 1991; London: Free Association, 1991

Hardy, Thomas, *The Return of the Native,* New York: Henry Holt, 1878; London: Smith, Elder, 1878

———, *Tess of the D'Urbervilles,* New York and London: Harper & Brothers, 1893

———, *The Woodlanders,* New York and London: Macmillan, 1887

Kingsley, Charles, *Glaucus, or, The Wonders of the Shore,* Boston: Ticknor and Fields, 1855; Cambridge, Macmillan, 1855

———, *The Water-Babies: A Fairy Tale for a Land-Baby,* London: Macmillan, 1863

Kipling, Rudyard, *The Jungle Book,* New York: Century, 1894; London: Macmillan, 1894

Lawrence, David Herbert, *Lady Chatterley's Lover,* New York: Grosset and Dunlap, 1928

———, *The Rainbow,* New York: B. W. Huebsch, 1915; London: Heinemann, 1915

———, *Women in Love,* New York: Viking, 1920

Lewis, Wyndham, *Unlucky for Pringle: Unpublished and Other Stories,* New York: D. Lewis, 1973; London: Vision, 1973

McEwan, Ian, *The Child in Time,* London: Jonathan Cape, 1987; New York: Penguin, 1988

Morris, William, *News from Nowhere,* Boston: Roberts, 1890

Orwell, George, *Nineteen Eighty-Four,* New York: New American Library, 1949; London: Secker & Warburg, 1949

Swift, Graham, *Waterland,* New York: Poseidon, 1983; London: Heineman, 1983

Webb, Mary, *Gone to Earth,* New York: Dutton, 1917; London: Jonathan Cape, 1917

———, *Precious Bane,* London: Cape, 1924

Wells, Herbert George, *The Island of Doctor Moreau,* New York: Stone and Kimball, 1896; London: Heinemann, 1896

Williamson, Henry, *The Henry Williamson Animal Saga,* London: Macdonald, 1960

———, *Tarka the Otter: His Joyful Water-*

Life and Death in the Country of the Two Rivers, New York and London: Putnam's, 1927

———, *Young Phillip Maddison,* London: Macdonald, 1953

Woolf, Virginia, *To the Lighthouse,* New York: Modern Library, 1927; London: Hogarth, 1927

———, *The Waves,* New York: Harcourt, Brace, 1931; London: Hogarth, 1931

Environmental Literature:
The English Descriptive Prose Tradition

Jeremy Hooker

The English descriptive prose tradition consists of diverse arts of seeing the environment. While writers had been making tours and
discovering England since Tudor times, the tradition was strongly influenced by a new aesthetics of landscape in the second half of the
eighteenth century. The ways in which writers
came to view the country were defined by visual
art, especially the contrasting models of Dutch
realism and idealized, classical landscapes.
Native artists were among the first tourists to
open up parts of England to travellers with a
taste for scenery. The descriptive tradition in the
eighteenth century was associated with the
manipulation of nature for human purposes. It
had links with landscape gardening, which
entailed reshaping the natural world in accordance with changing ideals of the relationship
between nature, or the wild, and the cultivated
environment of the gentleman's country house.
Throughout the tradition, descriptions of the
environment are not neutral, but imply values
and meanings; keywords such as landscape and
place and nature are the locus of complicated,
and often conflicting, feelings and ideas.

William Gilpin, through books based on his
sketching tours in areas such as South Wales,
Cumberland and Westmorland, and the Highlands in the 1770s, popularized the idea of the
picturesque. The idea had an enormous influence upon the Romantic taste in scenery; it also
affected, often through reactions against it,
much of the subsequent history of verbal and
visual description. As a way of seeing that pictures the world, and directs the seer to reassem-
ble what is seen according to certain artistic
ideals, the picturesque may conflict with respect
for nature as an object of scientific enquiry,
and with the reverence for Nature as a power
that is a defining characteristic of Romanticism.

Thomas Gray, in describing his tour in the Lakes
in his 1775 *Journal*, wrote with the knowledge
of a naturalist, but also displayed the art of a
connoisseur of beautiful scenery, which he
viewed in a Claude glass. The works of man fit
into such a view only if they accord with the
ideal. Wordsworth, in his *Guide to the Lakes*,
quotes a passage in which Gray says of the Vale
of Grasmere, "No flaring gentleman's-house nor
garden-walls break in upon the repose of this little unsuspected *paradise*, but all is peace."
Wordsworth exclaims that, if Gray were still
alive, he would "have lamented the probable
intrusion of a railway," and "swarms of pleas-
ure-hunters, most of them thinking that they do
not fly fast enough through the country which
they have come to see" (pp. 162–163). To
Wordsworth, who wrote his *Guide* "for the
Minds of Persons of taste" (p. 1), the Lake District vales are "temples of Nature, temples built
by the Almighty" (p. 162).

Problems that would recur in the subsequent
history of descriptions of the English countryside are implicit in Wordsworth's appeal to
Gray. The rise of urban and industrial society in
England, facilitated by the construction of the
railways, heightened the contrast between town
and country, and increased the attraction of the
latter as a source of peace and spiritual sustenance, which the Wordsworthian vision of
nature did much to foster in a period of declining faith in established religion. Easier access to
the country, from the towns, increased tension
between the privileged, the men of property and
of taste, and those who viewed the country as a
common culture belonging to the people as a
whole.

Love of place, embodied in careful study of
the entire life of a district, is central to the English descriptive tradition. The first and most

influential exponent of "parochial history," consisting "of natural productions and occurrences as well as antiquities," was Gilbert White, curate of Selborne in Hampshire. White was a man who shared the educated tastes of his time; he had a literary sensibility, and he was "an admirer of prospects," who lamented the absence of church spires "in my own country; for such objects are very necessary ingredients in an elegant landscape" (p. 68). More importantly, however, he was a pioneer, who observed nature closely, with a scientific detachment that harmonized with his love of the subject. *The Natural History of Selborne* consists of letters in which he shared his observations with two distinguished scientists, and is shaped subtly as a literary work. The varied district of Selborne was his microcosm of a nature in which many facts remained to be discovered: "It is, I find, in zoology as it is in botany: all nature is so full, that that district produces the greatest variety which is the most examined" (p. 63). And White made discoveries, in the "fullness" of the environment as a whole.

In more ways than one, White's classic study depicts a harmonious world, of which the observer, with his scientific methods and his sense of wonder, is a part. While White was embarrassed by his uncertainty whether swallows and martins migrated, or went into hiding during the winter, he did not doubt that they "obeyed the strong impulse . . . imprinted on their minds by their great Creator" (p. 72). His close attention to the entire life of a locality is White's greatest gift to writers who follow him in the prose tradition. Given the unsettling experience of the Victorian and modern periods, however, it is not surprising that, in the words of Donald Worster, "within a century after the publication of White's book, Selborne had become a symbol of refuge for the homeless mind of Englishmen and Americans" (p. 14).

William Cobbett, in his writings about life in rural England, was motivated in part by the need to look into the causes that unsettled people, literally, from their home ground. Cobbett was a farmer, who claimed to have "no idea of *picturesque beauty* separate from *fertility of soil*." He was also a political journalist, whose travels on horseback through the southern shires in the 1820s (the tours that resulted in the original edition of *Rural Rides*) enabled him to gather facts for his campaign against the system, developed during the Napoleonic Wars, which had pauperized the rural labourer, and replaced "a resident *native* gentry, attached to the soil," with "new

men," who look "to the soil only for rents, viewing it as a mere object of speculation" (p. 38).

Cobbett was sensitive to natural beauty, but perceived it also as a common right. Delighting in spring in woodland country, he says singing birds are "amongst the means which Providence has benignantly appointed to sweeten the toils by which food and raiment are produced." "These," he continues, "the English Ploughman could once hear without the sorrowful reflection that he himself was *a pauper* . . . Shall he never have the due reward of his labour!" (p. 64). Cobbett's rage against injustice toward others is the more moving in a man with a strong sense of self. Cobbett frequently sees himself as a boy in the country that he rides through—in the growth of an oak tree, for example, or in other little boys set to keep birds off the cherries. What he sees, therefore, is personal continuity, but in contrast to ruinous change, brought about by a system that in his view has damaged the relationship he once knew, between landowners and farmers and labourers, and between humankind and the land. Cobbett's political radicalism is an important element within the prose tradition. There is also a strong tendency for writers in the tradition to associate childhood with an ideal of the past, and to blend (or muddle) fantasy and reality.

Whereas Cobbett speaks vigorously on matters of common interest to other men and women, writers of diaries or journals speak first to the self, and the reader, when invited to share the experience, enters into an inner world. In the Romantic and Victorian periods, journal and diary and letters, and nature essay and sketch, are forms in which personal visions of the environment take shape and are communicated. Their importance reflects the isolation of the individual in communion with nature, and of the self communing with the self, which comes in the course of the nineteenth century to form a significant part of the modern experience. A number of writers who contributed to the prose tradition in these forms were primarily poets. They include John Clare who showed, in his letters and prose descriptions, a knowledge of his district as intimate as White's knowledge of Selborne; Coleridge, in his Notebooks, who sought in his perceptions of natural phenomena to understand the relation between nature and the human mind; and Gerard Manley Hopkins, whose precise and finely wrought prose "inscapes" are one of the most exquisite arts of seeing produced by any Victorian.

Dorothy Wordsworth's *Journal* is of major importance in the Romantic perception of nature, both in its inherent quality as a literary work, and in the influence of her way of seeing upon her brother's poetry. Coleridge was impressed by: "Her eye watchful in minutest observation of nature." Her prose descriptions have a vivid immediacy; she notes colors, sounds, effects of light, weathers, actions and processes, and responds with quick and sensitive feeling. Like later journal writers, such as Hopkins and Frances Kilvert, she seeks the precise word, or image, to convey her vital sensing of the natural and human life she sees around her. She asks scientific questions; and she also mixes gothic images ("ivy twisting round the oaks like bristled serpents," [p. 1]) with accurate observation. Her *Journal* records leisurely walks, alone or with William or friends; walks in which she seeks natural "bowers" from which to view the scene or prospect, but in which she also sees a working landscape, and looks tenderly on human beings as well as plants and other creatures. In her writing, elements of the picturesque consort with a much more dynamic vision; she is happy "we cannot shape the huge hills, or carve out the valleys according to our fancy" (p. 13). In this mood, she writes: "Above rose the Coniston Fells in their own shape and colour. Not Man's hills but all for themselves the sky and the clouds and a few wild creatures" (p. 115).

As well as seeing wild nature, Dorothy Wordsworth herself was seen as "wild." In "Tintern Abbey," Wordsworth paid tribute to "the shooting lights / Of thy wild eyes," and referred to her "wild ecstasies." De Quincey described her as "the very wildest (in the sense of the most natural) person I have ever known." Both woman and the wild nature to which Dorothy Wordsworth was likened were idealized, at the same time as they were marginalized in the nineteenth century. As woman became the ideal other, identified with home and the domestic virtues, nature was seen increasingly as a refuge from the urban and industrial world, rather than as a working part of the common culture.

Nathaniel Hawthorne, after visiting the Lake District in 1855, wrote: "On the rudest surface of English earth, there is seen the effect of centuries of civilization, so that you do not quite get at naked Nature anywhere. And then every point of beauty is so well known, and has been described so much, that one must needs look through other people's eyes, and feel as if he were seeing a picture rather than a reality"

(Frick, 37). This is an American writer's perception of "English earth"; the native tradition, exemplified by Gilbert White, finds nature in local detail. It is true, however, that lack of contact with "naked Nature," or the wild, was felt increasingly by English writers in the Victorian period. One response to the resulting claustrophobic atmosphere of an urban and industrialized society was to seek out marginalized groups and out-of-the-way places, which could be identified with freedom.

This can be seen in the writings of George Borrow, based upon his wanderings among gypsies, or his explorations in "Wild Wales," as he called his book published in 1862. Wild places, however, could also be places in the mind, and in this respect, too, Borrow represents an important development in the prose tradition. He creates in his books a persona, a colorful, larger-than-life figure, which accords with what Edward Thomas called Borrow's "country of his soul," his "imaginative country, the product of his studies and of his temperament"(*Literary Pilgrim*, 238).

Borrow was a great walker, and walking that plays an important part in the Wordsworthian poetic tradition also helps to define the forms as well as the subject (things seen in the course of a walk) of prose writings. In Borrow's case, the walker becomes a somewhat mythic figure, whose adventures introduce the reader to a mysterious country peopled by wilder or freer spirits. The very different tone and style of Mary Russell Mitford, in the sketches collected in *Our Village*, may be seen in the invitation: "Will you walk with me through our village, courteous reader?" (p. 3). Miss Mitford's walks are occasions for meeting and describing people, and while the title of the collection indicates the sense of community and neighborliness, which was part of its appeal for middle-class readers in a society that often failed to realize these ideals, her delight in life and human character is as vitalizing in its way as Borrow's adventures.

English writing about nature in the nineteenth century increasingly compensated for what it was felt Progress pushed to the margins or destroyed. As well as the sense of mystery associated with wild nature, this included spiritual values (both religious meaning found in a deified Nature and the inner realm of personal experience), and ideals of community that counteracted what Friedrich Engels and other political commentators saw as the atomized individualism produced by capitalism. With the

1859 publication of Darwin's *The Origin of Species* and the dissemination of the idea of life as a war for survival among competing species, the view of nature darkened, and at the same time the pressure upon writers to supply a compensating vision of the environment increased. The prose tradition was in any case a complicated one, in which scientific observation and mysticism were by no means necessarily antagonistic to one another.

As the realm of unexplored nature diminished, the Victorians with their passion for natural history discovered, through the microscope and in marginal locations, such as the seashore, ways of enlarging the wild. This was not always an arena for agonies of religious doubt. In the writings of Philip Henry Gosse and Charles Kingsley, for example, the "strangeness" of nature (in a rock pool, for example) excites admiration of "the handiwork of the ever blessed God" (Johnson, 281), and serves to provide moral lessons for fallen man. Kingsley looked back too, and in "The Fens," published in 1869 at a time when drainage had changed the area, lingered over "the wild nature, the mystery, the majesty . . . which haunted the deep fens for many a hundred years" (Johnson, 294). This idyll also exemplifies the way in which for some Victorians the discoveries of geology about formative processes underlying the landscape, and the age of the earth, increased their sense of mystery and majesty in the Creation. For many others, such as John Ruskin, the geologists helped to undermine natural theology.

There are two principal ways in which Ruskin's achievement is crucial to the prose tradition. The first is in his emphasis "that the greatest thing a human soul ever does in this world is to *see* something" (p. 404), and in his own descriptions of mountains and rocks and water and clouds. The second is in his rejection of the picturesque as false and immoral, a way of seeing that idealizes without regard to the human condition of the subject. Ruskin described landscape as "the ruling passion of my life" (p. 13); but from his studies of art and nature he developed a moral vision of the whole of human existence: "you cannot love the real sun, that is to say physical light and colour, rightly, unless you love the spiritual sun, that is to say justice and truth, rightly" (Hewison, 201). It was a vision that, working upon strains in Ruskin's personality, produced a nightmare sense of what man, through an economic system based on exploitation, was doing to himself and

to the environment in the second half of the nineteenth century. From Cobbett to Ruskin and William Morris and beyond, ideas of what is natural constitute a major element within radical criticisms of the social and political system.

Richard Jefferies was another Victorian writer who developed his art of seeing into a moral vision. Jefferies is the key figure linking the parish history of Gilbert White to later writers, and the conservation movement of the twentieth century. Born on a small farm at Coate in Wiltshire in 1848, Jefferies drew on his knowledge of the nature and rural life of his surroundings to establish himself as a journalist, and the author of such books as *The Gamekeeper at Home* and *Wild Life in a Southern County*. The relative success of these books and others of the same kind was due to the growth in the Victorian period of an urban middle-class readership, no longer "bound to the soil," as, in many cases, their ancestors had been, but attracted to the countryside as actual or armchair tourists. In his vivid descriptions of wild life, his depictions of rural customs and characters, and his analyses of the conditions of agriculture, Jefferies gave such readers what they wanted. From early on, Jefferies had a message, too. At the end of *The Amateur Poacher*, he wrote: "Let us get out of these indoor narrow modern days, whose twelve hours somehow have become shortened, into the sunlight and the pure wind. A something that the ancients called divine can be found and felt there still."

To Edward Thomas, growing up in the London suburbs in the 1880s, these words "were a gospel, an incantation" (*Childhood*, 134). Jefferies' nature mysticism achieved much fuller expression in his spiritual autobiography, *The Story of My Heart*. His mysticism, his way of seeing and his style had a considerable, and mixed, effect upon later writers in the rural tradition. Some, like Henry Williamson and, to some extent, Edward Thomas, identified with the isolation of the obscure genius, the "worshipper of earth" (Jeffries, *Landscapes*, 290) who also came to emphasize the gulf between the human mind and a designless nature. In another mode, Jefferies was an explorer of unknown England, a writer who drew a conscious parallel between contemporary explorations in Africa and his discoveries of wild life in hedges and ditches. Both W. H. Hudson (who was brought up on the Argentinian pampas, and moved to England in 1869) and Edward Thomas were to follow Jefferies in this mode, writing "rambling books." The phrase is one Thomas applied to books by Hudson, and it nicely denotes books, such as Hudson's *Hampshire Days* and *Afoot in England*, and Thomas's *In Pursuit of Spring*, describing what the writer had seen and thought in his journeys in the English countryside.

Initially, Jefferies had looked with a naturalist's eye at his human neighbours, as well as at wildlife. He launched himself as a spokesman for the farmers' interests with a letter to *The Times* in which he described "the Wiltshire agricultural labourer" with clinical detachment. Later, sympathy informed his vision. In his essay, "One of the New Voters," for example, Jefferies paints a remarkable picture of "a woman labouring in a harvest-field" (*Landscape*, 259). It is, indeed, a word-painting, but the aesthetic vision, quickened by Jefferies' feeling for ideal female beauty, penetrates to "the realities of rural life behind the scenes." As he demonstrates: "The wheat is beautiful, but human life is labour" (p. 260).

Jefferies is important to the prose tradition not only because of what he wrote, but also because of what others made of him. This is true of other writers too, especially White and Cobbett. It was Edward Thomas, in particular, who, in the years before the First World War, mapped the descriptive tradition. Thomas not only wrote books or essays about Borrow and White and Cobbett and Clare and others; he also made Jefferies over as a mythic figure, describing him, in relation to his landscape, as "the genius, the human expression, of this country, emerging from it, not to be detached from it any more than the curves of some statues from their maternal stone" (*Richard Jefferies*, 1). The myth expresses the longing of its maker: the young man from London, educated at Oxford, influenced by Walter Pater as well as Jefferies, who went to live in the country, as a writer, at a time when rural life was in decay. Thomas is important as a poet and a literary critic; his rambling books, such as *The Heart of England* and *In Pursuit of Spring*, invite adverse comment in comparison with both Jefferies's and Hudson's. Thomas's self-consciousness devitalizes his natural vision; he is not a naturalist, like Hudson; and he lacks the confidence of Hudson's animism and Jefferies's mysticism. It is however a strength of Thomas's prose writings about the country that he is able to analyze the weakness of his position. He knows that for him southern England is "a kind of home, as I think it is more than any other to those modern people who belong nowhere" (*South Country*, 7). He is aware that "only a rarefied conscious appreciation is made possible by detachment and the severing of all bonds of necessity" (*Country*, 31).

The question "where man belongs," in the title of one of Harold J. Massingham's books, is central to the prose tradition in the twentieth century. It begins earlier, of course, with writers who, like Clare and Jefferies, see their home ground with eidetic memory, and in the light of nostalgia, because they have moved (or have been removed) from it. Few writers after White and Cobbett write from a sense of their continuous existence in one district or region. George Sturt inherited a family business, a wheelwright's shop, that served his rural society. His writings, however, are those of an intellectual, who values the men who work for him because they "belong" to the tradition, as he does not; and who modernizes the business, and writes books looking back to rural life as he believes it once was.

Edward Thomas wrote: "*There is nothing left for us to rest upon,* nothing great, venerable, or mysterious, which can take us out of ourselves, and give us that more than human tranquillity now to be seen in a few old faces of a disappearing generation" (*Country*, 6). Respect and even reverence for the people of "a disappearing generation"—for shepherds and craftsmen for example—is strong in Thomas's country books, in Hudson's *A Shepherd's Life*, and in Sturt's *The Wheelwright's Shop* and books about "Bettesworth," and in H. J. Massingham's books. It is patently a genuine emotion, and it helps to produce valuable documentary accounts of rural life. In practice, however, it is often shadowed by a kind of primitivism, a way of seeing and feeling by which the writer projects onto his rural subject qualities, such as "rootedness," of which he feels he has been deprived, by civilization. V. S. Pritchett's description of George Orwell as "a writer who has 'gone native' in his own country" (Gervais, 158) applies equally to the tendency of writers in the tradition, such as Hudson and Massingham, to assess "native" types, and compare "countrymen" and "townsmen."

Through its use by F. R. Leavis and Denys Thompson in *Culture and Environment*, Sturt's idea of "the organic community" contributed to an influential critique of "mass culture." Like Sturt, Massingham wrote lovingly of country crafts and people; in numerous books, he wrote with knowledge and passion about English landscapes. Massingham deployed his archaeological and historical ideas to evolve a vision of the integrated region, in which land and people and religion form an interlocking whole. In *Remembrance*, he described his "ultimate disengagement from urbanism" as "the most important event in my life" (p. 4). His corresponding engagement was with an idea of "the organic life." Other modern uses of tradition may be seen in the non-fictional writings of the Powys brothers, John Cowper, Llewelyn, and T. F., each of whom, in his different way, bases his philosophy on a religious apprehension of nature.

A certain distance from the subject, implicit in the position of observer or onlooker, the man or woman who is an incomer to the country, characterizes by far the larger part of the prose tradition in the twentieth century. To it, we owe valuable documentary works, such as the books of George Ewart Evans, and Ronald Blythe's *Akenfield*. In almost every instance, the record receives a literary shaping; which was also true of Gilbert White's letters. Often, even when an invaluable record of past life in the country is written by one who participated fully in it, as in the case of Flora Thompson's books about Juniper Hill, collected under the title *Lark Rise to Candleford*, the author adopts a distancing technique, such as the projection of a semi-fictional persona.

Since the 1880s, and especially during the world wars, the tendency of English writers about the environment to express patriotic sentiments and explore the national idea has been pronounced. Edward Thomas was at pains to distinguish the England (and the Wales) he loved from Great Britain and the British Empire. One of the ways he did so was by compiling a wartime anthology, *This England*. Gathering the dead to one's cause is partly how a tradition is created; and national or personal crisis provides the motive. It is certain that the minds of readers were more receptive to the writings of Gerard Manley Hopkins after 1918 than they would have been during the Victorian period, when they were written. Something similar has to be said about the publication of Kilvert's *Diary* in 1938–40, when the young Victorian parson's untroubled and exuberant love of life shone out in the encompassing gloom.

Writing of Dorothy Wordsworth in 1966, Geoffrey Grigson expressed his belief that "a *pietas* towards England, or for an Englishman towards the world as environment, needs knowledge of her *Journals*" (p. 381). In some ways, Grigson does for appreciation of the En-glish rural tradition in his own time what Edward Thomas had done for it in his generation. Grigson uncovers hidden aspects of the tradition, and re-interprets it and helps to make it more accessible. He does so as editor and critic, in writing about Samuel Palmer, Clare, Thomas Hardy, Hopkins, and other writers and painters. At the same time, he continues the tradition, in books and essays in which he explores English places, showing a sharp eye for their peculiarities, and a considerable knowledge of natural history. Grigson writes his own Selborne, too, in *Freedom of the Parish*, in which he portrays the parish in which he was born and grew up, Pelynt in Cornwall, "as an organism, ancient but not devitalized; which has been one both of human beings and of the land surface which they mastered for their food" (p. 192).

It is true that Grigson, as he said of White, "liked to know the total history of his environment" (p. 374). This is a strong impulse in books, concerned in one way or another with the making of the land, written since the 1939–45 war: in, for example, Jacquetta Hawkes's *A Land*, W. G. Hoskins' *The Making of the English Landscape*, and Oliver Rackham's *The History of the Countryside*. It is also a driving force of the conservation movement, which has shaped, or influenced, serious English writing about the environment during the last quarter of the twentieth century.

The movement is animated by a far more critical attitude toward the descriptive tradition than that which we find at any other time in its history. This stems largely from Raymond Williams's *The Country and the City*. Williams, an independent Marxist, analyzes the literary ideas that have set country against city, instead of seeing them as connected, within the development of a capitalist economy. He writes also as a man with a strong sense of his family's working history, and with a primary attachment to his home landscape, under the Black Mountains, on the Welsh border.

Despite Cobbett, the prose tradition has produced writers with anti-democratic sentiments, anxious to preserve their cherished places from "invasion" by urban "hordes." George Orwell was an exception; in "Some Thoughts on the Common Toad" Orwell makes the point that "the pleasures of spring are available to everybody, and cost nothing" (p. 361). Richard Mabey, biographer of Gilbert White, and the organizers of Common Ground, Susan Clifford and Angela King, with whom Mabey edited *Sec-*

ond Nature, work in the spirit of Orwell, and of Williams's criticism of the tradition. Mabey has continued the exploration of "unknown" England in, for example, his study of the wildlife inhabiting urban wasteland. Another writer with a radical approach is Patrick Wright, who examines the part played by social class and political reaction in shaping England's "heritage" and symbolic landscapes.

What is missing from the Williams analysis is any real interest in the spiritual needs expressed in the religious and mystical elements of the tradition. A partial alternative may be found in Peter Fuller's adaptation of Ruskin to the late twentieth century. Drawing upon the new sciences, Fuller writes: "In the post-modern age, science is re-discovering the aesthetic and spiritual meanings of nature—and Ruskin's dream of a natural theology without God is becoming a reality" (p. 234). James Lovelock's model of Gaia, "in which the Earth's living matter, air, oceans, and land surface form a complex system which can be seen as a single organism" (p. vii), has affinities with intuitions and feelings that recur throughout the tradition. At the end of the twentieth century, awareness of the human environment as a whole, in country and city, and of its relation to life on Earth is stronger than ever among writers. In a situation of ecological crisis, White's scientific observation, Cobbett's concern for human conditions, and the art of seeing of Jefferies are among elements of the tradition that are inspiring new explorations of the total environment.

Selected Works and Further Reading

Allen, David Elliston, *The Naturalist in Britain,* London: A. Lane, 1976; New York: Penguin, 1978

Blythe, Ronald, *Akenfield,* New York: Dell, 1969; London: A. Lane, 1969

Borrow, George, *Wild Wales: Its People, Language, and Scenery,* London: J. Murray, 1862; New York: Scribner and Welford, 1888

Cobbett, William, *Rural Rides,* London: Cobbett, 1830; New York: Dutton, 1912

Coburn, Kathleen, ed., *The Notebooks of Samuel Taylor Coleridge,* New York: Pantheon, 1957; London: Routledge & Kegan Paul, 1957

Frick, Thomas, ed., *The Sacred Theory of the Earth,* Berkeley, California: North Atlantic, 1986

Fuller, Peter, *Theoria: Art and the Absence of Grace,* London: Chatto & Windus, 1988

Gervais, David, *Literary Englands,* New York and Cambridge: Cambridge University Press, 1993

Grigson, Geoffrey, *An English Farmhouse and Its Neighbourhood,* London: Max Parrish, 1948

———, *Freedom of the Parish,* London: Phoenix House, 1954

———, *Places of the Mind,* London: Routledge & Kegan Paul, 1949

———, *Poems and Poets,* London: Macmillan, 1969; Chester Springs, Pennsylvania: Dufour, 1969

———, *Samuel Palmer: The Visionary Years,* London: Kegan Paul, 1947

———, ed., *The Shell Country Alphabet,* London: Joseph in association with George Rainbird, 1966

Hawkes, Jacquetta, *A Land,* London: Cresset, 1951; New York: Random House, 1952

Hewison, Robert, *John Ruskin: The Argument of the Eye,* Princeton, New Jersey: Princeton University Press, 1976; London: Thames and Hudson, 1976

Hooker, Jeremy, *Writers in a Landscape,* Cardiff: University of Wales Press, 1996

Hopkins, Gerard Manley, *Selected Prose,* New York and Oxford: Oxford University Press, 1980

Hoskins, W. G., *The Making of the English Landscape,* Harmondsworth, England: Penguin, 1955

Hudson, William Henry, *Afoot in England,* London: Hutchinson, 1909; New York: Knopf, 1922

———, *Hampshire Days,* New York and London: Longmans, Green, 1903

———, *A Shepherd's Life,* New York: Dutton, 1910; London: Methuen, 1910

Jefferies, Richard, *The Amateur Poacher,* Boston: Roberts, 1879; London: Smith, Elder, 1879

———, *The Gamekeeper at Home,* London: Smith, Elder, 1878; Boston: Roberts, 1879

———, *Hodge and His Masters,* London: Smith, Elder, 1880; reprinted, New York and London: Quartet, 1979

———, *Landscape with Figures,* New York and Harmondsworth, England: Penguin, 1983

———, *The Story of My Heart: My Autobiography,* Boston: Roberts, 1883; London: Longmans, Green, 1883

———, *Wild Life in a Southern County,* Boston: Roberts, 1879; London: Smith, Elder, 1879

Johnson, E. D. H., ed., *The Poetry of Earth,* New York: Atheneum, 1966; London: Gollancz, 1966

Keith, W. J., *The Rural Tradition,* Buffalo, New York, and Toronto, Ontario: University of Toronto Press, 1974; Hassocks: Harvester, 1975

Leavis, F. R., and Denys Thompson, *Culture and Environment,* London: Chatto & Windus, 1933; Westport, Connecticut: Greenwood, 1977

Lovelock, J. E., *Gaia,* New York and Oxford: Oxford University Press, 1979

Mabey, Richard, *Gilbert White,* London: Century, 1986

———, *Home Country,* London: Century, 1990

Mabey, Richard, Susan Clifford, and Angela King, eds., *Second Nature,* London: Cape, 1984

Massingham, Harold J., *Remembrance,* London: B. T. Batsford, 1942

Merrill, Lynn L., *The Romance of Victorian Natural History,* New York and Oxford: Oxford University Press, 1989

Mitford, Mary Russell, *Our Village,* New York: E. Bliss, 1830; London: Whittaker, Treacher, 1830

Orwell, George, *The Penguin Essays of George Orwell,* Harmondsworth, England: Penguin in association with Secker & Warburg, 1984

Plomer, William, ed., *Kilvert's Diary: Selections from the Diary of the Rev. Francis Kilvert,* 3 vols., London: Jonathan Cape, 1938, 1939, 1940; New York: Macmillan, 1947

Powys, Llewelyn, *Somerset and Dorset Essays,* London: Macdonald, 1957

Rackham, Oliver, *The History of the Countryside,* London: J. M. Dent, 1986

Robinson, Eric, and Geoffrey Summerfield, eds., *Selected Poems and Prose of John Clare,* New York and Oxford: Oxford University Press, 1967

Ruskin, John, *Modern Painters,* New York: American, 1856; London: Smith, Elder, 1856; abridged ed., London: Deutsch, 1987

Sturt, George, *The Wheelwright's Shop,* New York and Cambridge: Cambridge University Press, 1923

Thomas, Edward, *The Childhood of Edward Thomas,* London: Faber and Faber, 1938; reprinted, Boston and London: Faber and Faber, 1983

———, *The Country,* London: T. Batsford, 1913

———, *The Heart of England,* New York: Dutton, 1906; London: J. M. Dent, 1906

———, *In Pursuit of Spring,* New York and London: Thomas Nelson, 1914

———, *A Literary Pilgrim in England,* New York: Dodd, Mead, 1917; London: Methuen, 1917

———, *Richard Jefferies,* Boston: Little, Brown, 1909; London: Hutchinson, 1909

———, *The South Country,* London: Dent, 1909; New York: Dutton, 1932

———, ed., *This England: An Anthology from Her Writers,* New York and London: Oxford University Press, 1915

Thompson, Flora, *Lark Rise to Candleford,* New York and London: Oxford University Press, 1945

White, Gilbert, *The Natural History of Selborne,* New York: Harper & Brothers, 1788; London: T. Bensley for B. White, 1789

Williams, Raymond, *The Country and the City,* New York: Oxford University Press, 1973; London: Chatto & Windus, 1973

Williamson, Henry, ed., *Richard Jefferies: Selections of His Work, with Details of His Life and Circumstance, His Death and Immortality,* London: Faber and Faber, 1937

Wordsworth, Dorothy, *Journals of Dorothy Wordsworth,* New York and London: Macmillan, 1904

Wordsworth, William, *Guide to the Lakes,* 1835; London: Henry Frowde, 1906; also published as *Wordsworth's Guide to the Lakes,* New York and Oxford: Oxford University Press, 1977

Worster, Donald, *Nature's Economy,* San Francisco: Sierra Club, 1977; Cambridge: Cambridge University Press, 1985

Wright, Patrick, *The Village That Died for England: The Strange Story of Tyneham,* London: Cape, 1995

The Idea of Nature in English Poetry

Neil Roberts and Terry Gifford

This chapter is concerned with the poetry of English writers up to the early twentieth century, and with the ways in which imaginative engagement with the natural world is shaped by a constantly varying idea of nature that is structured by a relationship to another term that may be spirit, or society, but most significantly art.

There are many possible starting points for a discussion of this topic. One might begin where Chaucer begins the *Canterbury Tales*, with a celebration, perhaps slightly tongue-in-cheek, of harmony between the seasonal cycle and the cycle of social and religious observance:

> Whan that Aprill with his shoures soote
> The droghte of March hath perced to the
>   roote,
> And bathed every veyne in swich licour
> Of which vertu engendred is the flour . . .
> Thanne longen folk to goon on pilgrimages.
>   (Chaucer, 17)

Or with Shakespeare, who in *King Lear* articulates much more disturbed and conflicting thoughts about nature, when Lear himself ("Hear, Nature, hear, dear Goddess hear!" I.iv.282) invokes retribution for Goneril's rejection of his patriarchal authority, while Edmund ("Thou, Nature, art my Goddess," I.ii.1) enlists an opposed conception of nature to validate his rebellion against that very authority.

Any artistic engagement with an idea of nature is bound, more or less explicitly, to reflect upon itself, since art and nature are terms that, like individual and society, presuppose each other and whose discursive lives are lived in a constantly shifting relationship, whether of antithesis, identity or transcendence. Thus in *The Winter's Tale* Perdita dislikes carnations because "There is an art which, in their piedness, shares / With great creating nature" (IV.iv.87–88) while Polixenes answers that "nature is

made better by no mean, / But nature makes that mean. . . . The art itself is nature" (89–97). And, later in the seventeenth century, Andrew Marvell's idealized garden of "The Garden" is brought into question by his "Mower Against Gardens" who alleges that man, by grafting, has made plants "as double as his mind" (Marvell, 105).

It must also be stressed that while the word nature always gestures toward a reality that transcends the cultural and the social, any particular idea of nature will have a social dimension. Thus Chaucer's pilgrimage figures a cross-section of society, in constant conflict, but united in a common aim. For Lear and Edmund nature is little more than a projection of their self-interested ideological predilections while, conversely, Polixenes's enthusiasm to "make conceive a bark of baser kind / By bud of nobler race" proves skin-deep when it is a question of his princely son marrying a shepherd's daughter. We may even suspect, in Marvell's Mower, an element of class hostility to the artifice of the rich man's garden.

This essay does not propose, in any rigorous sense, a history of the idea of nature in English poetry, but will examine a number of outstanding examples from different periods, and the shifts that occur between them. I will begin with a period, and a poet, in which the relationship between ideas of nature, art, and society is particularly strong and explicit, the early eighteenth century and Alexander Pope.

Pope's "Epistle to Burlington" offers advice on the use of riches. Throughout this poem the terms art, taste, sense, and nature are used with a sense of compatibility verging on identity. Its most memorable section is the satire on "Timon's Villa," a rich man's estate that accumulates every possible offense against Pope's linked values. A vulgar desire for grandeur prompts Timon to build and plant on a monstrous scale making "His pond an Ocean, his parterre a Down." Nature is ignored in the most obvious sense when "a Lake behind / Improves the keenness of the Northern wind." Nature is "inverted" with "Trees cut to Statues, Statues thick as trees," and facilities are created with no regard for their function, "With here a Fountain, never to be played, / And there a Summer-house, that knows no shade" (p. 592). This is, evidently, a conception of nature in which proportion is of the highest importance, and a conception of art that follows nature in the most literal and functional sense.

Perhaps the most interesting lines in the portrayal of Timon's Villa are these:

His Gardens next your admiration call,
On ev'ry side you look, behold the Wall!
No pleasing Intricacies intervene,
No artful wildness to perplex the scene;
Grove nods at grove, each Alley has a
  brother,
And half the platform just reflects the other.
  (p. 592)

The oxymoron "artful wildness" epitomizes the rhetoric by which the potential tensions between art and nature are subdued in Pope. We have seen that he scorns the artifice of a "Fountain, never to be played": nature must be consulted in everything, but nature, intriguingly, is not the same as reality. One of Timon's offenses is that the boundary wall of his estate is visible. An important purpose of the alliance of art, taste, sense and nature is illusion, to "perplex the scene" so that the owner of the estate can imagine, as later in the century William Cowper imagined Alexander Selkirk thinking, "I am monarch of all I survey" (p. 311).

A modern reader is also likely to be provoked by the complaint against a garden design in which "Grove nods at grove, each Alley has a brother, / And half the platform just reflects the other." This is exactly what many readers feel about Pope's verse, with the ubiquitous heroic couplet, rigorously end-stopped, and the frequent use of the caesura for effects of balance or antithesis. But what Pope does with verse actually corresponds quite closely to his principles: within a clearly ordered framework to create variety and the unforeseen. Despite the formality of verse structure his poetry often creates effects of lively, if polished, conversation, and if a passage such as this one contains stereotypically Augustan lines such as "Trees cut to Stat-

ues, Statues thick as trees," a few lines later Pope gives us the beautiful mock-elegiac plangency of "Un-water'd see the drooping sea-horse mourn."

It is no surprise that when, earlier in his career, Pope gives advice about writing in his "Essay on Criticism," he begins, "First follow NATURE" (p. 146). Nor is it a surprise that this entails the utmost respect for classical precedent, in which taste, sense and art are enshrined. The rules, exemplified in Homer and codified by Aristotle, were later discovered by Virgil to be identical to nature: "*Nature* and *Homer* were, he found, the *same*. . . . Learn hence for Ancient *Rules* a just Esteem; / To copy *Nature* is to copy *Them*." These rules were "*discover'd*, not *devis'd*," and Pope describes them, in a phrase that recalls "artful wildness," "*Nature Methodiz'd*" (p. 146).

Pope's poetic is not rigidly imitative and rule-bound. The idea of creative genius, and the sublimity of phenomena "Which *out of* Nature's *common Order* rise," has an important place, and "Great Wits sometimes may *gloriously offend*, / And *rise* to *Faults* true Criticks *dare not mend*" (p. 147). If, despite this, and despite the positive and optimistic conception of the relationship between art, the human mind, and nature that his poetry expresses and exemplifies, not to mention the extraordinary brilliance of his verse, most modern readers feel there is a significant barrier between themselves and Pope, this is surely because his idea of nature—and that of the world he represents—rested on an extremely narrow and historically unstable social and intellectual base. The integration of "*Nature Methodiz'd*" is available to the man whose riches as well as sense, taste and art enable him to create the antithesis of Timon's villa—an Earl of Burlington, as the poem dedicated to him of course suggests. To the poet it is available only if his education gives him access to those classical models of which it can he said that "To copy *Nature* is to copy *Them*."

Turning to Wordsworth, writing at the very end of Pope's century, and after the French Revolution, one has only to register the scene of his poetry to see that a fundamental shift in the social complexion of the idea of nature has taken place:

These plots of cottage-ground, these
  orchard-tufts,
Which, at this season, with their unripe
  fruits,

Among the woods and copses lose
  themselves,
Nor, with their green and simple hue, disturb
The wild green landscape. Once again I see
These hedge-rows, hardly hedge-rows, little
  lines
Of sportive wood run wild; these pastoral
  farms
Green to the very door; and wreathes of
  smoke
Sent up, in silence, from among the trees,
With some uncertain notice, as might seem,
Of vagrant dwellers in the houseless woods,
Or of some hermit's cave, where by his fire
The hermit sits alone. (p. 57)

In a sense this is no more real than the scenes of Pope's nature. It is a highly picturesque passage, which acknowledges its debt to poetic tradition in the word pastoral, applied to those farms that are "Green [not muddy] to the very door." The vagrants are conveniently out of sight. Nevertheless, it is a strikingly vernacular scene. This difference, however, masks continuities. The "hedge-rows, hardly hedge-rows, little lines / Of sportive wood run wild" are recognizably an image of "artful wildness" or "*Nature methodiz'd.*" Perhaps the most interesting difference is in the verse itself. Wordsworth conforms as rigidly to the iambic pentameter as Pope, but not only does his blank verse not rhyme, he seems as determined to avoid end-stopping as Pope is to observe it. The result is a remarkably fluid verse that often comes close to masking the metrical artifice that structures it. It is verse like this that by contrast can make Pope's couplets seem, to some readers, too much like Timon's groves and alleys.

Even more of a contrast is provided when Wordsworth articulates the significance that scenes such as this have for him. He owes to them

          that blessed mood,
In which the burthen of the mystery,
In which the heavy and the weary weight
Of all this unintelligible world
Is lightened:–that serene and blessed mood,
In which the affections gently lead us on,
Until, the breath of this corporeal frame,
And even the motion of our human blood
Almost suspended, we are laid asleep
In body and become a living soul. (p. 58)

If we have seen Pope obliterating the antithesis between art and nature, here we see Words-

worth dissolving what is at least for Christian culture an even more fundamental opposition, between the natural and the spiritual. He has "learned / To look on nature, not as in the hour / Of thoughtless youth, but hearing oftentimes / The still, sad music of humanity," and feeling "a sense sublime / Of something far more deeply interfused" (p. 59). Poetry such as this yields unusually little to interpretive analysis. Conceptually it is thin and, unless the reader is predisposed, unconvincing. What does carry conviction and is in a real sense the philosophical substance of the poetry is Wordsworth's extraordinary verse style, in which a predominantly abstract language is as it were given body by rhythm, and the "serene and blessed mood" is directly communicated to the reader's mind and, if the verse is read aloud, body: consider, as an obvious example, the effect of the line-break before "Almost suspended." The iambic meter is always present but at times hardly distinguishable, like the bodily rhythms, the breath and blood, on which it is based. It is by means such as this that poetry can appear to perform the miracle of dissolving the most fundamental oppositions: the signifier and signified, art and nature, body and soul.

It is no surprise that Wordsworth explicitly derives his poetic powers from his experience of nature, perhaps most famously in the opening of the *Prelude*:

For I, methought, while the sweet breath
  of Heaven
Was blowing on my body, felt within
A corresponding mild creative breeze,
A vital breeze which travelled gently on
O'er things which it had made, and is
  become
A tempest, a redundant energy
Vexing its own creation. (p. 158)

Wordsworth's evocations of nature as a nurturing power, not only physically but imaginatively and creatively, are so powerful and so well-known, that this view of nature is often thought of as characteristic of the period subsequently labelled Romantic. However, his greatest contemporaries had very different views of the relationship between nature and the poetic imagination. William Blake wrote in the margin of Wordsworth's poem "Influence of Natural Objects in calling forth and strengthening the Imagination in Boyhood and early Youth": "Natural Objects always did & now do weaken, deaden & obliterate Imagination in Me. Words-worth must know that what he Writes Valuable is not to be found in Nature" (pp. 821–822). For Blake nature was an inert material realm presided over by the deadening, measuring men-tality that he associated with Newton and Locke. Whereas Wordsworth's daffodils are flowers, natural objects, before they are any-thing else, Blake's rose and tiger owe very little to the study of flora and fauna: they are imagi-native symbols with an autonomous existence in the world of their respective poems.

Even more significant is the attitude to nature of Wordsworth's friend and collaborator Cole-ridge. In "The Rime of the Ancient Mariner" Coleridge wrote perhaps our language's greatest ecological fable, but "Frost at Midnight" and "Dejection: an Ode" suggest a very un-Words-worthian view of nature and imagination. In "Frost at Midnight" it is not the "owlet's cry" or "Sea, hill, and wood" that create, in Words-worth's words, "that serene and blessed mood, / In which the affections gently lead us on" but "the sole unquiet thing," a "film, which fluttered on the grate," an optical illusion created by the heat (p. 240). In "Dejection" the opposite of the Wordsworthian creative dynamic is even more obvious. The natural world is available to Coleridge as he looks at the evening sky, the clouds, moon and stars, but "I see, not feel, how beautiful they are!" (p. 364). Whereas Words-worth conceives of the promptings of poetic power as a "corresponding . . . creative breeze," Coleridge writes of "My shaping spirit of Imag-ination" (p. 366), which is suspended by the experience of dejection (or what would now be called depression). He could look at the beauties of the natural world forever but in vain because "I may not hope from outward forms to win / The passion and the life, whose fountains are within" (p. 365).

For many modern commentators the most significant poet of the Romantic period is not Wordsworth or Coleridge, nor the legendary sec-ond generation of Byron, Shelley and Keats, but a contemporary of the last three, John Clare. To some extent the modern vogue for Clare is moti-vated by the desire to rectify earlier comparative neglect, to some extent by political sympathies, since Clare came from the rural working class. Such motives are not tangential at a time when the canon, and previously accepted notions of the central and the marginal, are being examined and challenged. The rescue of Clare's poetry from relative obscurity does not merely add one

(quaintly vernacular) poet to the existing canon, or even topple Wordsworth from pre-eminence as the greatest poet of the English countryside. It raises questions about the very concept of nature poetry, and, therefore, Clare is appropriately central to an essay on this topic. In what sense is a passage such as the following nature poetry?

> The martin cat long shagged of courage
>   good
> Of weazle shape a dweller in the wood
> With badger hair long shagged and darting
>   eyes
> And lower than the common cat in size
> Small head and running on the stoop
> Snuffing the ground and hind parts
>   shouldered up
> He keeps one track and lies in lonely shade
> Where print of humans foot is scarcely made
> Save when the woods are cut the beaten
>   track
> The woodmans dog will snuff cock tailed
>   and black
> Red legged and spotted over either eye
> Snuffs barks and scrats the tree and passes
>   bye
> The great brown horned owl looks down
>   below
> And sees the shaggy martin come and go.
>   (p. 244)

Despite the dialect usages, unorthodox spelling and occasionally faulty sentence construction this is not illiterate or un-literary poetry. Clare had full possession of the English poetic canon, including eighteenth-century poets such as Thomson and Cowper, from whom his earlier work is derivative, as well as Pope, and of course his Romantic contemporaries, several of whom he knew personally. Perhaps his marginal posi-tion gave him a certain freedom of access to the canon, since his mature work is free from current mannerisms and would be hard to date with ref-erence to the prevailing styles of the age. What is most distinctive about poetry such as this is the perspective, the absence of what I have called, with reference to Wordsworth, the picturesque. It is close-up and detailed, the point of view shifts from the martin to the woodman's dog to the owl; later poachers and gypsies come on the scene. At no point, however, is the material of the poem shaped into a scene and given the special value of nature. In a poem such as this it is a question not so much of nature as of reality, the reality that happens to be at hand. A poem about a bird's nest is likely to shape itself into a nature poem because the nest will function as a synecdoche of all that is non-human. When, however, a poet writes (at a rough count) 24 such poems, each concerning a different bird, that kind of figurative status is weakened, and the poems increasingly seem concerned with the specifics of the nests themselves, without reference to a larger category, or to the oppositions that the concept of nature invariably brings with it.

It would be naive to suppose that Clare produced such poetry unselfconsciously, or without an eye to popular taste. It would also be misleading to suggest that, even in his most characteristic poetry, he never gives expression to the kinds of opposition I have been talking about: for example, "The Reed Bird" ends, conventionally enough, "Ah happy songster man can seldom share / A spot as hidden from the haunts of care" (p. 235). However, unlike most of the other poets discussed in this chapter, the poet's self is hardly ever at the center, constructing what he sees as a nature from which he derives moral, spiritual or imaginative sustenance. Indeed, one of his finest poems, "The Sky Lark," is surely in part a reflection on the liberties his Romantic contemporaries—here figured as "unheeding" boys—take with their bird subjects. There is an unmistakable sly implicit allusion to poems such as Shelley's "To a Skylark" and Keats's "Ode to a Nightingale." At the center of the poem is the lark's flight, described in familiar enough terms: "the skylark flies / And oer her half formed nest with happy wings / Winnows the air–till in the clouds she sings / Then hangs a dust spot in the sunny skies." This is all the boys see, not "dreaming" that birds capable of such flight "would drop agen / To nests upon the ground where any thing / May come at to destroy" (p. 216).

Nature poetry is nearly always, at least implicitly, religious. This is obvious in Wordsworth and Coleridge, and remains so in contemporary poets such as Ted Hughes and Peter Redgrove. However, this usually entails at least a loosening, if not abandonment, of attachment to the orthodox tenets of Christianity. The outstanding exception to this is the Victorian poet and Jesuit priest Gerard Manley Hopkins. His poetry is dedicated to the belief that "The world is charged with the grandeur of God" ("God's Grandeur," 70). His most memorable nature poems have a characteristic expository, almost didactic, structure, within which some of the most intense and concentrated verbal effects in English poetry are deployed. The Petrarchan

sonnet, with its division of octave and sestet, lends itself particularly well to this structure. Here is a characteristic opening:

> As kingfishers catch fire, dragonflies dráw fláme;
> As tumbled over rim in roundy wells
> Stones ring; like each tucked string tells, each hung bell's
> Bow swung finds tongue to fling out broad its name. (p. 95)

The intense sound-patterning in Hopkins's poetry is never decorative: indeed it is more likely to disconcert than to please the reader looking for familiar poetic sound-effects. This poem is his most explicit treatment of what he called inscape, the unique essence of things. The actions described in the poem are the reverse of contingent: the alliteration and internal rhyming are attempts to suggest an essential relationship between subject and predicate or, as the poem goes on to say,

> Each mortal thing does one thing and the same:
> Deals out that being indoors each one dwells;
> Selves—goes itself; *myself* it speaks and spells;
> Crying *Whát I dó is me: for that I came.*

One has constantly in reading Hopkins the sense of an experience, or a thought, for which he is having to invent the language: hence the characteristic disruption of word order and class-shift, and even the counter-intuitive stress-marks. The *Oxford English Dictionary* has no entry for "self" as a verb: Hopkins has, in effect, invented a concept in articulating his response to the natural world. Following the structure of the Petrarchan sonnet, the explicit religious statement comes in the sestet:

> I say móre: the just man justices;
> Kéeps gráce: thát keeps all his goings graces;
> Acts in God's eye what in God's eye he is—
> Christ—for Christ plays in ten thousand places,
> Lovely in limbs, and lovely in eyes not his
> To the Father through the features of men's faces.

It is a paradox of Hopkins's poetry that although his religious faith was undoubtedly vital to the intensity and individuality with which he experienced the natural world, and therefore to the originality and uniqueness of his work, the explicitly religious affirmation is often the least impressive part of the poem. Here, figures such as "the just man justices" and the alliteration in the final line are pale reflections of their equivalents in the octave. The necessarily abstract language of religion does not nurture Hopkins's sensuous and plastic art. As a result, one is often left wondering whether the function of the Christian conclusions of such poems is not to permit rather than to inspire a glorification of the natural world that might otherwise seem dangerously pagan: consider his celebration of "The Windhover" (kestrel) as "morning's minion, king- / dom of daylight's dauphin" (p. 73).

Hopkins's struggle to celebrate both the Christian God and the natural world is emphasized when seen against the background of more characteristic Victorian poets. This was the period in which the development of the physical sciences, above all evolutionary theory, raised the grim image of a blind, mechanistic nature indifferent to human life and values. As Tennyson wrote in "In Memoriam A. H. H." (1850),

> Are God and Nature then at strife,
>   That Nature lends such evil dreams?
>   So careful of the type she seems,
> So careless of the single life. (p. 397)

When he reflects further, the situation seems still worse, nature does not even seem to value the species: "She cries, 'A thousand types are gone: / I care for nothing, all shall go'" (p. 398). Man's trust that "God was love indeed / And love Creation's final law" is mocked, in the poem's most famous line, by "Nature, red in tooth and claw" (p. 399). Tennyson rejects this vision, but only because it seems too horrible to be true. Meanwhile for Matthew Arnold the ebbing of the tide, which in most cultural contexts might seem an obvious example of natural cyclicity, is a "melancholy, long, withdrawing roar," symbolizing the relentless ebbing of the "Sea of Faith," "down the vast edges drear / And naked shingles of the world" ("Dover Beach," 211).

Nature is problematic in a different and more intimate way for the female Victorian poet. Tennyson and Arnold's metaphysical anguish is undoubtedly deeply felt, but Christina Rossetti's remarkable fable "Goblin Market" centers the problem on the body in a way that no male English poet of the period approaches. The sisters Laura and Lizzie, of indeterminate age but living independently together, are solicited to buy fruit from "goblin men" with animal characteristics. Both the disturbing animal natures of the men and the seductive variety of the fruit are emphasized in extensive detail. The style of the poem is deceptively childlike, as if this material can only be handled in the guise of a children's story. Laura succumbs to the seduction of the fruit—

> She sucked and sucked and sucked the more
> Fruits which that unknown orchard bore;
> She sucked until her lips were sore (p. 165)

—losing the "open heart" that she had shared with Lizzie and falling into an "absent dream . . . longing for the night" (p. 167). Lizzie saves her sister by braving the goblins, letting them assault her and literally press the fruit on her without eating it, and returning to offer her fruit-stained body and lips to Laura as an antidote. The fable is an obvious reworking of the Eden myth, which might be described as the founding anecdote of Western civilization's alienation from nature. But despite appearances it is not a simple reversal, casting the male in the role of tempter. Throughout the poem there is a sense of the extraordinary and dangerous vulnerability of the female body and psyche to the addictive and destructive pleasures of nature and the senses: after eating the fruit Laura lies awake at night "in a passionate yearning, / And gnashed her teeth for baulked desire" (p. 169). The female body and female desire are still where the problem of nature is concentrated. The poem insipidly concludes representing the sisters as eventually "wives / With children of their own," but much more memorable is the way Lizzie's body is offered to Laura: "Hug me, kiss me, suck my juices / . . . Eat me, drink me, love me" (p. 174), implying that same-sex love is the antidote to the natural but destructive seductions of heterosexuality.

A poet's attitude to Nature, however, is not simply determined by gender. If a Christina Rossetti, writing from within a Christian worldview, centers the struggle of desire and alienation in the female body, the poet who of all Victorian writers was perhaps the most free from Christian preconceptions was also a woman, and Emily Brontë habitually wrote as if the realm of Nature and that of the spirit were interchangeable:

> High waving heather, 'neath stormy blasts
>   bending,

Midnight and moonlight and bright shining
    stars;
Darkness and glory rejoicingly blending,
Earth rising to heaven and heaven
    descending,
Man's spirit away from its drear dungeon
    sending,
Bursting the fetters and breaking the bars.
    (p. 33)

If "earth," or in older parlance "the world" is man's "drear dungeon," this captivity is not thought of in terms of nature: on the contrary, it is precisely the natural imagery of the first two lines that offers the promise of escape.

At the very end of the century, in a poem dated 31st December 1900, Thomas Hardy returned, as John Clare had done, to the bird imagery of the Romantics, in a poem whose title echoes the "Ode to a Nightingale," "The Darkling Thrush." The desolate winter scene characteristically "seemed to be / The Century's corpse outleant," as if it epitomized all the historical tendencies that made a Keats or a Shelley unthinkable in 1900, and Hardy's bird is "an aged thrush, frail, gaunt, and small, / In blast-beruffled plume." Nevertheless, it chooses to "fling his soul / Upon the growing gloom" and the poet takes it as a sign of "Some blessed Hope, whereof he knew / And I was unaware" (p. 137).

"The Darkling Thrush" exemplifies two characteristic tendencies of the poetry of the century to come: a more modest, low-key celebration of the natural world and the representation of the "blessedness" of Nature as intact but inaccessible to man. A good example of the first of these tendencies is Hardy's own "An Afterwards" that records precise observations such as "the May month flaps its glad green leaves like wings, / Delicate-filmed as new-spun silk" and "The dewfall-hawk comes crossing the shades to alight / Upon the wind-warped upland thorn" and hopes that the poet will be remembered as "a man who used to notice such things" (p. 521). A combination of these tendencies is the most characteristic note of the finest nature poet of the early twentieth century, Edward Thomas. In his poem "October," for example, he notes, "The gossamers wander at their own will. / At heavier steps than birds' the squirrels scold," but reflects,

        now I might
As happy be as earth is beautiful,

Were I some other or with earth could turn
In alternation of violet and rose,
Harebell and snowdrop, at their season due,
And gorse that has no time not to be gay.
    (p. 76)

The possibility that "some other's" happiness might be equal to the earth's beauty is touched on but passed over in favor of a much longer evocation of the perfect integration of death. As Hardy alluded with partial irony to Keats in his title so Thomas adapts Wordsworth's line, "The river glideth at his own sweet will" (Wordsworth, "Composed Upon Westminster Bridge," 136), and by omitting the word "sweet" alters the original smooth-flowing pentameter to a more tentative rhythm.

D. H. Lawrence addresses the alienation of man from nature more robustly in perhaps the most famous nature poem of the twentieth century, "Snake," a poem that echoes the aristocratic language with which Hopkins celebrated the kestrel: "I missed my chance with one of the lords / Of life." Lawrence (or more strictly the persona of the poem) missed his chance because, although like Hopkins his heart in hiding stirred at the visitation of the snake—

He reached down from a fissure in the
    earth-wall in the gloom
And trailed his yellow-brown slackness
    soft-bellied down, over the edge of the
    stone trough
And rested his throat upon the stone bottom,
And where the water had dripped from the
    tap, in a small clearness,
He sipped with his straight mouth,
Softly drank through his straight gums, into
    his slack long body,
Silently— (p. 128)

he listened to the "voice of my education" that told him that the snake was dangerous and "*If you were not afraid, you would kill him!*" (p. 129). He does not kill the snake but throws a log at it, which causes it to disappear precipitately into its hole. This is a familiar Romantic motif that echoes the killing of the albatross in "The Rime of the Ancient Mariner" and the vandalism of the boy in Wordsworth's "Nutting" who "dragged to earth both branch and bough, with crash / And merciless ravage" (Wordsworth, 70). There is an important difference, though, that marks Lawrence's poem as post-Romantic and even, one may say, post-Christian. The

Coleridge and Wordsworth poems both lend themselves to Christian interpretation as fables of original sin—indeed, in the case of "The Ancient Mariner" Coleridge himself did so in the marginal glosses written many years later. The protagonists' actions are unmotivated and individual, although implicitly representative of human nature. There is no suggestion of any authorized or ideological element in them. Lawrence's protagonist, however, is acting in accordance with the voices of his education, and although they refer explicitly to the snake's venomous character, there is little doubt that the traditional Christian identification of the snake as the enemy of God and man plays a part in the drama of the poem. The assault on nature is now seen as a socially validated action, with Christian sanction implicitly in the background. The representative of the natural world is seen as an alien (the poem's foreign setting is significant) who rarely visits and, when rebuffed, disappears into a "black hole" (p.130).

The contemporary poet who has most rigorously and consistently examined the way Western culture has become alienated from the natural world is Ted Hughes. He began by developing Lawrence's celebrations of the life force in creatures, deliberately choosing less conventionally comfortable creatures and perceptions that resulted in the accusation that he focused only on Tennyson's "Nature, red in tooth and claw." In fact the best of these early poems, like "An Otter," are more balanced in catching the creative-destructive dynamics in nature: "An otter belongs / In double robbery and concealment— / From water that nourishes and drowns, and from land . . ." The anti-pastoral impulse to shock his readers out of complacency, a Blakean "cleansing of the doors of perception," continued alongside an attempt in the epic visionary sequences of *Crow* and *Cave Birds* to reconnect a central figure, humbled of his hubris, with his creator, an elusive female figure. If any one poem can represent the climax of this process it would be the symbolic marriage in "Bride and groom lie hidden for three days," the pivotal poem of *Cave Birds*.

The range of Hughes's expansion of the notion of nature in English poetry includes his treatment of agricultural and industrial decay in his original landscape, the Calder Valley of West Yorkshire, as a natural process ("Dead Farms, Dead Leaves") in *Remains of Elmet*. In the book *River* his religious treatment of the river is more a case study than a metaphor for what is to be gained by a sustained engagement with one natural form. His personal practical responsibility for nature as a farmer is graphically charted in *Moortown*. More recently he has written, with varying degrees of success, poems that have commented directly upon conservation issues. His record of his own greening as a poet is published in Terry Gifford's *Green Voices* (pp. 131–132).

A contemporary of Hughes has been described by Terry Eagleton as "for long England's leading ecological poet *avant la lettre*, and [he] has now had the pleasure of seeing the letter catch up with him." Perhaps more than anyone writing in England today, Peter Redgrove might be called "the English poet of Gaia." He has written prose, with his partner Penelope Shuttle, about what they call the Black Goddess, those invisible forces to which we are still, just, attuned as sentient creatures, although in ways severely limited by our culture. For example, a poem like "The Big Sleep," the last of his selected poems, *Poems 1954–1987*, links the rhythms of the sea with first the pull of bees toward honey, then the magnetic forces of the earth, the pull of the moon, the effects of weather on dreams, and finally, all these forces on the pattern of procreation in the town of Falmouth. Trained as a scientist, Redgrove has researched his imagination to find a language for the world of spirit in its various forms. To Redgrove the notion of finding poetic images and insights in dream, or more properly reverie, is central to his way of apprehending the workings of Gaia. So his poems often cannot follow conventional grammatical structures, but might be described as following the logic, or more accurately the narrative grammar, of dream. In "The Big Sleep," the form feels its way toward an accumulating apprehension of "the big one," "the Dreamer" who, through the state of the tides, affects the subconscious sleeping life of the human inhabitants (and hence their waking lives), even to the extent of resulting in localized patterns of pregnancies. Often, Redgrove's poems seem to be working at the very edge of art's ability to articulate nature.

If the fields of forces present in particular places are important to Redgrove, they are not the only source of his poetry. But there is a long tradition of a poetry of place in Britain, which is why its literature can be best represented here in regional chapters. In Britain culture is to a large extent the result of landscape. In England one might point to the work of Norman Nicholson whose entire oeuvre is based upon his life in the town of Millom on the southern edge of the Lake District. The interaction between the industrial and the forces of nature in mountain, fellside, river and sea produces poems that veer from a childhood nostalgia for Millom, to a celebration of a supposed permanence in natural processes, if not in natural forms themselves. This longing for an ultimate, elemental absolute within place results in poems like "Shingle" or "Tide Out," which appear to be about the natural dynamics of change, actually lacking any tension between the elements because they are viewed from a perspective of slowed-down, comfortable (and comforting), geological time. The poetry often produces, contrary to its apparent intention, a static notion of nature against which human life is sentimentally humbled and, pace Hughes, disempowered from its responsibility for its interaction with the natural world.

The poetry of place has been both the critical and creative interest of the English poet Jeremy Hooker (who has contributed a chapter to this book). Born near Southampton, Hooker has also developed a poetry that explores cultural and historical interactions with place, as in his poem sequence "Itchen Water," for example. His first book, *Soliloquies of a Chalk Giant,* also reflects upon geological time, but with a more subtle awareness of making and unmaking both within nature and in our cultural engagement with it, specifically the form of the Cerne Abbas giant cut in the turf of the Dorset downs. The poem "A Chalk Pebble" uses a simple form to explore, with a deftness of touch, the meanings located in a symbolic figure that brings together the organic and the inorganic in nature. The giant's mythical notion of a pebble as the giant's egg is a hubris mocked by his chalk hand crumbling as it makes contact with the harder stone. So any possible hubris of human achievement in the making of the giant is undercut with quiet simplicity by the poem's ending:

The dead sponge mingles
With alchemical water
For the slow formation
Of a perfect stone.

The fact that every stone is, of course, perfect, is one of the ironies that Hooker's position of quietly reflective observer endorses in his best poetry. The danger is, perhaps, that his presence can at times be so quiet as to be apparently "letting the place speak for itself," that false deference toward place that pretends there is no art, and thereby no attitude, in simply descriptive nature poetry. This was the common stance of the Georgian poets who were published in the five anthologies called *Georgian Poetry* edited by Edward Marsh between 1912 and 1922. Wistful descriptive nature poetry by poets such as Rupert Brooke, A. E. Housman, W. H. Davies, John Masefield, Edmund Blunden, Walter de la Mare and others clearly used nature as a pastoral escape from the horrors of the First World War. It is perhaps the long memory of the Georgians in the culture, enervated by the spirited attack upon them in 1932 by F. R. Leavis, that has left the term nature poetry as a pejorative one in Britain today.

Far from wanting to be known as nature poets, those black and Asian poets who have invigorated English poetry for two generations now, are usually associated with the urban environment. But the fact is that they have brought an injection of new forms, rhythms, icons and symbols to English nature poetry. Theirs is very much a poetry of place and a poetry of attitude. James Berry came to England in 1948 and explicitly celebrates the presence of the Caribbean environment in London's markets in his poem "The Coming of Yams and Mangoes and Mountain Honey," which begins:

Handfuls hold hidden sunset
stuffing up bags
and filling up the London baskets.
Caribbean hills have moved and come.

Sun's alphabet drops out of branches.
Coconuts are big brown Os,
pimentoberries little ones.

James Berry can write in a variety of voices and this diversity is characteristic of these most recent additions to English poetry that engages with environment. Since leaving Guyana in 1977 to live in Brighton, John Agard and Grace Nichols have contributed quite different poetry to English life. Agard's work is typically playful, but with a political sting in the tail, often aimed at the racist English environment in which he finds himself. In "Palm Tree King" he accepts the role of foreign expert on palm trees and the exotic in order to turn his attention upon the effects of tourism on the Caribbean. Grace Nichols is also able to treat racism in England indirectly in *The Fat Black Woman's Poems,* but she also has a powerful sequence of poems remembering from England the relationship of women with the Caribbean environment. "Those Women" from *i is a long memoried woman* has a linguistic inventiveness that saves it from sentimentality in its evocation of women at work "in their own element":

How I remember those women
sweeping in the childish rivers
of my eyes

and the fish slipping
like eels
through their laughing thighs

An indication that there is more to come from the myths and symbols of Asian poetry is suggested by the very recent publications from Asian women in particular. A glimpse of just how different these notions of environment might be from traditional English nature poetry can be seen from Debjani Chatterjee's poem "Ganapati" in her collection *I Was That Woman*. The elephant-headed god of wisdom and of literature is the result of the union of the goddess of mountains and the outcast god of cemeteries. In his turn Ganapati married a banana tree, thereby unifying the animal and the vegetable. In the poem this comes to represent a challenge to human conceptions of boundaries and divisions. So, the writer says, in understanding this myth "we stretched our notions of humanity."

The lessons of Ganapati's life as told in this poem integrate what have come to be recognized as green or ecological notions of holistic acceptance of plant and animal, mountain building and cemetery haunting gods, creative and destructive forces in nature. Some indication of the range of green poems being written now in England should conclude this brief sampling of poetic notions of nature. What might be called didactic environmental poetry such as David Craig's "Against Looting" comments directly upon an issue, in this case drawing attention to the link between exploitation of the earth's resources and the exploitation of people. Heathcote Williams' popular long poem *Whale Nation*, on the other hand, comes close to suggesting that the whale is more worth saving than the human species. The self-centered greed of the species is cleverly exposed in the Brechtian fable of Philip Gross's poem "What This Hand Did." The future effects of our species upon the environment are imagined in Adrian Mitchell's apocalyptic poem "On the Beach at Cambridge." The sea level has risen,

in this poem, after a nuclear holocaust. The poem is in the voice of a bureaucrat newly emerged from a bunker and recording what he sees. A photograph of an oiled cormorant during the Persian Gulf War was the starting point for Tony Harrison's topical green poem "Initial Illumination," which was first published in the *Guardian* newspaper. Each of these poems might be called environmentalist in their use of art to engage with a nature that is now considered to be threatened in a way that makes Lear's worst vision a real possibility.

The apparent stability of the word nature is, like all such words, deceptive. As we have seen, the word can have different significance for different poets in the same period or even, in the case of *King Lear*, in the same text. It is not surprising then that even more radical shifts should occur historically. Yet, however unstable its meaning, the word and concept does not seem to become redundant: art continues to need something else against which to define itself, and that something else, in all its varying manifestations, remains one of poetry's central preoccupations.

Selected Works and Further Reading

Agard, John, *Mangoes and Bullets: Selected and New Poems, 1972–84,* London: Pluto, 1985

Arnold, Matthew, *The Poetical Works of Matthew Arnold,* edited by Chauncey Brewster Tinker and Howard Foster Lowry, New York and London: Oxford University Press, 1950

Berry, James, *Chain of Days,* New York and Oxford: Oxford University Press, 1985

Blake, William, *Poetry and Prose of William Blake,* edited by Geoffrey Keynes, New York: Random House, 1927; London: Nonesuch, 1927

Chatterjee, Debjani, *I Was That Woman,* Frome, England: Hippopotamus, 1989

Chaucer, Geoffrey, *The Complete Works of Geoffrey Chaucer,* edited by F. N. Robinson, Boston: Houghton Mifflin, 1933; London: Oxford University Press, 1957

Clare, John, *John Clare,* edited by Eric Robinson and David Powell, New York and Oxford: Oxford University Press, 1984

Coleridge, Samuel Taylor, *Poetical Works,* edited by Ernest Hartley Coleridge, New York and London: Oxford University Press, 1969

Cowper, William, *The Complete Poetical Works of William Cowper,* edited by

Humphrey Sumner Milford, New York and London: H. Frowde, 1905

Craig, David, *Against Looting,* Lancaster, England: Giant Steps, 1987

Gifford, Terry, *Green Voices: Understanding Contemporary Nature Poetry,* New York and Manchester, England: Manchester University Press, 1995

Hardy, Thomas, *Collected Poems of Thomas Hardy,* London: Macmillan, 1919; New York: Macmillan, 1925

Harrison, Tony, *A Cold Coming,* Newcastle-upon-Tyne, England: Bloodaxe, 1991

Hooker, Jeremy, *Soliloquies of a Chalk Giant,* London: Enitharmon, 1974

——, *A View from the Source: Selected Poems,* Manchester, England: Carcanet, 1982

Hopkins, Gerard Manley, *Poems of Gerard Manley Hopkins,* edited by W. H. Gardner, New York and London: Oxford University Press, 1948

Lawrence, D. H., *Selected Poems,* edited by Mara Kalnins, London: J. M. Dent, 1992

Marvell, Andrew, *The Complete Poems,* edited by Elizabeth Story Donno, Baltimore, Maryland, and Harmondsworth, England: Penguin, 1972

Mitchell, Adrian, *On the Beach at Cambridge: New Poems,* London: Allison and Busby, 1984

Nichols, Grace, *The Fat Black Woman's Poems,* London: Virago, 1984

Nicholson, Norman, *Selected Poems, 1940–1982,* London: Faber and Faber, 1982

Pope, Alexander, *The Poems of Alexander Pope,* edited by John Butt, London: Methuen, 1940; New York: Oxford University Press, 1942

Redgrove, Peter, *The Moon Disposes: Poems, 1954–1987,* London: Secker & Warburg, 1987

Rossetti, Christina, *Poems and Prose,* edited by Jan Marsh, Rutland, Vermont: C. E. Tuttle, 1994; London: J. M. Dent, 1994

Shakespeare, William, *King Lear,* edited by G. K. Hunter, Harmondsworth, England: Penguin, 1972; New York: Penguin, 1981

——, *The Winter's Tale,* edited by Ernest Schanzer, Baltimore, Maryland, and Harmondsworth, England: Penguin, 1969

Tennyson, Alfred, *Tennyson: A Selected Edition,* edited by Christopher Ricks, Harlow, England: Longman, 1969; also published as *Tennyson: A Selected Edition Incorporating the Trinity College Manuscripts,* Berkeley: University of California Press, 1989

Thomas, Edward, *Collected Poems,* London: Selwyn and Blout, 1920; New York: Seltzer, 1921

Williams, Heathcote, *Whale Nation,* New York: Harmony, 1988; London: Jonathan Cape, 1988

Wise, Thomas James, and John Alexander Symington, eds., *The Shakespeare Head Brontë,* Oxford: Blackwell, 1934

Wordsworth, William, *William Wordsworth,* edited by Stephen Gill and Duncan Wu, New York and Oxford: Oxford University Press, 1994

Nature Writing in Irish Literature

❧

James Mc Elroy

In his poem, "The Stolen Child," W. B. Yeats calls on the "human child" to forsake this world and turn to "the waters and the wild" (pp. 18–19). But "the wild" Yeats has in mind on this occasion, "leafy island," "flapping herons," "drowsy water-rats," "reddest stolen cherries," is not half as wild as he would like to believe. In actual fact, Yeats's topographical references to the "rocky highland" of Sleuth Wood, the "furthest" Rosses, and the "hills above" Glen-Car are so tame (the same goes for his talk of "moonlight glosses" and "dim grey sands") that "the waters and the wild" end up as part of an otherwise wistful colonial dream wherein Ireland, England's nearest hinterland, is envisaged as a kind of quaint ecological backwater.

Of course, the same Yeats who used such evanescent terms in "The Stolen Child" was himself convinced that there were some remote Irish locations—rugged, primitive, quintessential locations—where nature could be seen in "the wild." One such location was the Aran Islands that Yeats visited in the summer of 1896. When he returned from the islands he wrote that his "imagination was full of those grey islands where men must reap with knives because of the stone" (p. 299). Indeed, he was so taken by "those grey islands" that he urged John Millington Synge to leave Paris and "'Go to the Aran Islands. Live there as if you were one of the people themselves; express a life that has never found expression'"(p. 299).

The most immediate outcome of this exchange between Yeats and Synge was the appearance of *The Aran Islands* in 1907, a travel journal in which Synge recorded an existence he thought "perhaps the most primitive in Europe" (p. 53). More to the point, *The Aran Islands* was a journal in which Synge's obvious devotion to things "primitive" helped him, as the critic Robin Skelton has suggested, to reconfigure "the dreaminess" of Yeats (p. 40). And

one of the first things that helped in this reconfiguration was the simple fact that the inhabitants of these three small islands, Inishmore, Inishmaan, Inishere, knew what it meant to be part of nature in an inhospitable place—case in point, when Synge asked the locals if there were any trees on the islands, an exchange ensued in which his Irish-speaking hosts inquired if "'tree'" meant the same thing as "'bush,'" if so, they replied, there might be "a few in sheltered hollows to the east" (p. 52).

In any event, it was these bleak, carboniferous islands that Synge identified as one of Ireland's most primitive borders, where he celebrated the "wild pastimes of the cliffs" (p. 73). And while there certainly are some passages in *The Aran Islands* where he idealizes, much as he does in *The Playboy of the Western World*, *The Shadow of the Glen,* and *The Well of the Saints,* the values, the language, the perspective—the primitiveness—of Ireland's indigenous people, his account of the islands is something of a milestone insofar as it spawned several accounts, in both Irish and English, of life in a part of the world where isolation was equated with vastness—in the vernacular, "wilderness":

As I lie here hour after hour, I seem to enter into the wild pastimes of the cliff, and to become a companion of the cormorants and crows.

Many of the birds display themselves before me with the vanity of barbarians, forming in strange evolutions as long as I am in sight, and returning to their ledge of rock when I am gone. Some are wonderfully expert, and cut graceful figures for an inconceivable time without a flap of their wings, growing so absorbed in their own dexterity that they often collide with one another in their flight, an incident always followed by a wild outburst of abuse. Their language is easier than Gaelic, and I seem to understand the greater part of their cries, though I am not able to answer. There is one plaintive note which they take up in the middle of their usual babble with extraordinary effect, and pass on from one to another along the cliff with a sort of inarticulate wail, as if they remembered for an instant the horror of the mist. (pp. 73–74)

Synge was not, however, the only writer to visit the Arans. As it happens, a host of other writers visited the islands, among them, Lady Gregory, Ethna Carbery, and Emily Lawless, whose 1892 novel, *Grania: The Story of an Island*, was based on her observations of the same "grey islands." James Joyce was another writer who paid a visit to the Arans and wrote a brief article for *Il Piccolo della Sera* in which he referred to Inishmore as the island (translation in *An Aran Reader*) "that sleeps like a great shark on the grey waters of the Atlantic Ocean" (p. 108). As well as Joyce, there was also a curious assortment of personalities, Somerville and Ross, Antonin Artaud, Brendan Behan, Orson Welles, Patrick Pearse, who all made a trek, in part, ecopilgrimage, to check out "the wild pastimes of the cliffs." No less important, there was even an occasional filmmaker like Robert Flaherty, who, after a brief visit in 1931, decided to make *Man of Aran,* which was released in 1934 (for the record, it received mixed reviews from Graham Greene and several other critics).

All these visitors aside, it was not until Liam O'Flaherty released *Thy Neighbour's Wife* in 1923 that the first real native account of life on the islands appeared in print. O'Flaherty (an Irish speaker) knew, first-hand, the elemental attraction, harshness, at times violence of his native home and wrote some fine short stories that explore, or, to be more precise, observe nature in a much more "primitive" light than ever before. One example of this narrative primitivism is "The Wounded Cormorant" in which O'Flaherty describes a cormorant injured when a rock drops from a cliff ledge and cuts its leg. As a result, the bird, even though it survives for a short time, does not do so well when it finally makes it back to its so-called "comrades": "It flopped on to the ledge over their backs and screamed, lying on the rock helplessly with its wings spread, quite exhausted. But they had no mercy. They fell upon it fiercely, tearing at its body with their beaks" (pp. 109–110).

Here, as so often in O'Flaherty's short stories,

the author never dwells on death and destruction. Instead, he just observes how survival of the fittest, in this case, elimination of the weakest, takes its course. And this, in some measure, is what he also does in "The Hawk," where he follows a hawk as it is about to move in for the kill: "He circled once more above his falling prey, took aim, and stooped again. This time the lark did nothing to avoid the kill. He died the instant he was struck; his inert wings unfolded" (p. 348). This piece, however, does not end with the lark's death. As a matter of fact, all the action soon shifts to the hawk's nesting site where, almost out of the blue, a human intruder climbs down the steep ledge, steals the hawk's egg, and, in the struggle that ensues, knocks the hawk (who has taken to the wing in an effort to protect his nest) off target and makes it smash headlong into the rock face—drop, without a sound, to the "dark water" below: "Far away below the body of the dead hawk floated, its broken wings outstretched on the foam-embroidered surface of the dark water, and drifted seawards with the ebbing tide" (p. 352).

In both these stories nature is viewed as something perilous and unpredictable, something that measures life's outer limits. In fact, if we flick back to the last few lines of "The Cormorant" it is clear that the ocean's inscrutable ebb and flow often serves as a kind of metanarrative that gives the entire piece its sense of closure: "It fell, fluttering feebly through the air, slowly descending, turning round and round, closing and opening its wings, until it reached the sea. Then it fluttered its wings twice and lay still. An advancing wave dashed it against the side of the black rock and then it disappeared, sucked down among the seaweed strands" (p. 110).

It should be said, of course, that Ireland's ocean/island narratives are not confined to the Arans. Hence, it is important to recognize that there is an impressive store of pieces that were written on the Blasket Islands, the same Blaskets that Synge once described as quite unlike the limestone verges of the Arans (p. 247). Perhaps the best known of the Blasket narratives is Tomás Ó Crohan's *The Islandman*, Muiris Ó Súilleabháin's *Twenty Years A-Growing*, and, most famous of all, Peig Sayers's *Peig: The Autobiography of Peig Sayers of the Great Blasket Island* and *An Old Woman's Reflections*. The concept of nature contained in these pieces is, much as we might expect, dialectical: on some occasions, Sayers describes, as per the *Autobiog-*

raphy, her island home as "this lonely rock in the middle of the great sea" (p. 211); on other occasions, she writes, "Dead indeed is the heart from which the balmy air of the sea cannot banish sorrow and grief" (p. 177). But whatever line Sayers or her Blasket neighbors take, one thing is certain, as Eoin Mc Kiernan has written in his introduction to the *Autobiography*, the islanders themselves live in "no romantic mist" (p. 4).

While all these different narratives contain many of the things that people associate with Irish literature—the dreaminess of Yeats, the drama of Synge, the primitivism of O'Flaherty, the native language of Sayers—it is important to remember that Ireland's other narrative lines (and here we return to the mainland) also contain some things that reconfigure whatever nature narrative comes to hand. Among such narratives, George Russell, in poems like "The Dawn of Darkness," "The Earth Breath," "The Voice of the Waters," "The Memory of Earth," and "The Voice of the Sea" enters a view of nature as a kind of aesthetic mysticism—in "Dust," he writes, "I have touched the lips of clay" (p. 34). Much like Russell, many of Katharine Tynan's nature verses, "The Maker," "Dove's Weather," "After the Drought," "The Wayside Bank," "The Making of Birds," "Sparrow," "In the Wood," "Poplar," "The Silent Time," also include the kind of religious—aesthetic—qualities that W. B. Yeats acknowledges in a letter to her, dated December 21, 1888, where he insists, "The want of your poetry is, I think, the want also of my own. We both of us need to substitute more and more the landscapes of nature for the landscapes of art" (p. 76).

F. R. Higgins is another poet whose "landscapes of nature" were criticized on the grounds that their aesthetic base, in part Georgian pastoral, was either inauthentic, ineffectual or insincere. To a certain extent, much the same criticism was also levelled against Padraic Colum even though he (unlike Higgins) took some of Ireland's "English" pastorals and gave them a new look with "Crows," "Otters," "Night-Fliers" and "Dedication: to M. C. M. C." For the most part, though, Colum's devotion to Celtic Ireland meant nothing more than an immediate shift from certain Anglo-Irish pieties, for example, the arcadian qualities of "the waters and the wild," to something that was supposed to be ever so "Irish"—an arcadian realm known as *Tir na nOg* (in translation, "the land of the young").

This attempt by Colum to re-envisage Ireland as a paradise at some point before "The Fall," in political terms, long before England ever colonized Ireland, found a kindred spirit in the prosodic experiments (themselves based on Gaelic originals) of Austin Clarke who was reckoned to be a far more able poet than either Russell, Tynan, Higgins or Colum. The real truth, however, is that many of Clarke's poems are themselves uneven and rather sentimental. In fact, a lot of Clarke's nature poems, and this includes "A Strong Wind" and "On a Bright Morning," are much more sentimental than the autobiographical fragments he has on offer in *Twice Round the Black Church: Early Memories of Ireland and England* where he recounts childhood encounters with nature—the "animus in Nature"—on trips to the outskirts of Dublin: "There was an animus in Nature against which I had to struggle, for Dublin was far away and I was evidently in a region beyond the strict guidance of the catechism" (p. 59).

Someone else who deserves to be included in this article is Louis MacNeice. For even though MacNeice has never been dubbed a "nature" poet, he did put together some nice rural pieces in "Autumn Journal," "Nature Notes," "The Closing Album," "Turf Stacks," and "Western Landscape," while in "The Park," he pieced together an "Urban enclave" where "Children who never had seen the country" believe that the park is it, while those who had once known what real country looked like "ignore the void / Their present imposes" (pp. 494–495). Not half as urbane as MacNeice, John Hewitt (like MacNeice, an Ulster Protestant) was much less concerned about "Children who had never seen the country" than he was with Northern Ireland's topographical, or, as it is in the North, territorial struggles. A fact that is not lost on Seamus Heaney who writes in *Preoccupations: Selected Prose 1968–1978* that Hewitt's "attachment to his actual countryside involves an attachment to an idea of country: his cherishing of the habitat is symptomatic of his history, and that history is the history of the colonist" (p. 147).

More than all these writers, however, it was Patrick Kavanagh who redefined Ireland—redefined habitat—as a legitimate poetic subject. And in this singular mission Kavanagh took no prisoners; on more than one occasion he hurled insults at W. B. Yeats because Yeats, as he put it in *Collected Pruse*, "invented" writers like F. R. Higgins who wrote "bad poems about blackthorn sticks" (p. 225). In marked contrast, Kavanagh himself produced first-hand accounts of life along the Monaghan, Armagh, Louth border; published narratives of what it meant, as per his *Self-Portrait,* to eke out a living in the shadow of "watery little hills that would physic a snipe" (p. 9). And perhaps the most famous of all these poetic accounts is "The Great Hunger," a minor classic that offers a forthright account of life in the shadow of such "watery little hills."

First published in 1942, "The Great Hunger" is tied to the land in much the same way that John B. Keane is tied to it in his drama, *The Field,* where his lead character, "The Bull" Mc Cabe, announces that "Land is all that matters" (p. 16). But while it is true that Kavanagh, like Keane, is tied to the land in much of his work (the opening line of "The Great Hunger" reads, "Clay is the word and clay is the flesh") the land he is tied to is of a kind: the immediate use of "clay" reminds us that Kavanagh identifies with what Seamus Heaney, in *Preoccupations,* has called "the unpromising, unspectacular country-side of Monaghan" (p. 137). Perhaps even more important, it is at the heart of the "unpromising, unspectacular" that Kavanagh finds some things the Irish establishment never even countenanced circa 1942—prime example, when he takes the time to acknowledge, in marked contrast to most of his contemporaries, that the "goldfinches on the railway pailing were worth looking at" (p. 45).

At other points in his work, Kavanagh represents bird species like the corncrake as "A cry in the wilderness / Of meadow" (p. 16). And he is successful in such "wilderness" representations—this also applies to his treatment of Monaghan's native farmers—because the language he uses is "natural and spoken"; it is, in Heaney's words, never used as a "mark of folksiness" in the sense that Synge used language to describe his native subjects and their environment (p. 138). All of which puts Kavanagh in a unique position to celebrate, as he does in "Advent," the "spirit-shocking / Wonder in a black slanting Ulster hill" (p. 70). Far more to the point, Kavanagh's stomping ground is a small, ancestral parish where nature, as is evident in his poem, "On Reading a Book on Common Wild Flowers," might sometimes go unnamed, but seldom goes unnoticed: "The burnt saxifrage was there in profusion / And the autumn gentian—I knew them all by eyesight long before I knew their names" (p. 137).

These last lines, coupled with lines from "In Blinking Blankness: Three Efforts," where Kavanagh writes about "used up lanes / Waters that run in rivers or are stagnant," suggest that Ireland's otherwise brackish habitats are much more important to Kavanagh than we might imagine (p. 196). His genuine interest in the importance of unimportance (in part, the unnoticed flora and fauna that make up one of Ireland's ecological backwaters) brings with it an irredentist edge: it represents, however transposed, a measure of Catholic experience in rural Ulster where subsistence farms, themselves servile reminders of historical dispossession, survive against all the odds.

As it turns out, the same dependence on "Waters that run in rivers or are stagnant" also appears to characterize some of Kavanagh's later poems where he hopes, as he does in "Canal Bank Walk," that he can "Grow with nature as before"—turns to Dublin's canal banks as unrushed ("or are stagnant") backwaters. And for Kavanagh, at least, the natural connection between Monaghan and Dublin is as clear as the nose on his face: "For many a good-looking year I wrought hard at versing but I would say that, as a poet, I was born in or about nineteen-fifty-five, the place of my birth being the banks of the Grand Canal. Thirty years earlier Shancoduff's watery hills could have done the trick but I was too thick to take the hint" (*Self-Portait,* 26).

Kavanagh's use of these otherwise "unspectacular" materials—the "banks of the Grand Canal," "Shancoduff's watery hills"—made it possible for a whole generation of poets, among others, John Montague and Seamus Heaney, to extol the virtues of place, observe rural rituals, and revere—in the same breath, curse—the earth's natural processes. And, so, while it is perfectly reasonable to argue, as Heaney does, that John Montague inscribes certain "etymological" elements Kavanagh never bothered to think about, the fact remains that both Montague and Kavanagh grew up in an "unpromising, unspectacular" environment that was defined in accordance with a specific cultural and historical experience, an experience that helps to explain, among other things, Montague's preference for "low bushes and grass, / heatherbells and fern, / wrinkling bog pools" (p. 272). For it is among such "low bushes" that Montague enters a dark, divided land and describes, in rather bleak terms, what Irish dispossession is all about: "plaintive moorland," "small, whin-tough hills," "heathery gap," "ravaged hillock."

It should come as no surprise, then, that Montague views his natural environment as an inhospitable quarter: "Harsh landscape that haunts me, / Well and stone, in the bleak moors of dream, / With all my circling to return" (p. 9). Nor should it come as a great surprise that Montague identifies his vestigial homeland, in sectarian terms, Catholic stronghold, as "A high, stony place—bogstreams, / Not milk and honey—but our own" (p. 38). As much as Montague might criticize such "bogstreams," however, it is still clear that this "high, stony place" is a species habitat he would like to preserve and protect. A position he makes most clear, perhaps, in Section VII of *The Rough Field* where he decries the pollution caused by road construction that forms a toxic brown stain that "seeps" down and discolors "the grass, thickening / the current of the trout stream / which flows between broken banks" (p. 59).

Whereas Montague encounters his "Harsh landscape" (and it him) in the "current of the trout stream / which flows between broken banks," Seamus Heaney defines his townland as a "'place of clear water'" (*Selected Poems*, 58). Elsewhere, Heaney even goes so far as to claim that "To this day, green, wet corners, flooded wastes, soft rushy bottoms, any place with the invitation of watery ground and tundra vegetation, even glimpsed from a car or a train, possess an immediate and deeply peaceful attraction. It is as if I am betrothed to them" (*Preoccupations*, 19). But while it is undeniable that Heaney is "betrothed" to the sensuous draw—the "wet corners"—of nature in a wide selection of his pieces, "Blackberry-Picking," "Gifts of Rain," "Glanmore Sonnets," "The Otter," "Song," it is also undeniable that many of his poems are not a bit soft, for instance, poems that introduce us, as happens in "At a Potato Digging," to "A people hungering from birth / grubbing, like plants, in the bitch earth" (*Selected Poems*, 22).

This "bitch earth," with its Kavanagh turn of phrase and famished plants, finds even more chthonic sustenance in "Digging" where Heaney writes that "the curt cuts of an edge / Through living roots awaken in my head" (*Selected Poems*, 11). But there is a small problem here: the sensual betrothal of Heaney's language sometimes makes us forget that "Digging" is a poem about subsistence in and around "Toner's bog," and how, even on those occasions when the poet leaves subsistence behind, it leaves an indelible mark in its wake. What is more, in pieces like "The Early Purges" the same "curt cuts" are used to draw some critical lines—ecological, economic, environmental—between subsistence farmers and town dwellers who hold radically different views on how to control "pests": "'Prevention of cruelty' talk cuts ice in town / Where they consider death unnatural, / But on well-run farms pests have to be kept down" (p. 23).

Much the same kind of thing might also be said (although this requires an element of imaginative transposition) about the "Glanmore Sonnets" in *Field Work* where, quite apart from all the poem's luscious terms of phrase, Heaney identifies a number of "pests" that emerge from "the hiding places"—"Ferreting themselves out of their dark hutch" (p. 34). For example, the ninth sonnet in the Glanmore sequence defines "wilderness" (one of the poem's speakers asks, "Did we come to the wilderness for this?") in terms of animal and plant species that are, for better or worse, "pests." And notice how Heaney does this. All it takes is a casual observation that "Outside the kitchen window a black rat / Sways on the briar like infected fruit"—the unspectacular comes to life as "black rat," "briar," "infected fruit."

While it is obvious that such "infected" lines might not strike a lot of readers, in particular, North American readers, as the stuff of "wilderness," it is still important to recognize that this kind of dispossessive lead provides some of Ireland's poets with the "curt cuts of an edge." And not least among said poets is Michael Longley who has, with some real artistic success, managed to incorporate the insights of Kavanagh, Montague, Heaney, and reinforced these insights with the help of Wordsworth, Clare, and Lawrence. As a result, Longley's devotion to nature in "Kestrel," "Sandpiper," "Snow Bunting," "Otters," "Peregrine," "Goldcrest," "Flora," "Botany," "Badger," "Mole," not only gives nature pride of place as a literary subject, but, and this is just as important, puts the human species on notice; at the end of "The Ornithological Section" (*Poems 1963–1983*), he serves up an ominous reminder that "We come as ornithologists— / As taxidermists we depart" (p. 25).

Much as it would be wrong to overlook the poems of someone like Michael Longley, it would be unconscionable to overlook the poems of several Irish women who have put together some intriguing narratives over the last few years. Thus, while there is not enough space in this article to examine the works of Nuala Ní Dhomhnaill, Medbh Mc Guckian, Eiléan Ní Chuilleanáin, it is important to at least acknowledge their various contributions to nature writing in modern Ireland. No less important, it is time to re-read the "unwild" poems of Eavan Boland who has waged a virtual campaign on behalf of nature in the Dublin suburbs. Last, but not least, it is about time that we started to read—to recognize—women like Anne Peters and Evangeline Paterson who have had something to say about ecological issues in Ireland as when Peters writes, in "Progressions," about the "heedless mercenaries" whose "machines burn the air we breathe" (p. 20), or when Paterson writes, in "Non-Biodegradable," that a "tattered streamer of plastic, snagged / on the highest unreachable twig of hawthorn / signals distress" (p. 29).

Given these various developments in Irish literature over the last few decades, it is now clear that the Irish establishment must start to acknowledge how much its standard assumptions have had, and continue to have, a dramatic impact on how we define nature, wilderness, and the environment. Should this occur (and should is the operative word) it might then become possible to re-envisage Irish literature, in part, the "unpromising, unspectacular," as a literature where "the waters and the wild" come with a real "edge" and where many of the writers outlined above, not to mention people like Derek Mahon, Richard Murphy, Eamon Grennan, Thomas Kinsella, John Mc Gahern, turn England's nearest hinterland into an ecological subject the natives can now call their own: "A high, stony place–bogstreams, / Not milk and honey–but our own."

Selected Works and Further Reading

Boland, Eavan, *Collected Poems,* Manchester, England: Carcanet, 1995

Clarke, Austin, *Selected Poems,* edited by Thomas Kinsella, Winston-Salem, North Carolina: Wake Forest University Press, 1976; Dublin, Ireland: Dolmen, 1976

———, *Twice Round the Black Church: Early Memories of Ireland and England,* London: Routledge & Kegan Paul, 1962

Colum, Padraic, *Collected Poems,* New York: Devin-Adair, 1953

Grennan, Eamon, *Wildly for Days,* Dublin, Ireland: Gallery, 1983

———, *What Light There Is,* San Francisco: North Point, 1989

———, *As if It Matters,* St. Paul, Minnesota: Graywolf, 1992

———, *So It Goes,* St. Paul, Minnesota: Graywolf, 1995

Heaney, Seamus, *Field Work,* Boston and London: Faber & Faber, 1979

———, *Preoccupations: Selected Prose, 1968–1978,* Boston and London: Faber & Faber, 1980

———, *Selected Poems, 1965–1975,* Boston and London: Faber & Faber, 1980

Hewitt, John, *Collected Poems 1932–1967,* London: MacGibbon & Kee, 1968

Higgins, F. R., *Arable Holdings: Poems,* Dublin, Ireland: Cuala, 1933

———, *The Dark Breed,* London: Macmillan, 1927

———, *Island Blood,* London: John Lane, 1925

Kavanagh, Patrick, *Collected Poems,* New York: Devin-Adair, 1964; London: MacGibbon & Kee, 1964

———, *Collected Pruse,* London: MacGibbon & Kee, 1967

Keane, John B., *The Field,* Cork, Ireland: Mercier, 1966

Kinsella, Thomas, *Poems, 1956–1973,* Winston-Salem, North Carolina: Wake Forest University Press, 1979

Longley, Michael, *Poems 1963–1983,* Dublin, Ireland: Gallery, 1985; Edinburgh, Scotland: Salamander, 1985; Harmondsworth, England: Penguin, 1986; Winston-Salem, North Carolina: Wake Forest University Press, 1987

McGahern, John, *The Collected Stories,* London: Faber & Faber, 1992; New York: Knopf, 1993

McGuckian, Medbh, *Captain Lavender,* Oldcastle, Ireland: Gallery, 1994; Winston-Salem, North Carolina: Wake Forest University Press, 1995

———, *The Flower Master,* New York and Oxford: Oxford University Press, 1982

———, *Marconi's Cottage,* Oldcastle, Ireland: Gallery, 1991; Winston-Salem, North Carolina: Wake Forest University Press, 1992; Newcastle-upon-Tyne, England: Bloodaxe, 1992

———, *On Ballycastle Beach,* Winston-Salem, North Carolina: Wake Forest University Press, 1988; Oxford: Oxford University Press, 1988

———, *Portrait of Joanna,* Belfast, Northern Ireland: Ulsterman, 1980

———, *Single Ladies: Sixteen Poems,* Devon, England: Interim, 1980

———, *Venus and the Rain,* New York and Oxford: Oxford University Press, 1984

MacNeice, Louis, *The Collected Poems of*

Louis MacNeice, edited by E. R. Dodds, New York: Oxford University Press, 1967; London: Faber & Faber, 1979

Mahon, Derek, *Selected Poems,* New York and London: Viking, 1991

Montague, John, *Collected Poems,* Winston-Salem, North Carolina: Wake Forest University Press, 1995; Liverpool, England: Gallery, 1995

Murphy, Richard, *The Price of Stone and Earlier Poems,* Winston-Salem, North Carolina: Wake Forest University Press, 1985; also published as *The Price of Stone,* London: Faber & Faber, 1985

Ní Chuilleanáin, Eiléan, *Acts and Monuments,* Dublin, Ireland: Gallery, 1972

——, *The Brazen Serpent,* Oldcastle, Ireland: Gallery, 1994; Winston-Salem, North Carolina: Wake Forest University Press, 1995

——, *The Magdalene Sermon,* Meath, Ireland: Gallery, 1989; also published as *The Magdalene Sermon and Earlier Poems,* Winston-Salem, North Carolina: Wake Forest University Press, 1991

——, *The Rose-Geranium,* Dublin, Ireland: Gallery, 1981

——, *Site of Ambush,* Dublin, Ireland: Gallery, 1975

Ní Dhomhnaill, Nuala, *An Dealg Droighin,* Baile Átha Cliath, Ireland: Cló Mercier, 1981

——, *The Astrakhan Cloak,* translated by Paul Muldoon, Oldcastle, Ireland: Gallery, 1992; Winston-Salem, North Carolina: Wake Forest University Press, 1993

——, *Féar Suaithinseach,* Maigh Nuad, Ireland: An Sagart (St. Patrick's College), 1984

——, *Pharaoh's Daughter,* rev. ed., Winston-Salem, North Carolina: Wake Forest University Press, 1993

——, *Selected Poems/Rogha Dánta,* translated by Michael Hartnett, Dublin, Ireland: Raven Arts, 1988

Ó Crohan, Tomás, *The Islandman,* translated by Robin Flower, New York: Scribner's, 1934; London: Chatto and Windus, 1934

Ó hEithir, Breandán, and Ruairí Ó hEithir, eds., *An Aran Reader,* Dublin, Ireland: Lilliput Press, 1991

O'Sullivan, Maurice, *Twenty Years A-Growing,* New York: Viking, 1933; London: Chatto and Windus, 1933

Paterson, Evangeline, *Lucifer, with Angels: New and Selected Poems,* Dublin, Ireland: Dedalus, 1994

Peters, Anne, *Rings of Green,* Gerrards Cross, Buckinghamshire, England: C. Smythe, 1982

Russell, George, *Collected Poems,* London: Macmillan, 1913; Philadelphia: Biddle, 1916

Sayers, Peig, *Peig: The Autobiography of Peig Sayers of the Great Blasket Island,* translated by Bryan MacMahon, Syracuse, New York: Syracuse University Press, 1974

——, *An Old Woman's Reflections,* translated by Séamus Ennis, New York and London: Oxford University Press, 1962

Skelton, Robin, *The Writings of J. M. Synge,* Indianapolis, Indiana: Bobbs-Merrill, 1971; London: Thames and Hudson, 1971

Synge, J. M., *Collected Works: Volume 1: Poems,* edited by Robin Skelton, London: Oxford University Press, 1962; Washington, D.C.: Catholic University of America Press, 1982

——, *Collected Works: Volume II: Prose,* edited by Alan Price, London: Oxford University Press, 1962; Washington, D.C.: Catholic University of America Press, 1982

Tynan, Katharine, *The Poems of Katharine Tynan,* Dublin, Ireland: Figgis, 1963

Yeats, W. B., *The Collected Poems of W. B. Yeats,* London: Macmillan, 1934; New York: Macmillan, 1935

——, *Essays and Introductions,* London: Macmillan, 1959; New York: Macmillan, 1961

——, *W. B. Yeats: Letters to Katharine Tynan,* edited by Roger McHugh, New York: McMullen, 1953

Nature in Scottish Literature

Christopher MacLachlan

In the sixteenth chapter of Sir Walter Scott's first novel *Waverley*, the hero, Edward Waverley, enters the Highlands of Scotland for the first time, led there by a party of clansmen. At a pause in the journey, Scott describes the landscape and Waverley's romantic response to it.

The scene is dominated by mountains and water, with a frame of trees. It is a rather generalized picture, yet instantly recognizable to the modern reader as of the Scottish Highlands, perhaps because of the simple combination of limited elements. The sense of archetypical simplicity is enhanced by the indistinctness of the view, here partly obscured by night (in other versions of this landscape mist plays the same role). There is also a vagueness of topography; it is not clear whether the water in view is a river or a lake, nor does it seem to matter. As a consequence of the features just pointed out, nature here is rather empty—empty of human life, and empty of obvious meaning. There are mountains, trees, and water but no people here, apparently, and without them there is no clear significance to the picture. Who belongs here, and to whom does here belong? These questions are obliquely answered by noting another aspect of the passage, its mediation to the reader through the main character, who is straightforwardly a spectator, and takes up a position of detachment from it. Yet he uses it, quite consciously, for an aesthetic purpose, giving himself up to "the full romance of his situation" (p. 138). For Waverley, this scene of nature exists to provide him with a certain set of feelings, and so in a sense it belongs to him.

The early chapters of the novel have been at pains to define the hero as a man of feeling, so that it is almost with relief that he comes upon a situation in nature that allows him to practice the sensibility his literary education has given him. Waverley does what countless visitors to Scotland have done, especially after reading the Waverley novels: he goes to the Highlands to admire the scenery and feel a thrill of excitement from looking at it, an excitement based partly on a sense of strangeness and partly on ignorance, replaced by literary imaginings. In *Waverley*, Scott's first international prose best seller, the image of the Highlands as the image of Scotland is firmly fixed in the terms described above.

Robert Louis Stevenson, Scott's great successor in Scottish romance fiction, uses the same image in his fiction, notably in *Kidnapped*, in which David Balfour, accompanied by the Highlander, Alan Breck, makes an epic journey across the Highlands. To the elements present in Scott's version of the Highlands Stevenson adds the strain of being pursued across a bleak and empty land. The characteristic scenery is that of Chapter 22: "[t]he mist rose and died away, and showed us that country lying as waste as the sea. . . . A wearier-looking desert man never saw . . ." (p. 142). Weary to cross, no doubt, but again there is a spectatorial aspect to this description; we sit in our armchairs with the book in our hands and revel in this stark picture of nature, full of signs of violence and threat, but strangely fixed and passive to the gaze—an almost textbook version of the Burkeian sublime, terrific but not terrifying. Across this terrain our heroes are hunted, to escape back to civilization at the end.

It was Stevenson's own successor, John Buchan, who refined this version of the Scottish landscape to a definitive statement. Although the Scottish scenes in *The Thirty-Nine Steps* are set, not in the Highlands, but among the hills of the Scottish Borders, their effect is similar to that in *Waverley* and *Kidnapped*. Buchan's hero, Richard Hannay, flees to Scotland to avoid the consequences of finding a dead body in his London flat. The sense of release he feels when he reaches the Scottish moors is an open statement of the escapism inherent in the view of nature Scott, Stevenson and Buchan are presenting.

Buchan is also the most direct in suggesting that a hint of danger adds spice to the dish. As a result, the pace of his flight across the hills and moors is that much faster than David Balfour's in *Kidnapped*, and the sense of Scotland as a grand adventure playground, where men play deadly games of hide-and-seek, becomes that much more obvious in Buchan's novel. The game quality of Buchan's use of landscape becomes explicit in his later novel *John Macnab*, in which a group of gentleman-heroes, jaded by their normal lives, wager themselves against the landlords of three Highland estates in a trio of poaching adventures. Here the physical demands of deer stalking, in which man confronts nature, are real, but the human dangers are self-evidently factitious.

Although the fiction of Scott, Stevenson and Buchan may have fixed the image of the Scottish Highlands, it did not begin there. Scott himself, in the verse that preceded his novels, had adumbrated the idea. The first canto of *The Lady of the Lake*, for example, is full of description of mountain, lake and wood; but more significant is a passage, once famous as a familiar quotation, from the sixth canto of Scott's first poetic success, *The Lay of the Last Minstrel*, hailing "Caledonia," the "Land of the mountain and the flood" as "Meet nurse for a poetic child" (Canto Sixth, ll. 17, 18, and 20). But these lines are spoken in the voice, not of Scott himself, but of the Last Minstrel of the poem's title, and are meant as a lamentation for what will soon be lost.

This pose is certainly an echo of an earlier set of lamentations for the past by a bard who is the self-proclaimed last of his kind, the Ossian of James Macpherson's rhapsodic prose versions of what he claimed were the remains of ancient Scottish Gaelic poems, published in several volumes from 1760 to 1765. In Macpherson's repetitive sentences can be found the generalized natural elements that have become the standard features of the Scottish experience: mountains, mists, moors, lakes, rivers, rock, rain and wind, eagle and deer, with hardly a human being in sight, and those either doomed to early deaths or, dead already, haunting the land as ghosts. Whether directly describing the land of his Celtic heroes or using it as a source of metaphors, Macpherson endlessly recycles the same set of natural images, overlaid with suggestions of the numinous, and animated by active verbs into anthropomorphic but stupendous life. The Highlands become not just a tract of mountains

but a vast being, the personification of human ideals of endurance, nobility, unworldliness and constancy, as well as the medium for spiritual insight and uplift. This is why Scott calls them "Meet nurse for a poetic child" and thither sends his young heroes, in *Waverley* and the later *Rob Roy*, to complete their educations, a move Stevenson copies in *Kidnapped*.

Yet the nature of the Highlands in Ossian conceals another meaning. The controversy over Macpherson's sources reminds us that he had an ideological and political motive for his poems. His aim was to state the case for the Scottish Gaelic culture from which he came and that had been dealt a severe not to say mortal blow by the defeat of the Jacobite Rebellion of 1745–46 (the subject of *Waverley*). As a boy he had seen something of that event, and he had experienced its aftermath and the beginnings of the destruction of the clan system and with it the human ecology of the Highlands. The elegiac tone of the Ossianic fragments, although projected into the distant past, expresses a contemporary feeling, and the aggrandizement of ancient heroes is an attempt to restore the pride of a defeated people. As such it is deeply flawed by its own obliqueness and its overwhelming melancholy. The reader is diverted from a direct confrontation with what was happening after the Forty-Five toward a dream-vision of a past so distant as to seem disconnected from history. The elements of the Ossianic world that persist are those belonging to nature, the landscape itself. The poems repeat over and over a lamentation for the passing of the heroes, leaving only the hills and moors as their memorials. All that is left for the present and future is a landscape of memories. *Waverley*, with its subtitle, "Tis Sixty Years Since," takes up this nostalgia; *Kidnapped*, set in the period of retribution after the rebellion, so that the great event is already over, is written in the voice of a David Balfour who now has leisure to look back on his youth.

Both Scott and Stevenson, however, were aware of the submerged meaning of the Highlands they portrayed. Chapter 16 of *Waverley* contains more than just a romantic landscape. While Waverley indulges in the romance of the Highlands, Scott reminds us that to do so he must suppress the reason for his journey—the attempt to recover cattle stolen by Highlanders. As Scott several times makes plain in the novel, he knows that cattle theft, and the levying of protection money or blackmail against such theft (*see* Note F to the novel), are part of the complex economic system upon which the existence of the Highland clans depends. He knows that, from an economic point of view, the Jacobite Rebellion was partly a continuation of and partly an attempt to prolong this system. Yet this un-Romantic aspect of the Highlands is easily overlooked by readers, attracted like Edward Waverley by the romance of the situation.

Similarly, Stevenson builds into *Kidnapped* clear signs of the Highland Clearances, directly in his description of an emigrant ship (chapter 16), indirectly in his portrayal of an empty landscape. This emptiness is perhaps more accurate as a picture of the Highlands of his time than that of the young David Balfour, but the very vagueness about history here leaves the reader with the impression that the Highlands have always been a "desert," and therefore with no questions about how it became so. Such questions are not raised in *The Thirty-Nine Steps* (although they are in *John Macnab*, especially in chapter 8), but the structure of the book implies them. Hannay's adventures in Scotland are sandwiched between episodes in England, mainly in London, where the real events of the plot take place and are resolved. The Scottish scenes are exciting, but irrelevant to the defense of civilization (although Buchan sometimes hints that the freedom to enjoy the Scottish countryside is a mark of the civilization to be defended). Buchan's novel thus gives a strong clue to what has happened: Scotland has become a place out of touch with modern history, for all that it is steeped in the romance of Fingal and Bonnie Prince Charlie. Instead of history it has natural sublimity, age-old mountains, rushing torrents, ancient woods and the endless cycle of the seasons. The reason for its lack of history is that history has moved away to London, with the Union of the Parliaments of England and Scotland in 1707, against which, amongst other things, the Jacobite Rebellions were directed. The significance of the way nature appears in Macpherson, Scott, Stevenson and Buchan is that this way of seeking the essential Scotland, in visions of mountain and flood, develops after the end of Scotland as an independent nation, and nature is made to offer a kind of compensation for the loss of other expressions of national identity.

The move after the loss of independence to a compensating national image of apolitical, ahistorical natural wilderness was and is extremely popular, easily sweeping aside the signs of realism present even in the fictions that abet it. It is the stuff of Scottish tourism, itself launched by Scott (*The Lady of the Lake* created the touristic appeal of the Trossachs by its landscape descriptions), boosted by the decision of Queen Victoria and Prince Albert to build Balmoral Castle and still exploited in such recent forms as the 1995 film *Rob Roy*. This embracing of a permanent world of nature as the soul of Scotland survived the twentieth-century reaction against Victorian Romanticism, evident in the decline in Scott's reputation. Lewis Grassic Gibbon, in his trilogy *A Scots Quair*, strives to present a version of Scotland that is truer to the real toil of life, in field and factory, but his novels are rich in descriptions of nature, and ultimately cannot resist its pull. At one point his heroine, Chris Guthrie, must choose between keeping on her father's farm or leaving for the city and a career as a teacher. She decides in favor of staying on the land. Although by the end of the trilogy Gibbon sets out a political agenda for Scotland, involving a communist revolution, he also clings to his heroine's vision of the land, and she has the last word in the book. In an essay titled simply "The Land," Gibbon calls it "only half-inanimate" (p. 69) and, while graphically evoking the mind-numbing labor of agriculture (from which he had escaped himself), still he testifies to the land's fascination, in images of the seasonal round that echo those in "Sunset Song," the semi-autobiographical first part of *A Scots Quair*.

In their fiction Gibbon's female contemporaries seem to endorse his presentation of his heroine as close to nature. In *Open the Door!*, a novel by Catherine Carswell, friend of D. H. Lawrence, of the spiritual and sexual liberation of a young woman, the climactic ending takes place on yet another open moorland. The heroine, finally alienated by life in Glasgow and London, escapes to the countryside of her childhood holidays. She has bathed naked in a stream, slept rough, milked a cow for her breakfast and roamed across the heather, when she unexpectedly spots her half-estranged lover and races over the moor to embrace him with new commitment. The novel ends in imagery of sheaves and ripe seeds. Similarly, the heroine of Nan Shepherd's *The Quarry Wood* wanders at night in a fever of longing through the wood until she comes upon the man she wishes to give herself to. Silently they commune in the moonlight and the glow of dawning. Nature and darkness allow the expression of feelings silenced by everyday life.

Just as for Scott, Stevenson, and Buchan, nature offers an outlet for patriotic feelings that escape the impotence of Scotland's historical position, in these women's novels nature represents a sphere in which the aspirations society discourages can be expressed. The elements of natural landscape become a metaphorical language for the socially repressed feelings of women. Interestingly, a third, slightly later, novelist, Willa Muir, in *Imagined Corners*, has the younger of her two heroines indulge in just the same kind of swooning into nature that Carswell and Shepherd describe, until her older heroine talks her out of it with a wonderfully acerbic dismissal of nature as "an anachronism in the present stage of human development" (p. 245), before whisking her out of Scotland to Italy. It is tempting to see this as a prophecy of the career of the most famous Scottish woman novelist of the twentieth century, Muriel Spark, whose use of nature seems to exemplify Muir's suggestion that "one had to filch from her [Nature] the energy of one's own purposes" (p. 246). Certainly this seems true of Liz Lochhead's poem "What the Pool Said, on Midsummer's Day," in which the voice of nature becomes female and predatory, taking power over itself and others. But although Scottish women writers' exploitation of the rhetoric of nature parallels that of their male compatriots, it would be wrong to say it shares the patriotic purpose that interests, not to say obsesses, so many of the men.

Lewis Grassic Gibbon's version of nature as the bedrock of existence, shorn of his political activism, is handed on to later writers such as the poets Edwin Muir and George Mackay Brown, both from the Orkney Islands, off the north of Scotland, and perhaps therefore inclined to seek a vision of permanence, combining nature and the spiritual, to compensate for political marginalization—just as Macpherson did 200 years before. Although Mackay Brown's work is much concerned with the past, it is a mythic past, whose exact relation to the present is obscure, or even suppressed. Placing him in line with Macpherson, Scott, Stevenson, Buchan and Gibbon, we can perhaps see why—the difficulty of articulating the history of a nation that stepped aside from history in 1707. In this sense, nature, whether it is the grandeur of the Highlands or Mackay Brown's "green fables" (*see* Gifford, 33), is an escape route, a source of identity that instigates no program of action.

There is, however, another way in which nature appears in Scottish literature, and it brings us to Scotland's national poet, Robert Burns. He is of course as surrounded by myth as any Highland mountain, but this much is beyond dispute: that, unlike most writers, including Scottish writers, he was indeed born and brought up in close contact with nature in the raw, and he made that the subject of much of his verse. Burns was a creature of paradox and self-contradictions and it is impossible in a short space to do justice to the complexity of his achievement, not least because that often consisted of a disarming appearance of simplicity. His poems combine some of the most direct and unassuming descriptions of nature ever written with a lively awareness of the contemporary discussions of man and nature of his time. A notable example is "To a Mouse," which opens with a stanza, in rich Scots, descriptive of the mouse and the man, and moves on to a stanza, in formal, Latinate English, that states a theory of their relationship strongly reflecting the environmental thinking of his day (and ours). The poem goes on to explore the shared state of mouse and man in the face of nature's hardships, "the Winter's sleety dribble, / An' *cranreuch* cauld!" (ll. 35–36). The concept of nature that emerges is of a force that is harsh but indifferent, disinterested in the challenges it offers, inclined to favor neither the weak nor the strong, and too far above either to be malicious.

This is very much the constant view of nature in Burns. Several of his most important and personal poems, including "The Cotter's Saturday Night," "Tam o' Shanter," "The Vision," "Love and Liberty," and "Man was made to mourn," open with a contrast between the condition of humanity and the severity of winter weather as an image of adversity. Tam o' Shanter's tavern pleasures have to be paid for by his journey through a stormy and haunted landscape. Typically, Burns includes Tam's horse among the beings oppressed by this journey; for Burns there seems to be a division between animate beings, human and otherwise, and the rest of nature. Although Burns is anticipating Scott's description of Scotland as "stern and wild" he does not make of this an anthropomorphic reflection but instead presents live creatures as at the mercy of unfeeling nature.

Of course, nature sometimes smiles in Burns's poems, for example at the start of "The Holy Fair," or in many of the songs. Yet in other songs there is still a sense of division between man and nature. The forsaken lover in "The Banks o' Doon" is alienated from the "warbling bird," in "Afton Water" the singer begs the river not to disturb his Mary's sleep, and in one of the last songs, "Oh, wert thou in the cauld blast," love is the only shelter against adversity. Burns, then, while an accurate and sensitive observer of nature, is rarely a sentimentalizer of it, no doubt because of his struggles with the unforgiving soil of several unprofitable farms. But a glance at any illustrated edition of his poems, or some of the favorite portraits of the Bard, will soon show that his readers were far less clear-eyed. Burns rapidly became an iconic figure, the Ayrshire ploughman surrounded by rural devices, and the inspiration for a view of Scotland as a land of honest, hardworking country folk, living traditional lives in humble circumstances, well away from the pressure of modernity. The high point of this post-Burnsian sentimentality is the Kailyard movement of the nineteenth century, named after the kailyard or cabbage patch that was the symbolic location of much of this kind of fiction; the stories of Ian Maclaren are typical, as is the title of one of his collections, *Beside the Bonnie Brier Bush*. Well after Scotland had become one of the most urbanized and industrialized nations of the world its popular literature dwelt on the life of small farms in isolated glens, projecting an image of homeliness and conventionality, and a harmony between man and nature at the small-scale level of individuals and families.

Although Grassic Gibbon, and others, reacted strongly against the Kailyard, the leading voice of protest was that of Christopher Grieve, writing under the name Hugh MacDiarmid. His violent opposition to sentimentality led him to attack Burns himself and call for a return to the spirit of the sixteenth-century Scottish poet, William Dunbar. It would be rash to see Dunbar as a nature poet in any modern sense, although it is tempting to find in the use of natural description by his predecessor, Robert Henryson, in *The Testament of Cresseid* and his *Fables*, and by Gavin Douglas, in some of the prologues to the books of his translation of Vergil's *Aeneid*, an anticipation of Burns's clearheadedness about nature. In MacDiarmid's own early lyrics from the collection *Sangschaw* is found an attitude to nature that is almost metaphysical. Poems like "The Eemis Stane" and "The Bonnie Broukit Bairn" take a view of mankind and the earth that is detached and cosmological, and in "The Watergaw," which means a kind of indistinct rainbow, the natural imagery that is the mainstay of the poem has an aloof inscrutability.

This sense of nature as the prompter of difficult questions, and no easy answers, could be described as the inspiration for MacDiarmid's first long poem, *A Drunk Man Looks at the Thistle*, in which the ambiguous symbol of Scotland provides the center for an interrogation of humanity's place in the universe, and much else, of ferocious intellectualism. In the end the thistle remains an enigma, although MacDiarmid insists on the human imperative to question the non-human world, however hard it is to get an answer. In later poems he found a linguistic parallel to this indifference of nature in the use of abstruse scientific terms, in works like "In the Caledonian Forest" and "On a Raised Beach." In the latter especially, MacDiarmid's preference for a nature of hard indifference to mankind is forcefully expressed: "We must reconcile ourselves to the stones, / Not the stones to us." Truth to tell, few Scottish writers since MacDiarmid have tried to follow this lead. Instead, Scottish literature in the second half of the twentieth century has become strongly urban in theme and setting.

Terry Gifford has argued that nature is a social construct. "A personal notion of nature," he writes, "will always be in dialectical relation to socially constructed notions of nature. The poem is a site where writer and reader negotiate that dialectic of personal and social meanings" (p. 16). In the case of Scottish literature it is necessary to stress the role of the reader in this dialectic, for it was readers who insisted on the grand Romantic vision of Scotland that was discernible in Scott, ignoring his attempts to temper that vision with prosaic asides; and it was readers who chose to ignore Burns's cool attitude to nature and amplify instead his talent for recording the natural world. Thus it was that readers constructed the two views of Scottish nature this essay has been about, and against which twentieth-century writers, notably MacDiarmid, have struggled—with mixed success, since both kinds of nature image survive in Scottish culture today. Women writers, however, having begun this century adapting the language of the natural sublime to their own concerns, have since distanced themselves in their own way from the male traditions of nature as the essential soul of the nation (although to be fair, the writing of the 1980s by men as well as women has shown a turning away from nationalist worries, and from nature, too).

Another group of writers somewhat apart from the concerns of this essay are writers in Gaelic. The success of Macpherson's Ossian branded the Celtic culture of Scotland with misty otherworldliness, but in fact the Gaelic nature poetry of Macpherson's contemporaries was quite unlike that. Alasdair Mac Mhmaister Alasdair's "Oran an t-Samhraidh" (Song of Summer) and Donnchadh Bàn Mac an t-Saoir's "Moladh Beinn Dòbhrainn" (Praise of Ben Doran) are clear and precise in their depiction of nature in celebration of native Highlands. A century later, however, after the evictions and depopulation of the country in the Highland Clearances, the same landscapes become for their modern successor, Somhairle MacGill-Eain (Sorley MacLean), poignant reminders of whole communities that have disappeared. In "Hallaig" and "Coilltean Ratharsair" (The Woods of Raasay) there is the same directness of description as in eighteenth-century Gaelic nature poetry, but the elements of nature now stand for a powerful sense of loss.

This essay has so far avoided the term pastoral but I would like finally to mention that as a matter of fact Scottish literature includes the writings of a man who was not only a poet but also a real shepherd. James Hogg was brought up as a Border shepherd before being drawn into the literary world of Sir Walter Scott's Edinburgh, and among his writings can be found not only a collection of stories significantly entitled *The Shepherd's Calendar,* but also *The Shepherd's Guide: Being a Practical Treatise on the Diseases of Sheep, their Causes, and the Best Means of Preventing Them.* Hogg gained the sobriquet of "The Ettrick Shepherd," after the valley of his birth, and became caught up in the complex cultural games of the Scottish capital, but he was a man of acute insight. In his greatest novel, *The Private Memoirs and Confessions of a Justified Sinner*, there occurs an incident that raises the whole question of modern pastoral. The sinner, escaping from the law and realizing that his clothes, which identify him as an educated man of religion, will give him away, admits that " [I] exchanged clothes with a poor homely shepherd, whom I found lying on a hill side, singing to himself some woful love ditty. . . . I now supposed myself completely disguised; and I found moreover that in this garb of a common shepherd I was made welcome in every house" (pp. 226–227). He is even hired as a shepherd but "I had not . . . gone many times to the sheep, before all the rest of the shepherds told my master, that I knew nothing about herding, and begged of him to dismiss me" (p. 227).

Two things are evident from this highly symbolic episode in a novel full of such telling detail:

first, the intellectual hero's desire to retreat into a humbler social position (indeed, the sinner's change of appearance is one of the first signs that he is turning from the arrogant self-certainty that has led him to commit inhuman crimes); and second the failure of this attempt (an ironic comment on the literary trope of the pastoral retreat). Hogg, who had had his claims to serious literary regard undermined by insistence on his country background, indicates that it is no less difficult for a man of letters to go back to nature. Like Burns, Hogg shows a hard-headedness about the relations between man and nature, a tough-mindedness that appears intermittently in Scottish literature but always battles, as Hogg himself had to do, with a sentimental preference for a national myth of harmony between land and people.

Selected Works and Further Reading

Brown, George Mackay, *Selected Poems,* London: Hogarth, 1977

Buchan, John, *John Macnab,* Boston: Houghton Mifflin, 1925; London: Hodder and Stoughton, 1925

———, *The Thirty-Nine Steps,* edited by Christopher Harvie, New York and Oxford: Oxford University Press, 1993

Burns, Robert, *Robert Burns: Selected Poems,* edited by Carol McGuirk, New York and London: Penguin, 1993

Gibbon, Lewis Grassic, *A Scots Quair,* New York and London: Jarrolds, 1934

Gifford, Terry, *Green Voices: Understanding Contemporary Nature Poetry,* New York and Manchester, England: Manchester University Press, 1995

Hogg, James, *The Private Memoirs and Confessions of a Justified Sinner,* edited by John Wain, New York and Harmondsworth, England: Penguin, 1983

———, *The Shepherd's Calendar,* edited by Douglas S. Mack, Edinburgh, Scotland: Edinburgh University Press, 1995

MacDiarmid, Hugh, *Complete Poems of Hugh MacDiarmid,* edited by Michael Grieve and W. R. Aitken, 2 vols., New York and Harmondsworth, England: Penguin, 1985

———, *A Drunk Man Looks at the Thistle,* annotated ed., edited by Kenneth Buthlay, Edinburgh, Scotland: Scottish Academic, 1987

Maclaren, Ian, *Beside the Bonnie Brier Bush,* New York: Barse and Hopkins,

1894; London: Hodder and Stoughton, 1895

Macpherson, James, *The Poems of Ossian and Related Works,* edited by Howard Gaskill, Edinburgh, Scotland: Edinburgh University Press, 1996

Mitchell, James Leslie, *A Scots Hairst: Essays and Short Stories,* edited by Ian S. Munro, London: Hutchinson, 1967

Muir, Edwin, *The Complete Poems of Edwin Muir,* edited by Peter Butter, Aberdeen, Scotland: Association for Scottish Literary Studies, 1991

Scott, Walter, Sir, *Rob Roy,* edited by John Sutherland, Rutland, Vermont: Charles E. Tuttle, 1995; London: J. M. Dent, 1995

———, *Selected Poems,* edited by Thomas Crawford, Oxford: Clarendon, 1972

———, *Waverley,* edited by Andrew Hook, Harmondsworth, England: Penguin, 1972; New York: Viking/Penguin, 1985

Stevenson, Robert Louis, *Kidnapped; and, Catriona,* edited by Emma Letley, New York and Oxford: Oxford University Press, 1986

Toogood, Mark, "Nature and Nation: Ecology and the Reconstruction of the Highlands," *Scotlands* 3:1 (1996), pp. 42–55

Watson, Roderick, ed., *The Poetry of Scotland: Gaelic, Scots, and English, 1380–1980,* Edinburgh, Scotland: Edinburgh University Press, 1995

The Environment in Twentieth-Century Welsh Writing in English

Linden Peach

One of the striking features of Welsh writing in English is the extent to which literature is implicated in the cultural construction of the landscape. Jeremy Hooker has argued that it is "in a feeling for the land of Wales that Welsh writers in English with different and even opposing views . . . come close together" ("Natives," 38). Some of this "feeling for the land," even in the second half of the twentieth century, can be traced to a pre-industrial, rural Romanticism. In the period between the First and the Second World Wars, when Welsh writing in English first began to flourish, rural Romanticism was kept alive through the work of writers who are not much studied these days, such as Hilda Vaughan, whose sentimental stories were rooted in the Border counties, and Richard Vaughan who moved further back in time to chronicle the farming communities of southwest Wales. But some of the concepts and perspectives that have had the most profound effect on the depiction of nature in Welsh writing in English have their origins in the industrial rather than the rural writing of the period.

The period between the wars saw the emergence of fiction in south Wales that tried to give shape and explanation to the disaster that now overtook the area. As Dai Smith has pointed out, "The society which had been force-fed until all its shoots were luxuriant now withered" (p. 133). Among the more interesting and contentious works of the period are: Rhys Davies, *A Time to Laugh* and *Jubilee Blues*; Jack Jones, *Rhondda Roundabout* and *Black Parade*; Gwyn Jones, *Times Like These*; Lewis Jones, *Cwmardy* and *We Live* and Richard Llewellyn, *How Green Was My Valley*.

Traces of the often florid pastoralism of the earlier rural work are still to be found in writing based on industrial Wales. But often where the pastoral approach is reclaimed, it is altered and recontextualized by the impact of industrialization, not only on the landscape but on the way in which nature itself is mediated. This is especially evident in fiction written from an insider's view of industrial Wales as opposed to that in which the industrial environment is only a background. The distinction is succinctly made by Raymond Williams in his novel, *Border Country*: "The visitor sees beauty; the inhabitant a place where he works and has his friends" (p. 75). Williams's use of the word "beauty" suggests a perspective on the landscape mediated through canonical traditions of landscape art and writing. But the word "inhabitant" suggests the depiction of a landscape mediated through prolonged, first-hand involvement with it.

In Glyn Jones's short story, "I was born in the Ystrad Valley," from *The Blue Bed and Other Stories*, Wynn, the son of a collier, remembers the valleys of his boyhood:

> . . . one sees northward mountain ranges, tawny, muscular, leaking the whitewash of streams that weave in the distance . . . Here the river pools are clear beneath the lime cliffs and the down drench of the birches, and the valley boys bathe bare with swimming flesh chinaed in empty water. . . . Here no thick vein drains down under the side of the mountains, and no pulse beats in the earth of a deep hill . . . (p. 16)

Here what is important is the concept of nature that emerges literally in the binarism between the industrial and the unpolluted landscape. The environment is seen in pre- and post-lapsarian, almost Lawrentian, terms. The clear waters and nude swimming encapsulating a disappearing idyll suggests a sense of loss. But the unpolluted landscape has also been redefined by the industrial landscape to which it stands in opposition: it is now defined as a site of re-creation; a place where one can escape from work and recharge oneself spiritually.

Within this context, the way in which the mountain emerges as an important trope in Welsh writing in English about the environment is significant. For Wynn, like so many characters in south Wales fiction and poetry, the mountain affords a prospect beyond the narrow confines of the valley. But, as Hooker points out:

> Mountains are holy. They are places of temptation. A poet may look down from on high on the people in the valley, alienated, or knowing himself (sic) part of them. He may feel tension between the pull of the community below, and freedom to dream on the heights. ("Natives," 32)

How the mountains are perceived, then, is inseparable from the social psychology of the wider environment of work, oriented as David Smith says, in a discussion of Lewis Jones's fiction, on the pit, chapel, home, pub, square, shops and the bare elements of civic life (p. 54). The presence of the chapel is significant for what the mountain also affords, as Hooker says, is "a kind of negative religious vision." Alun Lewis in one of the best known poems from the mid-twentieth century, "The Mountain Over Aberdare" from *Raider's Dawn*, looks down from the mountain to see a community in the grip of economic depression: mourners "singing hymns? That drift insidious as the rain" and women hugging "Huge grief and anger against God" (pp. 87–88).

The view of nature that emerged in the binary divide between the industrial and the rural, then, was a combination of the actual, of psychological fantasy, of literary tradition, and a sense of cultural loss that proved significant for Welsh writing in English. Equally important proved the concept of nature that emerged in the proximity of the animate and inanimate. In "I was born in the Ystrad Valley," Wynn describes being trapped in a lane by a massive horse that pulls the coalman's cart:

> His driver had backed him there hard before I could get out of the way, all the brass and the jerking chains of his heavy harness crashing through my ears, his slipping shoes shining the hard black earth, and his stuck back

head furfolding the thick of his neck like a fern-spread. I stood in terror with my face close to the shaft chains and the wet skin of his flank . . . the black sweat smoking under the harness leathers of his back and his gaping collar . . . (p. 13)

In this passage, the distinction between the animate and inanimate is blurred. The strength and power of the horse is the product of its confinement in the shafts of the cart. At first Wynn does not notice the horse as flesh, but focuses on the harness that is animated by, yet also animates, the horse, and on the brass, the jerking chains, the collar and the shoes. Jones is beginning to explore here what happens to our concept of nature when it is altered through a new set of meanings, priorities and values generated by industrialization. It is significant that the horse is described in the kind of language that might be used to describe the power of a colliery: "jerking chains," "shaft chains," "black sweat," "smoking," "hard black earth." The sense of power and energy here is not solely the product of the young boy's appreciation of the animal. It is rooted in a concept of energy that comes from the industrial revolution: literally the harnessing of natural resources.

For Jones, industry is destroying the landscape: "The grey bleak hills lean up from the streets . . . everywhere without a daffodil or the huge suck of a tree" (p. 17). But there is a tension in his work because, as a boy and subsequently as a writer, he is fascinated by industrial machinery and processes. As Dai Smith points out, "there is a brooding fascination with the industrial glamour of the Valley-in-work that Glyn Jones transforms into a stunning wordscape" (p. 139). Although the natural world is described by Glyn Jones in sensuous and beautiful language, in some of the descriptions, nature, seen from the perspective of those who have a close proximity to industry, is framed in a way implicitly defined by industry. In "The Kiss" from *The Blue Bed and Other Stories*, a workman stares at a daisy:

> lifting up the yellow flat catchment of its flower to the sun, gathering the tilted warmth like a funnel, pouring a light-thread down through its thin stem to meet sap that rose up from roots leeching hungrily at the arterial earth. It was a perfect blossom . . . and the stem was powerful, flexible, a slender column twisting itself slowly round among the

crouching grasses, revolving upon the security of its roots like the ponderous gyring of some machine . . . (p. 117)

Here, the words associated with industry—"funnel," "column," "gyring"—are an indication of how nature is being understood increasingly as a process. The flower is implicitly a perfect product. Although the industrial-based language does not necessarily alienate us, any more than the workman in the narrative from the flower, it changes our view of it from a transitory, fragile thing. In Jones's account, the flower is part of a natural world that is dynamic and in flux.

There is a distinction to be made here between Jones's view of nature as a dynamic process and the similar concept that is developed in the work of Dylan Thomas. Thomas did not write about the rural environment as such very extensively, claiming to have little knowledge of Wales outside of Swansea. Although he wrote effectively about the family farm, Fernhill, in the first story in *Portrait of the Artist as a Young Dog*, in his early stories rural Wales is really only a means of anchoring a surrealist prose that is itself a combination of Gothic and Freudian fantasy. But like Jones's work, his poetry suggests new parameters in which we should see nature, especially our relationship to it.

As for Jones's characters in *The Blue Bed and Other Stories,* Thomas's experience of his own body is related to the impact of the natural world about him. His suburban upbringing did not divorce him from nature. "Especially when the October wind," for example, is rooted in the experience of blustery autumnal weather against the hillsides and seascapes of his Swansea home. As Ackerman points out, "in Thomas nature is always seen as an organic power, not simply as a source of metaphor as is usually the case in Yeats or Eliot" (p. 78). Although Jones writes about nature in a sensuous way, in Thomas's work physical and sensory perception is pre-eminent. The relationship of Thomas's own body to the dynamic processes of creation as a biological creative-destructive continuum is a recurring preoccupation. For Ackerman, this is clearly registered in "The force that through the green fuse drives the flower" from *18 Poems*, a poem that, as far as the realization of nature is concerned, lends itself to comparison with Jones's passage published only three years later. Jones's passage moves from the flower to the stem to the earth, signifying nature as a larger dynamic process, but returns to ponder the power in the stem and in the way in which it twists around the grass. Thomas's poem, however, begins with imagery of flowers and trees, but moves through imagery of rocks and water to a reflection on mortality and those notions of immortality that promise more than the biological concept of a return to first elements. Whereas Ackerman recognizes the development in "The force that through the green fuse drives the flower," he overlooks the enigma in the poem's opening lines:

> The force that through the green fuse
>   drives the flower
> Drives my green age; that blasts the roots
>   of trees
> Is my destroyer. (Davies and Maud, 13)

Stewart Crehan points out that the rapidity with which the first line of the poem is undermined suggests the way in which Thomas thought of language and imagery in his writing: that "each image must be born and die in another" (p. 49). Hence, Thomas's writing does not simply present us with a perspective on nature, but explores the concept of nature as a creative-destructive process in poetry that also pursues the implications of this concept for language and meaning.

Explorations of the fusion of the mechanical and the animate, an important but not much written about aspect of Welsh writing in English, can be traced from the work of Glyn Jones through to contemporary writers such as Robert Minhinnick. From the point of view of writing about the environment, Minhinnick's most important collections include *Native Ground, Life Sentences, The Dinosaur Park* and *The Looters*. In "Smith's Garage," Minhinnick describes how: "Only ivy's industry/ Survives the change" focusing on the way in which the plant has become entwined with the skylight and how a lorry chassis has found "bone-like fusions" with the earth (Butler, 47). Minhinnick himself has explained:

What interested me in writing the poem, what excited me and impelled me to write, was the extraordinary interaction between the natural world and the industrial in the garage. There were gear-wheels and fly-wheels scattered around the yard, all orange with rust. And they looked exactly like the enormous gilled fungi that sprouted there in the grass. . . . It was the rusted gear-wheels that delighted me, the exhaust systems trailing bindweed and couch-grass, the chalk marks of ancient lorry rotas viewed through a nest of webs. There was a harmony there, a sense of destiny fulfilled. And the physical reality seemed far more important than the theoretical possibilities of the scene. (Butler, 188)

This physical reality in which the boundaries between the inanimate and the animate are blurred as they are in Smith's Garage is one to which Minhinnick frequently returns or tries to create in his work. For example, in "The Brook" from *Life Sentences* eels are "black and vulcanized like bicycle tyres" (Butler, 52). In *The Dinosaur Park*, in "Snaps" "the small rockpools / Glitter like a switchboard" (p. 26); in "Images from Criesbach" meteorites are compared to "discs of light / On some computer screen" (p. 34); in "Born on the M4" a hawk is "a ruddy crucifix" (p. 39).

There is more here than a poet ransacking the world of machines for images with which to describe nature. Like Jones, Minhinnick is exploring new ways of looking at nature that emerge from its fusion with the mechanical and from the abolition of the traditional exclusiveness of the urban and the rural. Although Minhinnick is not an urban poet in the sense that John Tripp was, Tripp provides an interesting gloss on Minhinnick's work:

The urban and rural should have something positive to say to each other . . . But rural themes were always thought to be more "poetic" than urban ones, set among aerials and housing estates. The pastoral has had a fatal attraction for many Welsh poets, to the exclusion of all else—just as the clichés of pit and chapel have maimed other poets. (p. 190)

The environment in which most people live in Wales is a border country and Minhinnick, as Hooker says, is "a poet of borders or margins; between past and present, self and others, man and nature; and his landscapes are between industrial and rural Wales, or between polluted sea and polluted shore . . ." (*Presence*, 182). Minhinnick sees the distinctive cross-fertilization that he believes occurs in Wales as crucial to his own work and Welsh writing in English generally:

Wales is a country of strongly creative frictions, at least I feel they should be creative, especially for writers. The rural and the industrial, traditional industry and new technology, the English and the Welsh languages, a past representing an emphatic and unique cultural identity and a present in which that identity might become irreversibly eroded. (Butler, 187)

Machines, technology and the microchip are part of the world in which we live along with the natural environment. But they pose threats to the environment that Minhinnick who has worked for industry as well as for Friends of the Earth understands better than most. In *The Dinosaur Park* and *The Looters*, and especially in the latter, the destruction of the environment is mirrored in the breakdown of a sense of a social consensus and of community. Inhumanity extends in an ever-widening circle. The refrain that earth cannot sustain a search for resources is linked provocatively to increasing cruelty and inner hopelessness.

In "The Coast" from *The Dinosaur Park*, Minhinnick describes a shore that is polluted with glass and plastic objects buried in the sand. The poem is not simply a polemic against pollution, acknowledging also our need to be remembered and how time always erodes humankind's achievements. But in our present throwaway society, epitomized by plastic and brand names, the relationship to nature has changed. The coast, increasingly the site of a leisure industry, is evidence of a diminishing sense of responsibility to maintain the natural environment (p. 12).

The attention given to the interaction between machine and nature in the work of Jones and Minhinnick, acknowledging their insistence on the need to protect the natural environment, can be contrasted with the pastoral writing to which Tripp refers. But the most important advocate of "nature" over the machine in Welsh writing in English, R. S. Thomas, can hardly be called a pastoral poet. In work, labelled by Gifford as at best "reluctant pastoral" (p. 46), many aspects of the landscape appear to suggest anti-pastoral as in the opening lines of "A Peasant" that depict a windswept hillside where the peasant farmer, Iago Prytherch, "pens a few sheep in a gap of cloud" or churns "the crude earth" (*Selected Poems*, 3). In fact, Minhinnick has little time for what he sees as Thomas's "remote, politicized landscape, populated mainly by demons, sometimes by angels" ("Living," 12). But many of Thomas's poems, depicting difficult personal struggles, are much more complex than Minhinnick allows. His view of nature has to be seen within a religious context, especially his search for the presence of God in an apparently empty landscape.

As Tony Bianchi points out, Thomas is best known for a canon of some 50 poems within which about 10 are the most anthologized and the best known. Of these the majority—"The Welsh Hill Country," "A Peasant," "Welsh Landscape," "The Hill Farmer Speaks," "Cynddylan on a Tractor"—are from the first two collections dated 1946 and 1952. This is significant not only for the way in which Thomas is perceived as a poet but for the way in which Welsh writing in English is implicated in the cultural construction of the Welsh landscape. As J. D. Vicary has pointed out, while the early poems are steeped in particular places and observations of people, in the later poems the mediating contexts and occasions that provided the basis for Thomas's religious reflections are absent (pp. 56–57). Thomas's early poetry, as Bianchi says, associates the reader with a number of negatively inscribed positions concerned with outsiders, the machine, English or the public and entices them into accepting certain alternative values concerned with nature, Wales and history. The Welsh landscape, then, is a means to a Welsh culture located in a rural past. Hooker points out that as a figure in Thomas's poetry, Prytherch is extremely malleable, but he is consistent "as a survival and defender of an old, pre-industrial way of life in the countryside" (*Presence*, 131). Eventually, however, in "Too Late," Prytherch becomes the victim of "the cold brain of the machine," Thomas's hatred of which grows in his poetry.

Much of R. S. Thomas's early work is rooted in his experiences as a young curate in English Maelor and later in Manafon in Montgomeryshire. Thomas remembered that "Manafon was an eye-opener to me. . . . I can remember the lonely figures in the fields, hoeing or docking mangels" (Anstey, 138–139). In discussing the environment in Welsh writing in English, it is important to recognize that the work is often rooted in particular environments and that the creative tensions of which Minhinnick speaks occur in different ways, with different emphases and in different contexts throughout Wales. Welsh writing in English is closely implicated in the cultural construction of Welsh environments because specific contexts give the writing cultural relevance and it is important to recognize the authenticity of these contexts. A case in point is the way in which Merthyr, important to the work of poets such as Mike Jenkins and Leslie Norris, is often falsely perceived as a solely industrial environment. But in writing of his childhood, Leslie Norris who was brought up in pre-war Merthyr, although he has lived most of his life in England and Utah, recalls the proximity of the rural to the industrial. In his poetry, he remembers, rather nostalgically, having access to the Brecon Beacons, his aunt's farm on the hillsides overlooking the town, and bathing in the river. In order to appreciate the interaction of poet and landscape, then, we have to have the kind of knowledge demonstrated by Wynn Thomas. He points out that Merthyr is distinct from the Rhondda valley on the other side of the mountain in that it was an early and culturally indigenous industrial settlement so that "Merthyr writers themselves have therefore tended to present their relationship to the pre-industrial Welsh past rather differently, emphasizing the continuities as well as the discontinuities that constituted change in their case" (*Internal Difference*, 27).

A concomitant issue in discussing how literature in Wales is implicated in the representation of the environment is which Wales are we talking about? It is hard not to think of Wales as Waldo Williams did; "Ynof mae Cymru'n un. Y modd nis gwn" (In me Wales is single and united. I know not how.) But his viewpoint has been challenged by Wynn Thomas who rightly points out that Wales is a country of geographical differences and that "on the back of this one difference rides a whole host of others—historical, social, cultural, linguistic and so on. In the Welsh context, knowing your place can mean a great many things" (*Internal Difference*, xi–xii). The risk in discussing the internal distinctions and divisions in Wales is that we might impose a map on the country that makes sense in general terms—Thomas cites an attempt to divide Wales into a Welsh-speaking Wales, A Welsh Wales corresponding to the old south Wales coalfield, and a British Wales (p. xii)—but that bears little relationship to the specific environment in which a writer's particular work is rooted. The argument may be illustrated with reference to the recent work in English of Welsh women writers.

Since the 1970s, a number of prominent women poets—Gillian Clarke, Christine Evans, Ruth Bidgood, Hilary Llewellyn-Williams—have brought new dimensions to Welsh English-language writing about the environment. The emergence of so many prominent women writers on the environment is not a phenomenon peculiar to

Wales. But it has led some critics, such as Hooker, to ask whether there are "possibilities available to Welsh women poets, possibilities inherent in certain Welsh literary and cultural traditions, and offering alternatives to the influences of Anglo-American culture" ("Ceridwen's Daughters," 143). This is an interesting issue but we must be careful not to impose a false homogeneity on their work. The poets come from different parts of Wales and are implicated in their respective environments very differently. Not all the poets, for example, are equally concerned with the social or biological centering of conflicts concerning an explicitly female self. In fact, Deryn Rees-Jones believes that Ruth Bidgood, whose first collection *The Given Time* was published in 1972, is a marginal figure because her work is not directly linked to the struggles for equality and the need to validate women's needs and lives (p. 9). Gillian Clarke, on the other hand, in "Letter from a Far Country" employs a form of writing traditionally associated with women to explore an increasingly, albeit rather conservative, feminist view of traditional Welsh rural communities. In "Cofiant," she adapts the Welsh form of recording genealogy to reclaim the position of women in the Welsh environment.

For women writers, Gillian Clarke has so far proved the major presence and influence, especially through *The Sundial*, *Letter from a Far Country*, *Letting in the Rumour* and *King of Britain's Daughter*. In her short poems, based on events and observations in the rural environment in which she lives or on memories of her childhood, she appears as a reflective, intuitive poet who thinks in symbols. Her work is characterized by a sensuous, physical delight in the world to which she also brings concerns as a woman. This is evident in "Birth" where her own experiences of the pain and pleasure are evident in references to "the soft sucking / Of the new-born" and "the tugging pleasure / Of bruised reordering" (*Selected Poems*, 12). This is a distinctly female voice finding a balance between pain and pleasure. Although earlier in the poem there are references to buzzards overhead, it is still possibly a rather sanitized account compared to Christine Evans's description of birth in "First Lamb" that encapsulates the "struggling flesh . . . meshed in mucus" and the "afterbirth, a pendulum of blood" (*Looking Inland*, 40).

In searching for a sense of identity amidst the landscapes and traditions of the past, Ruth Bidgood keeps alive in Welsh writing in English a tradition that through the work of Edward Thomas and Thomas Hardy is as much English as Welsh. However, unlike R. S. Thomas, she is not seeking to reclaim a Welsh past that is accessed through nature, but, as is clear from collections such as *The Print of Miracle* and *Kindred*, she seeks to put her own present into perspective. While Bidgood seems often alienated by the otherness of the Welsh past, Clarke and Llewellyn-Williams reclaim Welsh history and legend. In "King of Britain's Daughter," Clarke employs the *Mabinogian* to structure and shape her memories of the family farm. Hilary Llewellyn-Williams's work, rooted in her study of Celtic legend, *I-Ching* and shamanism, fuses nature, Welsh legend and contemporary environmental concerns. Llewellyn-Williams's *The Tree Calendar* is an especially original work. The titular poem draws on the Druidic tree calendar as a way of exploring and defamiliarizing the landscape as it is implicated in the poet's life over a year. It offers a sensuous and imaginative recreation, but at times a very individual experience, of the rural environment.

It is outside the scope of this essay to analyze Welsh language writing on the environment that has obviously contributed significantly to the representation of nature in Wales. Many Welsh authors who write in English—such as R. S. Thomas, Gillian Clarke and Mike Jenkins—have learned Welsh or are familiar with Welsh language culture. Welsh influences are apparent in the syntax and rhythms of their writing, in their adaptation of Welsh forms, and in their subject matter. The "feeling for the land," a concern for community and a sense of the past, for example, are tropes to be found in the language of both literatures. Many Welsh language writers, as diverse as Gwenallt Jones, Waldo Williams, Robert Williams Parry, Gwyn Thomas, Saunders Lewis, Kate Roberts and Euros Bowen, have a presence in Wales of which no writer living there could be unaware. Moreover their work has been brought to a wider audience through translation—Clancy (1982 and 1991), Conran (1986), Jones and Thomas (1973), Davies and Davies (1993). An as of yet undeveloped, although potentially exciting, area of scholarship is the interconnection between Welsh writing in English on the environment and Welsh-language work. The importance of this kind of comparative approach has been admirably demonstrated by Jason Walford Davies's study of the influence of Welsh language traditions, including those of nature writing, on the work of R. S. Thomas. At times, as Wynn Thomas says, "scholars of Anglo-Welsh literature seem almost to conspire together with their Welsh-language counterparts to give the impression that the history of modern Wales can be neatly divided between the two literatures, with industrial experience being the monopoly of the Anglo-Welsh and rural life being the preserve of the Welsh" ("Hidden Attachments," 152). In this, albeit brief, survey of Welsh writing in English, I have argued that important perspectives on nature have been developed in literature emanating from both industrial and rural Wales. The same is true for Welsh-language literature where important contributions to the representation of the Welsh landscape are to be found in the work of writers, such as Euros Bowen and Kate Roberts, who have come from an industrial background.

The environment is clearly an important subject around which Welsh writing in English coheres but retains its diversity. Current scholarship has established important parameters within which future work might be developed such as the environmental diversity within Wales itself and the extent to which Welsh writing in English is rooted in complex and often idiosyncratic locales. But perhaps two of the most interesting, and least discussed, veins running through Welsh writing in English are: firstly, the concepts of nature that have emerged in the space that writers have opened between the conventional urban/rural and technology/nature dichotomies; and, secondly, the extent to which the literature is the product of being situated, as Minhinnick has said, at the confluence of a number of distinctive creative frictions in Wales.

Selected Works and Further Reading

Ackerman, John, *A Dylan Thomas Companion: Life, Poetry, and Prose,* Basingstoke, England: Macmillan, 1989; New York: St. Martin's, 1990

Anstey, Sandra, ed., *Critical Writings on R. S. Thomas,* Bridgend: Poetry Wales, 1982; rev. ed., Bridgend: Poetry Wales, 1992

——, *R. S. Thomas: Selected Prose,* Bridgend: Poetry Wales, 1983

Bianchi, Tony, "R. S. Thomas and His Readers," in *Wales, the Imagined Nation: Studies in Cultural and National Identity,* edited by Tony Curtis, Chester Springs, Pennsylvania: Dufour, 1986; Bridgend: Poetry Wales, 1986

Bidgood, Ruth, *The Given Time,* Llandybie, Wales: C. Davies, 1972

——, *Kindred,* Chester Springs, Pennsylvania: Dufour, 1986; Bridgend: Poetry Wales, 1986

——, *The Print of Miracle,* Llandysul, Wales: Gomer, 1978

Butler, Susan, *Common Ground: Poets in a Welsh Landscape,* Chester Springs, Pennsylvania: Dufour, 1985; Bridgend: Poetry Wales, 1985

Clancy, Joseph, trans., *Twentieth Century Welsh Poems,* Llandysul, Wales: Gomer, 1982

——, trans., *The World of Kate Roberts: Selected Stories, 1925–1981,* Philadelphia: Temple University Press, 1991

Clarke, Gillian, *The King of Britain's Daughter,* Manchester, England: Carcanet, 1993

——, *Letter from a Far Country,* Manchester, England: Carcanet, 1982

——, *Letting in the Rumour,* Manchester, England: Carcanet, 1989

——, *Selected Poems,* Manchester, England: Carcanet, 1985

——, *The Sundial,* Llandysul, Wales: Gomer, 1978

Conran, Anthony, trans., *The Penguin Book of Welsh Verse,* Harmondsworth, England: Penguin, 1967; also published as *Welsh Verse,* Chester Springs, Pennsylvania: Dufour, 1986; Bridgend: Poetry Wales, 1986

Crehan, Stewart, "The Lips of Time," in *Dylan Thomas: Craft or Sullen Art,* edited by Alan Bold, New York: St. Martin's, 1990; London: Vision, 1990

Davies, Cynthia, and Saunders Davies, trans., *Euros Bowen: Priest-Poet,* Penarth: Church in Wales, 1993

Davies, Jason Walford, "'Thick Ambush of Shadows': Allusions to Welsh Literature in the Work of R. S. Thomas," in *Welsh Writing in English: A Yearbook of Critical Essays,* vol. 1, Bangor, Wales: New Welsh Review, 1995

Davies, Rhys, *Jubilee Blues,* London: Heinemann, 1938

——, *A Time to Laugh,* London: Heinemann, 1937; New York: Stackpole, 1938

Evans, Christine, *Cometary Phases,* Chester Springs, Pennsylvania: Dufour, 1989; Bridgend, Wales: Seren, 1989

——, *Looking Inland,* Bridgend: Poetry Wales, 1983

Gifford, Terry, *Green Voices: Understanding Contemporary Nature Poetry,* New York and Manchester, England: Manchester University Press, 1995

Hooker, Jeremy, "Ceridwen's Daughters: Welsh Women Poets and the Uses of Tradition," in *Welsh Writing in English: A Yearbook of Critical Essays,* vol. 1, Bangor, Wales: New Welsh Review, 1995

——, "Natives and Strangers; a View of Anglo-Welsh Literature in the Twentieth Century," in *Writing, Region and Nation,* edited by James Davies and M. Wynn Thomas, Swansea: University of Wales, Swansea, Department of English, 1994

——, *The Presence of the Past: Essays on Modern British and American Poetry,* Chester Springs, Pennsylvania: Dufour, 1987; Bridgend: Poetry Wales, 1987

Jenkins, Mike, *A Dissident Voice: Poetry,* Bridgend, Wales: Seren, 1990

——, *Graffiti Narratives: Poems 'n' Stories,* Aberystwyth, Wales: Planet, 1994

——, *Invisible Times,* Chester Springs, Pennsylvania: Dufour, 1986; Bridgend: Poetry Wales, 1986

——, *This House, My Ghetto,* Bridgend, Wales: Seren, 1995

Jones, Alun, and Gwyn Thomas, eds., *Presenting Saunders Lewis,* Cardiff: University of Wales Press, 1973

Jones, Glyn, *The Blue Bed and Other Stories,* London: Cape, 1937; also published as *The Blue Bed,* New York: Dutton, 1938

——, *Selected Short Stories,* London: Dent, 1971

Jones, Gwyn, *Times Like These,* London: Gollancz, 1936

Jones, Jack, *Black Parade,* London: Faber and Faber, 1935

——, *Rhondda Roundabout,* London: Faber and Faber, 1934

Jones, Lewis, *Cwmardy: The Story of a Welsh Mining Village,* London: Lawrence & Wishart, 1937

——, *We Live: The Story of a Welsh Mining Valley,* London: Lawrence & Wishart, 1939

Lewis, Alun, *Raiders' Dawn and Other Poems,* New York: Macmillan, 1942; London: Allen and Unwin, 1942

Llewellyn, Richard, *How Green Was My Valley,* London: Michael Joseph, 1939; Garden City, New York: International Collectors Library, 1940

Llewellyn-Williams, Hilary, "Poetry of the Natural World," *Poetry Wales* 26:1 (1990), pp. 17–19

——, *The Tree Calendar,* Chester Springs, Pennsylvania: Dufour, 1987; Bridgend: Poetry Wales, 1987

Minhinnick, Robert, *The Dinosaur Park,* Bridgend: Poetry Wales, 1985

——, *Life Sentences,* Bridgend: Poetry Wales, 1983

——, "Living with R. S. Thomas," *Poetry Wales* 29:1 (1993), pp. 11–14

——, *The Looters,* Bridgend, Wales: Seren, 1989

——, *Native Ground,* Swansea, Wales: Triskele, 1979

Norris, Leslie, *The Girl from Cardigan,* Salt Lake City, Utah: G. M. Smith, 1988; Bridgend, Wales: Seren, 1988

——, *Selected Poems,* Chester Springs, Pennsylvania: Dufour, 1986; Bridgend: Poetry Wales, 1986

——, *Sliding: Short Stories,* New York: Scribner's, 1976; London: J. M. Dent, 1978

Peach, Linden, *Ancestral Lines: Culture and Identity in the Work of Six Contemporary Poets,* Bridgend, Wales: Seren, 1993

——, "The Imaginations Caverns: Identity and Symbolism in the Work of Gillian Clarke and Christine Evans," in *'Fire Green as Grass': Studies of the Creative Impulse in Anglo-Welsh Poetry and Short Stories of the Twentieth Century,* edited by Belinda Humfrey, Llandysul, Wales: Gomer, 1995

Rees, Ioan Bowen, *The Mountains of Wales: An Anthology in Verse and Prose,* Newtown, Wales: Gwasg Gregynog, 1987; rev. ed., Cardiff: University of Wales Press, 1992

Rees-Jones, Deryn, "Facing the Present: The Emergence of Female Selves in the Poetry of Ruth Bidgood," *Poetry Wales* 6:3 (1991), pp. 9–12

Smith, Dai, "A Novel in History," in *Wales, the Imagined Nation: Studies in Cultural and National Identity,* edited by Tony Curtis, Chester Springs, Pennsylvania: Dufour, 1986; Bridgend: Poetry Wales, 1986

Smith, David, *Lewis Jones,* Cardiff: University of Wales Press, 1982

Stephens, Meic, ed., *The Bright Field: An Anthology of Contemporary Poetry from Wales,* Manchester, England: Carcanet, 1991

Thomas, Dylan, *Collected Poems, 1934–1953,* edited by Walford Davies and Ralph Maud, London: J. M. Dent, 1988

———, *Portrait of the Artist as a Young Dog,* New York: New Directions, 1940; London: J. M. Dent, 1940

Thomas, M. Wynn, "Hidden Attachments: Aspects of the Relationship Between the Two Literatures of Modern Wales," *Welsh Writing in English: A Yearbook of Critical Essays,* vol. 1, Bangor, Wales: New Welsh Review, 1995

———, *Internal Difference: Twentieth-Century Writing in Wales,* Cardiff: University of Wales Press, 1992

———, ed., *The Page's Drift: R. S. Thomas at Eighty,* Bridgend, Wales: Seren, 1993

Thomas, R. S., *Collected Poems, 1945–1990,* London: J. M. Dent, 1993

———, *Selected Poems: 1946–1968,* London: Hart-Davis, 1973; New York: St. Martin's, 1974

Vicary, J. D., "Via Negative: Absence and Presence in the Recent Poetry of R. S. Thomas," *Critical Quarterly* 1 (1985), pp. 41–51

Williams, Raymond, *The Border Country,* London: Chatto and Windus, 1960; New York: Horizon, 1962

The Mountain in Twentieth-Century French Literature

Tamara L. Whited

Mountains have held no small importance in French life and literature—as borderlands, frontiers, and, in the case of the Alps, the cradle of Romanticism and the place where alpinism got its name. In the twentieth century, mountains have seen the loss of human population and the concomitant disappearance of a cultural memory of fantastic beings and unnameable forces. Different points in this rapid transformation can be discerned in novels by Jean Giono, a distinguished author who portrays a traditional alpine culture, and Roger Frison-Roche, a popular novelist who evokes the post-peasant alpine world. Despite differences in imagery, both authors portray the mountain as an environment with dual significance: the mountain models the entire existence of all its inhabitants, yet it remains a highly gendered space that promotes the education of men.

While Jean Giono looms large in the canon of twentieth-century prose writers, his earlier works can be placed within a narrower context of regional writing in France. Regionalism appeared on the French literary scene in the decade before World War I, the same era that saw the flowering of folkloric studies. Regionalism ranged from the conservative outlooks of René Bazin and Henry Bordeaux, who saw in Brittany and the Savoie, respectively, reservoirs of sanctity and traditionalism, to the lyrical, even mystical evocations of rural people and animals in the Provence of Henri Bosco and the Franche-Comté of Louis Pergaud. After the Great War Jean Giono, too, created a decidedly mythical and mysterious Provence in his own universalizing regionalism. Two of his novels, *Colline* and *Batailles dans la montagne*, reveal that Provence as well as Giono's particular way of crafting mountains.

Jean Giono's first published novel, *Colline*, won him critical acclaim and the American Brentano Prize. It is also the first volume of the "Pan" trilogy, in which Giono sought to associate the people and landscape of Provence with classical mythology by invoking Pan, Ceres, and Dionysus. *Colline* posits a dire confrontation between the inhabitants of a hillside hamlet and an elusive but overpowering natural force. The place carries the vestiges of a once vibrant human presence in the mountains above Manosque—Giono's northern Provençal birthplace and residence for nearly all his life. In this post–World War I setting, only four households remain in the hamlet, their members eking a traditional highlanders' living through which some wheat, olives, and fruit bring cash up from the valley. And the men's attitude toward the alpine environment—for theirs is the only attitude Giono depicts—is that of peasants, as well: the land is rude, the living is hard, wildlife is a nuisance.

The plot unfolds as a series of natural calamities that test the peasants' hardened mistrust of nature. Foreshadowing greater challenges, the novel presents an early scene in which one of the men, Gondran, kills a lizard that has startled him from a nap in his olive orchard. The act appears to be a matter of course, but suddenly shame overtakes Gondran, and, while mounding dirt over the lizard's crushed body, he imagines the affinity between the lizard's blood and his own:

Blood, nerves, suffering.
He made red flesh suffer, flesh like his own.
Thus, all around him, on this earth, do all of his gestures cause suffering?
(p. 50, my translation)

Odd thoughts for a peasant. Gondran has been pushed to them by his dying father-in-law, Janet.

Having survived a stroke, Janet becomes delirious and pours out an incessant stream of words warning Gondran and others of nature's invisible, in fact immaterial, reality. Snakes emerge from his fingers and speak to him: surely the old man has rounded the bend of senility. In any case, the younger men are loathe to listen too closely.

It is only later in the novel, and in altered circumstances, that the dying Janet articulates a new ethic, this time to Jaume, another man of the hamlet: "The earth isn't made for you, alone, for your use, without end, without asking the master's opinion from time to time" (p. 111, my translation). Janet soon names the master—not a deity but rather "*la grande force.*" As he holds Jaume in his verbal thrall, Janet also refers to the force as "the boss" and uses "he," but ultimately describes the force with feminine imagery. At the end of time, Janet foretells, humanity will be beckoned to sit in nature's lap:

My beautiful little man [*hommelet*], with beautiful fingers which take and squeeze, come here, my man, come see if you remember how one caresses with one's hands; that's the first thing I taught you when you were on my knees, a little one with your mouth full of my milk. (p. 118, my translation)

This image of humanity's return to its mythical origins recurs in other novels by Giono (Godin, 132); in *Colline* the author emphasizes the creative powers of the original elements— are not Pan's limbs made of earth, sky, water, and fire? But just as they regenerate, the elements can also strike in reprobation. By the time Janet pronounces his manifesto, a disaster has befallen the hamlet: the well has run dry. Evoking rural superstition, Giono has a black cat appear before the discovery is made; the inhabitants know full well that black cats have always appeared prior to a mishap. Jaume, then, interprets the *grande force* as evil and associates it with Janet, who scoffs at the men's inability to find water and refuses all advice.

The search for water takes the men to the mountain, La Lure, an actual place north of Manosque to which the novel's title refers. La Lure emerges as the keeper of the *grande force*; Janet tells the men that the hill is alive, and the hill promises water. This time it is another irrational character who leads them to water— Gagou the idiot, who had wandered into the hamlet one day and taken up residence.

Thus, the dying and the crazed perceive nature in ways inaccessible to the peasant mind, with its mixture of rationality, superstition, skepticism and fear. The tiny community continues to pay for its distance from nature as further disasters occur: Marie, a child, falls ill, and the hamlet is nearly consumed by fire, a fire that seems to come from the depths of La Lure. By now the reader can predict the dual responses. The peasant men fight the fire, while Gagou walks deliberately into it in an act of self-immolation. The hamlet saved, Jaume insists on the link between the "*force*" and Janet; he plans to kill the old man, who spares Jaume by dying promptly. But Jaume is able to kill a wild boar in a final symbolic act, nullifying his earlier hesitation when he had let a boar pass undisturbed through the hamlet. One senses that Gondran, likewise, is ready to return to killing lizards without qualms.

Colline concludes ambiguously. Old ways and ignorance appear to return, yet Giono has successfully drawn the reader into the peasants' difficult existence, and malice is clearly present in Janet's cackling disregard for a hamlet verging on destruction. In the mountains, the boundaries between creation and destruction blur; to give credit to Giono's characters, the men's victory can be read as a chastened resolve to continue living on and with the mountain and its unnameable force.

The theme of alpine malevolence comes to the fore in *Batailles dans la montagne*, published by Gallimard in 1937. Marking the end of Giono's "peasant cycle," this novel stands at the junction in the author's corpus: from the late 1930s Giono abandoned the peasant novel set in a mythical Provence and embraced history and classical mythology more directly. *Batailles dans la montagne* posits no contradictory values as in *Colline*: here the confrontation between people and alpine nature is apocalyptic. But like *Colline* the novel presents a strangely hermetic alpine society in the post–World War I era. Giono takes care not to over-naturalize his peasants, however; some of the characters are Piedmontese migrants. The peasants' sealed isolation is even more eerie than that in *Colline*, for several alpine communes have nearly been wiped out by a mammoth natural disaster. The reader expects the people of the valley to take notice, yet rescue arrives belatedly in the form of a gendarme and several soldiers; the gendarme largely blusters about the law, and one of the peasant men punches him out for his inopportune comments.

The chief interest of *Batailles dans la montagne* lies in Giono's vigorous—and lengthy—depictions of mountains bent on self-destruction; Walter Redfern sees Giono in his "quintessential role of demiurge, amassing and mashing turgid chunks of fictional landscape, reworking the world, improving on God" (p. 198). The human story in the novel traces an excruciating journey toward understanding and salvation, the latter term suggested by the name and actions of the novel's hero—Saint-Jean. How can a community rebound in the face of seeming apocalypse? Its key (male) members must begin by comprehending their predicament, a process as tortuous for the reader as for the characters. While the peasants acquire a non-technical knowledge of the disaster through dialogue and their travails, Giono reserves an explanation for the reader in a chapter entitled "The Glacier." Water has accumulated beneath a glacier, increasing in pressure, attacking the mountain from the inside, finally bursting from the snout of the glacier and causing a massive flood; meanwhile, a large slab of granite sliding along strata of clay and marl combines with rockfalls from the high peaks to create a dam; the icy, muddy water from the glacial burst thus gathers in a lake, in the midst of which a protruding island attracts the straggling survivors.

But most of this Giono evokes rather than makes explicit; he is far less interested in providing a geography lesson than in suggesting the powers that move mountains. His arresting strength as a nature writer lies in his ability to make subjects of natural phenomena; the mercurial alpine environment is indeed the central character in *Batailles dans la montagne*. With respect to this and other novels, Giono has been criticized for allowing his human characters comparatively few dimensions; most of them pale by their puniness, while a few saviors are marred by the simplicity of their superhuman heroism. These caveats aside, the reader can revel along with Giono as the author captures the mountain's wrath on more than one scale, from the massive cracking and breaking of rocks he calls a "detonation," to the insidious, drop by drop action of the tiniest torrential tributary. As central, overwhelming actor, the mountain cannot symbolize anything but itself; on the contrary, Giono has a bloodthirsty bull represent (among other things) the mountain's destructive force: the lone animal swims to the island and kills an old woman and two horses before Saint-Jean slaughters it, an episode announcing the hero's ultimate victory over the mountain.

Giono reserves his most lavish descriptions for water; the Ebron torrent, he states early in the novel, is the "spirit of the mountains and the forests" (p. 134, my translation). With its cascade of verbs and similes, the following depiction of subglacial water finding its way to the surface reveals Giono's efforts to get at the essence of alpine forces:

The water began to spout from all the fissures beneath the glacier. It looked for corridors and channels, passing through the slightest grooves, into the traces that mark the site of minuscule roots a thousand years old in the hollows of the granite. It finds them, enters, passes through, deviates, pushes, strikes, recoils, strikes, recoils, like the beating of blood in a man's wrist, shakes, splits, crushes, passes through, descends, rises again, twists, opens out, broadens like the boughs of an oak, twists, coils up, overtakes, forms knots, arranges itself like a beehive, splits the Muzelliers wall, leaps into the void like an arc of glass. (p. 283, my translation)

For the peasants, such uncontrollable vitality represents nature denatured; they had, after all, domesticated portions of the mountain through stockbreeding and the cultivation of grains and grapevines. They react to the disaster with a sense of injustice, a "great peasant reproach" that implores: "Who will work my vineyard, the earth, my life, who will live?" (p. 286, my translation). The water's "phosphorescent scalp" that now covers all the vineyards mocks the human efforts of centuries.

Although struggle overwhelmingly defines the relationship between peasants and nature, another ethic does emerge during the episode with the marauding bull, that of domestic "attachment." Joseph Glomore loses two of his precious horses to the bull's horns; appreciating Glomore's loss, Charles-Auguste helps push the carcasses into the water instead of preparing them for consumption, although food supplies on the island are running low. Glomore had loved his delicate, playful horses ill-adapted to the alpine environment, and Charles-Auguste calls this sentiment "attachment," without which "there are no men, no women, no beasts, no planets, nothing, not even nothing." (p. 378, my translation). Attachment is possible in the mountains, yet only through supreme and risky attempts at domestication.

Those attempts forever remain a battle, for, as Saint-Jean muses, all of nature has a tendency to absorb people. Putting mountains between you and the plains allows you to see more broadly, but the absorptive force increases in those "inhuman heights." Here is a peasant distrust that measures the "small grandeur of men" in comparison to the mountain (p. 490, my translation). To return the mountain to a state of precarious domesticity, Saint-Jean matches destruction with destruction: in a delicate operation, he packs his body with dynamite, rafts across the lake, and deposits the sticks in holes along the flank of the dam. The latter explodes, the lake drains with deafening noise, and Saint-Jean and his comrades witness "the birth of the world" (p. 576, my translation).

Batailles is epic in length, structure, and tone; whether or not Giono succeeded in creating a convincing epic, he achieved the rare literary feat of letting natural forces speak for themselves; this, and the author's evocation of peasants staking their livelihoods on the volatile mountain, recommend the novel.

French mountains and mountain life of roughly the same period appear quite different through the optic of popular literature. Born in 1906, Roger Frison-Roche, an alpinist, mountain guide, journalist, and explorer before he turned novelist, produced fiction that celebrated the splendors and rigors of the Alps, the Sahara, and the Scandinavian North. Two of his Alpine novels, *Premier de cordée*, translated into English as *First on the Rope*, and *La Grande Crevasse*, present adventure stories whose mountain-guide protagonists titillate readers with the appealing skill and daring exacted by the mountain. The initial, wartime popularity of Frison-Roche is easily accounted for: in a France ignominiously defeated by Nazi Germany, the heroism of virile young men—decidedly French, not Teutonic—exemplified the very model of social regeneration propounded by the Vichy government of Philippe Pétain. While educative and patriotic, these novels also delineate a recreative aesthetic of the mountain and reveal the mutations that the twentieth century has brought to the lives of alpine people.

Frison-Roche did not share Jean Giono's compulsion to get inside natural phenomena with words; instead, through the eyes of an alpinist-turned-writer, we see mountains that have essentially become sets of conditions that will determine the difficulty of particular ascents at particular times. One infers the mountain through the synecdoches of snow, ice, declivity, and weather. When Frison-Roche does refer to the whole in both *Premier de cordée* and *La Grande Crevasse*, he bounds his description by clichés: the mountains' "inhuman scale," "inexorable laws," and "never-ending drama" create an aesthetic of warmed-over sublime. Notwithstanding such predictable description, Frison-Roche emphasizes the mountains' unpredictability. The mountain is a supreme challenge that the guides must meet through technique, honed from a tender age, and technology, however basic—the simplicity of their ropes, pitons, and crampons only heightens the guides' prowess each time they maneuver around an overhang or cross over a crevice.

However, the mountain is a landscape no less privileged for being continually "conquered" by the young alpinists. The latter have special access to the mountain but are capable of loving it as well; the guides do gaze in silent reverence at times, they let out joyful yodels, and they become "one" with the mountain on sheer faces and in narrow passages (Frison-Roche employs the sensual phrase "*faire corps avec la montagne*"). *La Grande Crevasse* is itself a love story in which Zian, a Savoyard guide, and Brigitte, a Parisian woman, fall in love during an arduous climb and, given their striking differences that lowland life casts in high relief, remain linked only by the mountains. In Brigitte's mind, Zian and the mountain are parts of the same entity.

The lowland-highland opposition elsewhere receives its due. Tourists, from the lowlands, rarely rise above ineptitude and lack of appreciation for the "natives'" skills. Conversely, long stints among the high peaks impart superior qualities to the guides: alpine expeditions foster solidarity, overriding differences in family or village origin. When life is at stake, the "petty rivalries of the valley" evaporate (*Crevasse*, 51, my translation). The tourist station of Chamonix, at a mere 1,037 meters, forms the essential contrast with the heights in *Premier de cordée*. Indeed, the guides have even chosen a more arduous way to make a living than that of the alpine pastoralists, who have largely disappeared: the organic alp (an alpine pasture) and the inorganic rock oppose each other explicitly in *Premier de cordée*:

On one side, the smiling prospect of the alp, bounded by the elaborate candelabra of the larches, where the streams weave iridescent threads, where hazelcocks call under the sun-drenched alders; on the other, a polar region of ice and granite, over which now blew an icy wind. (*First on the Rope*, 216)

But who, after all, are these guides? Hardly superhuman impostors, they are in fact made-over peasants themselves. Herein lies the central, historical interest of these novels, their manner of bearing witness to the new economy of the mountains in the twentieth century. Pierre Servettaz, Zian Mappaz and the others are but local young men for whom agriculture and livestock can no longer provide a living. Alongside a generalized contempt for lowlanders lies the guides' deep sense of responsibility for their clients, stemming from both professional probity and an unspoken sense of economic dependence. In the French rural tradition, however, the guides are actually *pluriactifs*, people engaged in various economic pursuits to make ends meet. The mother of Pierre Servettaz, protagonist in *Permier de cordée*, fervently wants her son to give up his dream to become a guide and instead run the chalet, for tourists, left by her husband, who dies from a lightning strike on an exposed ledge. As we see in *La Grande Crevasse*, a sequel to the former novel, Pierre ends by doing some of both. Zian Mappaz gives ski lessons in the winter, cuts wood in spring and fall, and keeps a few cows. The guides have far from lost their peasant ways; they speak in alpine patois and transfer a culturally inherited fortitude to the spurts of intense stamina needed on the mountain face.

In a striking interlude in *Premier de cordée*, Frison-Roche depicts an *inalpinage*, the ritual trek in early summer to the alpine pastures to leave livestock in the care of shepherds. All of the guides appear to be implicated in this ancient relationship to the mountain, although they will spend the rest of the summer among the peaks with their clients. On the alp "they were no longer guides, they were barely even civilized; they had become once more, of their own free will, typical narrow-minded, heavy-featured mountain peasants" (*First*, 184). Zian Mappaz of *La Grande Crevasse* engages in the notorious peasant activity of poaching, which Frison-Roche excuses: "Poaching has always been the little sin of guides" (p. 190, my translation). The cultural fissures between Zian and his Parisian wife grow more difficult to span than the glacial crevices; Brigitte cannot adapt to mountain life and takes an extended leave from it. Yet she plans to return to the mountain while, unbeknownst to her, Zian has died uselessly in an accident, living just long enough after his rescue to call Nanette—the peasant girl he should have married—by his wife's name.

In the end, though, these young peasant/ guides are rationalists; they have left the spirited world of the mountain. As Pierre Servettaz declares in *La Grande Crevasse*, "There are no longer ghosts in our day" (p. 257, my translation). One needs only to recall the image of the portentous black cat in Jean Giono's *Colline* to see where these young men stand. Both authors mark the mountain as a place that challenges and educates men, yet their writings stand on opposite sides of a historical transition. That transition is not contemporaneous with the writings themselves, for Jean Giono tried to recapture a mountain mysticism and isolation that had already disappeared, while Frison-Roche was, if anything, forward-looking in planting his characters in the new alpine order.

Through these contrasts we can identify the contributions of Jean Giono and Roger Frison-Roche to French regional writing and, more broadly, to environmental literature. To the extent that regionalism has mythically rendered the landscapes and people of particular regions, the two authors differ tellingly in their emphases. Giono structures his novels around a spiritual conflict between nature and people; twentieth-century readers can identify the Romantic inheritance in Giono's mountains, which breathe sanctity and mystery, but the author further enhances their unnamed powers by means of minute description. In the novels of Frison-Roche, the unnamed forces are purely economic, the mountain entirely desacralized. This author, conversely, mythicizes his protagonists by endowing them with the physical and emotional qualities necessary for a heroic adaptation to twentieth-century exigencies. Reflecting the historical transition, a crevice in perception also lies between the hazards of rural domestication and those of a heroic alpinism driven by urban desires: on one side, Giono and the supernatural; on the other, Frison-Roche and the superhuman. Such an antithesis raises at least one broad question about the future meanings of mountains in literature. From what will they derive significance once stripped of their powers to enchant?

Selected Works and Further Reading

Bourgeois, René, "Elements pour une symbolique de la montagne chez Giono et Ramuz," *La Revue des Lettres Modernes* 652–657 (1983), pp. 11–23

Frison-Roche, Roger, *First on the Rope,* translated by Janet Adam Smith, London: T. Brun, 1949; New York: Prentice-Hall, 1950

——, *La Grande Crevasse,* Grenoble, France: B. Arthaud, 1948; Gallimard, 1975

Giono, Jean, *Batailles dans la montagne,* Paris: Gallimard, 1937; Gallimard/Folio, 1995

——, *Colline,* Paris: Grasset, 1929; reprinted, introduction by Brian Nelson, New York and Oxford: B. Blackwell, 1986

Godin, Jean-Cléo, "Entre la pierre et la boue: Jean Giono et les images de la vie," *La Revue des Letters Modernes* 735–738 (1985), pp. 123–136

Redfern, Walter, "Jean Giono," in *Dictionary of Literary Biography: French Novelists, 1930–1960,* vol. 72, edited by Catharine Savage Brosman, Detroit, Michigan: Gale Research, 1988

The Nature of German Romanticism

Deborah Janson

It is by now well established that German Romanticism cannot be pinned down to one all-encompassing definition, nor identified as the sum of its individual parts. Instead, each aspect of Romantic thought transforms and influences the other: an emphasis on individualism is replaced by an appreciation for community; a fascination with aesthetics leads to an interest in psychological obsessions; universal ideals give way to nationalism; and the desire to live in harmony with nature exists alongside the desire to dominate it. These manifold and contradictory aspects of Romanticism correspond to the varied ways nature is depicted in texts from the period (1795–1830), providing further proof of Romanticism's heterogenous character. Yet despite this potpourri of diverse elements, one thing can be said with certainty: in almost every Romantic work nature plays an active and central role. Whether as symbols of the human mind or as the real (or supernatural) setting for the protagonist's journey of personal development, nature elements are of such importance in Romantic literature that they frequently take on the status of characters, or subjects, themselves.

Many German Romantic texts call to mind the animistic view that all of nature is alive, and that all natural entities (animals, plants, streams, rocks, etc.) are articulate, able to communicate with each other and with human beings. These descriptions of nature talking reflect the belief that spirit resides in nature as well as the longing for communication between the human and non-human worlds. Such longing is also expressed in German Romanticism's best known symbol, the blue flower. Introduced in Novalis's *Heinrich von Ofterdingen*, this dream component consists of both human and plant organs. While the flower's transformation into a girl's face foreshadows the protagonist's union with his future bride, it also signifies the desire to merge the human and non-human realms and to overcome the established order of things.

With such importance placed on elements of the fantastic, it is not surprising that fairy tales became the Romantics' favorite genre. Both Novalis and Friedrich Schlegel praised fairy tales for their aesthetic and philosophical potential— their ability to simultaneously reflect diversity and oneness and to conjure up "dreams of that homeland that is both everywhere and nowhere" (Novalis, *Schriften*, II: 564).[1] The Romantics' preference for fairy tales was further strengthened by Johann Gottfried Herder's passion for developing a culture rooted in local native traditions, which in turn influenced Jakob and Wilhelm Grimm's efforts to record folk fairy tales that had been passed on orally. To promote a sense of German pride, the Romantics consistently chose the German Middle Ages (rather than ancient Greece or Rome) for their tales' settings. According to Simon Schama, the medieval landscapes of virgin oak and birch forest represented the sacred, heroic and communal life the Romantics attributed to early German tribes, and that they hoped to revive (p. 103).

This essay focuses on three Romantic fairy tales that express differing views on the relationship between human beings and the rest of nature, drawing on the work of ecocritics and ecofeminists for its theoretical basis.[2] Novalis's earliest tale, first written in 1798 and incorporated in his *The Novices of Saïs*, is juxtaposed against Ludwig Tieck's "The Runeberg," thereby addressing some differences between what has come to be known as Early and Late Romanticism. Although a contemporary of other Early Romantics—including his good friend Wilhelm Heinrich Wackenroder, the brothers August Wilhelm and Friedrich Schlegel, and Novalis—Tieck (born in 1773) possessed a psychological sensibility that anticipates later concerns. For example, like many late Romantic writers such as Clemens Brentano, Achim von Arnim, Joseph von Eichendorff, and E. T. A. Hoffmann, Tieck emphasizes the danger to the human psyche that an attempt to merge too closely with nature can hold. This focus contrasts with the early Romantic interest in the development and potential of the human mind as both an organ of nature's consciousness and as a microcosm of universal spirit. It is also in opposition to the desire to live in partnership with nature that is apparent not only in early Romantic texts but in the more difficult to categorize work of female Romantics such as Bettine von Arnim and Karoline von Günderrode. Von Arnim's tale "The Queen's Son," written in 1808, the last text to be examined in this chapter, foreshadows ecocritical concerns by expressing a desire to overcome the separation between the human and the non-human, or culture and nature.[3]

From an ecocritical perspective, the role the physical setting plays in a given piece of literature is very important, as is the way in which human culture is connected to the natural world. In German Romantic texts, mines and the forested mountains in which they are situated predominate, offering a clear example of just such a nature-culture intersection. The Romantics' frequent reference to mines illustrates the influence of place on the imagination, since a surprising number of Romantic authors, including Novalis, Joseph von Eichendorff, and Jean Paul Friedrich Richter, were trained as mining engineers, and chose to blend their then newly formed interest in geology with their philosophical and aesthetic views on life. Furthermore, their interest in the budding science of geology coincided with the general public's newly discovered passion for mountain climbing, which led naturally to excursions into mines and caves. Citing a Whitsuntide outing that Tieck and Wackenroder undertook in 1793, Theodore Ziolkowski writes: "The descent into a mine rapidly became a requisite of the walking tour that every German student undertook" (p. 22).

Since the twelfth century, German mining had been centered in the Saxon town of Freiberg. Its mining academy rose to world prominence in the Romantic era under the tutelage of Abraham Gottlob Werner, who taught there from 1775 until his death in 1817 and whose many students included Novalis. Werner is featured in two of Novalis's works: in *Heinrich von Ofterdingen* he assumes the role of the Bohemian miner who educates his listeners in

the wonders of mining, and in *The Novices of Saïs* he is the teacher who guides his students at a natural sciences academy to a clearer awareness of their place in nature. This teacher espouses views ecocritics hold today, such as the awareness that all of nature is interconnected, and that its diversity is to be revered. In a critique of usual scientific methods, the teacher asserts that what is needed to understand nature is "not the mere breadth and system of knowledge, not the gift of relaying this knowledge easily and purely to familiar concepts and experience and of exchanging peculiar, strange-sounding words for common expressions," but a sense of awe and respect for nature (p. 117). Hence, as William Arctander O'Brien points out in *Novalis: Signs of Revolution*, *The Novices of Saïs* blends the roles of nature lover, poet, and scientist, proposing a new, "self-reflective" and "poetic" science that recognizes its own plurality and subjectivity (pp. 206–208).

The fairy tale contained in *The Novices of Saïs* also teaches respect for nature. A youth named Hyacinth, originally a happy and contented person, becomes alienated from nature and from his beloved Rosebud after a stranger introduces him to worldly knowledge and leaves him a book "nobody could read" (p. 79). To cure Hyacinth of the melancholic state the stranger's visit has incited in him, the "odd old woman of the forest" hurls the book into the fire and instructs him to set out in search of "the mother of all things." After a long and arduous journey through diverse terrain that mirrors his changing inner condition, Hyacinth eventually finds himself in uncannily familiar yet extraordinarily wondrous surroundings. It is here that the heavenly goddess he has been searching for appears. As Hyacinth lifts the goddess's veil, Rosebud falls into his arms.

An ecofeminist reading of this tale cannot overlook the strong association between women and nature that it asserts. Whenever Hyacinth is alienated from Rosebud, he is also alienated from nature. For example, when the stranger's visit results in his paying Rosebud less attention, Hyacinth's ability to communicate with the neighboring plants, animals and rocks also decreases. It is not until he has achieved inner peace and is approaching the goddess's garden that nature's creatures begin to talk with him again. Furthermore, Rosebud's association with nature causes her to be portrayed as Hyacinth's opposite. She, like the world of nature around her, is stationary, whereas Hyacinth is actively engaged in a spiritual journey of self-discovery. Gordon Birrell comments: "This juxtaposition reinforces the symbolic interpretation of the two characters as Nature (passive, immobile) and Mind (active, questing), an interpretation that is further underscored at the conclusion by the revelation that Rosenblüte herself is the 'Mother of All Things'" (pp. 12–13).

Ecofeminists generally see the link between women and nature as based on domination and therefore as oppressive, maintaining that if men acknowledged that they were as much a part of nature as women, the exploitation of both women and nature might cease. In this regard their view differs from that of Novalis and other male Romantics who saw the association between women and nature as a means of overcoming the separation between nature and culture. To transcend the limitations imposed by culture (a realm they felt content to claim for themselves), male Romantics sought to merge with nature via love for a woman. The importance of love as a vehicle for achieving such a merger is apparent, for example, in Hyacinth's reunion with Rosebud, an occurrence that results in everlasting happiness for all.

The different stages in Hyacinth's life reflect Novalis's tripartite view of history: his childhood represents the first Golden Age where all creatures lived together innocently and harmoniously; his long journey represents the interim period in which human beings are alienated from the rest of nature (our current condition); and his reunion with Rosebud and the blissful life that follows it signifies the "infinite, boundless present" of the second Golden Age.[4] Presumably, if human beings could develop a sense of respect for and unity with nature, they would, like Hyacinth, have returned home. Thus Novalis's vision resembles the hope of many ecofeminists that human beings can in the future live in partnership with each other and the rest of nature in a way reminiscent of the alleged harmony of prehistorical (and prepatriarchal) societies. For both Novalis and late twentieth-century ecofeminists, the idealized conception of the past provides a model for an alternative vision of the future, a model that is based not only on an optimistic view of the human potential to change but also on a realistic assessment of the dire need for such change.

Rather than explicating a utopian theory concerning the importance of living in loving partnership with nature, Tieck's *Runenberg* emphasizes the necessity of separating "man" from nature. This is done by splitting the natural world into a dualistic configuration of mountains and plains, which in turn signifies the division between wilderness and civilization. The mountains are depicted as sublime, massive, and solemn, but also as a world alive with unpredictable movement, full of rushing streams, steep cliffs, jagged crevices, dark caverns, and sinister, supernatural beings. The plains, by contrast, are at times boring and uniform, but also comforting and serene. Whereas pagan forces rule in the mountain wilderness, the plains are controlled by the taming influences of Christian community.

Christian, the story's protagonist, is an impressionable and indecisive young man who is torn between his fascination for the mountains and his desire to lead a pious and peaceful family life. His dilemma intensifies when he absent-mindedly pulls at a mandrake root that is sticking out of the earth, breaking it in two. The root lets out a long and reproachful moan, a sound Christian later interprets as the pain of the decaying plant world. Plants are, he maintains, "the living corpses of earlier magnificent worlds of stone, they offer to our sight the most shocking putrefaction" (p. 96). By breaking the root, Christian inadvertently initiates an end to his relationship with the world of cultivated plants—of human civilization—while releasing supernatural powers residing in the ancient stone realm. Immediately following his thoughtless action a mysterious stranger from the stone realm appears. This figure plays an important role in Christian's ultimate rejection of human culture—first, by calling his attention to Rune Mountain, and second, by tempting him with the mineral kingdom's most powerful and corrupting influence: gold.

The contrast between wilderness and civilization is further strengthened by the juxtaposition of two very different women. One of these undresses before Christian's gaze in the ruins of an ancient castle on Rune Mountain, where she has been invoking the spirits of the ancient mineral realm. She is of "supernatural beauty," with long wavy black hair and limbs so powerful they appear to be carved out of marble. The other woman he meets in church, after reaching the safety of the Christian community that dwells idyllically in the valley below. This woman is "slender and blond," her blue eyes reflect "the most pervasive gentleness," her innocent countenance "the tenderest colors" (p. 89). At once pious and down-to-earth, this woman becomes

Christian's wife and the mother of his children. Yet he remains haunted by the memory of the castle woman all his life. She assumes many different forms, including that of the old lady of the woods to whom Christian finally becomes enslaved and who herself transforms at times into the ominous stranger.

In the end Christian descends into an abandoned mine, leaving his wife and children for the promise of eternal happiness among the heathen forces of the ancient mountain forest. While Christian does not doubt the correctness of his decision, the story's other human characters lament his loss of sanity, thus exposing to its readers the dangers that await those who renounce their Christian faith and its promise of transcendence.

With its portrayal of wilderness as a threat to human civilization, *The Runenberg* reflects a turning away from the early Romantic desires to live in partnership with nature and to attain universal consciousness. It foreshadows instead late Romanticism's dedication to the ideals of community and state and their foundation in conventional religion, as well as its focus on the supernatural's negative effect on the human psyche. For example, in E. T. A. Hoffmann's *The Mines at Falun*, a sensitive young man leaves his fiancée on their wedding day, having been lured to his death in a mining accident by a supernatural beauty who has promised him eternity in the stone realm. A similar but more optimistic scenario is depicted in Eichendorff's *The Marble Statue*, where the poetically inclined protagonist, Florio, temporarily forgets his love for the pure-hearted Bianca as he falls under the spell of a marble statue who at times transforms into the beautiful pagan goddess Venus. In the end Florio is rescued by the power of a pious Christian song that is used "to exorcise and tame the wild earth spirits that reach out from the depths to seize us" (p. 169).

Not wild earth spirits but human beings are perceived as threatening to Bettine von Arnim, who, although 12 years younger than Tieck, was philosophically much closer to the ideals of his generation than was he. This is apparent in her fairy tale "The Queen's Son," which, like Novalis's narrative about Hyacinth and Rosebud, criticizes the human tendency to abuse nature and laments the resulting alienation that exists between human and non-human animals.

The story takes place in the gardens of a medieval castle near the edge of a forest. This setting represents a border position between nature and culture, a position also assumed by the pregnant queen. Having failed to produce offspring after the normal nine-month term, the queen has been banished to the castle's back quarters by her angry husband. She remains pregnant for seven long years, carrying her heavy burden slowly through the lonely gardens, envious of the wild animals whom she sees raising their young in their "wild, rough way." She finally gives birth to seven sons, but her first-born is stolen by a she-bear. The queen begs the wild creatures to return him to her, but since they have never before been asked to comfort human beings, having instead only been persecuted by them, the animals cannot understand her pleas. In the end, the lost son returns with his furry companions and becomes "King of the animals and of humankind in spirit, without language" (p. 454).

This tale addresses the mutual alienation that exists between human and non-human animals, as well as the promise of harmonious cohabitation. In mentioning the persecution of other animals and their inability to comprehend human language, von Arnim blames Western culture for nature's silence. Her views thus resemble the ecocritical perspective expressed by Christopher Manes in "Nature and Silence," which states that unlike animistic societies, Western culture denies anyone who is not human the status of speaking subject. Quoting Hans Peter Dürr as saying "people do not exploit a nature that speaks to them," Manes notes that unfortunately the reverse of this statement is also true—that human beings do not give moral consideration to those with whom they do not communicate (p. 16). To speak in a language "free from an obsession with human preeminence," Manes supports the development of schools or monasteries that call to mind the natural sciences academy of Novalis's *The Novices of Saïs*, institutions "whose purpose is to promote an understanding of, reverence for, and dialogue with nature" (Manes, 25).

Bettine von Arnim proposes a slightly different route. Having abandoned any hope of getting human beings to see that they are not the planet's only speaking subjects, she unites nature and culture through spirit rather than language. She also posits woman—with her reproductive capabilities and motherly love—as a mediator between these two realms. This is illustrated by the queen, who gives birth to the possibility of harmonious cohabitation by producing a son capable of living in peace with the forest animals. Von Arnim thus differs from the writers of her generation who regard too close an association with "nature spirits" to be dangerous to one's sanity and standing in the human community. Whereas late Romantics tend to uphold the traditional and anti-ecological nature-culture dualism, writers of an "early Romantic sensibility," such as Novalis and von Arnim, instead share with spiritually oriented ecocritics the vision of a society that is based on cooperation between human and non-human nature, that is aware of the interconnections between all life forms, and that acknowledges the subjecthood of all beings.

Notes

1. Quoted in Birrell, 117. The translation is mine. I should point out that Novalis is a pseudonym for Friedrich von Hardenberg. Although he is better known by his pen name than by his given name, Hardenberg himself "set the pseudonym to print only four times, and never once used it otherwise" (O'Brien, 3).

2. Of particular relevance to this essay are Cheryl Glotfelty and Harold Fromm's anthology, *The Ecocriticism Reader: Landmarks in Literary Ecology*, and the work of various ecofeminists, including Riane Eisler, Susan Griffin, and Starhawk. Ecofeminism is a sub-category of ecocriticism. Some of its central tenets are discussed in this essay.

3. Bettine von Arnim never provided a title for this fairy tale, which she recorded in a letter to her husband, Achim von Arnim, in 1808. When it was first published by Reinhold Steig in 1913, it was given the title "Der Königssohn" ("The King's Son"). In translating it into English, Jeannine Blackwell changed the title to "The Queen's Son" because, as she explains, the tale is not primarily about the king's offspring, but is told from the perspective of the queen and is about her experiences as Mother. This perspective makes the story unusual for its time.

4. This phrase, included in the title of Birrell's book, is taken from *The Novices of Saïs* where it also serves as a description of the second Golden Age.

Selected Works and Further Reading

Arnim, Bettine von, *Die Günderode,* edited by Heinz Amelung, Leipzig, Germany: Inselverlag, 1914

————, "The Queen's Son," in *Bitter Healing:*

German Women Writers from 1700–1830: An Anthology, edited by Jeannine Blackwell and Susanne Zantop, Lincoln: University of Nebraska Press, 1990

Arnim, Ludwig Achim Freiherr von, and Clemens Brentano, *Des Knaben Wunderhorn: Alte deutsche Lieder,* Berlin: Arnimschen Verlag, 1845

Birrell, Gordon, *The Boundless Present: Space and Time in the Literary Fairy Tales of Novalis and Tieck,* Chapel Hill: University of North Carolina Press, 1979

Brentano, Clemens, "The Tale of the Myrtle-Girl," in *German Literary Fairy Tales,* edited by Frank G. Ryder and Robert M. Browning, New York: Continuum, 1983

Düerr, Hans Peter, *Dreamtime: Concerning the Boundary Between Wilderness and Civilization,* translated by Felicitas Goodman, Oxford: Blackwell, 1984; New York: Blackwell, 1985

Eichendorff, Joseph Freiherr von, "The Marble Statue," translated by Frank G. Ryder, in *German Literary Fairy Tales,* edited by Ryder and Robert M. Browning, New York: Continuum, 1983

Eisler, Riane Tennenhaus, *The Chalice and the Blade: Our History, Our Future,* Cambridge, Massachusetts: Harper & Row, 1987; London: Unwin, 1990

Glotfelty, Cheryll, and Harold Fromm, eds., *The Ecocriticism Reader: Landmarks in Literary Ecology,* Athens: University of Georgia Press, 1996

Griffin, Susan, with David Macauley, "On Women, Animals and Nature: An Interview with Eco-Feminist Susan Griffin," *American Philosophical Association Newsletters* 90:3 (1991), pp. 116–127

Günderode, Karoline von, *"Der Schatten eines Traumes": Gedichte, Prosa, Briefe, Zeugnisse von Zeitgenossen,* edited by Christa Wolf, Darmstadt, West Germany: Luchterhand, 1979

Heine, Heinrich, *The Harz Journey,* translated by Charles G. Leland, New York: Marsilio, 1995

Hoffmann, Ernst Theodor Amadeus, "The Golden Pot," in *Selected Writings of E. T. A. Hoffmann,* 2 vols., edited and translated by Leonard J. Kent and Elizabeth C. Knight, Chicago: University of Chicago Press, 1969

————, "The Mines at Falun," in *Selected*

Writings of E. T. A. Hoffmann, 2 vols., edited and translated by Leonard J. Kent and Elizabeth C. Knight, Chicago: University of Chicago Press, 1969

Hölderlin, Friedrich, *Hyperion and Selected Poems,* edited by Eric L. Santner, New York: Continuum, 1990

Kent, Leonard J., and Elizabeth C. Knight, eds. and trans., *Selected Writings of E. T. A. Hoffmann,* 2 vols., Chicago: University of Chicago Press, 1969

Manes, Thomas, "Nature and Silence," in *The Ecocriticism Reader: Landmarks in Literary Ecology,* edited by Cheryll Glotfelty and Harold Fromm, Athens: University of Georgia Press, 1996

Novalis, *Heinrich von Ofterdingen,* 1802; published as *Henry von Ofterdingen,* translated by Palmer Hilty, New York: Unger, 1964

———, "Hyacinth and Rosebud," translated by Gordon Birrell, in *German Literary Fairy Tales,* edited by Frank G. Ryder and Robert M. Browning, New York: Continuum, 1983

———, *Novalis Schriften. Die Werke Friedrich von Hardenbergs,* 3rd ed., edited by Paul Kluckhohn and Richard Samuel, Stuttgart, West Germany: W. Kohlhammer, 1977

———, *The Novices of Saïs,* 1800; translated by Ralph Manheim, New York: Curt Valentin, 1949

O'Brien, William Arctander, *Novalis: Signs of Revolution,* Durham, North Carolina: Duke University Press, 1995

Ryder, Frank G., and Robert M. Browning, eds., *German Literary Fairy Tales,* New York: Continuum, 1983

Schama, Simon, *Landscape and Memory,* New York: Knopf, 1995; London: HarperCollins, 1995

Schlegel, Friedrich, *Friedrich Schlegel's Lucinde and the Fragments,* translated by Peter Firchow, Minneapolis: University of Minnesota Press, 1971

Starhawk, "Power, Authority, and Mystery: Ecofeminism and Earth-Based Spirituality," in *Reweaving the World: The Emergence of Ecofeminism,* edited by Irene Diamond and Gloria Feman Orenstein, San Francisco: Sierra Club, 1990

Tieck, Ludwig, "Fair-Haired Eckbert," in *German Literary Fairy Tales,* edited by Frank G. Ryder and Robert M. Browning, New York: Continuum, 1983

———, "The Runenberg," translated by Robert M. Browning, in *German Literary Fairy Tales,* edited by Frank G. Ryder and Browning, New York: Continuum, 1983

Wackenroder, Wilhelm Heinrich, *Outpourings of an Art-Loving Friar,* translated by Edward Mornin, New York: Ungar, 1975

Ziolkowski, Theodore, *German Romanticism and Its Institutions,* Princeton, New Jersey: Princeton University Press, 1990

Environmental Elements in Maltese Literature: The Example of Dun Karm, Malta's National Poet

Oliver Friggieri

The history of Maltese literature reflects to a great extent the gradual emergence of a small nation in search of itself and eventually fully aware of its identity. The Romantic revival has meant to Malta much more than what it has meant to most other countries. It signified above anything else the need for the island to discover its own language and embark on the task of forming an indigenous literature, namely in Maltese, the traditionally downtrodden language derived from Arabic, spoken by all, written sporadically by quite a few.

The Historical Premise

Throughout the late nineteenth century and the first half of the twentieth, Maltese poetry and narrative prose profoundly contributed toward the ideal definition of Malta as a typically Mediterranean island. Poets like Gan Anton Vassallo, Dwardu Cachia, Dun Karm, Anastasju Cuschieri, Ninu Cremona, Guzé Delia, Mary Meilak, Gorg Zammit, Gorg Pisani, and Anton Buttigieg were constantly inspired by the natural elements that they believed to be the intrinsic justification for Malta's claim to nationhood. They almost politicized nature, interpreting natural beauty as the most direct document in merit of which the island could identify itself with the more respected countries. Novelists like Anton Manwel Caruana, Guzé Muscat Azzopardi, Guzé Galea, and Guzé Aquilina sought refuge in the remote past in order to go into detail in describing the countryside. Alleys, narrow streets, the village's main square, and farmhouses were gradually transformed into symbols of moral correctness, aspects of the island's age-long religious tradition.

The modern period, which can be traced back to the late 1960s, is characterized by the radical contestation of the thematic content of the whole Romantic period. The island is frequently conceived as a highly restricted space, symbolized by a cage, and refuge is normally sought in the open expanse provided by the sea. This is highly paradoxical since in substance both poets and novelists were still subtly being inspired by the idealization of the countryside that is so typical of all romantics. Poets like Victor Fenech, Achille Mizzi, Daniel Massa, and Mario Azzopardi are all frightened by the direct and indirect effects of rapid urbanization and violently deplore the destruction of land for building purposes. Novelists like Frans Sammut, Oliver Friggieri, and Alfred Sant set their plots somewhere midway between the traditional village and the modern city, thus striving to localize the identity crisis underlying the personality of their respective protagonists.

The pattern had been definitely set by Dun Karm, Malta's national poet, who standardized certain environmental elements, practically exhausting the subject and largely determining the mode by which subsequent writers were bound to treat environmental themes.

Nature as the Image of Divinity

Dun Karm Psaila, a humble and poor priest popularly and officially known as Dun Karm, is Malta's national poet. He is generally considered the best interpreter of his country's natural and historical heritage and identity. He was born in October 1871 in a small village, Haz-Zebbug, that was later to operate as a microcosm of the whole island in his poetry. His humble rural origin never played second fiddle to other aspects, and this fact may account for the paramount importance he gives to the landscape even in dealing with transcendental arguments. The island's natural identity provided him with a secure point of reference in the treatment of universal themes. When he died in October 1961 he was already revered as a major national figure.

In the late 1920s and throughout the 1930s Dun Karm reached the peak of his creative powers, principally owing to his transcending the particular and perceiving the universality that actually transforms routine into uniqueness and thought into intuition. In "Zaghzugh ta' Dejjem" (An Eternal Youth) he describes the sea in terms of its apparent immutability. All empirical experience conveys the idea that life is transient; change only leads toward utter destruction. Only the sea is static, supreme in its uniqueness. The Maltese archipelago, known for its relative serenity, is built up into an image of philosophical significance and timelessness is perceived in the local environment itself. The land is opposed to the sea, mobility to immobility, history to eternity. The purely descriptive motive soon becomes a point of departure for an inner voyage toward self-discovery.

The theme is best developed in "Il-Gerrejja u Jien" (The Drifter and I), composed in 1933 to recall two periods of deep depression that he went through when still very young. The poem is based on the description of a Maltese boat that goes through three different stages: the enthusiasm of the early morning, the maturity of midday, the expectation of death in the late evening. The three classical phases of human life (youth, adulthood, old age) are engulfed within the limits of one day. The sense of sight easily gives way to the sense of feeling, synesthesia being one of the most consistent psychological aspects of Dun Karm's poetry. The opening stanzas directly recall the normal condition of the Maltese sea:

Kif hammret fuq il-bahar
f'roghda ferrieha taz-zerniq id-dija,
u z-ziffa ta' filghodu
qajmet is-sigar ta' gnejniet mohbija,

rajtek, dghajsa hafifa,
tifrex il-qlugh ghal majistral sabih,
u, helu, taqbad triqtek,
taht ir-razan tat-tmun, ghal xejret ir-rih.
(Dun Karm, 275)

When crimson over the sea
trembled joyous the radiance of dawn,

and the breeze of daybreak
awoke the trees in hidden gardens,

I saw you, nimble skiff,
spreading your sails to the fair mistral,
and gently taking your way
under the rein of the helm, in the wake
   of the wing.
   (Arberry and Grech, 69)

The heat of the sun, the blue sky, and finally the "colourless veil" of the night play the role of physical aspects of a profoundly sad personal condition. The poet makes full use of the elements he is provided with by the environment to give an almost concrete coherence to what is spiritual, inner and undescribable. He is equally meditative and descriptive, but he is essentially sensory; he passes on from seeing to feeling. Psycho-physical situations of this sort, which abound in his works as well as in those of most other Maltese writers, are due to the influence exerted by the visual dimension of living on a tiny island.

The sea has eventually emerged as a major tourist resort, and it can be safely claimed that numerous images of Dun Karm have, at least subconsciously, been fully utilized for tourist advertising. But this is only to prove that the whole point in the poet's constant treatment of the sea is sorely missed. He is enchanted by its beauty and takes pains to describe its rhythmic movements, change of moods, subsequent calm and rage. The ocean embodies mystery, typifies solitude, and is finally conceived as final oblivion. The two closing stanzas of "Il-Gerrejja u Jien" are definitely a unique example of the extent to which Maltese environmental inspiration is actually philosophical, not empirical:

Hawn issa t-tnejn nitbandlu
qeghdin fil-qala jien u d-dghajsa tieghi,
ghaliex iz-ziffa raqdet,
u x-xemx ta' nofs in-nhar ma ghadhiex
mieghi:

nizlet, u biss xi hmura
ghadha titnikker fietla fuq l-gholjiet . . .
dal-waqt jinsatar kollox
fid-dlam tal-lejl . . . u jkun sultan is-skiet.
(Dun Karm, 276–277)

Here now we two are tossing
motionless in harbour, I and this skiff of
   mine,

because the breeze sleeps
and the sun of noonday is no more with me:

it has sunk, and only a glow
still lingers faintly above the hills . . .
soon everything is shrouded
in the darkness of night . . . silence reigns
supreme.
    (Arberry and Grech, 71)

It should be pointed out that fatality is closely associated with certain aspects of the environment in the whole of Maltese literature. Gan
Anton Vassallo, the major Maltese poet of the
nineteenth century, had already shown the way.
Melancholic, solitary, lamentive, he had already
shown in lyrics like "Lil Gannina" (To Gannina), "L-imsiefer" (The Migrant), and "Iz-Zghoz-
ija" (Childhood) how the physical aspect,
derived from a keen observation of the environment, could be integrated with one's own psychological condition. Dun Karm has remained
faithful to tradition even in this respect, and has
subsequently determined the way Maltese writers ought to transcend description through intuition. At its best Maltese literature is never purely
descriptive, although it deceptively looks so.

"Wied Qirda" (The Valley of Destruction) is
a Petrarchan sonnet Dun Karm also composed
in 1933. The valley is one of the most beautiful
to be found in Malta, a solitary spot seldom fre-
quented by either tourists or local residents. It
still fails to attract sufficient attention, in spite of
its highly picturesque, evocative character. A terrible battle took place there during the insurrec-
tion of the Maltese people against their French
occupiers in 1799, although it is only faintly
alluded to in the sonnet.

The sonnet is highly tense, consisting of a single complex-compound sentence. The octave is
constituted of a number of subordinate clauses
of time, and the sestet rises up toward its climax
through a sequence of main statements. The valley is somber, almost macabre, and its sheer
beauty is made subject to the metaphysical role
it now assumes. Transience is again, as in so
many other instances in Maltese literature, a
feeling one can only get through physical experience, which is mainly visual, and finally tactile.

The sense of movement in most Maltese environmental literature, which probably derives
from the fact that Malta is a small island, evokes
the passage of time in such a manner that immobility itself becomes ambiguous, indicative of
something else, its real opposite. Dun Karm is
preoccupied with two trees that abound in

Malta, the ash tree and the carob. They are so
frequently referred to in his poems as to become
archetypes. Their old age challenges and contradicts the truth that human life is relatively very
brief. The time factor is again conveyed through
aspects of nature. In their concreteness these
objects fail to instil a sense of permanence; they
defy time, whereas man, as a thinking substance,
becomes their inferior. Non-human nature is
superior and in beholding it humans can only
become more aware of their finitude:

Nisma' gol-fraxxnu u gol-harrub tal-plajja
bhal karba twila ta' min q'ghed ibati
u jigdem l-art fl-ugigh ta' l-ahhar firda;

u hsiebi jarga' lura lejn il-grajja
ta' min ghalina kien bil-bosta hati,
u nhoss ghaddejja l-Mewt minn fuq Wied
Qirda. (Dun Karm, 279)

In the plain, amid the ash-trees and the
    carobs,
I hear as it were the long sigh of one in
    anguish
biting the earth in the agony of the last
    parting;

and my thoughts go back towards the
    history
of those who committed many crimes
    against us,
and I feel Death passing over Wied Qirda.
    (Arberry and Grech, 83)

The tragic treatment of the environmental
theme does not exclude other approaches and
interpretations, although it is perhaps the most
important one in Dun Karm's work. He himself
dwells at length on the charm of typically sunny
days and "shining" nights. This time the elements of nature, always treated as vehicles of a
transcendental truth, convey the message that
life itself is actually worth living. What is generically termed optimism is not common to Maltese literature, or the whole of Mediterranean
culture for that matter. It would be more correct
to speak of a deep sense of inner contentment
derived from the contemplation of the landscape. It is, however, limited, subject to superior
criteria, which are not environmental at all.

"Nofs in-Nhar Sajfi" (Summer Midday) is a
sort of vignette typifying solitude as a source of
serenity. The moon is shining "tranquil over the
tranquil houses." One can only hear in the distance a watchdog barking. From a nearby gar-

den come the rustle and scurry of rats. The most intriguing aspect is provided by the shrilling of crickets that are now lulling people to sleep. The clock's warning, as the poet calls it, echoes over the whole village. The air is like a silvery azure linen sheet spread over one and all.

God himself is depicted as the supreme environmentalist in "Alla mhux Hekk" (God is not Thus). The underlying theme of the poem is the contrast between the inexhaustive creative power of God and the limited capabilities of an excellent painter. Landscapes are formed and rubbed off every day as night follows day, whereas a painter can only produce a fixed image of that same process caught in its instantaneousness. The artist has thought long and deep how to steal colors from the rose and other flowers, and his work has marvelled people, but that is as far as an artist inspired by nature can go. There now comes the descriptive component of the poem. Dun Karm describes sunset at Il-Wardija, one of the most beautiful natural places in Malta. In the summer sky there was "a fine spray of liquid gold and powdered topaz." The sea moved quietly "in a tremor of joy and love." The overall effect on the beholder immediately becomes metaphysical. Human genius is infinitesimal in contrast to the daily process of nature that produces the real source of a painter's visual inspiration. The artist has depicted "a setting sun that shall never set," but God performs hundreds of such wonders every day, and then he cancels them only to repeat them the next morning.

Theology is thus translated into a series of images that can be easily identified by the average inhabitant of Malta. Abstract concepts, such as the infinite wisdom of God, are thus illustrated through the charm of a well known landscape. In "Bjuda" (Whiteness) Dun Karm passes from the particular to the universal in a typically Aristotelian manner. He is struck by the intense whiteness of daybreak, over which there is the crimson that is bursting "aflame at the birth of the kindly sun." As in all other instances, whatever is abstract is transformed into an identifiable, sensory figure. Anthropomorphism is an underlying feature in Dun Karm's literary strategy and conceptual process. He glimpses whiteness again at noon, which now takes the shape of an "ornament of the highlands." Here the empirical experience comes to a halt and intuition takes over. Whiteness kindles in him love, the supreme law of nature, and finally transforms itself into a vision of the Virgin Mary.

"Gunju" (June) is inspired by one of the hotter months in Malta. The sun is burning forcefully and a fine breeze reminds us that the earth will soon be "roasting underneath our feet." June personifies the hope of ploughmen; the farmer will soon be repaid in abundance for his toil. In January men will be able to stay happy and sheltered in their homes. Nature will have worked its annual miracle. Similar motives recur in "Dell u Dija" (Shadow and Light), "Lis-Silla" (To the Clover), "Ward" (Roses), "In-Nissiega" (The Weaver), "Zjara lil Gesu'" (Visit to Jesus), and "Non Omnis Moriar." Typical aspects of the Maltese landscapes all gradually construct a unique system in which sensory perception leads to reflection on the fundamental ethical values embraced by most Maltese throughout history.

Autobiography itself is registered by means of the discovery of the local environment. "Inti ma Targax" (You Return Not) is an elegy to the poet's mother, an average village woman. The verdure returns "over the draught of autumn's dryness," as the sun reappears after winter. A fine breeze returns with all its fragrance amid blossoms and buds. On the contrary, his mother will never come again, and her sweetness and compassion are lost forever. Nature itself provides Dun Karm with the elements he uses to describe his mother. It is the same metaphorical strategy with which he defines Malta itself in his patriotic poems.

His resentment of urbanization, a sentiment that surfaces in various modern Maltese poets, is best declared in "Xenqet ir-Raba'" (Country Yearning) and "It-Tifla tar-Raba'" (The Country Girl). In both he derives a sharp contrast between traditional life in the village and the modern trends prevailing in the cities. He is actually contrasting nature with culture, echoing the romantic dictum "God made the country, man made the city." He would not tarry any longer in city streets, nor would he tread under his feet pitch and limestone. He only yearns for a small house "ornamented with the green of vine and orange-tree." In "It-tifla tar-Raba'" he vehemently advises a girl to keep aloof from urban culture, which he identifies with a sort of distortion of the natural process and the moral order derived therefrom.

The Inner Voyage Typified Through Nature

The long experience of Dun Karm as a poet in Maltese (he wrote exclusively in Italian until 1912, when he reached his forties) can be divided in at least three different phases. The first one is characterized by the exploration of the most immediate aspects of intimate life, such as family ties, personal solitude, the Maltese landscape, and by the classical commemoration of historical events. Lyrics like "Minghajr Omm" (Motherless), "idx-Dar" (The House), "Wahdi" (Solitary), and "Lill-Kanarin Tieghi" (To my Canary), mostly relying on the depiction of natural elements, illustrate the hidden anxiety of an apparently peaceful and calm spirit. Colorful descriptions of his surroundings, frequently resolving themselves into nostalgic vignettes, and an aptitude for subjectively involved narration already point toward what was to be his typical preoccupation: the quest for the sense underlying existence, itself a mystery perceived only mistakenly and approximately through empirical experience. He was only waiting for the right moment to look more deeply into nature to arrive at the central conclusion of all his poetry.

In the late 1920s and throughout the 1930s Dun Karm reached the peak of his creative ability by transcending the particular and perceiving the universality that transforms routine into uniqueness and rationality into intuition. "Zaghzugh ta' Dejjem" (An Eternal Youth), "Wied Qirda" (The Valley of Destruction), and "Naf u Nemmen" (I Believe and I Know), beside being sublimated expressions of the constant state of solitude the poet lived in throughout his life, are glaring examples of the way in which he gives a metaphorical shape to the conflict between the dictates of life and the force of violation, as well as to the need of reconciling human knowledge with a definite theological interpretation of existence. Although each lyric emphasizes some particular aspect and ignores another, this group constitutes a whole in which the physical environment and the metaphorical level are fused and reorganized according to the demands of a personal sensibility. The Maltese landscape again plays the leading role, a sort of rite of passage from the purely empirical to the essentially spiritual. In so doing he succeeds in giving universal, philosophical significance to a natural heritage that traditionally had been grossly underestimated. In so doing he anticipated by several decades the decisive role the natural heritage of the island was to assume when tourism became the most important industry in Malta.

Anxiety about the significance of being and the problem of evil, epitomized in death, imposed upon him the need of concentrating on a major work that affirms his truest world vision and automatically his firm belief that the natural environment is the most reliable source of knowledge of the unknown. "Il-Jien u Lil Hinn Minnu" (The I and Beyond Self), published in 1938 and since then universally acclaimed as his masterpiece, is his most valid contribution to Maltese poetry and evidence of his inner need to go beyond human experience in order to arrive at a spiritual justification of the mystery of being.

An inner condition of a disturbed self is immediately rendered poetically through the systematic construction of a physical itinerary. The Maltese landscape, mostly the one he knew best as a man hailing from Haz-Zebbug, is utilized for purely philosophical purposes. As always, Dun Karm betrays his rural origin and subsequently relates to the feelings of most Maltese, who still feel their country is essentially a village, namely a country whose primary resource is its natural heritage. The opening lines immediately set the rest of the whole long narrative poem:

> Hsiebi bhal aghma: biex isib it-trejqa
> itektek bil-ghaslug kull pass li jaghti;
> jimxi qajl qajl u qatt ma jaf fejn wasal;
> dalma kbira tostorlu l-kif u l-ghala,
> u d-dawl li hu jixtieq qatt ma jiddilu.
> . . . Min gol-Hondoq
> tad-dwejjaq kiefra jien ghajjat imbikki:
> Ghejjew ghajnejja thares bla ma tara,
> u qalbi nfniet. (Dun Karm, 128-129)

> My thought is like a blind man: to find the way
> he taps out with a stick every step he takes,
> shuffles slowly, never knowing where he has got.
> A dense darkness shrouds from him the how and why,
> and the light he yearns after never illumines him.
> . . . Out of the deep abyss
> of cruel anguish weeping I cried aloud:
> My eyes are weary of peering and never seeing,
> and my heart forspent.
> (Arberry and Grech, 147–149)

The thematic content is philosophical whereas the symbolic structure is wholly environmental. Throughout the poem Dun Karm establishes a set of relationships with various antropomorphically rendered elements of nature. The spiritual itinerary takes the shape of a weary walk in the countryside. Birds, trees, the sun, and the sea play decisive roles in determining the various stages experienced by the traveller. The contrast between the troubled condition of the soul and

married a fairy. Death is imagined in the ballad as a cosmic marriage with a fairy queen, a joyous osmosis between human and nature, cosmic and terrestrial, not an end but a continuation. Death becomes a moment of celebrating the return to nature, a wedding in which all the natural elements participate.

Sadoveanu changed the plot but the structure of the myth is still there. Much of the pleasure of the text comes from the nuances of retelling, which makes a connection with his *Ancuta's Inn* (*Hanul Ancutei*). Nechifor Lipan, shepherd in the mountains of Moldavia, has been missing from home for a while. His wife, Vitoria, decides that the agrarian calendar with norms about sheep traveling does not account for his absence. She goes to the police, then asks for the advice of a priest and a witch, looking for counsel from both the white and black spirits. None of these spiritual or secular authorities seems to be of any help, so the woman decides to start a journey, retracing the steps of her husband with his herds of sheep. Although accompanied by her son, it is Vitoria that leads the quest. The novel has been read as an initiation of the woman into the world outside of her household. She had traveled outside of her village in the mountains before, but this time she is the leader.

The quest could be seen as a banal detective-adventure story. Vitoria cunningly plays people against one another, discovers the murderers, and forces the truth out, and vindication is achieved. The reading is not very rewarding if we follow this simple path. The importance of Vitoria's quest is that she gives up all the external, social authorities and tries to read the answer within herself, through the signs of nature. From this perspective the novel is a means of communication between the inner and the external world. Once she leaves the mountains and her community and goes down to the towns in the fields, Vitoria encounters the emergent civilization, with telephone, post office and trains. Vitoria is not perturbed in any way by the new aspects of civilization. Although she cannot read and write, she communicates with the voice of nature. The mythical dimension doubles the detective story.

The woman tries to open herself to the messages in her unconscious. The dead husband comes back to her in her dreams, but he does not talk. Oral tradition, of which her son is removed and ignorant, is meaningful for Vitoria. She is performing during the journey: she pretends to be weak and naive, sheds tears in public and

communicates with other women in order to find out the details of her lost husband. This is only one of her voices, of her possible models of behavior. Inwardly, she tries to open herself to the signs of nature. Vitoria's worries about her husband start with premonitions manifested in nature: "The sun beat down from the Magura rock to the South and when Vitoria looked up, blinking, the fir-trees seemed to be darker than usual" (p. 20). In her world every element in nature is raised to the level of significance. The change of weather is a disturbance of the cyclical order of transhumance and an interruption of its archaic rituals: "Vitoria felt a cold rush of wind sweeping down from the mountains . . . she suddenly blinked, as though trying to shake off her drowsiness" (p. 22). She also has dreams invested with significance by oral tradition.

Vitoria's world view is inherited from ancient civilizations, in which there are assimilated Judeo-Christian elements. The world is defined as an ordered structure in which the temporal and seasonal rhythm of every event and gesture connected to agrarian practices and rituals is clearly established. There are unwritten laws that set the pastoral calendar, dominated by the alternative movement into the mountains in spring and down back to the community for winter. What Vitoria does all through her journey is try to decipher this rhythm backward. Moreover, there is a connection between realms that is open only for the ones initiated into uninterrupted traditional knowledge.

Communication with nature opens her to a kind of knowledge and sensitivity shared with the other beings: "The woman of the mountains felt the fragrance of the fresh water tickling her nostrils, quite like the beasts of the forest" (p. 66). It is a world where everything signifies, where the elements of nature cooperate in the adventure of the character and pass messages from a different realm. The special sense of communication depends on the woman's surrender of her consciousness to the voices expressed in nature. She reads the wind and tells her son "our orders are to halt here" (p. 70).

In the mythical approach of *The Hatchet* the people mirror their place, they share the same character:

The people who live in the shadow of the pines are strange people: quick tempered and fickle like the waters and the weather, enduring with fortitude both hardships and the stress of fearful weather, yet radiant in their joy and under the August heat. Eager for love and drink, they preserve traditions that date back to the beginning of the world. (p. 76)

The relationship between people and land is worked on throughout the novel. Its atemporal features are inscribed at the level of tradition. Automatisms, cyclical order and patterns of behavior seem to dominate the advance of the quest. Vitoria's behavior is coordinated according to spatial elements. Communication between woman and land is determined by her willingness to surrender herself to the rules of the land and to the signs in weather. Her destiny is determined by external elements. It is hard to decide whether in her quest Vitoria is an agent or is just led by signs although she deciphers and accepts.

Consider the early description of her motherhood log in the first pages of the novel: "From the seven children that God had blessed them with, only two had been left to them. The five other had died of measles or diphtheria, and their faces and names had been forgotten, becoming one with the flowers, the butterflies and the lambs born over the years" (p. 17). The image of children that have been lost and recuperated to nature, among plants and animals around the house, is not idyllic. Rather, it betrays a need to come to terms with the order of things as they are, open to suffering. It is important to retain this log of the lost children when we read *Ion*, where every woman's narrative would carry over a similar log. In *The Hatchet* the woman stands under the sign of acceptance of her destiny. Institutions do not seem to have interfered much in the life of the people of the mountains. Religion itself is present in its ritual rather than in dogma. Vitoria has learned to accept what happens to her as already inscribed in the story.

Vitoria fails to understand any need for change. She opposes her daughter, Minodora, in her tendency to adapt to new ways of life, and scolds her: "you no longer like our peasant skirt and blouse. . . . I never knew such things, nor did your grandmother, not mine either—and you shall live according to our way . . ." (p. 19).

The mountains secure the transmission of tradition without change, given the closure they offer:

secluded from the world of the valleys, generation after generation for hundreds of years had rejoiced when the days grew longer and a new year began. Here everything was as in the days of Burebista, the prince of long ago, for though the masters now were different and the language had changed, the men, customs and elements were still the same. (p. 41)

The tendency to conserve customs is seen in a positive light according to the mythic interpretation of the world. Vitoria carries out the function of correcting Lipan's murder back into the cycles of nature and place.

It is hard to attempt a reinterpretation of woman's position in traditional writing that claims its logic in a mythic interpretation of the world. Here people are bound to their place and woman's roles within house and community are strictly inscribed. Vitoria is a heroine who travels outside of her place, but in dealing with new people, situations and places she has to act according to the received available roles in the repertoire of behavior. She empowers herself by this free play between the possible roles. Nature itself takes part in the quest and gets transformed into an active system of signs the woman is supposed to read, in a communication made possible in the logic of the mythic interpretation of the world. However, the process of obeying the unwritten laws within a traditional community is not always seen in its positive aspects. Woman and land in a subsistence model characteristic of a primitive trading system are displaced and oppressed. The disturbance of the agrarian norms due to economic factors turns them both into mere resources.

The Marriage Contract in the Realist Mode

The land and the woman are bound together in a position of subordination in Liviu Rebreanu's *Ion*. The novel might be shocking if read outside the premise of the naturalistic view of the world to which Rebreanu was indebted. At the same time, it is important to notice that this view is not unique to Rebreanu in the tradition of Romanian literature. One of the first successful agrarian novels, *Moara cu noroc* (*The Mill of Luck and Plenty*) by Ion Slavici, is built on the same strong realist convention, in which woman and land determine the conflict.

My premise of analysis for *Ion* tries to read the text against the logic of the title that favors the man and recuperate Ana's story. The novel is built polyphonically, based on two separate levels that meet only incidentally or in periods of crisis. I shall refer to only one level, centered on the life of the peasants in the village rather on the part dealing with the village intellectuals—the school teacher, the priest and the authorities—and with explicit nationalist issues. The story is quite simple. Ion, a young man, is about to make his decision of marriage; he is trying to choose between a young good looking woman as poor as he is, and rather plain Ana, whose father is rich. Once he decides for the latter, he has to find a means to force her father's agreement. The means Ion resorts to is implied in the novel as cunning: he seduces Ana, gets her pregnant, then waits for the woman to be ostracized according to the traditional standards of the community. Most of the novel is consumed by the journey pregnant Ana makes between her father's and her husband's places, banished by each in a cruel negotiation that seems to bear no relationship to Ana herself. She is reduced to the status of labor source or is simply one detail in the marriage contract.

Woman and land are placed in the same position: they are part of a negotiation, reduced to objects of dispute. Criticism of the novel has always come back to the famous scenes where Ion goes out in the fields to see his land. The erotic imagery does not leave any doubt about the spirit of possession that drives him, in which land becomes an animate passion:

The sight of his land stirred his heart so strongly that he felt like dropping to his knees to hug it. It was so much the more beautiful because it belonged to him. The thick, lush grass, with its sprinkling of clover, was swaying languidly in the cool air of the morning. He could not restrain himself. He tore up a handful of grass and rubbed it eagerly between his palms. (p. 41)

The satisfaction of possession sets the land in a position of subordination. It is a passion shared by many characters in the novel. In fact Ion is not exceptional in the sense that all the other peasants represented act more or less like him. Land and women are appropriated for a sense that destroys their individuality. They are not valid in themselves: they are both permanently turned into something else. There are many passages in the book that present the displaced physical relationship between peasant and the land. Every time Ion is out in the fields, the tone of the novel changes. It is the only time when the rather flat realist-naturalist style gains poetic valences to express the passion for the land. The

romance in the novel, if any, takes place between man and the land.

The arbitrary rules of ownership have cut the fields into parcels; both the dead and the living try to dictate over the land, in a continuous process of interaction:

Under the soft down light, the whole land, dissected into thousands of small pieces by the needs and whims of a host of living and dead, seemed to be alive and breathing. The fields of maize, of wheat, of oats, the hemp-field, the orchards, the houses and woods all buzzed and whispered and rustled, speaking their own rough tongue, rejoicing in the flood of light and was steadily growing brighter, triumphant and fertile. (p. 43)

The rich enumeration betrays the perspective of a peasant in the details of the culture. Yet, Ion's response to the cosmic voice of the land in all its splendor comes back to the level of possession or even envy: "He heaved a deep sigh of humility and awe before the giant: 'Great God, how much land there is!'" (p. 43).

The land has been there for generations as a subject of passionate conflicts in which children turn against their parents, accusing them of having squandered the land. Woman and the land are set in the same position, never seen as individualities independent and self-determining. They are appropriated into a system, coveted or used, and their parallel destiny is marked throughout the novel. Recounting Ion's early passion for the land, the narrator stresses that "ever since, his love for the land had been greater even than love for his mother" (p. 43). Ion covets land in the same way he covets women. Moreover, his passion is doubled if the object of his desire belongs to someone else. One of the important legal cases he is involved in is caused by his having trespassed the border of his property. One day Ion gets out in the fields to plow and is seized by "uncontrollable craving" for his neighbor's land, so he ends by plowing into a couple of his furrows (p. 78).

Land and woman are equally objects of dispute, becoming more valuable in as much as they are claimed by someone else. They are both transmitted from father to husband. Again, the identification between woman and land as objects of property is such an obvious theme in this novel that it is hard to operate with feminist concepts. The basic terminology of oppression is explicitly used in the text. It seems that the theme of appropriation of woman in a typical labor, sexual and reproductive contract is overworked in a naturalist novel that claims itself as a faithful image of reality. The novel is written in the tradition of a male voice in a literature in which there is little canonical literature by women. That is why it requires a resistant reading to analyze the structure of the main female character. Ana's story takes over the focus especially in endless painful walks across the village. The scene of the community works against her, intensifying her suffering. In traditional communities there is no boundary between public and private, or at least the circulation between them is used as an extremely efficient means of punishment.

Clearly, Ion counts on the reaction of the community and the need for Ana's father to give up his pride and approve of the marriage contract. Ana is punished by all of them at the same time. As she waits for her father to come home after finding whose child it is, Ana considers the reactions around her; the initial question "What will he do?" gets complicated into a multiple "What will father do, what will Ion do, what will people do?" (p. 159). The woman is set at the mercy of the whole community around her. In this case there is revealed rather a negative aspect of community life, in contrast with the one analyzed in the mythic view represented in *The Hatchet*.

The scene in which Ana is beaten by her father in the yard, witnessed by the peasants crowded around, provides painful evidence for the way a community sanctions and approves of the rule of complete power the male has within the legal boundaries of his family:

> The shouts and cries that rang out from Vasile Baciu's yard soon brought the whole village to their feet. The women from the neighboring homesteads arrived with breathless haste, but halted terrified at the gate whence they only dared call out in an entreating voice: "Leave her, Bade Vasile, you're killing her. . . ." (p. 164)

Stopping in front of the gate defines a general attitude inscribed in the rules of rural power distribution within the household, as "every man is his own master in his farmyard, whatever he may be doing there and no stranger may interfere" (p. 164). The battering scene is not the only one in the text. A few pages later Ion beats Ana after he is legally married to her.

The negotiations for marriage themselves leave no trace of doubt as to the character of the contract to be signed. Ion sends pregnant Ana back to her father: "I have nothing to settle with you but with him we can settle things over and come to some arrangement, I should think, as between decent people. . . . How can we come to any settlement without bargaining? Who has ever seen a contract without a price?" (p. 168). There is no trace of romanticism in the settlement of marriage in this case.

The description of the marriage contract in the rural world is always a problem largely dwelt upon in the traditional Romanian novel. In this instance it seems that the negotiation itself becomes the topic. Land is an object of dispute and in the impoverished Transylvanian village marriage settlement becomes the only means of altering ownership. Sexuality becomes just another means in the repertoire of available behavior strategies. Ion knows what he is doing: he acts according to preimposed available models of a patriarchal society, of which he is completely aware. The stereotypes against the woman are voiced clearly: "Is it my fault that her belly is up to her chin? Is it my fault? It's her look out; if she hadn't liked it she wouldn't have had it. . . . After all, it wasn't me that asked her, God knows . . ." (p. 182).

The negotiations are endless and it takes the priest to organize a meeting in which all the injured parties involved have to trade the land and the woman. Taking pride in the fact that ever since he "shepherded the congregation, there had been no children out of the wedlock" (p. 185), the priest tries to control the negotiations. In the end he takes advantage of the lack of knowledge of the peasants and has them sign a final lease of the land for the benefit of the church.

Signing the marriage contract is a communal process of negotiation in which woman and land are seen as resources. The labor of production and reproduction in which the woman is involved is ignored by the process of negotiation. Ion's address, "And now you want me to feed your daughter too" (p. 189), synthesizes this prejudice against the labor value of the woman in the rural system. At this level the kind of subsistence labor the impoverished peasants are engaged in is a mark of the rural situation in the country in general, where the exploitation of the peasants through exaggerated taxes drives them to extreme behaviors. In another novel called *The Uprising (Rascoala)*, Rebreanu describes the mass revolt of the peasants in 1907, the largest form of protest caused by the desperate economic situation.

The systematic process of pauperization of the peasants between the two world wars is a general theme in most of the Romanian agrarian novels, the best example being *The Morometes (Morometii)* by Marin Preda. The difference in Preda's novel is that it was written during communism, so that all the messages are contradictory in themselves and ambivalent. The literature after 1944 tends to be more nuanced: social and economic aspects are often touched through the political code of a style akin to magical realism, as represented in the recently published anthology of stories *The Phantom Church and Other Stories from Romania*. Against the reference to the political reality of Romania during communism, any agrarian novel written about property becomes problematic. If we keep in mind the reality of the cooperativization forced upon the farming population between 1949 and 1962, any interpretation of the Romanian agrarian novel has to deal with the ambivalence of the messages. Traditional agrarian novels before 1940 get to be read as a sign of resistance. Ion's passion for land gets significance in a system dependent on the social and historical reality of the time.

Coming full circle in the presentation of the relationship between woman and land in *The Hatchet* and *Ion*, I want to stress the fact that the difference between the mythic and the realist modes does not necessarily erase the common reality of the analogous position of woman and land, as portrayed in the Romanian agrarian novel. The problem is that the language of oppression is quite graphic. Also, the gender division of labor marks the exploitation of woman and the underestimation of the value of her work. In each of these two novels the relationship between woman and land is determined according to various interpretations of nature and the values of community. In *The Hatchet* nature is a signifying system for an order beyond the human that has to be deciphered for the benefit of the woman in the quest. In *Ion* land and woman together have been completely translated into economic terms, as resources. The traditional community in both cases works equally through constraint and punishment, as well as being a resource of ancestral knowledge and providing support for the individual.

Past criticism of these two canonical novels

has not touched the patriarchal aspects of the joint exploitation of woman and land. Although the novels tell the stories of women, there is hardly any dramatized explicit voice to address the injustice the women experience. Neither is there such a voice in the Romanian criticism of the traditional novel to counterbalance its appropriation as the basis for the Romanian literary canon.

Selected Works and Further Reading

Bakhtin, Mikhail M., *The Dialogic Imagination: Four Essays,* edited by Michael Holquist, translated by Caryl Emerson and Holquist, Austin: University of Texas Press, 1981

Fârnoaga, Georgiana, and Sharon King, eds. and trans., *The Phantom Church and Other Stories from Romania,* Pittsburgh, Pennsylvania: University of Pittsburgh Press, 1996

Levitchi, Leon, trans., *Balade Popular Românesti/Romanian Popular Ballads,* Bucharest, Romania: Minerva Publishing House, 1980

Merchant, Carolyn, *Earthcare: Women and the Environment,* New York: Routledge, 1996

Mies, Maria, *Patriarchy and Accumulation on a World Scale: Women in the International Division of Labour,* Atlantic Highlands, New Jersey, and London: Zed, 1986

Preda, Marin, *The Morometes* [*Morometii*], translated by N. Misu, Bucharest, Romania: Foreign Language Publishing House, 1957

Rebreanu, Liviu, *Ion* [*Ion*], translated by A. Hillard, London: Peter Owen, 1965

———, *The Uprising* [*Rascoala*], translated by P. Grandjean and S. Hartauer, London: Peter Owen, 1964

Sadoveanu, Mihail, *Ancuta's Inn* [*Hanul Acutei*], Bucharest, Romania: Book Publishing House, 1954

———, *The Hatchet* [*Baltagul*], translated by Eugenia Farca, Bucharest, Romania: Minerva Publishing House, 1983

Slavici, Ioan, *Classics of Romanian Literature: The Mill of Luck and Plenty and Other Stories,* vol. 5, East European Monographs No. 351, edited and translated by Kurt W. Treptow, New York: Columbia University Press, 1994

Nature and Environment in Russian Literary Prose

Yuri Vedenin

Russian literature in general and Russian prose in particular have strong ties with the outer world and its natural component. The character of these ties enables one to presume that Russian literature is somewhat ecologically oriented and to find it manifested in the interest of Russian authors in the preservation of nature as the origin of all processes. Each epoch and writer has a particular relation to the environment, which shows itself mainly in the scale of world perception. Majestic pictures of nature are followed by unpretentious scenes confined to the house or the garden. Characteristics of the environment depicted vary. Nature can either be an enemy to the main character or an equal partner, or become itself the main character in a short story or even a novel. All of these differences are inextricably interwoven with literary processes, with the evolution of literary tastes, as well as the history of Russia and its place among the world's countries.

Early Russian Literature

The early period of Russian prose, from the eleventh through the seventeenth century, is characterized by the prevalence of translations, including chronicles, apocrypha and biblical scriptures. Sermons, precepts, lays, travelogues, satires, war narratives and various fictional genres emerged somewhat later. Lives of the saints were particularly popular. This variegated set of genres accounts for a vivid description of the surrounding world, including the settings of the Bible and the geography of Russia and its immediate neighbors. Russian chronicles provided detailed information on historical events and their scenery. For instance, *The Russian Primary Chronicle* depicts the geographical situation of the Kievan Rus, trade routes, the major Russian rivers, the Black Sea, and adjacent and remote nations and countries. Geographic realia and

scenery play an even more active role in *The Lay of Igor's Campaign*, where nature immediately participates in the narration through the solar eclipse being a bad omen on the eve of the battle or the dark clouds and blue lightning witnessing the tragic fighting. Moreover, the battle is hard not only on the warriors but also on the country; the narrator mentions such details as the earth rumbling, river streams being muddied, and the fields being covered with dust. Nature can be benevolent to people, however. It answers the prayer of Igor's wife Yaroslavna and helps the prince to escape from captivity with the aid of the sun and the wind. A majority of the characters have their natural counterparts: Igor is compared to the stoat, Vsevolod is likened to the aurochs, Boyan is called the nightingale, and the Cumans are perceived as dark clouds.

New expressive means were used in *The Lay of the Fall of the Russian Land* written in the thirteenth century. The narrator remembers Russia as it was before Mongolian invasion, its peaceful lakes and groves, its prosperous cities. Thus, nature becomes an integral narrative component and is described as humanity's habitat as far back as the Middle Ages. One can even trace certain difficulties pertaining to the deterioration of landscapes as a result of military campaigns and enemy invasions.

Russian Literature of the Eighteenth Century

Feofan Prokopovich, one of the first eighteenth-century Russian writers, mentions the majesty of Russia, its territorial growth, its new capital, St. Petersburg, as well as other countries, first of all Holland and France. It is worth noting that he calls Russia "The Russian Europia." He sometimes resorts to landscape description, for example, the island where a shipwrecked sailor Vassili finds himself is covered with "a great thick forest, with large moors and marshes." At the same time, nature is kept in the background as compared with the earlier literature, and the estrangement of humanity from it becomes more pronounced. As M. Chulkov puts it in "The Fair Cook," "I was neither acquaintance nor lover of the woods and fields, they were not enchanted with my beauty nor gave me anything."

In the late eighteenth century, however, nature rapidly regains importance. It becomes socially oriented, helping the author to show an attitude toward the state system and political realities of the period. On the other hand, self-sufficient landscape descriptions, the first signs of the purely aesthetic approach to literary creation, also appear. True, both trends can well be present in one and the same piece of literature. In his "Journey of V. I. T.," Nikolai Novikov recorded the hard life of peasants: "The unploughed fields, a poor harvest. . . . Low, straw-roofed huts. . . . The only street covered with mud and all sorts of sewage." Yet the same author uses different words with regard to wealthier people, such as the pleasant night coolness, birds singing, and the harmony of nature.

The late eighteenth century saw drastic changes in the attitude of Russian writers toward nature and its role in plot development. These changes are especially evident in the works of the Russian writer and historian Nikolai Karamzin. Landscape in his prose is not merely the character's habitat. Through it the author perceives his sensations, his attitude toward life and other people, and nature becomes an independent character. Karamzin varies the scale of his narration, yet humble, unpretentious scenes are evidently more to his liking. He admires the grass and flowers, examines "their slender stocks, their indented edges, their motley leaves," and wonders at their unexpectedly strong fragrance. Karamzin displays a new ideology of human-nature interaction opposing nature to artifacts and extolling it as the highest aesthetic value: "There is no pleasure for me where evidence of labor can be seen. A tree transplanted and cut is like a slave wearing a golden chain," he states.

The majority of the late eighteenth-century authors did not show any preference to particular areas or towns. They described Russia in general, its regions and cities. A significant feature of the time is not a mere emergence of new geographical sites but a pronounced interest in the urban milieu, primarily in the landscapes of St. Petersburg and Moscow. Thus, the scene of "Poor Lisa" is set in Moscow, in the vicinity of the Simonov monastery. He provides a minute description of the city and its suburbs. The literature of the eighteenth century provided a firm basis for a keen artistic perception of the environment. New ground was broken at the end of the century owing to a renaissance of various aspects of Russian culture, including the attitude toward nature. It is not for nothing that landscape architecture and painting come into full bloom in that period of history. These facts are indicative of ecological trends in Russian culture at that time.

Russian Literature of the Nineteenth Century

In the nineteenth century, Pushkin, Golgol, Leo Tolstoy, and Dostoevsky brought a worldwide fame to Russian literature. An active role of the environment and natural phenomena in the unraveling of the plot became a characteristic trait of their works. Pushkin created vivid descriptions of Russian landscapes that helped him to reveal emotional elements of the plot and were therefore closely connected with his characters and their milieu. He was particularly fond of describing natural phenomena, or rather their interaction with the main characters of his works. Pushkin masterfully used landscape description for rendering the mood of his narrations, as he does with the melancholy of "The Postmaster." In "Damsel Peasant," a light and joyful story, the environment is depicted quite differently from that in "The Postmaster."

Gogol was one of the first Russian prose writers to give vivid descriptions of Russian landscapes. The environment permeates his texts, often rivaling the main characters. With the aid of colors, movements, and sounds, he renders the beauty of the scenery through the state of a character enjoying gorgeous landscapes, as in "Fair at Sorochintsy." There are magnificent lines in Gogol's prose devoted to the description of Ukrainian summer, fall, and even winter. He masterfully describes Russian and Ukrainian landscapes: rivers, like the Dnieper and Psyol, and mountains, like the Carpathians. He was apparently the first Russian author to make a particular landscape the subject of an artistic description. At the same time, his description is perfectly true and meets all the requirements of scholarly analysis. It is also worth noting that Gogol was the first Russian author to provide a detailed description of a city, nay, of a single street, which is the Nevsky Avenue in St. Petersburg. The polyphony of the picture drawn of that street is also noteworthy. Nevsky Avenue appears before the reader as a multitude of characters, as an architectural ensemble, and as a daily changing theatrical performance. Gogol's interest in artificial landscapes is manifest throughout his literary activity, as his so-called "poem" "Dead Souls" testifies. One can see there both pictures of particular towns and landscapes the main character passes by during his journey. The description of rural estate landscapes, rendered in strict accordance with the personalities of relevant characters, is of particular interest.

Leo Tolstoy maintained and further developed many a tradition of Russian literature. Nature is not merely scenery for him; it takes an active part in the plot, entering into dialogue with characters. Suffice it to mention Andrei Bolkonsky's encounters with the oak, first a dying creature and then suddenly revived and crowned with young leaves. It was the second encounter that helped Prince Bolkonsky to gain a foothold in his new life. The workings of nature are usually related to the brighter, more optimistic trends in Tolstoy's works.

Unlike Tolstoy, Dostoevsky achieved his fame primarily through writing on urban matters. Nevertheless, his perception of the latter is permeated with nostalgia for rural landscapes and the countryside. While describing rural periods of his characters' lives, he uses such words as "a hot, clear and bright day," "immense stacks of wheat," and "a happy, joyful mood." He rejects the city outright and yet cannot do without it. As early as in his first novel, *Poor People*, the city is associated with foul weather, mud, and slush. It is hard to live in Dosteovsky's city. In this respect he differs considerably from the authors of the late eighteenth and early nineteenth centuries, like Batyushkov and Karamzin, who tended to admire cities, their majesty and beauty.

Travel notes came into vogue in the nineteenth century, although they had emerged in Russian literature as early as in the previous century. Among the first examples of this kind of literature were books by Karamzin and Dolgoruky, yet the most valuable contribution was made by Goncharov. He took part in a voyage around the world and described his impression in his novel *The Pallas Frigate*. For the first time in Russian literature a single book provided descriptions of various countries, their landscapes, cultures, and economies, as well as a most picturesque and poetic image of the ocean.

Yet another trend in Russian prose emerged in the early 1800s, which is books where Russian landscapes are the main characters. In the 1840s Sergei Aksakov wrote his books *On Angling* and *Diaries of the Fowling-Piece Sportsman* containing, besides traditional landscape descriptions, masterfully done portraits of fish, birds, and beasts. Animals in these books seemed to depict themselves and their habits. This trend soon gained wide popularity.

Russian Literature of the Twentieth Century

The early twentieth century is characterized by a growing interest in natural habitat and rural landscapes. At the same time, urban landscapes gradually encroach upon the domain of literature. The attitude toward the latter becomes more liberal. They no longer arouse either gloomy or rapturous feelings. The description of the receding of old Russia takes up a special place. In this respect, Russian writers' interests in Russian rural estates and their attempts at looking on the world from the window of an old country house or from an old neglected park are worth noting. The Nobel Prize–winner, Ivan Bunin, for instance, was a veritable bard of the receding gentry Russia.

The main trait of twentieth-century Russian literature, however, became its concern with ecology. Nature was perceived not only as an aesthetic category but also as a milieu indispensable for humanity as well. Various genres dealing with nature emerged. Certain writers devoted their work almost completely to the environment. The twentieth century saw many writers become Aksakov's followers. Among the most eminent ecologically oriented writers are Mikhail Prishvin and Ivan Sokolov-Mikitov, in whose works landscapes are self-sufficient characters engaged in a dialogue with the author. Particular attention is paid to philosophical problems and the intrinsic value of the flora and fauna. Even landscapes are depicted as living creatures with their specific character, behavior, and attitude toward one another. Leonid Leonov has played an important role in the ecological development of fiction. He was the first Russian writer to bring up the issue of the scientist's and the citizen's responsibility for nature: preservation. Konstantin Paustovsky occupies a particular place in Russian literature. For him nature is a kind of laboratory, where scientists, land-reclamation specialists, and foresters, that is, those who preserve and transform nature, are working. Paustovsky wrote most of his books in the 1930s through the

1960s, when the ideas of world transformation, including the draining of marshes, the construction of reservoirs and canals, the diversion of the flows of rivers, and other projects forming the so-called Stalin's plan of nature transformation, were extremely popular. The fact of this campaign influenced his work and he devoted a number of his books to poetically depicting projects that were later strongly criticized, such as the land-reclamation projects in Colchis and the construction of the Volga-Don Ship Canal. At the same time, he keenly perceived the beauty of the environment. He succeeded in demonstrating the unique character of seemingly very well known lands, such as Meshchyora lying not a long way from Moscow.

Vladimir Soloukhin became yet another pioneer exploring the Russian countryside. His book, *The Vladimir Country Roads*, deals with the landscapes and cultural heritage of Middle Russia. He is not only a writer depicting the beauty of the earth but also its defender. The main goal of the book is to show that the environment and traditional culture in the Vladimir region should be preserved and to tell the reader about the people who protect the land. Since the 1970s this very trend has become more influential and has acquired certain traits of the journalistic genre. A typical example of this genre is Valentin Rasputin's *Farewell to Matyora*, dealing with the annihilation of a village and the neighboring landscape drowned as a result of the construction of a hydroelectric power plant. Works of other authors who have devoted their literary activity to the preservation of traditional values of the Russian peasantry, namely Fyodor Abramov, Viktor Astafyev, Vassili Belov, and others, belong to this same trend.

The theme of nature occupies a particular place in children's literature as well. Vitali Bianchi's books have become classics of this original child-oriented ecological genre. His miniatures devoted to certain animals and fairy tales with insects and wild and domestic animals are still popular today. Bianchi owes much to his predecessor Prishvin, the author of many children's books on nature and a proponent of the necessity of a reverent attitude toward nature, as well as of the mystery of everything taking place in the forest, on the marsh, and other wild places.

Whether for adults or children, there exists a flourishing production of literary works treating nature and addressing ecological issues in Russia today. Many of these books address specific regions and local cultural values, while all of them speak to the importance of environmental concerns to the Russian people and a continuing Russian tradition of ecologically oriented prose literature.

Selected Works and Further Reading

Abramov, Fydor, *The Swans Flew By and Other Stories*, Moscow: Raduga, 1986

Arsenyev, Vladimir K., *Dersu Uzala*, translated by V. Shneerson, Moscow: Foreign Language Publishing House, 1957

Astafyev, Viktor, *Queen Fish: A Story in Two Parts and Twelve Episodes*, Moscow: Progress, 1982

——, *To Live Your Life and Other Stories*, Moscow: Raduga, 1989

Belov, Vassili, *Morning Rendezvous: Stories*, Moscow: Raduga, 1983

Bunin, Ivan A., *Stories and Poems*, translated by Olga Shartse and Irina Zheleznova, Moscow: Progress, 1979

Dostoyevsky, Fyodor M., *Poor People: A Novel and Stories of the 1840s*, translated by Olga Shartse, Moscow: Raduga, 1988

Gogol, Nikolai V., *Dead Souls*, translated by Christopher English, Moscow: Raduga, 1987; New York: Oxford University Press, 1998

——, *Diary of a Madman, Nevski Prospect*, translated by Beatrice Scott, London: L. Drummond, 1945

——, *Taras Bulba*, translated by O. A. Gorchakov, Moscow: Foreign Language Publishing House, 1955

Karamzin, Nikolai M., *Bednaia Liza/Poor Liza*, Letchworth, England: Bradda, 1963

Karinsky, Sergey, "Geographia iskusstva" [Geography of Fine Art], *Vestnik Moskovskogo Universiteta*, series 5, *Geographia* 2 (1990), pp. 27–33

Leonov, Leonid M., *The Russian Forest: A Novel*, 2 vols., Moscow: Progress, 1976

Lihachov, Dimitry S., *Poezia sadov* [The Poetry of Gardens], Moscow, 1983

Obruchev, Vladimir A., *Sannikov Land*, translated by David Skvirsky, Moscow: Foreign Language Publishing House, 1955

Panegiricheskaya literatura petrovskogo vremeni [Panegyric Literature of the Period of Peter the Great], Moscow, 1979

Paustovsky, Konstantin G., *Selected Stories,* translated by Vladimir Noskov, Moscow: Progress, 1974

Polyan, Pavel M., "Geographia I vdohnovlyayusshie resursy prirody" [Geography and Inspirational Resources of Nature], *Priroda* 3 (1978), pp. 51–63

Prishvin, Mikhail M., *A Selection,* Moscow: Raduga, 1985

Pushkin, Aleksandr, *The Tales of Ivan Belkin,* translated by I. and T. Litvinov, Moscow: Foreign Language Publishing House, 1954

Semenov-Tian-Shanskii, Veniamin P., *Raion I strana* [Region and Country], Moscow and Leningrad, 1928

Shirgazin, Oleg P., "Geographicheskoye prostranstvo 'Slova o polku Igoreve'" [The Geographic Space of "The Word About Igor's Regiment"], *Priroda* 3 (1993), pp. 84–92

Soloukhin, Vladimir, *Honey on Bread: Short Stories,* Moscow: Progress, 1982

Tolstoy, Leo, *War and Peace: A Novel,* translated by Rosemary Edmonds, Baltimore, Maryland: Penguin, 1977

Nature and Environment in Russian Poetry

Olga Lavrenova

Russian poetry reveals the interrelation between Russian nature and the world environment, between Russian culture and the Russian individual. This interaction is achieved through the understanding of nature and its elements as well as through reflections on its life and laws. Moreover, elements of nature are often used in Russian poetry as poetical symbols. Microlandscapes and their various states usually express the author's feelings. Large objects of nature, such as continents, oceans, mountain chains, and rivers, have their own symbolic significance in Russian culture. The symbolism of natural objects in poetry depends not only on the idea of their climate, relief, water level, and other physical characteristics, but also on the idea of a particular ethnicity, its culture, and the land with which it is associated. In Russian poetry small rivers, e.g., the Seine and the Neva, are closely related to the capitals lying on their banks, Paris and St. Petersburg. Therefore, in order to make an adequate interpretation of the treatment of an environment, one is bound to determine the place of anthropogenic formations, such as cities and nations in Russian poetry.

The national artistic consciousness and its interaction with nature are widely represented in the works of renowned Russian poets. In the eighteenth century, the key figures are Aniok Kantemir, Vassili Trediakovsky, Mikhail Lomonosov, Alexander Sumarokov, Gavriil Derzhavin, and Nikolai Karamzin.

A generalized description of the world is inherent to poetry. A synthetic world picture is built around large objects of nature while the same role is played by cities as an integral part of cultural space. The earth, conceived in terms of the universe and God's will, is also an important natural object in the eighteenth century, as nature was usually contemplated in that period within the context of God. Landscape motifs did not become self-sufficing until the late eighteenth century in the lyrics of Derzhavin and Karamzin. Derzhavin was the first to depict real landscapes, such as his own estate of Zvanka. Karamzin, who introduced motifs of discrepancy between one's mood and the state of nature, became a precursor of psychologism in landscape lyrics.

Russia's national landscape is conceived through poetically rendering its enormous expanses by means of enumerating every nook and cranny. This cataloging device is characteristic of Lomonosov and Derzhavin's poetry. The image of Russia is related to the consciousness of its stately power and to the glorification of its majesty. Russia's place on the map of the world is identified as the North, or more rarely, the Orient in many poems, with the Russian landscape often being conceived of as severe, icy, and rocky, as in the poetry of Lomonosov and later Konstantin Batyushkov. Russia's capital, St. Petersburg, is its ideological axis. A gleam of its glory falls on the Neva River, described by Russian poets in invariably glowing terms. Yet, in this century, detailed descriptions of objects of nature are rare; among them, the Volga River was the first to be sung by Karamzin.

Throughout much of the eighteenth century, images of the world can be divided into two groups: those of the European and the exotic worlds. The most widely mentioned European toponyms are Germany and France, as well as the Rhine and the Seine, which symbolize their respective countries. No European landscape, however, is ever described in detail. The only exceptions are those of antique landscapes, such as Castalia and Helicon, which can be accounted for by Russian translations of classical authors and the use of antique topics in Russian poetry. The exotic world and its nature are considered to be symbols of wealth abounding in gold and precious stones, with fertile soil and friendly climates, very much the "other" to the commonplace descriptions of icy Russia. Nature in India, Egypt, Libya, and other countries is rendered only in very general terms, mainly according to their characteristic climatic conditions. Vassili Tredyakovsky's phrase, "The heat sets the Libyan land blazing," is quite typical.

In the nineteenth century, the generalized perception of the outer world characteristic of the eighteenth-century poets was not wholeheartedly embraced by their successors. The new poetry encompassed minor objects of nature, both dimensionally and culturally, as well as towns. Leading poets of this period are Vassili Zhukovsky, Konstantin Batyushkov, Pyotr Vyazemsky, Yevgeni Baratynsky, Alexander Pushkin, Nikolai Yazykov, Mikhail Lermontov, Fyodor Tyutchev, Alexei Koltsov, Afanassi Fet, Alexei Tolstoy, Nikolai Nekrasov, and Vladimir Solovyov.

Diffuse vision supersedes generalization in this period's descriptions of nature. Landscape lyrics look more and more like landscape painting rather than natural philosophy. Descriptions of nature within the context of human activity emerge, as in the poetry of Koltsov. Philosophical perceptions of nature are characteristic of Lermontov, Tyutchev, and Solovyov, while Zhukovsky was the first to depict a fantastic infernal landscape in his poetry.

One sees Russian poets in this century beginning to perceive the national landscape from within. Pushkin and Vyazemsky became pioneers of poetically rendering a poor and plain Russian landscape. Baratynsky also depicts the poverty of Russian nature with a negative emotional coloring. In contrast, Pushkin creates, besides commonplace landscapes, rapturous pictures of various states of Russian nature. Later its majesty is glorified by Yazykov and Alexei Tolstoy.

A generalized, yet true, image of Russian nature was first created by Lermontov, who amalgamated traits of various local landscapes of Russia into a single image. The poet emphasizes the northern character of Russian nature and makes it the tenor of poetic descriptions of many a plain landscape with its unorthodox beauty and wretchedness. In fact, the North remains the principal poetic synonym of Russia.

While describing mainly the European part of Russia, authors tended to emphasize the regions that they knew best. Batyushkov describes the originality of Crimean nature. Pushkin and Lermontov (the latter was exiled to the Caucasus) were the first to sing romantic Caucasian nature. Glimpses of the Ukraine emerged in Pushkin's poetry owing both to his exile to Odessa and to the theme of his poem "Poltava," while Baratynsky, who was exiled to Finland, was the first Russian poet to describe Scandinavian landscapes.

The Caucasus became a romantic region for Russian poetry owing to its natural contrasts, as well as the original and somewhat hostile culture of the highlanders. This poetic stereotype, first recorded in the nineteenth century, has not changed much since then. Crimean landscapes depicted by Pushkin and Batyushkov are actually incarnations of classical nature. Proportioned and smoothed down by time, the old mountains of the Crimea remind the poets of Greek culture. As for a realistic interpretation of Crimean landscapes, one has to thank Alexei Tolstoy for that.

Yazykov and Nekrasov depicted the Volga landscapes. Nekrasov paid much attention to the Volga valley, its nature and way of life, juxtaposing melancholy landscapes with the grievous state of the peasantry. In his poem, "Who Can Live Happily in Russia?" Nekrasov creates, against the background of the Volga area, a symbolic geography of Russian life, mentioning the Terpigorevo (Hapless) district, the Neyelovo (Hungry) and Neurozhaika (Bad Harvest) villages, and the like. Siberia and its physical features are mentioned by Pushkin and Nekrasov in connection with the exile of the Decembrists.

In nineteenth-century poetry Russia is a country of two capitals. The image of St. Petersburg acquires a certain ambiguity implying both positive and negative connotations and the importance of Moscow is growing and noted. The Neva River share the fate of St. Petersburg being both loved and hated as a result. Images of the world remain semantically subdivided into the European and exotic worlds. Descriptions of local European landscapes, not associated with antiquity, emerge. The poetry of Batyushkov, a pioneer in European landscape description, encompasses the characteristic traits of the environments of northern Europe, Italy, and the Midi. He also establishes an antithesis between northern and southern nature. And an integral picture of Russian and European landscapes emerges in Vyazemsky's poetry.

Batyushkov brings forth in his poetry the theme of river camaraderie in Europe, while for many poets France and Italy are the most inspiring countries at this time. The environments of Italy form the focus of positive emotions in the synthetic image of the world created by Russian poetry. The two capitals, Paris and Rome, however, also carry negative connotations, the former symbolizing the harmful fits of civilization, as in Nekrasov's poetry, and the latter as the center of Roman Catholicism, as with Tyutchev and Nekrasov, or as representative of the Holy Roman Empire. Russian poetry in this century extensively explores the exotic world. Besides the generalized geographical characteristics of India, China, and Egypt, certain Central African regions and the most renowned cities of the Muslim world are treated, the former by Batyushkov and Lermontov and the latter by Pushkin and Lermontov.

In the early twentieth century, both poetry and its interaction with the outer world became more individualized. Many poets cherish an integral synthetic image of the world, embracing some hitherto ignored larger aspects of nature. Some of the major figures for this period are Valeri Bryusov, Konstantin Balmont, Innokenti Annensky, Maximillian Voloshin, Alexander Blok, Nikolai Gumilyov, Osip Mandelstam, Nikolai Klyuyev, Velimir Khlebnikov, Vladimir Mayakovsky, Sergei Yesenin, and Boris Pasternak.

In this period, poets once again perceive nature within the context of God and the universe, as with Bryusov and Gumilyov. Poetry revisits cosmic themes, enriching them with earthly reality. Bryusov, Khlebnikov, and Gumilyov fill nature with new and old mythologies, describing the mythical landscapes of Atlantis and Lemuria. The new generation of peasant poets, primarily Klyuyev and Yesenin, contended with staying within the boundaries of the earth and prayerfully contemplated nature. The genre of a natural philosophical hymn eulogizing the primeval might of nature also emerges, as in the poems of Balmont, while Mayakovsky and fellow futurists considered the environment as a phenomenon of secondary importance as compared with society and its technical achievements.

The image of Russia at the turn of the century is related to the idea of Messianism. It embraces both Russia's spiritual potential and the sensation of living at a turning point in history. The idiom, "Holy Russia," for example, is widely used at this time and it becomes identified as "Asia" rather than as the "North" in Bryusov, Yesenin, Gumilyov, Blok, and Khlebnikov. After the October Revolution the idea of spiritual messianism is transformed in the poetry of Bryusov and Mayakovsky into that of world revolution.

The national landscape is perceived by poets as reflecting the general mood of the time. The ideas of Russia's spiritual might can be seen in Klyuyev's likening of its landscape elements to churches, while a disturbing, wretched state of nature is associated with the critical situation of Russia during World War I by Mandelstam, Bryusov, and Mayakovsky. Yesenin reflects upon nature vanquished by its civilizations, while Klyuyev was the first to introduce the theme of ecological disaster in his poems.

Emphasis on the geography of certain areas can be accounted for by the poet's personal impressions. Khlebnikov, Mandelstam, Mayakovsky, Yesenin and Boris Pasternak provide lengthy descriptions of the Caucasus, while Klyuyev, Yesenin, and Voloshin depict northern and central Russia and the Crimea respectively. Khlebnikov was the first to show the Asian outskirts of Russia and the uniqueness of their cultures and nature. The Neva, having borrowed St. Petersburg's symbolism, becomes an emblem of Western culture in Russian poetry, while Moscow and its urban landscapes embody the Asianness of the country according to Mandelstam and Yesenin. The Urals, once the ultimate boundary of Russian civilization, turn into an inner territory, since the Russo-Japanese War triggered the acknowledgment by such poets as Bryusov, Khlebnikov, and Yesenin of easternmost Russian strongholds, such as Port Arthur, Mukden, and Liaoyang. The Caucasus, on the other hand, remain a romantic and exotic area in the early twentieth century, and Siberia regains its significance of vastness and hidden treasures, even though it is at times associated with exile, as in Blok and Mandelstam. Images of the rest of the world are greatly enriched with detailed landscapes of Africa and China in the poetry of Gumilyov, India and other tropical lands by Bryusov, while Yesenin depicted in his "Persian Motifs" Asian landscapes he had never actually seen, which makes them sound semimythical.

Poetry of the early twentieth century considered Europe to be old and representative of cultural heritage, and its nature is no longer described as classical. Metaphors, rather, abound in descriptions of European landscapes, making it extremely difficult to decipher the poets' attitudes toward them.

The ideas of an all-embracing integrity typical of many poets of the early twentieth century are expressed through global-scale listing. Klyuyev, for example, mentions lands "from Borneo to the sheep-skin Shuya," while Bryusov enumerates continents, and Khlebnikov lists a number of rivers symbolizing certain countries and cultures. India and the Orient are depicted as symbols of spirituality by Klyuyev, Gumilyov, and Khlebnikov, while the latter two used the landscape and culture of China in the context of originality and uniqueness. Within the synthetic image of the world, it is the United States, under the name of America, that stands out in the poetry of Bryusov, Yesenin, Khlebnikov, and Mandelstam, while Bryusov and Mayakovsky look to Mexico. The United States and its natural and anthropogenic details are sometimes mentioned by these poets as symbols of a somewhat inimical civilization.

In the early decades of the Soviet period, from the 1930s through the 1950s, the synthetic image of the world preserves its integrity, encompassing natural objects of various scales, from particular mountains to seas and mountain chains. The poetry of the period tends to emphasize earthly landscapes. The sun, the moon, and the stars can be but rarely encountered in landscape lyrics, with the only exception those of Nikolai Zabolotsky. Zabolotsky also works up natural-philosophical themes. His poetry in the 1930s is a kind of ecological utopia, where nature is embraced by the world of reason.

Mikhail Isakovsky and Alexander Tvardovsky are of peasant origin and perceive the environment from within rather than from without. Nature in their poetry is inextricably intertwined with people, their feelings, sensations and stages of life. The theme of nature and human labor is elaborated by both Tvardovsky and Zabolotsky, tinged with the sensation of human conquest. Such motifs are especially prominent in the poetry of Mikhail Svetlov, while, in contrast, occasional poems by Isakovsky and Zabolotsky treat the depredation of nature.

Russia is often seen in this period through the lens of the poet's home, such as the vicinity of Smolensk for Isakovsky and Tvardovsky, the Ladoga for Alexander Prokofiev, and through local landscapes, such as the Caucasus and the north for Isakovsky, the Far East and Siberia for Tvardovsky, Isakovsky, and Zabolotsky, the Urals and the steppes of Kazakhstan for Zabolotsky, the Caucasus, Central Asia, and the Ukraine for Nikolai Tikhonov. The once symbolic territories acquire their own distinctive traits owing to the realistic descriptions of these poets. No longer does Russia have a geographical synonym, such as the north or Asia, which had once been crucial for self-identification.

The ideological axis of the Russian cultural landscape moves decisively to Moscow, which has become the official capital of the country. Poets of this period tend to consider the city the original capital, Mother Moscow in Tvardovsky's poems, intimately related to a geographical substrate as "A Big Village" in Isakovsky's words. Poets such as Tvardovsky also tend to emphasize the importance of certain natural areas for Russian culture, calling the Urals, "Father Ural," and the Volga River, "Mother Volga."

In the 1930s Siberia had its natural resources described as "the peasant paradise" by Isakovsky. The exploitation of Siberia and the Far East, large-scale building sites, and other aspects of Soviet industrialization favored the inclusion of respective toponyms into verse eulogizing human conquest of immense spaces yielding untold wealth in the poetry of Tvardovsky and Isakovsky. Siberia and the Far East, however, only appear as places of exile in Tvardovsky's poem "Tyorkin in the Next World," published posthumously in the late 1980s.

There is no question of Russian messianism, of outwardly oriented spiritual and social impulses in this period. In the literature, the majesty of Soviet land becomes self-sufficient and inwardly oriented. As a result, images of the world are very scanty. With a few exceptions, as in the lyrics of Tikhonov and Zabolotsky, the details of the outer world are mostly just mentioned, without any detail. The synthetic image of Europe is still minutely elaborated, but it is chiefly with regard to the political situation and World War II. As a result, Germany becomes an object of topophobia and emotional rejection. In the late 1950s, the United States becomes yet another phobia and the object of political denunciations by poets like Isakovsky.

In the period of the 1960s through the 1980s, the global scale of the perception of the outer world returns, yet there seems to be no mention of geographical regions or mountain chains, which are replaced by continents, seas, countries, rivers, and cities. The outer world for the poets of this period, such as Arseni Tarkovsky, Bula Okudzhava, Yevgeni Yevtushenko, Andrei Voznesensky, Nikolai Rubtsov, Alexander Kushner, Bella Akhmadulina, Yunna Morits, and Yuri Kuznetsov, is extremely socialized. The whole world becomes habitual, lived-in, and devoid of symbolism. But at the same time, we again witness a prayerful attitude toward nature in the poetry of Akhmadulina and Kushner, with it perceived within a cosmic context by Tarkovsky and Voznesensky. Cosmic themes emerge amid earthly phenomena in Ms. Morits's verse, while Okudzhava brings back fairy-tale landscapes.

The theme of interaction between humanity and nature acquires new dimensions in this period. On the one hand, humanity is given a place in the focus of the universe and considered a mediator between the universe and the microcosm, according to Tarkovsky. On the other hand, nature is a measure of the "genuineness" or "naturalness" of people, their feelings, and actions, according to Yevtushenko. There also appears the theme of friendly ties between the nature of different countries in Yevtushenko and in Voznesensky, while Voznesensky, Yevtushenko, and Tarkovsky sound an increasingly resounding alarm of ecological disaster. In the poems of Okudzhava, nature begs humanity for mercy, yet in Kuznetsov's verse civilization remains ruthless. At the same time, humanity becomes aware of the tremendous might of nature, which has nearly exhausted its endurance in the representations of Kuznetsov.

The national Russian landscape is mainly perceived in this period through local ones. The majesty and wide scope of Russia are no longer sung. Rubtsov's lyrics, for instance, are focused on his native regions of the Archangel and Vologda. For many poets the harmonious links between humanity and nature are emphasized rather than human domination of nature.

The ideological and cultural aspects of the two capitals become almost nonexistent. The Siberian Asiatic Russia rivals the European Russia in poetic representation. Landscapes of Siberia and the Far East, as well as the Asian steppes, are minutely described by such poets as Yevtushenko and Voznesensky. Siberian and Far Eastern landscapes, in fact, are correlated not only with the theme of the "true man," but also with that of ecological disaster. A good case in point is Voznesensky's periphrasis of a folk song, "The Dead Sea of the Sacred Baikal." In the late 1980s Siberian and Far Eastern features, such as the Kolyma River and the city of Magadan, are mentioned in relation to the Gulag Archipelago in the poems of Yevtushenko and Voznesensky. Crimean and Caucasian landscapes are most widely represented in Morits's verse, while reflections on the dialogue between northern and southern, mainly Crimean and Caucasian, landscapes occupy a prominent place in Kushner's poetry. Images of the world are concentrated in Europe, Latin American and the United States, with the New World and its cities taking deep roots in the socialized verses of Yev-

tushenko and Voznesensky. Sparse descriptions of foreign landscapes serve often as a background for the depiction of social and political activities. And nature itself is politicized in such poems as Yevtushenko's "The Afghan Ant."

As Russian poetry approaches the end of the century, it reflects a deepening of concern about ecological problems and the necessity of reinvigorating a popular appreciation for the natural world that was under such industrializing assault during the Soviet period. At the same time, the economic problems besetting Russia and the kinds of attitudes toward nature as resource and capital prominent in free market economics are likely to intensify contradictory feelings among the people toward the exploitation and conservation of nature, a conflict likely to attract the attention of many poets in the coming years.

Selected Works and Further Reading

Afanasyev, Alexandr N., *Poeticheskiia vozzrieniia slavian na prirodu* [Poetic Perception of Nature Among the Slavs], 3 vols., Moscow: K. Soldatenkova, 1865–1869

Akhmadulina, Bella, *Stikhi* [Verses], Moscow: Khudojestvennaya Literatura, 1975

Annensky, Innokenti, *Stikhotvoreniia I tragedii* [Verses and Tragedies], Leningrad, U.S.S.R.: Sovetskii Pisatel', 1959

Balmont, Konstantin, *Sobranie liriki* [Collection of Lyrics], 6 vols., Moscow: V. V. Pashukanisa, 1917

Barakov, Victor N., *Chuvstvo zemli: "pochvennoe" napravlenie v russkoi sovetskoi poezii I ego razvitie v 60–80e gody* [The Call of the Earth and the "Back-to-the-Soil" School of Russian Soviet Poetry and Its Evolution in the 60s–80s], Kyzyl, Russia: Gosudarstvennyi Pedagogicheskii Institut, 1991

Baratynsky, Y. A., *Polnoe sobranie stikhotvorenii* [The Complete Verses], Leningrad, U.S.S.R.: Sovetsky Pisatel', 1936

Batyushkov, Konstantin, *Stikhotvoreniia* [Verses], Leningrad, U.S.S.R.: Sovetsky Pisatel', 1941

Belyi, Andrey, "Iz knigi *Poezia slova*: Pushkin, Tyutchev, I Bartynsky v zritelnom vospriyatii prirody" [Excerpts from the Book "Poetry of the Word": Pushkin, Tyutchev and Bartynsky's Vision of Nature], in *Semiotika*, Moscow: Raduga, 1983

Blok, Alexander, *Selected Poems,* translated by

Jon Stallworthy and Peter France, Baltimore, Maryland, and Harmondsworth, England: Penguin, 1974

———, *Stikhotvoreniia* [Verses], Leningrad, U.S.S.R.: Sovetsky Pisatel', 1955

Bryusov, Vladimir, *Stikhotvoreniya I poemy* [Verses and Poems], Leningrad, U.S.S.R.: Sovetsky Pisatel', 1961

Chelovek I priroda v sovremennoi literature [Man and Nature in Modern Literature], Krasnodar, U.S.S.R.: Znaniye, 1986

Derzhavin, Gavriil, *Stikhotvoreniia* [Verses], Leningrad, U.S.S.R.: Sovetsky Pisatel', 1957

Epshtein, Mikhail, *Priroda, mir, tainik vselennoi . . .* [Nature, Cosmos, the Treasury of the Universe . . .], Moscow: Vysshaia Shkola, 1990

Esenin, Sergei, *Selected Poems,* Derbyshire, England: Hub, 1979

Eventov, Isaak, "Chelovek I priroroda v lirike s. Yesenina" [Man and Nature in S. Yesenin's Lyrics], *Voprosy Literatury* 11 (1979)

Fet, Afanassi, *I Have Come to You to Greet You: Selected Poems,* London: Angel, 1982

———, *Stikhotvoreniia* [Verses], Moscow: Khudojestvennaya Literatura, 1970

Filippov, German, *Russkaia sovetskaia filosofskaia poeziia: Chelovek I priroda* [Soviet Russian Philosophical Poetry: Man and Nature], Leningrad, U.S.S.R.: Leningradskogo Universiteta, 1984

Gumilyov, Nikolai, *Stikhotvoreniia i poemy* [Verses and Poems], Leningrad, U.S.S.R.: Sovetskii Pisatel', 1988

Gunn, Genrikh, *Ocharovannaia Rus: Leskov, Nesterov, Blok, Rerikh, Khlebnikov, Remizov* [The Enchanted Russia:], Moscow: Iskusstvo, 1990

Isakovsky, Mikhail, *Stikhotvoreniia* [Verses], Leningrad, U.S.S.R.: Sovetsky Pisatel', 1965

Jincharadze, D., *Gruziya v sovremennoi russkoi poezii (70–80 gg.)* [Georgia in Modern Russian Poetry, the 70s–80s], Kyzyl, Russia: Gosudarstvennyi Pedagogicheskii Institut, 1991

Kantemi, Antiokh, *Sobranie stikhotovreny* [Collection of Verses], Leningrad, U.S.S.R.: Sovetsky Pisatel', 1957

Karamzin, Nicolai, *Stikhotvoreniia* [Verses], Leningrad, U.S.S.R.: Sovetskii Pisatel', 1958

Khlebnikov, Velimir, *Izbrannye stikhotvoreniia* [Selected Verses], Moscow: Sovetskii Pisatel', 1936

———, *Snake Train: Poetry & Prose,* Ann Arbor, Michigan: Ardis, 1976

Klyuyev, Nikolai, *Polnoe sobranie sochinenii* [Complete Works], New York: Chekhov Publishing House, 1954

———, *Stikhotvoreniia I poemy* [Verses and Poems], Leningrad, U.S.S.R.: Sovetsky Pisatel', 1977

Koltsov, A. V., *Stikhotvoreniia* [Verses], Moscow: Kniga, 1989

Kushner, Alexander, *Stikhotvoreniia* [Verses], Leningrad, U.S.S.R.: Khudozhestvennaia Literatura, 1986

Kuznetsov, Yuri, *Izbrannoe: Stikhotvoreniia I poemy* [Verses and Poems], Moscow: Khudozhestvennaia Literatura, 1990

Lavryonova, Olga, *Khudozhestvennoye prostranstvo russkoi poezii 18 veka* [The Artistic Space of the 18th-Century Russian Poetry], in *Geografiia iskusstva,* Moscow: Institut Naslediia, 1996

Lebedev, Evgenii, *Kontseptsiya mira I cheloveka v russkoi poezii 18 stoletiya* [The Concept of the World and Man in the Russian Poetry of the 18th Century], Moscow: Znanie, 1985

Lermontov, Mikhail, *Selected Poetry,* Winnipeg: University of Manitoba Press, 1965

———, *Stikhotvoreniia, Poemy, Maskarad* [Verses, Poems, Masque], Moscow: Kudozhestvennaia Literatura, 1969

Literatura I priroda [Literature and Nature], Moscow: Znanie, 1987

Lomonosov, Mikhail, *Stikhotvoreniia* [Verses], Leningrad, U.S.S.R.: Sovetsky Pisatel', 1935

Mandelstam, Osip, *Sobranie proizvedenii: Stikhotvoreniia* [Collection of Words: Verses], Moscow: Respublika, 1992

Nurmukhamedov, M. K., *Sredniaia Aziia v tvorchestve A. S. Pushkina* [Central Asia in A. S. Pushkin's Works], Tashkent, U.S.S.R.: Fan, 1988

Pigarev, Kirill, *Russkaia literatura I izobrazitelnoye iskusstvo: ocherki o russkom natsionalnom peizazhe serediny 19 veka* [Russian Literature and Fine Arts: Outline of the Russian National Landscape in the Mid-19th Century], Moscow: Nauka, 1972

Postnov, Iurii, *Sibir' v poezii dekabristov* [Siberia in the Decembrists' Poetry], Novosibirsk, U.S.S.R.: Nauka, 1976

Prokushev, Iurii, *Zhivoi lik Rossii: Razdumya, kritika* [The Living Image of Russia: Reflections and Criticism], Moscow: Khudozh Literatura, 1985

Shaitanov, Igor, *Mysliashchaia muza: "Otkrytie prirody" v poezii XVIII veka* [The

Intellectual Muse: "The Discovery of Nature" in the 18th-Century Poetry], Moscow: Prometei, 1989

Skatov, Nicolai, *Russkiye poety prirody* [Russian Poets of Nature], Moscow: Pravda, 1980

Sokhriakov, Iurii, *Priroda I chelovek (po stranitsam sovremennoi literatury)* [Nature and Man (Leafing Through Modern Books)], Moscow: Znanie, 1990

Trefilova, Galina, "Vremya vybora: Khudozhestvennoye osmysleniye vzaimootnoshenii cheloveka I prirody v sovetskoi literature" [Time of Choice: Artistic Perception of the Interaction of Man and Nature in Soviet Literature], *Voprosy Literatury* 1 (1981)

Zhukovsky, Vassili, *Stikhotvoreniia* [Verses], Leningrad, U.S.S.R.: Sovetskii Pisatel', 1956

The Theme of Nature in Russian Theater

Alexander V. Kamenets

Russian theater has its roots in prehistoric society and takes shape as a professional art in the seventeenth century. Russian theater grew out of the subsistence activity of Old Slavs and their corresponding rites and feasts. It is characteristic that such terms as theater and drama were widely recognized in Russian only in the eighteenth century. In the late eighteenth century the term comedy was still in use and throughout the same century theatrical performance was called *potyekha* (merrymaking). The folk term for theater was *pozorishche* (spectacle), while drama was called *igrishche* (playing). Those merrymaking and festive playings imitating subsistence activity performed educational and training functions, thus providing not only an aesthetic but also a pedagogical and ecological basis for Russian theater.

The beginning of agriculture saw the growth of the theatrical element of merrymaking due to the striving for understanding nature through ascribing to it certain qualities more proper to humanity. Merrymaking implied playing with images personifying nature; people anthropomorphically depicted it, seeking human traits in the habits of beasts and birds. It required a certain keenness of observation as well as creative abilities on the part of the performers. They had to create characteristic images of a certain natural phenomenon and then find the qualities relating it to human culture. Hence, complicated transformations of human beings into animals and plants and vice versa occurred. For instance, a beast can be represented as a boy or a girl and a hunting play can develop into a love or family theme.

Crucial points of subsistence activity were marked with feasts. The most important of them were celebrated during the winter solstice when a new agricultural year was coming into being; after the embrace of Christianity these feasts came to be called Yuletide. Then followed feasts marking the vernal equinox and the summer solstice. Early feasts were related to a pagan worship of the dying and resurrecting deity of vegetation. Annual withering of plants in fall, their death in winter, and their resurrection in spring were perceived through the life cycle of this deity.

Feasts were a conglomerate of merrymaking: playings, mummeries, maskings, dances, songs, and the playing of musical instruments. Puppets and men of straw embodying the deity were widely used. They were worshiped, then destroyed and finally revived in the name of nature resurrection. In the course of time, the deities were replaced by the tzar, general, landlord, merchant, and Father Superior, who were first worshiped and then held in derision. The procedure of unmasking the characters in order to restore the natural ecological values as well as the sincerity and unselfishness opposed to the morality of civilization became one of the characteristics of Russian theater as a social, artistic, and cultural phenomenon.

The said merrymaking played an important part in developing the subject and compositional peculiarities of Russian theatrical art. It can be clearly seen in the example of traditional folk round dances. Once they involved the whole of the clan. Up to the present, three main kinds of round dances have survived, the circular, the bilinear, and the unilinear, the latter being the rarest. The dances began with a prologue, which was the gathering of the dancers accompanied by the gathering songs and ended with the finale accompanied by the breaking up songs. The dances elaborated labor, love, family, military, and hunting themes.

The aesthetics of merrymaking and feasts was later used by the Russian theater for the demonstration and poetical representation of the patriarchal everyday life of the peasantry. At the same time, this aesthetics gave birth to many a plot based on a clash between the values of the peasantry and those of the city.

The *skomorokhs* (minstrels-cum-clowns), in whose art elements of pagan rites survived, took up a particular part in the evolution of Russian theater. The *skomorokhs* belonged to the following categories: 1.) the court *skomorokhs* cut off from their folk roots and nature, who did not leave a noticeable trace in theatrical art; 2.) the sedentary *skomorokhs* who lived both in town and in the country, who were mainly small landowners, craftsmen, and merchants who improvised at feasts and fairs; 3.) wandering *skomorokhs* who made up their repertoire regardless of festive occasions and, therefore, were actually professional actors. The sedentary *skomorokhs* later formed the folk theater of live actors, while the wandering ones monopolized the Punch-and-Judy, tame-bear, and peep shows, that is, the kinds of theater independent of the climate and seasonal conditions.

Nature in Russian Drama

The theme of nature was elaborated both by folk and professional theaters. The folk theater included such forms as the folklore drama, puppet plays and peep-shows, and interludes of the *balagan* jesters. The folk theater was constantly changing. In the late seventeenth century, cheap popular prints depicting jesters, *skomorokhs*, folk feasts and merrymaking, fairy-tale characters, as well as cheap books of stories, fairy tales, and satires, became popular with the general public. It was in this way that the original figurative and literary basis of the folk theater was taking shape. Since the early nineteenth century, the peep show illustrating fairy and historical legends had become an integral part of folk festivities, especially fairs. The pictures were displayed in a small box fitted with two magnifying lenses. The spectators peeped through the lenses, while the show manager rolled the pictures commenting on them. The historical and geographical drawings were accompanied by jesting and satirical catchphrases.

In the late nineteenth century the interludes of fair jesters made up a peculiar genre of folklore. The Punch show theater took shape at this time. The Russian Punch, called *Petrouchka* (see Stravinsky's famous ballet), is a sort of fool getting the better of the military man, the police, the merchant, the teacher, and other town officers, and, in his turn, meeting a violent death at the teeth of a hound or at the hands of the devil

or a brownie. In the concluding scene, *Petrouchka* is dragged off the stage only to spring back to life at the next show.

The analysis of the above-mentioned genres of the folk theater reveals the widespread motif of criticizing the official social roles through the "laughter culture"—to use Mikhail Bakhtin's term—of a village fool deliberately mixing up the generally accepted social hierarchy (as in the Old Slav pagan rite involving first the worship and then the dethroning of the vegetation deity). The Russian street theater occupied a major place in town festivities of the eighteenth century. The authorities, however, gradually drove the theater outside the town walls. Thus, the urban world outlook takes vengeance on its rural counterpart for the latter's mercilessly sober view of urban civilization.

The most elaborate genre of folk dramatists is the folk drama. Dramas were usually handed down orally from generation to generation. Some connoisseurs composed dramatic scenarios of sorts; they were collected elsewhere and played in the country, usually during Yuletide and sometimes during Shrovetide. Folk dramas had their specific features. Thus, the traditional folklore theme of noble highwaymen is treated as that of a free, uncivilized way of life, a means of restoring social justice in accordance with the peasant's outlook—see, for instance, plays showing highwaymen known under the general title of *The Boat*. Yet another widespread theme of folk drama is the mockery of muddle-headed landlords destroying their own estates and unable to enjoy the fruits of the earth, as in a series of satirical dramas titled *The Lord*. In professional drama the theme was later transformed into that of the degeneration of the gentry and the rejection of both urban morals and official statecraft.

Professional drama begins to elaborate the motif of nature in the seventeenth century. In the eighteenth century the theme was taken up by Aleksandr Sumarokov and Mikhail Lomonosov. They interpreted the traditions of French classicism in accordance with the Russian mentality emphasizing lyricisim and natural human passions, which can be seen in Sumarokov's historical tragedies *Khorev* and *Sinav and Truvor*, as well as in his comedies influenced by the folk drama, and in Lomonosov's tragedy *Tamira and Selim*.

This accounts for the longer life of sentimentalism in comparison with classicism in Russian theater. The former came into full bloom in the eighteenth and saw the beginning of the nineteenth century. Russian sentimentalists tried to establish a relation between personal virtues of landlords and their attitude toward their own estates (*see* Vladimir Lukin's drama *A Prodigal Reformed by Love*), as well as between the values of the peasantry's patriarchal way of life and their clemency, as in Nikolai Ilyin's dramas *Lisa or The Triumph of Gratitude* and *Generosity or the Levy*.

Dramatic exposures of reality within an ecological context made up a more stable tendency in drama. In this respect, one can cite the works of Denís Fonvízin (von Wiesen), who criticized the urban pseudo-education and serf-ownership from the point of view of folk culture and the morals of the peasantry in *The Brigadier*, *The Minor*, and *The Choice of a Tutor*. In the nineteenth century this trend was taken up by Ivan Krylov, who used devices of the Russian *skomorokh* style for criticizing the autocracy, as in his jesting tragedy *Podshchipa*, along with the richness of the folk language used for the criticism of both the Russian gentry's thoughtless admiration for foreign culture and the stupidity of Russian jingoists, as in his plays *Fashionable Shop* and *A Lesson for Daughters*.

Mikhail Zagoskin developed the "Bourgeois Gentilhomme" theme borrowed from Molière. The main character of his dramas is a certain Bogatonov, a perfunctorily educated landlord who, in his pursuit of whatever is in vogue, spoils the landscape of his own estate, as in *Bogatonov or A Provincial in the Capital* and *Bogatonov in the Country or A Surprise to Oneself*. Later the theme of the gentry uprooting themselves in their quest for city happiness was further elaborated by Alexander Sukhovo-Kobylin in his comedies *Krechinsky's Wedding*, *The Case*, and *Tarelkin's Death*. He depicts the bureaucratic machine as a bitter enemy of every living thing, especially of the people with provincial village minds, functioning solely with the view of making money. He traces the biological mutation of the officials losing all human traits and becoming mere functions.

Besides the ecologically oriented exposure trend, Russian drama was characterized by the Romantic representation of nature. This latter trend was represented primarily by Vladislav Ozerov's plays *Fingal* and *Dmitri Donskoy*. Breaking with the classicist tradition, he introduces changes of scenery, pantomime, ballet, and music as important components of the performance. Therefore, he regards nature not as a mere background but as a means of rendering his characters' states of mind and providing them with a Romantic halo. It is significant that contemporaries had difficulty in defining the genre of Ozerov's plays, while modern scholars call them "musical dramas." Also, renowned literary critic and author Vissarion Belinsky made his contribution to ecology from the point of view of romanticism. In his play *Dmitri Kalinin* the theme of one's natural right to personal happiness has anti–serf-owning connotations. The main character prefers to take his own life rather than lose his freedom.

The Masquerade, Mikhail Lermontov's famous drama, should be examined within the context of his romantic poems, such as "The Caucasian Prisoner," "The Demon," "Mtsyri," and others, where nature is regarded as an abode for solitary characters rejecting urban civilization and "children of highlands, woods and dales" are praised for preserving their individuality unspoiled by city morals. The drama shows the true character of high society cut off from natural human attachments proper to those unaffected by its hypocrisy.

Russian comic operas written by Mikhail Popov, Yakov Knyzhnin, Ivan Krylov, Nikolai Nikolayev, and Alexander Ablesimov are yet another unique theatrical phenomenon linking the professional stage to the Russian song and dance folklore, as well as to everyday rites. Russian vaudeville or comic sketches were related to the former genre. Their authors, including Dmitri Lensky, Fyodor Koni, Pyotr Karatygin, and others, tried to show a deep influence of the provincial milieu on their characters: petty officers, moderately well-to-do merchants, intellectuals of modest means, and such, who do not lose touch with folk culture and the traditions of small townships and villages.

The greatest Russian poet, Aleksandr Pushkin, made a significant contribution to raising ecological problems in drama. Contrary to the usual practice of his poems, nature is not the immediate subject of his plays. At the same time, he elaborates certain philosophical ideas concerning the indispensability of ecological values for one's morals regardless of one's social position. Such a philosophy is evident in such plays as *Boris Godunov*, *The Miserly Knight*, *Mozart and Salieri*, *The Stone Guest*, *The Pest Feast*, and *The Mermaid*. Thus the deep pagan idea of an imminent ecological revenge for one's villainy is the message of Pushkin's dramas.

The dramas by Alexander Ostrovsky broke

new ground in showing nature and ecological values. Depicting everyday life and morals of the merchants, he succeeded in visualizing a conflict between the natural and social sides of the characters. In his dramas, nature is an invisible judge passing a sentence on petty tyranny and sanctimoniousness, as in *Thunderstorm* and *The Forest*, the social insecurity of lovers and the impetus to build an ecologically oriented society, as in *Snowmaiden, Wolves and Sheep*, and *Let the Cobbler Stick to His Last*, and the folkloric outlook opposing philistinism, as in *Poverty Is No Sin*.

Moreover, Ostrovsky reveals an even subtler link between nature and society. In his dramas, nature is involved in the interaction of characters, playing the role of a go-between in conflicts. This role is often transferred to certain characters embodying ecological ethics based on natural affections, including friendliness, love, family affiliations, and clemency toward the weak and humiliated. The author also depicts characters breaking these rules and in accordance with the values of their social stratum displaying petty tyranny, greed, and sanctimoniousness. Thus, Ostrovsky can be called a founder of an ecologically oriented approach to social problems in Russian drama.

The nature-oriented approach played an important part in the emergence of psychological dramas. It can be seen in Iván Turgénev's *A Month in the Country*, and Anton Chekhov's *Ivanov, The Wood-Goblin, The Seagull, Uncle Vanya, Three Sisters*, and *The Cherry Orchard*. The ecological motif of betraying one's love for the sake of one's comfort is later conceived by Chekhov as the betrayal of their ideals by the Russian intelligentsia incapable of asserting their personalities through professional activity. Yet even professional activity (e.g., literary pursuits) cannot save Russian intellectuals if this activity is opposed to life and its ecological laws or becomes mere belles-lettres disregarding the established ethical norms, as in *The Seagull*. Chekhov's genius gave an insight into the clash between the gentry and the bourgeois cultures through their respective attitudes toward nature, either an enthusiastic and protective one or a propriety and transformational one, as in *The Cherry Orchard*. This opposition has survived and is still constantly revived, regardless of the social position of the opponents.

After 1917, Russian drama has mostly displayed the transformational approach both to nature and to the biology of humanity—breeding a new race of Soviet people. Ardent revolutionaries, promoters of industrialization, and war heroes come to the forefront of Soviet drama. Ecological issues are never raised prior to the end of World War II, when they become evident in plays devoted to the theme of war and patriotism, as in the work of Alexander Korneichuk, Konstantin Simonov, Leonid Leonov, Boris Vassilyev, and others, and to that of the working class, as with Alexei Arbuzov, Gennadi Bokarev, Ignati Dvoretsky, Alexander Gelman, and others. The attention of the playwrights is focused on the fight of "the man in the street" against soulless social and economic regulations, for his own dignity and the well-being of his family. Members of the so-called village prose school, Valentin Rasputin, Boris Mozhayev, Mikhail Vorfolomeyev, and others, are vehemently advocating the dying village in their dramas and stage adaptations of their novels.

However, a virtual ecological breakthrough was achieved by Aleksandr Vampilov, who imbibed the best traditions of Nikolai Gogol, Alexander Ostrovsky, and Anton Chekhov, and, in his turn, paved the way for modern dramatists. His characters inhabit a tragicomic space, typical of the playful folk self-consciousness, aware of the relative nature of any appraisal of reality. No statement can be taken at its face value. This expresses the spirit of the time, when words become an element of carnival mask disguising the character's true personality and often remaining unknown even to its owner. In every one of Vampilov's plays, the characters overcome the temptation to stick to their social masks in order to live up to their moral ideals. They do so through mimicking themselves wearing a particular mask in *A June Farewell*, through the demonstration of the tragic consequences of wearing it in *The Duck Hunt*, through mystification with the aid of an assumed social role in *The Elder Son*, through the opposition of the official mask and the human face in *Provincial Anecdotes*, and of the rural environment and the urban cast of character elements in *Last Summer at Chulimsk*.

Thus, Vampilov's dramas produce a sort of double reality, "a theater within a theater," which enables him to create a spirit of sincerity. Characteristically, one of the playwright's favorite devices is playing on the inherent carnival elements of reality, such as wedding parties, birthdays, imaginary funerals, and the like. As a rule, those feasts turn out a failure, opening the characters' eyes to the situation. Vampilov thereby reinterprets not only old pagan rites but also old Russian parodies showing the opposition of a false, yet official truth and true, yet unauthorized lie. Vampilov was the first post-revolutionary dramatist to introduce the motif of restlessness, a quasi-anti-sociality of his best characters, who are trying to remain their own selves in the face of uniformity imposed on them by society. He can be regarded as the continuator of the tradition of ecological ethics in drama. According to this ethics, love for living things is the ultimate criterion of morals.

In the post-Soviet period, the best performances advocate clemency and sympathy with the underdogs, people who did not make it in the rat race, in the face of the power cult, the administrative arbitrariness, and the striving for prosperity at any price. The survival of the inclination to friendship and love regardless of religious beliefs is being emphasized. God's fools of the Dostoevsky type and Chekhov-type intellectuals become the heroes. Turning to socio-ecological issues, theaters are thus setting the time that "is out of joint," restoring the humanitarian ecological values inherent in the Russian national character.

Selected Works and Further Reading

Arbuzov, Alexei, *It Happened in Irkutsk,* in *Three Soviet Plays,* Moscow: Foreign Languages Publishing House, 1961

Aseev, B. N., *Russkii dramaticheskii teatr ot ego istokov do kontsa XVIII veka* [Russian Theater from Its Origins to the 18th Century], Moscow: Iskusstvo, 1977

Bakhtin, M. M., *Tvorchestvo Fransua Rable I narodnaia kultura srednevekovia I renessansa* [The Works of Francois Rabelais and the Folk Culture of the Middle Ages and the Renaissance], Moscow: Khudozhestvennaya Literatura, 1965

Chekhov, Anton P., *The Cherry Orchard: A Comedy in Four Acts,* new version in English by Jean-Claude Van Itallie, New York: Grove, 1977

Dmitriev, Iurii, and G. A. Khaichenko, *Istoriia russkogo I sovetskogo dramaticheskogo teatra* [A History of Russian Theater], Moscow: Prosveshchenie, 1986

Eliash, Nikolai, ed., *Istoriya russkogo dorevolutsionnogo dramaticheskogo teatra* [A History of Pre-revolutionary Russian Theater], Moscow: Prosveshchenie, 1989

Folklornyi teatr [The Folk Theater], Moscow: Sovremennik, 1977

Fonvízin, Denís, *The Young Hopeful,* translated by G. Z. Patrick and George R. Noyes, in *Masterpieces of the Russian Drama*, edited by George R. Noyes, New York: D. Appleton, 1933

Istoriia russkogo dramaticheskogo teatra [A History of Russian Theater], 7 vols., Moscow: Iskusstvo, 1977–1987

Istoriia russkogo sovetskogo dramaticheskogo teatra [A History of Russian Soviet Theater], vol. 1, Moscow: Prosveshchenie, 1984; vol. 2, Moscow: Prosveshchenie, 1987

Lermontov, Mikhail, *Mikhail Lermontov: Selected Works,* Moscow: Progress, 1976

Ostrovsky, Alexander N., *Plays,* translated by Margaret Wettlin, Moscow: Progress, 1974

Pushkin, Aleksandr S., *Borís Godunóv: A Drama in Verse,* translated by Alfred Hayes, New York: Dutton, 1918; London: K. Paul, Trench, Trubner, 1918

———, *Little Tragedies,* translated by Eugene M. Hayden, Yellow Springs, Ohio: Antioch Press, 1965

Stanislavsky, Konstantin S., *An Actor Prepares,* translated by Elizabeth R. Hapgood, New York: Theatre Arts, 1936

———, *My Life in Art,* translated by J. J. Robbins, Boston: Little, Brown, 1924; London: Geoffrey Bles, 1962

Turgénev, Iván S., *A Month in the Country,* translated by George R. Noyes, in *Masterpieces of the Russian Drama*, edited by George R. Noyes, New York: D. Appleton, 1933

Russian Ecological Nonfiction

Yuri L. Mazourov

During the last 100 to 150 years, a relatively independent and large-scope school that can conditionally be named ecological nonfiction was formed in Russian literature. The school encompasses literary works dealing with natural phenomena and objects and nature conservation. Contrary to fictional prose, poetry, and drama, ecological nonfiction is based on actual facts and events and invariably reflects the current level of scientific knowledge of nature. Ecological nonfiction has evolved on the borderline between fiction and science. The former accounts for stylistic and genre originality, plot lines, graphic style, elements of fiction, and other literary devices resulting in works of literature. The latter provides the theme and the main ideas as well as the subject matter and contents of a literary piece.

In Russia the genre of ecological nonfiction emerges in the second half of the nineteenth century in the works of Russian explorers of the north, Siberia, Central Asia, the Far East, and foreign lands. Among the explorers are such renowned scholars as Pyotr Semyonov-Tian-Shansky, Nikolai Miklukho-Maclay, Nikolai Przevalsky, Grigori Potanin, Mikhail Pevtsov, Ivan Chersky, Ivan Mushketov, Alexei Fedhenko, Pyotr Kropotkin, Alexander Voyeikov, Pyotr Kozlov, and Vladimir Obruchev. Those scholars, geologists, geographers, land surveyors, biologists, and ethnologists described nature as such and nature creating either favorable or unfavorable conditions for economic and cultural evolution of human society. Being publicly oriented, they completed fascinating works full of information and originality. For instance, Semyonov-Tian-Shansky was an editor of the series, *Russia, A Complete Description of Our Homeland,* while Obruchev, a famous geologist, is known to the general public first and foremost as the author of the hitherto-popular novels *Plutonia* and *The Sannikov Land.* Owing to the talent of the writers, books by Russian explorers were a great success and thus promoted the emergence of the ecological nonfiction genre, all the more so because they were the only source of information on unexplored territories.

Later on, as information on terra icognita was piling up, travel books gradually went out of fashion as a source of knowledge, still remaining exciting classics. In the meantime, ecological nonfiction recruited volunteers from other fields, among them hydrologists, soil scientists, forestry specialists, glaciologists, physicists, and even philosophers, as well as journalists and professional writers. This diversification was due to the emergence of another ecological nonfiction trend, which was the description of mysterious and anomalous natural phenomena, such as volcanic activity, seismic disturbances, terrestrial magnetism, meteorites, ancient and endangered animal species, and other unaccountable phenomena.

Ecological alarmism has become a third major trend within ecological nonfiction. It appeared as far back as the late nineteenth century, owing to the realization of an imminent danger, the loss of the unique Russian chernozem as a result of human-inflicted deforestation of central Russia. It was only in the 1960s and 1970s, however, that this trend reached its climax, when it won over many well known journalists and writers, including such celebrities as Konstantin Paustovsky, Mikhail Sholokhov, Vladimir Soloukhin, Vassili Belov, and later on, Valentin Rasputin, Viktor Astafyev, Vladimir Krupin, and others. At present one can also discern such major trends of ecological nonfiction as science fiction, social and political journalism, essays, and some others to be outlined below.

Roots and Prerequisites of Russian Ecological Nonfiction

Nature has always been prominent in the environmentalistic Russian culture. This can be observed in Russian painting, music, folklore, and last, but not least, literature. It is due to literature and art that Russia is famous not only for its original culture but also for its magnificent landscapes and other environmental features. The tradition of including nature can be traced back to the very first Russian literary works. Thus *The Tale of the Downfall of the Russian Land*, a literary monument of the thirteenth century, begins with a lengthy description of the beauty and richness of Russian nature. Eventually, with the development of the country's numerous ethnicities, nature becomes the habitat of national cultures. Hence the emergence of ecological nonfiction as an independent genre of Russian literature was more than predictable.

A major prerequisite of the emergence of ecological nonfiction became a deep-rooted tradition of studying nature, the environment, natural resources and phenomena by Russian scholars, which was stirred up in the late nineteenth century. Russian historical literature is known to pay much attention to nature. The tradition was established by Karamzin's 12-volume *History of the Russian State*. Karamzin, a famous Russian sentimentalist, also wrote *The Russian Traveler's Diary*, yet he was primarily a historian. According to Pushkin, Karamzin had discovered early Russia just like Columbus discovered America. Karamzin interweaves Russian history and geography, holding the environment, among other subjects, responsible for the different fates of Slav tribes and other ethnic groups. The idea of geographical conditions affecting history was extensively elaborated by the Russian historian Sergei Solovyov, especially in his notable 29-volume *History of Russia*. He invariably proceeds from his motto: "the course of events is always dependent on geography." Vassili Klyuchevsky pays still more attention to the role of nature in Russian history. Several chapters of his monumental *Course of Russian History* treat the environment, such as landscapes, rivers, natural phenomena, and the like. He examines such an intriguing issue as the cult of nature among Old Slavs, suggesting an original theory of humanity's attitude toward nature, and is one of the first historians to mention the dangerous environmental consequences of human activity.

In the course of time the thesis of the interaction between nature and human history became widely recognized and applied not only to social but also to cultural history. *Essays on the History of Russian Culture* by Pavel Milyukov, a Russian historian, politician, statesman, and Foreign Secretary in the Provisional Government (March–November 1917), are typical in this respect. The lengthy and popularly written book is focused on the broadest spectrum of natural factors having influenced Russian culture. Among the issues raised, Milyukov's interpretation of the "History of the conception of man's dependence on nature" (vol. 1, part 1, essay 1) is of great interest.

A prominent place in ecological nonfiction is occupied by the works of Lev Gumilyov, who is considered one of the greatest twentieth-century Russian historians and geographers. Giving several ethnic groups as examples, he regards ethnogenesis as a natural-historical process and demonstrates close links relating history to the environment and the evolution of the biosphere. Sophisticated as they are, Gumilyov's numerous books are extremely popular both in Russia and abroad. This phenomenon is due to a certain extent to the literary talent of the author, the son of famous Russian poets Anna Akhmatova and Nikolai Bgumilyov, who had made their own contribution to the poetical vision of the environment. Lev Gumilyov's masterpiece, *Early Russia and the Great Steppes*, underestimated in academic circles, attracts the attention of the general public both by the originality of his concepts and his refined style.

Still another important prerequisite of the emergence of ecological nonfiction in Russia is the rapid progress of the natural sciences at the turn of the twentieth century. It was accompanied by the publication of books by prominent scientists, who happily combined scholarly and literary gifts. Pyotr Chikhachyov, a diplomat and an explorer, was probably the first career scientist to study humanity's transformation of nature. Alexander Middendorf, one of the first Russian ecologists, a famous explorer of North and Central Asia and the Far East, is well known for his book, *Notes on the Ferghana Valley*, which shows both the dynamics of the milieu and humanity's role in its drastic transformation in a standard Central Asian oasis. Lev Mechnikov wrote in collaboration with Nikolai Ogaryov and Nikolai Shevelyov a popular *People's Geography* and assisted the first great French geographer Elysee Reclus in his editing of the "Earth and Man" series. Mechnikov's own scandalous book, *Civilization and Historical Rivers*, is still a matter of debate among specialists in different fields of knowledge. Alexander Voyeikov, who had majored in climatology, later grew into a geographer and ecologist of the widest profile and conducted outstanding research on exploitation in Turkestan and on the Caucasian coast of the Black Sea. His classical paper, "Vozdeistvije Cheloveaka na Prirodu" (Man's Impact on Nature), was published in *Annales de Geographie* under the title "De l'influence de l'homme sur la terre," and thus acquired popularity abroad. Vassili Dokuchayev, a famous Russian soil scientist, ecologist, and geographer, issued books that became classics, *The Russian Chernozem* and *The Past and Present of Our Steppes*, and deeply influenced the theory and practice of exploitation in central Russia.

The above list of the authors who contributed to the development of ecological nonfiction and ecological education in Russia is far from exhaustive. There also was Dmitri Anuchin, a geographer, physical anthropologist, and ethnologist; Georgi Morozov, a forestry specialist and ecologist, a pioneer of steppe afforestation; Andrei Krasnov, a botanist and biogeographer, an organizer of botanical gardens in Russia; Georgi Kozhevnikov, a zoologist, an initiator of a network of national parks in Russia; Vladimir Vernadsmy, a geochemist, geobiochemist, and philosopher, the founder of the noosphere theory; and Lev Berg, a hydrologist, ichthyologist, and geographer; as well as others.

Russian ecological nonfiction is an original phenomenon of national culture. At the same time, it has imbibed much from foreign literature. It is not for nothing that George Perkins Marsh's famous book *Man and Nature*, the first solid work on the deterioration of the environment under the influence of human economy, was published in Russia as far back as 1866, only two years after it first came out in the United States. Russian was the first language into which it was translated. Many other classical books on ecology, such as Jean Dorst's *Avant Que Nature Meure* (Before Nature Dies), Barbara Word and René Dubos' *The Only One Earth*, Rachel Carson's *Silent Spring*, Barry Commoner's *The Closing Circle*, and Al Gore's *Earth in the Balance*, books by renowned naturalists, such as Bernhard Grzimek and Gerald Durrell, as well as the first reports of the Club of Rome and the committee headed by Gro Brundtland, have exerted a profound influence on the development of science and literature, on the enlightenment of the masses, and on the ecological policies pursued in Russia.

The perception of ecology in philosophy, religion, literature, and art is yet another prerequisite of the development of ecological nonfiction both in Russian and abroad. The works of Nikolai Roerich, the Russian artist, author, scholar, and traveler, who spent nearly half of his life abroad, are a striking example of such an influence. The cult of nature is one of the main themes of Roerich's paintings and writings, which have given a powerful impetus to the development of culture as a whole and of ecological culture in particular.

Ecological Popular Science

Popular science books on nature, including science fiction have an important inherent feature: they are ultimately aimed at teaching the reader to better understand his or her environment. Leonid Leonov, the author of the once famous novel *Russian Forest*, points out that "the one who understands nature is both noble and pure. He would not dream of committing a barbaric act; he is a graduate of 'the soul' university." All those writing on nature in Russia are likely to share this conviction. Books by Vladimir Arsenyev, such as *Debryakh Ussuriiskogo kraya* (In the Ussuri Jungle), dealing with his explorations in the Far East, which are classics of the genre, confirm Leonov's idea. One of Arsenyev's main personages, a native taiga dweller Dersu Uzala, the author's invaluable companion and helper during his travels through the thickets of the Ussuri region, has a keen perception of nature and is a bearer of a high spiritual and ecological culture, which has since become scarce and sought after.

Authors of popular science literature describe certain phenomena of nature or events pertaining to its perception, transformation or management using varied expressive means. Works of this genre are characterized by a combination of scientific ecological basis and fictional form. They are usually fairly lengthy and extremely diverse with regard to their themes and style. Nevertheless, certain trends of the modern popular science literature on nature can be distinguished.

Descriptions of the landscape of the country as a whole, or of its particular regions, sprang from the local lore, which flourished in Russia in the late nineteenth century, and has apparently the most impressive list of publications and authors to its credit. Among the best-selling authors of recent decades are the popular explorer Ivan Papanin, zoologist Pavel Marikovsky, biogreographer Okmir Agakhanyants, geographer and writer Yuri Yefremov, and writers Vitali

Shentalinsky and Vyacheslav Palman. Yefremov's masterpiece is his book ingeniously entitled *Priroda Moyei Strany* (My Country's Habitat). He provided his own verses for the epigraph, reflecting both the essence of his method and the driving force of his work: "I love it and know it, know it and love it. / And the more I know it, the more I love it." These lines could well be an epigraph to the bulk of Russian popular science literature and science fiction.

The description of foreign landscapes has one of the steadiest rates of popularity among popular science books. In spite of quite a few translations of foreign literature, books by Russian authors on foreign lands still enjoy a good reputation. One can cite such works as the repeatedly republished *Five Continents* by the famous geneticist Nikolai Vavilov, *Under the Tropics of Asia* by reputed biologist Andrey Krasnov, *In the Thickets of Central Asia* by renowned geographer Vladimir Obruchev, and *Polyot Bumeranga* (The Flight of the Boomerang) by Nikolai Drozdov, a well-known scientist and popularizer.

One of the first Russian books on certain natural phenomena, both typical and unique, mysterious and abnormal, was the work of the famous natural scientist and brilliant popularizer Konstantin Timiryazev, *The Life of Plants*, published in 1878. Then followed many editions of books by geologist Alexander Fersman on minerals, by his colleagues Alexander Gangnus on tectonics and seismic activity and Boris Vronsky on the Tunguska meteorite, by Vladimir Shcherbakov on the fabulous continent of Atlantis, by the philosopher Yuri Linnik on moors, by geographer Dmitri Oreshkin on glaciers, and the work of many others.

The management of living nature takes its roots in such marvelous books as *On Angling* by Sergei Aksakov and *Fishes of Russia* by natural scientist Leonid Sabaneyev. Both works are as entertaining as they are instructive. Among modern books on living nature management, those by Igor Akimushkin occupy a prominent place. His numerous publications, both original and fascinating, are focused mainly on the inextricable interweaving of life forms in the biosphere. With the aid of striking examples he shows that even minor damage of the fabric of a biological symbiosis can trigger a chain reaction of grave consequences inevitably leading to the impoverishment of life on earth. It is worth noting that, while foreseeing such possibilities, Akimushkin invariably suggests ways to avoid them.

Yuri Arakcheyev and Boris Vorobyev devel-

oped their own original ideas of nature preservation. Their books, published in the late 1980s, *Poskakh Apollona* (In Quest of Apollo) and *Vesyegonskaya Volchitsa* (The Vesyegonsk She-wolf) respectively, became a significant happening in the literature on nature. Notwithstanding their individual traits, both books are united by their militant anti-anthropocentrism. Wildlife is represented as an independent spiritual value, indispensable, if not salutary, for humans and humankind and infinitely mysterious, rather than as mere human habitat. The same theme is worked up by biologists Savva Uspensky, writing on the preservation of Arctic fauna, and Andrei Bannikov and Vladimir Flint, dealing with the preservation of rare and endangered animal species.

The history and actual problems of nature preservation in Russia are treated in numerous manuals and monographs. Owing to many decades of severe censorship, however, the majority of them merely echo the usual set of pseudo-optimistic information often having little to do with reality. Hence, the more valuable are those, unfortunately quite scanty, editions that reveal the unvarnished, if unflattering, truth about the state of nature preservation. Among theme are the splendid book, *Nam I Vnukam* (To Us and Our Grandchildren), by geographer David Armand and a number of publications by Yuri Yefremov, presumably one of the authors of the first Russian "Nature Preservation Law." The law, adopted in 1960, was fairly liberal for its time, although never properly enforced.

Among the publications of the 1990s, a brilliant polemical book, *Lukomorye, gde ono?* (Where Is the Land of Milk and Honey?), a book of fiction based on real events, by Felix Shtilmark, an eminent ecologist and writer, stands out. The author, who took an active part in the events treated in his book, gives his own vision of the dramatic history of nature and wildlife preservation in Russia, beginning from the 1920s. Paradoxical as it may seem, Shtilmark's book has not attracted much attention in Russia, either from the general public or literary critics, not to speak of governmental bodies. It appears that society is not ripe for facing the naked truth when it comes to its recent interaction with nature and the attitude to its cultural heritage.

Ecology in Soviet Russia by an American historian, Douglas Winer, although thematically close to that of Shtilmark's book, has gained a wider recognition. The book translated from English in 1991 as *Ekologiya Sovetskoy Rossiyi* deals with the history of nature preservation in the Soviet Union, including tragic events involving such notorious obscurantists as Lysenko and Prezent. The unbiased, scientifically correct and informationally rich book was welcomed by both the general public and critics.

Nature is more or less touched upon in a number of other branches of popular science. Among the relevant books, those on the place of nature in the history of civilization written by Boris Andrianov, Lev Bondarev, Rudolf Balandin, and Anatoli Chistobayev are worth noting. One can also cite books on the phenomenon of ecological culture written by such cultural anthropologists as Sergei Maksimov, Yuri Simchenko, Igor Krupnik, as well as books on the adventures of nature explorers by Zinovi Kanevsky, Andrei Kapitsa, Igor Zotikov, Alexander Shumilov, and others.

Ecological Journalism

Russian ecological journalism began with Dmitri Pisarev's *Essays on the History of Labour*. The author repeatedly brought up the subject of the place of nature in the life of a community and that of its transformation in the course of evolution of human civilization. His eloquent appeal to the general public for the study of the natural science he deeply appreciated was widely taken up and it profoundly influenced the formation of many a Russian scholar in the late nineteenth century. Philosopher Vladimir Solovyev, the author of *Beauty in Nature* and *The Enemy from the Orient*, made a valuable contribution to ecological journalism. The latter book is a striking example of philosophic perception of such an urgent ecological problem of the time as desertification, a perception prompted by the works of Dokuchayev and other natural scientists.

At the same time, ecological problems, latent for the time being, were not adequately perceived by the Russian society of the later nineteenth and early twentieth centuries, and, consequently, did not provide a considerable reaction of journalists and writers. True, newspapers and magazines did discuss the depredation of forests, the extirpation of wild animals, the anthropogenic soil erosion and, more rarely, pollution of reservoirs and the creating of national parks, but usually discussions were focused not on nature preservation but mainly on the economic, social, ethical, or aesthetic consequences of social vices. Writers, together with artists, scholars, and others, were apparently swept along with the general feeling of human conquest of nature.

In the post-revolutionary Russia of the late 1920s, social and political journalism, including writings on ecology, practically died out. Moreover, nature-oriented ideals were gradually replaced by anthropocentric ones. The latter helped with the ideological conversion of people to the ideology of struggling against the taiga, the tundra, deserts, rivers, seas, and nature in general. The conquest of nature is one of the main trends in the Soviet literature of the 1930s through the 1950s. Such recognized literary authorities as Maxim Gorky, who repeatedly used the expression "struggle against nature" in his publications, took part in the elaboration of the theme.

Thus encouraged by its spiritual and political leaders, Russia had been at war with its own landscape for several decades, striving to exploit the natural resources and to seize unrestricted power over nature. Alas, as the philosopher Nikolai Berdyayev pointed out, "bitter and ugly are the fruits of power over nature." The majority of scholars and writers never forgot it, yet the time to speak openly about it did not come until the 1950s, when Russian ecological writing came back to life, although relapses into old errors in both literature and economy took place until the late 1980s.

The renaissance of ecological writing in Russia is believed to be related to the echo produced by Vladimir Chivilikhin's book *The Earth in Trouble* and a number of other publications by the same author. Books and papers by Vladimir Soloukhlin, Oleg Volkov, Yuri Naguibin, Yuri Kazakov, Chingiz Aimatov, Sergei Zalygin, and other writers gave a strong impetus to nature-oriented trends in Russian society. The activity of the authors dealing with ecological problems had been until the late 1980s restrained by rigid censorship aimed at supporting the officially implanted myth of an inherent ecological harmony of socialism. The myth proved to be not only ideologically harmful but also physically dangerous for the country and its population, as the after-effects of the Chernobyl tragedy have proven. While overruling these restrictions, professional writers appealed to the readers' emotions using the magic of literature.

Scientists who appealed to their compatriots to abandon pernicious stereotypes of the cavalier attitude to nature were in a more difficult position, since they had to use only their professional tools, figures and facts. Nevertheless, owing partly to perestroika and glasnost, their numbers in the 1980s were considerably augmented. Such books on ecology as *The Turning Point*, the collected articles of Sergei Zalygin, *Chuvstvo Zemly* (The Feeling of the Earth) edited by Yuri Mazourov, *Ecologiceskaya Alternativa* (The Ecological Alternative), edited by Mikhail Lemeshev, as well as other books, were published in hundreds of thousands of copies by prestigious publishing houses. As a rule, scientists have been among the first to discuss the most urgent ecological problems of the whole country or of certain regions; for example, Fattei Shipunov and Grigori Galaziy have addressed the salvation of the Volga and the Baikal respectively, while Alexander Yanshin has opposed large-scale landscape transformations. Mikhail Lemeshev and Pavel Oldak have addressed ecodevelopment, while Aleksei Yablokov has treated ecological safety, Valentin Kotyug and Nikita Moiseyev have considered the steady ecological development of society, and Vladimir Kotlyakov and Valentin Katasonov the idea of harmonious exploitation. Wildlife conservation and national parks have been addressed by Nikolai Reimers and Felix Shtilmark. Dmitri Likhachev has devoted a number of his brilliant articles to the ethical aspect of human attitudes toward nature. Similar themes are dealt with by journalists writing on ecology, such as Mark Borozin, Anatoli Ivashchenko, Arkadi Melua, Oleg Poptsov, Yuri Chernichenko, and Viktor Yaroshenko.

Other Varieties of Ecological Popular Science

Among the varieties of the genre, such literary forms as the essay, developing on the borderline between newspaper reports and fiction, stands out. Writer Mikhail Prishvin, in whose works the theme of Russian landscapes and their preservation was dominant, became the founder of the this trend in Russian ecologei popular science. It was Prishvin's quotation, "By protecting nature your protect your own motherland," that became one of the main slogans of the Russian ecological movement.

Yet another writer, as well as poet and traveler, Sergei Markov, a devotee of the Russian cultural and natural heritage, did much for the elaboration of the genre of ecological essays. His works are focused on rendering our imperfect world habitable. Rendering the earth habitable implies, according to Markov, wildlife and landscape preservation. Characters in his essays, short stories, and novels, like the author himself, invariably act with this ideal in mind. It is noteworthy that the ecologically oriented Markov wanted, as his poem says, to be thought of as a "seeker of the water of life."

Mention of the present-day Russian ecological essay evokes primarily the name of Vassiliy Peskov, the author of such books as *Barefoot Through the Dew*, *White Dreams*, *The River of My Childhood*, and *Ptitsy na Provodakh* (Birds on Wires), published in numbers considerable even for Russia. Peskov's essays reach a wide audience owing to his longstanding cooperation with the press, first of all with the *Komsomolskaya Pravda* newspaper. In the genre of essays on nature the names of Rudolf Balandin, Ivan Vasilyev, Vadim Dyozhkin, and Alexander Yanshin, not to mention others, are also prominent.

Reference works for the general public occupy a particular place in the literature on nature. The need for them is called forth by nature-oriented trends in society, the growing interest in the preservation of the environment, and, last but not least, the growing responsibility of people for the preservation of Russia's natural heritage. Among such editions, the unprecedented *Slovar' Narodnokh Geograficheskik Terminov* (Dictionary of Folk Geographical Terms) by Eduard Murzayev, containing some 4,000 headwords, and *Prirodopolzovaniye. Slovar'-spravnochnik* (Nature Management: A Glossary) by Nikolai Reimers, covering nearly all of the main terms and notions of modern environment-oriented sciences, must be mentioned. Reimers has also published other reference books, including those in collaboration with Alexei Yablokov.

Certain serial reference books have gained a considerable popularity with the general public. Among them are the *Nature* series, including such volumes as *Mountains*, *Deserts*, *Reservoirs*, *Landscapes*, and the like; the *Geographer's and Traveler's Handbooks* series, and the seven-volume *National Parks of the USSR* series edited by Vladimir Sokolov and Yevgeni Syroechkovsky. Since these books, however, are not available in bookshops, the brisk demand for ecological popular science and reference books apparently exceeds the supply.

The Social Role of Ecological Nonfiction

The interest in ecological popular science has given an impetus to the emergence of the ecological press in Russia. One can mention such nationwide newspapers as *The Green World* and

Salvation, and numerous magazines, not to speak of the local press. Many a publishing house dealing, either wholly or partially, with ecological literature, has been established with *Geographgiz, Mysl, Progress, Mir, Nauka, Agropromizdat*, and *Lesnaya Promyshlennost* among them. The Nature Preservation Committee headed by Vladimir Krupin has carried out fruitful activity at the Moscow Branch of the Writers' Union.

Ecological popular science, having its own intrinsic value, is also playing an important role in the life of modern society, influencing the formation of public opinion on certain important social issues and the ecological culture of the population, thus promoting civic virtues. Documentary ecological publications have made a valuable contribution to the struggle against attempts to partially divert the flow of the Siberian and northern rivers to the southern regions of the country, against the construction of huge dams and reservoirs on a number of rivers, and against the depredation of forests in the North, the Altai, and the Far East.

In the 1980s, documentary ecological publications rendered great service to the cause of democracy. While breaking the once rigid taboos, including that on discussing the true ecological situation in the country, these publications favored the formation of new political movements and parties and ultimately the overcoming of stagnation. It is possible, however, that the main task of ecological literature is to satisfy the natural urge of human beings to communicate with nature, inter alia, by means of a good book. To cite Leo Tolstoy, "to be happy is to be with nature, to see it and to speak to it." Certainly, there exist other interpretations of happiness, yet one thing is unquestionable: human happiness and well-being are inconceivable without nature and a full-scale communication with it.

Selected Works and Further Reading

Akimushkin, Igor, *Nevidimye Niti Prirody* [Invisible Threads of Nature], Moscow: Mysl, 1985

Anuchin, V. A., *Osnovy Prirodopolzovaniia: Teoreticheskii Aspekt* [Bases for Using Natural Resources], Moscow: Mysl, 1978

Apresyan, Grant Z., *Esteticheskoye otnosheniye k prirodye v sotsialisticheskom obshchestvye* [The Aesthetic Attitude Toward Nature in Socialist Society], Moscow: Znaniye, 1981

Arakcheyev, Yuri, *V Poskakh Apollona* [In Quest of Apollo], Moscow: Mysl: 1985

Armand, David L., *Nam I Vnukam* [To Us and Our Grandchildren], Moscow: Mysl, 1964

Arsenyev, V. K., *V. Debryakh Ussuriiskogo kraya* [In the Ussuri Jungle], Khabarovsk-Vladivostok, U.S.S.R.: Knizhnoe Delo, 1928

Balandin, Rudolf K., and L. G. Bondarev, *Priroda I Tsivilizatsiia* [Nature and Civilization], Moscow: Mysl, 1986

Drozdov, N. N., *Polet Bumeranga* [The Flight of the Boomerang], Moscow: Mysl, 1988

Efremov, Iurii K., *Priroda Moei Strany* [My Country's Habitat], Moscow: Mysl, 1985

Gumilyov, Lev N., *Drevniaia Rus' I Velikaia Step'* [Early Russia and the Great Steppes], Moscow: Mysl, 1989

Khatskevich, Dina Kh., *Priroda kak esteticheskaia tsennost* [Nature as an Aesthetic Value], Moscow: Vysshaia Shkola, 1987

Lemeshev, Mikhail Ya., ed., *Ecologiceskaya Alternativa* [The Ecological Alternative], Moscow: Progress, 1989

Mazorov, Yuri, ed., *Chuvstvo Zemli* [The Feeling of the Earth], Moscow: Mysl, 1988

Murzayev, E. M., *Slovar' Narodnokh Geograficheskik Terminov* [Dictionary of Folk Geographical Terms], Moscow: Mysl, 1984

Peskov, V., *Ptitsy na Provodakh* [Birds on Wires], Moscow: Molodaia Gvardiia, 1982

Reimers, Nikolai F., *Prirodopolzovanye: Slovar'-spravnochnik* [Nature Management: A Glossary], Moscow: Mysl, 1990

Saushkin, Yulian G., *Istoriya I metodologiya geograficheskoi nauki* [History and Methodology of Geography], Moscow: Moscow University Press, 1976

Shtilmark, F. R., *Lukomorye, gde ono?* [Where Is the Land of Milk and Honey?], Moscow: Mysl, 1993

Uspensky, Savva M., *Zhivaya Arctica* [The Living Arctic], Moscow: Mysl, 1986

Voyeikov, A. I., *Vozdeistvie Cheloveka na Prirodu* [Man's Impact on Nature], Moscow: Geografgiz, 1949

Vorobyev, Boris, *Vesyegonskaya Volchitsa* [The Vesyegonsk She-Wolf], Moscow: Mysl, 1989

Winer, Douglas R., *Ekologiya Sovetskoy Rossiyi* [Ecology in Soviet Russia], Moscow: Progress, 1993

The Environment and Nineteenth- and Twentieth-Century Spanish Literature

Dale Pratt and Barbara Gordon

A critical analysis of the environment as imagined in nineteenth- and twentieth-century Spanish literature broaches the fundamental issues of reality and representation, industrialization and urbanization, "nature versus nurture," and individual versus society. Literary environments never merely provide settings for the narrative; rather, they mold the destinies of the characters, help fix the trajectory of the plot, set the tone, move the action along, and often serve as additional narratorial witnesses to confirm or undermine the reliability of the primary narrator. Thus, it becomes important to examine relationships between textual environments and the characters who inhabit them, as well as the connections and points of divergence between textual environments and the extra-textual counterparts they so often appear to imitate.

The nexus of nature and literature illustrates how context precedes and precipitates text. The environment within which a culture exists forms an ineluctable component of that culture's literary discourse; it invariably constitutes a contextual backdrop informing every text produced by that culture. Culture is always a loaded term, of course; semioticians Yuri Lotman and Boris Uspensky argue that culture is the set of processes by which the groups of texts traditionally denominated "culture" come into being. The semiotic mechanisms of accumulation, change of norms, and forgetting mix in varying proportions over time to create a cultural milieu. In a relationship much like that between the biosphere and the activities of the various species within it, culture provides the environment for the discourses of social life (Lotman and Uspensky, 211–215). Culture appears as a macro-set of numerous signifying systems against the background of non-cultural context (natural history, physical geography, bodily functions, etc.),

which constrains these signifying systems even as it serves as a screen upon which they can mean. Iberia's peninsular isolation from Europe, its proximity to North Africa, the height of its mountains, its varied ethnic groups, the species of plants and animals living there, its aridity in the south and its rain in the north are all non-cultural contextual elements that have forever colored Spanish literature, because they modulate the discourses of Spanish culture. Any map of Spain is a text, but the land that provides shape to that map forms part of its environmental context. The multifarious relationships between Spanish literature and the regions and peoples of Spain have evolved over the course of the nineteenth and twentieth centuries through the accumulation of literary intertexts, changes of literary norms (as in which tropes or rhetorical figures characterize relationships between humans and their environments), and the frequent forgetting or rejection of previous literary methods. Extra-textual environmental changes, especially the move from an impoverished agrarian society to the industrialized Spain of the later Franco years, also have profound effects on the ways literature approaches and receives influence from the environment.

Extratextual environments relate to the literary environments according to the literary operations of romanticization, objectification, camera-eye, mimesis, and irony. Most textual environments can appear only in certain historical periods and due to specific cultural constraints. For example, romantic prose writers like Serafín Estébanez Calderón and Ramón de Mesonero Romanos created *cuadros de costumbres*, which consist of tenuously connected scenes from rural life and extensive descriptions of the countryside. The majority of the *cuadros* treat the environments in which humans live on a non-symbolic, non-ironic level. They boast neither a well-constructed plot nor any significant symbolism; their textual environments do not point away from themselves to serve any larger end. Here synecdoches form the basic relationship between the characters and their environments: the characters and the land belonging to each other, the land providing ample territory and picturesque beauty for its inhabitants and the characters coloring the landscape with rustic humor, folklore and customs. Even in *La gaviota* (The Seagull), a late romantic novel by Fernán Caballer (Cecilia Bohl de Faber), the picturesque landscape of the first half of the book is significant to the plot only as a place-holder in a country-mouse/city-mouse dichotomy. In the writings of the other great early *costumbrista,* Mariano José de Larra, the urban environment in Madrid tends to function on a symbolic level. In "El día de difuntos de 1836. Fígaro en el cementerio" (The Day of the Dead, 1836. Fígaro in the Cemetery), the narrator walks through the streets of the capital and sees the buildings as great tombstones with epitaphs announcing the decline of Spanish culture. The architectural beauty and integrity of the buildings belie the economic and political ruin of the country. By ironically invoking the city's environment, Larra symbolically ascribes a hollowness to modern civilization in general. Later incarnations of *costumbrismo* appear in the Realist stories and novels of Pedro Antonio de Alarcón and José María de Pereda.

Romanticism in Spain finds its fullest expression in the theater. Angel de Saavedra, José Zorilla, Juan Eugenio Hartzenbusch, among others, created plays filled with dashing heroes, swooning heroines, medieval and Golden Age motifs, fervid action, and multiple changes of scenery. Natural and artificial landscapes often intrude into the plot. Zorilla's Don Juan escapes his pursuers by leaping into the currents of the Guadalquivir, a symbolic expression of his fluidity in personae (he figuratively and literally dons masks at every turn) as well as his inconstancy in love. He returns later to Seville to find the concrete remains of his adventures in the family cemetery filled with statues of his victims. Here the romantic hero surrounds himself with an artificial environment of his own creation. The statue of Don Gonzalo animates and attempts to drag Don Juan to hell, but in Zorilla's version the deceased Inés's intercession with God rescues him.

The Romantic universe is a realm of pathetic fallacies—metonymic relationships between nature and characters—where even the statues of the dead come to life seeking vengeance. According to Hans Eichner, the organicism of the Romantic world responds to various problems in the mechanical universe as envisioned since the time of Galileo and Newton. Eighteenth-century optimists argued that specific, fixed quantities of good and evil existed in the world, an idea that entailed the impossibility of any real social or individual progress. Romantic organicism tries to resolve this problem by imagining an imperfect Nature striving toward perfection (p. 15). Along with Nature's imperfection, however, comes its boundlessness, a feature potentially destructive of human subjectivity. In the sublime moment there arises in the subject a mental resistance to the chaos of nature's immensity. Humans perceive the infinite yet organize unity from chaos through their rational faculties (Kant, 100–102). Yet Spanish Romantic literature focuses mainly on experiencing the sublime and little on the consoling aftereffects of rational organization of the moment (*see* Rosenberg). Sublimity overwhelms frail beauty.

In Saavedra's play *Don Alvaro o la fuerza del sino* (Don Alvaro or the Force of Destiny), the eponymous hero, the son of an Inca princess and a Spaniard, must hide his lineage to maintain his honor and social class. Alvaro laments his loss of love and honor: "¡Qué carga tan insufrible/ es el ambiente vital/ para el mezquino mortal/ que nace en sino terrible!" [What an insufferable burden / is life's environment / for the wretched mortal / born to an awful destiny!] (p. 105). His mixed lineage forever frustrates his quest for respect within Iberian cultural codes; whereas had he remained in the Peruvian milieu he might well have belonged to the creole upper class. The Spanish setting creates the need for secrecy and hence the dramatic tension of the play. Pathetic fallacies dominate the final act, which begins in a convent as night falls and ends in a thunderstorm high on a mountaintop. Don Alonso, a vengeful brother of Alvaro's long-lost true love, slays his sister just as he dies from Alvaro's blow. Alvaro, now insane from finding and losing his love in an instant, hurls himself off a cliff. The natural sublimity of the setting and the great storm parallel the overarching destiny that destroys Alvaro and Leonor. The final words of the play, the *Miserere* sung by terrified monks, appeal directly to God for salvation from the sublime horror of fate metonymically associated with unconquerable nature.

The Romantic landscape in Enrique Gil y Carrasco's novel *El señor de Bembibre* (The

Lord of Bembibre) functions metonymically on two levels. First, the picturesque scenery of el Bierzo marks out the passions of the hero (again named Alvaro) and Beatriz, and eventually slays the heroine as nature's sublimity crushes her subjectivity. Second, the local medieval environment, filled with Roman ruins (and the future ruins of Templar castles) is history itself, encapsulating in past and present a political allegory of mid-century Spain. Near the end, the romantic heroine's health has steadily deteriorated. Beatriz's father recognizes the irony of the Romantic landscape appearing softened in the moonlight just as his daughter lies in the depth of her agony (pp. 354–355). Later, in broad daylight and in view of her hero's return, the rejuvenated Beatriz takes a short trip out onto a mountain lake. Here, though, the moon plays no softening light on the peaks, and the lake, no longer merely natural, becomes a frightening pathway to heaven (p. 371). The sky and its reflection appear as two abysses to the sick woman, and dissipate her fleeting happiness. Nature's immensity finds its counterpart within the heroine's soul, another abyss opened by the continual seesawing of hope and desperation. Nature cannot fill the void; instead, it enhances the sublime emptiness, and Beatriz feels lost on a limitless sea (p. 372). Spanish natural landscapes in the first two-thirds of the nineteenth century could inspire nostalgia for rustic lifestyles and wonder at the picturesque in the *cuadros de costumbres*, and evoke the sublime moment in the (near) obliteration of human frailty and finitude.

Whereas the fictional Beatriz dies in the distant fourteenth century, any reader familiar with northern Spain knows that the Bierzo area continues unspoiled today. The long and varied history of the land infuses itself into the generations of those residing in it. History is inescapable in Spain—major cities are built on the ruins of earlier Christian, Moorish, Visigothic, Roman or Celtiberian settlements. One telling scene in *Bembibre* occurs when from the abbey of Carracedo the abbot and Alvaro discern a veritable mountain of Roman ruins; the abbot tells Alvaro that just as with the Romans their pride will ruin the Templars (p. 106). The scene also serves as a heuristic for interpreting Gil's historical novel in light of nineteenth-century Spanish politics (*see* Picoche). The Templars need to ponder the fall of Rome, just as nineteenth-century Spaniards must reflect on the medieval civil wars and the suppression of the Templars as well as on the decay of the Romans.

Fifteen years after Gil y Carrasco's meditations on history, the publication of Darwin's *On the Origin of Species by Means of Natural Selection* forever changed literary conceptions of history, nature and the environment. Darwinism sees each species as the product of random accumulated variations within specific environments. Post-Darwinian literary environments necessarily function on symbolic and other levels because the environment invariably shapes the character of the struggle between individuals and species for niches suited for their survival. In the post-Darwinian universe, humans are but one species working in Nature, and natural environments necessarily assume a symbolic register absent from the metonymic Romantic landscapes. Whereas the physical environment represents but one portion of Romantic subjectivity, after the mid-nineteenth century it constitutes the fundamental element in the lives of human beings, determining (or in Catholic Spain, nearly determining) their proclivities, attitudes, actions and reactions. Romantic teleology no longer functions in the natural world with the advent of the Darwinian universe. No progress toward a divine finale occurs, and in literature no ultimate answer nor respite from the travails of nature and oppressive society obtains.

Realists Benito Pérez Galdós, Emilia Pardo Bazán, and Leopoldo Alas wrote novels that bestow characterhood on the physical settings of the texts. However, the determinism typically associated with naturalism does not exist in Spanish literature from this period. In Alas's *La Regenta* (The Regent's Wife), a park in the middle of the newly industrialized Vetusta symbolizes the natural world; the park's gigantic eucalyptus tree rivals the cathedral tower (symbol of the power of the chief priest). The natural world provides a powerful foil for the corruption of the Vetustan aristocrats, whose hypocritical discourse hastens their decay. In contrast, the buffoon-like Frígilis's close contact with the natural world and Darwinian theory permits him to conduct scientific experiments with real results. In *La Regenta*, nature provides the solid foundation for the enhancement of life otherwise unachievable in Vetusta.

In Pardo Bazán's novels, set in rural Galicia, civilization's urban comforts seem even more distant because of the overpowering closeness of the natural world. *Los pazos de Ulloa* (The House of Ulloa) and its sequel *La madre naturaleza* (Mother Nature) recount the aftermath of a petty nobleman's disregard of his city-bred wife in favor of a robust country servant. Each woman bears a child, but the aristocratic Nucha soon dies, leaving her daughter to become a pauper while Isabel's son will inherit the estate. Later as teens they fall ignorantly into an incestuous love affair that the natural world surrounding the manor seems inexorably to force upon them. Pardo Bazán closes *La madre naturaleza*, the most naturalistic of her novels, with the lines "Naturaleza, te llaman madre. . . . Deberían llamarte madrastra" [Nature, they call you mother. . . . They should call you stepmother] (p. 410). Nature is a cruel stepmother who allows her lost children to stagnate in rural Galicia as the sensuality of the natural world threatens to overwhelm human society. The outsider Gabriel suggests that Darwinistic laws predetermined the unhappy outcome of the novel: "en lo más sagrado y respetable que existe . . . en la Naturaleza" [in that which is most sacred and respectable . . . in Nature]. The austere priest Julián corrects him: "la ley de Naturaleza, aislada, sola, invóquela las bestias; nosotros invocamos otra más alta . . . Para eso somos hombres hijos de Dios" [let the beasts invoke the law of Nature alone; we call upon a higher law . . . For this reason we humans are the children of God] (p. 409). However, despite Julián's disclaimer, the novel's characters are neither children of God nor products of culture, but rather children of nature.

Pérez Galdós, nineteenth-century Spain's greatest novelist, infuses dozens of his novels with the urban environment of Madrid (for instance, many of the *Episodios nacionales, Miau, Tormento, La de Bringas, Fortunata y Jacinta*, the *Torquemada* series, *Tristana*, and *Misericordia*). Indeed, Madrid is the principal character of all Galdósian writing. Much like Darwin's theories of natural history, Galdós's fiction ensconces human characters within meticulously described environments. Madrilenian mores and hypocrisy find reflections in the architecture, in the hive-like business of the Royal Palace, in the urban renovation projects, in the dilapidated buildings of the poor districts, in the street, and in the trajectories of the (often ruined) lives of the characters themselves. Fortunata, a beautiful, impoverished young woman, suffers privations and indignities merely because of the squalor in which she was raised. Other previously wealthy aristocrats or white-collar workers fall into economic ruin in Madrid even though in provincial capitals they could have maintained their socio-economic status. Galdós's fiction never yields to strict determinism, although in many instances the poverty, disease and filth seem overwhelming.

Galdós's narrators and characters frequently comment on the role of the environment in the story. In *Tormento*, Agustín Caballero says "Cada hombre . . . es hechura de su propia vida. El hombre nace, y la Naturaleza y la vida lo hacen" [every man is the creation of his own life. Man is born, and Nature and life make him what he is] (p. 37). Caballero ostensibly belies his own aphorism at the novel's close when he unexpectedly takes a young lover and sets off on a tour of Europe. However, this apparent freedom and caprice have their origin in his many years' stay in America, far from the staid Spanish environment to which Caballero tries and fails to adapt. Much like Saavedra's mestizo Don Alvaro, Caballero's insertion into the peninsular environment occasions tension and sets up a potential tragedy. In this case, however, the American ideal of personal liberty, symbolized by the open spaces of Texas and northern Mexico, wins out over Spanish cultural norms.

The group of writers known as the "Generation of 1898" reiterated the idea from the later Realist works of Pereda and Pardo Bazán that true history resided in the land of Spain, or perhaps in the blood of all Spaniards. Novelists and essayists Miguel de Unamuno, Pío Baroja, José Martínez Ruiz, "Azorín," and poet Antonio Machado saw in Spain's environment the explanation for past glories and present woes as well as hope for the future. In the prologue to *Campos de Castilla* (The Castilian Countryside), Machado declares that the simple love of nature surpasses a love of art. Machado seeks to unite the people and their faith with the land: "mis romances miran a lo elemental humano, al campo de Castilla y al libro primero de Moisés" [my ballads look at the fundamentally human, at the Castilian countryside and at the first book of Moses] (*Poesías completas*, 79). Machado's poetry from this book onward leaves behind the motif of the solitary poet, to locate instead the concrete natural environment and the people from whom sprang the heroic epics (p. 79).

Unamuno reiterates the Romantic trope of metonymic resonances between land and people when he devotes a long essay in *En torno al casticismo* (About Traditionalism) to the influence of the land of Castile. The harsh, dry plateau inspires neither sensuality nor feelings of joy or comfort: "no evoca su contemplación al animal que duerme en nosotros todos" [the land does not evoke the contemplation of the animal sleeping within us] (p. 76). For Unamuno, a writer deeply concerned with the human spirit, the Castilian landscape is not "una naturaleza que recree al espíritu" [a nature that re-creates the spirit] (p. 76). Spain's malaise at the fin de siecle will find resolution in an examination of Castile itself. The history of the "land of castles" should not be the story of those castles and the elites that resided in them. Rather, the *intrahistoria* (intrahistory), the lives and traditions of the people of the tiny villages, tells the true tale and reveals the strength of the Castilian spirit that cannot commune with nature but is forever shaped by it (p. 79). In Unamuno's *San Manuel Bueno, mártir* (Saint Manuel the Good, Martyr), the priest Don Manuel sees a girl herding goats on a mountainside and exclaims: "Esa zagala forma parte, con las rocas, las nubes, los árboles, las aguas, de la naturaleza y no de la historia" [that girl forms part of nature's rocks, clouds, trees and waters and not part of history] (p. 47). Here contiguity with the land and its ahistoricity teach us about the goatherd and eternalize her.

Baroja treats the natural world more sardonically as he contemplates the wonders and dangers of modern technology and medicine. In *Paradox, rey* (Paradox, king), a group of shipwrecked Spanish colonists in Africa makes friends with natives and attempts to build a utopian society. The reforms include better agriculture, hygiene and care for the sick, but more importantly, radically altering the physical environment. Silvestre Paradox and his companions use explosives to create a lake for the natives. Spanish colonialism had recently suffered grave setbacks in the Western Hemisphere; nevertheless, the Spanish government maintained ambitions toward Africa. *Paradox, rey* underscores the power of modern technology to affect the environment. However, the characters never apply technology to the Spanish environment, but only to the seemingly pliant African jungle (which appears to change as readily as do its native denizens). When the French invade Paradox's fledgling state, they introduce weapons, diseases, bureaucracy and other ills. The African jungle quickly becomes a site upon which European colonial rivalries map themselves.

The preeminent twentieth-century Spanish philosopher, José Ortega y Gasset, provides a natural segue from late nineteenth-century concerns to the avant-garde of the 1920s and 1930s. Ortega declared in *Meditaciones del Quijote* (Meditations on Don Quijote) that "yo soy yo y mi circunstancia, y si no la salvo a ella no me salvo yo" [I am I and my circumstance, and if I do not save the latter I do not save myself] (p. 77). The natural and cultural environments surrounding any person condition (rather than determine) life's limits for that person, and yet also offer expansive possibilities to the soul. Ortega's astute essays on phenomenology and existentialism mark out culture as an environment at once artificial yet fundamentally united with the ambient natural world.

Avant-garde writers dismissed Realist objectivity and the highly intellectual novels of the Generation of 1898. They rejected mimesis, cultivated experimentation in technique and form, and avoided historical and overtly political themes in texts focused on beauty and infused with a jovial spirit. Imitation of the techniques of Italian cinema—close-ups, perspectivism—and themes such as jazz, sports, mass transit, and contemporary man prevailed as a certain superficiality permeated many of the works of the first third of the twentieth century. These techniques provided an impression of reality without the tediously mimetic flavor of the Realists. After Spain's civil war, however, the writers of the 1940s could not conceive of depicting the frivolity of the twenties and so turned toward individuals and their surroundings, their sociocultural sphere, and humans as historico-political entities. The reality of the war required a realistic look at contemporary men and women and their struggles to survive.

Following the Spanish Civil War, the Franco regime cultivated a language that exalted the grandeur of Spain despite the obvious devastation caused by the three-year conflict. The government attempted to elevate the cultural reality by casting Ortega's (liberal) rhetoric in the register of Mussolini's Fascist propaganda. On the radio and in the press, Spanish citizens received the message that Spain was thriving when the reality surrounding them bespoke the opposite. Writers like Nobel laureate Camilo José Cela and Carmen Laforet disintegrate or deconstruct the regime's fictional world by depicting urban life as desperate and bitter. Miguel Delibes and Ana María Matute perform similar tasks with novels and stories set in rural areas. Laforet's *Nada* (Nothing) portrays the stark post-war life of a family torn apart by politics, reprisals and hunger. The textual environment shrinks to the size of a tiny apartment in Barcelona, mirroring the dwindling possibilities for reconstruction or rapproachment.

Delibes's first novel *La sombra del ciprés es alargada* (The Cypress's Shadow is Long) similarly conveys deep pessimism about the ruin of Spain; the cypress's long shadow symbolizes death and pain. Other Delibes novels such as *Las ratas* (The Rats) also decry the impoverished life of rural peasants whose lands barely yield a harvest. Nevertheless, in other texts Delibes recounts the charms of rural life, such as *El camino* (The Way), which views rural life nostalgically through the eyes of an 11-year-old, and *Viejas historias de Castilla la Vieja* (Old Histories of Old Castile), a series of rural vignettes recalling the Romantic *cuadros de costumbres*. In his innovative novel *Parábola del náufrago* (The Hedge), Delibes shows the natural world–so often a refuge from political oppression–become the agent of the oppressor, when a giant hedge grown from specially engineered seeds beseiges the protagonist, who compares his situation with that of a castaway. Images of nature and hunting in *Los santos inocentes* (The Holy Innocents) recall the oppressive atmosphere on the large rural farms during the Franco years, as well as the desire for vengeance lurking in the hearts of the oppressed. They also hint at the opportunities that opened up for the lower classes when Spain industrialized.

In Cela's novel *La colmena* (The Hive), the inhabitants of Madrid, a teeming city of hive-like structures, exist in a seemingly chaotic world. But as with a natural beehive, organization and order underlie its complexity. Within the hive—Madrid—human relations weave together to form an interdependent society of family, friends, co-workers and lovers. Characters from various narrative threads gradually knit together the disparate stories. Shared experiences during the years of hunger and repression unite the people within their social environments. These events take place in a city where nature is conspicuous by its absence but culture dictates one's personal outcome. The rich abuse the poor, while the poor patiently endure and sometimes encourage their own oppression. Yet just as with bees in a hive, the castes comingle. The shoeshine in Doña Rosa's cafe pathetically allows the pretentious Don Leonardo Meléndez to mistreat him, but the culture has degraded Don Leonardo with all the others. In *La colmena* the different local environments run together as the streets of Madrid relate the cafe to Celestino's bar, later to Doña Celia's bordello, and on to the characters' apartments.

The marble tables of Doña Rosas's cafe—where many of the characters loiter or work—are made from tombstones (some even retain the epitaphs of the dead they originally memorialized). The symbols of the dead, whose flesh and bones return to nature, find their way into the hive, the land of the living dead, the war's survivors who in 1940s Madrid have nowhere to go, nothing to do. The novel's final fragment reiterates the cemetery motif. Martín Marcos leaves Madrid to visit the tomb of his mother. As he travels, he decides to leave behind his benighted past and begin again with whatever position he is offered. Ironically—for he is soon to be accused of murder—he finds himself happy with his future prospects and exclaims: "¡Hoy sí que estoy fresco y discurro bien! Debe ser el aire del campo" (p. 388) [Today I'm in really good form and put things well. It must be the country air (p. 248)]. But that air blows through the lifeless cemetery. Martín must choose between the relative sanctuary within the cemetery, or return to the death sentence awaiting him in Madrid. Once again, more than 100 years after Larra's *artículo de costumbre,* death fills the unnatural cemetery Madrid.

Postwar novels set in rural areas similarly invoke nature imagery to critique the war's aftermath. Ana María Matute's novel, *Primera Memoria* (School of the Sun), inverts the paradisiacal island environment of Mallorca, turning it into an infernal space. The young Matia feels torn between her wealthy, traditional grandmother's Nationalism and her father's Republicanism. Three environmental images in her memoir—the island, sun, and flowers—depict Nature itself affected by and representing the war. Matia's atlas speaks to her of distant places more pleasant than the island. Yet the island constitutes her reality, characterized by ominous descriptions of the clouds, sea, rocks and flowers: "miraba la tierra, y me decía que vivíamos encima de los muertos, y que la pedregosa isla, con sus enormes flores y sus árboles estaba amasada de muertos y muertos sobrepuestos" (p. 92) [I looked at the earth, and I told myself that we lived on top of the dead; that the stony island, with its enormous flowers and trees, was a mass formed by the piling up of corpses, corpses upon corpses (p. 100)]. Matia's sun rarely recalls peace, rather the violence and pain of the war. The flowers' aroma also lends an oppressive air to the novel; they personify rage and evil. Franco's rebellion transforms even the most beautiful Spanish vistas into lugubrious landscapes.

Luis Martín-Santos's *El tiempo de silencio* (The Silent Time) continues the post-war discourse on the sprawling degradation of Madrid and its surrounding slums and ends with the protagonist fleeing the city to take a medical position in a small town. An allusion to nuclear annihilation threatens the supposed refuge offered by the country (p. 291), foreshadowing the probable failure of the protagonist's bid to redeem himself as a country doctor. Martín-Santos also makes reference to the awful pollution of Madrid and environs, a literal and symbolic witness of the difficult quest for industrial modernity forced onto Spain and its people by Franco.

The twentieth-century version of the *cuadros de costumbres*, the *libros de viajes* or travel narratives produced during the late 1950s and 1960s, reported the abhorrent conditions of rural Spain. Due to the cultural environment, the *libros de viajes* differ radically from the *cuadros*. Jesús Fernández Santos, Antonio Ferres, Juan Goytisolo, and many others cultivated this genre that spoke to the masses in deflated, cruder language than did previous literature, and presented an objective way of observing, contemplating and exploring the forgotten villages of Spain. In an essay on aesthetics, Goytisolo castigates the Generation of 1898 for ignoring the stark realities of rural life in their romanticized encomia of Castile; for him, authentic Spanish literature must look at Spaniards and the landscape where they are born, suffer and die ("Tierras," 190). In discarding "artistic" renderings of rural life, Goytisolo follows the models of the Italian filmed documentary and other earlier travel narrators in providing an eyewitness account of the day-to-day degraded lives of the peasants of the forgotten provinces. Thus *libros de viajes*, visits from urban, sophisticated environments to backward rural areas, depend upon something alien to the rural landscapes: the camera-eye vision produced by twentieth-century technology. Still, these authors write to decry the poverty and inhumanity of the social hierarchy exploiting the peasants. They seek to show, not tell, that the environment is not that of a nineteenth-century Romantic novel, but the harsh reality of a raped land.

In Goytisolo's *Campos de Níjar* (Countryside of Níjar) and *La Chanca*, the eyewitness enumerates the problems he encounters among destitute peasants. The money needed to rebuild rural provinces must originate elsewhere; Spain cannot or will not support the rural towns but willingly exploits their resources. Improvements to roads or buildings happen only to facilitate exploitation. The dying land cannot reach out to its inhabitants. Similar travel narratives bespeak this devastation; the depletion of natural resources painfully announces the poverty and starvation still rampant even decades following the war.

Contemporary writers born in small towns after the war, like Julio Llamazares, Christina Fernández Cubas, and Adelaida García Morales, share a somewhat more optimistic view of humanity's place in nature. Although these authors have studied or worked in the city, their characters' rural lifestyles tend to unfold in small towns. In most post-war novels prior to García Morales's novel *El silencio de las sirenas* (The Silence of the Sirens), nature holds some evil or sinister sway over the people, an ability to thwart their existence. In this novel, however, nature finally suggests the edenic peace so long repressed by images of the civil war. To the outsider, nature is still inexplicable or unreasonable; its attraction-repulsion frightens the visitor unfamiliar with nature. The day the narrator María arrives, the sun shines on the most beautiful area she has ever seen. The next day, however, the clouds literally and metaphorically roll in on the dying town: it has nothing to offer the new generation. The symbiotic relationship between town and people leads to mutual infections and downward spiraling (reminiscent of Goytisolo's description of Níjar). The connection between the people and their town means that the loss of one devastates the other.

Elsa, the protagonist, takes long walks into the mountains, to places where the snow remains all year long. There, far from town, she finds peace. Later, María locates Elsa's body "rígida, inmóvil, adherida a la tierra y formando parte de la montaña, igual que sus plantas, sus árboles, sus rocas, sus piedras. . . . Y me pareció que ella vibraba ahora con la misma pulsación de la tierra" (p. 165) [rigid, motionless, clinging to the ground, become one with the mountains, the plants, the trees, the rocks and stones. . . . It seemed to me that she vibrated now with the pulse of the earth (p. 172)]. The urbanite María hesitates to leave Elsa in the mountains, so she buries her in a borrowed niche in the cemetery. She later regrets her mistake for having taken Elsa away from the frozen mountainside, the site most natural for her. In *El silencio de las sirenas*, humanity and nature become one; the struggle between them no longer matters.

Physical environments (non-culture) often resist textualization even as they provide contexts for the cultures producing literary texts. *Spain* the political entity differs drastically from the land of the Iberian peninsula. The maps in Matia's atlas, for all their pretty colors and neat lines, do not share three-dimensionality with their geographical referents. Just as Don Juan created an artificial environment (the statuary of victims), Francoist Spain created its own rhetorical landscape denying the realities uncovered by the *libros de viajes*. The truth underlying the artifice in both cases returns to haunt the creators. The cemetery imagery in Larra, Zorrilla and Cela refers to the ruins of individual human histories; the crumbled Roman buildings in *El señor de Bembibre* witness that whole societies perish while the land remains intact. Although nature can suffer pollutions and physical alterations (in *Paradox, rey*), and certainly undergoes rhetorical manipulations within literary documents, it typically represents an implacable force, sometimes loving and often malevolent. The changing character of these representations, from Romantic tropologies of metonymies to Realist symbolism and post–civil war allegorizing, reveals that Spanish cultural contexts imperfectly inflict themselves upon the environment that, in turn, radically shapes and continually changes the literature produced in Spain.

Selected Works and Further Reading

Alas, Leopoldo, *La Regenta* [The Regent's Wife], Barcelona, Spain: Biblioteca 'Arte y letras, 1884; rev. ed., edited by Gonzalo Sobejano, 2 vols., Madrid, Spain: Castalia, 1981

Baroja, Pio, *Paradox, rey*, Madrid, Spain: Hernando, 1906; New York: Macmillan, 1937; as *Paradox, King*, London: Wishart, 1931

Caballero, Fernán, *La gaviota* [The Seagull], 1849; edited by Carmen Bravo-Villasante, Madrid, Spain: Castalia, 1979

Cela, Camilo José, *La colmena* [The Hive], Barcelona, Spain: Noguer, 1951; as *The Hive*, translated by J. M. Cohen, New York: New American Library, 1954

Darwin, Charles, *On the Origin of Species by Means of Natural Selection*, New York: Modern Library, 1859; London: John Murray, 1859; facsimile of first edition, edited by Ernst Mayr, Cambridge,

Massachusetts: Harvard University Press, 1964

Delibes, Miguel, *El camino* [The Way], Barcelona, Spain: Destino, 1950; New York: Holt, 1960; London: Harrap, 1963

——, *Parábola del náufrago*, Barcelona, Spain: Destino, 1969; as *The Hedge*, New York: Columbia University Press, 1983

——, *Las ratas* [The Rats], Barcelona, Spain: Destino, 1962; London: Harrap, 1983

——, *Los santos inocentes* [The Holy Innocents], Barcelona, Spain: Planeta, 1981

——, *La sombra del ciprés es alargada* [The Cypress's Shadow Is Long], Barcelona, Spain: Destino, 1948

——, *Viejas historias de Castilla la Vieja* [Old Histories of Old Castile], Barcelona, Spain: Lumen, 1964

Eichner, Hans, "The Rise of Modern Science and the Genesis of Romanticism," *PMLA* 97 (1982), pp. 8–30

García Morales, Adelaida, *El silencio de las sirenas*, Barcelona, Spain: Anagrama, 1985; as *The Silence of the Sirens*, translated by Concilia Hayter, London: Collins, 1988

Gil y Carrasco, Enrique, *El señor de Bembibre* [The Lord of Bembibre], edited by Enrique Rubio, Madrid, Spain: Cátedra, 1991

Goytisolo, Juan, *The Countryside of Níjar; and, La chanca*, translated by Luigi Luccarelli, Plainfield, Indiana: Alembic, 1987

——, "Tierras del Sur," in *El furgón de cola*, Paris: Ruedo Ibérico, 1967

Kant, Immanuel, *Kant's Critique of Judgement*, translated by John Henry Bernard, London: Macmillan, 1914; New York: Hafner, 1964

Laforet, Carmen, *Nada* [Nothing], Barcelona, Spain: Destino, 1945; New York: Oxford University Press, 1958; London: Weidenfeld and Nicolson, 1958

Larra, Mariano José de, "El día de difuntos de 1836. Fígaro en el cementerio" [The Day of the Dead, 1836. Fígaro in the Cemetery], in *Artículos de costumbres*, edited by Luis F. Díaz Larios, Madrid, Spain: Espasa-Calpe, 1989

Lotman, Yuri, and Boris Uspensky, "On the Semiotic Mechanism of Culture," translated by George Mihaychuk, *New Literary History* 9 (1978), pp. 211–232

Machado, Antonio, *Poesías completas* [Complete Poems], edited by Manuel Alvar, Madrid: Espasa-Calpe, 1979

Martín-Santos, Luis, *El tiempo de silencio*, Barcelona, Spain: Seix Barral, 1961; as *Time of Silence,* New York: Harcourt, Brace, 1964; London: J. Calder, 1965

Matute, Ana María, *Primera memoria,* Barcelona, Spain: Destino, 1973; as *School of the Sun,* translated by Elaine Kerrigan, New York: Columbia University Press, 1989; London: Quartet, 1991

Ortega y Gasset, José, *Meditaciones del Quijote,* edited by Julián Marías, Madrid, Spain: Revista de Occidente, 1957; as *Meditations on Quixote,* New York: Norton, 1961; London: Norton, 1963

Pardo Bazán, Emilia, *La madre naturaleza* [Mother Nature], Madrid, Spain: V. Prieto, 1910

———, *Los pazos de Ulloa,* Madrid, Spain: S. Bernardo, 1886; as *The House of Ulloa,* New York and London: Penguin, 1990

Pérez Galdós, Benito, *Tormento,* Madrid, Spain: La Guirnalda, 1884; as *Torment,* London: Weidenfeld and Nicolson, 1952; New York: Farrar, Straus & Young, 1953

Picoche, Jean-Luis, *Un romántico español: Enrique Gil y Carrasco (1815–1846)* [A Spanish Romantic: Enrique Gil y Carrasco], Madrid, Spain: Gredos, 1978

Rivas, Angel de Saavedra, duque de, *Don Álvaro: o, La fuerza del sino* [Don Alvaro or the Force of Destiny], edited by Alberto Sánchez, Salamanca, Spain: Anaya, 1959

Rosenberg, John R., "The Fall from the Beautiful: An Aesthetics of Spanish Romanticism," *Revista de Estudios Hispánicos* 24:2 (1990), pp. 83–101

Unamuno, Miguel de, *En torno al casticismo* [About Traditionalism], Madrid, Spain: F. Fé, 1902

———, *San Manuel Bueno, mártir, y tres historias más* [Saint Manuel the Good, Martyr, and Three Other Stories], Madrid, Spain: Espasa-Calpe, 1931

Zorilla, José, *Don Juan Tenorio,* edited by José Luis Gómez, Barcelona, Spain: Planeta, 1984

Section 3:

Asia and the Pacific

200 Years of the Australian Desert in Literature

Roslynn D. Haynes

Cultural appreciation of the Australian desert areas as evidenced in oral tradition of the indigenous peoples is immensely old, predating European settlement by many thousands of years, but until recently the Aboriginal understanding of the desert was ignored by Euro-Australians. Arriving with the cultural baggage of long-established ideological responses to the notion of deserts, derived from Africa and the Middle East, Europeans at first tried unsuccessfully to apply these concepts before evolving a new mythology with cumulative images that over 200 years have provided a major focus of Australian literature, art, consciousness and national identity.

Contributing to the lure of the desert for Europeans was the strong sense, deriving from the Judeo-Christian tradition, of its ambivalent otherness. On the one hand, an enduring reminder of the Fall and expulsion from Eden, the desert also offered the means of spiritual purification. Three of the predominant responses recorded by the explorers of the Australian desert, namely terror at its starkness, awe at its immensity, and fascination at its wildness, align precisely with the sensations of *mysterium,* *tremendum,* and *fascinans* identified by Rudolph Otto as accompanying the experience of the numinous. On the other hand, the desert was peculiarly a man's place: we know of no Desert Mothers. Thus, for European settlers, an important aspect of the desert was its masculine ethos and its association with sexual abstinence and rejection of women, offering a manhood free from the restraints of female presence.

For nineteenth-century European settlers an element of fascination attached to the unknown heart of Australia. Shrouded in mystique, it remained the last terra incognita and from the 1840s to the first decade of the twentieth century successive expeditions set out optimistically from the coastal settlements to cross the continent and discover some hypothetical central oasis. In a country that had experienced no battles on its territories other than the undeclared war waged against the Aborigines, explorers provided attractive substitutes for national military heroes, and were honored accordingly. Indeed, Australian literature of the desert has been as inextricably entwined with these figures as Aboriginal legends are with the ancestors of the Dreaming.

Intriguingly, the most highly mythologized heroes of Australian exploration, Edward John Eyre, Charles Sturt, Ludwig Leichhardt, Robert O'Hara Burke and William Wills, are those who could only be considered failures in terms of conquering the land, since they either failed to find the fertile land they so passionately sought, or died during their expeditions. Because most of the explorers were drawn from the officer class of the British army and thus trained to regard their endeavors as a military campaign, the expeditions were conceived in terms of a classical struggle, in which they themselves were the protagonists and Nature, as represented by the desert, was cast as antagonist. The nation's subsequent need to lionize its heroes perpetuated this vilification of the land in quasi-personal terms as harsh, treacherous and unrelenting.

The land was also characterized as female and virginal, waiting to be conquered and pos-

sessed. Such gendering of the land was not confined to desert exploration; it provided a common metaphor, identifying the alien terrain with
the alien sex, and thus constituting it as doubly
Other, but the imagery of sexual conquest, and
terms such as "unveiling "and "penetrating" the
"inner recesses" of the land are particularly frequent in narratives of desert exploration.

After the first-hand accounts of exploration
came the literary responses of those who, with
singularly few exceptions, had never been to the
desert. These writers inherited a landscape in
which the figures of the explorers were inscribed
as an integral and dominant element, the desert
itself being cast in the supporting role of antagonist in a contest, which, although entirely secular in reality, was fictionalized in semi-religious
terms.

Henry Kendall's 1861 poem, "Leichhardt," is
concerned not merely with a daring explorer, but
one sanctified even further by his devotion to science and, most significantly, his intriguing disappearance. Yet, in order to establish the full
extent of Leichhardt's heroism, the desert is further condemned by contrast with the fertility of
Germany. Burke and Wills, leaders of the disastrous Victorian Exploring Expedition of 1860–
61, who through their own incompetence died
of starvation, were immediately valorized, in literature as in art. Among the first in the field were
Henry Kendall's poems "Oh, Tell me ye Breezes"
and "The Fate of the Explorers, Burke and
Wills," which invoke the attributes most commonly associated with the desert—immensity,
loneliness, monotony, silence and antiquity.
"Deserts weird and wide . . . Deserts lonely;
lying pathless, deep, and vast, / Where in utter
silence ever Time seems slowly breathing past."
The power of these images lay in their implications for the fragility and transience of European
civilization perched precariously on the rim of
the world's most arid continent.

Also widely attributed to the desert was a
timeless quality, amplified by the realization of
its great geological age and reference to its silence. In his 1879 poem "In the Desert" Ernest
Favence, one of the few poets to write from
first-hand experience, constructs a silent, timeless, female land like a "dull grey sea, that had
no seeming bound" where "My footfall first
broke stillness that had reigned / For centuries
unbroken."

By the end of the nineteenth century, however, the mood had swung against the early inland
explorers. For assertive nationalists they were
too imperialist in their intentions, and their failures came to be seen, not as sanctification, but as
evidence of British effeteness. Sanguine expectations associated with imminent independence
from Britain at Federation (1901) pictured the
desert as succumbing to new technology, about
to yield treasures of gold and artesian water, and
this optimism issued in numerous adventure stories in the style of S. Rider Haggard's *She*. However, as these hopes, also, withered, the desert
virtually disappeared from Australian literature
for nearly four decades. When, at the end of the
1930s, it reappeared, it was associated with two
diverse impulses: interest in Aboriginal culture
and delineation of a uniquely Australian counterpart of T. S. Eliot's waste land.

Despite some detailed anthropological studies and Katharine Susannah Prichard's controversial novel *Coonardoo* set on a cattle station in
the far northwest and dealing with the emotional relationship between a white man and Aboriginal girl, there was virtually no literary
interest in Aboriginal tradition as a viable culture or in the desert as the national image until
the formation of the Jindyworobak Club,[1]
founded by Rex Ingamells in Adelaide in 1938.
The Jindyworobak writers, the majority of them
poets, determined to forge a unique Australian
culture derived from the spirit of place, and,
more controversially, to assimilate Aboriginal
myths of the Dreamtime or *Alcheringa*[2] as an
integral part of such a synthesis. Ingamells's
manifesto included "A clear recognition of environmental values" and an "understanding of
Australia's history and traditions, primeval,
colonial and modern." In his Introduction to
The Jindyworobaks Brian Elliott compares the
Jindyworobaks to the English Romantic poets
but concludes:

> They had *some* of this impersonal detach-
> ment [of a ritualistic poetical system]. . . . it
> appears to be something absorbed from the
> landscape, the 'environment', or 'spirit of the
> place', and in this respect a response of their
> own to something that had great importance
> in the Aboriginal mind. . . . Every location,
> every feature of the visible landscape was
> inhabited with mystical, mythical and
> totemistic presences—places where mythical
> events had occurred, where the wandering
> ancestors had rested. (p. xxx)

Although this mystical experience of place could
be accessed anywhere, some of the most charac-

teristic Jindyworobak poems are situated in the desert as the place of last and least European contact and one where only Aborigines were fully at home. In "Uluru, An Apostrophe to Ayers Rock," Rex Ingamells, one of the first to use the Aboriginal name, celebrates his experience of realization at "Uluru of the eagles": "Arrival is more than physical: it is / the dreaming at the inner shrine."

Despite their missionary fervor, the success of the Jindyworobak experiments was limited, partly because there was no single Aboriginal culture or language to use, and Aboriginal words did not work well in metric verse developed for English words. Moreover, because the Aboriginal lifestyle was not that of their readers, there was inevitably a sense of observing a primitive Other from a distance. However, if their movement lapsed, the expression of a spiritual dimension particularly accessible in the desert was to re-emerge in a popular vein in the 1980s. An unexpected resurgence of interest in the desert came through Australian poets' integration of the discourse of Modernism. The literal wasteland at the heart of the continent was taken to symbolize the barrenness of soul of a materialistic nation. A. D. Hope's 1939 poem, "Australia," was one of the first to enunciate this connection and also to associate the desert with potential for spiritual growth: "Yet there are some like me turn gladly home / From the lush jungle of modern thought . . . / . . . / Hoping if still from the deserts the prophets come." James McAuley's *paysage intérieur* "Envoi" draws similar parallels between the infertile land and the spiritual sterility of its inhabitants, again without precluding the possibility of limited renewal: "Beauty is order and good chance in the artesian heart / . . . / Though the reluctant and uneasy land resent / The gush of waters, the lean plough, the fretful seed." Although inclusive of a psychological correlative, these images still depend on the basic notion of the desert as unrelieved barrenness. The immediate catalyst for recognition of its greater complexity and apocalyptic potential came, not from literature, but from art and involved a new reading of the explorer figure. The central desert, the "dead heart" becomes "the Interior" with all the resonances of Joseph Conrad's sense of a "heart of darkness."

Sidney Nolan's symbolist paintings of the explorers Burke and Wills, rendered with scant regard for history but much interest in the relationship between explorer and the land, stimulated both an appreciation for the aesthetic and literary potential of the desert as archetypal setting, and a new curiosity about the psychological motivation and spiritual state of the once-revered explorers. In accordance with Modernist skepticism, these former heroes were recast as complex, tortured beings, selfish martyrs obsessed with fame. In such revisionist portrayals the significance attributed to the desert necessarily changed also from evil antagonist to a tabula rasa on which the explorers inscribed the extension of their psyche. The literary counterpart of Nolan's explorer paintings was Patrick White's best known novel, *Voss*, with its suggestion of a psycho-spiritual pilgrimage occurring in parallel with the physical journey of exploration. The character and expedition of Voss have strong echoes of the German explorer Ludwig Leichhardt, who disappeared without trace during his third expedition, but in White's treatment he becomes the prototypical egoist, determined to secure eternal fame by conquering the desert and finding spiritual enlightenment. To a potential follower he describes his mission in terms of both exultation and death-wish: "In this disturbing country . . . it is possible more easily to discard the inessential and to attempt the infinite. You will be burnt up most likely, you will have the flesh torn from your bones, you will be tortured probably in many horrible and primitive ways, but you will realize that genius of which you sometimes suspect you are possessed, and of which you will not tell me you are afraid" (pp. 35–36). Diverse readings of the novel suggest that White finally leaves it uncertain whether his protagonist is eventually humbled by his experiences or arrogantly seizes martyrdom. To achieve this ambiguity, White casts the desert in a Janus role. Barren and beautiful, demonic and inspiring, it both impedes the explorer's physical progress and endangers his soul with its lures of self-transcendence and self-destruction, yet simultaneously offers spiritual rebirth through rejection of materialism.

Francis Webb's poems "Leichhardt in Theatre" and "Eyre All Alone" also employ revisionist treatments of the desert explorers. In the latter, based on incidents from the life of Edward Eyre, the desert is more symbolic than in *Voss*, revolving around an almost wholly intellectual experience. Eyre's former pieties and securities are thrown into doubt, thereby permitting either spiritual growth or decline. Webb's note on the poem that the hero's greatest discovery is not a stock route but himself could stand as epigraph of most mid-century treatments of the Australian desert.

Randolph Stow, poet and novelist, also expresses this ongoing national consciousness of the many explorers' lives claimed by the desert. In 1969, he wrote in "The Singing Bones": "No pilgrims leave, no holy-days are kept / for these pilgrims who died of landscape. Who can find, / even, the camp-sites where the saints last slept?" Stow's novel, *Tourmaline*, where, again, the desert topography symbolizes the landscape of the mind, offers his most sustained analysis of how the desert informs national character. Tourmaline, an isolated mining town in the Western Australian desert, symbolizes the individual eternally estranged: "There is no stretch of land on earth more ancient than this. And so it is blunt and red and barren, littered with fragments of broken mountains, flat, waterless. Spinifex grows here, but sere and yellow, and trees are rare, hardly to be called trees" (p. 7). Tourmaline and its inhabitants are regularly threatened, actually and symbolically, with oblivion in desert dust storms: "I walked out, into the thick red wind. It was like swimming under water, in a flooding river. Dust sifted into my lungs; I was drowning. . . . There was no town, no hill, no landscape. There was nothing. . . . There was no town, no landscape. What could this be if not the end of the world?" (pp. 220–221).

Replaying the nineteenth-century pursuit of water and gold in the Centre, Stow's story concerns the quest for water by an itinerant diviner who offers to find water at Tourmaline; but his search is fruitless, producing only gold. Stow provided a key to the novel's meaning in his poem sequence "From the Testament of *Tourmaline*: Variations on Themes of *Tao Teh Ching*," indicating that the desert is the setting for a contest between Christianity and Taoism. Thea Astley's novel, *An Item from the Late News*, set in the dust bowl of a western Queensland mining area, also employs symbolic resonances of the desert as a place of material and spiritual privation, paradoxically inhabited by both saints (in the person of Wafer who has divested himself of all possessions except one) and sinners (whose avarice stops at nothing, even gang murder).

The 1980s and 1990s saw a further literary reshaping of the Australian desert as the locus of Aboriginal culture and environmental values, often presented in strongly didactic terms and endowed with unique spiritual insights. Thus in Bruce Pascoe's *Fox* the desert signifies both the locus and the means whereby the protagonist,

Fox, on the run from the police, discovers his Aboriginality and regains the spiritual illumination available to his people. The true desert, as opposed to the regions desecrated by white settlers, is characterized as ancient, immense and unchanging, as symbolized by the ancient trees, patterns of bird life and the rituals of the indigenous inhabitants. Pascoe insists that this identification with Nature cannot be made through an act of will. Aboriginal knowledge is conceptual rather than perceptual, derived not from observation but from initiation into traditions that are intimately linked with the idea of the sacredness of the land.

Similarly, Brad Collis's *Soul Stone* describes the pilgrimage of a Catholic priest, Simon Bradbury, into the desert wilderness where he learns from the Aboriginal elders the spiritual meaning present in the land. Collis's characters are authorially judged by their response to the desert. Nearly all the Euro Australians hate and fear the desert, because it threatens their acquisitiveness, but to the novel's moral heroes it is the source of truth. Making a personal retreat in the Great Victoria Desert, Simon experiences through the process of initiation "wonderful mysteries . . . a tangible spiritual dimension; a dimension that was a product of this land" (pp. 363–364). His sermon in the cathedral on his return to Perth, which outrages his bishop and bewilders his white congregation, enunciates his epiphanic experience: "'I discovered a wonderful truth and beauty; a knowledge that we here are blessed to dwell in such an ancient land that is suffused with spiritual presence. . . . [God] comes from the land . . . this ancient unspoiled land. . . . Listen to the land and its people . . . seek out the songlines that only they can teach'" (p. 415).

In Australian literature of the 1990s the desert is almost exclusively the preserve of Aborigines. Astley's novel represents one of the very few instances where a non-Aboriginal person is permitted to embody the spiritual enlightenment associated with sojourn in this modern wilderness.

Notes

1. The name "Jindyworobak" was derived by Ingamells from the word "Jindy-worabak" meaning "to annex, to join," which he found in the glossary of James Devaney's *Vanished Tribes* (1929).

2. *Alchera* or *Alcheringa* (the adjective) is the Aranda-language word for what is most often

known as the "Dreamtime." Ingamells came across it when reading Spencer and Gillen's seminal work, *The Arunta,* a new edition of the earlier and little read *The Native Tribes of Central Australia* (1899).

Selected Works and Further Reading

Astley, Thea, *An Item from the Late News,* New York: University of Queensland Press, 1982; Harmondsworth, England: Penguin, 1984

Collis, Brad, *The Soul Stone,* Rydalmere, Australia: Hodder & Stoughton, 1993

Elliott, Brian, ed., *The Jindyworobaks,* St. Lucia, Australia: University of Queensland Press, 1979

Favence, Ernest, "In the Desert," *Queenslander* (May 3, 1879); reproduced in *The Poets' Discovery: Nineteenth-Century Australian Verse,* edited by Peter Pierce, Carleton, Australia, and Portland, Oregon: Melbourne University Press, 1990

Hope, A. D. "Australia," in *Collected Poems, 1930–1970,* London: Angus & Robertson, 1972

Kendall, Henry, *Selected Poems,* edited by T. Inglis Moore, Sydney, Australia: Angus & Robertson, 1957; also published as *Selected Poems of Henry Kendall,* Sydney, Australia, and London: Angus & Robertson, 1975

McAuley, James, "Envoi," in *Selected Poems,* Sydney, Australia: Angus & Robertson, 1963

Pascoe, Bruce, *Fox,* Fitzroy, Australia: McPhee Gribble/Penguin, 1988

Prichard, Katharine Susannah, *Coonardoo,* London: J. Cape, 1929; New York: W. W. Norton, 1930

Spencer, Baldwin, Sir, and Francis J. Gillen, *The Arunta: A Study of a Stone Age People,* London: Macmillan, 1927

Stow, Randolph, *A Counterfeit Silence,* Sydney, Australia: Angus & Robertson, 1969; London: Angus & Robertson, 1977

———, *Tourmaline,* London: Macdonald, 1963; New York: Taplinger, 1983

Webb, Francis, *Collected Poems,* Sydney, Australia: Angus & Robertson, 1969

White, Patrick, *Voss,* London: Eyre & Spottiswoode, 1957; New York and Harmondsworth, England: Penguin, 1960

Early Perceptions of the Natural History
of Australia in Popular Literature

Nick Drayson

It has been suggested that Australia lacks a tradition of intimate nature writing, and that it has still to find its Edward Hoagland or Annie Dillard (Grant, 30–34). This is wrong. Books by Australian contemporaries of Hoagland and Dillard, such as Graham Pizzey's *A Time to Look*, Barbara York Main's *Between Wodjil and Tor*, Vincent Serventy's *Dryandra: The Story of an Australian Forest* and Robin Hill's *The Corner: A Naturalist's Journeys in South-Eastern Australia* are written in a personal, intimate style that not only shows deep understanding of the natural world but also brings out its beauty. They are the modern nature literature of Australia. But these books did not arise de novo. Nature writing in Australia has a rich past. This chapter examines the genesis of Australian natural history writing and explores some of the main themes found there—notably the tension between strangeness and beauty in this wide brown land.

A literature of Australian natural history has been accumulating since the earliest written descriptions of this land. From the first matter-of-fact observations of European voyagers, through the journals of English immigrants who saw Australia as a strange place yet one that could only be understood in terms of the science and arts of European civilization, a deeper understanding and affection for the nature of Australia has evolved.

To Europeans Australia is a new country, but it is an old land. It is a land whose features have been worn flat by time. Its few ancient mountains are now hardly more than hills, its rivers meander so slowly that most of the water evaporates before it reaches the oceans. In this ancient southern land has evolved a flora and fauna very different from that of the north.

The flora of Australia is based on the elements it inherited when the southern supercontinent of Gondwana finally split up about 60 million years ago. Shaped by poverty of soil and dryness of climate, it is dominated by eucalyptus and other thick-leaved trees and shrubs. Australia's fauna also largely derives from Gondwana, especially its mammals. Apart from the many species of bats and a rich rodent population probably derived from Asia, Australian terrestrial mammals are mostly marsupials, bearing small young that feed and grow safe within their mother's pouch. The Australian bird fauna is more complex, with Gondwanan elements represented by the flightless emus and cassowaries but also with many pan-tropical taxa such as parrots; with their bright plumage and loud calls, parrots are one of the most conspicuous elements of the Australian avifauna.

Conspicuousness has always been an important trait in the study of natural history. Birds and mammals are conspicuous, although they comprise only a small fraction of total animal species and of the Australian fauna in particular (Australia, roughly the same size as the United States, has fewer than half the number of terrestrial mammals). But they are the animals most obvious to humans and therefore the subject of most natural history writing. This chapter, therefore, will focus mainly on the plants, birds and mammals of Australia.

Although the fundamentals of climate, geology and biogeography are largely responsible for the natural history of Australia today, humans have also been an important influence. Humans have been in Australia for at least 50,000 years. By their use of "fire stick farming" they have greatly influenced the vegetation, and hence the fauna, of the continent. For millennia Aboriginal Australians have used fire to encourage feed for game animals (this practice, as well as hunting, may have combined with climatic changes to cause the extinction of the extensive marsupial megafauna that existed in Australia up to about 10,000 years ago). Plants and animals are, and probably always were, of great importance to Aboriginal culture. But few written records of their knowledge exist: this chapter will necessarily concentrate on perceptions of Australian natural history by visitors and settlers from Europe.

The earliest European visitors to Australia were seafarers, who although well-travelled saw Australia through European eyes. They naturally named the strange animals of the new continent after those with which they were familiar. Thus in 1629 the Dutch sailor Francisco Pelsaert landed on the Abrolhos Islands off Western Australia and found "cats"—although cats in which "the female carries a pouch, into which you may put your hand; inside this pouch are her nipples, and we have found that the young ones grow up in this pouch with the nipples in their mouths" (quoted in Whitley, 11). These were in fact Tammar Wallabies (*Macropus eugenii*). In 1699 the English buccaneer William Dampier landed several times on the northwest coast of Australia in search of water and saw "Heath, much of a kind we have growing on our commons in England. . . . a Sort of Raccoons, different from those of the West Indies, chiefly as to their Legs; for these have very short Fore-Legs; but go jumping upon them as the others do" (Dampier, 108).

Dampier's "raccoons" were in fact Banded Hare-wallabies (*Lagostrophus fasciatus*), but Dampier was describing the flora and fauna of the new continent in terms of the already familiar, either from England (heath) or elsewhere (raccoons, from the Americas). This form of description, using the names of familiar animals to describe the new fauna, was common to most early descriptions of Australian natural history.

It was used extensively by James Cook and his botanist companion Joseph Banks on their visit to the east coast in 1770. At Botany Bay (near what is now Sydney) they saw "an Animal something like a Rabbit" and recorded "a variety of very Beautiful birds, such as Cocatoos, Lorryquets, Parrots, etc., and crows Exactly like those we have in England" (Cook, 248, 260). However, Banks soon realized that the flora and fauna of the new continent were unique, and although James Cook found no difficulty in naming Australian birds after birds with which he was already familiar (the avifauna of Australia is mostly endemic at the species level but many of the most obvious birds—parrots being a notable

example—have similar relations in other parts of the world), he had problems with the mammals. In Botany Bay the party had already caught tantalizing glimpses of unusual mammals; further north in Queensland Cook saw an animal "the full size of Grey Hound," but one that was so different from anything he had seen before he could not find an existing name. Instead he used the native name, "Kangooroo" (Cook, 281, 294).

The use of an Australian native name was important. It was an implicit recognition that these animals had no place in the existing systems of naming and describing natural history. However, the recognition did not extend to all new species. Cook later used the word "opossum" to describe the only other marsupial he encountered (the Common Ringtail Possum, *Pseudocheirus peregrinus*), a word that had originally entered the English language from North America. Subsequent naming of Australian animals continued to be from both Aboriginal (wombat, koala, kookaburra) and non-Aboriginal sources (emu, cockatoo, native cat).

These earliest European visitors to Australia were well-travelled and used to novelty. With the arrival of the first convicts and their guards at Botany Bay in 1788 came a different type of immigrant, to whom Australia was not only more strange, but also hostile. Brought here against their will, and with little experience of foreign lands, these newcomers at first found Australia a difficult and threatening environment. But as the colony grew and prospered it soon became clear that although Australian plants and animals may have been strange and unsuited to the agricultural demands of the settlers, they were not particularly dangerous. Strange, useless and harmless, the natural history of Australia soon came to be held in mild contempt. In the early nineteenth century this became exemplified by the notion that Australia was "a land of contrarieties."

Australia's geographical position at the antipodes had long caught the imagination of people in the northern hemisphere. It was summer in Australia when it was winter in Europe, night was day, the cold winds came from the south. To these opposites were added the perceived peculiarities of its natural history. Barron Field, an English lawyer who came to the colony as judge in 1816, listed some of them

> Australia is the land of contrarieties, where the laws of nature seem reversed . . . where the swans are black and the eagles white; where

the kangaroo, an animal between the squirrel and the deer, has five claws on its fore paws, and three talons on its hind legs, like a bird, and yet hops on its tail; where the mole . . . lays eggs, suckles its young, and has a duck's bill; where there is a bird . . . with a broom in its mouth instead of a tongue; . . . where the pears are of wood . . . with the stalk at the broader end; and where the cherry . . . grows with the stone on the outside. (pp. 461–462)

These descriptions are all based on real Australian plants and animals, but seen as being "contrary" to the norm. Once Field's idea of Australia as a "Land of Contrariety" took hold it had a tenacious grip. From then on it was found in many descriptions of Australia, and was added to and elaborated upon throughout the century.

But although the natural history of Australia was strange to many European eyes, it was not without interest to the naturalist. From early days descriptions of Australian flora and fauna—in both scientific and popular publications—had appeared in a steady stream in Europe, usually based on dried, stuffed or pickled specimens. But as Barron Field had written of Australia, "her zoology can only be studied and unravelled on the spot, and that too only by a profound philosopher" (p. viii). One man eager to be that "profound philosopher" was George Bennett, a surgeon and friend of the great British anatomist Richard Owen, who arrived in Australia in 1832. As well as publishing in medical and scientific journals, Bennett wrote popular accounts of his travels. These were widely quoted and referred to during his own lifetime and have been described as "classics of nineteenth century natural history literature" (Newland, 57).

Although Bennett brought a more scientific vision to interpreting the nature of Australia, he was still blinkered by the attitudes and prejudices of his time. Whereas he could appreciate the beauty of individual flowers, Australian forests were "dull" and "gloomy," its trees "curious" and "peculiar" compared to those of Europe and Asia. But Bennett appreciated plants and animals more for their scientific than aesthetic value. To him they were specimens, and although Bennett thought of his specimens not as individuals but as parts of a whole, the whole was not nature—it was science. Lynn Merrill has suggested that in nineteenth century Britain the aesthetic of natural history was dialectical,

"moving from particulars to panorama and back again" (p. 56). For George Bennett in Australia, it was science rather than nature that provided the "panorama" against which the particular specimens could be viewed. With nature perceived as contrary and even ugly, this was a major influence on much early writing about the natural history of Australia.

To some degree George Bennett bridged the gap between the professional and the amateur naturalist that developed during the middle of the nineteenth century (for Britain, *see* Allen; for Australia, *see* Moyal and Mozley Moyal), later popular writers, however, were more firmly in the amateur camp. One such was the poet Louisa Meredith, who arrived in Australia in 1839 and over the next 50 years published several books describing its wildlife. Like Bennett she was an able botanist, but Meredith's descriptions differed markedly from his. Her poetry was strongly influenced by the English Romantic tradition, and her natural history observations were also tinged with the Romantic and the anthropomorphic. Australian flowers were transformed into fairies, Australian birds became people (e.g., p. 47). Again, the natural history of Australia was transmuted through European perception.

Before her arrival in Australia Meredith had done much to popularize the study of natural history in England; during the subsequent decades its popularity grew (*see* Barber and Merrill). When bank clerk and amateur naturalist Samuel Hannaford arrived in Australia from England in 1852, he soon realized that the country offered great scope for such an amateur, and for a writer. He wrote what were the earliest field guides to the flora and fauna of Australia.

Hannaford's books were very much in the tradition of British popular seaside natural history writing exemplified by the English clerics Philip Gosse and Charles Kingsley, whose frequent references to Nature as God's handiwork so closely reflected the Natural Theology of William Paley (e.g., Gosse, foreword). Like Kingsley, however, Hannaford was eager to assure his readers that natural history was not, as some had suggested, "effeminate" (Kingsley, 40). Although Hannaford acknowledged that "Ladies, by the bye, are always capital collectors, accurately discriminating between species, and sure to find the prettiest and most delicate of everything" (p. 103), his ideal naturalist was a man.

Charles Kingsley had written that the ideal naturalist was "strong in body; able to haul a dredge, climb a rock, turn a boulder, walk all day . . . eat or drink thankfully anything . . . pull an oar, sail a boat, and ride the first horse that comes to hand; and, finally, he should be a thoroughly good shot, and a skilful fisherman and, if he go far abroad, be able on occasion to fight for his life" (p. 43). Hannaford strongly approved of this ideal, although as a provincial bank clerk he could never hope to realize it. One man who did was Horace Wheelwright. Australia had always been a man's country, and when Wheelwright arrived from England in 1852 during the first frenzy of the great gold rushes of Victoria, men were arriving from all corners of the world to search for yellow metal in the harsh conditions of the Australian bush. Wheelwright wrote about his experiences of that time when, living in the bush, he shot game to sell in the booming city of Melbourne. In *Bush Wanderings of a Naturalist*, Wheelwright started a different strand in Australian natural history writing—natural history for men.

Wheelwright was fascinated by the animals of Australia, but along with detailed descriptions of Australian fauna he included information on how to find, kill, skin and cook it. And because in nineteenth century Australia such "sport" was no work for women, women were excluded from Wheelwright's world and his writing.

Yet despite his utilitarian, and what some see as "masculinist" approach to the natural history of Australia (*see* Griffiths), Wheelwright was aware of its aesthetic value. He enjoyed the study of ornithology and loved the songs of Australian birds (Wheelwright, 137). Wheelwright denied, like Meredith and many other writers before, the popular conception that Australia was the land of scentless flowers and songless birds (this was a recurring theme in nineteenth-century descriptions of the natural history of Australia, often linked with the notion of "contrariety"). In his artless way, Wheelwright helped created a new art of natural history literature in Australia.

Previous writers had also found beauty in the Australian bush, despite cultural preconceptions. Bennett may have treated the plants and animals of Australia as scientific specimens, Meredith as characters in Romantic poems, but still their writing revealed something of the essential beauty of Australian nature. As the century progressed, this appreciation became more marked. The natural history of Australia came to be seen in Australian terms

There were many underlying social and his-

torical influences on this change of attitude. Society in Australia had gone from a convict/military regime, through expansions fueled by agricultural and pastoral settlement and the boom times of the gold rushes, into a more solid, civilized maturity. The centenary of European settlement was celebrated in 1888, and with an increasingly native-born white population, Australian society was more self-confident. This confidence was exemplified in natural history writing. Rather than seeing the plants and animals of Australia as inferior and contrary, a new generation of writers were able to appreciate the beauty of their natural history with Australian eyes. Notable among these was Donald Macdonald.

Macdonald was born near Melbourne in 1859. He became a reporter and journalist, but was best known for his nature writing in various Melbourne newspapers. A collection of this writing was published in 1883 as *Gum Boughs and Wattle Bloom, Gathered on Australian Hills and Plains*. The very title of this book bespoke its self-conscious and self-confident Australian identity—"for the Gum is more correctly a Eucalyptus, and the Wattle an Acacia" (p. vi).

Macdonald considered himself neither scientist nor naturalist, but saw in nature the same beauty that in England had been described by Richard Jefferies and in the United States by Henry David Thoreau, both of whom Macdonald read and admired. "Personally," he wrote, "I claim to be nothing more than a bush loafer, with the time and mood occasionally to give an eye and ear to Nature;—what Robert Louis Stevenson called that strange American, Thoreau, a skulker—and not within a hundred miles of being a scientist" (p. 248).

Macdonald's importance to natural history writing in Australia was twofold. He was mentor to later writers such as Charles Barrett and Alec Chisholm and had a strong influence on their writing (*see* Griffiths), but more importantly Macdonald's own writing showed a new maturity in Australians' attitude to their own country. He wrote in a deliberately literary rather than journalistic style, which not only added its own aesthetic element to Australian natural history writing but helped Australians appreciate that their own flora and fauna was not something to be denigrated or scorned—that it could be treated with not only affection but respect.

Macdonald's descriptions of flora and fauna of Victoria, whether on the wide plains of the

Murray River, in the dense coastal forests, or in the restricted confines of the Melbourne Botanical Gardens, were celebrations of a beauty that was uniquely Australian. They were well received. Macdonald and his protege Charles Barrett were so highly regarded in the late nineteenth and early twentieth centuries that one literary critic even compared their descriptions of the natural history of Melbourne with Gilbert White's seminal English book *A Natural History of Selborne* (Bernard O'Dowd, quoted in Griffiths, 365). Macdonald above all helped break the bonds of colonialism in popular perceptions of Australian natural history.

This chapter has examined some of the writing and themes of natural history writing that developed in Australia up to the twentieth century. This century has also seen great developments in the genre. But apart from a few casual references in historical and literary studies and a handful of anthologies (Chisholm; Pollard; Pizzey, *Graham Pizzey*), the literary wealth of Australian natural history has never been fully investigated, nor even defined. I am currently engaged in writing a book on the genre, as well as compiling a bibliography and an anthology. As I hope to show in this chapter, it is an area well worth exploring.

Selected Works and Further Reading

Allen, David Elliston, *The Naturalist in Britain: A Social History,* London: A. Lane, 1976; New York: Penguin, 1978

Barber, Lynn, *The Heyday of Natural History, 1820–1870,* Garden City, New York: Doubleday, 1980; London: J. Cape, 1980

Bennett, George, *Gatherings of a Naturalist in Australasia: Being Observations Principally on the Animal and Vegetable Productions of New South Wales, New Zealand, and Some of the Austral Islands,* London: J. Van Voorst, 1860

———, *Wanderings in New South Wales, Batavia, Pedir Coast, Singapore, and China: Being the Journal of a Naturalist in These Countries, During 1832, 1833, and 1834,* 2 vols., London: Bentley, 1967

Chisholm, Alec Hugh, ed., *Land of Wonder: The Best Australian Nature Writing,* Sydney, Australia: Angus and Robertson, 1964

Cook, James, *The Journals of Captain James Cook on His Voyages of Discovery,* 4 vols., Cambridge: Hakluyt Society, 1955–1974

Dampier, William, *A Voyage to New Holland,* London: James Knapton, 1703

Field, Barron, ed., *Geographical Memoirs on New South Wales; by Various Hands . . . Together with Other Papers on the Aborigines, the Geology, the Botany, the Timber, the Astronomy, and the Meteorology of New South Wales and Van Diemen's Land,* London: J. Murray, 1825

Gosse, Philip Henry, *The Ocean,* London: Society for Promoting Christian Knowledge, 1845; also published as *The Wonders of the Great Deep, or, The Physical, Animal, Geological, and Vegetable Curiosities of the Ocean,* New York: J. W. Lovell, 1880

Grant, Peter, "A Half Open Door," *Island* 53 (1992), pp. 30–34

Griffiths, Tom, *Hunters and Collectors: The Antiquarian Imagination in Australia,* New York and Cambridge: Cambridge University Press, 1996

———, "The Natural History of Melbourne: The Culture of Nature Writing in Victoria, 1880–1945," *Australian Historical Studies* 23:93 (1989), pp. 339–365

Hannaford, Samuel, *Jottings in Australia; or, Notes on the Flora and Fauna of Victoria: With a Catalogue of the More Common Plants, Their Habitats, and Dates of Flowering,* Melbourne, Australia: James J. Blundell, 1856

———, *Sea and River-side Rambles in Victoria: Being a Handbook for Those Seeking Recreation During the Summer Months,* Geelong, Australia: Heath & Cordell, 1860

———, *Wild Flowers of Tasmania: or, Chatty Rambles Afloat and Ashore, Amidst the Seaweeds, Ferns, and Flowering Plants: with a Complete List of Indigenous Ferns, and Instructions for Their Cultivation,* Melbourne, Australia: F. F. Bailliere, 1866

Hill, Robin, *The Corner: A Naturalist's Journeys in South-Eastern Australia,* Melbourne, Australia: Lansdowne, 1970

Kingsley, Charles, *Glaucus: or, The Wonders of the Shore,* Boston: Ticknor and Fields, 1855; Cambridge: Macmillan, 1855

Macdonald, Donald, "A Flake of Wild Honey," *The New Idea* (November 6, 1903), pp. 427–429

———, *Gum Boughs and Wattle Bloom, Gathered on Australian Hills and Plains,* London: Cassell, 1887

Main, Barbara York, *Between Wodjil and Tor,* Melbourne, Australia: Jacaranda, 1967

Meredith, Charles, Mrs., *Notes and Sketches of New South Wales: During a Residence in That Colony from 1839 to 1844,* London: John Murray, 1844

Merrill, Lynn L., *The Romance of Victorian Natural History,* New York: Oxford University Press, 1989

Moyal, Ann Mozley, *A Bright & Savage Land: Scientists in Colonial Australia,* Sydney, Australia: Collins, 1986; new ed., New York: Penguin, 1993

———, ed., *Scientists in Nineteenth Century Australia: A Documentary History,* Melbourne: Cassell Australia, 1975

Newland, Elizabeth Dalton, "Dr. George Bennett and Sir Richard Owen: A Case Study of the Colonization of Early Australian Science," in *International Science and National Scientific Identity: Australia Between Britain and America,* edited by Roderick W. Home and Sally G. Kohlstedt, Boston and Dordrecht, The Netherlands: Kluwer Academic, 1991

O'Dowd, Bernard, "Wood-Wind and Wattle Breath," *The Socialist* (November 1, 1908)

Pizzey, Graham, *Graham Pizzey Introduces Stories of Australian Birds,* Melbourne, Australia: Currey O'Neil, 1983

———, *A Time to Look,* Melbourne, Australia: Heinemann, 1958

Pollard, Jack, comp., *Birds of Paradox; Birdlife in Australia and New Zealand,* Melbourne, Australia: Lansdowne, 1967

Serventy, Vincent, *Dryandra: The Story of an Australian Forest,* Sydney, Australia: A. H. and A. W. Reed, 1970

Wheelwright, Horace William, *Bush Wanderings of a Naturalist; or, Notes on the Field Sports and Fauna of Australia Felix,* New York and London: Routledge, Warne, & Routledge, 1861

Whitley, Gilbert Percy, *Early History of Australian Zoology,* Sydney, Australia: Royal Zoological Society of New South Wales, 1970

Ecological Restoration and the Evolution of Postcolonial National Identity in the Maori and Australian Aboriginal Novel

C. Christopher Norden

The restoration of degraded ecosystems appears as an integral element of a broader program of cultural recovery in many Native and Third World literary traditions, including those of the Maori of New Zealand and the Aboriginal peoples of Australia. As represented by indigenous novelists, the twinned process of cultural and environmental recovery includes the reclaiming of traditional homelands; a return to a traditional, sustainable, and locally constituted economic base; and the reuniting of scattered or diasporic families, clans, and tribes. Protagonists often evolve from alienated, detribalized individuals into culture heroes, restoring landscape, physical infrastructure, and also interrupted bonds within the tribal community as components of a unified and fundamentally unparseable process of recovery. Enabling these evolutionary returns to more functional and traditional forms of cultural practice is the restoration of an orally based narrative tradition, with various forms of written narrative figured as useful tools for the articulation and recovery of oral values and cultural forms.

First novels by three well known Maori writers, Witi Ihimaera's *Tangi*, Patricia Grace's *Mutuwhenua: The Moon Sleeps*, and Keri Hulme's *The Bone People*, offer variations on a common syntax of alienation, homecoming, and ecosystemic restoration. In each novel, a Maori protagonist returns from a period of alienated self-exile, and in so doing fulfills an ancient prophecy foretelling the return of a restorationist culture hero. An incarnation of a founder or creator, the returning culture hero will restore the culture's eroded spiritual base by reaffirming ritually articulated bonds of interdependence between individual, community, and landscape.

Significantly, this reaffirmation of culture does not occur on a solely rhetorical level, but involves the actual rehabilitation of degraded land and of an ecosystem shown to include human as well as animal communities, and the land itself. The apotheosis of the culture hero's act of restoration, then, is the transformation of a waste land back into a holy and fertile homeland capable of providing long term sustainability in both economic and spiritual senses.

In terms of its international reception, the Australian Aboriginal novelistic tradition is largely the province of one major writer, Mudrooroo (formerly Colin Johnson). A number of Aboriginal writers concerned with the role of environmental restoration in the process of cultural recovery, however, have succeeded in finding broad audiences both in Australia and abroad, including memoirist Sally Morgan; short story writer Archie Weller; memoirist, short story writer and poet Oodgeroo Nunukul (Kath Walker); poet, historian, and cultural critic Kevin Gilbert; and poet, playwright, and prose author Jack Davis.

In several important ways, the Aboriginal novelistic tradition parallels the Maori tradition in terms of the development of an internationalized, environmentally and ecologically based narrative counter-tradition. Several of Mudrooroo's novels represent a return to a cultural metaphysics that is fundamentally contrary to the set of assumptions regarding individual identity that motivates the Anglo- European modernist novelistic tradition. In so doing, Mudrooroo both refutes and seeks to correct a broad range of assumptions about what constitutes progress, both historically and in modern times. This is most particularly true of Mudrooroo's radically revisionist history of the colonization of Australia, a novel entitled *Doctor Wooreddy's Prescription for Enduring the Ending of the World*, which simultaneously rejects colonial European metaphysics and politics while pointing to traditional Aboriginal ecologies of wholeness and sustainable use, sacred hunting and harvesting of food, and, importantly, ritualized roles for human beings as sustainers and stewards of the world. In each instance, Mudrooroo demonstrates the crucial role played by an uninterrupted narrative tradition as the sole means by which these values are transmitted, preserved, and made sacred. The apocalyptic "ending of the world" experienced by tribal cultures under colonialism thus alludes not only to physical genocide, but also to a cultural genocide that is itself a direct function of denarrativization, or the loss and interruption of narrative tradition.

Rather than denoting cultural and historical redundancy, moral diminishment, and the impossibility of genuinely heroic action, Maori and Aboriginal cosmologies share in common with many other orally based Native traditions the belief that the present day individual must ritually reenact the creative deeds of his or her culture's founders—its culture heroes—if the culture is to survive and thrive in the present day. This ritual reenactment occurs both in cultural terms, as narrative performance, with oral storytelling or dance serving to recount and resurrect tribal history, and also in directly ecological terms, as stewardship of traditional homelands.

While the Anglo-American modernist tradition of the early to mid-twentieth century offered a degraded, absurdist, even nihilistic version of the pastoral relationship between human beings and natural landscapes, the seeming triviality, redundancy, and unimportance of the detribalized and denatured modern individual is figured as a soluble historical and cultural dilemma in many modern day indigenous narratives. Modern Maori and Aboriginal narratives and rituals emphasize, in much the same way as do their counterparts in performed ritual and oral storytelling, the importance of each tribe member in maintaining the health and wholeness of family, culture, and homeland, ecosystems of which that individual is a necessary and irreplaceable part.

Mudrooroo's *Doctor Wooreddy's Prescription*

Not coincidentally, both Aboriginal and European cultures hold land to be the single most important factor in a society's ability to achieve collective happiness and success. But as Aboriginal novelist, critic, and scholar Mudrooroo graphically illustrates in his novel *Doctor Wooreddy's Prescription for Enduring the Ending of the World*, a dialectical worldview based on a pernicious myth of absolute cultural difference and animated in the form of a militarized colonial enterprise has the unfortunate effect of turning tools of mutual aid and common understanding, such as language, technology, and religion, into weapons potentially fatal to indigenous cultures, native ecosystems, and the people and animals that inhabit those ecosystems. The key to overcoming absolute difference, and thereby initiating dialogue on the subject of sustainable modes of living, lies not in a forced and imperfect reconciling of Native and colonial metaphysics, he argues, but rather in the discovery of a common interest in the preservation of the land as a fundamental and potentially boundless source of the good life.

Novels such as *Doctor Wooreddy's Prescription* are potential agents of cultural transformation and healing for both Native and non-Native members of a transitionally post-colonial society; in laying bare the historical processes by which Aboriginally owned land was denarrativized and reinscribed with a colonial mythos and ideology, Mudrooroo sets the stage for a renaissance of cultural narrative focusing on the land. Non-indigenous readers are left to speculate whether such a return to the land-based roots of human narrative tradition must of necessity be cessationist, or whether it might eventually include both Native and postcolonial non-Native traditions and values, set not in conflict but rather in dialogue. In fact, the dialogical or multi-voiced nature of *Doctor Wooreddy's Prescription* and specifically Mudrooroo's representations of traditional oral community suggests the possibility of dialogue across cultural lines. Most tribally derived models of oral culture involve the creation of a collective identity based on mutual well-being and common interest, while at the same time allowing local and even individual idiosyncrasies and differences to exist and flourish.

Doctor Wooreddy's Prescription is first and foremost a critique, an indictment of colonial practices of physical and cultural genocide, yet its primary rhetorical objective is that of community-building. This community building impulse is directed both to the reanimation of an Aboriginal community that has been fragmented by centuries of colonial history, and also to the establishment of a long-deferred postcolonial dialogue between Aboriginal and non-Aboriginal Australian cultures founded on mutual respect, cooperation, and, importantly, common interest solutions to root problems often displaced by a primary emphasis on the enduring symptomatic problems of white paternalism and black victimization.

Cultural differences, and specifically the institutionalized concepts of land ownership and resource management, are seen as at root political, and thus relative and changeable rather than metaphysically ingrained in the deepest fundament of a culture's collective psyche. By bringing issues of property ownership and land management out of the realm of the metaphysically absolute, a realm that broaches no discussion or negotiation, and putting them into the realm of the metaphysically relative, the realm of the ethical and the political, the Aboriginal novel opens a door to dialogue that had been previously held shut by a bolt of absolute cultural difference. Once cultural readings of the good life come open to debate and redefinition, a collectivized good life based in part on Aboriginal recovery and stewardship of sacred lands becomes a possibility. Again, the historical novel plays an important role in facilitating such a sense of community. Disseminated to a Euro-colonial audience, detailed accounts of genocidal practice often serve to discredit national founding myths invested in the false idea that colonial nations were carved out of uninhabited territory.

Mudrooroo's novel argues that the historical process of colonization involves parallel dislocations for both Aboriginal and colonial peoples, in which the sacred, narrative-based, and ritualized relationship between human culture and natural environment is broken: "Before, uneventful time had stretched back towards the known beginning. Now, it seemed that something had torn the present away from that past" (p. 5). At the same time, Mudrooroo holds opens the possibility that a subsequent narrative reconstruction of Australian national culture may come to include not just Aboriginal voicings of the origin and nature of the land, but also multiculturally voiced readings of a spiritually animated landscape not unlike those that served as the philosophical and religious foundations of Aboriginal culture prior to, during, and after its holocaust.

Doctor Wooreddy's Prescription features several embedded narratives clearly intended to evoke the oral creation stories that are the spiritual foundation of Aboriginal tribal culture, narratives keyed to the physical landscape of the tribe's homeland: "'Those birdmen, those two messengers from Great Ancestor, did not fly off into the sky. They stayed on in our country and you will see the marks of their camping places . . .'" (pp. 6–7). Here as elsewhere, Mudrooroo points to the absolute importance of an intact narrative tradition for the survival of any culture, whether orally based or literate. Without this connection to the land, the past, and to its own sense of community, a tribe or society is reduced to atomized, alienated individuals, each of whom is left to experience alone an apocalyptic "ending of the world."

Critiquing his first two novels, *Wildcat Falling*, and *Long Live Sandawara*, Mudrooroo states that "they lack a basic underpinning of community . . . this is what Aboriginal novels should be aiming for, I think, to have the feeling of community; not existing in isolation, bourgeois isolation, as an individual" (p. 31). Given its potential ability to critique and resist institutional narratives of control and central authority, the dialogic novel (multivoiced, polyphonic, or "heteroglossic," to use Mikhail Bakhtin's term) seems particularly well suited to enacting a critique of colonially imposed psychological individualism, this being a necessary first step in the reconstruction of a collectively constituted Aboriginal and/or Australian national identity.

Patricia Grace's *Mutuwhenua*

While postcolonial narrative often seeks the recovery or restoration of lost or repressed history, subaltern writing such as Mudrooroo's concerns itself with the retelling of colonial history from the perspective of colonialism's indigenous victims. A related trope in indigenous postcolonial narrative is that of ecological restoration, focused particularly on the restoration of the indigenous culture's stewardship role relative to the natural world. This stewardship role, we come to understand, is instrumental in the recovery of meaning for tribal and non-tribal individuals alike. As the problem of alienated modernity is commonly represented by both Native and non-Native writers in terms of urbanization, atomization of both consciousness and conscience, and loss of place, so is the solution to this crisis often found in a recovery of a lost sense of ecologically based tribal or collective identity.

In a manner reminiscent of Zora Neale Hurston's *Their Eyes Were Watching God*, Maori author Patricia Grace's novel *Mutuwhenua: The Moon Sleeps*, another novel of a minority woman's coming of age, exile, and eventual homecoming, begins with the image of several related species of trees indigenous to New Zealand. But unlike Hurston's pear tree, Grace's trees signify not just metaphorically, but also literally, biologically. Grace's ti kouka, ngaio, and macrocarpa trees symbolize the dreams and aspirations of her Maori protagonist Ripeka, who as "Linda" hopes to find a happy life with her new Pakeha (white) husband. In addition, Ripeka's trees also suggest family integrity; cultural unity and continuity; and, finally, ecological health and land stewardship: "The ti kouka had been brought down from the bush when my father was a small boy; in front of it stands a ngaio tree that was planted at the time I was born" (p. 1). We are encouraged to see landscape not simply as a mirror or a projection of the human mind—its fears, desires, and ambitions—but in fact as a participant in the ongoing dialogue that constitutes a living culture, a dialogue about the land and its relation to the humans and other species that live on it.

Grace's trees do function metaphorically, to denote the work of maintaining continuity and unity in a family and a culture, yet at the same time, she suggests that this condition of cultural health is intimately related to the health of the land itself. Ripeka identifies herself with the ngaio tree, which seems evenly shaped and unremarkable at first: "'Not until you get in close to it do you discover the pained twisting of its limbs and the scarring on the patterned skin, but even so it is a quiet tree. I was named after it'" (p. 1).

Nature—the green world in its physical and biological sense—is the ground on which culture flourishes, and as human communities care for their homeland, so do individuals thrive as members of a stewardship-based culture. Ripeka sees in the thick roots of an old macrocarpa tree a living metaphor for continuity in human families: "'. . . without its strength against the wind that licks through the gully there, the others—the ti kouka and the one that gave me the name—would not have taken root and flourished'" (pp. 1–2).

It may be said that the novel as we know it takes as its province the interval between knowledge and action, the lag time between knowing the truth intuitively and finally being able to act on that truth. Looking back on her suburban

marriage and her time away from her family, Ripeka acknowledges that her self-exile took place despite her awareness of a higher order of value based on family and a culturally based spiritual connection to the land: "'. . . I've always known that land can love its people and always understood the reciprocity between people and land'" (p. 110).

The acts of restoration that provide closure to Grace's circular narrative of departure and return are twofold. Ripeka and her cousins Toki and Hemi, each a missing but necessary part of an incomplete family, culture, and ecosystem, are all restored to their proper places. But Ripeka knows that it is her foretold destiny to live away from her immediate family and homeland as a cultural emissary, as an incarnation of the mythological Rona, who clings to the roots of a ngaio tree as she is carried away by the moon, thus carrying the tree up with her, roots and all.

In preparation for her return to a bicultural life with her husband, Ripeka enters into a period of active stewardship, ensuring a permanent connection to the land and to the son she is temporarily leaving. She plants a ti kouka tree, content in the knowledge that both boy and sapling will be nurtured and cared for best in the homeland to which she herself will soon return (p. 152–153).

Witi Ihimaera's *Tangi*

In Witi Ihimaera's *Tangi*, it is a funeral rather than a wedding that brings the urbanized Maori protagonist home, but as in Grace's *Mutuwhenua*, it is the ritual invocation by both novelist and his characters of a lost and fugitive wholeness of family, tribe, and homeland that sets the deep plot of cultural and ecosystemic restoration in motion. Returning home to Waituhi for his father's *tangi*, or funeral, Tama Mahana reflects on the spiritual poverty of his life in urban Wellington. In a passage reminiscent of Quentin Compson in William Faulkner's *The Sound and the Fury*, Tama realizes that as an urbanized individual, his cultural and familial identity has been radically circumscribed, even atomized: "'I am alone. Time has caught me unaware and taken my father away. Strange really . . . that time should seem to pass only where you are'" (pp. 44–45).

Returning home for his father's funeral, Tama reconstructs his lost ties to family and homeland by first participating in a traditional Maori burial and mourning ritual, or *tangi*, a multi-day ceremony involving the entire extended family or clan. In addition, Tama reaffirms his spiritual bond to his family's land, recalling how his father had previously taught him about the literal identity between a family and its homeland: "Our own place . . . . This was our home, our family. . . . This was Waituhi, our whanau, our family. And we had come home" (p. 112).

The ritual of the *tangi* is itself a culturally prescribed process of restoration and rebuilding; it emphasizes parallel restorations of both narrative tradition and physical infrastructure, calling for a systematic remembering and telling of family history and genealogy, and a many handed refurbishing of both the Mahana clan's traditional meeting house, Rongopai, and the land on which this building stands. Significantly, this restoration involves a return to traditional Maori decorations and symbols, which had been covered over or altered by younger clan members. Again, Tama articulates the identity between family and place, and the inclusiveness of Maori culture and ecology: ". . . for me, Rongopai is like my father. Home. The place of the heart. The centre of my universe" (p. 115).

After this restoration is underway, we witness through Tama's eyes a blooming not only of culture, but of the land itself. Awake in the night while his kin sleep in and around the meeting house, Tama hears a passerby, whistling in the distance: "It is the song of the earth renewing. Of clear streams trickling over parched earth and leaves rustling in the wind. It is the plough turning the fields, the indefinable aroha between earth and man" (p. 181).

For many American readers, parts of Ihimaera's *Tangi* will likely evoke Emerson, Whitman, and the transcendentalist writers of the mid-nineteenth century. An interesting question regarding Native novelistic and poetic traditions concerns the degree to which particular writers have intentionally evoked and played off of either transcendentalist rhetoric, for models of spiritual connectedness, or off of Anglo-American modernist writers for models of alienation from nature, community, and traditional culture.

Like Patricia Grace's Ripeka, Ihimaera's Tama Mahana understands that he must spend a period of his life away from his family before coming home for good. Tama also looks to Maori legend for strength, and understands that he is reenacting the origins of his race, sojourning for a period of time in a world of darkness, in this case a Pakeha society largely ignorant of the spiritual relationship between the land and

its people, before entering into the Maori "world of light."

When Tama returns to Wellington, the terror of modernist isolation (and that terror's narrative syntax also) is bracketed by a deeper spiritual knowledge, by an evocation of both the form and the content of traditional Maori orality: "For a moment, I pause on the steps of the railway station. I am half in light, half in darkness. Shadow and light, my future. It is raining heavily . . ." (p. 203). But the clipped, prosaic sentences quickly become poetic as Tama wills himself to remember a collective identity that supersedes that of a displaced individual: "My mother was the Earth. / My father was the Sky. / They were Rangitane and Papatuanuku, the first parents . . ." (p. 204).

Evoking the cyclical time of orality, Ihimaera enacts a shift of cultural metaphysics, offering in so doing a strong refutation of modernist nihilism, which claims the loss of meaning in present day life to be epistemological and universal rather than merely social or political, and thus peculiar to certain cultural formations. In a Maori cosmology based on the continuous ritual reenactment of creation, ontogeny—or the development of the individual—recapitulates cosmogenesis, or the creation of the world. By this view, individual lives in the present moment are not at all meaningless, diminished relative to a lost or decayed heroic tradition; instead, the modern day individual has both the opportunity and the duty to participate in the literal and ongoing recreation of both culture and cosmos. In addition to offering a sense of cultural, ecological, and even political empowerment, such narratives tend to make exciting and enjoyable reading, and can easily be allegorized or adapted to the circumstances of non-Native readers, including especially those of young adult audiences.

Keri Hulme's *Bone People*

Keri Hulme's 1984 novel *The Bone People* constitutes in one important respect a reworking of Grace's and Ihimaera's earlier narratives. Hulme acknowledges that the modern Maori culture hero's destiny involves both the restoration of culture and homeland, and also self-sacrifice directed toward Maori/Pakeha reconciliation. In the case of Hulme's mixed-race Maori protagonist Kerewin Holmes, however, this sacrifice does not involve a prolonged exile in the outside world. Rather, Hulme presents something of a deep ecology of cultures in which the hard-won goal of intercultural openness and trust stands as prerequisite to the restoration of individual cultures and homelands.

Hulme begins the novel with a solitary Kerewin, self-sufficient culturally and aesthetically (she paints and sculpts, has a substantial personal library, and plays her own compositions on a guitar), and self-sustaining economically and even ecologically (she has money such that she need not work for a living, and harvests from the sea much of what she needs in the way of food). But Kerewin lives in a tower, outside any circle of human community, a strong suggestion that her life may be incomplete and indeed unnatural.

Using the figure of Simon, a blondheaded deaf-mute orphan who in effect adopts Kerewin simply by arriving at her door one day, Hulme twines together cultural recovery, ecological restoration, and bicultural reconciliation. Despite his frequent provocations and violent outbursts, Kerewin's compassion for and loyalty to the disturbed boy may be read allegorically to suggest a deeper Maori tradition—an ecology of cultures, human beings, and landscape strong enough to possibly resocialize and reacculturate Pakeha society and New Zealand's national culture in the direction of a less self-destructive way of life. Read in this way, *The Bone People* stands as a persuasive argument for the ecological restoration of habitat as a key element in the restoration of functional and sustainable cultural forms.

Kerewin's gradual resocialization of Simon involves a relearning of trust on the part of both characters, a slow and often frustrating process in which she teaches the boy to care for himself, for others, and for the idea of home in its various emotional, material, and ecological dimensions. Hulme suggests that a reciprocal trust between individual and the land itself is axiomatic, an original, biologically rooted contract from which all other bonds of loyalty derive, including those of family, culture, and nation. Kerewin's act of heroic restoration in the novel, partly directed toward rebuilding long-neglected sacred Maori architecture, is less a function of individual strength or will, and more simply a releasing of power immanent in the land itself: "She touched the threshold, and the building sprang straight and rebuilt, and other buildings flowed out of it in a bewildering colonisation" (p. 428).

Kerewin first conceives of her role as a restorationist culture hero in a dreams; as the dreaming Kerewin reconstructs her family's sacred architecture, so does she also envision a simultaneous restoration of the land and its inhabitants: ". . . strangely clad people, with golden eyes, brown skin, all welcoming her . . . . The land is clothed in beauty and the people sing" (p. 428). On the strength of this prophetic dream, Kerewin initiates the rebuilding of her extended family's *marae*, or meeting hall, and in so doing revitalizes and restores both family and culture as well.

But the very act of physical restoration implies a corollary return to a traditional cultural metaphysics of collectivity as well. Kerewin's radically individuated sense of self, initially presented as a self-destructive pathology, is in a real sense cured or resolved by the work of restoration: "We have not just a hall, but a marae again. The fire's been relit, and I sink gracefully back into oblivion having lit it" (p. 432).

Mudrooroo's *Doctor Wooreddy's Prescription*, Witi Ihimaera's *Tangi*, Patricia Grace's *Mutuwhenua*, and Keri Hulme's *The Bone People* concur in one important respect: the classic modernist problem of the individual's alienation from family, community, and culture is shown at root to be the result of alienation from one's traditional land base. In each novel, the problem of Native alienation is mirrored by a non-Native national identity that is at once racially exclusionary, strongly invested in a denial or at best a selective acceptance of its own history, and at the same time increasingly cognizant of its own fragmentary, incomplete nature. In much the same way that the alienation of detribalized and urbanized Native people is traceable to a loss of deep connectedness to community and homeland, so too is the latter day psychological and spiritual alienation of their former colonial masters traceable to similar historical dislocations of individual, community, and homeland. Translated into the tribal cultural metaphysics of the contemporary Native novel, the alienation of Anglo-American modernism appears not to be universal or transcendentally necessary at all. Instead, modernist alienation is seen from a tribal perspective as representing a particular historical and political moment, a lapse in cultural continuity directly traceable to the loss of a ritual-based relationship between individuals, their communities, and the land itself.

Keri Hulme suggests that at one time both Pakeha—meaning European—and Maori cultures defined themselves and their place in the cosmos in similar terms, according to structurally similar ritual and narrative expressions of the relationship between nature and culture. Due to specific historical corruptions, dislocations, or ruptures, however, dysfunction and alienation have become the norm for both groups. In the case of Maori culture, this rupture is located in the experience of colonization, while in the case of Pakeha culture, the rupture is perhaps located in the dehumanizing and demonstrably unsacred morality of colonizing, a process necessarily involving the objectification of both natural world and indigenous inhabitants.

As ritually articulated narratives of multicultural identity, colonial national mythologies have understandably fallen victim to their own repressed origins, and have yet to fully recover from the experience of self-willed dislocation. Positing a role for ritual restoration of degraded landscape in the articulation of a mature postcolonial national identity depends upon a simple premise, namely that ecological restoration is something more than simply a set of technical corrections made to a degraded landscape. Rather, restoration involves a relearning–indeed a renarrativizing–of traditional ecologies of human community and natural world, with the end result being the restoration of a traditional balance between individual, community, and land base. Ecological and cultural restoration are two sides of the same coin: both are equally necessary elements in the development of a national identity capable of acknowledging its own conflicted history while at the same time being strengthened rather than factionalized by its diversity.

Selected Works and Further Reading

Bakhtin, Mikhail, *The Dialogic Imagination: Four Essays,* translated by Michael Holquist and Caryl Emerson, edited by Michael Holquist, Austin: University of Texas Press, 1981

Davis, Jack, et al., eds., *Paperbark: A Collection of Black Australian Writings,* Portland, Oregon, and St. Lucia, Australia: University of Queensland Press, 1990

Faulkner, William, *The Sound and the Fury,* New York: Random House, 1929; London: Chatto & Windus, 1930

Gilbert, Kevin, *Because a White Man'll Never Do It,* Sydney, Australia: Angus & Robertson, 1973; New York: Angus & Robertson, 1994

Grace, Patricia, *Mutuwhenua: The Moon Sleeps,* Auckland, New Zealand: Longman Paul, 1978; New York: Penguin, 1986

Hulme, Keri, *The Bone People,* Wellington, New Zealand: Spiral, 1983; London: Hodder and Stoughton, 1985; New York: Penguin, 1986

Hurston, Zora Neale, *Their Eyes Were Watching God,* Philadelphia: J. B. Lippincott, 1937; London: J. M. Dent, 1938

Ihimaera, Witi Tame, *Tangi,* London: Heinemann, 1973

Ihimaera, Witi Tame, and D. S. Long, eds., *Into the World of Light: An Anthology of Maori Writing,* Exeter, New Hampshire, and Auckland, New Zealand: Heinemann, 1982

Johnson, Colin, *Doctor Wooreddy's Prescription for Enduring the Ending of the World,* Melbourne, Australia: Hyland House, 1983; New York: Ballantine, 1986

——, "White Forms, Aboriginal Content," in *The Post-Colonial Studies Reader,* edited by Bill Ashcroft, Gareth Griffiths, and Helen Tiffin, New York and London: Routledge, 1995

Morgan, Sally, *My Place,* New York: Seaver, 1987; London: Virago, 1988

Walker, Kath, *Stradbroke Dreamtime,* Sydney, Australia: Angus & Robertson, 1972; London: Angus & Robertson, 1982

Weller, Archie, *The Day of the Dog,* Boston and Sydney, Australia: Allen & Unwin, 1981; London: Allen & Unwin, 1992

——, *Going Home: Stories,* Boston and Sydney, Australia: Allen & Unwin, 1986

Modern Japanese Nature Writing: An Overview

Shogo Ikuta

It is difficult to provide a definite outline of the various discourses on nature in Japanese literature, not only because nature writing has not yet been widely accepted as an independent literary genre and we have no criteria by which to elucidate it, but also in a more fundamental sense because there have been so many writers and poets in Japan who have touched upon the topic of nature in their own works. We can even say that almost every literary work has some description of nature in it. When we discuss traditional Japanese art and culture in general, we often refer to *ka-chō-fū-getsu*, a term that literally means "flowers, birds, winds, and moon." This term indicates the way generations of Japanese people have responded to nature, and suggests that nature has been the matrix for the making of civilized society. Indeed, most Japanese regard themselves as nature lovers and have flattered themselves to believe that they are very sensitive to the natural environment. So it is not surprising that there are many and varied discourses on nature in Japanese literature. We can even declare that whenever we read a literary work, we find some references to nature in it.

Furthermore, readers will certainly notice in Japanese literature some characteristically Japanese elements that are quite different from those in American nature writing. The most remarkable one is in regard to the sense of place or sense of belonging. In the United States, such nature writers as Gary Snyder, Wallace Stegner, Wendell Berry, Barry Lopez, and John Daniel consider this to be one of the most important themes, and they deal with its implications repeatedly. Japanese writers, however, do not seem to have any trouble locating this sense in what they write. Or, rather, the sense of place has been so acknowledged by writers as something inherent in the Japanese mentality that sometimes they are not even aware that it is latent in their own writing. In other words, writers represent an emotional attitude common to all Japanese people wherein they are intuitively confident that they belong where they can obtain a self-containedness by establishing an intimate relation with nature. Here lies the essential part of the Japanese sense of place.

This sensibility appears even among those poets and writers who led lives as hermits and wanderers and rejected secular wealth and social status. Such well-known haiku poets as Matsuo Bashō (1644–94) and Taneda Santoka (1882–1940), for example, actually spent their lives in this way. And yet their attitudes were also relevant to this commonly held sense of place, because they believed that the invaluable world of nature remained for them even after they had dismissed all else. Nature is not something to be worked upon, but rather a heartwarming home. Thus, the traditional view of nature was clearly illustrated by a sense of place that can be called Japanese pastoralism. It will not be possible to fully understand the various Japanese discourses on nature unless we recognize the fact that pastoralism has been the underlying basis of Japanese literature. Harmonious relations between humans and nature have historically been taken as a self-evident truth.

To explain the place of nature and Japanese pastoralism in Japanese literature, it is relevant to mention some climatic and cultural background. Japan, an island country, is in the temperate region and has a rich natural environment with very clear cyclic changes of four seasons. The society has developed on the basis of agriculture, mainly that of rice. These have been the most important factors influencing people in acquiring their way of life and in establishing their emotional outlook. Their outlook did not demand of them an oppressive working upon nature, but rather, efforts to find out how to coexist with it. Discourses on nature can be better understood when seen against this background.

Since early times, observing what was around them—wildlife as well as other natural phenomena—people developed keen senses regarding nature, and accumulated deep knowledge of it, and in this sense Shōeki, discussed in the following chapter, stands squarely in a long Japanese tradition. Although there were very few systematic studies made into nature in the past, many creatures were well known and were often entered into peoples' journals. Popular knowledge of natural history as a cultural heritage seems to have reached a high level. Out of such everyday experiences have come some excellent scientific achievements in the years since Shōeki's death by scholars like Makino Tomitarō, a taxonomic botanist; Minakata Kumagusu, a renowned natural historian; and Imanishi Kinji, an ecologist.

As the term *ka-chō-fū-getsu* suggests, the sense of the moment's beauty and the delicate nuances of nature that are present before human eyes exists not only in the traditional forms of short poetry—waka and haiku—but also in passages in other literary works. Furthermore, Japanese pastoralism basically remains unchanged even in this age of environmental disruption and industrial pollution. If we limit our discussion to the literary situation of the modern period since the Meiji Era, we can see some traces of new elements added to traditional writing on nature—notably the impact of Western literature and especially the works of Wordsworth and other Romantic poets upon Japanese writers. Strangely enough, however, the Western elements have not so much changed the fundamental character of the Japanese writing, but have served rather to reinforce it. For example, Japanese readers are inclined to regard Wordsworth as just an innocent poet who spent his life wondering without trying to examine social aspects or the problems of the self and nature. In a way, this attitude seems to reflect the basic sense of what Japanese nature writing is about.

Two representative figures who show the characteristics of modern Japanese writing on nature are Nojiri Hōei and Yoshida Genjirō, although they have been largely forgotten today. It is interesting that their careers shared a number of points in common: both of them studied English literature and worked for some time as teachers of English. They were both fascinated by Wordsworth, as well. Nojiri's best known work is *Hoshi* (Stars, 1941) and Yoshida's is *Kotori no Kuru Hi* (Days with Birds, 1921), but they also wrote many other essays including travel journals and occasional thoughts on life. Although they are now neglected and regarded as minor writers, their works were very poplar at the time. This popularity was due to their speculative discourses beautifully expressing the traditional Japanese sensibility toward nature, adopting at the same time the poetic imagination of the Romantics.

In their essays there is a strong yearning for seclusion and wandering in pursuit of a poor, but spiritual life. "I wandered lonely as a cloud" was their motto. What had motivated their longing was, again, that characteristically Japanese sense of belonging. They believed that wherever they were, their identity could be established and recognized only through heartfelt communion with nature. Thus, both Nojiri and Yoshida repeatedly narrated their blissful encounters with birds, mountains, and stars as if they had found their own homes in the world of nature. Whatever they saw in the world of nature, distinctions between the gazer and the gazed-upon disappeared, such that there was only a sense of deep affection and unity. Their essays, numerous as they are, illustrate the characteristic world of Japanese pastoralism.

Apart from the essays of Nojiri and Yoshida, the themes and topics found in Japanese discourses on nature are manifold. Even scientists have often written about the joys of their studies of natural phenomena and wildlife, as well as of their experiences in nature. As there is a great number of such essays, it is impossible to deal with them in detail, but let us mention just one example—mountaineering essays, which appeared mainly from around 1900 to before and after World War II—in order to see how nature itself is foregrounded in traditional pastoralism. This genre may well correspond to that in American nature writing. In the past, high mountains in this country were worshipped as sacred places, and only a few people, if any, dared to climb them for the purpose of religious training. But triggered by the climbing of Japan's Southern Alps by the English missionary Walter Weston in 1892, modern alpinism came to be gradually established in Japan. Along with the growing enthusiasm for climbing among the educated class, mountaineering essays and journals were published successively.

Kojima Usui is one of the most conspicuous writers in this genre. Kojima had read Wordsworth and was influenced especially by the essays of Ruskin. As an excellent nature writer himself, Kojima depicted the beauty of the mountains and his invaluable personal experiences in climbing. His numerous essays include an unfinished voluminous work, *Nihon Arupus* (Japan Alps, 1908–15), and, following the advice of Weston, he also published a magazine, *Sangaku* (Mountains), thereby contributing to the flowering of the contemporary mountaineering essay in Japan. He traveled once to the United States, where he climbed the Sierra Nevada, and was deeply impressed by the life of John Muir. Among other writers of the genre were Tabe Shigeharu, Fukada Kyûya, and Kushida Magoichi. Many of these writers had a knowledge of Western culture and literature as their intellectual background. While describing their delightful conversations and communion with mountains and their spiritual exuberance, their essays are filled with a sense of awe and wonder toward the landscapes that they encountered for the first time in their lives. However, because most of the high mountains in Japan have recently become easily accessible, the unknown has become the well-known. And this may well explain in part why this genre seems to be on the decline.

In order to give an overview of the present situation of nature writing in Japan, we need to mention the deplorable condition of nature. As witnessed in the case of Minamata disease, the rapid economic growth and industrialization of this country has resulted in serious environmental disruption and pollution. This condition has not so much brought about a crisis in the traditional relations between humans and nature as it has come to threaten the very extinction of the harmonious pastoral world, such that it seems that this world cannot retain its wholeness and is becoming a lost paradise. In this condition nature writers have had to face the difficult task of reassessing the pastoralism that they inherited, and, needless to say, of questioning its future. We can name some of the writers who have been grappling with this problem: Kawai Masao, Kaikō Ken (Takeshi), Takada Hiroshi, Miki Taku, and especially Ishimure Michiko. Kawai, a distinguished zoologist, has written excellent essays on civilization and the relations between humans and nature. He also writes impressive essays describing his encounters with wildlife. Kaikō, once a correspondent of the Vietnam War, often sharply criticized the ways of humans while reporting on his delightful fishing trips around the world. His works, which focus on human desolation, are bitter in tone, although at the same time they strike the reader with their profound warmth.

Takada, in responding sensitively to the miserable state of environmental disruption, has tried to reevaluate forgotten discourses on nature in the past in order to recover the dialogue between humans and nature in our time. Miki continues to tell of the significance of encounters with small creatures like insects living around humans. Reading his essays, we are reminded of the fact the we very often overlook even what we should be familiar with in the world of nature. Ishimure, mentioned also in the "Conservation Movement in Japanese Literature" chapter, is Japan's most important nature writer today. She describes the breaking up of her peaceful world, a seaside village in Kyushu, by methylmercury pollution. She deplores the way that all the members of the community—humans, other living creatures, and the sea—have been made to suffer miserably. Nonetheless, her sorrow, personal as it is, contains a strong appeal to civilized societies to meditate on what humans are and what we should do to stop the crisis. Ishimure's sense of place and her recognition of the importance of community offers a perspective from which contemporary Japanese nature writing can reestablish itself.

Notions of ecology and ecosystems have gradually been introduced into Japanese society and, reflecting the uprise of the global conservation movement, some ecoconscious writers have started exploring the possibilities of building a new culture. Among these are Ikezawa Natsuki and Imafuku Ryuta, who question the meaning of nature in the postmodern world. We can also name writers, such as Noda Tomosuke and Ashizawa Kazuhiro, who emphasize living in nature. Uchiyama Takashi and Hoshikawa Jun have also written impressively on nature.

In the mid-1990s nature writing has come to receive increasing attention in the Japanese literary world. Such literary magazines as *Folio*, *Eigo Seinen* (the Rising Generation), and *Eureka* have had special issues devoted to nature writing. There have been several anthologies of nature writing published for Japanese students (Slovic, 1995; Noda and Yamazato, 1997; and Itoh and Slovic, 1997). Although so far the focus has been primarily on American nature writing, this attention, along with the active work of the Association for the Study of Literature and Environment—Japan (ASLE—Japan), has helped to strengthen the recognition of the genre. This work has given support to its wider acceptance among Japanese writers, critics, and readers, and to the continued development of nature writing in this country. Thus, although nature writing has just begun to be accepted as an independent literary genre in Japan, it now seems that we are in a good position to develop and evaluate it, and to establish its significance among contemporary readers.

Selected Works and Further Reading

Ashizawa Kazuhiro, *Irving wo yonda hi* [The Days I Read Irving], Tokyo: Ozawa Shoten, 1994

Fukada Kyūya, *Nihon hyaku meizan* [One Hundred Famous Japanese Mountains], Tokyo: Shinchōsha, 1964

Hisamatsu Senichi, *The Vocabulary of Japanese Literary Aesthetics,* Tokyo: Centre for East Asian Cultural Studies, 1963

Hoshikawa Jun, *Chikyū seikatsu* [Our True Nature], Tokyo: Tokuma Shoten, 1990

Ikezawa Natsuki, *Hahanaru shizen no oppai* [Mother Nature's Breast], Tokyo: Shinchōsha, 1992

Imafuku Ryuta, *Yasei no tekunolojī* [Technology of the Wild], Tokyo: Iwanami Shoten, 1995

Ishimure Michiko, *Kugai jodo: Waga Minamatabyo,* Tokyo: Kodansha, 1972
——, *Paradise in the Sea of Sorrow: Our Minamata Disease,* translated by Livia Monnet, Kyoto, Japan: Yamaguchi Publishing House,

Kaikō Ken (Takeshi), *Opa!* [Opa!: A Fishing Tour in the Amazon], Tokyo: Shūeisha, 1978

Kawai Masao, *Shōnen dōbutsushi* [A Boy's Natural History], Tokyo: Fukuinkan Shoten, 1976

Kojima Usui, *Nihon arupusu* [The Japan Alps], 4 vols., Tokyo: Maekawa Bun' eikaku, 1913–1916; reprinted, Tokyo: Iwanami Shoten, 1992

Kushida Magoichi, *Yama no panse* [Private Thoughts on Mountains], 1957; reprinted, Tokyo: Shūeisha, 1990

Miki Taku, *Umibe no hakubutushi* [A Natural History of the Seaside], 1987; reprinted, Tokyo: Shogakukan, 1996

Noda Ken-ichi and Katsunori Yamazato, eds., *A Sense of Place: An Anthology of American Nature Writing,* Tokyo: Kenkyusha, 1997

Noda Tomosuke, *Kawa e futatabi* [On the River Again], Tokyo: Shogakukan, 1993

Nojiri Hōei, *Hoshi* [Stars], Tokyo: Kōseisha, 1941

Slovic, Scott, ed., *Worldly Words: An Anthology of American Nature Writing,* Tokyo: Fumikura, 1995

Slovic, Scott, Shoko Itoh, and Masami Yûki, eds., *Other Nations: Animals in American Nature Writing,* Tokyo: Tsurumi Shoten, 1997

Tabe Shigeharu, *Yama to keikoku* [Mountains and Valleys], Tokyo: Yama to Keikoku Sha, 1929; reprinted, Tokyo: Iwanami Shoten, 1993

Takada Hiroshi, *Ki ni au* [Encounters with Trees], Tokyo: Shinch sha, 1989

Uchiyama Takashi, *Mori no tabi* [Journey into the Woods], Tokyo: Nihon Keizai Hyoronsha, 1996

Yoshida Genjirō, *Kotori no Kuru hi* [Days with Birds], 1921; reprinted, Tokyo: Sinchōsha, 1957

Pre-Modern Japanese Nature Writing:
The Example of Andō Shōeki

✿

Ken Akiyama and Bruce Allen

Three representative poems from the *Manyoshū*, the *Kokinshū*, and *haiku* provide illustrations of the long tradition of Japanese poets and writers who share an awareness of nature.

The first is an example of a *tanka,* or short poem, from the *Manyoshū*:

> In the east, over the field, I see the dawn
> glow rise; I look back—the moon has
> declined.
> (Kakinomoto No Hitomaro)

Next is an example of a *chōka* or long poem from the *Kokinshū*:

> Waters we dipped from,
> wetting our sleeves,
> are frozen now—
> will the breezes of this—
> first day of spring unbind them?
> (Ki No Tsurayuki)

The third example is that of a *haiku*:

> The Mogami River has poured the hot sun
> into the sea.
> (Matsuo Bashō)

In fact, as these examples suggest, the most obvious basis of unity among Japanese poets of all periods is the close relation that they show for the manifestations and processes of nature.

In Japanese pre-modern nonfiction writing about nature, the work of one writer, Andō Shōeki, deserves particular attention, because of its growing relevance and importance for scholars of the literature of nature and ecological thought.

The tremendous scope of the life work of Andō Shōeki spans his careers as, in turn, a Buddhist monk, a doctor of medicine, and then, finally, a pioneering ecological activist-philosopher. At the age of 15 Shōeki became a Zen monk of the Sōtō sect and continued his religious studies until the age of 30 (Andō was his family name and Shōeki his pen name). But soon after his confirmation as having attained enlightenment, he gave up the monastic life. He then began to study medicine, aiming at a career he judged to be of greater help to people. After completing more than 10 years of medical study, he returned to his home in the Tōhoku region of northeast Japan, hoping to finally begin practice as a physician. By all accounts, until this time, despite whatever ferment may have been brewing within, outwardly Shōeki remained a quiet, well-mannered scholar-professional—hardly an outspoken radical critic. But upon his return to the countryside in the early 1740s, he underwent a radical change in both beliefs and manner.

What brought about this change was his experience in finding his homeland in the midst of a severe environmental crisis. He witnessed extreme agricultural collapse, attended by widespread famine, suffering, and death. This devastating experience forced Shōeki into a profound examination of all he had studied and believed. He declared all his earlier skills—whether medical, philosophical, or religious—to be almost totally worthless in attending to the problems about him. The cause of the disaster, he came to believe, lay in government agricultural and development policies, and in peoples' destructive relationships with the land. In short, what he faced—and in time came to explain as such—was a profound ecological collapse. No one around him, however, saw the problem in this way. As in the past, people blamed the weather, the gods, fate, faulty performances of rituals—all excuses that Shōeki was to increasingly speak out against as being escapist and based on charlatanism and necromancy. But his critique did not end simply in outrage and blame. He began to analyze why all was failing so badly. Unflinchingly, he placed the blame squarely on humans and their unnatural systems, but then he also moved on to propose practical measures to avoid such disasters in the future.

In his efforts to explain his ideas, Shōeki wrote some 101 volumes. The main body of his work consists of nonfiction essays and discourses on the natural world, society, and ecological relationships, but it also contains many satiric fables based around animals' lives, which are reminiscent of the fables of both Aesop and, even more so, of Jonathan Swift. These writings, however, were to remain virtually unknown outside the circle of Shōeki's few followers until they were rediscovered at the turn of the twentieth century. Even then they did not begin to receive widespread study until after World War II, and their core ecological ideas have only more recently begun to receive primary attention. Andō Shōeki himself stated quite prophetically that he wrote "for the benefit of readers of 100 years hence" (quoted in Norman, 10). In fact, it took his writing well over 200 years to find a readership. The reason for this delay was that his ideas were far too dangerous for his own times. For, among other things, he radically rejected the feudal order. What was more, he proposed practical alternatives to it and he even started an experimental community to realize his ideas. After his death, his writings were never distributed and in time were lost. But even if his works had been better distributed, there was little audience at that time to understand the thoroughly ecological core of his thought.

To summarize some of the most important aspects of Shōeki's later ecological work, we can refer to the following four points:

1.) A thoroughly ecologically based philosophy that modeled ideal human and social relations on principles observed in nature. His philosophy was organic, egalitarian, and activist. It was, he claimed, totally his own and without precedent. It rejected the hierarchical philosophy of Confucianism and its manifestations in feudalism, replacing it with equality not only among classes but also among the sexes, coupled with harmonious relations between all animals, plants, and the earth itself. Shōeki's philosophy

stressed an active personal responsibility to change society—in contrast to the passivity he believed characterized Taoism. Similarly, it rejected what he called the "morbid pessimism" and "lazy" aspects of Buddhism. He rejected the dualism of the predominant Sino-Japanese cosmologies in favor of a conception of continuous flux of all matter and energy alike.

2.) An insistence on the primacy of cultivation of land as providing the foundation of society. Shōeki claimed that the first essential for regaining a society that can live in accord with nature is the re-establishment of a free and unfettered farming class. He came to see most of the clerics, scholars, politicians, doctors, and merchants as "drones, parasites, and idle gluttons," who lived divorced from their basic responsibility for cultivation of the land.

3.) An insistence that the ravages of nature are not at root nature's fault, but, rather, humans'. This charge was backed by his proposing practical, empirically based methods to avoid such problems through living in accord with the principles of nature.

4.) Finally, a deep concern for the effects of language on peoples' relationship to nature. Shōeki believed that written language in particular had led humans to an estrangement from nature, and therein to oppressive social organization. He argued that written language could easily create a prison of estrangement. Finally, he proposed a way out of this prison.

The great importance that Shōeki places on the linguistic problem derives from his central claim that nature and the body are fundamentally one. On this point he writes, "The mouth and tongue are activated by the workings of energy in the human empty and full organs, and pronounce the words Heaven-and-Earth, but this is nothing other than Heaven-and-Earth itself articulating its own name through the medium of a human being, which is composed of Heaven-and-Earth" (quoted in Yasunaga, 54). Shōeki uses the key term "Heaven-and-Earth" approximately as we use the word "nature" today. He insists that in earlier times—and still potentially at present as well—humans could communicate with all elements of nature. He asserts that we can both receive and understand messages from nature, and then communicate back with them. For example, on this point, he writes: "There is nothing in Heaven-and-Earth, among human beings, birds, beasts, creatures, fish or plants that does not produce sounds. Nor is there any sound that we human beings cannot understand" (quoted in Yasunaga, 15). Repeatedly, he stresses that nature is not unknowable. Unfortunately, however, humans have come to think of themselves as separate. Shōeki then goes on to search for the reasons why humans have grown so estranged from our native perceptual abilities. His answers lie partly in our unnatural social and governmental systems. But he finds that at the root of these social aberrations lies our linguistic estrangement from the world of nature. In turn, he traces this estrangement to the development of written language. He describes the writing of complicated Chinese ideographic characters as a kind of "fetishism" that is causing the loss of peoples' ability to hear and respond to the sounds of the nonhuman world. He boldly claims: "With the invention of characters began the obscuring of nature" (quoted in Norman, 40). He decries the fact that along with this process humans' original cyclic conception of time has been changing to a new, estranging linear one (Yasunaga, 86). As a remedy for these losses, Shōeki calls for a reintegration of the oral tradition of language.

Particularly in his later works, Shōeki at times directs some rather strong negative blasts against the effects of written characters. But it seems that what he railed against primarily in regard to written language was the problem of its use in fostering codified systems of ideology that were replacing oral language—rather than against the use of writing itself. In fact, he was extremely interested in written characters, even if he was sometimes rather zealous in his writings that criticized them. There is, of course, an obvious paradox to be noted in the fact that he wrote more than 100 volumes on this subject, using those same written characters that he criticized. But the main thrust of his criticism was against the way in which written language had come to dominate culture and to replace the wisdom of the oral tradition.

As a sort of compromise form of writing, Shōeki advocated the use of the native Japanese phonetic syllabary, known as *kana*. He argued that since this phonetic syllabary was based on actual spoken sounds it, therefore, was more natural than the complex abstract Chinese ideographs. Shōeki felt that moving away from ideographic writing to phonetic characters could help bring people back to a greater connectedness to the natural world. Beyond his later critiques of written characters, what comes through in the overall scope of his writing on language is an appeal for the need to broaden our use of language by reviving the oral tradition, which in the past had kept us more connected to the nonhuman natural world. In the last years of his life, Shōeki returned to his birthplace in Akita Prefecture. There he persuaded the peasants to adopt his ideas and to start an experimental community. He convinced them to give up their religious affiliations and to institute the egalitarian, agricultural, ecologically based society outlined in his teachings. Yet such a nonreligious, classless community, which existed as but a tiny pocket within a still completely feudal world, was likely to survive only as long as its inspiring leader lived. After his death, Shōeki was declared persona non grata by the shogunate. His loyal peasant followers, however, erected a stone pagoda in his memory. They in turn were accused of deifying him—a striking, if not wholly surprising, irony.

Despite and beyond the fate of Andō Shōeki's brief experimental community, today, after 250 years of slumber, his writings have taken on a new life. Finally, they have found both readers and a climate in which their ecological ideas may be understood and built upon.

Selected Works and Further Reading

Norman, E. Herbert, *Andō Shōeki and the Anatomy of Japanese Feudalism,* reprint edition, Washington, D.C.: University Publications of America, 1979
Sato Hiroaki and Burton Watson, *From the Country of Eight Islands: An Anthology of Japanese Poetry,* Seattle: University of Washington Press, 1981
Yasunaga Toshinobu, *Andō Shōeki: Social and Ecological Philosopher of Eighteenth Century Japan,* New York: Weatherhill, 1992

Nature in Modern Japanese Literature: Fiction, Nonfiction, and Poetry

🌿

Takashi Kinoshita and Masataka Ota

Fiction

Meiji Era (1848–1912)

As a result of Japan's contact with Western culture in the middle of the nineteenth century, the word *Nature* was first introduced and translated as *shizen* in Japanese. At that time there was no concept for nature that indicated sky, earth, mountains, grass, trees, and so on, as the objective natural things. Up to that time, the word had been used mainly in the text of the philosophy of Lao-tze and Chuang-tze: the basic attitude was that human beings had to accept the movements of the sun and the moon, and the changes of the climate in the forms of winds and rain. And this was often mixed with the Buddhist concept of *jinen*, which means "the nature of the self that is not dependent." Moreover, there was a dominant concept indicating the exclusively abstract and artificial nature (since the Heian era, almost 1,000 years ago), which had been transformed by the traditional view of beauty into the refined, conventional style called *ka-chō-fû-getsu* (literally, "flowers, birds, winds, and the moon").

The first works that showed the influence of the Western view of nature were Kitamura Tōkoku's essays: "Naibuseimeiron (On the Inner Life, 1893) and "Emaruson" (Emerson, 1894). Under the influence of Ralph Waldo Emerson's transcendentalism, Kitamura (1868–91) found his salvation in throwing himself into the far-off history and the eternity of earth and heaven. And his thought deeply influenced Shimazaki Tōson (1872–1943) and his description of nature. Shimazaki's novel *Yoakemae* (Before Dawn, 1829–35) is a good example of this influence.

The works of Miyazaki Koshoshi (1859–1919) are full of fresh emotions that are a mixture of a Christian view of nature and Miyazaki's simple lyricism. And under the influence of both Emerson and the mystic Romanticism of William Wordsworth, Kunikida Doppo (1871–1908) wrote a book of short novels, *Sorachigawa no kishibe* (The Shore of the Sorachi River, 1902), the background of which is the severe nature of Hokkaido at the age of reclamation. And in his famous book, *Musashino* (1901), he described a landscape around a small suburban village in the Tokyo of those days. These two books represent his nature writing.

Longing for the modern Western culture, Japanese writers in the Meiji era accepted Christian or mystic views of life. What they were interested in was not modern materialistic civilization, but, rather, the Romantic inclination toward the mystery within nature. That is to say, just as Wordsworth found God in nature in the Lake District, they tried to find such spiritual elements in the nature surrounding them. Yet "the God of Creation" that they tried to discover was almost always indistinguishable from those of Shintō, Taoism, Buddhism, or Christianity. And they could see the force of human nature as a part of Nature through Walt Whitman's praise for the flesh and sex.

Also under the influence of Lev Nikolaevich Tolstoy who saw "the life of Eternity" in the base of every religion, Tokutomi Roka wrote his collection of essays *Shizen to jinsei* (Nature and Life, 1889). He led a rural life in an agricultural village near Tokyo, and called himself "an aesthetic farmer." Although he published *Mimizu no tahakoto* (Idle Chatter of an Earthworm, 1913) in the Taishō era, he did not have such a deep spiritual concept as Wordsworth or Kunikida Doppo.

Taishō Era (1912–26)

In Japanese literature between the Taishō era and the early Shōwa era, the first writer to show a unique view of nature was Miyazawa Kenji. He was born in Iwate prefecture, the northeastern part of the main island of Honshu. Having studied agriculture and forestry at Morioka Agricultural High School (now Iwate University), he started teaching at a local agriculture school, and became deeply interested in literature, fine arts, music, religion, science, and so forth. He also devoted his life to practical agricultural activities, such as improving the quality of manure. He was a natural scientist, man of letters, and naturalist. He was the pioneer of modern Japanese ecologists.

The climate of Iwate was so severe that the north-northeast cold and damp wind often caused cold-weather damage, bad crops, and famines. Seeing the distressed farmers, he did his best to help them. As a natural scientist, he was very keen at astronomy, geology, animals, plants and minerals, so that he could not keep looking objectively on such a severe nature. Therefore, his view of nature in his tales and poems was not that of the nature that could be objectified, and accordingly it was very different in quality from the traditional aesthetic. He used to tell his friends that "Human beings are also a part of Nature," and his works express both the oneness of human beings with nature and the interchanges or mutual sympathy between the two: "I'm indeed a part of the core of water, light, and wind. I feel it means that the entirety of water, light and wind is myself" ("Taneyamagahara no yoru" [The Night on the Plain of Mount Tane, 1924] in *Haru to ashura*).

This kind of identification with nature can typically be seen in the preface to his own book of tales, *Chû mon no ōi ryōriten* (The Restaurant of Many Orders, 1924):

> These tales of mine are all given by rainbows or moon light in the woods or fields or on railway roads. When I pass alone by the blue woods of oak in the evening or stand trembling in the wind of November mountain, truly I cannot help feeling like that. Indeed, I wrote that I could not help feeling that these kinds of things really happened.

His tales, which were "all given" by nature, enter into the eternally moving nature like religious persons, and talk and interact with clouds, winds, lights, or trees, flowers, stones, insects and animals. The next few lines from his unfinished masterpiece, "Ginga tetsudō no yoru" (The Night of the Galaxy Railway," circa 1924), may be said to express the author's clear inner world identified with the galactic system in his highly "transparent" language:

> The pebbles of the galaxy were all transparent; surely they were crystals, topazes, or those with rumpled folds, or corundums which emanate blue pale lights like mist from its edges. Jovanni ran to the strand and put his hands into the water, but the mysterious water of the galaxy was much more transparent than hydrogen.

This oneness of the transparency with nature penetrates all of the literary works of Miyazawa Kenji. As he says, "to live rightly and strongly is to be aware of the galactic system being in oneself and to be willing to accept it." That oneness comes from his unique religious belief and philosophy that humans are a part of nature, living in and being supported by nature surrounding them.

Shōwa Era (1926–89) and Heisei Era (1989–)

In his speech accepting the Nobel prize in literature, Kawabata Yasunari, the first Japanese winner of this award, who expressed the aesthetic of the ancient Monarchic Age in his works, talked about Japanese traditional aesthetic. His aesthetic was not so different from that of conventional *ka-chō-fu-getsu*. But it was Nakagami Kenji (1946–92) who suggested consciously for the first time that behind this view of nature that supported the traditional aesthetic was a suppressed, different nature. His view was totally different from the view of nature that the Japanese traditionally had held until then.

Using the nature of his native place (Kishu), as the stage of his novels, such as *Misaki* (A Cape, 1975), *Karekinada* (1977) and *Sen-nen no yuraku* (A Thousand Years of Pleasure, 1982), Nakagami drew on his own complex family relationships as a material to seek out the secrets of the conflict caused by blood relations. In *Kishū: ki no kuni ne no kuni monogatari* (The Story of the Country of Trees and Roots, 1978), he tries to prove that historically the whole of Kishū has been the whirling place of "the discriminating and the discriminated" since the beginning of the reign of Jimmu, the most ancient emperor. Kishū is located in the south of such central places of authority and power as Kyoto and Nara. There are not many plains in the peninsula although one finds many mountainous spots where political refugees would be sent or would go to hide. Kishū was, as it were, the nation of darkness, a kind of upside-down nation, the place where the discriminated in the power system dwelled. Having this kind of history, the nature of Kishū has nothing to do with the beautiful landscape, as is reflected in the conventional depiction of nature. It is, rather, a landscape that makes humans stand still to pray; in other words, it is humanly uncontrollable, full of bright things and overwhelming force. Facing this nature, humans are sure to be deprived of their qualification as its controller, the ruler, or the one who discriminates against it.

Against the artificial and dominated nature of *ka-chō-fū-getsu*, and also against the nature that is loved but deprived of its essential life under the central power (the so-called "emperor system"), the nature of Kishū is supposed to be the opposite of the conventional and politically powerful; it is a natural environment where the wild gods dwell, overwhelming human beings. And this nature bears a political tint. It is the peninsula itself where the dead souls dwell as the supernatural beings who lost against the political world of the central power.

Poetry

Meiji Era (1867–1912)

Since early times the Japanese have always felt close to nature. In the long history of poetic writing, one can find various types of expressions concerning nature: nature on which human consciousness is projected through their words and ways of seeing things; nature that heals human grief; nature that is a metaphorical vessel for Buddhist ideas, and so forth. Epistemologically, however, up until the Meiji era a distinction between the outer nature and their inner-world nature was not so clear, and the concept of nature as the entity that contains humans was too natural for them, and, as a result, it was difficult for the Japanese to see nature objectively. In general, their attitude toward nature has come from the animistic world view, and their basic way of thinking is as polytheistic as ever.

The revolutionary change of society in the early Meiji era also affected the literary writing of nature. The newly introduced concept of the Western Nature made writers rediscover the traditional concept of Japanese Nature and pushed writers and poets to become aware of the necessity of seeking a new relationship between these two ways of seeing nature. Various imports from the Western culture and civilization such as Romanticism, natural science, machinery, Christianity, and the theory of evolution began to be reflected in literary works, and especially the writing about nature started over using the methods of "observation" or "sketch," trying to absorb the diverse important aspects of the Western culture.

On the early stage of modern poetry, it was Kunikida Doppo who responded sensitively to the drastic changes in the early Meiji era. In his famous poem, "Sanrin ni jiy sonsu" (There is Freedom in Mountains and Forests), he writes, "Where is my dear old home? There I was a child of mountains and forests." The poet as an adult deplores his lost childhood, when he could enjoy the freedom in his beloved nature. This reminds the reader of Wordsworth's line, "A wilderness is rich in liberty."

Another poet of the early Romanticism who reveals a strong affinity with nature is Shimazaki Tōson. His "Chikumagawa ryojyō no uta" (Song of Travel to the Chikuma River) begins with these lines: "Near the old castle of Komoro, / under the white clouds, a traveler feels lonely, / No green chickweeds sprout, / nor fresh grass to sit upon. / The light snow covers the hill like a silver blanket, / melting and flowing in the sun." And in the middle of the poem the poet ponders over his life in the eternity of nature: "Yesterday it was as it was, / today it'll be as it must be, / why should I then fussily / worry about tomorrow?" Thus, his troubled soul is healed by the love for the river and by the river itself.

This kind of early Romantic vein is also found in the poetry of Irako Seihaku. In a symbolic lyric "Hyōhaku" (The Wandering), he depicts a wanderer in the valley of his native place who, remembering his deceased parents, returns to the heart of his joyful childhood. Among those traveling poets, the name of Kanbara Ariake should be mentioned. He identified his ego with nature symbolically and wrote *Shunchōshō* (Songs of Spring Birds, 1905).

Taishō Era (1912–26)

Now the influence of Walt Whitman could be seen here and there, and a movement of idealism for the reinvigoration of life was born. Some praised anti-intellectualism and wildness, and some sought the mystic vision of nature like that of William Blake.

Takamura Kōtarō was a disciple of Auguste Rodin, but he also wrote many good poems. In "Dōtei" (A Journey), Takamura writes: "There's no path before me, / and a track will be found behind me. / Oh, Nature, / Father, / You, so wide, who let me stand Spirit / for this distant journey, / for this distant journey." Here he pleads with the severe and infinite nature for its creative force of life. Another important poet, Muroo Saisei, overflowed with a sense of innocence, instinctive wildness, and unconstrained feeling. His poem "Sabishiki haru" (A Lonely Spring) expresses the cry of the pure heart.

Noguchi Yoneōjirōō began to write poems in the United States and came home as a famous international poet, but his Japanese reader could not fully understand the romantic and metaphysical ideas that he expressed in his works. In "Sanjyō no ippon matsu" (Lone Pine Tree on the Mountain), for example, he wrote about his lofty solitary ego in nature. But there is also a modest line like this: "I'm only a piece of humble flesh in front of nature." In those days, there were many other poets who depicted their inner nature: Yamamura Bochō, a Christian priest, published *Kaze wa sōmoku ni sasayaita* (The Wind Whispered to Trees and Plants, 1918). Hagiwara Sakutarō, who is usually regarded as a great urban poet, wrote many symbolic visionary poems of the mystic inner life, describing nature and his own inner world. Kitahara Hakushū asserted "the life of all things in the universe" as "the heart of nature." In the poem "Karamatsu" (Larch), he discovers joy in the diversity of nature.

Although his first volume *Haru to ashura* (Spring and Ashura, 1924) was published in the year following the Kantō Great Earthquake (1923), Miyazawa Kenji, who was then an almost unknown local poet, was discovered only in the next era, and today is thought of as one of the most popular and important poets in Japan. He tried to fuse his unwavering Buddhist faith (of the Nichiren sect) with the newly introduced knowledge of science, and tried to live together with nature through the daily practice of agricultural life. His religion taught him that everything that exists, seen or unseen, is to be saved, so that he was able to reach the delightful state through interacting positively with the universe. And then there is Kusano Shinpei, an eccentric poet, who uniquely wrote most of his humanistic poems through the cosmic consciousness of frogs.

Shōwa Era (1926–89) and Heisei Era (1989–)

During the first two decades of the Shōwa era, totalitarianism made the so-called Tennō-sei (Emperor System) the absolute authority, and led the people into the disastrous World War II. Culturally, importation from the Western world had already become almost up-to-date, and also an environmental consciousness began to sprout in Japanese society. But the growing nationalism pushed away the literature of the proletariat or that of modernism into silence. In such a depressing social situation, Itō Shizuo started his poetic career influenced by Hölderlin and sharpened his ability to see nature in terms of life somewhat like that of Rilke. As for Miyoshi Tatsuji, who was popular and famous for his masterly expression of Japanese obscure emotion, we have to admit with some reluctance (because of his propaganda poems during the war) that it was he who actually completed the re-forming of the poetic tradition in writing about nature. In him, one may see a watershed that divided modern Japanese poetry.

Experiencing great hardship in the war, poets could not talk about the reality without thinking about the inhuman aspects of human nature; they rejected the sentimental obscurity that could be easily misused for politics, and sought for new voices and styles. In such a direction Nishiwaki Junzaburō began to write about the relationship between humans and nature without adding any symbolic meanings to it. After his long silence during the war, this scholar-poet published *Tabibito kaherazu* (No Traveler Returns, 1945), which expressed the essential loneliness of human existence as a part of nature. After this volume, he tried to show his unique view of nature, which was very different from that which aims at conquering nature. We can perhaps say that Tamura Ryūichi learned much from Nishiwaki's attitude toward nature (*see* his collected volume *Shigo* [Dead Languages], translated into English in 1984).

In the Heisei era, the new genre of nature writing was introduced from the United States. Naturally, it is still too early to measure its impact on contemporary Japanese poetry.

Tanka and Haiku

Before many types of Western poetry were introduced into Japan in the Meiji era, there had been three main forms of poetry in Japan: *waka* (tanka's former name), *hokku* (haiku's former name) and *kanshi* (Chinese-style poetry). The poetic elements, however, had permeated most of prose writing from essays to historical tales; this means that the Japanese had always talked about human beings in relation with nature.

Japanese tanka is a very short lyric in which the poet expresses his/her exclamatory confession in the writing of natural phenomena. Before the Meiji era an emotional aesthetic approach was dominant, but Masaoka Shiki, who changed the name of the genre, insisted on putting the poet's subtle feeling into the writing of nature. In general, tanka expresses the subjective feeling much more strongly than haiku. Before World War II there were many representative tanka poets, such as Yosano Akiko, Nagatsuka Takashi, Saitō Mokichi, Wakayama Bokusui, and Ishikawa Takuboku. One of Ishikawa's tanka goes as follows: "Nothing to say / in front of the mountain of home village, / I am grateful to the mountain of home." Among the tanka poets after 1945, Mae Toshio has talent. He lives on a mountain as a woodsman and writes about his mythical experiences in the folk background of the place.

The Japanese *hokku* was derived originally from *waka*, and haiku (the name changed also by Shiki has a much shorter form). Generally, in contrast with tanka, the less subjective expression is aimed at in haiku. One unique characteristic is the rule that every haiku must have a seasonal word (*kigo*) that gives the reader the feeling or atmosphere of nature. Although its aesthetic consummation had been achieved by Matsuo Bashō, Shiki tried to break the convention influenced by Bashō and fashionable in the former age, and stressed the method of the pictorial "sketch." After Shiki's early death, Kawahigashi Hekigoō accomplished the reformation in haiku, radically casting away the conventions of *kigo*, and strove for more dynamic descriptions of nature. On the other hand, Takahama Kyoshi tried to retain the traditional taste and attitude toward love of nature. After many efforts and conflicts these two dominant currents are still flowing in Japanese haiku poetry.

Selected Works and Further Reading

Hirakawa Sukehiro and Tsuruta Kin-ya, eds., *Animizumu o yomu: niho bungaku ni okeru shizen, seimei, jiko* [Reading Animism: Nature, Life, and Self in Japanese Literature], Tokyo: Shinyōsha, 1994
Irako Seihaku, "Hyōhaku" [The Wandering], Tokyo: Kujyaku-Sen, 1906
Itō Shuntaro, ed., *Nihonjin no shizenkan: Jyōmon kara gendai made* [Japanese View of Nature: From the Jyomon Period to Modern Science], Tokyo: Kawade Shobo Shinsha, 1995
Kanbara Ariake, *Shunchōshō* [Songs of Spring Birds], Tokyo: Hongoshoin, 1905
Kitahara Hakushû, "Karamatsu" [Larch], Tokyo: Suibokusha, 1923
Kitamura Tōkoku, "Emaruson" [Emerson], 1894; in *Tōkoku zenshu* [The Complete Works of Tōkoku], Tokyo: Iwanami Shoten, 1973
———, "Naibuseimeiron" [On the Inner Life], 1893; in *Tōkoku zenshu* [The Complete Works of Tōkoku], Tokyo: Iwanami Shoten, 1973
Kunikida Doppo, *Musashino,* Tokyo: Min'yusha, 1901
———, "Sanrin ni jiyūsonsu" [There Is Freedom in the Mountains and Forests], in *Jyojyo Shi,* 1897
———, *Sorachigawa no kishibe* [The Shore of the Sorachi River], 1902; in *Nippon no bungaku* [Literature of Japan], vol. 5, Tokyo: Chû K ronsha, 1971
Miyazawa Kenji, *Chūmon no oi ryōriten,* Tokyo: Nihonkindaibungakukan, 1969; as "The Restaurant of Many Orders" in *Once and Forever: The Tales of Kenji Miyazawa,* translated by John Bester, Tokyo, New York, and London, Kodansha International, 1993
———, *Ginga tetsudō no yoru,* Tokyo: Kadokawa Shoten, 1958; as *Milky Way Railroad,* Berkeley, California: Stone Bridge, 1996
———, *Haru to ashura* [Spring and Ashura], Tokyo: Sekineshoten, 1924
———, *Miyazawa Kenji zenshū* [Complete Works of Miyazawa Kenji], Tokyo: Chikuma Shoten, 1980
Miyoshi Yukio, *Kindai nihon bungaku shi* [The History of Modern Japanese Literature], Tokyo: Yûhikaku, 1975
Muroo Saisei, "Sabishiki haru" [A Lonely Spring], in *Jyojyō shōkyokushū,* Tokyo: Kanjōshisha, 1918
Nakagami Kenji, *Karekinada,* Tokyo: Kawade Shobo Shinsha, 1977
———, *Kishū: ki no kuni, ne no kuni monogatari* [Kishū: The Story of the Country of Trees and Roots], Tokyo: Asahi Shinbunsha, 1978
———, *Misaki* [A Cape], Tokyo: Bungei Shunjû, 1976

———, *Sennen no yuraku* [A Thousand Years of Pleasure], Tokyo: Kawade Shobo Shinsha, 1982

Nishiwaki Junzaburō, "Tabibita karazu" [No Traveler Returns], Tokyo: Chikumashobo, 1953

Noda Utarō, ed., *Sekai-meishishū taisei. Nippon 17: II* [The World's Famous Poems 17: Japan II], Tokyo: Heibonsha, 1959

Noguchi Yonejirō, "Sanjyō no ippon matsu" [Lone Pine Tree on the Mountain], in *Chinmoku no chishio,* Tokyo: Shinchosha, 1922

Oōka Makoto, *Beneath the Sleepless Tossing of the Planets: Selected Poems, 1972–1989,* translated by Janine Beichman with the author, Honolulu: University of Hawaii Press, 1995

———, *1900-nen Zen'ya gochōtan: Kindai bungei no yutakasa no himitsu* [Various Aspects Around 1900: The Secrets of the Richness in Modern Literary Activities], Tokyo: Iwanami Shoten, 1994

Shimazaki Tōson, "Chikumagawa ryojyōno uta" [Songs of Travel to the Chikuma River], in *Rakubaishû,* Tokyo: Shunyōdo, 1901

———, *Yoakemae* [Before Dawn], Tokyo: Shinchōsha, 1900

Takamura Kōtarō, "Dōtei" [A Journey], in *Dōtei,* Tokyo: Sangabo, 1941

Tamura Ryūichi, *Dead Languages: Selected Poems, 1946–1984,* translated by Christopher Drake, Rochester, Michigan: Katydid, 1984

Tokutomi Roka, *Mimizu no tawakoto* [Idle Chatter of an Earthworm], Tokyo: Keiseishashoten, 1913

———, *Shizen to jinsei* [Nature and Life], Tokyo: Min'yusha, 1900

Yamamura Bochō, *Kaze wa sōmoku ni sasayaita* [The Wind Whispered to Trees and Plants], 1918; Tokyo: Hakujitsusha, 1924

Yoshida Seiichi, *Hyōshaku gendai shiika* [Modern Poetry Annotated—Tanka and Haiku], Tokyo: Obunsha, 1966

———, *Kindaishi* [Modern Poetry], in *Nihon bungaku kyōyō kōza III* [General Lectures on Japanese Literature III], Tokyo: Shibund , 1950

The Conservation Movement and Its Literature in Japan

Tsutomu Takahashi, Sadamichi Kato, and Reiko Akamine

Although Japanese literature in general is closely associated with seasonal cycles and natural descriptions, there is no specific genre corresponding to American nature writing. With haiku, tanka, and even modern novels, nature is one of the main themes, and yet these writings somehow lack a taxonomy of addressing natural events objectively and speculating upon the relationship between humans and the natural environment. In other words, Japanese literature writes, sings, and even dramatizes nature, but it is not about nature in itself. Even the concept of nature writing has been recently imported from the United States as a cultural and critical trend.

There have, however, been a few instances of literary enterprises speaking for the cause of the environment, with whatever significance they have in the canon of Japanese literature. These works, or documents, usually deal with some specific case of industrial pollution; they are strongly political and even propagandistic in scope and orientation; and they often speak for citizen's movements calling for and demanding necessary reforms and compensation. Somehow analogous to the rise of the counterculture movement and its influence upon American nature writing, environmental literature in Japan emerged as a direct consequence of the social struggle against the existing political systems. Especially, the conservation movement in the 1960s and the 1970s contemporaneously interacted with the social turmoil of the citizens' and students' movements; and the literature of environment inevitably carries political and proletarian dimensions.

The Conservation Movement in the Prewar Period

The serious destruction of the natural environment in Japan practically started with the Meiji restoration, which succeeded the largely feudalistic society of the Tokugawa shogunate. When the new government started to accelerate industrial modernization at the turn of the twentieth century, there broke out serious cases of industrial pollution and natural destruction. Above all, mine pollution was deadly, because the major heavy industry in the Meiji era was mining. In the 1890s, Furukawa's copper mine in Ashio in central Japan contaminated the Watarase River and the neighboring farmlands with heavy metal runoff and toxic waste; and in the 1910s, Sumitomo's copper mine in Besshi and Kuhara's mine in Hitachi seriously damaged the crop harvest with the release of sulphurous gases. Furukawa, Sumitomo, and other large corporations, to make matters worse, were closely associated with the government's officials and their efforts of national improvement; and the political discourse was often dominated by a production-oriented leadership in complete disregard for the natural environment, a tendency that was further aggravated by Japan's two major wars with China and Russia.

Tanaka Shozo, a former Diet member, impetuously protested at the cost of his life and career against the Ashio Mine Poisoning Case and left behind an enormous amount of documents, speech manuscripts, and political writings. Tanaka, fighting with a few remaining villagers (he desperately appealed to the emperor himself), serves as a model for the leader of a grassroots struggle against political authorities in defense of the environment. Tanaka's life story and the incident of Yanaka village, the final stronghold of their protest, have been illustrated by both historians and fiction writers.

Arahata Kanson, a socialist writer, wrote *Yanakamura metsubō-shi* (The Collapse of Yanaka Village, 1902); Oshika Taku published

Watarasegawa (The Watarase River, 1941) and its sequel *Yanakamura jiken* (The Incident at Yanaka Village, 1957); and more recently, Saburo Shiroyama, a contemporary novelist, depicted the last days of Tanaka and the aftermath of their protestation in *Shinsan* (Bitterness of Life, 1961).

Another important conservationist in the Meiji era is Minakata Kumagusu, botanist, folklorist, and philosopher, who introduced the notion of ecology and acted upon it in Japan. In modernizing and reforming the nation, the Meiji govenment adopted centralization policies, often sacrificing the interests of local communities and their natural environments. Minakata was desperately opposed to the government's policy of amalgamating local shrines, causing serious damage to the sacred forests as well as the lifestyles of local communities. In his prolific and internationally acclaimed career as a botanist and ecologist, he published *Junishi-kō* (Study on the Twelve Zodiac Animals), 50 articles in *Nature,* and 323 articles in *Notes and Queries*, all of which are included in *Minakata kumagusu zenshu* (The Collected Works of Minakata Kumagusu, 1971–75). Minakata's idea of ecology has been very influential and has inspired many scholars, naturalists, and environmentalists of today. The numerous books on Minakata include Tsurumi Kazuko's *Minakata kumagusu* (1981), Kousaka Jiro's *Shibarareta kyojin* (A Bound Giant, 1987), Nakazawa Shinichi's *Mori no barokku* (Baroque in the Forest, 1992), and Yoneyama Toshinao's *Kunio to kumagusu* (Kunio and Kumagusu, 1995).

These acts of protest in the Meiji era should not be interpreted as sporadic cases of individual acts of conservation, but rather as incisive criticism of Japan's modernization process, which was completely based on the homocentric principles of national improvement and industrial development. Their protests have now been reevaluated and recognized as the prototypes of contemporary environmental movements in Japan.

The Conservation Movement in the Postwar Period

The second wave of the conservation movement came in the 1960s and the early 1970s when the nation was confronted with the deadly outcome of the rapid industrialization in the post-war period. From beneath the unprecedented growth of the national economy emerged various cases of *kōgai* (industrial pollution); and the nationwide contamination of the sea, air, and rivers made Japan one of the most polluted countries in the world. From the late 1950s, the victims began to protest sporadically in the polluted regions, and in the 1960s the environmental contamination became a nationwide concern, not only because of the much-publicized diseases resulting from the pollution, but also because people found themselves imminently threatened by air and water pollution. In 1970, the Diet held a special session on environmental pollution called *Kōgai Kokkai* (the Pollution Diet); the Environment Agency was established in 1971; and the Environmental Conservation Act was issued in 1972. The sensational rise of environmental awareness championed the four major lawsuits concerning the Minamata Disease, the Niigata-Minamata Disease, the Itai-Itai Disease, and the Yokkaichi asthma case, and ultimately led to legal victories and financial compensation.

The theme of a grass-roots movement with regard to industrial pollution is best seen in Ishimure Michiko's *Kugai jōdo* (1967; *Paradise in the Sea of Sorrow: Our Minamata Disease*, 1990), which depicts the Minamata Disease, the most tragic and extensive sea water pollution, which is now internationally known through Eugene Smith's photography titled "Minamata." The Minamata Disease consists of syndromes of neurological disorder caused by methylmercury from industrial waste. Ishimure's book comprises both fiction and historical documents, describing how the peaceful villages of the seashore, people's lives, and even their memories are devastated by the contamination and the deceitful manipulation of the victimizing corporation. As is seen in her title, the author emotionally identifies herself with Minamata patients, leading for years an isolated struggle for their assistance and simultaneously criticizing the corporation, the government's policies, and the whole modernization process in the twentieth century. The book is significant not only as a historical record of industrial pollution, but also as the first instance of a literary enterprise in which the writer was seriously involved and confronted with an environmental crisis.

In the early 1970s there were two significant incidents concerning the literary representation of environmental problems. One is the reappraisal of Tanaka Shōzō, the Meiji activist; and the other is the publication of *Fukugō osen* (Multiple Contamination, 1975) by Ariyoshi

Sawako. Amid the controversial disputes over industrial pollution, the Ashio Mine Poisoning Case was reconsidered as the prototype of a citizens' movement, not only because of the protest guided by the strong leadership of Tanaka, which aroused the nation's concern, but also because the incident highlighted the picture of the political and economic authorities systematically overpowering the poor villagers. *The Complete Works of Tanaka Shōzō* was newly compiled in 1970; and Arahata's *Yanakamura metsuboshi* and Oshika's *Watarasegawa* were respectively reissued in 1970 and 1972. Also Nishino Tatsukichi wrote *Shousetsu: tanaka shōzō* (Tanaka Shozo, A Novel, 1972).

In 1975, Ariyoshi Sawako wrote *Fukugō Osen* (Multiple Contamination), a documentary novel investigating various effects of chemicals upon humans as well as the natural environment. Apparently influenced by Rachel Carson's *Silent Spring*, Ariyoshi publicized the dangers of food chemicals and insecticide, provoking the public on the issue of chemical contamination. In its afterword, Ariyoshi wrote, "I just wanted to help advertise the facts that researchers and pioneers have already warned against so that more people would know the reality." First serialized in a major newspaper, the novel created a sensation nationwide, awakening the readers to the imminent threats in their living environments. Ariyoshi's novel functioned as a catalyst for the consumers' movement, and evidently accelerated the popularity of health food and organic farming.

The Conservation Movement as a Global Issue

With the Oil Crisis in 1973 and the economic depression that followed, the conservation movement somehow receded, and it was not until the middle 1980s when the media sensationalized the global environmental issues that people's awareness of conservation was rekindled. The citizens' awareness and participation became no longer restricted to particular cases of industrial pollution in particular regions, but became more pervasive and individualized. Through the media the people were awakened to the global issues of the environment, such as acid rain and destruction of the ozone layer, on the one hand; and on the other, they realized the importance of conserving their own local environment and closely watching for regional development and natural destruction. Accordingly, the conservation movement in Japan has now changed in cause and

emphasis: the target of its protest has shifted from waste problems of private industries, for which legal guidances and regulations have been formulated, to evidently excessive developments and construction often carried out by force by local governments and public investment.

Among many works of environmental conservation are Amano Reiko's *Mansa to nagaragawa* (Mansa and the Nagara River, 1990), Nebuka Makoto's *Shirakami-sanchi* (Shirakami Mountains, 1995), and Shigeru Kayano's *Kamuiyukara to mukashibanashi* (Yukar, the Ainu Epic and Folktales, 1988). Amano for years led the movement against the government construction of an estuary dam in the Nagara River; unfortunately, the dam has been built. In her *Mansa to nagaragawa* she depicts the life of a fisherman and emphasizes the importance of the local ecosystem, as well as the lifestyle of villagers and townspeople within the watershed. Nebuka is concerned about the preservation of the wild beech forest in the Shirakami mountains in northern Japan, which has been designated as a World Heritage.

Kayano depicts how closely the Ainu, native Japanese living in Hokkaido, have lived with their gods and wild natural systems around them. Kayano is one of the few remaining Ainu who has protested against the construction of a dam upon their traditional sanctuary on the Saru River in the northern island of Hokkaido.

In the late 1980s and the 1990s, there also emerged other types of writing directly or indirectly related to the conservationist movement. One is the popularity of so-called outdoor literature, which deals with worldwide adventures, fishing, camping, and canoeing. Writers like Kaikō Ken and Shiina Makoto explore the possibility of writing about and filming the natural environment. Although not as consciously political as the activists cited above, these writers emphasize the importance of restoring an original and spontaneous relationship with nature and trying to regain native wisdom from it. Apparently, their works reflect and also reinforce the contemporary cultural trend of "back to nature."

The other type of writing is represented by incisive criticism of the contemporary culture and its social values. Nakano Koji's *Seihin no shisō* (The Idea of the Poor and Pure Life, 1992) recaptures the traditional theme of "plain living and high thinking" in Japan and sharply criticizes the highly practical and materialistic values of the society. Takada Hiroshi's collections of essays, *Shizenshi* (Nature Writing, 1995), also gives us a contemporary conservationist view of the domestic as well as global enviromental issues. Recent nonfiction essays like Tasaka Toshio's *Yûkari bijinesu–tai shinrinhakai to nippon* (Eucalyptus Business–Destruction of Thai Forests and Japan, 1992), Toyama Yukio's *Sabaku o midorini* (Green Campaign for Deserts, 1995), Tsurumi Yoshiyuki's *Tōnan Ajia o shiru* (To Know Southeast Asia, 1995), and others demonstrate that Japan's conservation movement and the people's awareness are internationally expanding.

Selected Works and Further Reading

Amano Reiko, *Mansa to nagaragawa* [Mansa and the Nagara River], Tokyo: Chikuma Shobo, 1990

Arahata Kanson, *Yanakamura metsubōshi* [The Collapse of Yanaka Village], Tokyo: Meijibunken, 1963

Ariyoshi Sawako, *Fukugō osen* [Multiple Contamination], Tokyo: Shinchosha, 1975

Ishimure Michiko, *Kugai jōdo: Waga Minamatabyo,* Tokyo: Kodansha, 1972; as *Paradise in the Sea of Sorrow: Our Minamata Disease,* translated by Livia Monnet, Kyoto, Japan: Yamaguchi Publishing House, 1990

———, *Story of the Sea of Camellias,* translated by Livia Monnet, Kyoto, Japan: Yamaguchi Publishing House, 1983

Kaikō Ken (Takeshi), *Kaikō takeshi zenshū* [The Complete Works of Takeshi Kaiko], Tokyo: Shinchōsha, 1991–1993

Kayano Shigeru, *Kamuiyukara to mukashibanashi* [Yukar, the Ainu Epic and Folktales], Tokyo: Shogakukan, 1988

Kosaka Jiro, *Shibarareta kyojin: Minakata Kumagusu no shogai* [A Bound Giant: The Life of Minakata Kumagusu], Tokyo: Shinchōsha, 1987

Minakata Kumagusu, *Minakata kumagusu zenshu* [The Collected Works of Kumagusu Minakata], Tokyo: Kangensha, 1951

Mishima Akio, *Bitter Sea: The Human Cost of Minamata Disease,* translated by Richard L.

Gage and Suzan B. Murata, Tokyo: Kosei, 1992

Nakano Koji, *Seihin no shisō* [The Idea of the Poor and Pure Life], Tokyo: Soushisha, 1992

Nakazawa Shinichi, *Mori no barokku* [Baroque in the Forest], Tokyo: Seika Shobo, 1992

Nebuka Makoto, *Shirakami-sanchi* [Shirakami Mountains], Tokyo: Nihon Kotsukosha, 1995

Nishino Tatsukichi, *Shōsetsu tanaka shōzō* [Shōzō Tanaka, a Novel], Tokyo: Sanichi Shobo, 1972

Oshika Taku, *Watarasegawa* [The Watarase River], Tokyo, 1941; reprinted, Tokyo: Shinsensha, 1972

———, *Yanakamura jiken* [The Incident at Yanaka Village], Tokyo: Shinsensha, 1972

Shiina Makoto, *Kusa no umi* [The Sea of Grass], Tokyo: Shueisha, 1992

Shiroyama Saburo, *Shinsan* [Bitterness of Life], Tokyo: Chuokoronsha, 1962

Smith, W. Eugene, and Aileen M. Smith, *Minamata,* New York: Holt, Rinehart, and Winston, 1975; London: Chatto and Windus, 1975

Takada Hiroshi, *Ki ni au* [Encounter with the Tree], Tokyo: Shinchosha, 1989

———, *Shizenshi* [Nature Writing], Tokyo: Tokuma Shoten, 1994

Tanaka Shōzō, *Tanaka shōzō zenshū* [The Complete Works of Shōzō Tanaka], Tokyo: Iwanami Shoten, 1977

Tasaka Toshio, *Yūkari bijinesu: tai shinrin hakai to nihon* [Eucalyptus Business: Destruction of Thai Forests and Japan], Tokyo: Shin Nihon Shuppansha, 1992

Toyama Masao, *Sabaku o midori ni* [Green Campaign for Deserts], Tokyo: Iwanami Shoten, 1993

Tsurumi Kazuko, *Minakata kumagusu* [Minakata Kumagusu], Tokyo: Kodansha, 1981

Tsurumi Yoshiyuki, *Tonan ajia o shiru* [To Know South-East Asia], Tokyo: Iwanami Shoten, 1995

Yoneyama Toshinao, *Kunio to kumagusu* [Kunio and Kumagusu], Tokyo: Kawade Shobo Shinsha, 1995

Contemporary Environmental Writers
of South Korea

Yong-ki Kang

As in other East Asian countries, many Korean ancient poets could be classified as nature writers. A considerable number of writers, who lived especially around the middle period of the Chosun Dynasty (1392–1905), would chant of life in nature. The salient poets among them are Chul Jung and Sun-do Yoon. Such a rich tradition of nature writing nurtured a literary background for the twentieth-century nature poets of Korea. In South Korea, however, literary concerns about environmental issues started to emerge as the nation became industrialized in the 1960s. As often pointed out, the industrial development of South Korea was made a national priority in those days when the Korean people fought against poverty after the Korean War. Especially as the 1970s set in, the nation accelerated industrialization, transforming its production mode from heavy and chemical industries to light ones. Owing to a nationwide motivation for economic development and an industrialization-driven education system, South Korea recorded an unprecedentedly high speed of industrial development over the years. The nation has had to pay a counter-price for its economic enrichment, however: people have often witnessed environmental accidents and have begun to suffer from many kinds of pollution. Finding the machine devastating the land and the human mind as well, writers in the 1960s and 1970s could no longer enjoy the beauty of nature without ecological care.

Kwang-sup Kim deserves attention as a leading eco-poet of South Korea, whose poetry goes beyond the mere description of natural beauty or life in nature. In his poem "Sungbook-dong Beedoolkee" (Pigeons of Sungbook-dong) that was published in *Wolganmoonhak* (Monthly Literature) in 1968 and appears in a high school textbook, Kim criticizes the inhumane industrialization and urbanization of the country by sympathizing with pigeons who have lost their habitat owing to the heat of development. The pigeons expelled by the industrialist culture may symbolize people in Seoul, who suffer from eco-destruction and the loss of their own humaneness.

In the genre of the novel, environmental issues tend to accompany the problem of class discrimination. In *Nanjangeega-Sosaolin-Jagen-Gong*, which was published in 1978, Se-hee Cho stimulates the reader's sympathy for the poor who suffer from various abuses and forms of oppression at the hands of the economically and politically privileged class over the marginalized. Even though Se-hee Cho clearly embodies a conflict between the Kims or Ji-sup and the top managers of Engang, he rarely creates a harmonious character who can enact a dialogical solution between the two opposing sides. What concerns the author is, as Byung-ik Kim comments at the end of the novel, "helping us to realize our own deterioration and feeling of psychological pain" (p. 294). Some years later, Se-hee Cho treated the same topic as in the above novel. In *Sigan-Yuhang*, a collection of short stories published in 1983, Cho criticizes the monstrous power of the machine and more seriously deplores the mechanization of the human mind. In a story entitled "We Never Knew That," the narrator reproves onlookers who cannot do anything when they know of the work speed-up forced on women workers, which has happened in the Engang Fabric Company.

Along with cutting words about labor exploitation, the author explicitly criticizes the oppression of nonhuman beings. In "A Dying River," he depicts how much we have already exploited our ecosystem: "We have already killed many things. (We) killed the sunlight, the moonlight, the starlight, the Milky Way, street trees, flowers, butterflies, bees, dragonflies, and even fireflies" (*Sigan-Yuhang*, 144). Although Cho sternly criticizes the inhumane exploitation of working class people and nonhuman beings, he is unable to suggest any alternative mode of life that may constitute an alternative to the industrialist culture. All he does is expose the reality.

While Se-hee Cho is concerned with the problem of city dwellers' dehumanization, Soon-tae Moon's literary taste leads him to the lost life of country people. A nostalgia for the lost pastoral life and country people haunts his literary theme around the end of the 1970s. As the government promoted the structural transformation of the South Korean economy from agriculture to heavy industry, it often forced country farmers to move to big cities. Having lost their home-places and beloved neighbors, farmers, not compensated enough for their lost fields and houses, moved nearer to cities without being armed with any industrial technology to sustain themselves and their families in the new world. Moon's stories catch the painful nostalgia of these people for the lost home villages and simple lifestyle there. In other words, Moon dreams of the survival of a preindustrialist mode of life, which is embedded in Korean traditional country life.

Moon's medium-length story, *Kohyangeero-Kanem-Baram*, well describes the sadness of innocent farmers who have lost their rural homes and drift on the surface of urban life. It also depicts their passionate desire to regain the lost pastoral life. The story takes its model from a true story of people who lived in a country village located in Chonnam Province in the south-western part of Korea. As Jangsung Dam was built, a number of villages were drowned. Moon fictionalizes the real situation in one of his stories. When the dam swallows a village named Noroomok (the neck of deer), most indigenous farmers move to nearby towns or cities. The elder Duk-bo and his daughter, whose house stands on the high hill side of the village, decide to remain there. Nobody who has left the home-place can possibly accommodate himself or herself to the urban lifestyle. In the mean time, the elder Duk-bo waits for the villagers who are expected to visit Noroomok on Choosuk (the biggest holiday of Korea, which falls on August 15 of the lunar calendar) and hold Kulippae (a traditional music and dancing festival of Korea). Nobody but Do-sam shows up that day. Because he is so disappointed and depressed, Duk-bo

drowns himself in the monstrous, artificial lake. A significant point is that at the very moment of committing suicide, Duk-bo hears the sound of *jing* (a Korean percussion instrument [gong] that produces a resounding tone when struck with a rice straw–padded stick). This sound represents the Korean spirit inherited from the preindustri-alist culture, centering the motif of Moon's literature as well. As it turns out, the author has written a novel under the title of *Jingsori* and published it in 1980.

In *Jingsori*, Chil-bok inherits the elder Duk-bo's spirit. Chil-bok, a resident of Bangwooljae, which is one of the drowned villages, has been very proud of his skillful playing of the *jing*, since he painfully learned it from his father. When all of the villagers leave their beloved place, Chil-bok keeps his *jing* with him. When-ever he suffers from depression, he strikes the instrument and experiences a mysterious solace. The sound of the *jing* moves the company head of Chilbo Stock and even Pan-do Son, who is the most wicked character that Moon has ever created in fiction. The mysterious power of the sound of the *jing* revives a hidden but never van-ishing nostalgia for their lost home.

Chil-bok's *jing* sound also helps all beings, as well as humans, to recover their own essentiali-ty. The narrator depicts the sound: "the sound is so mysterious as if coming down from the heav-en that it has beautifully washed the minds of all living beings" (p. 60). Thus, the sound gives Chil-bok a spiritual power strong enough to overcome the various kinds of hardships that he faces in his city life. The sound of *jing* is, in short, a voice of resistance against the urbanized and industrialized mode of life and a persistent stimulation toward the recovery of every being's own nature.

Suk-young Hwang's *Sampo-Kanen-Kil* should be included in the same kind of category as Moon's nostalgic stories. Even if the main character, Mr. Jung, is psychologically depressed by the mechanization of his city life as a con-struction worker, he has cherished a hope com-ing from an expectation that he has a country home to return to. When he decides to leave for his hometown of Sampo and is on the way to that place, he happens to meet Young-dal, a handyman. Unlike Mr. Jung, he does not have any memory of his home place. Although Mr. Jung has left his country home, he can be happi-er than Young-dal because his home place is still alive in his mind. Sick and tired of his city-drift-ing over the years, Young-dal decides to follow

Mr. Jung and stabilize his life at Sampo. Finding that a tourist hotel is under construction at his home place, however, Mr. Jung loses the advantage of nostalgia, and "he suddenly realizes that now he is in the same hopelessness as Youngdal's" (40). The commercial development has devastated the origin of Mr. Jung's nostalgia. Perhaps Mr. Jung also falls into the same group of lonely people who have to be solaced by Chilbok's mysteriously resounding *jing*.

Both Soon-tae Moon and Suk-young Hwang question industrial developmentalism by describing how helplessly people who have lost their home places drift on the surface of inhumane city life. Nothing can fill up the empty mind of those people whose life stages are separated from their indigenous soil, field, water, and humanity. Because Moon and Hwang's narratives focus on the psychological conflict of displaced people, however, they rarely draw attention to the crying voices of nonhuman beings. In other words, their view of nature does not avoid anthropocentrism per se.

Won-il Kim's *Doyosaeye-Kwanhan-Myungsang* provides a significantly different environmentalism from the above two writers. It also goes beyond Se-hee Cho's human-centered standpoint. It amalgamates humanism and an ecosystem-driven view of nature. Between the two standpoints, the author weaves a sense of tension by juxtaposing two contrasting groups of characters and dispersing the point of view. This story starts with Byung-sik's point of view. Byung-sik, who has failed the college entrance exam, leads a life of pleasure without any sense of direction. He humiliates his brother Byung-kook, who is expelled from the most competitive university in South Korea owing to his direct involvement with a labor movement, and now lives in his hometown Dongjin-eup, enacting a private investigation of the disappearance of snipe birds that once inhabited the mouth of Dongjin River. Belying the worldly expectations of his mother, the elder son Byung-kook devotes himself to the protection of the seasonal birds endangered from the river pollution generated by the Sukyo Plant of the Sungchang Fertilizer Company. Finding out that the water pollution has caused snipes to leave Sukyo Stream, he files a charge with the authorities against Sungchang. His efforts to save the river and snipes end with his frustration over the conspiracy between Sungchang and the authorities. His father shares the same ecological awareness as Byung-kook. Whereas Byung-sik and his mother favor mate-

rialism and industrialism, Byung-kook and his father are idealists from an ecological perspective, but social misfits from a materialistic perspective. Significantly enough, Byung-kook's view of nonhumans goes beyond anthropocentrism. When he discovers a flock of snipes at the delta of Dongjin River, which he used to see in his hometown before the Korean War, he is very pleased "as if he met his parents, siblings, or sweetheart, who has been away for a long time" (p. 234).

The author avoids using an omniscient point of view, relying instead on the differing points of view of his characters so that he invites readers into the presented conflict. The first chapter out of the four is depicted from Byung-sik's viewpoint while the second and the third are respectively described from Byung-kook's and his father's perspectives. In the fourth chapter, what has finally happened to the characters is simply sketched in the third person. The readers are, thus, allowed to meditate on the oppression of Sukyo Plant workers as well as the disappearance of the snipes. Won-il Kim seems to attribute the cause of social evil to individual responsibility as much as to systematic wrongdoings. Published in 1979, this story offered the first nonanthropocentric view of nature in South Korean fiction.

Since Kwang-kyoon Kim in poetry, some South Korean poets have questioned GNP-centered industrialism and its ecological destruction. As in fiction, no environmental writer of South Korea has a consistent career as an ecopoet. Witnessing the mechanization of the human mind and various kinds of pollution, they have developed their concerns on environmental topics. Some of them have transformed their voices from chanting the pastoral life to protecting the integrity of the natural environment of the country. Others have moved to ecoconsciousness from the democratization movement of South Korea, which occurred in the 1960s through the 1980s.

Imbued in the Taoist-Buddhist tradition of Asia, Dong-kyoo Hwang has persistently sung the virtue of life in nature since the 1950s. His literary themes show a metaphysical treatment of the ways of nature, depicting mysterious communications between humans and nonhumans, or longings for a life perfectly harmonized with nature. A poetic sequence, *Poonjang* ("Wind Funeral"), which consists of 52 poems, represents his position as a pastoralist poet. The first poem starting with a blunt request "Give me a wind funeral when I die" closes it with the reinforcement of the request: "Covering my body with wind as if with a blanket, / Without makeup or salvation" (*Akehreel-Josimharako*, 43–44). The narrator never problematizes industrialist culture even though he chants the wonders of life, as in "Poonjang 21." The last poem, "Poongjang 52," could be read as a typical piece of Hwang's nature poetry. The narrator says that he would like to exchange "hello" with a supporting pole of Mooryangsoojun in Boosuksa (a wooden building of Boosuk Temple that was constructed in the middle of the Korea Dynasty), take the place of it, and stand there, letting himself be exposed to fine snow. And then he hopes to be cleaved without regret (*Misryung-Ken-Baram*, 102). Throughout most of his later poems, he is concerned with how he would harmonize himself with the rhythm of nature.

As most of the concerned critics say, Hwang lacks socio-political considerations in most of his poetry. Over the deficiency of political concern, Jong-ho Yoo warns that "it might cause a trivialization of human beings to read them without a consideration of their social situation" (*Akehreel*, 114). In a comment on *Molwoondaehang*, Joo-yen Kim complains that Hwang's poetry during the end of the 1980s through the start of the 1990s does not go beyond mysterious thoughts and expressions. Certainly, most of Hwang's poems should be classified as nature writing. However, he has recently drawn attention to the environmental predicament of the country. Now he sympathizes with a cricket who cannot find a secure place in an apartment building so that it does not sing. The cricket has nowhere to sing because of light coming from the television (*Misryung*, 40). In "SOS," the narrator deplores the fact that the Han River cannot freeze in winter (p. 59). He also says that "I saw the moaning earth in a dream last night" (p. 62). Except for a handful of poems, however, Hwang's poetry traces back to the nature writing tradition of Korea as in the Chungnokpa poets or many other Taoist-Buddhist writers of this century.

While Dong-kyoo Hwang and many other Korean poets can be labeled nature writers, Hyun-jong Jung and Ji-ha Kim have so persistently dedicated no less than half of their literary works to criticizing the industrialist culture and its eco-destructive effects that each deserves the title of environmentalist poet. Both of them chant the wonder of life while resisting the culture of death. Employing the deconstructionist method, Jung and Kim point out the violence of reason and its ecologically negative effects. However, they show a difference in their literary scope; while Jung's poetry focuses on the subversion of industrialist language and his latent proposal for the reinvigoration of preindustrialist culture, Kim recommends *sangmyungsasang* as the ecologically sustainable mindset.

Even in the budding period of his poetry writing, Jung desired the primitive world where birds sing and flowers bloom. The word "island" is a metaphor of such a lost world: "There is an island between people / I would like to go to the island" (*Nanen-Byulajussi*, 68). To Jung, it is dangerous to privilege one particular cultural value or knowledge. The worshipping of any "-isms" or human being leads to death, cancer, or AIDS (*Han-Ktosongee*, 18). Going to the island alludes to liberation from various knowledges and -isms, especially those that are fundamentally anthropocentric. Thus, he says that knowledge favored by humans is sad. The poet senses that human-centered knowledge involves the oppression of nonhumans as well as human beings.

Jung's subversive voice against the mainstream culture does not remain as political inertia. His words are full of desire to transform the industrialist mind. He believes that the transformation of mind makes it possible to realize interconnected relations not only among humans themselves but also between humans and other beings: "You live because you let me live / Because I let you live, I live. // Oh, a change of mind!" (p. 39). Often, his poetry is directly political as in "If the Corrupted Part Is Active" (p. 45). The voice of cultural resistance establishes the thematic ground of his poetry, and in such a resistance hope and hopelessness cross each other.

Certainly, Jung's poetry offers a fresh shock to the anthropocentric culture. Indeed, most of us are not aware that contemporary humans are intoxicated by the industrialist culture just as we do not realize that we are addicted to rice (*Nanen*, 96). Although he thoughtfully questions the materialist culture, however, Jung does not offer any alternative way of thinking. His critical concern is given to a deconstruction of the mainstream culture. What he does is not suggesting how we can reach a transformation of our mindset but deconstructing the industrial developmentalism and desiring "the primitive world" (*Han*, 83).

A Lotus Prize–winning poet and social

activist, Ji-ha Kim widens the scope of Korean environmental literature and complexifies its thematic matter. In the 1960s and 1970s, Kim actively participated in the democratization movement of South Korea. Owing to that activity, he was imprisoned for five years. According to his confession, one day he experienced a sort of epiphany in the dark cell; one morning he unexpectedly found tiny, cute, and unnamable grasses on the small window frame of the cell. He said that the little but lively green grasses helped him to appreciate the great wonder of *sangmyung* (living things or being alive). After being released from prison and suffering from the aftermath of his imprisonment, he organized *Hansalim* (interbeing), a nation-wide association of environmental protection, transforming himself from a democratization poet and activist into a peace-loving ecologist and eco-poet.

Ji-ha Kim's poetry is, above all, a record of his passionate life. As Woo-chang Kim observes, "even though he has an ideological tendency, it is not the one systematically delivered from outside of the established concept but something newly thought of and internalized through the process of his own examination and first of all through his own life experiences and political resistance" (*Joongsimye-Kyorowoom*, 122). Since the early 1980s, he has transformed himself into an agent for nonhuman beings as well as a spokesperson for marginalized humans, declaring that he would live in order to listen to the crying sounds of all beings, to the sounds of death. To the poet, the death of one thing means his own death because "I am / dirt // and . . . the endless sea or universe" (64).

His neologistic word *aerin* indicates a comprehensive aspect of his *sangmyungsasang*. The concept of *aerin* is so elusive that each critic gives a different definition of it. One reads it as a combination of Christian love and Buddhist compassion. To Min-yup Sung, *aerin* is the overcoming of dualism—a complementary unification of two opposite forces such as "life and death, spirit and body, good and bad, happiness and sadness, high and low, light and darkness, men and women," and so forth (*Aerin II*, 96). Although its concept is uncertain like Tao, at least, the poet expresses his intention of synthesizing different cultural values between East and West. In fact, he wrote a series of poems titled as *Aerin*. The poet himself struggles to catch the concept of *aerin*: "Where are you, Aerin / before or after Korean Liberation Day, Korean War, or the April Revolution of South Korea, / or before

or after that before or after that, And before or after that" (*Aerin II*, 25). The poet furthers its meaning as "anything round, smooth, and soft / Whatever is light, bright, and clean" (p. 41). But he never fixes the concept, rather, he suggests that the eyes of *aerin* have, although not revealing enough, a potentiality like twinkling eyes in a stormy cloud—a still unheard thunder (p. 75).

Aerin is equivalent to *sangmyungsasang*, which is based on *donghaksasang*, a complementary synthesis of Confucianism, Buddhism, Taoism, and Korean geomancy. Its central idea is that "there arises the mysterious and eternal universal life inside of the human being" (*Nim*, 126). In sum, Kim proposes *hoochunkaebyuk* (a great transformation of culture). It is not a total rejection of the traditional culture but a great revision of it, a change of individual mind, and a revolutionary transformation of socio-political systems. He believes that without such a general transformation, but concrete enough as well, we cannot possibly face our environmental crisis.

Recently, women have tended to participate in various aspects of the environmental protection movement more actively than men. Ji-ha Kim even claims that such movements should be enacted more seriously by women than by men. A woman poet, Mi-hyeu Bak attempts to asociate female sexuality with the wonder of *sangmyung* in her poetry, *Erosye-Banji*. Jin-ha Ko and Kyung-ho Lee have edited and published a collection of eco-poetry, *Saedlen-Wae-Noksaekbyulel-Thernanenka*. In this book, they have collected 22 male and female eco-writers including Sang-byung Chun, En-Ko, Hyung-ki Lee, Kyung-rim Shin, Hyun-jong Jung, and Ji-ha Kim. Jong-chul Kim initiated the journal *Noksaekpyungron* in 1991 and has published a number of ecological essays and poetry.

In terms of environmental literature, South Korea tends to produce more poets than fiction writers. Although critical voices of fiction writers were strong in the 1960s through the 1970s, we rarely see any other stories published in the late 1980s and 1990s. In poetry, however, a number of poets are increasing their anti- or post-industrialist voices. And in tune with their active participation in environmental protection movements, many women writers are expected to release their oppressed voices as a powerful agent of nonhumans' unheard voices as well as of their own. Moreover, South Korea has significant potential for generating a complex environmentalism because it has not only experienced the heat of industrial developmentalism but also is a cultural and political, as well as geological, borderland.

Selected Works and Further Reading

Bak Mi-hyeu, *Erosye-Banji* [The Ring of Eros], Seoul, South Korea: Minemsa, 1995

Cho Se-hui, *Nanchangi ka ssoaolin chakun kong* [A Little Ball Launched by a Dwarf], Seoul, South Korea: Munhak Kwa Chisongsa, 1978

——, *Sigan Yohaeng* [A Journey into Time], Seoul, South Korea: Munhak Kwa Chisongsa, 1983

Hwang Sog-yong, *Samp'o kanun kil* [A Road to Sampo], Seoul, South Korea: Simji, 1987

Hwang Tong-gyu, *Akehrel-Josimharako?* [Watch out for the Crocodile?], Seoul, South Korea: Munhak Kwa Chisongsa, 1986

——, *Miriryong k'un param* [A Big Wind of Misiryung], Seoul, South Korea: Munhak Kwa Chisongsa, 1993

——, *Molundae haeng* [Bound for Molwoondae], Seoul, South Korea: Munhak Kwa Chisongsa, 1991

Jung Hyun-jong, *Han-Kotsongee* [A Flower Blossom], Seoul, South Korea: Moonhakwa-Jisung, 1992

——, *Nanen-Byulajussi* [I Am Uncle Star], Seoul, South Korea: Moonhakwa-Jisung, 1978

Kim Chi-ha, *Aerin,* Seoul, South Korea: Silch'on Munhaksa, 1986

——, *Joongsimye-Kyorowoom* [Pain in the Center], Seoul, South Korea: Sol, 1994

——, *Moro Nuun Tol Puch'o* [The Stone Buddha Lying on Its Side], Seoul, South Korea: Nanam, 1992

——, *Nim* [The Beloved], Seoul, South Korea: Sol, 1995

Kim Won-il, *Doyosaeye-Kwanhan-Myungsang* [A Meditation on Snipes], Seoul, South Korea: Nanam, 1985

Ko Jin-ha and Lee Kyung-ho, eds., *Saedlen-Wae-Noksakbyulel-Thernanenka* [Why Do Birds Leave the Green Star?], Seoul, South Korea: Dasanglebang, 1991

Moon Soon-tae, *Kohyangeero-Kanen-Baram* [A Wind Blowing into Home], Seoul, South Korea: Changjakwa-Bipyung, 1977

Environmental Literature: A Chinese Perspective

Wu Dingbo

Literature embodies the human desire to express and share experiences in life, and the major themes in literature are always closely related to the major concerns of such experiences. As the environment becomes the focus of attention worldwide and humanity's struggle with pollution and resource depletion a fundamental social issue today, a voluminous body of environmental literature and nature writing has emerged. It has led to a new field of philosophy known as environmental ethics, the ethics of human treatment of nonhuman realities and of humanity's relationship with nature. The steady increase in the publication of environmental literature and nature writing and the attendant increase in environment-related literature courses in colleges not only promotes public awareness of environmental problems but also provides one of the essential sources for studying the relationship between humanity and nature.

Environmental writing is a transformative literary mode. It intends to pave the way to a new consciousness that denies the prevalent anthropocentric, exploitative world view, and to a new consciousness that may eventually affect the harmony between humanity and nature. Judging from the worsening environmental conditions today, it seems that it will take a long time to realize this noble intention. There is no denying that the prevalent world view today remains anthropocentric and exploitative. Since 1949, the celebrated sayings in China have been: "What joy it is to struggle with heaven! What joy it is to struggle with Earth! What joy it is to struggle with human beings!" and "We don't wait for Nature's giving; we go and take it from Nature." Only in recent years have we occasionally heard the slogans of "Declaring war against environmental problems," "maintaining ecological balance," "cherishing natural resources," and "preserving the water of life."

Human beings conduct nuclear tests and build nuclear power plants without adequate provisions for waste disposal. They launch satellites and spacelabs without adequate provisions for their retrieval. Unchecked scientific exploration and technological exploitation and neglect of environmental protection in extending industrial production have done and are still doing irreparable damage to nature. Unavoidably, humans themselves bear the consequences today of their beliefs in unrestrained exploitation of nature: air, water, and noise pollution; extinction of countless species of plants and animals; clearcutting of the rainforests; global warming; genetic engineering; soil erosion and desertification; and human over-population. These are all symptoms of the modern disease of anthropocentrism.

To challenge this exploitative world view, environmental literature has emerged as the times require. It not only critiques previous cultures and brings in a new way of perceiving humanity-nature relationships, but also often offers alternatives to the anthropocentrism that dominates modern thought and contemporary culture. It calls for ecocentrism to replace anthropocentrism, demanding that humanity be decentered and the ecosphere take the center stage. Environmental literature manifests a laudable consciousness of environmental protection and ecological balance in nature.

The modern writers of the late twentieth century can never have the good fortune to enjoy nature as their ancestors, who produced a large body of Chinese nature poetry over many centuries, did. On the contrary, they must live in an increasingly deteriorating environment. As China focuses on the rapid development of its economy, modern science and technology of all kinds are being applied to an almost unscrupulous extent in order to raise productivity as high as possible and to create as much material wealth as possible. Along with the current prosperity comes pollution and depletion of resources, which have caused serious environmental problems. With a strong sense of responsibility and a deep love for nature, contemporary writers of sharp observational skills and deep insight have produced environmental literature to call for environmental protection. Among them Liu Guixian, Zhao Xinshan, and Zhou Yuming are most outstanding.

Liu Guixian is an editor of *Gongren Ribao* (Workers' Daily) in Beijing, and is also a member of the Chinese Writers' Association. He began his literary career in the 1970s and has published many essays, short stories, novellas, and nonfiction works comprising nearly 3 million words. When his literary reportage, "Zhongguo de shui wuran" (Water Pollution in China), appeared in *Sanyuefeng* (March Breeze), a literary magazine, in February 1989, he was hailed as the pathbreaker of China's environmental literature. In October of 1989, the Kunlun Press in Beijing published his nonfiction work *Shengming zi yuan de weiji* (Crisis of the Source of Life), and in 1993 the Huaxia Press turned out his nonfiction *Shuihun* (The Soul of Water). With his success in exploring environmental themes in literature, Liu has become the mover and shaker for environmental literature in China today.

Crisis of the Source of Life is generally regarded as his representative work. This is a full-length work of nonfiction on the subject of water pollution and water resources. The vivid and truthful narrative is made panoramic with detailed and authoritative materials quoted from both ancient and modern, both Chinese and foreign, sources. The author compares the water control of Yu the Great in the twenty-first century B.C. with the widely controversial present-day South to North Water Transfer Project. He relates the current extensive development mode of township enterprises with the pollution in the four great rivers and five great lakes in China. He parallels the forest fire on the Great Xingan Mountain in China with the desertification in the "blue Sahara belt" in Africa. he comments on acid rain, the population explosion, and other environmental issues. It is the author's noble intention to raise public awareness of a global water crisis so that precious water resources can be better conserved and the water crisis can be averted for present and future generations.

Zhao Xinshan is a professor at the Shanghai Science Academy and Zhou Yuming is an editor of *Weihui Daily* in Shanghai. Their collaboration in exploring environmental themes has pro-

duced two nonfiction books, *Bi tiankong geng guangkuo* (Broader Than the Sky) and *Diqiu zai kuqi* (Earth Is Sobbing). Zhao and Zhou published *Earth Is Sobbing* at their own expense. The book consists of four parts: Proclamation of the Three Poles (the South Pole, the North Pole, and Mount Everest): a Nonfiction; Green Footprints: an Opera; The Daughter of Earth—Li Yueshi: A Sketch; and Give me Back the Beautiful World: An Essay. This mind-expanding book shows the authors' desire to minimize human interference with the rest of nature. With their passionate love for nature and for humanity, they reveal the serious damage modern civilization has inflicted upon nature, warn people of the worsening conditions in their environment, and urge the governments and people all over the world to speed up environmentally related legislation and to improve supervision in law enforcement.

Among the famous women writers of environmental literature and nature writing are Shen Rong of Beijing, Zhang Kangkang of Heilongjiang, and Li Yueshi of Hong Kong. Shen Rong is a member of the Chinese Writers' Association. Her novel *Sihe* (A Dying River) is based on her personal experience while she was gathering material for creative writing in the countryside. This novel eulogizes the people's efforts for pollution control of the Mata Lake in Huantai county, Shandong province. Zhang Kangkang, the vice-chairperson of the Heilongjiang Writers' Association, has written literary works on environmental subjects, calling for rational exploration of natural resources and for scientific maintenance of ecological balance. Among her works are *Yueliang guilai* (The Moon Came Down) and *Dandan de chenwu* (The Slight Morning Fog). Li Yueshi is an environmentally conscious writer, photographer, and explorer. She has been to the South Pole, the North Pole, Mount Everest, and more than 80 cities on the seven continents. In her books and photo albums she not only shows the beauty of nature but also the deteriorating environmental conditions. Wherever she goes, she always urges people to establish a relationship that defends nature's independent wild integrity and does not merely preserve nature to sustain human life. People should learn how to live appropriately in a particular place and time so as to preserve and contribute to nature. *Baise liliang* (White Force) is one of her best-known photo albums with impressive pictures and touching captions.

During the 1980s, many notable writers, such

as Wang Meng, Liu Xinwu, Wang Anyi, Liang Xiaosheng, Zhang Jie, and Cong Weixi, showed great concern for the serious problems of environmental pollution. They proposed to develop environmental literature in China as a means to call for all people to protect our own ecosystems. As a result, the Chinese Society of Environmental Literature was founded in 1991, with Gao Hua as its secretary-general. Many well known writers in China today have participated in the society. *Luye* (Green Leaf) emerged in early 1992 as China's first magazine devoted to environmental literature, with Gao Hua as the executive vice-editor-in-chief. So far, this bimonthly has carried more than 1,000 works of environmental literature contributed by more than 100 writers.

For decades, Gao Hua has worked as an editor, first of the army's newspaper, then of the literary supplement of *China Environment News*, a newspaper, and now of *Green Leaf*. Although she herself is a member of the Chinese Writers' Association and her literary works focus on environmental issues, her major contribution to the field is her persistent and tireless efforts as an editor. Most notably, she has edited in collaboration with others a "Green Leaf" series, which has produced four books to date. Three of these works are collections of material originally published in the literary supplement of *China Environment News* from 1988 to 1990. *Luse sanzhongzou* (Green Trio) is a collection of 30 works of literary reportage and 16 short stories, *Lu caodi, lu caodi* (Green Grassland, Green Grassland) is an anthology of 73 light essays, *Caoye ji* (Leaves of Grass) contains 59 short-short essays, while *Chunfeng wujia* (Priceless Spring Breeze) is a collection of 31 pieces of literary reportage and 39 light essays, all of which were prize winners at the National Green Sanming Cup Contest of Environmental Literature held in Beijing in 1990.

Discoursing about environmental literature in *Diqiu–Nuren* (Earth–Women), Gao Hua estimates that "more than 6-million-character works, including fiction, poetry, essays, and literary reportage have been published in China in the past ten years" (p. 23). They include the following books of prose: Wang Xuewu's *He ziang qing* (Feelings for the Crane Farm), Li Xianyao's *Tianzhi jiaozi* (God's Favored One), Ceng Fanhua and Li Delu's *Shennongjia zhiye* (The Shennongjia Area Wilderness), Yang Zhaoxing's *Shapotou–shijie qiji* (Shapotou–World's Miracle), Jing Ping's *Luge* (Green Songs), and Liu Fang's *Liu Fang luse sanwen xuan* (Selections of Liu Fang's Green Prose); and the following books of poems: Chen Zhiyuan and Qi Shuping's edited collection *Huhuan* (Call) and Ceng Fanhuan and Xiao Hua's *Luxue* (Green Studies). Also, as a tradition in China, nature poems appear in daily newspapers all over the country. They are numerous and scattered, but rarely collected into books. No one seems to enjoy the laurel of China's nature poet today, but Gu Gong, Li Songtao, and Kuang Man do produce excellent verses on nature and environment from time to time. And occasionally, Liu Xinwu, Li Guowen, Ye Nan, Yuan Heping, and Zhang Yang present fiction; Cong Weixi, Li Xianyao, Feng Mu, and Wang Cengqi offer light essays; Huang Zongying, Yu Tianbai, Sha Qing, and Chen Zufen contribute literary reportage. It is also noteworthy that one-act dramatic presentations on environmental issues are frequently produced and are often screened for national television. A national contest for such performances was held in Beijing in 1995 and the winners were aired nationwide. It is a pity that these one-act humorous plays have not yet been collected into books.

The Chinese writers of environmental literature and nature writing remain a small contingent, but they are people with visionary and prophetic insight into human life and human relationships with nature. They take it as their social responsibility and historical mission to promote public awareness of the country's environmental protection. It is their common belief that the enhancement of the human ability to reconfigure nature will only instigate materialism and insatiable consumption. Consequently, the fine qualities of human nature that have been formed in the long process of cultural history will be replaced by rapacity and ruthlessness. They hold that humanity and nature form the material basis for the spirit of a civilization. Environmental writing has exerted an increasing impact as time goes on, and along with the heightening consciousness of the importance of environmental protection, environmental literature and nature writing will develop and prosper in the twenty-first century and leave their mark on the nation's literature.

Selected Works and Further Reading

Birch, Cyril, and Donald Keene, eds., *Anthology of Chinese Literature,* New York: Grove, 1965; Harmondsworth, England: Penguin, 1967

Ceng Fanhua and Xiao Hua, *Luxue* [Green
Studies], Beijing, China: Huaxia, 1992
———, and Li Delu, *Shennongjia zhiye*
[Shennongjia Wilderness Area], Beijing,
China: Kunlun, 1990
Chen Zhiyuan and Qi Shuping, eds., *Huhuan*
[Call], Beijing: China Environmental Science
Press, 1990
Chinese Society for Environmental Sciences,
ed., *Diqiu-Nuren* [Earth-Women], Beijing:
China Environmental Science Press, 1995
Dong Liu, "Renzhen" [Be Conscientious],
Xinmin Evening Paper (February 27, 1996),
p. 15
Huang Zongying, *Xiao muwu* [Little Log
Cabin], Fuzhou, China: Fujian Science,
1995
Jing Ping, *Luge* [Green Songs], Shenyang,
China: Liaoning People's Press, 1993
Li Xianyao, *Tianzhi jiaozi* [God's Favored
One], Beijing: China Environmental Science
Press, 1992
Li Yueshi, *Baise liliang* [White Force], Hong
Kong: Album, 1991
Liu Fang, *Liu Fang luse sanwen xuan*
[Selections of Liu Fang's Green Prose],
Changsha, China: Baihua, 1993
Liu Guixian, *Shengming zi yuan de weiji* [Crisis
of the Source of Life], Beijing, China:
Kunlun, 1989
———, *Shuihun* [The Soul of Water], Beijing,
China: Huaxia, 1993
———, "Zhongguo de shui wuran" [Water
Pollution in China], *March Breeze* 2 (1989)
Shen Rong, *Sihe* [A Dying River], Beijing,
China: Writers' Press, 1985

Wang En-pao and Wang Yüeh-hsi, eds., *100
Chinese Classical Prose Writings in English*,
Beijing, China: Beijing Language Institute,
1990
Wang Xuewu, *Hexiang qing* [Feelings for the
Crane Farm], Beijing: China Environmental
Science Press, 1988
Yang Chaofei and Gao Hua, eds., *Caoyeji*
[Leaves of Grass], Beijing: China
Environmental Science Press, 1990
Yang Zhaosan and Gao Hua, eds., *Lu caodi, lu
caodi* [Green Grassland, Green Grassland],
Beijing: China Environmental Science Press,
1990
Yang Zhaosan, Yang Chaofei, and Gao Hua,
eds., *Chunfeng wujia* [Priceless Spring
Breeze], Beijing: China Environmental
Science Press, 1991
Yang Zhaoxing, *Shapotou—shije qiji*
[Shapotou—World's Miracle], Beijing,
China: Kunlun, 1990
Yu Chaoran and Gao Hua, eds., *Luse
sanzhongzou* [Green Trio], Beijing: China
Environmental Science Press, 1990
Zhang Kangkang, *Dandan de chenwu* [The
Slight Morning Fog], Beijing, China: Chinese
Youth Press, 1982
———, *Yueliang guilai* [The Moon Came
Down], Beijing, China: Chinese Youth Press,
1984
Zhao Xinshan and Zhou Yuming, *Bi tiankong
geng guangkuo* [Broader Than the Sky],
Chengdu, China: Sichuan People's Press,
1992
———, *Diqiu zia kuqi* [Earth Is Sobbing], Hefei,
China: Anhui Literature and Art, 1994

Ecological Consciousness in the Contemporary Literature of Taiwan

Yang Ming-tu

In the twentieth century, ecological problems have become a main concern of human beings all over the world. People are concerned not only with their own environment, but also with other living organisms and the whole ecological system on earth. Studies of ecological balance, fauna and flora, and ecological poetics are now no longer marginalized but have emerged as a new paradigm in the academic field. Lester W. Milbrath, for example, asserts that the study of how to achieve a harmonious coexistence between human beings and nature has become one of the sectors of cultural studies. In Taiwan, ecology writers like to describe wildlife, warn people about man-made dangers to nature, and offer strategies to protect wetlands, nature parks and the fauna and flora. Studies of ecological consciousness in literature, however, have not yet become very common, although in 1995 National Taiwan University published a special issue on ecological literature in *Chung Wai Literary Monthly*, and a conference on ecology and postcolonialism took place in 1997. It is with this awareness that this chapter discusses ecological consciousness in the contemporary literature of Taiwan.

Taiwan Ecology: Past and Present

Taiwan was well known for its natural beauty, vigorous ecology, and admirable ecosphere. Yu Yung-ho praised its vivacious wilderness with such a description as "Trees are lush and green, old vines intertwine . . . myriad songbirds sing in trees" (quoted in Yamazaki and Nogami, 118). Lien Hun called it "a beautiful island in the graceful ocean" (p. 197). An historian admired its striving state of nature, saying that "Formosa is a real natural world paradise" (quoted in Tu Hsin-tzu, 39). Chen Yu-feng in his *Shen tai tai*

wan (Ecological Taiwan) also quotes such eulogies (pp. 150–151).

Most of its vigorous ecology and natural beauty, however, are gone now. A foreign report indicates that "20 per cent of the farmland is polluted by industrial waste, and 30 per cent of the rice crops contain unsafe levels of heavy metals" (quoted in McClintock, 264). Local investigation shows that old growth trees have been removed in large numbers from the mountains and in the past 40 years as many as 43 million square meters of forest has been destroyed (Chen Yu-feng, 120–121). Lin Chun-yi, an ecologist-scholar, says that Formosa as a synonym for beautiful island can no longer be applied to Taiwan with 70 percent of its inhabitants crowding each other in smoky and disordered cities (pp. 20–25). Other ecologists confirm Lin's statement with additional remarks that the condition of rivers and streams here is terrible with their beds clogged by soil erosion from hills being clear cut for farming, with their waters uninhabitable for fish and mollusks due to chemicals, and 17 out of 42 species of previously abundant fish in the Tamsui river having disappeared (Hsiao Hsin-huang, 30). These disheartening reports make the fact undeniable that Taiwan is no longer a paradise.

In the face of continued deterioration, ecologists, sociologists, arborists, and literary writers all express their concerns about the fate of the estuaries, swamps, forests, birds, and mountains. They work hard to impart to local people foreign ecological concepts, write to awaken ecological awareness, and launch movements and convene conferences to exchange ideas for improvement. Publishers are cooperative, knowing that publishing such books can make "a contribution to the protection of Taiwan's ecology, so that more people will better know Taiwan, discover lives therein, value its land . . . respect nature" (Chen Ming-ming, 3). The result is that more and more scientific ecological reports are available to the public. Of those that focus on Taiwan, the following are the best among them: *Tai wan: 2000* (Taiwan: 2000) and *Quan min cen yu qiang jiu he chuan* (All People Come to Save the Rivers) edited by Hsaio Hsin-huang, *Huan uo tzi ran* (Give Me Back Nature) and *Lan tian liu shui* (Blue Sky/Green Water/Pure Land) by Lee Chieh-mu, *Shui di kai fa chong tu he tiao he: liu-ian guo jian yu shui zi yuan yan tao hui lun wen ji* (Conflicts and Coordination in the Exploitation of Water Resources: Anthology of Papers Presented to the Seminar on the Six-year National Construction and Water Resources) edited by Chang Shih Chiao, and *Shui shi ji: shui yuan uyong xi fa zhan yan tao hui lun wen ji* (The Age of Water) by Ou Yang Chiao-hui.

In addition to the the above four books, some parts of *Guan du sheng ming: gan dou men zao ze gu si ran zhi* (Kuan Tu Shu Min: A Record of Nature in the Swamp in Kuan Tu) edited by Liu Ke-hsiang and others, some of the articles in *Chai shan zhu yi* (The Principle of Chai Shan) edited by Tu Hsin-tzu, and *Tai wan hong shu lin dao you* (Guide to Nature: Taiwan's Mangrove) by Kou Chi-yung, can also be regarded as scientific ecological reports. These works, like Lee Chieh-mu's books, concentrate on a comparison of the present bad ecological situation of the places studied with their past viability. Like Lee, these authors enjoy serving people as ecological remedial teachers, but Lee is more theoretical while the others are more practical. They not only confer frequently to draw up feasible plans for environmental improvements but also offer them to the authorities concerned. *Chai shan zhu yi* records the life and death of plants and animals in Kaohsiang's *sho shan* (Mountain of Longevity), while the other two books record shellfish, vegetation, insects, and migratory and sedentary birds in the wetlands. The authors of these articles are very enthusiastic and not so dry as the authors of *Tai wan: 2000* and the other books of its group. They write with a nostalgia for the past beauty of the landscape, and describe real things of nature. Therefore, they do not sound anthropocentric at all.

Travel and Historical Reports

Travel and historical reports with ecological interest are increasing in number and are now readily available to readers. Among the most important ones are Hung Yin-shen's *Tai wan xian min de jiao yin* (The Footprints of the Ancestors in Taiwan), Liu Ke-hsiang's *Tai wan jiu lu ta cha ji* (Retracing and Investigating Old Trails in Taiwan), his *Heng yue fu er mo sha* (Crossing Formosa), and his *Hou sha tan xian* (Adventures into the Back Mountains), and Yin Ping's *Hai yang tai wan* (Oceanic Taiwan).

The first four books are both travels and archaeological studies of the historical development of ancient trails that aborigines, foreign adventurers, and early settlers used to take in old times. They are ecologically significant, mainly because the writers shift their focus constantly from historical facts onto the senses of organisms, the endangered fate of wildlife, and the wretched sight of the exploited landscape along the routes. In this way they take readers endearingly into a natural world that had hitherto been a mystery to them, and generously share with the readers their "happy experiences in nature" (Liu Ke-hsiang, *Hou sha*, 49), their resentment of illegal trappers, developers, and farmers, and their anxiety over further mutilation threatened by encroaching civilization.

The next three books describe the flora and fauna respectively of different places. *Tai wan hong shu lin dao you* is somewhat like *Guang su sheng ming* in that it also records plants, birds, insects, and shellfish. But this book concentrates on several estuaries with luxuriant mangrove in Taiwan. It introduces people to the estuaries from one to another like a tour guide. In this respect, it is similar to Liao Hung-chi's and Liao Mei-chu's books, which are the best to be found so far about the flora and fauna in eastern Taiwan. These three books are all concerned about the ecology of the places they describe. Such ecological comments as "the scene . . . is beautiful. . . . However, it is a pity that people carelessly dump garbage, which damages the view tremendously" (Liao mei-chu, 120, my translation), are common in all three books.

Hai yang tai wan, although not so archeologically oriented, expresses anxiety as deep and irascible as that in Liu Ke-hsiang's books over the present pale countenace and murky future of Taiwan's environment and ecology. The places it surveys are partially different from and partially overlapping those of *Kuan tu shu min* and *Tai wan hong shu lin dao you*. It examines estuaries, coasts, rivers, harbors, and coastal villages. Each of its nine chapters begins with a historical narration of the development of a place, continues with passages of an objective description of different kinds of pollution in the place, which proves fatal to the wildlife and harmful to human inhabitants, and ends with a suggestion to all of the people concerned for rectification of the problems.

Yin's narration is tinged with nostalgia like that of Liu Ke-hsiang for the past ecological glory. It is also filled with sadness at the present destructive encroachment of capitalism. Yin is able to arouse sympathy even from nonchalant readers for the damaged areas and wretched victims nearby in nature. In one place, she tells a story about a boy littering his own town foolishly, ridiculously, and willfully. Readers feel irritated and even resentful, for not a person there cares, and neither the foreign investors or the government cares. Yin does not burst into tears at the indifference of the people, yet her heart bleeds, for she in many places expresses her protest against people taking willful garbage-dumping for granted, saying that the deep-rooted evil habit of Taiwanese people is an unforgivable sin that aborts attempts by environmentalists to make the island clean and inhabitable (pp. 88–89).

Generally speaking, Yin is anthropocentric in her book. But this does not mean that she is not aware of Arne Naess's deep ecology concept that "present human interference with the nonhuman world is excessive, and the situation is rapidly worsening" (Naess and Sessions, 49). She frequently shows herself to be a person of deep ecology. A good example is that when she describes the migratory birds in the hands of hunters, she tells the reader that she has more concern for nature than for human interests (p. 135).

Ecological Essays

"Ecological essays" here means compositions that are anayltical, interpretative, critical, or reflective. They treat ecological problems and present views in an objective way most of the time, yet are not dry in style and tone as are some general scientific or academic papers. Ecological essays in this definition are numerous and are published unceasingly every day in a variety of media, but here I will only discuss those that appear in books.

The ecological essays of Lin Chun-yi in *Zi ran de hong deng* (The Red Light of Nature) and *Tai wan gong hai he shi liao* (When Can the Pollution of Taiwan Be Stopped) deal with sundry pollution problems in Taiwan. Some of these essays are highly scientific while others are introductory articles about Western ideas of ecology, such as those of American ecological move-

ments, Thoreau's concept of nature, and deep ecology. The rest of the essays are Taiwan-oriented. They are very useful for environmental movements in Taiwan, for they not only supply objective knowledge and solid facts about severe pollution, as *Taiwan 2000* does, but also present strategies either for resistance to further devastation or for amelioration.

Along with Lin Chun-yi, other essayists concerned with the ecology of Taiwan are Hung Shu-li, Chen Yu-feng, Wang Chia-hsiang and Lee Chieh-mu. Hung Shu-li has written *Shou wang de yu* (A Vigilant Fish), Wang Chia-hsiang *Zi ran dao gao* (A Prayer for Nature), Chen Yu-feng *Ren yu zi ran de dui jue* (The Duel Between Man and Nature) and *Sheng tai wan* (Ecological Taiwan), and Lee Chieh-mu *Huan uo tzi an* (Give me Back Nature) and *Lan tian liu shui* (Blue Sky/Green Water/Pure Land), already discussed in an earlier section.

These essayists have many things in common. One, they are outspoken in expostulating human indifference to capitalists' violation of the rights of nature and activities harmful to wildlife. Two, they are nature lovers who argue vehemently against the utilitarian state of mind of the authorities concerned and the avarice of businesspeople. They regard the conspiracy of utilitarianism and avarice as an evil hub from which all kinds of nefarious practices originate and ulcerate the environment of Taiwan in the form of national policy, myths of economic prosperity, and anthropocentric legislation. Three, they announce unflinchingly that it is time to exert oneself to the utmost to rescue wilderness, to preserve as many areas as possible for natural parks, and to elighten people to a variety of healthy ecological concepts.

Among these essayists, Chen Yu-feng is the most prolific. In his articles in *Ren yu zi ran de dui jue*, such as "Lu she xuan ian" (Green Manifesto), "Sheng tai bu he tquo ju i" (Ecosabotage), "Geng ie di shuen lin ian ge di da di" (Weeping Forests and Castrated Lands), "Jiou jiou uo men di shuen lin" (Save Our Trees), and "Shi jie u ran tzai chiu tzai tze li" (Here Is the Afflicted Area of All the World's Pollution), and in the essays in the four parts of *Shen tai tai wan*, respectively entitled "Nature Literature," "Chronicle of ecological disasters and signals of danger," "Land ethics," and "The crisis of urban ecology and a turn for the better," Chen proves himself to be a resolute and adamant guardian of nature. He investigates mountain disasters, propagates land ethics, fights to prevent rare animals from becoming extinct, castigates the government's faulty policies and urges legislative action for nature preservation, and upholds local autonomy and decentralization as most helpful for disaster-rescue operations, while disparaging bureaucratic red tape and hierarchical chains of command as heinous impediments (Chen Yu-feng, *Ren*, 59–60). His contribution to the maintenance of Taiwan as a beautiful island is a benchmark in the history of Taiwanese ecology protection movements.

As Chen frequently advocates *ecosabotage* in his essays and pleads earnestly with people to subvert such governmental projects as those that bias people against ecology in favor of deforestation, exploitation of swamps, nuclear power plants, and public facilities in national parks, he, like the other essayists, is a deep ecologist more than a shallow one. His concept of ecology is in conformity with the seven points of Arne Naess's deep ecology, upholding the concept of ecological egalitarianism and the principle of diversity and symbiosis as a way to keep nature viable.

Just like Chen Yu-feng, both Hung Shu-li and Wang Chia-hsiang write with deep ecological consciousness and are very ecocentric. *Shou wang de yu* contains many articles about migratory birds that can be regarded as nature writing. But in many of the other essays, Hung expresses her very special critical ideas on ecological noninterference, human-made pollution, and ecosystem balance with a view toward solving Taiwan's problems. In "Environmental Philosophy—A Contemplation," she pleads with people to build natural parks and keep wetlands untouched. In "The Wetlands Near Estuaries," she relates that the unspoiled wetlands are a signifier of the glory of nature, for there all plants and animals can maintain a well-balanced ecosystem. Besides, she shows that human stupidity in polluting swamps and estuaries is the main cause for the death of birds (p. 98). In such articles as "The Coast," "Naturalistic Literature," and "Grapigel Island," she explicates to readers the meaning of ecological non-interference (p. 102), and scolds human interference as anathema. Her ecological belief here reminds one of John Muir's view as shown in his call to "Think Like a Mountain."

Wang Chia-hsiang is worthy of mention, too. Like Chen Yu-feng and Hung Shu-li, he too is concerned with nature parks and cannot bear to see nature being ill-treated by people who put capitalism and material gains above everything else. Like his fellow ecologists, Wang tries his best to inculcate in public servants and common people ideas of deep ecological ethics. Feeling a strong affinity with nature and eager to let others share his ecological, aesthetic, and spiritual view of nature, he implores irresponsible and avaricious people to stop interfering with nature and attempts to persuade government authorities to keep the wilderness free from contamination by urbanization projects. In undertaking such persuasion he adopts an indirect strategy. He shows government officials and citizens the value of wilderness as indispensable to the health of citizens, camouflaging his ecocentrism in utilitarianism, and thus subverting from within for the purposes of environmental protection.

Nature Writing

Many writers in Taiwan dedicate themselves to nature writing, by which I mean pieces of writing that record the phenomena of nature and the activities of birds, insects, plants, and other living organisms in the wilderness. In nature writing, the attitude of the author is to treat the flowers and the animals as sisters and brothers, while philosophizing as Thoreau did in "Walking," *Walden*, and *Faith in A Seed*; expressing concern about the endangered ecology as Leopold did in *A Sand County Almanac*; and symbolizing what is observed in nature as something holy and mysterious as Annie Dillard did in *Pilgrim at Tinker Creek*. While avoiding the pathetic fallacy, they aim to learn from nature and to show its ethereal beauty to people. Aesthetic quality without the pathetic fallacy is important here. It functions both to prevent manufacturers' accusations that such writers are upholding nature over human beings and it enables ecologists to inspire people's love of nature, to declare the rights of animals, and to convince people to respect nature instead of disregarding it.

Fortunately, nature writers in Tawian include Chin Hen-piao, Liu Ke-hsiang, Wang Chiahsiang, Tu Hsin-tzu, Hung Shu-li, and Shen Chen-chung, who can all write effectively in an aesthetic way. Chin Hen-piao displays this skill splendidly in *Jiu jiu re dai tu lin* (Save the Tropical Rain Forests). He is a scholar-arborist, and a translator of several important books, including Eric Hansen's *Stranger in the Forest: On Foot Across Borneo*, Henry David Thoreau's *Faith in a Seed*, and J. E. Lovelock's *Gaia: A New Look at Life On Earth*. Through long years of translating and immersing himself in foreign ecological books, he is able to make his knowledge of plants easily understandable to students and children. He has made *Jiu jiu re dai tu lin* a very informative and entertaining book. He uses pictures to illustrate what he writes, as well as simple words, poetic phrases, and a simple structure to convey a profound ecological message. Chin in some places is utilitarian and very anthropocentric, for he tends to discuss tropical plants from a consumer's point of view with emphasis on their medical and nutritional values, but this utilitarianism does not necessarily mean that his book cannot instill a love of nature in readers' minds, since the reasonable use of plants and animals is justifiable.

The merit of Shen Chen-chung's *Lao ying di gu shi* (The Story of Eagles) is that of realism. In order to write this book, he penetrated a dense forest in the mountains for many days, watching the daily lives of eagles and listening to their cries, distinguishing the implications of their nuances. He also records their skills in mating, food seeking, egg laying, nest building, as well as crises of survival from lack of food, scarcity of mates, and the traumatic phenomena of illness and death. While his description is strikingly real, realism is not the only merit of the book, as Shen writes with love. In recording his observations, he forgets himself as a man entirely. His position and the position of the birds become identical, the subject collapsing into the object and the two becoming one entity. In this magical transformation, the feelings of the eagle, its love of life, its ecstasy of soaring in the sky, and its fear of death caused by trappers, deeply move the heart of the reader. In this way, Shen upholds the beauty of birds and nature and encourages people to love them as he himself does.

Liu Ke-hsiang writes as superbly as the preceding two authors. As he does in other categories in this chapter, Liu gains readers' admiration for being so prolific in nature writing. In this category, he is well known for such books as *Zi ran liqing* (A Journey in Nature with Love), *Xiao lu shan zhi ge* (The Song of the Little Green Hill), *Xiao lu shan zhi jing ling* (The Genius of the Little Green Hill), *Xiao lu shan zhi wu* (The Dance of the Little Green Hill), and *Shan hwang ma jia shu* (Letters from Shan Hwang Ma). The Little Green Hill books are about the vegetation, birds, and insects he finds in the hills, ponds, ditches, and river banks in the Taipei basin and its surrounding hills. Like Chin Hen-piao, he draws sketches and uses photos to illustrate the flora and fauna to make the book substantial, aesthetic, and attractive. These three books are also informative and can serve as an excellent encyclopedia of wildlife in the vicinity of the Taipei metropolis. In the Green Hill books, Liu's attitude is very detached. He believes that living organisms can adjust themselves for a balanced ecology and that we need not interfere with them, for in a caption of a picture of newly grown lush grass on a wasted bank, he shows the reader that what they need to do with nature is to let it be as they are appreciating its dynamic vivacity.

In his other two books of nature writing, *Shan hwang ma jia shu* and *Zi ran li qing*, Liu's style is graceful and smooth and his tone is as religiously tranquil as Annie Dillard's in *Pilgrim at Tinker Creek*. Here he sometimes records objectively and at other times reflects meditatively, regarding himself as a part of the world of which he writes, like Shen Chen-chung. This attachment is best expressed in "Song of a Giant Tree," which is a short piece inserted in *Shan hwang ma*. In this song, Liu is so sympathetic to an ill-treated tree that he regards it as his fellow citizen, his "old friend." He takes care of it after saluting it, and prays that everything goes well with it (p. 62).

As far as attitudes toward nature are concerned, Wang Chia-hsiang is similar to Liu Ke-hsiang in many respects. He writes with attachment, with detachment, and even metaphysically. The first type is most noticeable in "Ze ji yu nan ji" (A Fowl's Entrapment in the Swamp), in *Zi ran dao gao*. Here he tells of the life of water fowl and their struggle for survival in a world of foul weather and uncertainty. In one place he describes a bird, observing how it lives and how it moves from one bush to another, and then records these activities. His description is heart stirring for, like Shen Chen-chung and Liu Ke-hsiang, he feels anxious when the bird gets entangled in a predicament, feels relieved when it succeeds in solving the trouble, but feels gloomy again when he sees some other fowl perish.

Wang's second attitude shows itself in "Zhu jian xing chang di huang ye" (A Wilderness is Coming into Being), in the same book, where he tells how a wasted islet reclaims its vitality and becomes a paradise regained for wild animals. The connotation here is that as long as people stop polluting and "harassing a once-disturbed place, it will soon revive"; so noninterference is the best way to let nature thrive. As for his third attitude toward nature, it is reflected vividly in such articles as "Dong tian" (Winter), "Wo kan dao shu di guang yu yin" (I Have Seen the Light and Shadow of Trees), "Lin shen bu zhi chu" (The Depth of the Forest is Unfathomable), and many others in *Zi ran dao gao*. In these articles, Wang writes like a philosopher, as Thoreau did in *Walden,* or as the Zen Buddhists say that "the wilderness and the forest give people peace all the time. In the woods people will have ever-deepening wisdom" (Wang Chia-hsiang, 31), and like an educator deep in his thinking about "environmental education" (p. 35). His philosophical dimension is quite valuable.

In brief, all the nature writers currently popular in Taiwan either writer reflectively or realistically. They may write with attachment, detachment, or philosophically. But they have never upheld humanity over nature. They ask people to respect the right to life of flora and fauna in the wilderness by means of articles that move the hearts of readers through their graceful style and intellectual depth, as well as through compassion toward nature.

Ecological Fiction and Drama

Ecological fiction and, especially, drama, are the weakest areas of ecological writing in Taiwan. Up until now, it seems that no one except Lin Chun-ji has published plays related to ecology. Lin has written two short plays, "Alice in the Wonderland" and "Walking Past the Land of Sadness," both included in *Tai wan gong hai he shi liao* (When Can the Pollution of Taiwan Be Stopped). The first play ironically treats the "wonderland" as a miserable world where a queen and her people slaughter rare animals, pursue material life at the expense of nature, and dump garbage at will. As the antagonists to the duchess, her son and the wild animals represent environmental protectors. After various struggles for power, the prince wins the conflict. He and his comrades proceed to purify the "wonderland" of its pollutants and show that the dream of making the wonderland into a real paradise is not impossible. Lin's second play is a religious ritual, where the singers interchange their opinions in the form of a dialogue. One half of the dialogue praises God for the creation of the fertile soil rich in food for human beings. The other half rebukes the folly, ignorance, and blasphemy of abusing what Providence provides. Together, the singers and angels encourage each other at the end to take good care of the natural resources and to pray to God for forgiveness. Being too simple in setting, plot, and characterization, these two plays lack dialectic complexity, dramatic diversity, and changeable philosophical depth. They are ecologically sound, however. Their simplicity suits the purpose of publicity, for they are written to act as media for propagating concepts of ecology to common people, laborers, and environmentalists on the street, instead of serving the interests of manufacturers or entertaining a materialistic elite in the grand theater. The theme of the two plays encourages people to protect rare animals while revealing the law of nature that the land supplies food and comfort only when it is kept unspoiled and viable.

In the genre of ecological fiction, there are four noteworthy authors: Yang Ming-tu, Wang Chia-hsiang, Liu Ke-hsiang, and Chen Yu-feng. Yang Ming-tu has written a collection of fables called *Shui Tui Tzu Fables*. It contains several stories about the folly of human beings. Most of these stories are not of ecological interest, but some stories, such as "Shit Civilization," "We Want Security," "The Right Time Is Over," "Whatever Is Nature Is Good," "Ignorance Is a Sin," and "Damned Indoctrination," are directly related to animals and nature. The themes of these fables are that nature is better than civilization, natural resources should not be polluted, and folly and ignorance on the part of environmental destroyers cannot be used as excuses for exoneration from punishment.

Wang Chia-hsiang has written four tales called "The Stories of Animals" and collected them in *Wen min de huang ye* (The Wilderness and Savagery of Civilization). The first of these tales treats a mongoose whose mother dies in a trap. The second is about a mouse who grows, migrates, mates, and reproduces from spring to winter. The third is about how a male leopard saves a female leopard from a trap in the jungle and his mating with her after their thrilling adventure. The fourth is about how a domesticated crane learns to return to nature and survive there in the wilderness. These four stories have two themes in common: animals feel at home more in the wilderness than in human habitats and human beings are most harmful to nature, although the law of the jungle is at work all the time among animals in the wilderness.

In the small circle of ecological fiction, Liu Ke-hsiang is the most admirable in content and in scale. Among his novels, *Feng niao pi nuo cha* (The Wind Bird Pinuocha) and *Zhou tou jing he lian mo mo* (The Whale Called He Lian Mo Mo) are the most interesting. They are new in Taiwan. *Feng niao pi nuo cha* is a beautiful novel about eagles as migratory birds. It shows us many things: the dignity of birds, the importance of experience, suffering, pursuit, and the adaptation of the life of a bird, on the one hand, and the necessity of mutual help in a community, the beauty of nature in all seasons, human cruelty to nature, the replacement of the Darwinian concept of survival of the fittest by the concept of the survival of coexistence as a new form of biospherical relationship, and human beings' noxious destruction of shallow areas and egocentric disturbances of animal habitats, on the other hand. Although this novel is different from Shen Chen-chung's *Lao ying di gu shi* due to the fact that the latter is a piece of realistic nature writing and the former is a work of the imagination, Liu and Shen present a common theme. Both express the idea that animals are equal to human beings in many things, including survival skills, adaptation, abilities of love and reproduction, and the will for achievement. Both seem to say that human beings have no right to obliterate the existence of other beings.

Liu's *Zhou tou jing he lian mo mo* is the same as his other novel as far as the theme of harmonious symbiosis among humanity and other animals is concerned. In this novel there are beautiful images of human beings in harmony with wildlife, especially a whale in a shallow estuary. In order to present such harmony, the author interlaces episodes of the life of the whale with those of an old nature lover and his grandson, who sojourn in a hut nearby the estuary. The plot reaches its climax when a symbiosis is expressed through mutual understanding between the whale and the nature lovers. Here, Liu arranges an episode in which the leading human characters play a symphony for the whale to listen to and to stir up its desire for survival in order to stimulate its energy to swim back out to the ocean.

If Liu is successful in depicting a world of harmonious relations between humanity and other creatures, Chen Yu-feng also shows us a dream of harmonious symbiosis. But his is a broken dream. In his short story, "I wei ri ben lao ren jun da lin dao" (An Old Japanese and the Chun Tai Forest Road) included with his essays in *Shih hie u ran chiu tzai je li* (Here Is the Afflicted Area of All the World's Pollution), Chen tells the story of a Japanese arborist with a strong love for trees. This Japanese who used to be fascinated by a hinochi woods in Taiwan returns to Japan. Many years later, he returns to visit the woods, but when he arrives and visits the place where the trees used to grow beautifully, it is barren with the trees destroyed long ago. The story reaches it climax when the arborist cannot bear the terrible sight of "the dead land" (p. 227), collapses to the ground, and wails with grief. The scene is so heartrending that the author cannot but abandon himself to despondence. The story touches readers, for what is seen is not an arborist as a subject weeping over some object lost, but a man-tree grieving at the eternal disappearance of his tree-fellows. Chen presents a broken dream of the happy cohabitation of humanity and nature.

Ecological Poems

It seems as if few poets in contemporary Taiwan are concerned about ecological problems, although there are six poets worthy of discussion here. First there are the two poets, Yu Su and Chiang Hsin, who are not ecologists. Both of them, however, have each written a poem to express their anxiety about environmental insecurity. Yu Su's poem, "u ran" (Pollution), provides a picture of polluted air and noise as gruesome as what Lin Chun-yi presents in his essay, "The Crisis of the Metropolis" in *Zi ran de hong deng*. The visual and auditory images are dreadful. Compared with this terrible pollution, Chiang's description of chemical pollution is equally hideous. His poem, "Duo lu lian ben" (Polychlorobiphnyl) reminds the reader of a chemical disaster in Taichung, which is described in Lin Chun-yi's essay, "Polychlorobiphnyl–The Mad Dog in the Environment" (*Tai wan*, 67–77). It is a disaster from which the victims contract incurable life-long diseases. While these poems are anthropocentric, their importance lies in their shocking effect. As Picasso's *Guernica* overwhelms people with its depiction of Nazi destruction, Yu's and Chiang's poems bring people into an awareness of how severe the pollution is in Taiwan and how urgent is the need for people to immediately treat that pollution.

Different from Yu and Chiang, Pai Chia-hua is less preoccupied with the killing effects of pollution. He is more interested in presenting nature as a dynamic animated subject. His poem, "The Breath of Trees," treats trees as a symbol of life in nature. Trees in this poem are not merely biological matter; they are a signifier of spiritual value. They give the poet a feeling of relaxation, a space for getting refreshed, and a dream of harmony between nature and people, in which they become one entity, as in Shen Chen-chung's *Lao ying di gu shi*.

Liu Ke-hsiang is much more complex than Pai Chia-hua. He shows the harmony between nature and people in a poem called "The Song of the Little Green Hill," included in the collection of the same name. In it, butterflies, flowers, children, shoots, new leaves, and spring itself are all young and vigorous. They spread out as in a grand celebratory rally of the glory of life. They grow together, mutually nourishing, all equal without hierarchy and discrimination. In a series of poems included in *The Song of the Wind Bird*, however, his harmonious picture of humanity and nature has been threatened by vicious human power. The peaceful atmosphere of the seashore in which birds used to feel easy is now disturbed and made uninhabitable by construction.

Walis Nokan is the only aboriginal poet among our contemporary ecological writers. His "Hui bu luo luo!" (Rejoining the Tribe) is a narrative poem composed of five stanzas. Each of the first four stanzas tells of the return of an aboriginal youth from his or her workplace to the tribe living amidst nature. The four characters in these stanzas are all exhausted. Their work in the city, as teacher, singer, laborer and clerk respectively, has produced in them a realization that naure is better than civilization, and that so-called civilized cities are nothing but a nightmare to them. The poet uses a refrain, "Seeing him/herself vanishing inch by inch" (pp. 68–69), to symbolize the persistent invasion of the aboriginal culture and the natural world in which they live by capitalism. The last stanza compares the journey back home to the upstream swimming of bruised and exhausted salmon to their birthplace. There is a note of sadness that the disillusioned people who return may not find in the tribe what they have lost, for the wilderness is no longer what it once was. The ecological interest of this poem consists of three points: it shows the destruction of wild nature caused by commercialism; it draws the reader's attention to the fact that unspoiled nature cures while cities kill; and, it hints that the natural areas that belong to the aborigines have been violated by Japanese imperialism and other colonizers.

Among these six poets, Cheng Kwei-hi, a member of the *Li* Poets' Association, is the most dynamic ecological writer. His "Kuei lan ji hua" (The Ulcerating Flower) is much more complex than the poems previously discussed. Published in the *Chung Wai Literary Monthly*, in a special issue on ecological consciousness and nature writing, this poem is composed of verse, a prose description, a story, a dialogue, and a live recording of a political demonstration. It expresses its concern for nature without considering humans as masters over nonhuman subjects. The verse, "Pin guo iu di pi"(An Apple and the Surface of the Earth), is the dominant part of the work and the main force unfolding the rest of the poem into action. Its theme is that the world of nature in Taiwan has been cut into pieces by external evils in the way that the skin of an apple is peeled by a knife. The first part, "Sheng ming di an liou" (The Source of Life), begins with a description of the vigorous ecology in Taiwan, which was formed naturally and admired and respected in the past, and ends with a warning that the beauty so formed and so admired by our ancestors should be kept from destruction by this generation and future ones. The second part, "Ma ka dau zu ta shie ie ben" (The Tribe of Ma Ka Tao Running in Blood at Night), is a story of the plunder of the land by pirates and politicians, and a history of the murder and enslavement of aborigines by invaders. The third part, "Shi chiu lian kung di tu di" (The Land Losing Its Face), accuses some writers of neglect of Taiwain's ravaging by colonizers and their infatuation with colonizing culture. And the last part, "Jie ian hua" (Blossoms Bloom From the Released Martial Law), reports a political demonstration in which a speaker shouts and seeks out the beautiful trees, rivers, and skies, which have been long lost in Taiwan.

"Kuei lan ji hua" as a literary work on ecology is significant in many ways. It presents a chronicle of Taiwan's colonization, in which its landscape, fauna and flora, and people have been first neglected and then trodden down, and its flowers will not bloom fully again until the time after decolonization, which is symbolized by the end of martial law. It also calls on people not to forget the original beauty of the island, but to cure the wound of nature in order to give new life to the island. Urbanization, commercialism, and political struggles can only play havoc with Taiwan's ecology, and the illusion of foreign culture is not helpful in reconstructing Taiwan's ecology and its inhabitability. All in all, Cheng Kewi-hi and Walis Nokan's poems are important in Taiwan's ecological literature. In addition to the theme that nature should be protected from deterioration, they show that colonizers often destroy the ecology of the colonized, and drain the colony of its natural resources.

Conclusion

In conclusion, I would like to mention that anthropocentrism, ecocentrism, the spirit of deep ecology, and the concept of shallow ecology have all found expression in Taiwan's contemporary literature. *Tai wan: 2000* reflects an anthropocentric concern for the human living environment. Such anthropocentric concern is also found in most factual ecological reports. In nature writing, the authors are more ecocentric in their consciousness. They incessantly accuse human beings as the destroyers of wilderness and identify themselves with nature in their wildlife descriptions. The case is the same for poetry, although there are those who show anthropocentric concerns, while others are more ecocentric, and with some it is difficult to judge their position based on the poetry alone. It does not appear that any writers in Taiwan treat nature as a Gaia, while only Lin Chun-yi has treated nature religiously as a place too holy to deserve devastation, and so sacred that human profanities will inevitably be punished, while veneration will be rewarded with bliss. Liu Ke-hsiang's story of the whale depicted trees as being holy, and Chen Yufeng has related a tribal legend about holy nature in his article, "Bao yu zhong de du deng yi jin ji" (Totems and Taboos in Ecological Protection) (*Ren*, 32). But neither writer has fully developed the theme into a more profound story. Similarly, relatively little work has been done with myths and religious mysticism, while only Walis Nokan and Cheng Kwei-hi have so far addressed colonialism's impact on nature.

Among all of the ecological writings discussed in this chapter, Cheng Kwei-hi's "Kuei lan ji hua" shows the most literary sophistication. Far different from other works, it conveys a deep concern for Taiwan's nature through a complex multi-genred structure; it is ecospherical, spiritual, artistic, and, therefore, extraordinarily rich and thought provoking. But while his work is outstanding today, it is important to bear in mind that contemporary nature writing and ecological literature are in the early stages of their development. The work done so far shows great promise for literature's contribution to

changing human consciousness toward nature in contemporary Taiwan.

Selected Works and Further Reading

Chang Shih-Chiao, ed., *Shui di kai fa chong tu he tiao he: liu-nian guo jian yu shui zi yuan yan tao hui lun wen ji* [Conflicts and Coordination in the Exploitation of Water Resources: An Anthology of Papers Presented to the Six-Year National Construction and Water Resources Seminar], Taipei, Taiwan: Shi Bau Uen Hua, 1995

Chen Ming-min, "Zi ran gong tuan shu xi shu ban yuan" [Why We Publish the Natural Park Series], in *Shou wang de yu* [A Vigilant Fish], Taipei, Taiwan: Morning Star, 1992

Chen Yü-feng, *Ren he zi ran de dui yue* [The Duel Between Man and Nature], Taipei, Taiwan: Morning Star, 1992

——, *Sheng tai Taiwan* [Ecological Taiwan], Taipei, Taiwan: Morning Star, 1996

Cheng Kewi-hi, "Kuei lan ji fa" [The Ulcerating Flower], *Chung Wai Literary Monthly* 23:12 (1996), pp. 68–70

Chiang Hsin, "Duo lu lian ben" [Polychlorobiphnyl], in *Dang dai zheng zhu wenxue lun* [On Taiwan's Contemporary Political Literature], edited by Cheng Min-li, Taipei, Taiwan: Shi Bau Uen Hua, 1994

Chin Hen-piao, *Jiu jiu re dai tu lin* [Save the Tropical Rain Forests], Taipei, Taiwan: Shi Bau Uen Hua, 1994

Dillard, Annie, *Pilgrim at Tinker Creek,* New York: Harper's, 1974; London: Jonathan Cape, 1975

Hansen, Eric, *Stranger in the Forest: On Foot Across Borneo,* Boston: Houghton Mifflin, 1988; London: Century, 1988

Hsiao Hsin-huang, ed., *T'ai-wan: 2000 nien* [Taiwan: 2000], Taipei, Taiwan: Commonwealth, 1993

Hsiao Hsin-huang and Ke Shan-chi, eds., *Quan min cen yu qiang jiu he chuan* [All People Come to Save the Rivers], Taipei, Taiwan: Shi Bau Uen Hua, 1995

Hung Shu-li, *Shou wang de yu* [A Vigilant Fish], Taipei, Taiwan: Morning Star, 1986

Hung Yin-shen, *Tai wan xian min de jiao yin* [The Footprints of the Ancestors in Taiwan], Taipei, Taiwan: Shi Bau Uen Hua, 1993

Kou Chi-yung, *Tai wan hong shu lin dao you* [Guide to Nature: Taiwan's Mangrove], Taipei, Taiwan: Da Shu Uen Hua, 1995

Lee Chieh-mu, *Huan uo tzi ran* [Give Me Back Nature], Taipei, Taiwan: Chien-wei, 1995
———, *Lan tian liu shuei* [Blue Sky/Green Water/Pure Land], Taipei, Taiwan: Chien-wei, 1995
Leopold, Aldo, *A Sand County Almanac and Sketches Here and There,* New York: Oxford University Press, 1949; London: Oxford University Press, 1968
Lien Hun, "Tai wan tung shi shiu" [Introduction to the General History of Taiwan], *Gu jin wen xuan* [A Selection of Ancient and Modern Literature] 1:43 (1952), p. 197
Lin Chun-yi, "Tai wan gong hai wen ti" [The Problems of Pollution in Taiwan], in *Tai wan gong hai he shi liao* [When Can the Pollution of Taiwan Be Stopped], Taipei, Taiwan: Independence Evening News, 1992
———, *Zi ran de hong deng* [The Red Light of Nature], Taipei, Taiwan: Independence Evening News, 1991
Liu Ke-hsiang, *Feng niao P'i-no-ch'a* [The Wind Bird Pi Nuo Chai], Taipei, Taiwan: Independence Evening News, 1994
———, *Heng yüeh Fu-erh-mo-sha* [Crossing Formosa], Taipei, Taiwan: Independence Evening News, 1989
———, *Hou sha tan xian* [Adventures into Back Mountains], Taipei, Taiwan: Independence Evening News, 1993
———, *Shan hwang ma jia shu* [Letters from Shan Hwang Ma], Taipei, Taiwan: Morning Star, 1984
———, *T'ai-wan chiu lu t'a ch'a chi* [Retracing and Investigating Old Trails in Taiwan], Taipei, Taiwan: Yü-Shan, 1995
———, *Xiao lu shian zhi ge* [The Song of the Little Green Hill], Taipei, Taiwan: Shi Bau Uen Hua, 1993
———, *Xiao lu shan zhi jing ling* [The Genius of the Little Green Hill], Taipei, Taiwan: Shi Bau Uen Hua, 1993
———, *Xiao lu shan zhi wu* [The Dance of the Little Green Hill], Taipei, Taiwan: Shi Bau Uen Hua, 1993
———, *Xhou tou jing he lian mo mo* [The Whale Called He Lian Mo Mo], Taipei, Taiwan: Shi Bau Uen Hua, 1993
———, *Zi ran li qing* [A Journey into Nature with Love], Taipei, Taiwan: Shi Bau Uen Hua, 1992
Liu K'o-hsiang et al., eds., *Guan du sheng ming: gan dou men zao ze gu zi ran zhi* [Kuan Tu Shu Min: A Record of Nature in the Swamp in Kuan Tu], Taipei, Taiwan: Morning Star, 1994
Lovelock, James E., *Gaia: A New Look at Life on Earth,* New York and Oxford: Oxford University Press, 1979
McClintock, Anne, "The Angel of Progress," in *Colonial Discourse/Postcolonial Theory,* edited by Francis Barker, Peter Hulme, and Margaret Iversen, New York: St. Martin's, 1994; Manchester, England: Manchester University Press, 1994
Milbrath, Lester W., *Envisioning a Sustainable Society: Learning Our Way Out,* Albany: State University of New York Press, 1989
Naess, Arne, and George Sessions, "Platform Principles of the Deep Ecology Movement," in *The Deep Ecology Movement: An Introductory Anthology,* edited by Alan Drengson and Yuichi Inoue, Berkeley, California: North Atlantic, 1995
———, "The Shallow and the Deep, Long-Range Ecology Movement: A Summary," in *The Deep Ecology Movement: An Introductory Anthology,* edited by Alan Drengson and Yuichi Inoue, Berkeley, California: North Atlantic, 1995
Ou Yang Chiao-hui, ed., *Shui shi ji: shui yuan uyong xu fa zhan yan tao hui lun wen ji* [The Age of Water], Taipei, Taiwan: Shi Bau Uen Hua, 1995
Pai Chia Hua, "The Breath of Trees," in *Ba shi nian shi xuan* [Selected Poems of 1992], edited by Chang Mo and Hsiang Min, Taipei, Taiwan: Xian Dai Shi Ji Kan She, 1994
Shen Chen-chung, *Lao ying ti ku shih* [The Story of Eagles], Taipei, Taiwan: Morning Star, 1993
Thoreau, Henry David, *Faith in a Seed: The Dispersion of Seeds and Other Late Natural History Writings,* edited by Bradley Dean, Washington, D.C.: Island/Shearwater, 1993
Tu Hsin-tzu, ed., *Chai shan zhu yi* [The Principle of Chai Shan], Taipei, Taiwan: Morning Star, 1993
Walis Noka, "Hui bu luo luo!" [Rejoining the Tribe], *Chung Wai Literary Monthly* 24:8 (1996), p. 68
Wang Chia-hsiang, *Wen ming huang yeh* [The Wilderness and Savagery of Civilization], Taipei, Taiwan: Morning Star, 1980

————, *Zi ren dao gao* [A Prayer for Nature], Taipei, Taiwan: Morning Star, 1992

Yamazaki Shigeki and Nogami Kyosuke, *1600–1930 T'ai-wan shih* [The History of Taiwan: 1600–1930], Taipei, Taiwan: Wu Ling, 1988

Yang Ming-tu, *Shui Tui Tzu Fables,* Taipei, Taiwan: Bookman, 1996

Yin P'ing, *Hai yang T'ai-wan* [Oceanic Taiwan], Taipei, Taiwan: Commonwealth, 1994

Yu Su, "U ran" [Pollution], in *Chuang shi ji shi nian shi xuan* [A Selection of Epoch-making Poems During the Past Forty Years: 1954–1994], edited by Lo Fu and Shen Feng-chi, Taipei, Taiwan: Chuang Shi Ji Shi She, 1994

Two Centuries of Environmental Writing in India

Kamala Platt

This study focuses on a small portion of the literature in English that demonstrates the figurative and empirical battles over India's natural environments, in particular, her forests. To write about Indian literature in English is a politicized act that privileges those who speak, write and read the British colonizer's tongue. To write of Indian Environmental Literature in English may, however, be a transgressive translation that exposes the forked tongues of the colonizer, native apologist, and post-colonial corporate entrepreneur who have shaken the Indian subcontinents' respectful relations with its natural environment on material, economic, cultural and spiritual planes; it simultaneously opens communication between India's forest peoples and their potential allies.

Even with the limitation of my focus on English-language texts, there is a large body of literature that could be discussed since human relations with the forest play a major role in much pre-Colonial Indian thought. Dating back to the Upanishads, nature writing continues as a consistent theme in the nineteenth and twentieth centuries. I could write of the mimetic Indian nature references originally evoked in the Sanskrit, or of the Indian-British dichotomy in nature writing citing the "dark threat" represented in the caves and the people of India in E. M. Forster's *A Passage to India* or Rudyard Kipling's imperialist adventure tales, travel narratives such as Colonel Burton's *Tigers of the Raj* or the man-eating-tiger adventures of passionate jungle lover Jim Corbett. British fiction writers, overall, added support—albeit sometimes ambivalent support—to the colonial project.[1] There were writers from the West who wrote against some aspects of the British attack on the forests. For instance, Jim Corbett made a name for himself as a killer of man-eating tigers and as a lover of Indian forest communities, who was often misunderstood by his fellow English

countrymen.[2] Interesting gendered comparisons could be made by examining British women writers such as Rumer Godden, whose work has been noted for its "lyric response to nature" (Godden, cover-jacket). However, such writers tacitly, if not flagrantly, supported the paternalistic colonialist relationship to Indians and most seldom recognized the Indian intellectual and spiritual traditions of reverence for and wisdom about its forests. I could research the split between East and West in the perception of nature, as that dichotomy is played out in India, where centuries of respect for the cyclical aspect of the universe and humanity's place in, rather than above, nature have predominated.

I could write of the nature writing in the South Asian Diaspora, of Indian nature writing in Britain or Trinidad, Guyana, Kenya or South Africa, of expatriates, exiles and cosmopolitan Indians like A. K. Ramanujan and Meena Alexander, whose work has synthesized Indian nature philosophy in the contexts of other continents. I could expand on brief but pervasive references to nature writing in Indian twentieth-century classics, such as Rabindranath Tagore's poetry and R. K. Narayan's fiction. Tagore held to the paradoxical concept of *jībān-debatā*, a "dual sense of involvement in and detachment from" both his work and nature writ large; thus "the diversity and extravagance of his art was but a reflection of the extravagance of Nature itself" (Radice, 35). This belief is evident in Tagore's poetry; for example, in the following line from "In Praise of Trees," the poet addresses the trees with admiration for the trick he has seemingly learned from them: "You processed light's / Hidden wealth to give color to light" (Tagore, 92). This mimetic characteristic applied also to the form of Tagore's poetry; for instance, he felt that "the rhythms of art . . . were a reflection of the rhythms of nature" (Radice, 36). He was particularly drawn to write about the dry plains of West

Bengal where he started the educational ashram Santiniketan (Radice, 25).

I could write of nature writing on the South Asian subcontinent including Pakistani, Bangla Deshi, Nepalese, and Tibetan writers. Twentieth-century Indian jungle and forest writing for children might be addressed; children's nature stories span years and continents from Dhan Gopal Mukerji's *Kari the Elephant, Jungle Beasts and Men* and *Hari The Jungle Lad*, in the 1920s; the Jaico Books series of the 1950s with such titles as Suresh Vaidya's *Ahead Lies the Jungle* and Col. Kesri Singh's *The Tiger of Rajasthan*; and the Young India Library books such as Ramesh Bedi's *Elephant Lord of the Jungle*, to the contemporary picture book *The People Who Hugged the Trees*. The recent international collaboration by Deborah Lee Rose, a science writer at the University of California–Berkeley, and Swedish artist Birgitta Säflund, depicts the Rajasthani folktale about Amrita Devi leading 300 people to save khejri trees.

I will not, however, cover any of these extensive, important, but nearly neglected issues. Instead, I have chosen to address briefly three areas of South Asian nature writing that describe (respectively) the effects of British colonialism on India's forest communities; nature themes originating in paradigms of Independence—for instance, the Chipko movement and the dichotomies of nature thought between Gandhi and Nehru; and contemporary literature that examines indigenous tribal, peasant, and women's and men's issues in relation to their forest home and the invading postcolonial outside world. The role of gender in relationship to nature serves as an important comparative factor in each of these arenas.

Environmental Degradation and Colonialism: Interconnected Legacies

Within the current rubric of postcolonial studies little attention has been paid to the ecological repercussions of the colonizer's attack on the environments of the colonized. However, a recent rich body of socially engaged poetics historically links environmental degradation with colonialism, imperialist capitalism and structural prejudice, demonstrating that an understanding of the socio-ecological results of colonial policies and actions is essential to India's cultural presence in a postcolonial present. As Vandana Shiva, Gail Omvedt, Ramachandra Guha, Madhav Gadgil, Mahasweta Devi, Nina Sibal, and others have

recently demonstrated, environmental racism is one legacy of European colonialism that has not diminished in the postcolonial context.

In *This Fissured Land: An Ecological History of India*, Madhav Gadgil and Ramachandra Guha "argue that British colonial rule marks a crucial watershed in the ecological history of India" (p. 5). Vandana Shiva links eco-colonial issues to gender issues, suggesting an irrevocable bond of mutual sustenance between women (and often all native forest peoples) and the forests. Her now classic text *Staying Alive*, like *This Fissured Land,* contrasts the ecological ideologies and conditions in pre-British India with subsequent colonial and postcolonial Indian ideologies and conditions. Pre-British ecological principles, often spread through oral tradition, sustained a symbiotic relationship between people and forests through "'local production for local use'" (Gadgil and Guha, 39). The preservation of sacred groves and ancestral sites of forest peoples in India (for example, the *aurans* in Rajasthan and *Devaranyas* of the western ghats) have been a mechanism for continual and sustainable forest maintenance (Shiva, 68; Gadgil and Guha, 23, 29). Familial relationships with nature objects encouraged respect and the forest helped people meet spiritual needs (Gadgil and Guha, 20). Taboos and proscriptions often promoted resource conservation and helped avoid environmental collapse (Gadgil and Guha, 22, 24). For instance, harvesting would often be curtailed when resource densities fell. Pasture was held in common ownership while herds were private property; contrary to Garret Hardin's classic (Western) assumptions in "Tragedy of the Commons," in India the system of common ownership protected the land. For centuries, religion and mythology—especially Hinduism, Jainism and to a less-publicized extent, tribal religions—have been important aspects of a generalized Indian view of nature in literature and life. The Upanishads are possibly the first extensive environmental writings in India. National and regional festivals still celebrate the cyclical renewal of nature that is tied to mythological/religious traditions. For instance, Holi (Phagwah) takes place in March to commemorate the sacrifice of Holika, who saved her nephew Prahalad from fire, allowing for the regeneration of the crops (after the wrath and vanity of the subsequently humbled king had passed). "The streets are filled with a moving mosaic of riotous colours" as people throw dyes upon one another (Haniff, 4).

Vandana Shiva demonstrates early examples

of a loosely defined "feminine principle" in Aranyani, goddess of the forest who is identified with a hymn in the Rig Veda (Mackenzie, 74); in the Aranyakas' (forest texts) in which the Earth mother is a tree mother (Shiva, 56); and Amrita Devi, the woman who led the first Chipko movement. Vandana Shiva shows through her examination of written and oral tradition that Indians have had a long-standing reverence for their forests and that that reverence has often been integrally related to the "feminine principle." Furthermore, "women as foragers were critical in managing and renewing the diversity of the forest" (Shiva, 60). The public domain of the forest was open to women and the gendered public and private spheres that held throughout modernization in the West were less stratified in India prior to the eighteenth-century wave of European colonialism. Furthermore, Shiva substantiates the native aspect of the bond she has identified by pointing to a wide range of (male) Indian writers who created literature about the relations between humans and nature in the national context during the British occupation: for example, J. C. Bose, the scientist; Mohandas K. Gandhi, the political activist; and Rabindranath Tagore, the poet. Each wrote extensively on the forest homescape. Tagore wrote of the forest "as the language of liberation," and in creating a contrast between the West and India, and between urban and rural, he argues that "culture that has arisen from the forest has been influenced by the diverse processes from species to species, from season to season, in sight and sound and smell. The unifying principle of life in diversity, of democratic pluralism, thus became the principle of the Indian civilization"(in Bandyopadhyay & Shiva, 67).

Recent work contradicts the commonly held mischaracterization that the British brought scientific forest management to India (Shiva, 58); rather, they brought environmental injustice through a charade of so-called preservation that was essentially a cynical prejudiced land grab:

When the British colonised India, they first colonised her forests. Ignorant of the wealth of knowledge of local people to sustainably manage the forests, they displaced local rights, local needs and local knowledge and reduced this primary source of life into a timber mine. Women's subsistence economy based on the forest was replaced by the commercial economy of British colonialism. (Shiva, 61)

The management and utilization of forests became possibly the "most important aspect of the ecological encounter between Britain and India," largely because Britain needed teak, sal, and deodars for its railroads and for building navy ships (Gadgil, 118). British military needs for teak brought about an eighteenth-century proclamation switching the right to teak trees from local governments to the East India Company. The shift in models created a shift in normative structures in forest communities from a forest-centered normality toward "normalcy dictated by market values" (Shiva, 69–71).

Its own forests already devastated by 1860, Britain became the world leader in deforestation, and the destruction of forest was used by Britain to symbolize political victory (Gadgil & Guha, 118). The ideology of domination was constructed as an absolute grant to further penetration and confiscation of Indian resources: "'The right of conquest', thundered one forest official, 'is the strongest of all rights—it is a right against which there is no appeal'" (quoted in Gadgil and Guha, 126). In the wake of British forest control, local communities lost access to land they had utilized for centuries, and the face of the land changed, often irreparably. Deforestation affected not only the land and the social and economic relations of the residents but entire ecosystems: flood and drought began to plague many of the areas where the polycultural ecologies had been upset.

Deleterious forest policy did meet with forest satyagrahas that spread across India as protests against British commercial reservations of forests.[3] Villagers removed what they needed from the forests in civil disobedience (Shiva, 66). However, since the late nineteenth century the forestry department has remained India's largest landlord and the "edifice of colonial forestry has been taken over by the government of independent India" (Guha, 6). Environmental racism has been extended from colonial India connecting the very structure of independent India, and the forest has become another site of skirmish over Indian economic independence many decades after political independence was won. Community-based systems continue to be delegitimated and the ideology of the market, not of nature, venerated (Gadgil and Guha, 44–45).

Literary Resistance to Forest Destruction

As the struggles for forest/forest peoples' rights have evolved there have been literary voices of resistance; the forest-centered aspects of colonialism have been addressed extensively in fiction by writers such as Mahasweta Devi and Nina Sibal. For instance, Mary Oraon, the protagonist in Mahasweta Devi's short story "The Hunt" offers an alternative model of capable resistance for both women and the forest under the siege of a feudalism, born of colonialism, and global capitalism. Both she and the planted timber are the result of Australian colonization in the region. Parallel plots are narrated in "The Hunt"—one tells Mary's revenge against sexual patriarchy; the other plot develops around the illegal cutting of the sal forest by an outside contractor who lies, cheats, and bribes in order to carry home an immense profit from forest he has no right to cut. The contractor is Mary's stalker. In order to retain her relationship with the man, whom she has chosen to marry, Mary uses the Jani Parab, the women's hunt, "to make the biggest kill"—the contractor (*Imaginary Maps*, 17). She thereby adheres to the symbolic ritual. "What Mary did that day has been done in that area again and again" (*Imaginary Maps*, viii). The tribal songs are their documentation of history and through their songs Mahasweta learned the story of "what [Mary] had done on Jani Parab day in order to marry the Muslim boy" (*Imaginary Maps*, xxviii). However, the significance goes beyond Mary's own self-determination in romance and revenge for harassment: "She resurrected the real meaning of the annual hunting festival day by dealing out justice for a crime committed against the entire tribal society" (*Maginary Maps*, xxviii).

As Mary prepares for her own marriage that will follow the hunt, she also prepares grounds for a marriage of gender and ecology issues. After the contract broker insults Mary with his unsolicited attentions, she uncovers the extent of his crimes and reveals them to the people he has cheated. Her detective work and organizing have prepared the local community—from the landowners on whose "property" the sal forests stand to the manual laborers who carry the cut lumber—to resist the illegal deforestation that is taking their resources without fair remuneration.

In another example of constructive resistance to ecological struggle, the incorporation of the historical Chipko Movement into a postmodernist bildungsroman is played out in Nina Sibal's *Yatra: The Journey*. The protagonist, Krishna Kaur, embarks on a pilgrimage for environmental justice that takes her through the area where the Chipko Movement is active; there she "received the secret of *angwaltha* from the *Chipko* women, their spirit of love reaching her as she walked through the *Deva Bhumi* of Uttarkhand on her *padyatra* (p. 168, italics in original). The novel begins with Krishna's return to India from an activist-business trip to London: "[h]er short visit had been useful in terms of the contact she had made in the Forestry Commission. And an international environmental foundation had committed funds for an important river project in the Gharwal Hills" (p. 1). But environmental concerns are rarely mentioned for the next 154 pages. At that midway point in the 300-page text, readers are given a narration of Krishna's *padyatra* (journey by foot), which is a pilgrimage to Chipko activism (p. 155). The novel foregrounds gender issues in the Chipko Movement:

> After all, at its heart, the Chipko Movement is very feminist. It consists essentially of a string of spontaneous confrontations, triggered and managed by women of the region, in which none of the so-called leaders were present. In some cases they were struggling against their own men who saw their immediate economic interests tied up with the decisions of the district administration.... Their men sold off the forest, its destruction would have meant the women walking at least another five kilometres every day to fetch fuel and fodder. The women won and saved the forest....
>
> (p. 156)

Sibal's portrayal of Amrita Devi is brief, but important in that it lays out a precedence in protecting the forest "by any means necessary," including the sacrifice of their own lives. Her followers mythologize Krishna, "the woman of the trees," like Amrita Devi, whose story Krishna evokes (p. 163). Krishna tells her audience:

> I will end with a small story. In the year 1730, a *saka* was offered by a band of Vishnois of Khejadli village in Jodhpur, Rajasthan, when their forest was invaded. They were led by Amrita Devi. She tied the first sacred thread round a tree and offered her head, saying that it was too cheap for the price of a tree. Three hundred and sixty-three men and women hugged the trees to save them, and they were hacked to death. (p. 158)

The historical Chipko Movement, like its fictional representation, has built its demonstrations and its name on the myth of Amrita Devi. The movement's success was recently heralded in *India Magazine*: "Chipko, the unique ecological movement, led by the women of Garhwal to save trees, has assumed folkloric status" (Jawahara 30). The contemporary "folkloric status" has precedent in the actions of the Vishnois martyrs to save the sacred *khejri* trees. With that event begins the recorded history of Chipko, which means "to embrace" (Shiva 67). The myth serves as a creative source of political action, centuries later.

Krishna's *padyatra* culminates in the joining together of the pilgrimage and the local organizing forces of students as well as voluntary organizations to campaign and demonstrate to stop a tree auction that has been scheduled "to award a contract for the felling of 20,000 trees" (p. 165). Through their local educational efforts, the people are successful in protecting the trees by shutting down the auction, promoting a ten-year ban on tree cutting, and initiating research to further understand what would go into maintaining a sustainable forest. Thus Krishna's pilgrimage and, indeed, the text as a whole weaves together personal and community discourses of self-determination and resistance to reveal structures of environmental degradation as well as patriarchal domination in both political and personal realms. Sibal's use of fiction as a "creative source of political action" toward green justice suggests a parallel to the movement's utilization of myth depicted in fiction.

Paradigms of Independence: Postcolonial Ecologies

The roots of the present focus on ecology in literature and politics lie partially in the Indian Independence Movement. Antje Linkenbach traces ecological perspectives to Gandhi's gram raj (village rule), which has been used continuously by leftists and militants. Gandhi's perspective was at odds with Nehru's socialist industrial model of modernization that was to end "all exploitation of nation by nation and class by class" (p. 64). For Nehru, political freedom would be followed by economic freedom, villages were backward, village life was irrelevant to modernization and nature was a resource for industry. However, for Gandhi, economic freedom was a precursor to political freedom, and

economic freedom would be achieved through decentralized village-based economies in collaboration with nature, and independence was a chance for a revival of the moral character of "Indian tradition and civilization" that critiques the West and claims universal relevance (Partha Chatterjee in Linkenbach, 64). Gandhi is seen now as "a kind of early 'Green,' a forerunner of the ecological movement, the root of an alternative socialism in India; indeed, much of today's Indian environmentalism refers back to Gandhi" (Omvedt, 12).

Gandhian strategies not only led to the Chipko movement, they helped shape Chipko's success. Two decades of poetics and praxis has enabled the Chipko andolan to establish itself as a new social movement with successful environmental resistance strategies. Mira Behn, an important precursor to the contemporary Chipko Movement,[4] was a European Gandhian disciple during and following the Independence Movement who moved to the Garhwal hills in the 1940s to continue village reconstruction on the Gandhian model. A mimeo by Mira Behn describes how she discovered environmental destruction due to forestry: "The sight of these disastrous floods led me each summer to investigate the area north of Pashulok whence they came. Merciless deforestation as well as cultivation of profitable pines in place of broad-leaf trees was clearly the cause" (p. 69).

Mira Behn's eco-sociological research determined the reasons for the environmental degeneration: "Mira studied the environment intimately and derived knowledge about it from the local people. From the older ones she learnt that, earlier, Tehri Garhwal forests consisted largely of oak"; she also learned that Garhwali folktales and folksongs repeatedly described two species—*banj*, an oak, and *kharik*, a hackberry, that had largely disappeared from the region. Mira Behn felt that a primary reason for environmental problems might be that the *banj* and mixed species forests were being replaced with the more exportable pine. She wrote about her ideas and also passed them directly to her younger co-worker, Sunderlal Bahuguna, who would become one of the main Chipko activists (Shiva, *Staying Alive*, 69–70).

Mira Behn was not the only woman in the region writing about the threats to its well-being. Another foremother of the Chipko movement was Sarala Behn, also a Gandhian European relocated in India, who started an ashram dedicated to education and empowerment of hill women (Jain, 173). In 1978, in *Blueprint for Survival* Sarala explained Chipko's demand:

> The main role of the hill forests should be not to yield revenue, but to maintain a balance in the climatic conditions of the whole of northern India and the fertility of the Gangetic Plain. If we ignore their ecological importance in favour of their short term economic utility, it will be prejudicial to the climate of northern India and will dangerously enhance the cycle of recurring and alternating floods and droughts. (Shiva, *Staying Alive* 72)

Chipko activists believe the forests sustain society; thus society must sustain the forests. Short term economic interests should be considered secondary. Such lessons, which countered the imposed industrial model of preservationism were still ancient wisdom to many peoples.

Sunderlal Bahuguna describes the role of environmental action in everyday Indian life: "People in the West imagine the ecological movement was born in the West. It was not university professors nor political leaders who gave birth to it, but village women, because this message is inbred in their hearts. They had no formal education, but they worshipped the tulsi plant, the sacred symbol of the flora. My mother was illiterate, but after taking her bath, she always watered the tulsi plant" (p. 9). Chipko has been an outgrowth of this very foundational relationship to nature. Not surprisingly, people use their literature and folk culture to further forest causes. Chipko poetics narrate popular protests in which women win their battles through performative acts/arts such as embracing the trees to interrupt the cutting, and singing responses to the local pro-development men's retorts. The first documentation of the use of Chipko in the 1970s is marked in a famous poem by "Chipko poet," Ghanshyam Raturi, which calls for embracing trees in order to "save them from being felled. / The property of our hills. / Save it from being looted" (Jain, 173; Shiva, *Staing Alive*, 73). Such poems became the logos of the movement, and were often "performed" by groups of youth, women and men in demonstrations and rallies; thereby, the forests were protected with word, song, symbol and, when necessary, bodies.

Bahuguna attributes success to the "political folk song" giving "more than 50 percent of cred-

it for the popularity of this movement to the folk-singers" (Weber, 90). The folk poet Ghan Shyam Sailani composed the following Garhwali song that schoolchildren sing to demonstrate the bond between trees and water "Do not axe these oaks and pines, nurture them, protect them. From these trees the streams get their water and the fields their greenery. Look how the flower smiles in the forest" ("The Response," Bharat Dogra, et al.).

Chipko poetry helped "the movement spread through the totally decentred leadership of local women, connected to each other not vertically, but horizontally—through the songs of Ghanshyam Raturi, [and] through 'runners' like Bahuguna, Bhatt, and Negi, who carried the message from one region to another" (Jain, 173). Bahuguna describes the related campaign against eucalyptus take-over.[5] "We walked over the hills, using songs to take the message to the people. There is a song that says, 'If you see a eucalyptus tree, pull it out, because it spoils the others; it takes too much water, and is a friend of the capitalist'" (p. 10).

In the Chipko andolan, feelings were split toward the ban that curtailed all forest cutting, including what was being done for local needs (Linkenbach, 75). Not only does the debate resemble the earlier one between M. K. Gandhi and J. Nehru over two visions for independence, it begins to examine the visions of indigenous peoples in India whose forest-centered perspectives have been largely ignored.

Indian Postcolonial Identities and Ecologies

In "Poet, Lover, Birdwatcher" Nissim Ezekiel, a definitive figure in twentieth-century Indian poetry, parallels birdwatching and pursuing a love interest from a heterosexual male poet's perspective. (The poet's gender is suggested by the pronouns in the poem). "To force the pace and never to be still / Is not the way of those who study birds or women"(Haq, 82). Ezekiel's poem is not about male exploratory conquests; it is not about conflict, so much as about quest. For Ezekiel, the places one must go to find "rare birds"—"Along deserted lanes and where the rivers flow" or along shorelines—are akin to deep grounds of one's being (Haq, 82). Ezekiel chronicles a process of self-exploration that occurs through relationship with human, aviatory, and mythical beings. "Poet, Lover, Birdwatcher" does not present a radical rewriting of heterosexual relations. However, the poem does present a model of masculinity that is an honest alternative to patriarchal domination; as the poet demonstrates in his last lines, such a process of "patient love relaxing on a hill" produces miracles inside the poet-man (Haq, 82). A place that spawns such miracles, a place that is learned of only through relationship with the natural, as well as the human, world may also be the seedbed for egalitarian relations between men and women.

Rabindranath Tagore builds upon a similar concept in several short stories about female-male relationships. S. B. Mukherji argues that "Tagore would insist on looking at love with the same eyes with which he looked at nature" (p. 71), and in both poetry and fiction the two themes are often synthesized. Five of Tagore's stories begin the collection *Of Women, Outcastes, Peasants, and Rebels: A Selection of Bengali Short Stories* translated by Kalpana Bardhan. Bardhan anthologizes stories that show "the parallels, the connections, and the points of intersection between the oppression of women in India and that of peasants, untouchables, and other stigmatized groups" (p. 31). She does not speak of choosing stories that also voice the domination of nature and, in particular, the "natural environment" upon which the "stigmatized" groups depend. However, in many of the Bengali stories in this collection, societal oppressions are presented in relation to the domination of nature, through metaphor and/or experience.

In "The Living and the Dead" a sense of the constructedness of death and life are examined. The story is carried forward by the weather, most often the monsoon storms that accompany the woman, Kadambini, who believes she has died and thus presumes she has become a ghost. In one instance, "[t]he rain-soaked wind blew in and put out the lamp, immediately filling the room with the outside darkness. Kadambibi stood inside the room, with the continuous sound of rainfall surrounding her, enveloping her. Grimly she said, 'I'm still Kadambini, [your] childhood friend . . . , even though I exist as dead'" (p. 59). Finally Kadambini, who has realized she is not dead, suicides by jumping into the pond in the rain in order to "prove that she was not dead before" (p. 61). The sound of her death interrupts the storm as the head of the house hears "the splash quite clearly through the pervasive sound of rain, just as the storm has interrupted her live appearances earlier. The rain, which has created an eerie feeling to accompany Kadambini's "ghostly" appearances to others, continues day and night surrounding her death.

In "The Girl in Between" a middle-aged man's erotic awakenings when he takes a young second wife are explained in an entomological metaphor: "The insect born and matured inside a ripe mango never had to search for its lovely nectar; it never knew the intense desire to savor its sweetness. Release that insect in a spring garden in bloom and then watch its eagerness: how it keeps hovering around the half-open rosebud; how a bit of the flower's perfume and a bit of its nectar intoxicate it for more, and more!" (p. 76). The most extensive nature imagery, which extends beyond metaphor, occurs in the bridegroom-protagonist's narration in another short story "Haimanti"; he watches in ineffective empathy as his young and idiosyncratically self-defined wife is slowly worn down by the torments of his family. She comes from a rural life where she lived alone with her father and did not learn to be the relentlessly docile and un-opinionated bride his middle class urban family expected. When they find out that she does not come with the wealth they presumed her father had, she becomes a scapegoat for their anger. The young bridegroom does not learn of his wife's suffering from her, but is told of the tormenting by his younger sister who witnesses it. He also observes what Haima does not vocalize when he sees her inside looking out on the natural world to which she had once had free reign: "I saw Haima sitting at one of the windows [with iron bars], sitting very quietly, looking to the west, where a *kanchan* tree in the Malliks' garden was covered with pink bloom. . . . A curtain lifted in my mind. . . . Never before had I seen so clearly this depth of her sadness" (p. 93). The freedom "outside and inside" with which Haima has grown up is reachable only through her relation to nature. Her husband believes that it is only nature that can give Haima back what she has lost when he asks "Was there any freedom inside me that I could give her? She knew that [her husband had no sense about the environment of her past freedom and thus could not retrieve it for her] very well. That was why, sitting at the barred window, she silently communicated with the sky, That was why in the middle of some nights I woke up to find her . . . on the roof . . . looking at the star-filled sky" (p. 93).

The epistle-writer-narrator of "Letter from a Wife" also finds critical revelations in both nature and the love of a young and tormented woman. Here the woman-nature parallels create opportunities for pro-active decision making. The "glow-ing red leaves," that sprout each spring on the "ugly bare branches" of "a lowly *gaab* tree, right beside an open drain in the desolate surroundings of her in-laws' house are the image that allows the letter-writer to see that "hearts too bloom in the most inhospitable surroundings at the touch of a spring breeze that comes from some unknown heaven, not exactly down the winding lane as in the case of the *gaab* tree" (p. 102). The writer's heart blooms, as well as the young woman who loves her: "it was her love that somehow made me see myself in a new light. . . . I found myself beau-tiful as a free human mind, in being my natural self" (p. 102). Later, after the suicide of the abused younger woman, she writes "alone by the sea" having come to full realization of this other "identity, which is [her] relationship with the uni-verse and its creator" that gives her the "courage to write . . . as [herself], not as the second daugh-ter-in-law of your family" (p. 96). As she com-pletes the letter, she sees her new life before her as the "vast ocean" and the "clouds of Asarh gath-ered to give the rain of life." She sees both the "boundless sky" and "how boundless the glory of human destiny can be" (p. 109).

The impasse of young women bound by soci-etal patriarchal protocol to unbearable and inhumane conditions is represented in conjunc-tion with the subjugation of nature, decades after Tagore's short stories were written. Mahasweta Devi's stories, like most of Tagore's, were originally written in Bengali. In *Imaginary Maps*, Spivak remarks that "the stories in this volume are not only linked by the common thread of profound ecological loss, the loss of the forest as foundation of life, but also of the complicity, however apparently remote, of the power lines of local developers with the forces of global capital." In engaging environmental issues, one must contend with global capitalism; likewise, as Mahasweta demonstrates, in rural India ecology is linked with bonded labor and the "displaced space" where woman, indigenous peoples and forest have been conscribed by feu-dal and capitalist control.

Mahasweta Devi and Spivak explain that in India, the bonded labor system had its origins under British rule: "They [the British] created a new class, which took away tribal land and con-verted the tribals into debt-bonded slaves" (*Imaginary Maps*, xii). The three stories in *Imag-inary Maps,* which are dedicated "for all indige-nous peoples of the world," take place in indigenous communities whose environmental

rights and needs have been long ignored both within India and externally. They illustrate the links of colonial and feudal exploitations of indigenous peoples. In examining women's dis-placement and sometimes almost complete and literal deterritorialization, Mahasweta never portrays women solely as victims; they are sur-vivors and they are often the initiators of exten-sive resistance to their oppression. For instance, a character by the name of Sanichari, usually an "herbal medicine woman"/social/health worker appears in many of Mahasweta's stories. Sanichari's profession as an herbalist aligns her with the forces of nature and she draws on her extensive knowledge of the complex intercon-necting of natural forces; this is precisely the knowledge that has not been acquired by outside "developers" who fail to recognize the ecologi-cal demise that their "development" projects bring (*Imaginary Maps*, 199).

Mahasweta's short story "Dhowli" can be read as a "tragic" love story that demonstrates that ties to the economic hierarchies and patri-archy are stronger than the bonds of affect or "love" but a parallel reading could find that "Dhowli" narrates a woman's regression to the point where her body has become means for "absolute sexual and economic exploitation." The contrast between these interpretations raises important questions about the position of women's subjectivity in the context of the ideolo-gy of heterosexuality. One might contemplate the ramifications of a shift from the passive paradigm of "woman as nature" to a view of "relationship and nature as a space of interaction—an active habitat for woman and man." At several points issues are raised that are salient to the links between feminism and environmental justice.

In "Dhowli" Mahasweta engages a "natural-ized" construction of sexuality as well as a "materialist" construction of sexuality and the two seem at odds. The naturalized paradigm is created through a description of nature with anthropomorphic characteristics that parallel the "nature" of Dhowli's sexual encounters. Dhowli and Misrilal consummate their mutual attraction for the first time in the forest that plays a role in convincing Dhowli to become involved with Misrilal: "The forest in the early afternoon is primitive, gentle, and comforting. The Misra boy's voice was imploring, his eyes full of pain and despair. Dhowli was unguarded in mind and body. She gave in" (*Of Women*, 192). As the relationship develops, the forest continues to set the tempo: "In the solitude of the forest, the Misra boy was dauntless, telling her of his plans, and his words seemed to mingle with all the myths associated with the old forest, taking on an enchanting and dreamlike quality" (Spivak, *In Other Worlds*, 192).

In Dhowli's period of waiting after Misrilal has been sent away by his family, the forest takes on an aura of foreboding: "The woods looked horrible to her, the trees looked like ghoulish guards, and even the rocks seemed to be watching her" (*Of Women*, 194). When Dhowli first considers suicide she intends to use pesticide: "She knew that she could fall asleep forever with the poison for killing maize insects" (*Of Women*, 187). In contemplating death by a synthetic anti-natural element, a pesticide, Dhowli figuratively equates herself—the human shunned by her lover and subsequently her community—with the creatures of nature that are despised and thus poisoned by men. Descriptions of nature are suspended in the middle of the narrative, but return at the end when Dhowli has been sentenced to become a "public whore" and is on the bus to the city, having been exiled/evicted from the village by her lover:

> The sun rises, and Dhowli watches the sky, blue as in other days, and the trees, as green as ever. She feels hurt, wounded by nature's indifference to her plight. Tears finally run from her eyes with the pain of this new injury. She never expected that the sky and the greens would be so impervious on the day of turning Dhowli into a public whore. Nothing in nature seems to be at all moved by the monstrosity of what is done to her. Has nature too gotten used to the Dhowlis being branded as whores and forced to leave home? Or is it that even the earth and the sky and the trees, the nature that was not made by the Misras, have now become their private property? (*Of Women*, 205)

Nature plays the role of surrogate lover: it is at the "imperviousness" of nature, not of Misrilal, that Dhowli is brought to tears. Yet nature plays a further role in this passage: in questioning the motives for Nature's indifference Dhowli draws attention to the connections between gender abuse and the economic and environmental subjugation of "feudal capitalism."

In "Paddy Seeds" Mahasweta politicizes the modernist trope of the regenerative forces of nature by mapping it over feudal capitalism, environmental racism and other class, caste, and eth-

nicity issues. Paddy (rice) seeds are of figurative and literal importance to the story "Paddy Seeds" just as they are literally the traditional bulk food sustenance of much of India, including the central northeastern plains that is the site of most of Mahasweta's work. Vandana Shiva empirically illustrates what Mahasweta critiques. She shows that paddy seeds, and other seed grains, are the latest sites of contested territory to fall victim to a global "capitalist patriarchy." Seed grains developed over the centuries as sites of production that are most compatible with local conditions have been "village commons"; these agricultural banks are being invaded by multinational corporate capitalism. "Patents are central to the colonization of plant regeneration and, like land titles, are based on the assumption of ownership and property. . . . Ownership and property claims are made on living resources, but prior custody and use of those resources by farmers is not the measure against which the patent is set"(Shiva, *Close to Home*, 133).

Gayatri Spivak finds an answer for "the internationality of ecological justice in that impossible undivided world" that can be potentially reached through learning what she names "ethical responsibility in singularity" or in "its simple name 'love'. . . . Nature, the sacred other of the human community, is, in this thinking, also bound by the structure of ethical responsibility of which I have spoken in connection with women's justice" (*Imaginary Maps*, 200).

As Gayatri Spivak suggests, the protagonist in each of Mahasweta Devi's stories creates a part of the model that is needed to promote the "impossible global justice" that is posited as an impossible imperative. In the environmental literature from India that is discussed in this essay, an "impossible [environmental] justice" is figuratively, if not literally sustained; the precolonialist vision of human ecological relations is being re-examined in India's twentieth-century literature. Perhaps in the twenty-first century the developing literary models will spread throughout India's forests.

The author would like to thank Pramila Venkateswaran, Neela Bhattacharya Saxena, and Ralph Nazareth for sharing poetry, essays, and ideas.

Notes

1. *A Survey of Anglo-Indian Fiction* lists more than 1,000 works of fiction by the English on India (Beliappa, 11).

2. In the jungle adventures described in *Man-eaters of Kumaon* and *The Temple Tiger*, Jim Corbett writes with an admiration for India's forests and forest peoples and for their adversaries, the tigers who had developed deviousness, most often through damaging encounters with humans; however, Corbett does not recognize the extensive damage done by the domination of human colonizers.

3. *Satyagraha* translates as "truth force" or nonviolent resistance/civil disobedience as popularized by Mahatma Gandhi preceding Indian independence.

4. "Behn" is an honorific term meaning "sister," often adopted by Gandhian women workers.

5. Eucalyptus was introduced broadly in India as a fast-growing commercial crop with devastating effects on polycultural forests and the people who depend on them.

Selected Works and Further Reading

Bahuguna, Sunderlal, and Jeremy Seabrook, "Right Livelihoods: Chipko Movement," *Earth Ethics* (Winter 1996), pp. 9–10

Belliappa, K. C., *The Image of India in English Fiction: Studies in Kipling, Myers, and Raja Rao,* Delhi, India: B. R., 1991

Corbett, Jim, *Man-Eaters of Kumaon,* New York: Oxford University Press, 1944; London: H. Milford, 1944

———, *The Temple Tiger, and More Man-Eaters of Kumaon,* Bombay, India: Oxford University Press, 1954; New York: Oxford University Press, 1955; London: Oxford University Press, 1957

Gadgil, Madhav, and Ramachandra Guha, *This Fissured Land: An Ecological History of India,* New York: Oxford University Press, 1992; Oxford: Oxford University Press, 1993

Godden, Rumer, *Mooltiki; and Other Stories and Poems of India,* London: Macmillan, 1957; also published as *Mooltiki; Stories and Poems from India,* New York: Viking, 1957

Haniff, Bebe, unpublished paper, 1996

Jain, Shobita, "Standing up for Trees: Women's Role in the Chipko Movement," in *Women and the Environment: A Reader: Crisis and Development in the Third World,* New York: Monthly Review, 1991; London: Earthscan, 1991

Jawahara, "A Chipko Journey," *The India Magazine of Her People and Culture* 13:10 (1993), pp. 30–41

Linkenbach, Antje, "Ecological Movements and the Critique of Development: Agents and Interpreters," *Thesis Eleven* 39 (1994), pp. 63–85

Mahasveta Debi, "Dhowli" and "Paddy Seeds," in *Of Women, Outcastes, Peasants, and Rebels: A Selection of Bengali Short Stories,* edited and translated by Kalpana Bardhan, Berkeley: University of California Press, 1990

———, *Imaginary Maps: Three Stories,* translated by Gayatri Chakravorty Spivak, New York: Routledge, 1995

Mukherji, S. B., *The Poetry of Tagore,* New Delhi, India: Vikas, 1977

Omvedt, Gail, *Reinventing Revolution: New Social Movements and the Socialist Tradition in India,* Armonk, New York: M. E. Sharpe, 1993

Shiva, Vandana, ed., *Close to Home: Women Reconnect Ecology, Health, and Development Worldwide,* Philadelphia: New Society, 1994; London: Earthscan, 1994

———, *Staying Alive: Women, Ecology, and Development,* London: Zed, 1988

Sibal, Nina, *Yatra: The Journey,* London: Women's Press, 1987

Spivak, Gayatri Chakravorty, *Outside in the Teaching Machine,* New York: Routledge, 1993

Tagore, Rabindranath, *Selected Poems,* translated by William Radice, New York and Harmondsworth, England: Penguin, 1985

Weber, Thomas, *Hugging the Trees: The Story of the Chipko Movement,* New York and New Delhi, India: Viking, 1988

Section 4:

Africa and the Arab World

War and Environment in African Literature

❦

Christine Ombaka

Throughout human civilizations, war and military violence have remained uniquely topical themes in the arts and literature precisely because war profoundly evokes strong emotions arising from gruesome human massacres, physical suffering, and mental anguish that war victims experience during and after the war. Indeed, civilians and non-combatants in the theater of war have always to run to the bushes or to foreign lands for safety. More tragically, if they ever return from their hiding places after the war, they are likely to find their property destroyed. On the other hand, if they are captured by the enemy they are likely to be killed, ill-treated or enslaved.

In many respects, therefore, war is all-embracing, affecting the whole human population as well as the natural environment. Human massacre, pollution of air and water, the accumulation of wastes, desertification and the disappearance of non-renewable resources, and refugee problems are the major by-products of war that are inexorably linked. These afflictions cannot be ignored because not only are they interlinked into seamless causes and effects but also they are fundamentally some of the emotionally moving images of war that have created imprints in the human psyche and have continued to haunt the imagination of artists born during or after a war. Literature, as well as the other arts, it has been argued, possesses great powers through words and images that can effectively be used to condemn war or celebrate peace.

Against this background, therefore, this chapter discusses the African attitude toward war and the environment as depicted and portrayed in African literature. Through a corpus of different literary genres, the chapter discusses trends, perceptions, and the changing outlooks of African writers toward war and the environment and provides a context in which the writers can be considered important and indispensable environmental educators who have emerged as a significant force in the protection of nature and human survival.

It can be argued that artists have celebrated courage and heroism during wartime because they have been fascinated by gallantry, heroism, and power (see Jones, Introduction). They have depicted war scenes with overflowing emotions and have thrilled the hearts of their audiences with heroic stories meant to instill courage and bravery in the young to whom the stories have been narrated by the evening fire. Not only did such legends and heroic tales in the past celebrate heroes as warriors and conquerors but they also became dramatic microcosmic representations of the battles that existed in human history which could continue to the present day.

According to the history of the African people, warfare was glorified and almost was a daily pastime. During state functions kings, emperors, and rulers celebrated their military exploits with the masses commemorating their heroic acts of war in song and dance, myths, and praise poems. Kwambana Nketia writing about Akan poetry argues that in the Akan oral performance, allusions are made to past successes in war, particularly the decapitations of enemy chiefs and potentates (p. 23). During such festivals, the chief was praised through song and dance for having delivered the old and young from the ravages of war.

Additionally, poems and songs were used to remind the chief of his roles and responsibilities as a statesman and a war leader upon whom the people collectively depended for protection, peace, and progress. At the same time, such poems and songs were intended to remind the chief of his former enemies or the enemies of his predecessors and to encourage him to face war as bravely as his ancestors had done. Therefore, in the African traditional society, artists composed military songs, poetry, and chants to praise and incite both their kings and warriors to take up arms and defend their communities. The poems and songs acted as psychological stimuli to them.

The question of bravery and warriorhood is, indeed, explored in Chinua Achebe's novel *Things Fall Apart,* where he depicts aggressiveness, heroism, and destructiveness as the hallmark of manhood. Achebe characterizes Okonkwo, one of his principal characters, as a great warlord in the land who had brought honor to his village. Okonkwo was also admired for being economically successful, having several wives and barns of yam in his household. At 20 or so he had had two titles and was proud to be the first to bring five human heads home. As a result of such feats, Okonkwo became a symbol of strength and bravery—a role model whose impressive acts of heroism and fearlessness had earned him a distinguished and respected position in the community. Achebe further portrays the Umofian clan as fearless and militaristic in nature. In the first place, he characterizes the Umofians as having been badly provoked by the cold-blooded murder of the wife of one of their clan members by the people of Mbaino.

As the war between the two clans (Umofia and Mbaino) becomes imminent, however, the Oracles of the Hills and Caves avert it, arguing that the people have no strong case for it. In other words, the oracles call for general efforts at disarmament and warn the people against engaging in a war that would be seen to be a war of blame. In this respect, the people have the choice of reaching peace and reconciliation after the oracles have warned them. The choice made by the Umofian community is to seek compensatory damages for injuries already suffered. The Mbaino people on their part are only too glad to pay compensation and avoid the impending war at all costs because of the age-old belief held in

the community that the Umofians possess powerful magic and medicine that were thought to be the most potent of all.

Thus, the Mbaino accept the peace proposals and quickly pay compensation in the form of a virgin woman to be given away to Udo as a direct replacement for his slain wife, while the ill-fated Ikemefuna is given away to the Umofian clan to be killed and sacrificed as the traditional gods demanded. The chief aim in this peaceful and compensatory negotiation is to achieve improved relations between the two clans. But more important is the belief in the oracles, magic, and medicine that were important mythical systems, and no serious attempt to achieve peace could ignore them as a means of establishing order in the society.

Similarly, Ngugi wa Thiong'o in *The River Between* shows us that Makuyu and Kameno have had leadership wrangles of long standing and that war between the two clans is imminent. Likewise, the war is averted because of the ancient belief held in the community that the Agikuyu people are blood brothers and sisters who according to the Agikuyu creation mythology have sprung from a common origin— Gikuyu and Mumbi. The gist of the argument is that since the Agikuyus have a common ancestor, they have no business engaging one another in unnecessary war but should foster the noble objectives of peace, reconciliation, and cohesion instead.

Indeed, Achebe, Ngugi, and many of the first generation of African writers derived their inspiration from traditional lore, indigenous customs, and the oral traditions in their attempt to demonstrate the fact that Africa had a culture she could be proud of, but also that the society had a close relationship with nature and the place of religion and cultural norms within it. They showed that in the traditional African societies people had a close relationship with the land whose use or misuse was viewed in close association with myth, ritual, religion, and other symbolic configurations. These cultural norms either imposed exemplary restraint in the utilization of the land or enhanced extensive damage of the land. The role of religion in the protection of nature is clearly depicted in Ngugi's *The River Between,* which presents the view that the Kameno hills and surrounding environs, including Mount Kirinyaga, were sacred areas, the abode of the god Murungu. Ngugi emphasizes that the sacredness of the hills was understood within the context of traditional creation mythology, that is, the story surrounding the origin of the Kikuyu tribe. According to this mythical tale, two very important proposals were made: first, the original ancestral parents, Gikuyu and Mumbi, and their creator, Murungu, sojourned on this hill en route to Mukurwe wa Gathaga, and while they were there, Mumbi and Gikuyu gave birth to nine daughters who, in turn, bore many children later to compose the Agikuyu tribe.

Secondly, and most importantly, the myth made clear that the gods gave the people maximum freedom to utilize various resources, including land and soil, which were to constitute the main interest of the tribe. Land and soil were to be the core of the community's economy; therefore no generation was ever to lose contact with it or give it away to strangers. Instead, they were to jealously guard it, protect it and efficiently utilize it as a source of food for themselves and the whole of posterity. Thus in *The River Between* the god is reported to have spoken of resource use and healthful production, giving the land to both "man and woman. . . . to rule and till" and to "hand it down" (p. 9).

The myth encased the right to live in Kameno hills and further gave the people sovereign right to possess and utilize their tribal resources throughout the labor process as a strategy for survival. Thus, not only was everyone to engage directly in the labor process but also to protect the land against wanton destruction for the benefit of future generations. The Agikuyu genesis story indicated that the biophysical environment was the natural basis of the Agikuyu's existence with religion governing it. For Murungu, the creator, is represented as issuing this instruction before the Fall, that is, before outside pollutants or colonialists—commonly referred to as the butterflies—invaded and degraded the land. In general, the myth explained not only the origin of land ownership by the Agikuyu community but also dictated the manner in which it was to be utilized according to the way history, evolution, and progress were imagined to have taken place.

But we must next ask the question: how did the African writers respond to colonialism and the white man's presence in Africa, where land alienation became sensitive and intensely pertinent in the definition of black and white relationships? Writers noted with great concern that the African traditional life was falling apart as a result of the onslaught of the colonialism and military conquest that depleted Africa to its very roots. Writers did not hesitate to capture this vio-

lent encounter and the way people perceived and reacted to the white man's arrival. This experience was aptly captured in Ouologuem's *Bound to Violence*, Achebe's *Things Fall Apart,* Kalu Okpi's *The Warriors*, and a host of other works that depicted the social forces and the violent coming of the white man in an ancient and proud African society. In these works, the artists recounted the history of their people and presented colonial conquest as a violent and destructive experience with the white man using firearms to subjugate and dehumanize the Africans. Achebe, for instance, narrated that the white man wiped out the people of Abame on one market day in retaliation for the murder of one of their missionaries—who had come to explore the terrain and pave the way for the rest of the missionaries. In one of their organized punitive expeditions, the white man opened fire and exterminated the entire people of Abame who were not only taken unaware but were unarmed themselves. Abame was obliterated. The inescapable fact is that Achebe depicted colonialism as a history of environmental transformation and a calamity that saw the African people terminated physically and socio-culturally. With Abame annexed, people massacred, and the land taken away, the colonial world became a question of environmental concern as it touched squarely upon the vital interests of human existence. But more importantly, it symbolized the violent history Africa was undergoing and ensured economic misery and degradation for generations to come.

Similarly, Ngugi wa Thiong'o in *The River Between* presents this violent conquest by probing into the distant past through myth, legend, and historical fact. He narrates that, although there were occasional tribal conflicts and confrontations in the primitive past, the situation was not as destructive as during the colonial era. In other words, the clashes that had existed did not go into full scale violence. It was the intrusion of the colonialists that disrupted the smooth life that the Gikuyu had lived. When the white man came to Africa, they robbed the people of their God-given land and posed as a great threat to the people's source of livelihood. Already, they had captured Nairobi, Muranga, Siriana Missionary Center, Kiambu, and Tumutumu and were gradually moving further inland to capture more land while displacing the people and destroying their cultural life in the process. What worried the people most was precisely what these new changes portended.

The African writers were sensitive to the fact

that colonialism represented grave inequalities that affected the basic means of production. Family land was taken away by the white minority who had taken over the greatest portion of the best land—the so-called White Highlands. They had appropriated for themselves the best part of land without considering the fact that the Africans had already owned the land from time immemorial. Later, the issue of land alienation became a major theme in African writing because, as Ngugi argued, the loss of ancestral land to the white settlers constituted a life- and livelihood-threatening phenomenon. Land constituted the principal aspect of economic life, and, according to the Agikuyu tradition and indeed Africans in general, it was not to be misused or given away to strangers. Land was bound up with the way people perceived and evaluated their surroundings. No wonder in his novel *Weep Not, Child* Ngugi's "Where did the land go?" becomes a disturbing question. Without land to satisfy material needs the African people were doomed to a miserable existence as squatters. Therefore, the Mau Mau war in Kenya emerged because of the land crisis. Land was stolen, and, according to Ngugi in *Homecoming*, this thieving remained the key to Kenya's problem as it was to all the colonies of Central and Southern Africa. The transfer of land from the African to the colonial masters provoked the people to take up arms and fight the white man and to resist colonial domination.

This resistance is demonstrated in Okpi's novel *The Warriors*, where Chief Igbonku the great warrior of Abam faces a fierce battle against colonial invasion. His army of spearmen are the pride of Abam manhood, and they are ready to defend their motherland without fear of death. They believe that as warriors of the society they are assured honorable positions by the sides of their forefathers in the underworld. This belief motivates them to face the white invaders bravely besides having strong military advisers and high priests with whom they were to fight the likes of Captain Pallock who epitomized the invading colonialists.

In general, the African artists writing on the European invasion have been concerned with demonstrating that colonization was violent and was equally matched with violent resistance from Africans. Despite fierce and heroic resistance against foreign domination, the Africans still lost the war because of the vast military superiority of European weapons. The loss of war spelled the beginning of barbarous colonial

rule in Africa that perpetuated and institutionalized discriminatory practices and subjected the black people to more and more restrictions on their mobility and their right to seek a livelihood in fertile lands. Indeed, they argue that an armed struggle was a necessary part of the total liberation struggle and was in keeping with the philosophy of human rights. Political liberation was seen to be related to economic growth and national ecology in many respects. First, land on which the Africans were relegated to live and to till was poor and infertile. It degraded and impoverished them, as Alan Paton portrays in *Cry, the Beloved Country*. He expresses the idea that the land apportioned to the Africans by the white masters was so bare and so unproductive that the maize hardly grew to the size of a man. His argument is that the Africans were so impoverished that they were forced to migrate to urban areas in search of food and shelter. The effect of this movement was that cities began to fill with people living in slums. The wretchedness of the people also has become a major theme of many African writers as they argue against poor political and economic systems.

The feeling of political liberation and economic empowerment began to emerge but it became more intense and urgent toward the end of World War II. All of a sudden, the Africans were awakened to their situation and therefore immediately after the war, there was a general nationalistic upsurge in the whole of the European colonies in Africa. Correspondingly, artists began to write poems and songs to inspire the people to take up arms and liberate themselves from the shackles of the colonial regimes. In so doing, literature of the period became so militant that it came to be known as protest literature. These were mainly political literary works that were written to expose all the evils and injustices that the colonial governments were inflicting upon the black race as a whole and to incite resentment and rebellion.

According to B. A. Ogot, a distinguished historian, the Mau Mau movement had first been associated with squatter agitation by the Africans who either were unable to meet their needs in crowded urban and rural areas or were made landless as a result of alienation. Apart from being landless, they also faced the brutality of the colonial administration. Their resistance to such treatment later exploded into the 1952 Mau Mau liberation war. The experience of the Mau Mau war subsequently led to an outpouring of Mau Mau literature.

The works of Meja Mwangi, namely *Carcase for Hounds*, the treatment of the story of Dedan Kimathi in novels and plays such as *The Trial of Dedan Kimathi* by Ngugi wa Thiong'o and Micere Mugo, and a collection of Mau Mau poems and songs, *Thunder from the Mountain* by Maina wa Kinyatti, came to give an artistic picture of the struggle for independence in Kenya. Kinyatti's songs, for example, are said to have been used as weapons to politicize and educate the Kenyan workers and peasant masses and to prepare them for an armed struggle.

Indeed, Mau Mau liberation songs were sung at various political rallies, at home, in the guerrilla bases, in detention camps, and in prisons as a medium of political education and sensitization. The songs expressed the people's hatred toward the imperial powers and recounted land as one of their major grievances. The songs "Struggle For Our Land," "Why Sell Your Land," "The General Cry in Gikuyu Land," and a host of others in Kinyatti's anthology stated that land was one of the most salient grievances within the anti-colonial movement. For instance, the song "Struggle For Our Land" in particular urged the people to struggle for land thus:

Struggle for land!
Because the land was ours
But was taken from us (p. 16)

Mau Mau artists became stern advocates of liberation and encouraged the people to sacrifice their lives and families in order to liberate their motherland. They felt that gallantry was no longer necessary in the liberation struggle. What mattered most was courage, bravery, and an unquenchable fighting spirit, which would earn them freedom and respect from other races. Therefore, Mau Mau literature demonstrated a spirit of armed resistance and a commitment to war and bloodshed as a means of bringing peace and development to the African people. This commitment was so strong and so religious that the poets appealed to the gods, *Ngai*, to give them strength and courage so as to overcome European oppression. They prayed in the mountains, kept night vigils, and took an oath of allegiance as an expression of their total commitment to the African cause. This commitment was further expressed in such poems as "Let Us Die If Need Be." Other guerrilla songs and mobilization songs in the anthology appealed to the masses to join the Mau Mau movement, sac-

rifice their lives for their land and also seize the moment for the affirmation of black power. On the other hand, artists pledged to deal ruthlessly with African traitors.

In *Carcase for Hounds*, Meja Mwangi depicts the Mau Mau warrior General Haraka and his troops as taking an oath of allegiance to keep the Africans loyal to one another throughout the Mau Mau movement. Psychologically, the oath gave them strength and a feeling of solidarity that enabled them to pillage, burn homes, and cause terrible carnage within European administrative outposts. Fear of General Haraka, the writer further demonstrates, created a mass exodus toward Mount Kenya. This means that displacements and general fear caused by Mau Mau warriors also affected the African people themselves. But the most important argument in the novel is that the Mau Mau fighters did not care very much what destruction they heaped on the people and the physical environment. Indeed, what mattered most to them was the belief in the liberation struggle–a belief that even the threat of death could not weaken (*see* Ngugi, *Homecoming*). Therefore, to a great extent, the Mau Mau created a state of violent savagery in their quest for political and economic liberation. Political and economic challenges were viewed as interdependent and integrated causing major tensions between the white colonizers and the colonized blacks.

Elsewhere in Africa this attitude toward war and violence also recurred time and again especially in Angola, Mozambique, and Guinea, where apartheid regimes caused terrible havoc. Many Africans went to detention, others died in police cells, on the gallows, in the towns, in the villages, and in the streets as victims of armed agents of the state. Accordingly, the literary output of the region came to express a tone of anger and ferocity as found in an anthology of poems, *When Bullets Begin to Flower*, edited by Margaret Dickinson. This is a collection of militant poems against the British, French, and Portuguese colonizers. Artists expressed their grievances and pledged to take up arms to liberate themselves because they were oppressed and inhumanely treated, as in Agostinoh Neto's poem "Contract Workers." Similar poems, like "A Militant's Poem," pledged revenge and warned that the people would open all the prisons, set free all the African prisoners and destroy the colonial tyrants in order to be politically and economically free. So long as land was taken away and the economic development of the people adversely affected, the African artists were compelled to resist such exploitation and they constantly dwelt upon the theme of war as a justifiable means of liberating themselves.

In this collection, *When Bullets Begin to Flower,* harsh mistreatment and exploitation by the apartheid regimes are further echoed in "Song of Agony" and Viriato da Cruz's "Black Mother," which recounted the suffering of African slaves working in cane plantations, paddy fields, the coffee farms, and cotton fields in various parts of the world. Noemia de Sousa's "Black blood," "We shall not mourn the dead" by Helder Neto, and "To point a moral to comrade" by Mercelino dos Santos praised the role of Frelimo soldiers in the liberation struggle, their devotion, determination, and courage in the face of difficulties, and their quintessential love for Africa—their motherland.

Within the process of the militarization of poetry, songs, novels, memoirs, autobiographies, music, and jazz, artists demonstrated courage and a fighting spirit in ways that their writings came to be associated with the revolutionary movements. They were fighting to put a stop to the atrocities committed by the white governments and to oppose the entire concept of the Bantustan (homeland). In South Africa, Alex Laguma depicts the poverty and squalor of slum life and the underprivileged in his famous novel *A Walk in the Night.* Peter Abrahams' *Mine Boy* depicts industrial filth and the poor conditions of laborers in the mines. Many artistic works of the region became increasingly assertive and questioned the appalling conditions of the apartheid system and what it stood for, including its diabolical impact on the black man and the environment in which he lived.

Thousands of blacks had been killed under the apartheid system, including Steve Biko, the Black Consciousness ideologist whose sad story is told in an anthology of liberation poems, *Malibongwe*, and a novel, *Cry Freedom*, which was later made into a popular film. These works epitomized the struggle for freedom and social justice and portrayed artists' visions and concerns about human degradation. More significant was the infamous Soweto uprising of 1976 that saw innocent schoolchildren massacred by the police state in what appeared to be a peaceful demonstration against the introduction of the Afrikaans language in the education system. The brutal murder was artistically captured in *Malibongwe*, the novel *Children of Soweto* by Mbulelo Mzamane, and two popular films,

Sarafina and *Graceland*. In outrage, artists captured this terrible scene in their works and condemned the shameful human carnage. This included pop singer Miriam Makeba. She sang *Soweto Blues*—a heartrending song in the film *Graceland*—a song that recounted the incident and accused the state of "finishing the nation."

Indeed, artists depicted and satirized the diabolical conditions of apartheid and expressed the urgency to strike against the state. The poem "A Soldier at War" in Barry Feinberg's anthology *Poets to the People* assured patriots that the moment to strike had come as the poet states:

This is the moment patriots!
to strike with the spear, to pierce
the heart of domination, this citadel
   of inhumanity (p. 126)

It is important to emphasize that African writing during this period of colonial rule demonstrated that artists had become political and nationalistic. Literature, especially poems and songs, projected the alternative revolutionary voice of the people who used them as instruments of political expression and condemned the outrageous and brutal systems of foreign domination. The picture that emerges is that of writers identified with the social and economic needs of the continent and pledged to advance the cause of nationalism. However, as Nkosi argues in *Tasks and Masks*, artists in South Africa and most parts of Africa where oppressive systems reigned had to produce their work underground and smuggle it out of the country as they attacked the government of the day. Other revolutionary writers and critics of the day were either killed or imprisoned while yet others fled into exile for expressing their strong stance against the status quo.

By the second half of the twentieth century, African liberation wars had become nastier with the arming of various tribal factions traditionally known to be hostile to one another. Having been kept under brutal and repressive colonial rule for so long, the Africans generally believed that political independence would automatically be a means to solving their economic problems.

Thus, Patrice Lumumba, the premier of Congo Kinshasa (now Zaire) and heroic martyr, in an electrifying speech marked with extraordinary irony and self-honesty promised that, as new African leaders, they were going to end all injustices they had suffered under colonialism and see to it that all citizens would enjoy fundamental liberties. He further pledged that the new African leaders were "going to rule not by the peace of guns and bayonets but by peace of the heart and will" (Ayittay, 98). Indeed, Lumumba and other Pan-Africanists, namely Nkrumah, Nyerere, and Padmore, had become unquestioned leaders of non-violence as they pledged juridical independence based on political equality, social justice, peace, and human dignity for the new African nations. Consequently, when independence came in each and every country, the African masses celebrated it with unbounded euphoria. Micere Mugo, a Kenyan poet, was to express this euphoria in her poem "We will Rise and Build a Nation" where she highlighted the fact that the African masses had not only been excited in rebuilding their countries, but had trusted their leaders and "garlanded them with embracing hearts" (p. 68). This political stance was particularly ironic in that, immediately after independence, Lumumba and Nkrumah were assassinated and robbed of the chance to lead their countries through the visionary post-independence period.

Secondly, the African masses began to experience worse predicaments than during the colonial period, as appropriately predicted or prophesied in Margaret Laurence's novel *This Side Jordan*. In this novel, one character, Victor Edusei, expresses fears and doubt over the future of Ghana's independence. In a pessimistic manner, he comments to another character: "You put your faith in Ghana, don't you? That new life. . . . You wait until after independence. You'll see such oppression as you never believed possible" (p. 117). Similarly, Achebe's Mr. Green of *No Longer at Ease* and Ngugi's Mr. Thayer of *Weep Not, Child* are quite convinced that the whole African leadership simply will not work. True to these words, since independence, African countries have experienced more civil wars, ethnic bloodbaths, injustices, oppression, wanton destruction, and military coups than they did during the colonial era. Wars and military coups have followed one after another despite these countries having been committed to peace and development at independence. Therefore, the period after independence has seen a prolific school of writers who have made it their business to record the happenings of the day.

Of great importance is that writers are more interested in depicting the post-independence wastelands than in singing the glories of the past, as was the case with the Senghorian school of Negritude. Scanning through the literary works of the post-independence era, one is inclined to find problems of poverty, corruption, degradation, and the abuse of power in such works as Achebe's *A Man of the People* and *No Longer at Ease*, Ngugi's *Petals of Blood*, and Armah's *The Beautyful Ones Are Not Yet Born*, which concern themselves with the ills and degradation of African political leadership and the painful definition of African independence.

But more than this, writers have realized on the whole that the Africans have not only been betrayed by their black leaders but cruel military dictatorships, coups d'état, civil wars, brutality, repression, and flagrant violations of human rights under the one-party dictatorship have become more widespread on the continent, especially in Nigeria, Uganda, Zambia, Malawi, Zaire, Kenya, Ethiopia, Somalia, Sierra Leone, Rwanda, and Burundi.

Cyprian Ekwensi wrote about the Biafra war of 1967 in *Survive the Peace*, while Okot P'Bitek's *Song of Prisoner* and "Song of Soldier," John Ruganda's *The Floods*, and Alex Mukulu's *30 Years of Bananas* depicted Idi Amin Dada's military dictatorship and Ngugi's *Petals of Blood* provided political commentary on Kenya's repressive situation. Writers of the post-independence period argue that, since independence, conditions in Africa have not improved but worsened. The continent has become more poor and violent than at the dawn of independence. Disgusted by the gruesome suffering of the masses during the 30-month-old Biafra war, Ekwensi was to depict in the most harrowing details scenes of genocide and the fear and desperation of fleeing refugees in Nigeria as a newly independent nation. Seeing the problem in context, Ekwensi contends that the Biafra war was a potential extension of the Cold War by the superpowers and their transfer of weaponry and war technologies in developing countries.

Novelists of the Biafra war, namely Kalu Okpi in his novel *Biafra Testament*, Achebe in *Girls at War and Other Stories* and his collection of poems *Beware, Soul Brother*; Okpewho in *The Last Duty*; Eddie Iroh in *Toads of War* and *Forty-Eight Guns for the General*; and others in this category are war artists whose interest was to expose the strains of the Biafra war on the people and the physical landscape.

Complex internal factors, such as ethnicity, religion, culture, economics, and the depletion of limited resources all inspired and perpetuated this conflict. Thus Ekwensi and the other Biafran artists could not help but to expose the general degradation of the war. Equally important, according to Ekwensi, was that war created pollution arising from shelling, air raids, and explosions. In addition there were the fleeing refugees described as "streams of silent people fleeing mainly on foot, with head loads. Men, women and children, sliding past like so many black ghosts." In *Girls at War and Other Stories*, Achebe also depicts the common person as the sufferer, the victim of war and political upheavals, while the engineers and military leaders partied.

The Biafra war could be likened to the 1996 Zairian and Goma wars, the 1994 ethnic bloodbaths in Rwanda and Burundi, and the infamous military dictatorship during Idi Amin's reign of terror between 1971 and 1979, as well as to ethnic genocide in Somalia, Sierra Leone, Liberia, and Ethiopia. The literary works reflect events in post-independence Africa and sad scenarios of war and militarism typically associated with independent black Africa.

John Ruganda, a Ugandan playwright, in his drama *The Floods* depicts episodes of murder, disappearance, destruction, and crackdown on human rights in post-colonial Uganda. Concerned with the political tyranny during Idi Amin Dada's regime, Rugands dramatizes the tragedy of this unforgettable episode. Buogo—the Ogre and the principle character in the play—personifies Idi Amin. In acts of systematic murder and terrorism the Ogre uses soldiers to create chaos. There is military lawlessness as the soldiers become the enemy of the people, plundering the country's resources, raping women, and killing innocent people at will, such that the whole realm resembles a slaughterhouse. According to Ruganda, Uganda was polluted in that it was barricaded with blood. The bodies of those who had been massacred were cast into Lake Victoria to be devoured by crocodiles. We are told of truckloads of civilians driven to their deaths over cliffs at the point of bayonets.

Similarly, in his "Song of Soldier," an extract of a song he began to write but never completed, the late Okot P'Bitek examined the destructive role of the military in Africa and the leaders who "enjoy blood" and the "freedom to kill." With an underlying touch of cynicism, P'Bitek was angry at the irresponsibility and unwillingness of the state to promote peace and harmony among human beings. His satire became the weapon to attack the Ugandan military dictatorship. Everything from destruction to wanton chaos was a common sight, but the crimes and atrocities committed by the dictator were too chilling even to witness, as "mad jets tore the sky in fury / scattering death across the land" (p. 111). The situation became so hopelessly gruesome that even animals were affected. They were stunned into silence, as we are told that "Cows gazed with bleary eyes / Goats huddled together / Sheep lowered their heads to the ground" (p. 113).

Like Ruganda, P'Bitek is disillusioned with the African political dictatorship, the orgy of ethnic bloodletting, and the general insecurity in the land. Like a war correspondent, he set out to make the people aware of injustices being done to them by their black brothers. Artists have attempted to wage a crusade against these senseless civil wars and arouse the masses to this plundering so that they could combat the situation. But this has been met more with apathy than enthusiasm. Most people at this critical time can only escape to other countries as refugees rather than try to overthrow the system. Many writers have been determined to show the manner in which the African world is, alas, wasted, a continent where even dead bodies are indecently assaulted.

Not only have the common people been subjected to the tyranny of repressive military governments where innocent people have either been mercilessly murdered in cold blood or detained or sent into exile, but also activist writers have been murdered. Environmental artist Ken Saro Wiwa was assassinated by the Nigerian Military government of Sani Abacha in November 1995. Saro Wiwa had protested on behalf of the Ogoni people against pollution and environmental degradation caused by the Shell Oil Company, but the government of Sani Abacha became intolerant of his criticism and silenced him. Murdered with eight other Ogoni leaders, Saro Wiwa, the author of *Saro Boy* and other works, attempted to mobilize his Ogoni people against the government through songs (*Africa Today*, 10).

It can be argued that within the dynamics of military regimes in Africa, artists have pointed out that there has been an intimate and symbiotic relationship between human and physical environments. Lake Victoria, the second largest freshwater lake in the world, for example, was considered a dumping ground for dead bodies killed by Uganda's military government. Ruganda in his satires depicted the lake as so polluted by dead bodies that fish disappeared. And the few that were caught were not even fit for human consumption because human fingers and flesh were found inside them. Ruganda appeared to argue for the protection of the lake and the need to maintain it as a valued environment at the same time that he exposed Idi Amin's atrocities.

Little-known Kenyan youth have also written poems on the African crisis and presented them at the Annual National Music and Drama Festivals, which culminated in an anthology of poems entitled *Youthful Voices*. Very significant environmental issues are captured as in the poem "Ethiopian Crisis." The poem personifies a young Ethiopian boy miserably clad in thin loincloth and desperate for water in drought stricken Ethiopia. The misery of the boy is not only the result of the pestilence of drought and hunger but also of the war and violence that have engulfed the Horn of Africa. "The Siren Sound of War," another poem in the same anthology, argues that the causes of the African crisis lie in "Lust for power, appetite for destruction / Is the story the bombs do tell / Violence, fear, utter devastation" (p. 44).

The question as to who or what is responsible for African violence and environmental degradation can be said to be as a result of lust for power and selfishness. The African leaders have mismanaged Africa and are responsible for the war, hunger, and poverty that have become commonplace. But the poems "Faceless Horror," "Refugees Crisis," and "The Civil War," also in the same anthology, give us the view that Africa is in a state of perpetual war with bombs constantly exploding and people running from place to place in search of food, shelter, and security. What is left of the land according to Kittobe the poet is nothing but "wailing women, crying children and whining animals."

In conclusion, the African artists have vividly captured the long tradition of war from the colonial period to the present and pointed out that the innocent Africa has not only been sinned against by European imperialists but that she too has been a sinner herself. The artists have used folklore, poetry, narratives, songs, and film to expose Africa's violent history and have emphasized that poor political leadership and senseless warfare have been responsible for depleting human resources and the surroundings in which they live. In other words, they have been concerned with the predicament of humankind and the natural world in a hostile social environment and have deplored the political systems that perpetuated such predicaments as found within the colonial, apartheid, and neocolonial systems that Africans have undergone historically. These writers reflect a sense of commitment to the protection of humanity and a respect for all of the rest of creation.

In their quest for human protection, the artists have used the gun, the pen, and the platform to fight these forces of destruction. Artists such as Achebe, Okigbo, and Ekwensi had been at the battlefront during the Biafra war. Agostinoh Neto, an outstanding poet and politician, was active in the Angola liberation war, while Denise Brutus, Ezekiel Mphalele, Alex Laguma, Ngugi wa Thiong'o, Micere Mugo, and many others wrote terse political novels and poems that saw them forced into exile. This included pop singers like Miriam Makeba, who used the song as a medium for political expression. Indeed, many of the artists who seemed to advocate peace and a respect for nature have believed that Africans can build a future that is more prosperous, more just, and more secure. In this way, they have contributed immensely and significantly toward environmental protection and the promotion of global harmony between humanity and nature.

Selected Works and Further Reading

Abrahams, Peter, *Mine Boy,* New York: Collier, 1946; London: Faber and Faber, 1946

Achebe, Chinua, *Beware, Soul Brother: Poems,* London: Heinemann, 1972

———, *Girls at War, and Other Stories,* London: Heinemann, 1972; Garden City, New York: Doubleday, 1973

———, *A Man of the People,* New York: John Day, 1966; London: Heinemann, 1966

———, *No Longer at Ease,* Greenwich, Connecticut: Fawcett, 1960; London: Heinemann, 1960

———, *Things Fall Apart,* London: Heinemann, 1958; Greenwich, Connecticut: Fawcett, 1959

Africa Today 2:3 (May/June 1996)

Armah, Ayi Kwei, *The Beautyful Ones Are Not Yet Born,* Boston: Houghton Mifflin, 1968; London: Heinemann, 1969

Ayittay, George B., *Africa Betrayed,* New York: St. Martin's, 1992

Beier, Ulli, and Gerald Moore, eds., *Modern Poetry from Africa,* Harmondsworth, England: Penguin, 1963; new ed., Baltimore, Maryland: Penguin, 1966

British Council, ed., *Youthful Voices: Poems*

from Kenyan Schools, Nairobi: Longman Kenya, 1992

Dickinson, Margaret, ed., *When Bullets Begin to Flower: Poems of Resistance from Angola, Mozambique, and Guiné,* Nairobi: Heinemann Kenya, 1989

Ekwensi, Cyprian, *Survive the Peace,* London: Heinemann Educational, 1976

Feinberg, Barry, ed., *Poets to the People: South African Freedom Poems,* London: Allen and Unwin, 1974; enlarged ed., Exeter, New Hampshire, and London: Heinemann, 1980

Jones, D. L., ed., *War Poetry: An Anthology,* New York and Oxford: Pergamon, 1968

Kinyatti, Maina wa, ed., *Thunder from the Mountains: Mau Mau Patriotic Songs,* London: Zed, 1980; Trenton, New Jersey: Africa World, 1990

Kittobe, Jem, *Black Jesus and Other Poems,* Nairobi, Kenya: East African Literature Bureau, 1978

La Guma, Alex, *A Walk in the Night,* Ibadan, Nigeria: Mbari, 1962; as *A Walk in the Night and Other Stories,* Evanston, Illinois: Northwestern University Press, 1967; London: Heinemann, 1967

Laurence, Margaret, *This Side Jordan,* New York: St. Martin's, 1960; London: Macmillan, 1961

Molefe, Sono, ed., *Malibongwe: ANC Women, Poetry Is Also Their Weapon,* Sweden: African National Congress, c. 1985

Mugo, Micere Githae, *My Mother's Poem and Other Songs,* Nairobi, Kenya: East African Educational, 1994

Mukulu, Alex, *30 Years of Bananas,* Nairobi, Kenya, and Kampala, Uganda: Oxford University Press, 1993

Mwangi, Meja, *Carcase for Hounds,* London: Heinemann Educational, 1974

Ngugi wa Thiong'o, *Grain of Wheat,* London: Heinemann, 1967

———, *Homecoming: Essays on African and Caribbean Literature, Culture and Politics,* New York: Lawrence Hill, 1972; London: Heinemann, 1972

———, *Petals of Blood,* London: Heinemann, 1977; New York: Dutton, 1978

———, *The River Between,* Portsmouth, New Hampshire, and London: Heinemann, 1965

———, *Weep Not, Child,* London: Heinemann Educational, 1964; New York: Collier, 1969

Ngugi wa Thiong'o, and Micere Mugo, *The Trial of Dedan Kimanthi,* London: Heinemann, 1976

Nketia, Kwabena, "Akan Poetry," in *Introduction to African Literature: An Anthology of Critical Writing from Black Orpheus,* edited by Ulli Beier, London: Longman, 1967

Nkosi, Lewis, *Tasks and Masks: Themes and Styles of African Literature,* Evanston, Illinois: Northwestern University Press, 1967; Harlow, England: Longman, 1981

Ogot, B. A., "Politics, Culture and Music in Central Kenya: A Study of Mau Mau Hymns, 1951–1956," in *Some Perspectives on the Mau Mau Movement,* edited by William R. Ochieng and Karim K. Janmohamed, Nairobi: Kenya Literature Bureau, 1977

Okpewho, Isidore, *The Last Duty,* London: Longman, 1976

Okpi, Kalu, *The Warriors,* Basingstoke, England: Macmillan, 1994

Ouologuem, Yambo, *Le Devoir de Violence,* Paris: Éditions du Seuil, 1968; as *Bound to Violence,* New York: Harcourt Brace Jovanovich, 1971; London: Heinemann Educational, 1971

Paton, Alan, *Cry, the Beloved Country,* New York: Scribner's, 1948; London: Jonathan Cape, 1948

P'Bitek, Okot, *Song of a Prisoner,* New York: Third Press, 1971

———, "Song of Soldier," in *Artist, the Ruler: Essays on Art, Culture and Values,* Nairobi: Heinemann Kenya, 1986

Ruganda, John, *The Floods: A Play,* Nairobi, Kenya: East African Publishing House, 1987

Saro-Wiwa, Ken, *Sozaboy: A Novel in Rotten English,* New York and Harlow, England: Longman, 1994

Long Live the Fresh Air! Long Live!
Environmental Culture in the New South Africa

Julia Martin

My first idea for this chapter was to collect and analyze eco-literature: recent South African plays, poetry, and fiction that raises or responds to environmental issues as one of its main concerns, or explicitly promotes an ecological philosophy or worldview. Working with Lannie Birch, my excellent research assistant, I wrote for information to about 100 people in environmental non-governmental organizations, trade unions, community organizations, and cultural institutions, as well as individual writers and activists. We telephoned, faxed, consulted library databases, worked in archives, and altogether conducted about 25 interviews. Quite soon I gave up the idea of producing a representative survey, and realized that the most I could hope for with this chapter would be to give a taste of the range of material available. Part one discusses a fairly wide range of interpretations of what counts for environment in the material we collected, and part two is a more specific focus on reinventions of African tradition in cultural responses to ecological crisis.

Although there is a sense in which all texts are writing, and a documentary is as cultural an object as a poem, I have narrowed the field to a more conventional understanding of literary culture. The project looks at material produced for speakers of English during the recent years of transition: from apartheid government to the new democracy, from the cultural discourses of people's struggle and resistance to those of reconciliation and empowerment. With one exception, all the examples I discuss here have appeared since the release of Nelson Mandela and the unbanning of major political organizations in 1990. Although "the environment" may still appear marginal to most South Africans, this transitional period has seen a significant broadening and redefinition of environmental

priorities: the white middle-class conservationism that was associated with the previous government has in many contexts been challenged by progressive models that more people are able to support. These changes are reflected in literary culture so that, in recent years, environmental literature has begun to emerge as a significant (if still quite embryonic) new direction.

In all genres, by far the majority of explicitly environmental work is aimed at children. Funders are more likely to support theater that is guaranteed a youth audience. This means that drama/theater in education work tends to predominate, and after that, the developing genre of children's fiction. If theater is the readiest medium for presenting the public/political dimensions of the subject, poetry (unfunded and marginal as it is) has tended to enable more personal/philosophical exploration. Prose fiction is then situated somewhere between them on the personal/political continuum. In all this, the availability of funds and the expectations of funders and audiences are very significant in determining not only genre and subject matter, but also the manner in which the subject is addressed.

What Is the Environment? What is Nature?

Instead of predetermining what counted for environmental material, I decided to use the range of work I received to reflect on people's assumptions about environmental priorities. Inevitably these assumptions serve different interests. A related issue concerns who or what is seen to be responsible for environmental degradation. Much of the material blames "Man" or "human beings," and there are several courtroom dramas that depict "mankind on trial." This approach tends to obscure the inequities of race, class, and gender that make some of "us" more effectively exploitative than others. This part of the chapter will look at three quite general and overlapping ways of defining "the environment" in the material I studied: Firstly as conservationism, wilderness, the wild; secondly in terms of specific green issues, both local and global; and thirdly with regard to eco-politics and eco-philosophy.

Conservation, Wilderness, the Wild

Much of the cultural material either represents environmental priorities in terms of conservationism, promotes a wilderness ethic or celebrates "wildness" in some way. In some cases this emphasis reproduces the very ideology that has alienated the majority of South Africans from wildlife conservation. In *Tikki's Wildlife Adventures*, the protagonist lives in a game park where his father is a game scout. While Tikki's encounters with animals are described in detail, the social space in which they arise is represented in a way that naturalizes the hierarchic, authoritarian (racist?) relations between white warden and black game scout and his family. The narrative is focalized from within the game reserve, so that poachers, an upstream village, and even the previous inhabitants of the land are represented as problematic outsiders. This is precisely the attitude that conservation authorities are now trying to undo, through participatory management by local people. The book is a mild example, but it is one of a series, and has been endorsed by the Wildlife Society.

Dale Kenmuir's *Sing of Black Gold* is a much harder book (the word "hard" appearing repeatedly) in which successful conservationism, specifically saving rhinos, is equated with militaristic, macho values. Employing fairly dubious methods learned in the Zimbabwe bush war, game ranger Tom Finnaughty leads a "military-style operation" against poaching in the course of which poachers are shot dead, rhinos saved, corrupt and ambitious black officials exposed, and humble black men rewarded. The novel's version of conservationism tends to stereotype women, and to promote an idea of woman-as-nature. The single woman in the novel is initially described as "the tomboy type, but with all the feminine trappings, and with a mind of her own" (p. 89). Later when glimpsed bathing in the river, she comes to "epitomize and symbolize the way he felt about nature . . . as precious and alluring as the visual wonder of a beautiful

woman" (p. 132). Although the narrative dismisses the equation of rhino horn with potency, the male battles it describes have a lot to do with phallic power. The prize in such contests? Promotion, further authority and woman/nature.

In the children's fiction we collected, conservationist discourse is often related to the language of "wild and free," with variations on the theme of setting free a wild animal. In some cases, this emphasis is in seemingly unconscious contradiction with the distinct unfreedom in the interactions between people. In Eileen Molver's *Guardian of the Mountain,* the white game ranger's son Mathew and his initially overwhelming desire to possess the lammergeyer chick he has rescued is gradually overcome by his love for it. When he sets the bird free, he suddenly understands "what conservation was all about" (p. 87). It's an important if slightly trite lesson, but in presenting it Molver makes use of several unexamined stereotypes that, to a large extent, undermine these assertions of the value of freedom. These include the uncritical representations of Mathew's boring, myopic, unliberated mother, and of Tolo, the faithful, reliable black retainer ("game guard"—a term that has now been replaced in the Parks Board for ideological reasons) who initiates the young white male protagonist in the ways of the wild. The novel values his view of conservation, but his subordinate status is unquestioned, his voicelessness in the white adult world, specifically the Parks Board, represented as natural.

If racist and patriarchal stereotyping are often "what conservation really means," there are happily a number of other examples that explore wildness as the source of many freedoms. In *The Shadow of the Wild Hare,* Marguerite Poland presents the trope of setting free a wild animal as a profoundly liberating rite of passage. Rosie rescues a very rare wild hare, tries to tame it, and ultimately returns it to the wild. Apart from the hare itself that she comes to observe closely, she learns about wildness from two marginal people whom she, along with others in the white farming community, had particularly feared and ridiculed. Jacoba Pandoer, the "mad," cross-eyed woman, tells Rosie the painful story of how, as a child, the white community took her away from the "Boesman" family she loved, forcing her to live in a Children's Home. The reader is drawn into recognizing correspondences: "You cannot tame something if that is not the thing it wants. . . . They locked me up, once" (p. 73). To learn about the hare, Jacoba sends Rosie to the terrifying jackal trapper, a "Boesman," who teaches her that the animal cannot live if its *isithunzi*—translated as shadow—has died. The hare is *Dhau*, "the child of the old people and like them he is almost gone" (p. 38). Housed among Rosie's rabbits and pet lamb, *Dhau* has lost his *isithunzi*. If she wants to restore his life, Rosie must keep *Dhau* in the dark where he likes to be alone, feed him wild plants, and give him back to the wild at new moon. This she does, discovering in the process that people have *isithunzi* too. Wildness, freedom, darkness, shadow, spirit, Bushmen, magic, madness; the novel effortlessly draws the wisdom of silenced knowledge into the foreground, and then returns it to the dark.

Green Issues

A second frame for defining environmental priorities is in terms of "green issues," specifically pollution control and waste management. With regard to local problems, issue-specific plays or stories aimed at promoting local action tend to be favored by corporate sponsors. For example, SAPPI Waste Paper has made extensive use of Drama in Education in promoting recycling. As part of the War on Waste (W.O.W) program thousands of schoolchildren have watched theater that promotes the message "Don't dump, recycle!" In plays such as *Pulling Green Strings*, and *War on Waste SAPPI*, W.O.W. recycling is associated with the forces of goodness, cleanliness and light, marshaled in a war (or a "mission") against the evil, dirty darkness of dumping. The dark forces are generally won over by the end of the play, and the audience directly or indirectly encouraged to become "warriors" too by participating in the W.O.W. program.

While the development of a culture of recycling is surely a prerequisite for an environmentally sustainable society, material of this kind is very questionable. Like other "green" corporate initiatives, such programs are both an exercise in containment and the source of further profit. In response to the growing public awareness of "green issues," they absorb people's potential energy for radical environmental activism, and provide the comfort that "at least I'm doing something," while detracting attention from the industrial-capitalist sources of the problem. In this case, the irony is astonishing: recycled pulp from paper collected by children inspired by the W.O.W "mission" is sold to none other than

Dirty Dumper himself—the notoriously polluting SAPPI paper mill.

In terms of global green issues, there have been several plays for children that aim to raise awareness of issues such as toxic waste, ozone depletion, deforestation, etc. While they may offer a valuable perspective on global problems, it would be more useful and provocative if connections were drawn between these issues and local eco-social problems. Otherwise, the audience for such material is limited to those middle- and upper-class children whose immediate environment is sufficiently privileged to make "thinking globally" a possibility.

Eco-Politics and Eco-Philosophy

Whereas it can be in the interests of corporate-sponsored material to discourage audiences from questioning the political and economic sources of eco-social suffering, a small body of more "community-based" cultural work has explored specific problems as a catalyst for just such questions. In 1991 the traditionally left-wing Community Arts Project Theatre Company performed *It's Hip to Be Green*, a piece of street theater about littering and recycling. And in 1992, the community theater group Action Workshop produced *The Reddening of the Greens* (directed by Ithumeleng Wa-Lehulere) which, as the title suggests, presented the "green" problem of industrial pollution from the perspective of a Gramscian analysis of hegemony. The action is situated in a "place of waiting" at a gathering of five people who have recently died, directly or indirectly as a result of mercury pollution from the Thor Chemical plant in Natal. Reflecting on their experience, the play promotes the view that ecological and socialist analysis should be mutually informing: "Yes, the Greens need the Reds, and the Reds need the Greens" (Action Workshop, 7). The statement is reminiscent of the slogan "Ecologise Politics! Politicise Ecology!" that informed Eco-Programme's National Conference on the Environment the previous year.

The timing of these initiatives is surely significant. The ANC, SACP and PAC had been unbanned in 1990, and Nelson Mandela and other political prisoners released. It was a time when the political activism of the 1980s seemed to have achieved at least some of its goals, while the left-wing discourse that had motivated it had not yet been rewritten in the interests of the New South Africa. Progressive ecology was beginning to emerge as an alternative to conservative conservationism. So after a 1980s history of concentrating on protest theater, CAP could say it was "hip to be green," and in 1992 Action Workshop was in a position to bring an explicitly "red" discourse into conversation with "the Greens."

Although this transitional moment is possibly now over, there is still some valuable work being done on the politics of specific environmental problems, perhaps most prominently through the medium of educational comics. With titles like *The River of Our Dreams,* and *The Mystery of the Dangerous Drums,* comic books from the Storyteller Group use illustrated narratives to explore issues such as toxic waste and river pollution for mass distribution. Environment/development issues are shown to be inextricable from social justice priorities, such as literacy and the empowerment of women, which are integral to the empowerment of the community. Through stories of young people working together to solve community problems, the comics use a dialogic medium to promote the idea that ordinary citizens need to take collective responsibility for monitoring environmental abuse, since the polluters certainly won't. Instead of presenting an explicitly left-wing agenda, the material promotes the concepts of empowerment and co-operation (and implicitly reconstruction and development) that have become powerful watchwords in the mid-1990s discourse of transformation in South Africa.

Among the most provocative cultural work in this field is that which broadly promotes an eco-political/philosophical worldview without being issue-specific. It is also the most difficult to categorize. Andrew Buckland's play *Bloodstream* opens with a tree, breathing. A man appears, singing about "TimberLumber." He sees the tree ("the last tree. Left. Remaining. On the planet," [p. 2]) and begins to chop. The tree shouts "STOP!!" and the dispute is brought before the universal court of karma. The court decides to help the tree change the man's mind (his name is R. Soul) by inserting the tree in microscopic form into R. Soul's bloodstream where he begins a journey in search of the mind. It's a difficult quest because the mind and the entire toxic, polluted corpus is being controlled by the fascist forces of the Conscious Intelligence Army (CIA). Finally, once the personality micro chip, "the great 'I,'" has been disconnected, the Higher Brain Functions awake from their sleep to explain to the corpus that "You all make up the

mind of this body" (p. 15) and that the only way to decide the tree's fate is for all the organs to vote. The tree wins, and the play ends with a delightfully repentant and ecologically sensitive human, who says "we" instead of "I", and has decided to become a forester.

Buckland's verbal and gestural wit is a marvelous medium for establishing correspondences: between the environmentally exploitative "timberlumber" attitude, the chattering "I" that asserts its tyrannical authority as boss of the human body through the mechanisms of the U.S. Central Intelligence Agency, and the political and economic interests that disempower the majority of people in our society. In place of these oppressive relations, the play presents an alternative in the mutuality of tree and human, body and mind, proposing meditative awareness instead of the chattering "I", and asserting the rights of the marginalized. In extending the concepts of oppression and liberation in this way, the familiar rhetoric of political struggle is delightfully recycled: "Viva! The Body Politic Viva!" (p. 6), and "Long Live anatomical democracy. Long Live!" (p. 15).

Michael Cope's poetry and fiction is another body of work that promotes an ecological view in conversation with discourses of socio-political-psychological-spiritual liberation. For example, "Tea Ceremony" from *Scenes and Visions* turns the act of attention that the traditional Japanese ceremony embodies into a meditation on interconnectedness. Through structural patterns of repetition and parallelism, the poem evokes the unseen—silenced, marginalized—ecological and social systems that bring a cup of tea into being; such as the growth of the bud, the workers who harvested the tea, the water flowing as rain and rivers, and the plumbers and builders who piped it in to the house. The attention moves outward from the minute and the particular to the big Earth ecosystem: "To the oceans and the sun, / the great trade winds, and the world's turning, I pay homage" (p. 69). I've read the poem to students and environmental activists, and there is always a strong appreciation of the way it uses sacramental language, such as "homage" to material systems, to challenge habitual lack of seeing, while situating the most ordinary activity in an eco-social context that is vast. One might say that it deconstructs the idea of cup as entity in order to affirm its connectedness with all living systems.

Finally, Douglas Livingstone's poetic sequence *A Littoral Zone* reflects on his work as a bacteriologist assessing microbial changes in the water quality of the marine environment off the coast near Durban. Precisely situated in this location, the speaker launches "futile, / scientifically delivered blows at sullage" (p. 10). In tough, ironic, tender, compassionate observations of people, animals and ecosystems, and recurrent demonstrations of human cruelty and ignorance, this major poet conveys a sense of relentless activity in "rapt attendance on the sea's health" (p. 48). The work may be hopeless, yet it needs to be done. Working along the littoral zone between land and sea, city and wild, the scientist is a poet exploring thresholds, edges, the in-between. The poems are situated somewhere between despair and dogged resilience, between loss of faith in religious discourse and an awed love of "creation."

Numerous poems question the Judeo-Christian absolutes, while refusing the polar opposite certainties of nihilism, and negotiating instead something between irony and the sacramental. In "A Visitor at Station 21," the speaker's reflections on proofs and deconstructions of God in Western philosophical discourse is repeatedly interrupted by an awareness of his immediate environment, and of what is appearing in his peripheral vision: "In one corner of a cornea / a delicate duiker doe appears: / . . . The sun strokes me" (p. 53). The debate is well-reasoned, but reason is not enough, and the poem ends with another order of awareness: the doe in full view, alive. Whereas a great deal of South African eco-literature draws uncritically on Judeo-Christian concepts of salvation, Livingstone situates the idea of saving the Earth in a wider perspective. In a sense the sea needs no saving. It is the sea whose life, and our concern for it, saves us.

Reinventing African Tradition

In an attempt to establish "the [African] roots of conservation," South African nature conservation authorities have recently begun to draw on practices associated with the totem system, traditional healers, and the ancestors. A similar emphasis is emerging in the work of writers and performers who see African forms and world views as being more environmentally friendly than those inherited from colonial culture. In other parts of the world, such as Australia, North America and India, eco-culture has interpreted pre-colonial, indigenous traditions for similar purposes. Ironically, some of the work I collected for this project makes use of this material—for example, the speech attributed to Chief Seattle—but fails to make the connection with local sources. So interviewing people around the country, I was quite excited at the creative potential of a fairly recent reinvention of African tradition among cultural workers as an alternative to the philosophical models that have informed the eco-social disasters of First World development. It's potentially problematic too, of course: essentialist, romantic stories of a pre-colonial past, or reified notions of "tradition" aren't helpful for anyone. But this does not mean we need to reject the whole package.

Working with Traditional Forms

Many people are reinterpreting traditional forms. Gugu Ngobese, a drama student at the University of Natal who is also principal of a rural school, has initiated a movement to "Bring Nomkhubulwane to the Fore." *Nomkhubulwane* is the name of the Zulu goddess who presides over rain and the fertility of fields and people, perhaps the Great Goddess. Working in the Impendle region, Ngobese has documented stories from old people in order to reconstruct the (ancient, almost forgotten) rituals associated with the goddess, and encouraged young people to create new songs, improvisational dramas and rituals. The result is an annual festival, and ongoing cultural practice that aims to renew respect for people's bodies, sexuality and the land. It is significant that the project, while recovering pre-colonial, pre-modern, pre-apartheid practices, seems committed to a contemporary, gender-sensitive reinvention, rather than promoting an idea of tradition as immutable object. As the history of Inkatha has shown in the same geographical region, invoking uncritical allegiance to "Zulu culture" may be a powerful traditional weapon in mobilizing support for conservative, authoritarian leadership. By contrast, the *Nomkhubulwane* project potentially empowers ordinary people, particularly women. Recovering a previously silenced orientation toward the goddess, it implicitly questions the militaristic, hierarchic, macho versions of Zulu tradition with which people in Natal are all too familiar.

Now is the time to revive traditional storytelling. I've heard this from many people in cultural organizations previously associated with political resistance. Implicit in this attempt to reconnect with the origins of African theater and performance seems to be a rejection of values associated with television consumer culture and the First World-dominated media. Although the content of the stories varies considerably, much of the material is either directly or indirectly concerned with relationships between human beings, animals, and the environment. Zanendaba Storytellers is a non-governmental organization founded in 1992 which is involved in developing a culture of storytelling through schools, community organizations and tertiary institutions. In the organization's poetic manifesto, storytelling is simultaneously "wisdom / from the ancestors," and a golden heritage "Given to us with love / By our all embracing / Mother Earth" (*Zanendaba Newsletter*, 2). About 30 percent of their work is explicitly environmental storytelling, emphasizing the importance of respect for the Earth and all living beings, but the whole project acknowledges the world as potential teacher and storyteller. Zanendaba's emphasis on the healing and empowering possibilities of storytelling arises appropriately in the post-struggle years of Reconstruction, at a time when the proceedings of the Truth and Reconciliation Commission have been working from a very similar premise.

African storytelling has also informed environmental drama in recent years. Bheki Mkhwane is an actor involved in, among other things, an annual project that produces plays and runs theater workshops in about 20 rural schools in Northern Natal. This work, which is explicitly concerned with environment and development issues, draws on traditional storytelling forms. During our interview over tea, Bheki kept changing: chirping, whistling, grunting, flying, he became a little bird, an elephant, a baboon. "You really need to live the spirit of the animal. . . . it's quite different from posing as an animal. . . . theatre for me is a kind of ritual," he said, describing the imaginative experience that the project teaches as a way into environmental awareness. Where North American eco-culture has reinterpreted a Native American concept of "animals as persons," this approach reinvents old styles of storytelling so that "Hey, I can be a car, or a pneumatic drill" as well as an animal or a tree. According to Mkhwane, his work in this field shaped the style of acting now associated with Theatre for Africa, a prominent and controversial environmental theater company. Under the direction of Nicholas Ellenbogen, the company has since 1990 produced a variety of plays promoting conservation and sustainable

management. The work has attracted good audiences and considerable funding, both nationally and internationally, as well as some criticism. The problems seem firstly to do with questions of ownership and control of the work and the funds it raises. Secondly, there seems to be a failure to address the potential compromises and contradictions involved in corporate sponsorship of environmental art. Finally, some have rejected the company's representation of African society, and its claims to being an authentically African theater. While some of the criticism might be due to sour grapes, the problems it highlights with regard to commercially successful "African" environmental art are surely instructive.

A Sacramental World View

For several writers and performers, African world views and/or philosophy offer a valuable way of understanding ecological interconnectedness. For example, the poet Mazizi Kunene has long emphasized the importance of African spiritual tradition in facilitating a sacramental relationship between human and non-human beings. Piwe Mkhize, writer, actor and cultural organizer, takes a more postmodern and explicitly politicized approach. In our interview he emphasized that African tradition should be affirmed critically—he rejects the traditional sexism of Zulu males—and non-exclusively—as a Hindu, he identifies correspondences with the concept of *ubuntu* and universal love. His *Back to Nature* is a contemporary morality play on environmental issues. Personifications of water, plant, etc. give speeches addressed to their common enemy, man [sic]. The message of interdependence, reverence and sustainable use is conveyed with reference to pre-colonial practice ("your ancestors," "ancient practice"), and the elements of nature are rallied to action in the rhetoric of recent political struggle: "Viva Comrade Animal, Viva!. . . . Long live the fresh air, long live!. . . . Forward with the struggle for the purification and preservation of all the elements of nature, forward!" (p. 16). The Voice of the Unseen instructs them to educate man to go "back to where he belongs . . . back to nature" (p. 19), which they do in speeches that are interspersed with Zulu traditional dance.

Mkhize's environmental discourse is constructed out of contemporary political and non-sectarian religious discourses as well as that of traditional African practice. The play suggests that our contemporary crisis is simultaneously an eco-social-spiritual one. So going "back to nature" refers at once to natural ecosystems, the wisdom of pre-modern practices, non-hierarchic social organization, and "original nature" (p. 12).

Finally, when I interviewed Marguerite Poland, she discussed her sense of affinity with San-Xhosa-Zulu worldviews in terms of interpreting a tradition that, as an anthropologist, she sees as dynamic rather than static. For example, she described having "reinvented" the concept of *isithunzi* to mean "freedom of spirit" in *Shadow*. Like Mkhize's, this approach makes an implicit distinction between a conservative and essentialist traditionalism and informed reinventions that is particularly useful for progressive ecological culture.

So much for a short introduction. A more detailed discussion of environmental literary culture in South Africa would need to investigate what is happening in the literatures of the other 10 official languages, and to consider many other questions, such as the significance of Judeo-Christian influences on the discourse, the multiple responses to the issue of didacticism and the silences about women and sustainability. Perhaps more importantly, the subject demands that one finds ways of making research available in other forms: if we can make it accessible, eco-criticism is a valuable networking, bibliographic and critical tool for activists, writers and performers.

Selected Works and Further Reading

Action Workshop, *Information Booklet,* Cape Town, South Africa, July 1992

Buckland, Andrew, *Bloodstream,* Johannesburg, South Africa: Market Theatre, 1992

Cope, Michael, "Tea Ceremony," in *Scenes and Visions,* Plumstead: Snailpress, 1991

Cox, Fran, *Pulling Green Strings,* Loft Theatre Company, Durban, South Africa, January 1994

Kenmuir, Dale, *Sing of Black Gold,* Pretoria, South Africa: De Jager-Haum, 1991

Livingstone, Douglas, *A Littoral Zone,* Cape Town, South Africa: Carrefour, 1991

Mazibuko, Khosi, personal interview (July 30, 1996)

Mkhize, Piwe, *Back to Nature,* unpublished manuscript, 1995

——, personal interview (July 25, 1996)

Mkhwane, Bheki, personal interview (July 23, 1996)

Molver, Eileen, *Guardian of the Mountain,* London: Viking, 1991

Ngwenyana, Martin, *War on Waste,* Whirly Gig Productions, Gugulethu, South Africa, Arbor Day, 1995

Phiri, Z. D., *Tikki's Wildlife Adventures,* Cape Town, South Africa: Houston, 1995

Poland, Marguerite, personal interview (July 23, 1996)

——, *Shadow of the Wild Hare,* Cape Town, South Africa: David Philip, 1986

Storyteller Group, *The Mystery of the Dangerous Drums,* Johannesburg, South Africa: Storyteller Group, 1994

——, *The River of Our Dreams,* Johannesburg, South Africa: Storyteller Group, 1991

Theatre for Africa, information booklet, Cape Town, South Africa, 1996

Wa-Lehulere, Ithumeleng, director, *The Reddening of the Greens,* Action Workshop, Grahamstown Festival, Grahamstown, South Africa, 1992

Zanendaba Newsletter, Johannesburg, South Africa, 1996

Ecological Postcolonialism
in African Women's Literature

Juliana Makuchi Nfah-Abbenyi

In *Elle sera de jaspe et de corail* the Cameroonian writer, Werewere Liking states:

Vraiment, Lunaï est un village fatidique.
Ce sont les différences qui caractérisent ce vingtième siècle dit-on. Des différences qui se côtoient de manière si inharmonieuse qu'il a fallu inventer l'écologie: Des super-puissants à côté du tiers-monde les villes à côté des bidons-villes les riches à côté des pauvres. . . . Tant de misère juste à côté de tant d'opulence c'est inharmonieux à vomir c'est disharmonique à crever . . . (pp. 44–45)

[Really, Lunaï is a fateful village.
Differences are characteristic of this twentieth century people say. Differences that co-exist in such an inharmonious way that ecology had to be invented: Superpowers side by side the third world cities side by side shanty towns the rich side by side the poor. . . . So much misery alongside so much opulence it's inharmonious one could vomit it's disharmonious to death. . . .]
   (my translation)

Ecology had to be invented, Werewere Liking maintains. "Why this invention?" one might ask. Liking's statement posits a reality that has either been lost, forgotten, or ignored. It claims a time when people knew their environment. They understood it, respected it, treasured the interdependence and harmonious co-existence with it. Then the seeds of "disharmony" in the form of differences, whether ideological, cultural, political or economic, were planted, nurtured, and have grown deep roots. This "disharmony" is clearly asserted not only by the content of Liking's statement but is also conveyed through her style of writing itself: one that defies conventional syntactic and grammatical norms; that transgresses traditional rules of writing as it combines poetic, prosaic, and dramatic forms of expression throughout the text, inscribing an intertextuality that is unique. It is one that aptly captures the chaos about which she speaks.

Liking's fictional village, Lunaï, sometimes stands for her native land, but often symbolically represents Africa, and the world at large. Lunaï embodies the almost total degradation and/or amnesia into which its peoples seem to bury themselves each waking day. They slumber and wallow in this atmosphere of total chaos, whether physical, psychical, or spiritual, as their world falls apart. It is because of their inability or refusal to acknowledge or to integrate traditional ways of knowing with technologically oriented values that "ecology" had to be invented, an invention that would supposedly rid the world of its environmental hazards. The people of Lunaï must therefore snap out of this general state of (dis)ease in order to save themselves, their environment, in short, their humanity. They can achieve this goal by taking the plunge, reimmersing themselves in their traditions and recreating the healthy relationship once shared with their universe.

Liking's text highlights the major issues that other African women writers also address in their writing, as well as the impact of these issues on the lives of their people, and especially, on women's lives. These writers show that African women's roles (and sometimes men's roles), which are often linked to the land, have seen drastic changes following the movement from colonialism, through independence, to the postcolonial era that have (re)shaped African societies, histories, and cultures. They contend that women's lives have tended to be the most affected by these local and global shifts.

Buchi Emecheta's *The Joys of Motherhood* is a case in point. Although we hear the patriarchal Nwokocha Agbadi in this novel scornfully declaring that "only lazy men who could not face farm work went to the coast to work, leaving the land which their parents and great-great-grand-parents had worked and cared for" (p. 37), it is the women like Nnu Ego and Cordelia who have married these "lazy men" who complain bitterly, and are constantly comparing life in urban Lagos with life in rural Ibuza. Their complaints are grounded by the fact that when their husbands become part of and are consumed by the (post)colonial economy, the women resent how their positions, roles, and influence are substantially eroded by their non-ownership of land and/or farms in Lagos. As Nnu Ego laments, "In Ibuza, women made a contribution, but in urban Lagos, men had to be the sole providers; this new setting robbed the woman of her useful role" (p. 81). The contribution that women made to the income and welfare of the family partially came from their work on the land thus promoting an acceptable sexual division of labor and creating a balance in gender relations. If Agbadi's criticism of "lazy men" who run away from the land and farm work in favor of modern, (post)colonial "menial" jobs (like becoming cooks or washer men for white men and women) not only robs them of their "manhood," thus redefining concepts of masculinity within Ibuza society and culture; displacement and non-ownership of land and/or farms not only represents the loss of a vital source of power for women, it also reshapes their gender roles and concepts of womanhood and femininity as well. In the minds of the Agbadis and the Nnu Egos, therefore, the urban setting destroys an important and essential link to one's land, one's home, and one's identity. They see the new relation to the urban environment as more destructive and less gratifying than constructive. Although one might argue that working on the land and assuming familial responsibilities does not necessarily always empower women—especially when they are treated as the mules of the earth, for instance, in Delphine Zanga Tsogo's *Vies de femmes* and *L'Oiseau en cage*—African women's writing does show that women and children are those who are the most adversely affected by the (post)colonial relation to the urban environment.

Calixthe Beyala paints just such a picture in *The Sun Hath Looked upon Me* and *Your Name Shall Be Tanga*. She portrays children as those who are primarily crushed by the weight of the migration to, and the living conditions in, urban slums. Through the eyes of her teenage heroines, Ateba Léocadie and Tanga, we are shown how life in the ghettos "kills" children, smothers their dreams, and engenders total disillusionment and often death. Beyala points out how unwary, ignorant, irresponsible, and/or morally bankrupt adults, parents, politicians (who themselves equally wallow in the malaise of post-colonial politics of survival) often watch helplessly as the children fester in poverty, illiteracy, homelessness, delinquency, crime and prostitution. Rural exodus has created untold imbalances that are progressively destroying the environment, contaminating children and especially young women. It is deplorable that local governments have been unable to help children in the stifling milieux that have become fertile ground for the daily violence perpetrated on their minds and bodies. Beyala claims to write for the ordinary people of the ghettos and she maintains that they are the ones who will bring true change to Africa. They are the future of the continent. She therefore points an accusing finger specifically at politicians who, after riding the waves of independence, have lagged into incompetence with the resultant gross mismanagement of their national resources.

Paralleling such incompetence is the corruption of these politicians and post-colonial leaders, as is comically, sarcastically, and cynically portrayed by Aminata Sow Fall in *The Beggars' Strike*. Fall exposes yet another ugly side of post-colonial politics and denounces the dexterity with which power-hungry individuals exploit this global invention called "ecology" with its global economic backing (tourism, development, aid from the so-called first world to the so-called third world) for their own selfish benefit.

The first sentence of *The Beggars' Strike* reads, "This morning there has been another article about it in the newspaper: about how the streets are congested with these beggars, these *talibés*, these lepers and cripples, all these derelicts" (p. 1). The streets of the Capital, we are told, are crying out to be cleansed of these dregs of society, "these parodies of human beings." The Director of the Department of Public Health and Hygiene decides to launch an "effective plan of campaign" to rid the Capital of this plague that stands in the way of hygiene and the city's progress. But Mour Ndiaye is also motivated by other personal and political reasons: "We are now the ones responsible for the destiny of our country. We must oppose anything which harms our economic and tourist development," he tells his personal marabout, Serigne Birama (p. 18). Birama remains unconvinced by this argument and resents the further marginalization of the beggars for reasons of so-called "economic development." His skepticism is well-founded given that the beggars "invade" the Capital because there is a relation of give and take between them and the city folk. City folk give alms to the beggars not out of the goodness of their hearts, not necessarily because religion demands that they give to the poor, but "out of an instinct for self-preservation" (p. 22). They need the beggars' wishes for long life, their wishes for prosperity, their prayers to drive away bad dreams, bring hope, and so they give, "so that they can live in peace" (p. 38).

Ndiaye's enthusiasm, therefore, is fueled by personal political ambition and his ability to exploit first/third-world politics grounded in something as elusive as "economic development." For the question remains: "Who benefits from this monster labeled development?" The campaign to harass the beggars is not undertaken because Ndiaye has the control of "congestion" or the need to limit the destruction of the environment thus promoting its protection at heart. His campaign is geared toward a tourist economy that needs to be developed and maintained. It is therefore the interests of the select, well-to-do foreign tourists and the local politicians like Ndiaye that "justify" this brutal action and not those of the local inhabitants themselves on whose backs ecological imperialism is being practiced. Local and exogenous power and economic politics therefore collude, further marginalizing already dispossessed numbers of African peoples. How, therefore, can one speak of development, of the benefits and values of this global politic called "ecology," of "protecting the environment," when those who inhabit that environmental space, whether geographic and/or political, are either used as bait, or blatantly excluded from the construction and implementation of policies that govern their land and, consequently, their lives?

Fall clearly discounts such policies/politics and their bearers/enforcers by subverting the entire process itself and putting the power in the hands of the dispossessed. Under the leadership of a woman, Salla Diang, and without the help of the likes of the Ndiayes, the beggars very cleverly solve the problem of "congestion" by moving to the Slum-Clearance Resettlement Area on the outskirts of the city. The tables are turned, for those who were formerly tracked down, flogged, and beaten like dogs, gleefully orchestrate their revenge on ruthless, power-hungry politicians like Mour Ndiaye (if only he had listened to Birama, the "uneducated" traditional leader!). The city folk now have to seek the beggars out and the cycle of dependence is reversed. By moving out of that overcrowded location, the beggars reclaim their identity, their dignity, and assert their humanity. Their ultimate revenge comes when Ndiaye himself is thwarted as the beggars follow Salla's order to continue their strike. "Don't budge from here. No one is to budge from here ever again! Tomorrow, we shall see that he bites dust!" (p. 86). By not returning to the Capital, they rob Ndiaye of the possibility of carrying out the one and only act of benevolence that would have guaranteed him the one thing he had been scheming for all along—an appointment to the post of vice president.

When Ndiaye begins to learn the invaluable lesson of interconnectedness, of the correlation between modern politics and economic development (administrative posts/tourism) and the link between traditional voices and values (Birama/beggars—"who have been here since the time of our great-great-grandparents" [p. 15]), it is almost too late to repair the damage that his campaign has already done. His statements, "We have to find some way of letting them get back their rights as citizens . . . create some organisations to which they can be assimilated . . . carry out a vast campaign of rehabilitation on their behalf . . ." (p. 94), stand in jarring opposition to Birama's question, "You waged war against the beggars . . . Who won?" (p. 66, all ellipses in the original). Ndiaye's inability to recognize the dialectical relation between culture, religion, economics and politics; his refusal to combine socio-cultural values with modern values in order to combat and effectively deal with the (dis)ease that "economic development" poses for his people becomes the tool of his own undoing.

But beyond much of the gloom that "development" and mismanagement breed in postcolonial Africa, there is hope, as Bessie Head demonstrates in *When Rain Clouds Gather* and *A Question of Power*. It is the coming together of traditional/local ways of knowing and modern science/technologies that can best guarantee a productive but protected environment in African and third-world countries where the drive toward modernization and so-called "progress and civilization" is pushing the limits of environmental degradation and the survival of its people. Their survival will continue to hang in the balance unless "progress and civilization" also means learning to aggressively combine local and exogenous ways of knowing.

Bostwana became Bessie Head's adoptive country, a hospitable place she could call home after she fled South Africa where she had faced rejection, humiliation, dispossession and virulent racism (Head, *Serowe* and *A Woman Alone*). The strong bonds of love and belonging that she developed in Botswana are captured in her novels. The name of the village in *When Rain Clouds Gather* is Golema Mmidi, which means "to grow crops" (p. 28), while the name of the village in *A Question of Power* is Motabeng, which means "the place of sand" (p. 19). It is no accident that the titles of these novels speak of the weather, of crops, of the land, of the environment, and their relationship with the people. Head's fascination with the land and its people comes through as she portrays the intricate webs that are woven between women and men, and between collaborative ventures involving local farming methods and modern scientific methods adapted to the land based on studying the weather and the environment itself. We are told in *When Rain Clouds Gather* that while men are cattle drovers, the women are the agriculturalists. The women are the tillers of the earth and are on the land 365 days of the year: "No one ever worked harder than Botswana women, for the whole burden of providing food for big families rested with them" (p. 104). The arid nature of the land, coupled with unpredictable weather patterns, and women's central role in farming, lead Gilbert Balfour to believe that perhaps, "all change in the long run would depend on the women of the country and perhaps they too could provide a number of solutions to problems he had not yet thought of" (p. 43). They would be women like Paulina Sebeso, who would rally the others and "help open the way for new agricultural developments" (p. 75).

But gender ideologies, and cultural and tribal land practices intertwine in complex ways, raising problems that could stand in the way of new agricultural developments. For instance: although women are the backbone of agriculture, programs for improved techniques in agriculture "were only open to men" (p. 34); the tribal land tenure system, whereby "ownership of the land was vested in the tribe as a whole" (p. 38), posed the problem of fencing parts of the land for controlled grazing. Eating habits grounded in culture and prejudice add (an)other dimension to development. For instance, although the discovery of a drought-resistant millet would not only increase the quantity and add diversity to the

Motswana diet, they would rather not eat this millet because it is consumed by the "inferior" Bushman of the Kalahari desert. The solutions to these many and varied problems are carefully laid out by Head in the novel. With the help of the women, and later with the collaboration of the men, Gilbert is able to launch some of the projects and find solutions that are uplifting for himself, the people, and their environment.

Projects are planned in such a way that the ecology is taken into consideration every step of the way. For instance, ways are sought to bring cattle production and crop production together—fencing the land and controlled grazing on cooperatively owned feeding grounds thus preventing overstocking and the spread of diseases. This method also increases the number of better fed beasts thereby increasing their cash value and, consequently, reducing the hardship and the labor of cattle rearing. Cash crop farming like growing Turkish tobacco is practiced alongside subsistence farming. The digging of boreholes and the making of reservoirs provide each home with water, and a network of small dams are built for irrigation purposes. The philosophy that guides the efforts made through collaborative work and incentives, "the materials were simple and the costs kept low" (p. 136), clearly underlines Head's belief that only when development projects in post-colonial African societies have the interests of the people at heart can these actually have any impact or meaning for all the parties concerned. Ultimately, this interrelationship of respect for the environment, while improving productivity, must have as its aim the "uplift of the poor," consequently uplifting the women whose major role it is to carry the burden of feeding the land. Therefore, "communal systems of development which imposed co-operation and sharing of wealth were much better than the dog-eat-dog policies, take-over bids, and grab-what-you-can of big finance" (p. 156).

Head builds on the idea of communal uplift once again in *A Question of Power*. In Motabeng, Youth Development work groups, represented by young, intelligent, enthusiastic men like Small-Boy and women like Kenosi, provide instruction on the basic tenets of productivity. They construct local industries projects; adapt agriculture to water conservation methods; practice crop rotation following a prescribed formula for success and continued productivity of various kinds of crops and products. Whatever the Motabeng community does is geared toward turning the "people's attention to their natural resources," thus breaking the cycle of dependence on "the goods of the rich manufacturers in South Africa and Rhodesia" (p. 69).

If turning to one's natural resources breaks the cycle of dependence that is not only economic but political, Head posits yet another element in this novel, that of turning to the land as an elixir to feed one's soul, as medicine to heal that which ails one's mind, one's body, as a means to discover and cherish one's and another's humanity (p. 158). "It is impossible," Elizabeth muses, "to become a vegetable gardener without at the same time coming in contact with the wonderful strangeness of human nature" (p. 72). Elizabeth's displacement and her search for a place to belong are captured in the words of the Schoolmaster of Motabeng: "I suffer, too, because I haven't a country and know what it's like. A lot of refugees have nervous breakdowns" (p. 52). Only her connection to the land saves her from literal death when Elizabeth suffers the same fate. Her relationship with Tom and, more importantly, with Kenosi and the garden help her free herself from the physical, psychological prisons, and the mental horrors that are a legacy of her childhood (her white mother's madness and suicide in the asylum where she was locked up for having a child with a black stable boy; the many times Elizabeth was locked up in school on the mere suspicion of her "inherited" insanity) and her growing up in apartheid South Africa. A place, she says, where it was "like living with permanent nervous tension, because you did not know why white people there had to go out of their way to hate you or loathe you" (p. 19).

During the three years of her "journey into hell and darkness" (p. 190), of the almost total collapse of her body, Elizabeth battles the demons that threaten to claim her, body and soul, as her life hangs in the balance while her inner and outer worlds collide. Her anxiety about her work in the garden with Kenosi "would jerk her awake" and bring her swimming back to reality (p. 169). Working with Kenosi serves as potent treatment for her condition, for, "[a]s far as Elizabeth was concerned she was to look back on . . . the Kenosi woman's appearance as one of the miracles or accidents that saved her life" (p. 89). Her work with Kenosi offers her healing that is physical, mental, spiritual and metaphysical (she is often in total contemplation, absorbed by her surroundings). In her quiet but stubborn and respectful attitude, Kenosi never mentions Elizabeth's illness, never invokes the evils that plague her

friend's entire existence. Kenosi would sit with Elizabeth, eat with her, chat with her son, and her only reproaches to her friend are made in relation to the garden:

"You must never leave the garden," she said. "I cannot work without you. People are teasing me these days. They say: 'Kenosi, where's your teacher? You are not in school.' People have never seen a garden like our garden. . . ."

Elizabeth struggled to an upright posture. The way this woman brought her back to life and reality! (p. 142)

Kenosi's words say how much their work and their lives are dependent on each other's. But most of all, Kenosi teaches Elizabeth that even in her world of distorted realities, other human beings can be/are dependent on her. She is an important and useful member of Motabeng village. The land, their work, their relationship, bring them together, giving them a sense of belonging, a sense of hope that must and does save Elizabeth. No wonder the last sentence of *A Question of Power* emphatically states: "As [Elizabeth] fell asleep, she placed one soft hand over her land. It was a gesture of belonging" (p. 206).

Belonging to the land, therefore, gives one an identity and a history that is deeply grounded in a culture as well. It is such a history that Nyasha in Tsitsi Dangarembga's *Nervous Conditions* craves. One that she needs to fill in the gaps of what she has lost or revise the "lies" taught by her Anglo-Saxon education. Nyasha's struggle is one of combating the "Englishness" that has erased her Shona self, her African history, and has made her forget who she is. She resents the hybrid she has become and she desperately seeks to redefine her identity. Unlike Nyasha who rebels against those and the discourses of (post)colonialism that threaten to destroy her sense of (Shona) self, Tambudzai does not lack that groundedness in her history. The advantage that Tambu has is one she has gleaned from her grandmother during their work sessions on the land.

Women like Tambu's grandmother are storytellers and custodians of history. Their knowledge of the land and of history is shared, thus making the acquisition of both forms of knowledge complementary for children like Tambudzai. She learns invaluable lessons about her family, the history of her people "that could not be found in the textbooks" from her grandmother. It is important to note how the grandmother subverts work on the farm and uses it as a platform for instruction and the construction of self, for whenever Tambu would plead for more (his)stories, Mbuya, as if teasing her grandchild with the bait, would say, "More work, my child, before you hear more story." And then, "[s]lowly, methodically, throughout the day the field would be cultivated, the episodes of [her] grandmother's own portion of history strung together from beginning to end" (pp. 17–18). It is her relationship with her grandmother, her stories, and their farm work, that give Tambu a sense of belonging, a strong sense of identity. She does not therefore have the same kind of struggle Nyasha has to (re)learn the forgotten. Not forgetting is Tambudzai's trump card. Knowledge of her history better prepares her to confront (an)other colonizing history, to resist assimilation and those oppressive discourses of (post)colonialism that almost consume her cousin, Nyasha. Learning, even if through farm work from Mbuya, more importantly, knowing her self will save her, a point that Werewere Liking also makes throughout *Elle sera de jaspe et de corail.* The people of Lunaï are pitiful because they have reneged on their histories and their traditions. They can only heal as a people when they reclaim and revalue local and traditional knowledge that they must then correlate with imported, modern ways of thinking. Liking optimistically posits that when men and women live in harmony with each other, with their environment and the cosmos, only then shall the new race of people that she maintains, will be of jasper and coral, be born.

Selected Works and Further Reading

Beyala, Calixthe, *The Sun Hath Looked upon Me*, translated by Marjolijn de Jager, Portsmouth, New Hampshire, and Oxford: Heinemann, 1996

——, *Your Name Shall Be Tanga*, translated by Marjolijn de Jager, Portsmouth, New Hampshire, and Oxford: Heinemann, 1996

Dangarembga, Tsitsi, "Interview," in *Talking with African Writers*, Portsmouth, New Hampshire: Heinemann, 1992; London: James Currey, 1992

——, *Nervous Conditions*, London: Women's Press, 1988; Seattle, Washington: Seal, 1989

Emecheta, Buchi, *The Joys of Motherhood*, New York: G. Braziller, 1979; London: Heinemann, 1979

Fall, Aminata Sow, *The Beggars' Strike, or, The Dregs of Society*, translated by Dorothy S. Blair, Harlow, England: Longman, 1981

Head, Bessie, *A Question of Power*, London: Davis-Poynter, 1973; New York: Pantheon, 1974

——, *Serowe: Village of the Rain Wind*, London: Heinemann, 1981

——, *When Rain Clouds Gather*, New York: Simon & Schuster, 1968; London: Gollancz, 1969

——, *A Woman Alone: Autobiographical Writings*, Portsmouth, New Hampshire, and Oxford: Heinemann, 1990

Liking, Werewere, *Elle sera de jaspe et de corail*, Paris: Editions l'Harmattan, 1983

Mateteyou, Emmanuel, "Calixthe Beyala: entre le terroir et l'exil," *The French Review* 69:4 (1996), pp. 605–615

Nfah-Abbenyi, Juliana M., *Gender in African Women's Writing: Identity, Sexuality, and Difference*, Bloomington: Indiana University Press, 1997

Zanga Tsogo, Delphine, *L'Oiseau en cage*, Paris: Edicef, 1983

——, *Vies de femmes*, Yaoundé, Cameroon: Editions CLE, 1983

Symbolic and Intersubjective Representations in Arab Environmental Writing

Maysa Abou-Youssef

In the Arab world, tradition, under the umbrella of religion, dominates the Arab vision of who they are and where they belong. Religion, primarily Islam, offers a way of connecting disparate parts of experience and a way of feeling connected, of feeling the interrelatedness of woman and man to their natural surroundings. Interrelatedness, the sense of belonging, has a survival value that takes many shapes: extended families, tribes, kingdoms, and nations. In the Qur'an, God creates humans and nature as completions for each other. Separately each is incomplete; together they form an ideal harmony. In the modern Arab world, however, both religion and nature have been too often taken for granted. Only at points in which there is a sense of loss or incompleteness has nature been invoked as a power, either in its presence or absence.

A second factor influencing Arab writing about the environment is the distinction between city and country life. Within most Arab countries, the increasing urbanization in the twentieth century has cut people off from the land and nature. Thus a number of poets and prose writers have used natural settings to explore the sense of alienation and remoteness that individuals suffer and the political ramifications of colonization and, more recently, westernization in their societies.

A third important factor in determining the shape of the environment in Arab writing is the distinction between male and female writers. Traditionally in surveys of Arab writing, women have been associated with poetry, and men with more realistic prose. In this brief survey of Arab environmental writing, however, I will reverse the usual categories and discuss selections from Arab male poets and female prose writers, in order to force a reinterpretation of the usual modes of categorization. Within the Arab culture, male writers are expected to be realists, while female writers are thought to deal with nature romantically. Nature is expected to be but a conventional symbol. This essay will argue that the environment is used by male writers more as a symbolic tool, to express political and personal agendas. Female writers, however, have achieved an intersubjective response to nature that is, in its way, more realistic than that of males.

But what does this environmental literature consist of? Among male poets, nature has been used to express the sense of alienation and a search for self, escape, and more recently the quest for a national identity. Consumed by politics, Arab writers have turned to polemic, using nature as a tool for expressing and asserting their political stands. In all of these modes of writing in which nature is used, communication is through nature, not with nature. Female writers, on the other hand, are in a different position in the structure of Arab society. Women are expected only to agree, in silence, with the assumed logic of the male voice. Being seen as tools themselves, women writers have rejected the pragmatic employment of nature and have welcomed nature for a partner in a community-centered discourse. Attempting to speak their own concerns, women first spoke to nature, seeing in nature a reflection of their situation. Nature was the secret, understanding ear to their confessions. From there, women moved to a concern for nature itself, and finally have seen themselves interconnected in ways that men have not been able to achieve.

In poetry, true environmental literature has emerged, indirectly, only in the last of three periods in the development of modern Arabic literature. The first neoclassical period, 1830–1910, was an age of translation and adaptation, reflecting more or less the West's impact on the East. The second, the interwar Romantic and nationalistic period, was dominated by a radical search for the self. This period between 1920 and 1960 was ruled by the rise of national frustrations, a sense of injustice, and a constant resistance to imperialism. Until 1945, poets avoided direct attacks on their colonizers by mirroring their world as imperfect and vague, lacking identity. Influenced to a great extent by Freud and Jung, Arab poets searched for the soul, a difficult, confusing task. In the third period, following World War II, writers reflected the political turmoil of clashing loyalties and ideologies on all levels, from the individual to the national. Political agendas, shaped by religion, colonization, and independence movements, prepared the ground for literature in general and environmental literature in particular. Pan-arabism and anticolonialism were strongly motivating political forces.

The Romantic use of nature as a mirror of man's alienation and an image of his search for self—including the self as poet—is seen in the works of the prolific Egyptian poet Ahmad Zaki Abu Shadi (1892–1955). The founder of avant garde poetry (the Apollo group), Abu Shadi started the Romantic movement. In symbolic and idealistic poems, Abu Shadi preserved the Arabic tradition, using formal language yet creating rhythmical innovations in free verse. In a qasida, which is the most common Arab verse form, titled "The New," he introduces the new poet who refuses the classical tradition of fitting the words to the rules and initiates a trend where the poet frees his rhyme scheme as part of an awareness of nature. After attacking the old style of poetry he describes the poet's task:

He studies the existence he traced to his limits, then decides,
roaming with the world, asking for her inspiration, so she judges and unveils inspiration's drapes,
sending into existence, from his free poetry, honest gifts and his creativity.
(Badawi, 71; my translation)

The poem embeds Abu Shadi's call for an idealistic poet who converses and acts with nature as part of the process of freeing himself.

Once Abu Shadi faced the country's political corruption, and feeling unrecognized, he left for England and then settled in the United States. At the same time, his poetry, which had been Romantic, became more philosophical. Even his political poetry focused on his personal feelings about life. Many of his poems became open-ended questions with no answer, such as "Oh Universe," in which he asks the Universe:

Isn't my soul mirror'd in you,
And am I not your mirror too?
You are both whole and part of me . . .
(Haywood, 169)

Taking a humanistic approach, Abu Shadi opened the path to self-recognition through questioning nature and the world around him. Yet the nature Abu Shadi invokes is described only in abstract, non-realistic terms.

Similarly, the rebellious Egyptian poet Abd El Rahman Shukri (1886–1958) attacked the malaise of intellectuals, rationalizing the use of nature as an ideal imaginative perfection. In "Bird of Paradise," he addresses the Bird:

. . . in your singing the soul poetry there is neither fakery nor vagueness
So don't follow the steps of others, for there isn't in humanity a person
Who could replace you by poetry, for in it we are brothers.
(Badawi, 58; my translation)

As Abu Shadi calls on the Universe, Shukri addresses the Bird of Paradise, seeking her attendance. Unable to connect with people in the real world, he invokes the bird, in its imaginative and, ironically, abstract paradise, as the real way to understanding.

While the Romantic poets were concerned with nature only in an abstract, symbolic way, contemporary poets have used a more realistic nature as a tool to express the search for self. For example, the Mahjar poets are well-exemplified through Ilya Abu Madi and Michael Naima. In Abu Madi's liberationist poems, man is the measure of all and poetry reflects the continual divine discontent and indecision. His way out is nature. He addresses the sea with a series of questions, concluding:

And you and I
Are but a drop
In the fathomless deep.
(Orfalea and Elmusa, 79)

While this poem still exemplifies Romantic abstraction, in "Be a Balm," Abu Madi calls on the nature around him to express his sarcastic despair:

> Turn your attention from the thorns
> to the garden flowers,
> and forget the scorpions when you see the
>   stars.
>   (Orfalea and Elmusa, 80–81)

Naima, the founder of the Arab Writer's Union, was also a pessimist. In "My Brother," he writes:

> Brother, if the farmer returns to till his land,
> . . . .
> Our waterwheels have dried up
> And the foes have left no seedling except the
>   scattered corpses.
>   (Orfalea and Elmusa, 59)

At the point of ultimate loss, however, nature can offer a refuge, a point for recovery of self. In "Autumn Leaves," Naima writes:

> Dress our earth!
> Touch, leaf to leaf,
> . . . .
> Go back to the arms of the earth.
>   (Orfalea and Elmusa, 60–61)

From self-recognition Naima moves to a direct call to reach for the earth, to its creatures and plants. While nature in these more recent poems is still Romantic and somewhat symbolic, the poems show an awareness of an actual physical environment: scorpions and waterwheels are part of the landscape of their remembered homeland in Naima's "My Brother." Moreover, nature is seen as a proper object for man's attention ("Dress our earth") and a place for humans to find solace ("Go back to the arms of the earth").

Becoming aware of the potential for nature to offer both an image of, and a cure for, human alienation, Palestinian poet Mohammed Maghut writes of a barren nature that yet offers man a sense of connection. In "Dream," he writes:

> There on the blue sands we will lie
> And sleep silently till daybreak,
> . . . .
> For the desert was in our hearts.
>   (Khouri and Algar, 203)

For Romantic and post-Romantic poets, therefore, the natural environment serves as a tool for imaging a sense of alienation and loss, but also, with the later poets, the possibility of an interconnectedness. The desert might be barren, but "the desert was in our hearts."

Environmental writing takes its strongest form in political statements, perhaps because of the devastating effects on the environment wrought by political forces. Colonial and capitalist expropriation of the land have showed no concern for the environment. The cedar forests of northern Jordan were clear-cut early in the century for use as railroad ties. In Egypt, farms were replaced by tenements and factories; even the Nile mud was, until recently, appropriated for bricks. A series of wars, including the Arab-Israeli conflicts since 1948, has rendered vast stretches of land unlivable. The Israeli government has even used anti-environmental actions as provocative political moves, such as the heavily symbolic uprooting of ancient family olive trees in Palestine. The environmental effects of the American counterattack in Kuwait and bombings in Iraq will be felt for generations. Within such a context, Arab writers have connected politics and the environment in a number of ways.

Poetry in Lebanon and Syria, for example, has long been consciously aware of environmental neglect and the effects of the class struggle. Bishara Abdallah El Khuri wrote "The Poor" in 1914 as a call for the lower classes to rebel against the rich. The poem claims a connection between nature and the poor; both have been forced to yield their being to the rich: "Sweet smelling plants which in your gardens grow, / Who planted them for you if not the poor?" (Haywood, 179). More recently, Nizar Qabani's poetry has also shown a social and political concern. In a reviving call of awakening to his nation, Nizar writes, addressing children:

> O rain of spring,
> O saplings of hope,
> You are the fertile seeds in our barren life . . .
>   (Khouri and Algar, 191)

Lebanese poet Adonis (born Ali Ahmad Said in Syria) sees in the loss of nature a loss of a sense of Lebanese identity. In "The Crow's Feather," he writes:

> Beirut didn't flower . . . and here are my
>   fields

Beirut didn't bloom, and here is the spring
Of nothingness and sand over my fields.
  (Badawi, 185; my translation)

Iraqi poets have also been politically active. nature voices their political beliefs. The socialist Abd el Wahab al Bayati, for example, writes, "The earth remains, and men too remain, / The plaything of the shadows" (Khouri and Algar, 117–119). Badri Shaker El Sayab is another Iraqi voice vibrating despair and discontent with the human condition. In "Before the Gate of God," he writes:

I am weary of my last spring
I see it in the pollen, the marigold, the rose
I see it in every spring, traversing frontiers
  (Khouri and Algar, 85)

In "For I am a Stranger," a nationalistic appeal seems to go unanswered:

If I shake the branches
Only decay will drop from them
. . . .
Stones—no fruit
  (Khouri and Algar, 89)

The poem reflects the disturbance of the natural order and the need for revolution; yet at the same time there is little chance that the revolution will succeed.

Other Arab poets have pursued similar political agendas; the future of the people is connected with the future of the land. The Sudanese poet Mohammed El Fayteri, in "Sad Saturday Night," laments the ruin of the African landscape and people: "[The cactus] stretches above us its hard branches / Covering with them shroudless corpses" (Khouri and Algar, 155). Likewise, the Tunisian, Muhamed El Arousi El Matwi asks humans to reconnect with the earth: "My soil am I: / Into this world I came to it of yore . . . I belong to it" (Haywood, 188). Palestinian writers as well, such as Mahmoud Darwish, locate a sense of identity in the land: "Our land is not barren and bare; / Every land must start somewhere" (Haywood, 190). Finally, Jabra Ibrahim Jabra again connects the nation with Palestine and the environmental identity of her "green land":

Among the olive trees of our valleys,
And in the ripeness of the fields
We wait for the promise of July . . .
  (Khouri and Algar, 227)

For male Arab poets, and prose writers as well, therefore, the environment exists primarily in a semiotic position as a sign for something else: a search for self, an image for alienation, a symbol of escape, a nostalgia, or, in a political sense, a sign of the effects of war and colonization and a symbol of national unity. Even the works cited at the conclusion of this section, in which descriptions of the land seem to promise a connection, a "joyous dance amidst the harvest," always reach beyond the calling forth of the environment to create a political message.

For Arab women writers, the case is different. In Arab cultures, as perhaps in all cultures, interrelatedness is threatening. It takes an effort to reach out to other people, yet it is impossible to deny their presence. This motivates the attempt to cover the other, to attempt to erase the other by veiling it. Both nature and women are threatening reminders of human interrelatedness. By placing a veil upon women and nature, men have defined them as commodities. The Arab proverb, "Woman is a downward creature," links women and the natural world. Women were physically veiled and nature was metaphorically veiled, as we have seen in the case of Arab male poets, turning nature into a political sign, covering its identity. This philosophy helps men retain power; it is easier to veil a threat than to face it. In the Arab culture, Nature has been misread as "what God created for man to use" rather than as a complementary force for completion of self. Women have been misappropriated in the same way. Significantly, the Arab woman writer, placed in this position with nature, has been best able to explore this attempt at control, expose it, and offer critiques of it.

Although this veiling could be seen as humiliating, Arab women have used the veil as an opportunity to dignify their "downward" position by becoming at one with nature. Throughout the Arab culture, women are, for males, closely associated with nature. First, they are seen as wild and constantly demand taming. There is also a romantic view of woman as an object of nature to be possessed by the man, such as a rose. And the peasants expect that women should be associated with agriculture, but again, for possession by the man. Women, however, see their position in connection with nature differently. They recognize that they have their own world that men do not understand, a world of connections. Women accept the interrelatedness that men reject and attempt to veil.

This sense of interconnectedness is seen

throughout writings by Arab women, from the early works of Aisha el Taimuri, Hind Nofal, and Mai Zeyada, to works by contemporary writers such as Hoda Naamani and Nawal el Saadawi, and takes three primary forms. Arab women writers have used nature to explore their interrelatedness and their oppression. First, recognizing how culturally prescribed discourses misposition women and nature, these writers use nature as a trope to represent their dislocation. Nature, similarly oppressed, mirrors their condition. While the mirror passively reflects their status, in a second mode, nature is a companion in suffering. Whereas in the first mode, nature is an image or mirror, in the second mode women accept nature's reality, although the reality is separate from theirs. In a third mode, women embrace nature, fully accepting their interrelatedness, transforming their position into a oneness with nature.

Fadwa Tuqan, a Palestinian writer, exemplifies the first mode, using nature as a trope to express an awareness of woman's position. "Difficult Journey, Mountainous Journey" implies, even in its title, the correlation of nature with a feeling of loss and domestic seclusion imposed by a patriarchal system. Tuqan uses the Palestinian landscape to mirror her condition: "On the one hand, there was my mother's warmth, gentleness and softness, and on the other, Sheikha [her spinster aunt] was like a desert without trees or water" (Badran and Cooke, 36). While the natural landscape mirrors her sense of desolation, Tuqan uses animals to image her sense of confinement: "I lived amidst thoughts sown in writing, but I was isolated from the world itself. As I matured into a woman, I was like a wounded animal sterile in its cage" (Badran and Cooke, 27).

Alifa Rifaat of Egypt also uses nature to mirror her condition. As noted above, women are, in the Arab culture, associated with wildness and the need to be tamed, as Tuqan images herself like a caged animal. "Who Will Be the Man," a short story based upon a day of circumcision, the ultimate taming of women, opens with a peaceful scene:

I'll try to describe my ordeal. It was a humid morning. Clouds of mist flooded the fields and transformed the four wild rose trees outside my window into little guardian angel birds. I awoke to their joyful chirping in celebration of life and looked down upon our fields stretching away into infinity. (Badran and Cooke, 74)

Since she is about to undergo the most unnatural of operations, nature's beauty and its inculcation as a guardian are in ironic contrast to her position.

Similarly, the first Arab female writer to call for woman's emancipation, the Egyptian writer Huda Shaarawi, uses nature to exemplify her loss of self. In her autobiography, Shaarawi recounts her reaction to her wedding feast, in which a grove of trees was cut down to make a place for the wedding party. The felling of the trees becomes an image of her loss of self, of dignity, and of innocence: "I wept for my trees. I wept for my childhood and for my freedom. I saw in this barren garden a picture of life: the life I would live cut off from everything that delighted me and consoled me in my melancholy childhood" (Badran and Cooke, 47). She and the trees are both subjected to a process of being cut by her husband. Both are subjugated to the patriarchal system of the culture that values barrenness over the garden.

The garden image is also used by the nineteenth-century Egyptian feminist Aisha al-Taimuriya as a model for women's education:

And it is a strange sight indeed, to see a planter of seedlings who neglects to prepare the ground properly and then expresses chagrin at the crookedness of the branch which represents the outcome of his planting the seedling. If men watered their seedlings from the vessel of knowledge and understanding, then at a time when they are enduring the load of heavy burdens, they could lean on firm, upright branches. (Badran and Cooke, 132)

While the images Tuqan, Rifaat, Shaarawi, and al-Taimuriya use are to some extent conventional reincarnations of a Romantic spirit, at the same time they are also local or regional, real in the way that Shaarawi's fallen trees were real. This mixture of convention and the real is seen in the works of contemporary Saudi writer Khairiya Saqqaf. Expressing isolation and entrapment, she writes, "Alone, I was torn. . . . It did not affect any of my brothers, because I was the light butterfly, you [her father] cut my wings, and so I fell to the earth, crushed into the mud and sin" (Badran and Cooke, 87). The images describing her mother, however, are drawn from the Gulf region:

The Gulf: it was my identity . . . its ocean was that gorgeous world that had begotten my mother, she ate its fishes, adorned herself with its pearls, pouring its love, its taste and eternal adoration into us.

Her heart was a pearl. . . Her eyes were two forests of palm trees! I have never forgotten this identity.
(Badran and Cooke, 88).

Saqqaf moves from seeing her identity reflected in nature, to feeling a part of nature, a sense of interconnectedness. When this occurs, nature becomes a positive image and even a positive force in her life: "Her [the author's] life was shrivelling. . . . Her name was melting. . . . Spiders around her were weaving a fence protecting her from dissipation" (Badran and Cooke, 89). Reversing the conventional association of spiders with fear and darkness, the spider becomes a positive figure, offering protection from her fear of being expelled from the Gulf (as her mother was not born in Saudi Arabia, she and her daughter were always under the threat of expulsion).

Saqqaf goes beyond nature as a mirroring image and shows a direct concern for nature (the second mode) as well as for her position: "Father, I wish I could have carried your faults and hers . . . I wish I could have been a sponge to erase the depths to gather the remains of bitterness that had spilled on the earth and with which you had nurtured my heart . . . and the earth . . . the word . . . and . . . time . . ." (Badran and Cooke, 89; ellipses are in the original). She identifies with the absorbent sponge to cleanse her own life and the earth as well.

Whereas Saqqaf uses nature as a positive force, for May Muzaffar, a contemporary Iraqi writer, nature stands for the clear reality that of which men are unaware and that is, because of the structure of society, unattainable. In "Personal Papers," she writes:

The sun is bright above our heads. The sun is playing with me and warming me up. . . . I must say I do not like the ice. . . . It is not like when you look at the desert and you see that in it are hidden secrets, and the setting sun on the sand dunes form signs of an unknown world. (Badran and Cooke, 184)

The Lebanese writer Emily Nasrallah, in "September Birds," describes a storm:

This is where nature has its primeval power; people laugh with the sun; they tremble with the thunder; their bodies crumble into dust storms; they cleanse their hearts with the purity of snow. (Badran and Cooke, 148)

Both writers immediately respond to the environment. For Muzzafar, even the forbidding environment of the desert encourages a personal response. For Nasrallah, nature as nature, not as sign, is significant.

In the third mode of writing on the environment, Arab women go beyond seeing nature as a human context, to a sense of deep interconnectedness with nature. For Egyptian writer Sakina Fouad, nature transforms. In "The Pasha's Beard," a dream vision in which she speaks to her dead grandfather, she imagines herself an aloe plant on her grandfather's grave, promising, "out of my tree, I will bring into flourish all that I loved and wished" (Samaan, 198). Egyptian Zeinab Sadek, in her story "Sparrows," has the main character commune directly with the birds: "Sparrows are part of her life. She complains to them about her sorrows, tells them about her joys, celebrates with them the coming of spring, and always wonders about the strange things with which they build their nests. . . . Why doesn't she act like sparrows?" (Samaan, 132). She has to learn to build her life with what she has, not with what she wishes for or imagines.

I will end this description of Arab writers and their use of the environment by turning to the Iraqi poet, Nazik el Malaikah. In "Who Am I," she opens her poem conversing with the night, responding to the question that becomes the poem's title:

I am its secret—anxious, black, profound
I am its rebellious silence
I have veiled my nature, with silence . . .
(Khouri and Algar, 79)

For Arab writers, nature has, to a large extent, been veiled. Wrapped in conventions and symbolism, nature has been kept silent. Romantic writers have seen nature as a setting for the search for self. Recent poets have used nature for political purposes. In the works of Arab women writers, however, there have been points at which nature has been seen and given voice. The veil has been lifted.

Selected Works and Further Reading

Badawi, M. M., comp., *An Anthology of Modern Arabic Verse,* London: Oxford University Press, 1970

Badran, Margot, and Miriam Cooke, eds., *Opening the Gates: A Century of Arab Feminist Writing,* Bloomington: Indiana University Press, 1990; London: Virago, 1990

Haywood, John, *Modern Arabic Literature, 1800–1970,* London: Lund Humphries, 1971; New York: St. Martin's, 1972

Khouri, Mounah, and Hamid Algar, eds., *An Anthology of Modern Arabic Poetry,* Berkeley: University of California Press, 1974

Orfalea, Gregory, and Sharif Elmusa, eds., *Grape Leaves: A Century of Arab American Poetry,* Salt Lake City: University of Utah Press, 1988

Sam'an, Anzhil Butrus, ed., *A Voice of Their Own: Short Stories by Egyptian Women,* Giza, Egypt: Foreign Cultural Information Department, 1994

Section 5:

Latin America and the Poles

Brazilian Art and Literature: Oswald de Andrade's Contribution to Global Ecology

Marcos Reigota *

In 1922, a "Modern Art Week" was held in the São Paulo Municipal Theater, bringing together intellectuals, writers, poets, painters, musicians, and sculptors whose purpose was to break away from the classical and academic models then generally predominant in Brazilian culture. Influenced by European vanguard movements at the beginning of the century, the young São Paulo intellectuals sought to promote a Brazilian art that was both contemporary with that which was being done in the cultural capitals of the world and reflective of the rapid modernization of Brazil and especially of São Paulo. The intellectuals and artists who participated in the "Week of '22" affirmed on different occasions that this event could have taken place only in this city, as a result of its economic development, rapid social and cultural transformation, and its political context, strongly influenced by liberal, anarchistic and communist ideas.

Among persons of note who contributed to the conception, organization, and execution of the "Week of '22" was Oswald de Andrade. His literary, journalistic, and academic activity and his political activism are intimately influenced by his radical, polemical style and by his amorous relationships, especially his association with the painter Tarsila do Amaral and the writer Patricia "Pagu" Galvão. Andrade was born in the city of São Paulo in 1890 and died there in 1954. Thus, he lived during the period in which the city was transformed from a quiet, provincial city into one of the largest, most industrialized cities in the world.

After the tumultuous and polemical modernist week, Oswald de Andrade left for Paris where, together with his wife Tarsila do Amaral, he became acquainted and lived with Blaise Cendrars, Pablo Picasso, Erik Satie, Jean Cocteau, Fernand Leger, Brancusi, and others.

In this city, he would publish, in 1924, "The Manifesto and Brazil Wood Poetry"[1] with drawings of Tarsila do Amaral and explicit references to the commentaries of Cendrars. These works mark the beginning of the author's departure from the principal ideas of modernist week, and contain the first signs of what would come to be the "anthropophagy movement," the beginning of Brazilian post-modernity.

Brazil Wood Poetry and Manifesto

Both the "Manifesto" and its complement, "Brazil Wood Poetry" (Andrade, *Pau-Brasil*) are constructed with phrases and slogans that call to mind rapid, cinematographic images which reinterpret the history of the country told by its colonizers, indigenous peoples, intellectuals, modernist poets, slaves, European immigrants, etc., illustrating the rapidity of the moderniza-

*Translated by Christopher C. Lund. The author is grateful for the collaboration of Albert Von Braunn (Zurich) and of his assistants, Nirave Caram and Tatiana Grasso.

tion of Brazil, with a special focus on that of São Paulo. In the "Manifesto," Oswald de Andrade proposes to eliminate from Brazilian poetry all those aspects foreign to the cultural underpinnings of the Brazilian people, the landscape, the residue of their colonialist heritage from their history, and the Parnassian aesthetic.

In a conference at the Sorbonne in 1923, Andrade analyzed the panorama of Brazilian culture, outlining the principle points that he would vigorously attack in his manifesto. On this occasion, he called attention to the necessity of abandoning, in art as well as in literature, the memory of classical forms, "the obsession of the Arcadians with their shepherds—always the Greek myths or the imitation of European landscapes—with their comfortable roads and their well-behaved fields, all this in a land where Nature is rebellious, light is vertical, and life is in full construction." For him, contemporary Brazil was far from the Arcadian scene and much closer to the "howitzers of elevators, the cubical skyscrapers, and that informed solar laziness," developing a Brazilian subjectivity and a Brazilian style all its own, where time is reserved for leisure, sexuality, spirituality, celebration, and fellowship, yet not ever forgetting the substance and objectivity required by industrialization that demanded "all that was necessary in terms of chemistry, mechanics, economics and ballistics. Everything digested" (*Estética e Politica*, 37–38).

He was of the opinion that Brazilian society ought to have as parameters two types of apprenticeship: a ludic-natural one inherited from the forest cultures, and a techno-intellectual one, more pertinent to the modernist model of education. These sources of knowledge are important in the measure that they are digested, lived, tried, recreated; and applied in diverse locales, without an imposed hierarchy of values. To the "Manifesto," Oswald de Andrade adds the poem "Brazil Wood," in which the same themes are repeated in different passages throughout its 10 parts. They are independent and complementary: the poem elucidates, probes, and underscores the ideas first presented in the manifesto.

The poem begins with the arrival of the Portuguese, "on the occasion of the discovery of Brazil," describing what would have been the impression of the European eye that first beheld the beauty of the indigenous women and of nature. From that moment on begins the "History of Brazil," chronicled by Pedro Vaz de Caminha, reporting to the king of Portugal, in classical Portuguese, that in this indigenous society every-

one is cared for and it is without beggars. Soon after, the French arrived and the Capuchin monk Claude D'Abbeville records in French the same ecstasy that the Portuguese experienced upon discovering the abundance of natural resources, and the health and beauty of the natives.

The beginning of the colonization of Brazil is represented by historical protagonists and explorers and adventurers who, like Fernao Dias Paes, spared no effort, indulged in recklessness, and committed crimes in order to find the gold and precious stones they sought. Jesuits found the city of São Paulo; it begins to prosper thanks to the presence of those protagonists and to the indigenous folk of the region who (in the poem) also begin to express themselves in Portuguese, committing the pronunciation errors inevitably associated with an imposed apprenticeship, and creating a decidedly "Brazilian" language.[2]

Like indigenous men and women, other protagonists and marginalized social groups begin to acquire voices; the slaves express themselves using a style even more farfetched, probably influenced by their owners. The rural ambience of the sugar cane cycle is gradually substituted by bucolic coffee plantations, whose owners make fortunes overnight, become sophisticated, and are seduced by liberal, republican, and abolitionist ideas.

Fortunes earned from coffee impose a new economic elite, new habits and social, cultural, and political mores based upon European models. The accumulation of capital makes possible the beginnings of industrialization, which in turn demands, besides a well-educated upper class, the development of a basic infrastructure which permits new activities to be pursued. With this, electricity, means of communication (the telephone), and transportation are introduced, as well as Oswald de Andrade himself, who becomes one of the protagonists of his poem. At the same time that he speaks about himself, the author describes the transformations that São Paulo is undergoing in advertising campaigns, the cultural mixing, the racism and prejudice against ex-slaves, and the new cities that are springing up in the state of São Paulo as the proliferation of coffee plantations opens new frontiers.

The moments of the country's social and economic transformation are not bothered by moments of celebration, where Carnival is the best expression of the "religiosity of the race," bringing together different social groups, from the "women and girls of good families" to the general population. The period of economic well-being permits the poet and his lover to travel to Paris where they are able to afford and try every delicacy available in the city. Upon their return to Brazil, they tour the hinterland trying to find its present history in the Baroque cities of Minas Gerais, whose architectural richness is what remains from the colonial period when the region supplied the gold that would empower the development of the industrial revolution in England. For the last trip reported in the poem, Andrade's choice is again Paris, now not as an uninitiated tourist, but as a traveler who, on his errands, collects fragments that explain to himself and to others moments of history, of international relations, and of reciprocal influences.

The return to Brazil begins with a parody of the popular Parnassian poem "Song of Exile," by Gonçalves Dias, in which he exults over the flora and fauna, while Oswald de Andrade substitutes a nostalgia for the tropical landscape with a nostalgia for the cosmopolitanism of São Paulo. But before actually arriving in what is "sometimes called the Chicago of South America," the Lloyds of Brazil freighter stops at a number of cities along the Brazilian coast. Here the poet renews acquaintance with landscapes, different persons, and friends. But as he goes, undetected, through Customs, he manages to smuggle in nostalgia for Paris.

In the texts entitled "Brazil Wood," the author establishes a constant dialogue/confrontation among different cultures and their different representations. In order to achieve his purpose of founding a notion of specificity for the country in a context of autonomy, originality, and modernity, he uses external aesthetic and theoretical references, not with the intention of comparing Brazil according to these criteria, but rather as tools that, once appropriated, would make possible a deconstruction of the official history, told by white, academic colonizers and conservative poets and enable him to reconstruct it in the most varied interpretations through the marginalized who had been beaten, forgotten, abandoned, or exterminated, documenting—without nostalgia—bygone social possibilities and reconstructing the utopias still alive and awaiting investigation.

"The Anthropophagy Manifesto"

"The Anthropophagy Manifesto" (Andrade, *A utopia*) was written in 1928 and received its name because of a painting, "Abopuru," by Tarsila do Amaral. Although Oswald de Andrade was its principal mentor and missionary, other intellectuals, like Tarsila do Amaral and the writer Raul Bopp, participated in its development. The Manifesto marks a definitive break from the principal ideas of the "Week of '22" and became the point of departure for a clear division among the principal Brazilian intellectuals who participated in the modernist movement.

Unlike the Modernists, the anthropophagi produce and spread aesthetic and political ideas that are more radical in an attempt to found a "Brazilian culture" and not a "national culture" (with over-optimistically patriotic and nationalist elements) as was the case with the Modernist movement. In this manifesto, the word anthropophagy is launched with the objective of attacking or provoking the imagination of the reader through the disagreeable association with all that cannibalism implies, "transformed into a permanent potential of mankind" (Nunes, "A antropofagia," 15)

The slogan is "Life is a devouring," and only the cannibal can devour everything that he admires and rejects, incorporating and recreating everything around him. One of the more famous slogans of the manifesto is "Tupy or not Tupy. This is the question."[3] Using the well-known phrase from Shakespeare with both irony and reverence, he places Hamlet's doubt into the context of the quest for affirmation of Brazilian identity at the same time that it explains and calls attention to the ethnocide of the Tupy and of other ethnic groups in Brazil.

Indigenous culture plays an important role in "The Anthropophagy Manifesto," underscoring its presence and extermination, its evangelization and its resistance to same, its influence and importance in the formation of the country, and the contempt and paternalism with which it is seen by the elite. The Manifesto plays with the fictitious idea spread through the official history of the "discovery" of Brazil, inverting the sense of the word, and shows that the Europeans, when they arrived, did not discover new lands that until then had not existed and were beyond their ethnocentric vision. Rather, what they discovered was that there were other possibilities and a life and social organization far superior to theirs. They discovered that true "paradise" was in Brazil, where everyone lived without clothes, without guilt, and without Bibles.

The clash of cultures brought about strong mutual influences. Oswald de Andrade tries to interpret how the native culture was affected as well as how European culture was affected. He writes: "without us Europe would not even have had its poor declaration of human rights." He gives little importance to the much-praised letter on human rights because he considers superior the basic principles of the indigenous social structure, in the fact that "we already had communism . . . the relationship and distribution of moral well being and of dignified well being"; much "earlier than the Portuguese discovered Brazil, Brazil had discovered happiness." The process of history shows that a culture with a more advanced technology dominates one that is nature based. The supremacy of a technical culture over a natural one brings with it ethnocide, the predatory exploration of natural resources, and the Christian sense of guilt.

The representation of the indigenous peoples, although somewhat idealized, is far from the Romantic notion of the "noble savage" found in the works of Goethe and Rousseau. It is closer to and reflects that of the "indigenous cannibal" described by Montaigne: a man proud of himself and his race, a man with an elevated and profound worldview (*weltanschaung*), who devours, in a complex ritual, his opposite—objects for which he feels revulsion, admiration, pleasure, and respect. In an anthropophagous perspective, some things survive—fragments and diffuse elements of national culture—and bring with themselves their own vital force, by way of the "devouring" of the dominant culture, thus refusing a well-behaved assimilation.

Oswald de Andrade proposes neither a return to the supposedly harmonious natural past, nor a pure and simple rejection of technological development. As he had already written in the Brazil Wood "Manifesto," he stresses the contributions of the forest and of the school, maintaining a utopian perspective of anthropophagous synthesis of them both. In this case, the thesis is natural man, the antithesis is atomic man, and the synthesis is historico-natural man, with technology seen in its function as liberator, making possible leisure-freedom from slavish, tedious, and alienating work—in a society where matriarchy had prevailed, in which "happiness was the acid test" (Andrade, *Estética*, 103–104).

The Manifestos and Global Ecology

After the Brazil Wood and the anthropophagy manifestos, Oswald de Andrade and his group continued to develop political, aesthetic, and theoretical aspects of the anthropophagy proposition. Shortly before his death, he tried to give philosophical and academic substance to anthropophagy in the thesis he defended in a competition for a professorial position in the Department of Philosophy at the University of São Paulo. Its title was "The Crisis of Messianic Philosophy." His desired academic activity never came to fruition, and the anthropophagy movement became ostracized for a time. It returned forcefully, however, in 1967–68 with the young artists and intellectuals who drove the movement known as "Tropicalism."

As heirs to anthropophagy and Brazilians of their own time, in the watershed year of 1968 they were also in tune with what was happening in other parts of the world. Among them were Helio Oiticica, TomZé, Caetano Veloso, Gilberto Gil, Gal Costa, Nara Leão, Rita Lee, Torquato Neto, José Carlos Capinam, Glauber Rocha, and José Celso Martinez. Their political positions, their revolutionary esthetic, and their artistic work provoked the wrath of the military leaders (many were imprisoned and/or exiled) and contempt from the intelligentsia on the orthodox and nationalist left. Today, they "export poetry," as Oswald de Andrade had urged in his Brazil Wood "Manifesto" and are known and recognized in the principal vanguardist cultural centers.

The multi-media artist, Helio Oiticica, through one of his performances entitled "Tropicalia," began a movement by that name, better known through its musical manifestations, which sought to create the image of the birth of a multicultural nation where one is "black, Indian, and white, all at once,"—taking to task elitist, academic ideas about good taste by incorporating into his music creative elements from popular and suburban culture and "hillbilly stuff" (Salomão, 3). In Helio Oiticica's propositions, the influences of Oswald de Andrade are clear, and they are made even more explicit by the composer, Caetano Veloso: "we take our example from the idea of anthropophagy . . . in which you eat everything that comes from anyplace in the world and make of it what you want; the idea is to eat everything that comes along and produce something new" (Dunn, 101).

Among those involved in the tropicalist movement, Gilberto Gil and Jose Carlos Capinam are those who have had the most involvement with ecology. The composer Gilberto Gil participated actively in the debates (and shows) which took place in the "Global Forum of the

NGOs (non-governmental organizations)," during the United Nations Conference on Development and Environment held in Rio de Janeiro in 1992, and he has lent his prestige and presented his ideas in many ecological activities in Brazil and beyond. The poet, Jose Carlos Capinam, organized in Salvador-Bahia, in May, 1996, the first conference on "Art and Ecology" that brought together a number of names associated with these aesthetic movements, as well as many renowned ecologists.

Oswald de Andrade's texts have been constantly reedited, translated, staged, and studied by theoreticians of literary criticism and of the sociology of culture. However, analyses with an ecological basis, as far as I know, remain unpublished. The ecological interpretation of the Brazil Wood and anthropophagy manifestos must be done in the context of Andrade's complete work, particularly as this work filters and reflects the interests of global ecology from cultural, political, and social points of view—implicitly and explicitly present in the images, phrases, and slogans of the Andrade texts.

One must keep in mind that these fragments have an autonomy of their own, and when they are included in flexible and unordered wholes, like the manifestos, one must keep in focus the constant dynamic of demolition, deconstruction, and creation of ideas—a characteristic of the Oswald de Andrade style,[4] which seeks "the chain of images that connect the dense poetic intuition to the schematized philosophical concept, just this side of any system, per se, and just beyond pure artistic creation" (Nunes, "A antropofagia," 39).

One of the most important aspects of contemporary ecological thought is the notion of interdependent spheres: biological, social, political, economic, and cultural. Thus, ecological identity is by definition international, multiple, and diverse, seeking to break down frontiers between nations and nationalities and hierarchies of knowledge and culture. Through a homogenization of social and economic models, the growing global ecological awareness continues to break down colonialist and neo-colonialist politics, and all the classical cultural, social, economic, political, and scientific paradigms. Complex issues like climate change, ozone depletion, biodiversity loss, nuclear arms, acid rain, demographic growth, etc., concern the inhabitants of the whole planet, in spite of national boundaries.

Global ecology is also concerned with the question of multiculturalism, relationships between species and generations, the value and contribution of different forms of knowledge, the political participation of inhabitants and marginalized groups which have no representation, etc. In this new planetary context in which ecology acquires the status of a high political priority, "multiple voices"[5] seek to be heard and reclaim spaces in which to present their options and alternatives in the search for solutions to both local and global problems. These solutions acquire political force and the possibilities of breakthrough and of breaking the monopoly of dominant discourses when they utilize their own forms of expression, profoundly connected to their own identities of ethnicity, of gender, of sexuality, of generation and of race, in which cultural heritage and specific knowledge and lifestyles, allied with the quality of their social representations, reflect what "was digested" and recreated in their historical developments. In the process of global interdependence, social relations do not occur only among equals, but predominantly among opponents and adversaries. Hence its difficulty and its richness, since any voice becomes valid only when in confrontation or in dialogue with the "other," which is not a model to be followed or copied, but rather an opponent, a reference, a mirror, or an interlocutor to be "devoured."

The end of the twentieth century and the beginning of the third millenium see contradictory moments of breaching and closing both objective and subjective frontiers amid the homogenization of world culture, on the one hand, and the refusal to establish contacts or dialogue with differences, on the other. In the context of these misunderstandings and anachronisms, the Andradian manifestos make important contributions to the serious focus of multiculturalism, without seeming too exotic or folkloric, in the formulation of a planetary culture which is both singular and plural.

The recent emergence upon the scene of ethnic groups such as the Yanomamis, who up until now have been completely isolated from that which has been accepted as civilized, is a reminder of what America must have been like before its colonization. The tribe's emergence and clash with a twentieth-century world is a reminder of its vulnerability (and that of others); the Yanomamis may, ultimately, find the same destiny as the Aztecs, Guaranis, Incas, Maias, Tupys, Tupinambas, etc. The tribe's presence recalls the notion of the "noble savage," and of the "primitive savage that impedes progress." But now, in the light of its own incipient power of articulation in the media—in international organizations, in churches, in political parties, in the non-governmental organizations, in universities, and in artistic circles—the cities and the citizens of Brazil and of the world again find themselves before Hamlet's dilemma in its anthropophagous expression "Tupy or not Tupy."

The manifestos emphasize the richness of the multicultural formation of Brazilian society, far from the ambiguities of pacific miscegenation, without hyperbolic nationalism, rejecting all aesthetic exoticism as well as colonialist and neo-colonialist ideas. They are, therefore, texts which help to comprehend the present course of our planetary civil society, where the principal challenge is to guarantee specific identities with a basis in solid national, ethnic, and religious parameters, and to construct a new global identity—multiple, fragmented, flexible, and in permanent flux—which will enable the survival not only of animal and plant species, but also of cultures and peoples. Marginalized social groups in different parts of the world are reclaiming their voice, their citizenship, and their right to exist and to express themselves in the tradition that they have inherited, learned, and lived, destabilizing international political and cultural systems, redefining arenas of political participation supported in the solidarity, in the exchange, and in the apprenticeships (or by the lack of them) of different origins, including those "of the forest and the school."

Anthropophagi circulate (either in groups or individually) on the frontiers of production, communication, and symbolically dominant power, yet they are at the center of international politics seeking the spaces where they can "digest" as much as possible, where they can present and develop their alternatives, staying in tune with their time, demanding and constructing a planetary society that is more just, more equitable, and ecologically sustainable. Oswald de Andrade, if he were alive, would provide a banquet!

Notes

1. The term Brazil Wood (Paul Brasil) comes from a tree of this name that existed in great quantities along the Brazilian coastline before the arrival of the Portuguese and eventually was used to name the country.

2. A language spoken even today, especially by inhabitants of rural Brazil.

3. Tupy is the name of one of the principal indigenous groups that inhabited the Brazilian coast. They were exterminated during the colonial period. The pronunciation in Portuguese of "Tupy" is similar to "to be."

4. This interpretation follows the ideas of Gianni Vattimo.

5. The concept of "multiple voices" has been developed by Professor Mary Jane Spink, of the Pontifical Catholic University in São Paulo.

Selected Works and Further Reading

Andrade, Oswald de, *A utopia antropofágica,* São Paulo, Brazil: Secretaria de Estado da Cultura de São Paulo/Editora Globo, 1990

——, *Anthropophagies,* Paris: Flammarion, 1982

——, *Estética e Política,* São Paulo, Brazil: Globo, 1991

——, *Obra escogida,* Caracas, Venezuela: Biblioteca Ayacucho, 1981

——, *Pau-Brasil,* São Paulo, Brazil: Globo/Secretaria de Estado da Cultura de São Paulo, 1990

——, "Sentimental Memoirs of John Seaborne," *The Texas Quarterly* 15:4 (1972), pp. 112–160

——, *Seraphim Grosse Pointe,* Austin, Texas: New Latin Quarter Editions, 1979

Art d'Amérique Latine, 1911–1968, Paris: Musée National d'Art Moderne/Centre Georges Pompidou, 1992

Boaventura, M. E., *A vanguarda antropofágica,* São Paulo, Brazil: Atica, 1985

Cendrars, Blaise, *Le Brésil; des hommes sont venus,* Monaco: Documents d'art, 1952

Dunn, C., "Caetano Veloso: Tropicalismo revisitado e TomZé: O elo perdido do tropicalismo (entrevistas)," *Brasil/Brazil: A Journal of Brasilian Literature* 7:11 (1994), pp. 99–120

Jackson, K. David, *A prosa de vanguarda na literatura brasileira: Oswald de Andrade,* São Paulo, Brazil: Perspectiva, 1978

Justino, M., *Modernité au Brésil à travers l'ouvre de Tarsila do Amaral, Ione Saldanha et Hélio Oiticica* (Ph.D. diss., University of Paris), 1991

Maltz, Bina, et al., *Antropofagia e tropicalismo,* Pôrto Alegre, Brazil: Editora da Universidade, Universidade Federal do Rio Grande do Sol, 1993

Nunes, Benedito, "A antropofagia ao alcançe de todos," preface to *A utopia antropofágica,* written by Oswald de

Andrade, São Paulo, Brazil: Secretaria de Estado da Cultura de São Paulo/Editora Globo, 1990

———, *Oswald Canibal,* São Paulo, Brazil: Perspectiva, 1979

Reigota, Marcos, *Ecologia e globalizaçao,* São Paulo, Brazil: Brasiliense, forthcoming

———, *Meio Ambiente e representação social,* São Paulo, Brazil: Cortez, 1994

Salomão, Waly, *Hélio Oiticica: Qual é o parangolé?,* Rio de Janeiro, Brazil: Relume Dumará, 1996

Schama, S., *Paisagem e Memoria,* São Paulo, Brazil: Cia das Letras, 1996

Vattimo, Gianni, *Oltre l'interpretazione: il significato dell 'ermeneutica per la filosofia,* Rome: Laterza, 1994; as *Beyond Interpretation: The Meaning of Hermeneutics for Philosophy,* Stanford, California: Stanford University Press, 1997; Cambridge: Polity, 1997

Xavier, Ismail, *Alegorias do subdesenvolvimento: Cinema novo, tropicalismo, cinema marginal,* São Paulo, Brazil: Brasiliense, 1993; as *Allegories of Underdevelopment: Aesthetics and Politics in Modern Brazilian Cinema,* Minneapolis: University of Minnesota Press, 1997

Zürich, Kunsthaus, *Bilderwelt Brasilien,* Bern, Switzerland: Benteli Verlag, 1992

The Caribbean: Colonial and Postcolonial Representations of the Land and the People's Relationships to Their Environment

Seodial Deena

From a colonial perspective, the nineteenth century is seen as a period of historical adventurism, a period of world exploration from which emerged numerous travelogues, diaries, letters, and reports describing, in a mysterious and exotic manner, the land and people of the New World. Whether these conquistadors were Spanish, British, French, Dutch, or Portuguese, they were primarily white Europeans who were curiously intrigued and fascinated by what they perceived as the dark worlds of Asians, Indians, and Africans. Within this periodic frame, writers like Joseph Conrad, Graham Greene, Rudyard Kipling, Coral Ballantyne, and others motivated and influenced by these expedition stories, sailed to many of these new regions and wrote voraciously about the peoples and their landscapes. Dictated by the hunger, thirst, and even lust for exotic descriptions and narratives from the European audience, these writers' works merely reinforced the myths and legends previously depicted by the colonizers, for example Conrad's depiction of Africa as evil and Africans as savages. According to Chinua Achebe, Conrad's "*Heart of Darkness* projects the image of Africa as 'the other world,' the antithesis of Europe and therefore of civilization, a place where man's vaunted intelligence and refinement are finally mocked by triumphant bestiality" (p. 252).

Later, another group of writers, such as E. M. Forster and H. D. Lister, would build on such dehumanizing depictions, devaluing the colonized and their environment. Homi Bhabha sums up the effects of the former and latter's colonial representation in the following manner:

> In shattering the mirror of representation, and its range of Western bourgeois social and psychic "identifications," the spectacle of colonial fantasy sets itself as an uncanny "double." Its terrifying figures—savages, grotesques, mimicmen—reveal things so profoundly familiar to the West that it cannot bear to remember them. It is in that sense, and for that very reason, that "the horror! the horror!" said in the heart of darkness itself, and the "Ou-boum" of the empty Marabar caves will continue to terrify and confound us, for they address that "other scene" within ourselves that continually divides us against ourselves and others. (pp. 119–120).

It was not until the beginning of the latter half of the twentieth century that a recognizable body of literature began to emerge from the Caribbean, and this body of literature had the magnanimous task of debunking the colonial myth of negativity of the Caribbean land and its peoples. It also had to forge a pioneering path of discovery and definition against the onslaught of both black and white American criticism. Emerging from rumor and legend of "sailors, saltfish merchants, displaced criminals, yellow-fever victims, slaves in the canefields, Maroons in the bush": "the men and women who laid the foundations of Caribbean societies in sixteenth and seventeenth centuries" (Dance, 1), Caribbean literature was viewed as cheap and low-class. But after half of a century of focusing on neglected subjects like ordinary people, landscape, and environment, this region has produced several excellent writers of international renown and a literature Nobel Prize winner.

Although most of the writers from the Caribbean had the opportunity either to live in or visit another country, namely England and later the United States of America and Canada, their memories of the Caribbean and its peoples remained freshly intact. Whether writing from England, the United States, Canada, or the Caribbean, these writers use the rich, tropical landscape of the Caribbean as setting and the socio-political and historical struggles as major themes. As a result, much of Caribbean Literature explores the importance of belonging to a place, and when the feeling of belonging is destroyed, a person's identity crumbles. One can understand the writers' dilemma since most of them emerged in the forties and fifties, when a great wave of migration occurred. Living in foreign countries, Caribbean writers experienced alienation and displacement, and their experiences filter into their writings, consciously or unconsciously. For the most part it is done consciously since literature becomes a means of evaluating and re-evaluating not only their homelands but also themselves. While the narrators of V. S. Naipaul's *Miguel Street* and George Lamming's *In the Castle of My Skin* are reflective and analytical about their departure from the Caribbean, Moses and Ralph Singh, through story telling, oral and written, re-evaluate their shipwrecked lives in England. And these narrators reflect the nostalgia and self-analysis of the authors.

Displacement results from the historical and cultural struggles of the region. The occupation of various areas of the region at different periods by the Spanish, Dutch, French, and British has left much historical fragmentation. The practice of slavery and indentureship has further complicated the wholeness of the region. Additionally, since most of these writers lived or live in foreign countries and experienced or experience alienation, loneliness, and loss of culture, their writings reflect this displacement. Jean Rhys's Rochester is very much displaced in the Caribbean as Antoinette is in England. The West Indians in England, as described by Samuel Selvon's *The Lonely Londoners*, experience displacement. They lose themselves, their culture, environment, and their sense of community. Although Moses tries to revive and foster the community spirit, by allowing fellow West Indians to meet, eat, and sleep at his apartment, the community still disintegrates because of the absence of their environment. This is one of the inevitable consequences they suffer for living in a foreign, large city. Thus they become fragmented, and out of fragmentation they live crippled lives. But their nostalgia for their warm, beautiful islands juxtaposed with a cold, frigid England forges a self-analysis that parallels re-evaluation from the first wave of migrated Caribbean writers. Moses, the narrator and contemplated writer, reflects:

> I does wonder about the boys, how all of we come up to the old Brit'n to make a living, and how the years go by and we still here in this country. . . . How after all these years I ain't get no place at all, I still the same way, neither forward nor backward. . . . From winter to winter, summer to summer, work after work. Sleep, eat, hustle pussy, work, Boy, sometimes I sit there and think about that. . . . I want to go back to Trinidad and lay down in the sun and dig my toes, and eat a fish broth and go Maracas Bay and talk to them fishermen, and all day long I sleeping under a tree, with just the old sun for company. (pp. 129–130)

Antoinette in Jean Rhys's *Wide Sargasso Sea* desperately tries to escape from the negation of her life, to assert her individual identity. She tries to answer the parrot's questions, "Who's there? Who are you?" But her quest for identity encounters patriarchal domination, and in some ways her plight reflects a similar fate for the Caribbean because of the cultural and political domination from metropolitan countries. Through the loss of a sense of place or the failure to identify with the Caribbean landscape, her identity is destroyed. Antoinette loves the Caribbean, especially Coulibri and Dominica, but due to patriarchal and colonial interference from Mason and Rochester, she is uprooted from both places. Of course Mason's marriage to Annette is central to the riot at Coulibri, the parallel of Eden (p. 19), and this riot drives the family from their fallen paradise. Antoinette's effort to remain at Coulibri is thwarted by a "jagged stone" from Tia. However, she clings to this place: "As I ran, I thought, I will live with Tia and I will be like her. Not to leave Coulibri. Not to go. Not" (p. 45). Later, in brooding nostalgia, she tells Rochester about the intensity of her love for Dominica and Coulibri: "'I love it [Dominica] more than anywhere in the world. As if it were a person.' 'But you don't know the world,' I teased her. 'No, only here, and Jamaica of course. Coulibri Spanish Town" (p. 89).

Colonial and postcolonial Caribbean writers have depicted their land and environment in a reverential, personified, and intimate manner, a harmonious and symbolic setting for their characters and actions. This personification creates a rather complex and interesting mosaic relationship between the peoples and their landscapes. On one level, the colonizer rapes the land, sets out to conquer violently the environment, and encounters hostile resistance. He uses his social, political, and economic authority/power to condemn the landscape as evil and destructive; whereas the colonized respects the land and environment, celebrates their energy and beauty, and draws strength from their fountains of life. Antoinette is strong and passionate in the Caribbean landscape that consists of hot sun, green vegetation, and fresh running streams. She is in harmony with this colorful landscape that contains her "tree of life," thereby supplying her with life (p. 19). Antoinette colors her roses in green, blue, and purple, and writes her name in "fire red" (p. 53). But for the wounded and fragmented Rochester, "everything is too much. . . . Too much blue, too much purple, too much green. The flowers are too red, the mountains are too high, the hills too near. And the woman is a stranger" (p. 70). His failure to control and dominate the landscape renders him powerless: "I wanted to say something reassuring but the scent of the river flowers was overpoweringly strong. I felt giddy" (p. 83), but it also symbolizes his inability to celebrate the colorful and passionate personality and sexuality of his wife. Threatened and terrified by the landscape, a fearful Rochester "broke a spray off and trampled it into the mud" (p. 99), and his cold and callous way of destroying the landscape symbolizes the way he destroys Antoinette in order to control her. His greedy thirst/lust cannot be satisfied because his colonial perspective associates his hatred to Antoinette and her landscape:

> I hated the mountains and the hills, the rivers and the rain. I hated the sunsets of whatever color, I hated its beauty and its magic and the secret I would never know. I hated its indifference and the cruelty which was part of its loveliness. Above all I hated her. For she belonged to the magic and the loveliness. She had left me thirsty and all my life would be thirst and longing for what I had lost before I found it. (p. 172)

This heavenly place, where Antoinette belongs and where she wishes to stay (p. 108), has been made into a hell by Rochester: "But I loved this place and you have made it into a place I hate. I used to think that if everything else went out of my life I would still have this, and now you have spoilt it. It's just somewhere else where I have been unhappy, and the other things are nothing to what has happened here" (p. 147). Carole Angier describes the implication of this destruction. She points out that "in destroying this place for Antoinette, Rochester precipitates her madness because he has destroyed her sense of hope, of belonging, of ownership, autonomy, and ultimately her own sense of personal power" (p. 154). The magnitude of Antoinette's destruction forces her confession to her destroyer: "I hate it now like I hate you and before I die I will show you how much I hate you" (p. 147).

Derek Walcott, in *Another Life*, talks about the task of setting down the landscape and naming it. Walcott nostalgically recreates the Caribbean landscape, particularly St. Lucia, with the rich congruence of painting imageries, figures, and theories. *Another Life* opens with the young artist (Walcott) striving to sketch the landscape at sunset and ends with the maturing writer, Walcott. The journey-motif becomes a vehicle for the poet's exploration of the beauty and fire of St. Lucia, coconut walks of his father's paintings, history and oppression, freedom and romance, his beloved Andreuille who lives at the water's edge, Simmons and his studio, privilege and aspiration, and frustration and fulfillment. *Another Life* also describes, celebrates, and reevaluates Walcott's life, art, love, landscape, language, history, the Caribbean, struggles of a few people, and spiritual resilience present in the human heart. Walcott looks at the standard view of Caribbean history and sees that colonization has depicted a distorted history filled with numerous gaps. In telling Caribbean history, the absence of facts renders the story as the hollowness of a coconut shell, thus, his intention is to provide autobiography, which he decorates with art and love, as an alternative to history, the accumulation of dead facts or the writing of a juiceless grocery list. Through autobiography, Walcott aims at the whole truth, which is multifaceted, and in the poem he transmits his personal experience into art, providing an artistic vision and form through a synthesis of writing and painting.

Wilson Harris, a trained government surveyor, draws upon his "close experiences with nature and landscape, and with the men of different races and classes who were his surveying crews and who were isolated with him in the jungle or on riverbanks for considerable periods of time" (Boxill, 187–188). Further, Harris's travels from Guyana to England and North America become a movement of re-evaluation in time and space of his own relationship to the land and landscape he revisits in the settings of his works. His most famous work, *Palace of the Peacock*, depicts Donne, captain of a multiracial crew, as the colonizer who is obsessed with the conquest of the legendary El Dorado, the lost city of gold. His lust for gold parallels his lust for Mariella, the Amerindian woman, who harmonizes with the land and landscape to destroy not only the process of colonization but also the colonizer and his crew. Hena Maes-Jelinek argues that

> not only do the outer and inner psychological landscapes coincide and real landscape features spatialize inner states of mind, the concrete and the intangible often overlap as again and again the surface reality is breached to reveal the tormenting obsessions of the crew with power or wealth, with Mariella, the native woman (at once sexual object, symbol of the land and the spirit of the place, and ambivalent muse), to reveal also the mixture of terror and beauty they experience in their journey towards death and rebirth. (p. 450)

In fact, Wilson Harris is the only West Indian author who has devoted much of his work to an elevating representation of native West Indians/Indians/Amerindians, who are closest to the land and environment. H. G. deLisser's *The Arawak Girl*, Edgar Mittleholzer's Kaywana trilogy (*Kaywana Blood*, *Kaywana Stock*, and *Kaywana Children*), and Michael Gilkes' *Couvade* are three of the few authors who include the Amerindians in their works. Since the colonizers/Europeans "virtually eliminated" the natives, "the small communities which survive in Dominica and Guyana today are regarded as marginal to the society," and for this reason the little fiction in which they appear "either registers them as de-tribalised individuals in the towns ('Bucks') or portrays them as exotic groups in the interior" (Ramchand, 51). But Harris' works, particularly *Palace of the Peacock* and *Heartland*, place the Indians at the center of colonial and postcolonial representations of the land and the peoples' relationships to their environment. According to Ramchand, Harris places Indians at the center of "three of his basic themes in fiction: the unity of all men, the theme

of rebirth, and the search for ancestral roots. At the same time, the author from Guyana makes the 'historical' Indian come alive in a way that no other West Indian novelist or historian has been bold enough to imagine" (p. 51).

The Guyanese land and landscape function like the gods in Greek literature to defend the poor and oppressed, the vanishing Amerindians in *Palace of the Peacock*, the poor East Indian laborers in *The Far Journey of Oudin*, and the descendants of runaway slaves in *The Secret Ladder*, and destroy the oppressors, namely the Europeans. Jungle and river falls in particular become ravenous wolves ready to devour the colonizers. Through the use of history and myths and legends from the Amerindians, Harris's *Palace of the Peacock* "recreates quintessentially the repeated invasion of Guyana after the Renaissance, the abortive meeting between the conquerors and the Amerindian folk and, symbolically, the exploitation of land and people from time immemorial" (Maes-Jelinek, 449).

Michael Anthony's *The Year in San Fernando* forces us to see the landscape in a new way, a way that causes us to identify with it and appreciate it. He brilliantly describes the cane fields, seasons, and rural and urban areas in a manner that depicts, foreshadows, and influences not only the social and political struggles of the character, but also the growing consciousness of Francis, the protagonist. Francis's closeness with nature parallels that of Tiger, the protagonist in Selvon's *A Brighter Sun*. American technological and materialistic pursuits of building a road at the naval base "changes the landscape and destroys the community's garden plots" (Fabre, 112), but they also mature Tiger's consciousness and wisdom of embracing farming.

In Caribbean literature, the concept of the strong mother figure features significantly, especially in relation with the land and the peoples' relationship with the land. The mother bears the responsibility of the family because the father is either dead or away from the home. In most cases an extra-marital relationship keeps him away from home, and in other cases he escapes into drunkenness. The result of this scenario promotes the mother as a heroine, for as a single parent she raises her family in a black working-class setting. Many Caribbean novels are set in the working-class tradition, and so the mother emerges as a figure of strength.

Antoinette's mother becomes insane in *Wide Sargasso Sea*. In fact, she becomes so depressed by her first husband's death, the periods of separation from her second husband, and the chaotic slavery situations that she offers Antoinette very little help. However, Christophine, the black house servant, becomes Antoinette's mother and a figure of strength. In times of problems, she turns to Christophine for counsel, strength, and help. With Christophine by her side she grows stronger in confidence, but Rochester becomes threatened and insecure, so he sends the servant away. Without Christophine, Antoinette crumbles spiritually, socially, and psychologically. She cannot cope with her man-made problems.

Jean Rhys' characterization of Christophine convinces us of the strength of the mother figure. Although the writer provides little physical description of her, she makes the servant's presence, power, and philosophy radiate throughout the novel. One hears the rhythm of her speech as powerful as one feels her presence as she advocates her feminist theory for Antoinette's survival: "Get up, girl, and dress yourself. Woman must have spunks to live in this wicked world" (p. 101).

In *The Year in San Fernando* Francis's father is dead and Ma labors as a domestic servant for a better future for her children. She seizes the opportunity for Francis to go to San Fernando to help the ailing Mrs. Chandles. She sees this as a good opportunity for her son to obtain a good education and escape from the poverty with which she has to cope. When he visits Francis in San Fernando and she prepares to leave, she earnestly encourages him to "Stay and take in education boy. Take it in. That's the main thing" (p. 67). Similarly, Sophia Adams, in *Moon on a Rainbow Shawl*, also labors as a domestic servant to support her family, especially to help Esther to take the island scholarship. Although her husband, Charlie Adams, is not dead or separated from her, he becomes useless because his cricketing career has been strangled by the authorities and he has no job. Charlie responds to his disillusionment by absenting himself from home most of the times and by getting drunk the rest of the times.

In *Miguel Street* and *In the Castle of My Skin* the two boys who are the narrators grow up without fathers. Both mothers strongly battle with the social and economic hardships to educate their sons for a better future. The mothers may severely punish their children out of frustration or from fear that the boys may stray from the right path of life, but they also know how important it is for the next generation to

escape the aftermath of slavery and colonialism. All these mothers also recognize that education is the key to deliverance from the region's poverty. G's mother bathes him naked while the other children climb on the fence and laugh. She lashes him to inculcate desirable behaviors, and even at eighteen when G prepares to leave the island for a job on another island, she spends hours lecturing to him about life. Similarly, the strong discipline of the narrator's mother in *Miguel Street* keeps him on the moral path of life and brings him success. Once she beats him so badly that he runs away to B. Wordsworth. He cries and decides not to return home, but with Wordsworth's help he returns a wiser boy.

The mother figure in Caribbean literature represents the symbol of origin, roots, and the land. In most cases the writers illustrate the Caribbean man's relationship with the land by exploring the man's relationship with his mother. Since most of the writers write from a foreign land with a sense of nostalgia, they feel a special sense of responsibility to explore the complications of a West Indian's departure from his mother or land. At the end of Michelle Cliff's *No Telephone to Heaven*, Clare Savage has rejected her father's hypocritical obsession with his white color for her mother's wish: "I hope someday you make something of yourself, and someday help your people" (p. 103). After a futile search for home in America and England, Clare returns to Jamaica, the land of her mother and grandmother's burial, where she is killed fighting for her people, but where her body becomes one with the land: "Clare's body is burned into the land by machine-gun fire, and as she loses consciousness, she slips from language into the preverbal, preliterary sounds of a land before meaning, language, or symbolic use" (Raiskin, 203). On another level, Christopher's identification with the land insists that he obtain a piece of land and bury his grandmother, although she has been dead "thirteen Chrismus" ago. He doesn't think it will hurt "the fat brown man in the big fat bed wrapped in flowers" (p. 47) to give him a piece of land. But colonial greed from this suburban family refuses Christopher any land and results in their massacre.

Caribbean literature depicts the colonizer as the white male who exploits the land and the woman, and destroys or threatens to destroy the relationship between the woman and the landscape. The women, as mothers whose wombs produce fertility and life and wives whose love and romance anoint the bruised and battered bodies of colonized men, are in harmony with the landscape. And from this relationship they draw strength, healing, and inspiration. Kitty's burial homage to her mother's body links her with her roots, identifies her with her homeland, and foreshadows her commitment to the land; a commitment that will cause her to deny America and her family for Jamaica and one that will not allow her to leave for treatment in Miami:

> When she dressed her mother's body, it was the first time she remembered seeing her mother's nakedness. The secret thing which had been hidden from her for thirty years became hers. . . . The breasts full—the nipples dark—were stiff with lifelessness, and she caressed them. From somewhere came an image of a slave-woman pacing aisles of cane, breasts slung over her shoulder to suckle the baby carried on her back. She kissed her mother on her eyelids and rubbed coconut oil across her body, into the creases and folds, softening the marks of childbearing and old age. (pp. 71–72)

Perhaps the strongest statement in favor of Caribbean environmental literature is depicted in Walcott's *Ti-Jean and His Brothers*, where the colonizer is also the planter, old man (Papa Bois), and the devil, whose nature and function are death and destruction: "The thief cometh not, but for to steal, and to kill, and to destroy" (John 10:10). Bolom concludes that the devil, his master, is responsible for evil, death, and destruction (p. 99). He has no respect for the land, landscape, and the animals. Gros Jean and Mi-Jean are defeated and destroyed by the devil because they rely on their own strength, physical strength and book knowledge, respectively, and they disregard their mother's counsel to respect the environment (pp. 103, 104, 116). Gros Jean and Mi-Jean are victims of postcolonial deception and foolishness propagated through a colonial education, but Ti-Jean's common sense and respect for his mother, symbol of the land, elevate him to that status of David's defeat over Goliath. Ti-Jean seeks his mother's prayer and counsel, heeds her words, and respects and compliments the creatures of the forest (pp. 135–137). His victory over the colonizer/planter/devil results from his harmonious relationship with his environment, the creatures of the forest, and his deep commitment to the land, mother.

This analytical and re-evaluative approach by Walcott and other Caribbean writers becomes a useful dialogue to stimulate the exploitation of history and imagination for progress and growth. As Caribbean writers, those mentioned and others like Martin Carter, Olive Senior, Louise Bennett, Jan Carew, Jamaica Kincaid, Ismith Khan, and Edgar Mittleholzer evaluate and re-evaluate representations of the land and the peoples' relationships to their environments; they demonstrate intriguing shifts in perspectives, but they forge a new creation. Harris, in *The Whole Armour* and *Palace of the Peacock*, depicts that history is a system of words, not facts, and that the Caribbean is not the first land of slavery for the Africans, but that they were already slaves in Africa. Edward K. Brathwaite, in *The Arrivants*, a book of poetry, also explores this question of confrontation of the past. His re-evaluation of himself and his people influences the division of the book into three sections: "Rites of Passage" deals with the journey of Africans from Africa to the Caribbean as slaves, "Masks" takes us back to Africa to explore the culture and living conditions of the Africans, and "Islands" depicts slavery in the Caribbean. V. S. Naipaul uses a universal approach to evaluate and analyze himself and the Caribbean through his satire, sarcasm, irony, humor, and fictional autobiography. Along with the above, he employs caricature in presenting the "complex fate of the Caribbean," while Wilson Harris, John Hearne, George Lamming, Andrew Salkey, and Samuel Selvon pursue the rebuilding of the native's cultural image (Bhatnager, 30–31), and each uses different techniques.

Derek Walcott's re-evaluation focuses on the socio-political, economic, and cultural struggle that results from the Caribbean cultural pluralism. Walcott's artistic and dramatic approach incorporates his mulatto metaphor to depict the freshness and uniqueness of the Caribbean, while Lamming uses a Marxist approach to focus on the working class and their struggle to regain the land and save their environment from capitalistic corruption and exploitation. He believes that the working class will overthrow the oppressors. Michael Anthony forces his readers to look at the Caribbean from a different point of view, and then he asks about the future of the postcolonial Caribbean. With such diversity of fictional and historical representations, nationhood and regionalism take shape. Indigenous Amerindians relate sacredly to the earth as their mother and God; Africans and Indians—emerging from slavery and indentureship, respectively—use the land and environment to fashion a new culture and belief, and at the same time their culture and belief shape the landscape; and Europeans exploit and destroy the land and environment. History informs, vision and imagination create, and "with this prodigious ambition one began" ("What the Twilight Says," 4). Wilson Harris's 1983 *The Womb of Space* with its appropriate subtitle *The Cross-Cultural Imagination* captures not only Harris's intention, but other Caribbean writers' ambition of re-evaluation and creation:

> The paradox of cultural heterogeneity, or cross-cultural capacity, lies in the evolutionary thrust it restores to orders of the imagination, the ceaseless dialogue it inserts between hardened conventions and eclipsed or half-eclipsed otherness, within an intuitive self that moves endlessly into flexible patterns, areas or bridges of community. (p. xviii)

Selected Works and Further Reading

Achebe, Chinua, "An Image of Africa: Racism in Conrad's *Heart of Darkness*," in *Heart of Darkness,* written by Joseph Conrad, edited by Robert Kimbrough, New York: Norton, 1988

Angier, Carole, *Jean Rhys: Life and Work,* Boston: Little, Brown, 1990; London: Andre Deutsch, 1990

Anthony, Michael, *The Year in San Fernando,* London: Andre Deutsch, 1965; Portsmouth, New Hampshire: Heinemann Educational, 1970

Bhabha, Homi K., "Representation and the Colonial Text: Critical Exploration of Some Forms of Mimeticism," in *The Theory of Reading,* edited by Frank Gloversmith, Totowa, New Jersey: Barnes & Noble, 1984; Brighton, England: Harvester, 1984

Bhatnagar, O. P., "Commonwealth Literature: Genesis and Bearings," in *Indian Readings in Commonwealth Literature,* edited by G. S. Amur, V. R. N. Prasad, B. V. Nermode, and N. K. Nihalani, New Delhi, India: Sterling, 1985

Boxill, Anthony, "Wilson Harris," in *Fifty Caribbean Writers: A Bio-Bibliographical Critical Sourcebook,* edited by Daryl Cumber Dance, New York: Greenwood, 1986

Brathwaite, Kamau, *The Arrivants: A New World Trilogy,* New York and London: Oxford University Press, 1973

Carter, Martin, *Poems of Succession,* London: New Beacon, 1977

Cliff, Michelle, *No Telephone to Heaven,* New York: Dutton, 1987; London: Methuen, 1988

Dake, Finis Jennings, *Dake's Annotated Reference Bible,* Atlanta, Georgia: Dake Bible Sales, 1961

Dance, Daryl Cumber, ed., *Fifty Caribbean Writers: A Bio-Bibliographical Critical Sourcebook,* New York: Greenwood, 1986

Fabre, Michael, "Samuel Selvon," in *West Indian Literature,* edited by Bruce King, Hamden, Connecticut: Archon, 1979; London: Macmillan, 1979

Harris, Wilson, *The Far Journey of Oudin,* London: Faber and Faber, 1961

———, *Heartland,* London: Faber and Faber, 1964

———, *Palace of the Peacock,* London: Faber and Faber, 1960; Boston: Faber and Faber, 1988

———, *The Secret Ladder,* London: Faber and Faber, 1963

———, *The Whole Armour,* London: Faber and Faber, 1962

———, *The Womb of Space: The Cross-Cultural Imagination,* Westport, Connecticut: Greenwood, 1983

John, Errol, *Moon on a Rainbow Shawl: A Play in Three Acts,* New York: Grove, 1958; London: Faber and Faber, 1958

Lamming, George, *In the Castle of My Skin,* New York: McGraw-Hill, 1953; London: Michael Joseph, 1953

Maes-Jelinek, Hena, "Wilson Harris," in *International Literature in English: Essays on the Major Writers,* edited by Robert Ross, New York: Garland, 1991; London: St. James, 1991

Naipaul, V. S., *Miguel Street,* New York: Vanguard, 1959; London: Andre Deutsch, 1959

———, *The Mimic Men,* New York: Macmillan, 1967; Harmondsworth, England: Penguin, 1967

Raiskin, Judith L., *Snow on the Cane Fields: Women's Writing and Creole Subjectivity,* Minneapolis: University of Minnesota Press, 1996

Ramchand, Kenneth, "Aborigines: Their Role in West Indian Literature," *Jamaica Journal* 3:4 (December 1969), pp. 51–54

Reid, Victor Stafford, *Sixty-Five,* Jamaica: Longmans, Green, 1960

Rhys, Jean, *Wide Sargasso Sea,* New York: Norton, 1966; London: Andre Deutsch,1966

Selvon, Samuel, *A Brighter Sun,* London: A. Wingate, 1952; New York: Viking, 1953

———, *The Lonely Londoners,* New York: St. Martin's, 1956; London: A. Wingate, 1956

Walcott, Derek, *Another Life,* New York: Farrar, Straus and Giroux, 1973; London: Jonathan Cape, 1973

———, *Ti-Jean and His Brothers,* in *Dream on Monkey Mountain, and Other Plays,* New York: Farrar, Straus and Giroux, 1970; London: Jonathan Cape, 1970

———, "What the Twilight Says: An Overture," in *Dream on Monkey Mountain, and Other Plays,* New York: Farrar, Straus and Giroux, 1970; London: Jonathan Cape, 1970

Ecology and Latin American Poetry

❧

Roberto Forns-Broggi

Nature is always present in Latin American poetry. However, it is true that we can notice an enormous development in the second part of the twentieth century and its challenging reading of human and non-human realities is not yet recognized by critics. Probably the reason for this lack of attention has been the readers' expectation of socio-political demands, the weight of which in the daily life of Latin Americans is still tremendous. But the growing presence of ecological destruction has made some writers more sensitive about the survival of this planet and has caused them to incorporate a long-term perspective into their writing and actions.

Thus Homero Aridjis (Mexico) became one of the world's major environmental activists as a founder and president of the Group of 100. As Angel Flores indicates, the group originally consisted of artists and intellectuals who battled against Mexico City's enormous pollution problems. The battlefield broadened, however, until it encompassed all of Mexico and the world (p. 53). Aridjis' poetry is full of urban images, such as endangered and faded trees, and the city as humanity's funeral. One of his best books, *Imágenes para el fin del milenio & Nueva Expulsión del Paraíso* (Images for the End of the Millennium & New Expulsion from Paradise), contains 38 short and precise poems under the title "trees" about this apocalyptic perspective: "In this Century / the Ax of evil / turns against the idea of a tree" (p. 124, my translation).

In the past decade one finds not only books entirely dedicated to this subject of the deterioration of the planet, but also anthologies, manifestos, and other publications about that crucial fight for the preservation of biological and cultural diversity, such as *Artistas e intelectuales sobre el ecocidio urbano* (Artists and Intellectuals about Urban Ecological Disaster) edited by Aridjis and Fernando Cesarman; a government forestation publication, *El árbol en la poesía guatemalteca* (The Tree in Guatemalan Poetry) edited by Francisco Rubio; the annual manifesto and anthology *El planeta en el espejo: Poetas por la tierra* (Planet in the Mirror. Poets for the Earth), published in Peru since 1991; the "Library of Ecology," a collection of more than 14 books published by Editorial Planeta, directed by Guillermo Sabanes (Argentina); or the manifesto *Sociedad para la liberación de las rosas* (Society for the Liberation of Roses, Peru).

According to Octavio Paz (Mexico) universal destruction and pollution will be the framework of the next millennium. In *Arbol adentro* (A Tree Within) the pollution of the city is one of the most critical poetic subjects. In the 1990s Latin American writers talk about pollution of consciousness, the problems of health and safety (Hopenhayn, 54, 25), and the ultimate human cruelty (Vitale, *Léxico* [Glossary], 85): the pernicious lack of love "which is coming with reproachful / rumor of the eruption of extermination / of all the volcanoes in the Andean Mountains" (Bintrup, *En tierra firme* [On Firm Ground], 71, my translation); and, nevertheless, the vivacious celebration of nature in the collective memory (Urzagasti, *La colina* [The Hill], 13–14). Where everything has a price, but nothing has value, this poetry shows a countercultural consciousness that is diverse and imaginative, but not well known by the common people, except in the cases of really strong indigenous traditions in an ecological perspective.

In analyzing these trends toward ecological poetry, one should take account of the work of two great poets of nature, Pablo Neruda (Chile) and Jorge Carrera Andrade (Ecuador). Neruda is better known as a public figure, but his attachment to nature is unbelievably diverse and suggestive. Neruda's poetry is as vast as Nature itself: in *Crepusculario* from 1923 the poet contemplates with admiration the world as matter;

in *Residencia en la tierra* (Residence on Earth) his surrealistic perspective provides new angles in a chaotic way; in *Canto general* nature is political, epic, and mythical; in his three books of *Odes* it is joyous and appreciative, and in the rest of his work, as Manuel Durán and Margery Safir indicate, "alternately imaginative and contemplative" (p. 33). In *Extravagaria* the celebration of being close to the sea and the land is heard in Neruda's passion for stars and his earthly destination. Durán and Safir pointed out that nature is "a life force overpowering the feeble impermanence of human existence, and in the posthumous works the poet seeks, in solicitude, contact with this force. Man's life is fleeting. Nature is the source" (p. 73). When Neruda wants to speak, he is thinking of flowers, stones, waves, animals. But first of all, he wants to listen to what nature has to say: "I shall be busy all week, / I have to listen incessantly" ("Bestiary," *Extravagaria*, translated by Alastair Reid, 283).

Carrera Andrade is another prolific poet who showed admiration and an incredible love for animals and flowers in experimental short poems like the haiku, as well as in commemorative poems of cosmic connections (*Obra poética completa*). Carrera Andrade writes: "Friendship of things and beings / in appearance separate and distinct, / but interwoven in their cosmic existence" ("Weapons of Light," *Selected Poems*, translated by H. R. Hays, 121). After the 1920s, his poetry continues to reveal the importance of the visual scrutiny of nature in order to participate in the natural transformations of life, but at the same time a foreboding perspective is gaining more strength, the appearance of disconnections is more real. Even though Carrera Andrade's poetry is not as universal as Neruda's, in the late books he insists on the importance of indigenous cultural treasures, such as "Quipos" (33 short poems in *Obra poética*) to show the sensual links of things and beings in the cosmos.

There are other poets of the countryside, such as Carlos Pellicer (Mexico). His poems reorder the elements of nature to construct a new reality that allows for the transformation of humanity. From this rural perspective other poets, most of them migrants to the big cities, have written books and poems that express indigenous points of view in the Indian languages, such as José María Arguedas (Peru), who also wrote ethnographic studies, recompilations, novels, and stories in Spanish but with a strong influence of Quechua, and William Hurtado de Mendoza (Peru) who has published his poems in bilingual

editions. Even in a narrative poet such as Eleodoro Vargas Vicuña (Peru), there is a cosmic sense of creation in the sensuality of earthly transformations ("A Grain of Salt," from the series "The Crystal in Which You can See Yourself," *Ñahuín*), where natural eyes are the spectators of animals and flowers that carry on the ritual of life and death. These writers represent the will of rescuing the ecological wisdom of ancient cultures that continues in legends, myths and traditions.

In Central America, we can find the same spirit of resistance against oblivion. Two poets are important in this regard: Pablo Antonio Cuadra (Nicaragua) and Laureano Albán (Costa Rica), who clearly are opposed to the typical idea of nature from the Anglo-Saxon twentieth-century poetry where the natural world is conceived as shattered, fragmentary, and painful. The Nicaraguan poet developed a refined mixture between indigenous traditions and Oriental and Greek mythologies. His cosmic orientation is well expressed in his brief but powerful book *Siete árboles contra el atardecer* (Seven Trees Against Sunset). Unity is the answer in different ways, such as with "The Ciruela," the tree that closes and opens wounds: "It closes them with its bark when they are war wounds. / It opens them with its fruit when they are love wounds" (Anton and Frederickson, 34). Albán universalizes even more this cosmic aim in *Viaje interminable* (The Endless Voyage) where the poetic subject of the dominant discourse is disintegrated in natural beings such as flowers. In *Geografía invisible de América* (Invisible Geography of America) the search for a cosmic perspective lies in indigenous traditions and gods (Popol Vuh, Chilam Balam, Sololá), and in many more other memories about the human fate in this new region where colonizers lose their souls confronting soil, stone, wind, water, sun, and tree.

Yet many poets who developed a spirituality from nature have to be rescued from obscurity, such as Oscar Castro (Chile) whose *Rocío en el trébol* (Dew in the Clover) shows a joyful and clear integration with the beings of the valley, even though it stems from a naive and pure religious sensibility. We can say almost the same for the revolutionary poets who pursued leftist utopias in the 1960s where nature was an ally, such as Javier Heraud (Peru), author of beautiful poems about the propagation of Autumn and rivers, symbols of nature's brotherhood in the search for justice; and Otto René Castillo (Guatemala) in whose work the consciousness of death is present in alliance with nature. Along these lines there are well known poets such as Juan Liscano (Venezuela), whose 1950s poetry shows the human struggle against the desert of injustice, while his late poems persist in confronting modernity with a cosmic view.

Another decisive writer is Ernesto Cardenal (Nicaragua), whose work has been politically influential in Latin America and throughout the world since the 1960s. His poetry is a powerful denunciation against capitalistic insensitivity and ecological disasters. History and myth become interwoven in *Quetzalcóatl* where a Mesoamerican god is the symbol of natural forces, the unity of humanity with god and agriculture. One of his recently published works, *Cántico cósmico* (Cosmic Canticle), develops connections between science, ethics, primitive cultures, ecology and political activism.

Gioconda Belli (Nicaragua) and Rosario Murillo (Nicaragua) develop the theme of the fecundity of the earth as it complements the physical and spiritual dimensions of women. Belli, for example, insists in her first books on her body consciousness with the branches of trees to look for love and justice, forging a national sense from her bonds with human and non-human tangibilities, returning to her natural roots in order to repeat the vital cycle and to create life: "You are fertile and earthy again / fill the veins of liquid fire that you believed turned off / like calm rivers" (*El ojo de la mujer* [Woman's Eye], 99, my translation). This feminine position shows a disintegration of the identity of woman, who becomes an agent of nature. Even though this is not the principal subject, it is an important point of reference for Central American women poets that is also a key to interpretation. The feminine self changes into nature in the erotic poetry of Ana María Rodas (Guatemala) and in the complaining voice of Claribel Alegría (Nicaragua-El Salvador).

Much of Latin American poets say something fascinating about nature even though nature is not their major subject. Such is the case of great poems about animals, such as those by José Emilio Pacheco (Mexico) compiled in *An Ark for the Next Millennium* and some texts by Antonio Cisneros (Peru) where natural beings become lessons from history. About the sea Pacheco wrote a beautiful book, *Los trabajos del mar* (The Works of the Sea), and there is also a refined young poet, José Luis Rivas (Mexico), whose phantoms and other memories of the sea fuse images of birds, sun, doves, and privateers

with readings of English poets such as John Donne, T. S. Eliot and others in *Raz de marea: Obra poética (1975–1992)* (A Little Touch of Tide. Poetic Work [1975–1992]) and *Luz de mar abierto* (Light of Open Sea). His personal tone appears in very short poems such as "Without storm coming / in clear sky / Lightning!" (*Raz de marea*, 218, my translation).

The same attitude toward cosmic connections is present in the work of many poets, such as Luis Cardoza y Aragón (Guatemala), Rafael Maya (Colombia), Enrique Molina (Argentina), Alfonso Javier Rojas Wiesand (Mexico), Jaime Sabines (Mexico), Juan Sánchez Peláez (Venezuela), Ida Vitale (Uruguay), and others; it is impossible to mention a complete list here.

Some attitudes become crucial to understanding the importance of nature in the poetic perspective. For example, Nicanor Parra (Chile) uses black humor to develop an acid sarcasm against urban disdain of nature. Sometimes a subtle irony is enough for him to be sarcastic: "Pedestrians / anonymous / heroes / of / the / ecology" (*Poemas para combatir* [Poems to Fight], 265, my translation). Nature is also the cardinal point of the poetic reflections by Roberto Juarroz (Argentina). His *Vertical Poetry* (1958–95) insists on the importance of looking for a change of mentality. Nature, including human beings, is made by cycles of death and life, light and shadow. Many "vertical" poems go deeply into a view of the human related to the non-human, constructing a new mentality far from modern urban stereotypes. Living in the city is a paradox that defies any credibility in imagination. In the city, he claims, "we betrayed the water" (*Duodécima* [Twelfth], 40, my translation), we live a flat life, without profiles; it is necessary to remodel the human house. According to Juarroz, to arrive at a new perspective depends on the reader's active imagination rather than on textual images. Juarroz proposes not only a critique of "urban rationality" but also a profound review of poetry as a way of existence: "But in the rootedness as well as in the exile / we still are without knowing our function, / perhaps because we ignore the function of the earth" (*Duodécima*, 34, my translation).

Other poets like Jesús Urzagasti (Bolivia) write poems that demand an attitude and sensibility in a very active alliance with nature, where the voice of the trees takes over the poetic (*see* Mitre, *El árbol*, 254–255; Urzagasti, *La colina*, 32–33, 69). Urzagasti wants to keep his memories about nature through a language inhabited

———, *Antología* [Anthology], Buenos Aires, Argentina: Editorial Nueva America, 1986

———, *Cántico cósmico,* Managua: Editorial Nueva Nicaragua, 1989; 2nd ed., Madrid, Spain: Editorial Trotta, 1993; as *Cosmic Canticle,* translated by Jonathan Lyons, Willimantic, Connecticut: Curbstone, 1993

———, *Epigramas,* translated by K. H. Anton, Boulder, Colorado: Lodestar, 1978

———, *Golden UFOs: The Indian Poems/Los ovnis de oro: Poemas indios,* translated and edited by Russell O. Salmon, Bloomington: Indiana University Press, 1992

———, *Homage to the American Indians,* translated by Monique and Carlos Altschul, Baltimore, Maryland: Johns Hopkins University Press, 1973

———, *Quetzalcóatl,* bilingual ed., translated by Clifton Ross, Berkeley, California: New Earth, 1990

Cardoza y Aragón, Luis, *Poesías completas y algunas prosas* [Complete Poems and Some Prose], Mexico: Fondo de Cultura Económica, 1977

———, *El río: Novelas de caballería* [The River: Novel of Chivalry], Mexico: Fondo de Cultura Económica, 1986

Carrera Andrade, Jorge, *Obra poética completa* [Complete Poetic Works], Quito, Ecuador: Editorial Casa de la Cultura Ecuatoriana, 1976

———, *Secret Country, Poems,* translated by Muna Lee, introduced by John Peale Bishop, New York: Macmillan, 1946

———, *Selected Poems of Jorge Carrera Andrade,* bilingual ed., translated and introduced by H. R. Hays, Albany: State University of New York Press, 1972

Carrión, Alejandro, *Agonía del árbol y la sangre,* Biblioteca de Autores Lojanos 2, Loja, Ecuador: Editorial Universitaria, 1948

Castillo, Otto René, *Let's Go!/Vamonos patria a caminar,* bilingual ed., translated by Margaret Randall, New York: Cape Goliard, 1971

Castro H., Guillermo, *Los trabajos de ajuste y combate: Naturaleza y sociedad en la historia de América Latina* [The Works of Adjustments and Combats: Nature and Society in Latin American History], Ciudad de La Habana, Cuba: Casa de las Américas, 1995

Castro Zagal, Oscar, *Rocío en el trébol* [Dew in the Clover], Santiago, Chile: Nascimento, 1950

Chase, Alfonso, *Obra en marcha: poesía, 1965–1980* [Work in Progress: Poetry, 1965–1980] San José: Editorial Costa Rica, 1982

Chirinos Arrieta, Eduardo, *Abecedario del Agua y otros poemas musicales* [Alphabet of the Water and Other Musical Poems], forthcoming

———, *Rituales del Conocimiento y del Sueño* [Rituals of the Knowledge and the Dream], Madrid, Spain: El Espejo del Agua, 1987

Cisneros, Antonio, *At Night the Cats,* bilingual ed., edited and translated by Maureen Ahern, William Rowe, and David Tipton, New York: Red Dust, 1985

———, *The Spider Hangs Too Far from the Ground,* bilingual ed., translated by Maureen Ahern, William Rowe, and David Tipton, New York and London: Cape Goliard, 1970

Clement, Jennifer, *El próximo extraño/The Next Stranger,* bilingual ed., translated by Consuelo de Aerenlund, Mexico City, Mexico: Ediciones El Tucan de Virginia, 1993

Collinson, Helen, ed., *Green Guerrillas: Environmental Conflicts and Initiatives in Latin America and the Caribbean: A Reader,* London: Latin American Bureau, 1996; New York: Black Rose, 1997

Corcuera, Arturo, *Noé delirante* [Delirious Noah], Lima, Peru: La Rama Florida, 1963

Coria, Neftalí, *Cuaderno para detener un río* [Notebooks to Stop a River], San Angel, Mexico: Consejo Nacional para la Cultura y las Artes, 1990

Cruz Alvarez, Félix, *Entre el río y el eco* [Between the River and the Echo], Mexico City, Mexico: Juan Pablos Editor/Universidad Autónoma Metropolitana, 1989

Cruz Vélez, Danilo, "La ciudad frente al campo" [The City in Front of the Countryside], *Ciencia política* 23 (1991), pp. 101–109

Cuadra, Pablo Antonio, *The Birth of the Sun: Selected Poems, 1935–1985,* translated by Steven F. White, Greensboro, North Carolina: Unicorn, 1988

———, *Seven Trees Against Sunset,* translated by K. H. Anton and Todd Frederickson, *Another Chicago Magazine* 19 (1989), pp. 31–49

———, *Siete árboles contra el atardecer y otros poemas* [Seven Trees Against Sunset, and

Other Poems], San José, Costa Rica: Libro Libre, 1987

———, *Songs of Cifar and the Sweet Sea,* translated and edited by Grace Schulman and Ann McCarthy de Zavala, New York: Columbia University Press, 1979

Di Paolo, Rossella, *Piel alzada* [Raised Skin], Lima, Peru: Editorial Colmillo Blanco, 1993

Durán, Manuel, and Margery Arent Safir, *Earth Tones: The Poetry of Pablo Neruda,* Bloomington: Indiana University Press, 1981

Espinosa, María Fernanda, *Tatuaje de selva* [Jungle Tattoo], Ecuador: Abrapalabra Editores, 1992

Flores, Angel, *Spanish American Authors: The Twentieth Century,* New York: H. W. Wilson, 1992

Galeano, Eduardo, *Uselo y tírelo: El mundo del fin del milenio, visto desde una ecología latinoamericana* [Use It and Throw It Away: The World of the End of the Millennium, Seen from a Latin American Ecology], Buenos Aires, Argentina: Planeta, 1994

González Rojo, Enrique, *Confidencias de un árbol* [Confidences of a Tree], Lecturas Mexicanas 53, Mexico City, Mexico: Consejo Nacional para la Cultura y las Artes, 1991

Granda, Euler, *Bla bla bla: poesía* [Blah, Blah, Blah: Poetry], Quito, Ecuador: Editorial Universitaria, 1986

———, *Un perro tocando la lira y otros poemas* [A Dog Playing the Lyre and Other Poems], introduction and notes by Sonia Manzano, Quito, Ecuador: Libresa, 1990

———, *Poemas con piel de oveja* [Poems with Sheep Skin], Quito, Ecuador: Casa de la Cultura Ecuatoriana "Benjamín Carrión," 1993

Harris, Tomás, *Zonas de peligro* [Dangerous Zones], Concepción, Chile: Ediciones Literatura Americana Reunida, 1985

Heraud, Javier, *Poesía completa* [Complete Poetry], prologue by Javier Sologuren, Lima, Peru: Peisa, 1989

———, "Six Poems by Javier Heraud" ("The Poem," "At Home," "Only," "Something," and "The River"), in *The Tri-quarterly Anthology of Contemporary Latin American Literature,* edited by José Donoso and William A. Henkin, New York: Dutton, 1969

Hernández Rodríquez, Rafael, *Cantos a la naturaleza cubana* [Songs to Cuban Nature],

La Habana: Unión de Escritores y Artistas de Cuba, 1978

Hopenhayn, Martín, *Escritos sin futuro* [Writings Without a Future], Santiago, Chile: Editorial Contrapunto, 1990

Hurtado de Mendoza S., William, *Mateo Llaqta,* Lima, Peru: Lluvia Editores, 1987

———, *Pacha Yachachiq* [Poems About the Land], Lima, Peru: Universidad Nacional Agraria La Molina, 1992

———, *Poesía quechua: Selección para niños* [Quechuan Poetry: Collection for Children], Lima, Peru: Lluvia Editores, 1990

Juarroz, Roberto, *Duodécima poesía vertical* [Twelfth Vertical Poetry], Buenos Aires, Argentina: Ediciones C. Lohlé, 1991

———, *Vertical Poetry,* bilingual ed., translated and introduced by W. S. Merwin, San Francisco: North Point, 1988

———, *Vertical Poetry: Recent Poems,* bilingual ed., translated and introduced by Mary Crow, Fredonia, New York: White Pine, 1992

Lezama Lima, José, *Poesía completa* [Complete Poetry], La Habana, Cuba: Instituto del Libro, 1970

———, "Un puente, un gran puente" [A Bridge, a Great Bridge] and "Peso del sabor" [Weight of Taste], translated by Willis Barnstone, in *Toward an Image of Latin American Poetry,* bilingual ed., edited by Octavio Armand, Durango, Colorado: Logbridge-Rhodes, 1982

Liscano, Juan, *Antología poética: 1942–1991* [Poetic Anthology: 1942–1991], Caracas, Venezuela: Monte Avila Editores Latinoamericana, 1993

———, "Moraleja" [Maxim], "Presagios del peligro" [Omens of Danger], and "Zona Tórrida (Fragmento)" [Torrid Zone (Fragment)], translated by Thomas Hoeksema, in *Toward an Image of Latin American Poetry,* bilingual ed., edited by Octavio Armand, Durango, Colorado: Logbridge-Rhodes, 1982

Lizalde, Eduardo, *Rosas* [Roses], Mexico City, Mexico: El Tucán de Virginia, 1994

Love, Glen A., "Revaluing Nature: Toward an Ecological Criticism," in *The Ecocriticism Reader: Landmarks in Literary Ecology,* edited by Cheryll Glotfelty and Harold Fromm, Athens: University of Georgia Press, 1996

Loynaz, Dulce María, "The Calm," "Time," "Sea Surrounded," "Futile Flight, Futile

Fugue," "Snow," and "The Cloud,"
translated by Alan West, in *These Are Not
Sweet Girls: Latin American Women Poets,*
Secret Weavers Series Volume 7, edited by
Marjorie Agosin, Fredonia, New York:
White Pine, 1994

———, *Homenaje a Dulce María Loynaz: obra
literaria, poesía y prosa, estudios y
comentarios* [Homage to Dulce María
Loynaz: Poetic Work, Poetry and Prose,
Studies, and Comments], edited by Ana
Rosa Núñez, Miami, Florida: Ediciones
Universal, 1993

McKibben, Bill, "Text, Civility, Conservation,
and Community: On Nature Writing and
Common Ground," *Wild Earth* 6:2 (1996),
pp. 5–6

Maya, Rafael, *La tierra poseída* [The Possessed
Land], Bogota, Colombia: Canal Ramírez,
1964

Milán, Eduardo, *Nivel medio verdadero de las
aguas que se besan* [Half True Level of
Kissing Waters], Madrid, Spain: Ave del
Paraíso, 1994

———, "Una poética crítica" [A Critical
Poetic], *La Gaceta* 305 (1996), pp. 42–43

———, *Resistir: Insistencias sobre el presente
poético* [Resisting: Insistences About the
Poetic Present], Mexico City, Mexico:
Consejo Nacional para la Cultura y las
Artes, 1994

Mires, Fernando, *El discurso de la naturaleza:
Ecología y política en América Latina* [The
Discourse of Nature: Ecology and Politics in
Latin America], Santiago, Chile: Editorial
Amerinda, 1990

Mistral, Gabriela, *A Gabriela Mistral Reader,*
translated by María Giachetti, edited by
Marjorie Agosin, Fredonia, New York:
White Pine, 1993

———, *Selected Poems of Gabriela Mistral,*
translated by Langston Hughes,
Bloomington: Indiana University Press, 1957

Mitre, Eduardo, ed., *El árbol y la piedra:
Poetas contemporaneos de Bolivia* [The
Tree and the Stone: Contemporary Poets
of Bolivia], Caracas, Venezuela: Monte
Avila Editorial Arte, 1986

Molina, Enrique, "Como debe de ser"
[The Way It Must Be], "Los trabajos de la
poesía" [The Labors of Poetry], and
"Mensaje secreto" [Secret Message],
translated by Naomi Lindstrom, in *Toward
an Image of Latin American Poetry,*
bilingual ed., edited by Octavio Armand,

Durango, Colorado: Logbridge-Rhodes,
1982

———, *Orden terrestre* [Terrestrial Order],
Buenos Aires, Argentina: Seix Barral, 1995

Montalvo, Berta G., *Donde se ocultan las
sombras* [Where the Shadows Are Hidden],
Colección Neblina haikú No. 2, Calarcá,
Colombia: Publicaciones Literarias Kanora,
Asociación Colombiana de Haikú, 1995

Mora, Tulio, *Zoología prestada* [Borrowed
Zoology], Peru: Tarea Ediciones, 1987

Moro, César, *Obra poética* [Poetic Work],
edited by Ricardo Silva-Santisteban, Lima,
Peru: Instituto Nacional de Cultura, 1980

Murillo, Rosario, *Angel in the Deluge,*
Pocket Poets Series No. 50, translated by
Alejandro Murguía, San Francisco: City
Lights, 1992

La naturaleza en el espejo. Poetas por la tierra
[Nature in the Mirror. Poets for the Earth],
Lima, Peru: Red Nacional de Acción
Ecologista Perú-Centro de Comunicación y
Cultura para la Mujer, 1995

Neruda, Pablo, *Art of Birds,* translated by Jack
Schmitt, Austin: University of Texas Press,
1985

———, *The Book of Questions,* translated by
William O'Daly, Port Townsend,
Washington: Copper Canyon, 1991

———, *The Elementary Odes of Pablo Neruda,*
translated by Carlos Lozano, introduced by
Fernando Alegría, New York: Las Americas,
1961

———, *Extravagaria,* bilingual ed., translated by
Alastair Reid, London: Jonathan Cape,
1972; New York: Farrar, Straus and Giroux,
1974

———, *Five Decades: A Selection (Poems:
1925–1970),* edited and translated by Ben
Belitt, New York: Grove, 1974

———, *Fully Empowered,* translated by
Alastair Reid, New York: Farrar, Straus
and Giroux, 1975; London: Souvenir, 1976

———, *The Heights of Macchu Picchu,*
translated by Nathaniel Tarn, London:
Jonathan Cape, 1966; New York: Farrar,
Straus and Giroux, 1967

———, *Late and Posthumous Poems,
1968–1974,* bilingual ed., edited and
translated by Ben Belitt, New York: Grove,
1988

———, *Neruda's Garden: An Anthology of
Odes,* selected and translated by María
Jacketti, Pittsburgh, Pennsylvania: Latin
American Literary Review, 1995

————, *A New Decade; Poems: 1958–1967,* bilingual ed., edited and introduced by Ben Belitt, translated by Ben Belitt and Alastair Reid, New York: Grove, 1969

————, *New Poems (1968–1970),* edited and translated by Ben Belitt, New York: Grove, 1972

————, *Pablo Neruda: A Basic Anthology,* compiled and introduced by Robert Pring-Mill, Oxford: Dolphin, 1975

————, *Pablo Neruda: The Early Poems,* translated by David Ossman and Carlos Hagen, New York: New Rivers, 1969

————, *Residence on Earth,* translated by Donald Walsh, New York: New Directions, 1973

————, *Selected Odes of Pablo Neruda,* bilingual ed., translated and introduced by Margaret Sayers Peden, Berkeley: University of California Press, 1990

————, *Selected Poems,* edited by Nathaniel Tarn, translated by Anthony Kerrigan, London: Jonathan Cape, 1970; New York: Dell, 1972

Neruda, Pablo, and César Vallejo, *Neruda and Vallejo: Selected Poems,* edited by Robert Bly, translated by Robert Bly, John Knoepfle, and James Wright, Boston: Beacon, 1971

Nigh, Ronald, and Nemesio J. Rodríguez, *Territorios violados: Indios, medio ambiente y desarrollo en América Latina* [Raped Territories: Indians, Environment, and Development in Latin America], Mexico City, Mexico: Dirección General de Publicaciones del Consejo Nacional para la Cultura y las Artes/Instituto Nacional Indigenista, 1995

Núñez, Ana Rosa, *Crisantemos/ Chrysanthemums,* Colección Betania Poesía, bilingual ed., Madrid, Spain: Editorial Betania, 1990

————, *Escamas del Caribe (Haikus de Cuba)* [Caribbean Fish Scales (Haikus of Cuba)], Miami, Florida: Ediciones Universal, 1971

Nye, Naomi Shihab, *The Tree Is Older Than You Are: A Bilingual Gathering of Poems & Stories from Mexico with Paintings by Mexican Artists,* New York: Simon & Schuster Books for Young Readers, 1995

Ortiz, Juan L., *En el aura del sauce* [In the Willow Aura], 3 vols., Rosario, Argentina: Editorial Biblioteca, 1970

Pacheco, José Emilio, *Album de zoología* [Zoo Album], selected by Jorge Esquinca, 2nd ed., Guadalajara, Mexico: Universidad de Guadalajara/Xalli, 1991

————, *An Ark for the Next Millennium: Poems,* translated by Margaret Sayers Peden, Austin: University of Texas Press, 1993

————, *City of Memory and Other Poems,* bilingual ed., translated by Cynthia Steele and David Lauer, San Francisco: City Lights, 1997

————, *Don't Ask Me How the Time Goes By: Poems, 1964–1968,* translated by Alastair Reid, New York: Columbia University Press, 1978

————, *Los trabajos del mar* [The Works of the Sea], Mexico City, Mexico: Ediciones Era, 1983

————, *Signals from the Flames: Selected Poetry of José Emilio Pacheco,* translated by Thomas Hoeksema, Pittsburgh, Pennsylvania: Latin American Literary Review, 1980

Parra, Nicanor, *Chistes para desorientar a la poesía (policía)* [Jokes to Mislead the Poetry (Police)], selected and introduced by María Nieves Alonso and Gilberto Triviños, Madrid, Spain: Visor, 1989

————, *Ecopoemas* [Ecopoems], Santiago, Chile: Gráfica Marginal, 1982

————, *Emergency Poems,* translated by Miller Williams, New York: New Directions, 1972; London: Boyars, 1977

————, *Poemas para combatir la calvicie* [Poems to Fight the Baldness], compiled by Julio Ortega, Mexico: Fondo de Cultura Económica, 1994

Paz, Octavio, *Arbol adentro,* Barcelona, Spain: Seix Barral, 1987; as *A Tree Within,* translated by Eliot Weinberger, New York: New Directions, 1988

————, *The Collected Poems of Octavio Paz, 1957–1987,* edited and translated by Eliot Weinberger, additional translations by Elizabeth Bishop, Paul Blackburn, Lysander Kemp, Denise Levertov, John Frederick Nims, Mark Strand, and Charles Tomlinson, New York: New Directions, 1987

————, *La otra voz: Poesía y fin de siglo,* Barcelona, Spain: Seix Barral, 1990; as *The Other Voice: Essays on Modern Poetry,* translated by Helen Lane, New York: Harcourt Brace Jovanovich, 1991

Pellicer, Carlos, *Primera antología poética* [First Poetic Anthology], Mexico: Fondo de Cultura Económica, 1969

Perazalonso, Carlos, "La monarca" [The

Monarch], *Revista de la Universidad Autónoma de México* 504–505 (1993), p. 19

El planeta en el espejo. Poetas por la tierra [Planet in the Mirror. Poets for the Earth], Lima, Peru: Red Nacional de Acción Ecologista Perú-Centro de Comunicación y Cultura para la Mujer, 1994

Puentes de Oyenard, Sylvia, *Rosa exigida* [Required Rose], Montevideo, Uruguay: Puentes, 1977

Rivas, José Luis, *Luz de mar abierto* [Light of Open Sea], Mexico City, Mexico: Vuelta, 1992

———, *Raz de marea: Obra poética (1975–1992)* [A Little Touch of Tide: Poetic Work (1975–1992)], Mexico City, Mexico: Fondo de Cultura Económica, 1993

Riveros, Juan Pablo, *De la tierra sin fuegos* [From the Land Without Fires], New York and Concepción, Chile: Ediciones del Maitén, 1986

Rodas, Ana María, *El fin de los mitos y los sueños* [The End of Myths and Dreams], Guatemala, Guatemala: Editorial Rin-78/Tipografía Nacional, 1984

Rodríguez Monegal, Emir, ed., *The Borzoi Anthology of Latin American Literature,* translated by Eliot Weinberger, 2 vols., New York: Knopf, 1977

Rojas, Gonzalo, "Carbón" [Coal] and "La palabra" [The Word], translated by Christopher Maurer, in *Toward an Image of Latin American Poetry,* bilingual ed., edited by Octavio Armand, Durango, Colorado: Logbridge-Rhodes, 1982

———, *Del Relámpago (Poemas)* [From the Lightning (Poems)], Mexico: Fondo de Cultura Económica, 1981

———, *Río turbio* [Confused Ray], Madrid, Spain: Hiperión, 1996

———, *Schizotext and Other Poems/ Esquizotexto y otros poemas,* translated by Russell M. Cluff and L. Howard Quackenbush, New York: P. Lang, 1988

Rojas, Wiesand, and Alfonso Javier, *Poesía de la naturaleza* [Poetry of Nature], Toluca, Mexico: Coordinación General de Comunicación Social: Tinta del Alcatraz, 1993

Rubio, J. Francisco, *El arbol en la poesía guatemalteca* [The Tree in Guatemalan Poetry], Guatemala: CENALTEX/Ministerio de Educación, 1987

Ruíz Gómez, Darío, *Geografía: poemas* [Geography: Poems], 1977

Sánchez Peláez, Juan, *Un día sea: antología* [Will Be a Day: Anthology], Caracas, Venezuela: Monte Avila, 1969

Serrano, Pío E., *Poesía reunida* [Collected Poetry], Madrid, Spain: Instituto de Cooperación Iberoamericana, Ediciones Cultura Hispánica, 1987

Sologuren, Javier, "Acontecimientos" [Events], "Te alisar, Amor, las alas" [Love, You Smooth Your Wings], and "Sinrazón" [Wrongness], translated by Mary Barnard and Willis Barnstone, in *Toward an Image of Latin American Poetry,* bilingual ed., edited by Octavio Armand, Durango, Colorado: Logbridge-Rhodes, 1982

———, *Hojas de herbolario* [Leaves of Herbalist], Lima, Peru: Jaime Campodonico, 1995

———, *The Hour/La hora,* translated by Elizabeth Doonan Kauffman, Maryland: La Yapa Editores, 1990

———, *Vida Continua: Obra poética, 1939–1989* [Continuous Life: Poetic Work, 1939–1989], Lima, Peru: Editorial Colmillo Blanco, 1989

Soto Vélez, Clemente, *Obra poética* [Poetic Work], San Juan, Puerto Rico: Instituto de Cultura Puertorriqueña, División de Publicaciones y Grabaciones, 1989

Sullivan, Mary-Lee Lewis, *Presencia de la naturaleza en la obra de cinco poetas comprometidos de América Latina* [Presence of Nature in the Work of Five Engaged Poets of Latin America] (Ph.D. diss., Boston University), 1990

Tapscott, Stephen, ed., *Twentieth-Century Latin American Poetry: A Bilingual Anthology,* Austin: University of Texas Press, 1996

Teillier, Jorge, *Muertes y maravillas* [Deaths and Wonders], Santiago, Chile: Editorial Universitaria, 1971

Urzagasti, Jesús, *La colina que da al mar azul* [The Hill That Reaches the Blue Sea], La Paz, Bolivia: Editorial del Hombrecito Sentado, 1993

Vallejo, César, *The Black Heralds,* bilingual ed., translated by Richard Schaaf and Kathleen Ross, Pittsburgh, Pennsylvania: Latin American Literary Review, 1990

———, *César Vallejo: The Complete Posthumous Poetry,* translated by Clayton

Eshleman and José Rubia Barcia, Berkeley: University of California Press, 1978

———, *Obra poética completa* [Complete Poetic Work], Lima, Peru: F. Moncloa Editores, 1968

———, *Poemas Humanos/Human Poems,* bilingual ed., translated by Clayton Eshleman, New York: Grove, 1968; London: Jonathan Cape, 1969

———, *Trilce,* translated by Rebecca Seiferle, edited by Stanley Moss, Buenos Aires, Argentina: Editorial Losada, 1990; Riverdale-on-Hudson, New York: Sheep Meadow Press, 1992

Vargas Vicuña, Eleodoro, *Ñahuín: Narraciones ordinarias, 1950–1975* [Ñahuin: Ordinary Stories, 1950–1975], 2nd ed., Lima, Peru: Milla Batres, 1978

———, *Zora, imagen de poesía* [Zora, Picture of Poetry], Cajamarca, Peru: Departamento de Publicaciones de la U.N.T.C., 1971

Velásquez, Lucila, *El árbol de Chernobyl/The Tree of Chernobyl,* translated by Jaime Tello, Caracas, Venezuela: Monte Avila Editores, 1989

Verástegui, Enrique, et al., *Sociedad para la liberación de las rosas* [Society for the Liberation of Roses], Lima, Peru: Ediciones Amantes de País, 1994

Vitale, Ida, "Ecológica" [Ecological], in *Léxico de afinidades* [Glossary of Affinities], Mexico City, Mexico: Editorial Vuelta, 1994

———, *Jardín de Sílice* [Garden of Silica], Caracas, Venezuela: Monte Avila Editores, 1980

———, *Sueños de la constancia* [Dreams of the Persistence], Mexico: Fondo de Cultura Económica, 1988

Volkow, Verónica, *Arcanos* [Mysteries], Mexico City, Mexico: Consejo Nacional para la Cultura y las Artes, 1996

———, *Los caminos* [The Roads], Mexico City, Mexico: Ediciones Toledo, 1989

Watanabe, José, *Historia natural* [Natural Story], Lima, Peru: Peisa, 1994

———, *El Huso de la palabra* [The Spindle/Use of the Word], Lima, Peru: Seglusa Editores/Editorial Colmillo Blanco, 1989

Zapata, Miguel Angel, *Lumbre de la letra* [Glow of the Letter], Lima, Peru: Ediciones El Santo Oficio, 1997

———, *Poemas para violín y orquesta* [Poems for Violin and Orchestra], Mexico: Premià, 1991

Zurita, Raúl, *El amor de Chile* [Chile's Love], photos by Renato Srepel, Santiago, Chile: Montt Palumbo, 1987

———, *Anteparadise,* bilingual ed., translated by Jack Schmitt, Berkeley: University of California Press, 1986

———, *Canto a su amor desaparecido* [Letter to His/Her Missing Love], Santiago, Chile: Editorial Universitaria, 1985

———, *Purgatorio, 1970–1977* [Purgatory, 1970–1977], bilingual ed., translated by Jeremy Jacobson, Pittsburgh, Pennsylvania: Latin American Literary Review, 1985

Seeing Green: 500 Years of Writing the Amazon

Timothy Gaynor

This essay seeks to record some of the changing significations ascribed to the Amazon in a literary history stretching from discovery to the late twentieth century. At the time of the discovery, the authority of the Catholic church was at its height. The Moorish bastion of Granada had fallen to Christendom and the Inquisition was preoccupied with extending the church's hegemony. Such a strident church would not allow for gaps in its essentially Ptolemaic cosmology, even though the experience of contemporary explorers insisted that there was in fact a gap of continental proportions. Faced with an entirely new world, Renaissance explorers were compelled to fill it with figures drawn from already extant bodies of knowledge. Such was the contemporary state of knowledge that the Amazon entered literature using bestiaries, mythologies and medieval romances as reliable guides.

The Amazon was itself named for the one-breasted tribe of warrior women from Greek mythology who, it was believed, peopled the green fringes of the great river upon which the early explorers sailed. So compelling was this belief in mythological wonders that the conquistador Pedro de Orellana's followers actually reported being attacked by a party of Amazons. The dense, mythological investment in the region also gave to it the city of El Dorado, reputed to lie deep in the jungles of what we now call Venezuela. Parties of adventurers continued to search for the fabled city of "the Golden One" right up until the close of the eighteenth century. Isabel Allende traces the enduring legend of El Dorado in the opening page of her novel *Eva Luna*. The Amazon is described appropriately as an "enchanted region where for centuries adventurers have searched for the city of pure gold the conquistadors saw when they peered into the abyss of their own ambitions" (p. 1).

Anthony Pagden, the historian of European encounters with the New World, considers some of the key problems that faced early travellers when it came to recording their experiences and discoveries. "[T]he difficulty was," he writes, "how to distance [their] account of a new and seemingly bizarre world from those described in romances of chivalry. Readers in Spain frequently confused what they read about America with what they had read about in *Amadís of Gaul* and *Palmerín of England*" (p. 62). The Peruvian novelist Mario Vargas Llosa suggests in an essay, "Fiction and Reality," that this confusion in some way contributes to the fantastic literature of the present century. It is described as a kind of literary patrimony that has shaped the Latin American imagination ever since, giving rise to a literary tradition that is still touched by the fabulous. The rich imaginings of such works as Gabriel García Márquez's *One Hundred Years of Solitude*, while drawing on magical elements in indigenous culture, also gesture toward the fabulous narratives of early Spanish and Portuguese conquerors. In this much praised novel, the Spanish Galleon that José Arcadio Buendía finds marooned in the jungles of Macondo is a reminder of an era in which the rich fabulation of a European tradition made landfall.

The traces of the genres that encoded the region in terms of the medieval imaginary can be followed through subsequent European literature of the Amazon. The Edwardian novelist W. H. Hudson was clearly influenced by the region's archive in his novel *Green Mansions: A Romance of the Tropical Forest*. The novel opens rather coyly with a reminiscence of friendship between two old colonial hands. Out of this recollection emerges the strange tale of Abel, a colonial adventurer lost alone among savage tribes in the farthest reaches of the Guyanese Amazon. On hearing a sing-song and ethereal voice filtering through the dense forest, Abel becomes aware of the presence of Rima, a magical woodland sprite. In a gesture suggestive of the romances of chivalry, he falls hopelessly yet chastely in love with her. True to the codes of chivalry their love is a forlorn affair. It is doomed to endless deferrals only occasionally brightened by intense bouts of psychosomatic illness. Just as the romance appears to be stranded in its own conventions, the narratological demands of the colonial text intrude. These require that the heroine die through the connivance and treachery of the savage native tribes. This event in turn allows for the hero to resolve the flagging romantic narrative through the imposition of his colonial authority in a final vengeful bloodbath. While the novel is a confused and in many ways distasteful read, its resolution usefully discloses the manner in which the enchanted Amazonian archive rests on a substrate of colonial violence.

Hudson was not alone among his peers in using the somewhat fantastic literary heritage of the Amazon in tandem with contemporary themes. Sir Arthur Conan Doyle, perhaps best known for his sleuth Sherlock Holmes, also made a memorable imaginative foray into the Amazon. *The Lost World*, first published in 1912, is difficult to place as a genre as it combines the elements of the colonial adventure yarn with a contemporary interest in science and the gothic. Like Hudson's text it opens in the upper echelons of Edwardian society in a discussion between gentlemen. Ed Malone, Lord John Roxton and their irascible companion Professor Challenger plan an expedition to a remote Amazonian plateau where dinosaurs are believed to roam. In the course of the story they reach their destination and encounter more than enough dinosaurs to silence their detractors back in England. They do battle with a triceratops, spy on a "rookery" of pterodactyls and, perhaps more tellingly for this enquiry, fight a giant water-serpent unknown to palaeontology. In its heady mixture of science, colonial adventure and the fabulous, the novel places the Renaissance obsession with the Amazon as a topos of mythological wonders in the early years of the twentieth century.

This set of chimerical associations persists in other genres that, while not ostensibly as fantastic, emphasize the Amazon's natural hazards in an almost mythopoeic way. A typical example would be Willard Price's adventure book for boys *Amazon Adventure*, which exaggerates the perils posed by Amazonian fauna to an absurdly hyperbolic degree. In this text the Amazon is a phantasmagoria of man-eating piranhas and anacondas that lie in wait to devour the hapless adventurers. Needless to say, the resourceful boy heroes see their way through this challenge while their "native" menservants perish horribly. This emphasis on the Amazon as a domain of egregious natural perils is shared by much travel writing. The English traveller Redmond O'Hanlon begins *In Trouble Again*, the account of his journey to the Amazon in the late 1980s, with an alarming chapter on the region's hazards. These hazards, while drawn from stolid and empirical works of natural history, yet reek of the Bestiary. The assortment of exotic diseases, killer fish and lethal snakes cited are woven with unreliable anecdote into a familiar kind of fantastical narrative.

Literary texts are not the only media that share this interest. Much popular film also delves into this decidedly phantasmagoric archive. The low-budget masterpieces *Piranha* (directed by Joe Danate, 1978) and *Killer Fish* (directed by Antonio Margheriti, 1978) both borrow serendipitously from it, variously cooking up an improbable bouillabaisse of B movie mayhem. Such works as these seem to conflate the discourses of natural history with those of earlier fantastical narratives, to produce a more contemporary but just as heavily stylized set of Amazonian discourses. In adventure, disaster movie, and even travel, the Amazon is not so much a place as a topos, a region of the imagination.

While the most common elements of this topos have been explored here, it is interesting to record an ancillary network of lesser designations accorded the region in the Western imaginary. In a substantial number of texts, the Amazon is used variously as a topos for alterity. The form that this otherness takes depends on the work in question. Werner Herzog's novel (and film) *Fitzcarraldo* is the tale of a visionary adventurer, driven by a dream to see opera performed in the heart of the jungle. Stripped to the narratological essentials, the story is really one of madness and obsession, in which the egregious and untamed Amazon functions as a correlative of the protagonist's extreme state of mind. Similarly, the Amazon has been taken as the other to regulated bourgeois sexuality in Cecile Pineda's pastiche magical realist text *The Love Queen of the Amazon*. The narrative's connection with the region itself is very slight. It betrays no knowledge of Amazonian geography or culture, but uses it as a topos of egregious, unbounded female sexuality. The Amazon is perhaps the only imaginative zone in which to locate Anna Magdalena Figueroa, whom the author hopes to be the most legendary whore in literature.

There is another strand to Amazonian literature that is perhaps more prevalent at the time of writing. The genre of environmental literature seeks to celebrate the Amazon as an exemplar of primordial nature (and of primitive tribal man as a subset of this category), threatened by the forces of industrial society. Works such as George Monbiot's *Amazon Watershed: The New Environmental Investigation* and Marnie Mueller's *Green Fires* begin from the apodictic premise of the value of the area in terms of sublime nature. This is exemplified–in a much cruder way—by the minor genre of the Amazonian environmental movie, such as *The Emerald Forest* (directed by John Boorman, 1985) and *Medicine Man* (directed by John McTiernen, 1992), which set out to celebrate the Amazon as a green paradise threatened by loggers. This change within discursive paradigms does not simply mark a final true knowledge of the region but has in fact a discursive genealogy as particular in its own way as those already described. The remainder of this essay seeks both to explore Romantic environmentalism as a genre and call into question the appropriateness of its assumptions.

The idea of the Amazon as a pristine natural environment owes to the Enlightenment shift in the structures of knowledge, which replaced the discourses of mythology with those of an incipient scientific modernity. The Amazon entered its second literary phase within the discourses of the great naturalist explorers—most notably the Prussian naturalist Alexander Von Humboldt—who set out to claim the region for the Linnaean system of taxonomy. The collection and classification of all species by genus replaced their assumed existence on hearsay, their erstwhile basis in medieval knowledge. Von Humboldt's interest in the natural world was also significantly colored by a burgeoning Romantic zeitgeist exemplified in his friendship with Schiller. As Mary Louise Pratt states, Humboldt's essentially descriptive work as a naturalist was shaped by his "emphasis on harmonious and occult forces [which] aligns him with the spiritualist aesthetics of Romanticism" (p. 124). Just as Von Humboldt was throwing the cognitive net of taxonomy over the Amazon, so Schiller's aesthetics claimed it for the European imagination. Whereas to the conquistadors the Amazon was a dense woods without semantic importance, to the new Romantic readership the wild beauty of

the Amazon became its most salient feature. The current environmental interest in the Amazon owes much to the axioms of Romantic thought. The Amazon is still a topos of the Romantic sublime, valued above all for its egregious natural attributes and its more picturesque peoples.

If travelers' tales captured the Amazon's terrain for Romanticism, Jean-Jacques Rousseau captured its inhabitants for the same cause. The Noble Savage became a theme that persists throughout Amazonian literature and lends a Romantic tinge to contemporary concern for the Amazon. Most films, novels, travelogues and magazine articles share an unexamined fascination with tribal peoples. The character of this interest is epitomized in Alejo Carpentier's *The Lost Steps*. The novel's protagonist is a musicologist who leaves the cacophonic modernity of New York in search of the simple musical tradition of a remote Amazonian tribe. As he travels farther up river in a dugout canoe, he goes further back in time toward a primal utopia where man lives without alienation. Mario Vargas Llosa's novel *The Storyteller* also seeks to find a resolution to the problems of contemporary Western society in the tribal cultures of the Amazon. Whereas the Cuban Carpentier sought to explore alienation in materialist terms, Vargas Llosa is preoccupied with a more Derridean conception of alienation as the lapse from speech into writing. The novel's protagonist, a Peruvian investigative journalist disillusioned with the inauthenticity of mass-media forms, goes in search of an Amazonian tribe with a vital oral tradition. The schema of Vargas Llosa's novel places the written tradition of the West in opposition to a spoken tradition of the primitive that is suggestive of the phonocentrism at work in Rousseau's *Essay on the Origin of Languages*. The way that Vargas Llosa uses tribal Amazonians in support of a phonocentrist refusal of writing is echoed in Petru Popescu's extraordinary work of travel writing, *Amazon Beaming*. Popescu's text purports to tell the true story of the author's expedition to the Amazon and his telepathic relationship with a remote tribe. This literally unspoken relationship inaugurates a form of pure communication unmediated by language.

The disparate texts that make up the literature of the Amazon share one thing in common; they create, restate and redefine the Amazon as a topos within the ambit of resolutely Western interests. What of the Amazon, and of Amazonian's themselves? How well are the region and its peoples served by the Western discourses that have given such strident account of the region in the last 500 years? The contemporary anthropologist Stephen Nugent is unequivocal. He argues that the archive of Amazonian discourses has provided "a constant background of mystification against which more discrete—and perhaps significant—factual matters appear drab and un-compelling" (p. 140). Nugent's view begins to suggest that the region's history has been displaced by these accounts and yet remains to be written. Amazonia, he writes,

is filtered for our consumption through a series of image grids which successfully distract the eye: Amazonia comes across as a nature preserve, a tropical forest, home of the noble savage, the toucan, the howler monkey, the electric eel, the head-hunter—a long list of compelling exotica. And most people would rather watch monkeys at play than pop-eyed infant beggars at work. (p. 2)

The discursive agenda that has looked to the Bestiary and to the Romantic sublime to account for the region has ignored the historical forces that have shaped it and its peoples. The history of the cities of the Amazon, such as Belém, Manaus and Recifé and the marginal peoples who live in them has yet to be written. Similarly, the struggles for land in the Amazon between a disadvantaged peasantry and a powerful land owning class is largely absent from the literature of the Amazon. Nugent is interested in these "out-of-focus Amazonians [who] appear when needed as guides, when laundry has to be done . . . but they are almost incidental, populating the transitional zone between airport and the Amazonian Indian theme park" (pp. 17–18).

The Brazilian novelist Marcio Souza is a rare exception in this tradition who writes about the "out-of-focus" Amazonians of the riverine cities in his novel *The Emperor of the Amazon*. The novel explores the way that the Amazon has been disavowed by history in the continuing insistence upon it as a natural domain. In the novel the grotesque figure of Sir Henry Lust tries to prove that the Teatro Amazonas (an actual neo-baroque masterpiece in Manaus) is the work of extraterrestrials. As Souza comments, "Sir Henry could not conceive of the Teatro Amazonas as the work of any human force. Much less the product of semi-civilized natives, notorious for their racial inferiority and incapacity for logical ratiocination" (p. 84). Souza's

novel satirizes a discursive tradition that has consistently refused the majority of Amazonians any historical legitimacy.

The hidden history of Amazonia is also described in the last testimony of Chico Mendes, the murdered leader of the Brazilian rubber tappers union. His testimony, published as *Fight for the Forest*, describes the dealings of the rich and powerful families that had divided up the Amazon between them. His descriptions of the harsh lives of the tappers, their maps of the forest and their debts at the company store begins to draw the vast green domains into the ledger books of capitalism, materializing the history that has so long been absent from Amazonian discourse. It suggests that the Amazon needs to be explored through a different set of textual guides. It is perhaps more meaningful to set aside Bestiaries, novels and texts of adventure travel and understand the Amazon through works such as Jackie Roddick's *The Dance of the Millions* and Sue Branford's *The Last Frontier: Fighting Over Land in the Amazon*, since they give account of the factors that affect the environment and the lives of all within it.

Selected Works and Further Reading

Aldrovandi, Ulisse, *Monstrorum historia*, Bologna, Italy: Typis Nicolai Tebaldini, 1522

Allende, Isabel, *Eva Luna*, Barcelona, Spain: Plaza y Janés, 1987; New York: Knopf, 1988; London: Hamish Hamilton, 1989

Branford, Sue, and Oriel Glock, *The Last Frontier: Fighting over Land in the Amazon*, Totowa, New Jersey, and London: Zed, 1985

Branford, Sue, and Bernardo Kucinski, *The Debt Squads: The US, the Banks, and Latin America*, Atlantic Highlands, New Jersey, and London: Zed, 1988

Cahill, Tim, *Jaguars Ripped My Flesh*, New York: Bantam, 1987; London: Penguin, 1989

Carpentier, Alejo, *The Lost Steps*, New York: Knopf, 1956; London: Gollancz, 1956; as *Los Pasos Perdidos*, Mexico: Cía. General de Ediciones, 1959

Derrida, Jacques, *Of Grammatology*, translated by Gayatri Spivak, Baltimore, Maryland: Johns Hopkins University Press, 1976

Doyle, Arthur Conan, *The Lost World*, New York and London: Hodder and Stoughton, Wyman and Sons, 1920

García Márquez, Gabriel, *Cien años de soledad*,

Buenos Aires, Argentina: Editorial Sudamericana, 1967; as *One Hundred Years of Solitude,* translated by Gregory Rabassa, New York: Harper & Row, 1970; London: Jonathan Cape, 1970

Herzog, Werner, *Fitzcarraldo: The Original Story,* San Francisco: Fjord, 1982

Hudson, W. H., *Green Mansions: A Romance of the Tropical Forest,* New York: Putnam's, 1904; London: Duckworth, 1904

Humboldt, Alexander Von, *Views of Nature,* London: H. G. Bohn, 1850; reprinted, New York: Arno, 1975

Mendes, Chico, *Fight for the Forest: Chico Mendes in His Own Words,* London: Latin America Bureau, 1989

Monbiot, George, *Amazon Watershed: The New Environmental Investigation,* London: Michael Joseph, 1991

Mueller, Marnie, *Green Fires: Assault on Eden: A Novel of the Ecuadorian Rainforest,* Willimantic, Connecticut: Curbstone, 1994

Nugent, Stephen, *Big Mouth: The Amazon Speaks,* London: Fourth Estate, 1990; San Francisco: BrownTrout, 1994

O'Hanlon, Redmond, *In Trouble Again: A Journey Between the Orinoco and the Amazon,* London: Hamish Hamilton, 1988; New York: Atlantic Monthly, 1989

Pagden, Anthony, *European Encounters with the New World: From Renaissance to Romanticism,* New Haven, Connecticut:

Yale University Press, 1993; London: Yale University Press, 1994

Pineda, Cecile, *The Love Queen of the Amazon,* Boston: Little, Brown, 1992; London: Hamish Hamilton, 1992

Porter, Dennis, *Haunted Journeys: Desire and Transgression in European Travel Writing,* Princeton, New Jersey: Princeton University Press, 1991

Pratt, Mary Louise, *Imperial Eyes: Travel Writing and Transculturation,* New York and London: Routledge, 1992

Price, Willard, *Amazon Adventure,* New York: J. Day, 1949; London: Jonathan Cape, 1951

Roddick, Jacqueline, *The Dance of the Millions: Latin America and the Debt Crisis,* London: Latin America Bureau, 1988

Rousseau, Jean-Jacques, *Oeuvres Complètes,* Geneva, Switzerland, 1782

Souza, Marcio, *Galvez: Imperador do Acre: Folhetim,* Rio de Janeiro, Brazil: Marco Zero, 1976; as *The Emperor of the Amazon,* New York: Avon, 1980; London: Sphere, 1982

Vargas Llosa, Mario, *El Hablador,* Barcelona, Spain: Seix Barral, 1987; as *The Storyteller,* translated by Helen Lane, New York: Farrar, Straus, Giroux, 1989; London: Faber and Faber, 1989

———, "Latin America: Fiction and Reality" in *Modern Latin American Fiction: A Survey,* edited by John King, London: Faber and Faber, 1987

The Arctic in Literature

Sheila Nickerson

It is an area for which there are no clear boundaries or definitions. For some, it is the land above the Arctic Circle, an imaginary line at 66°, 33′ north latitude. For others, it is what lies beyond the reach of trees or what is held by permafrost: an identity of temperature. It belongs to no one country but comprises numerous nationalities, languages, and cultures. When viewed from above on a circumpolar map, it appears to circle a bull's eye center, the North Pole. But that, too, is an imaginary point of wavering location. Mathematical calculations fix a more exact point—the Geographic North Pole. Far to the south and east of that invisible spot hovers the North Magnetic Pole, which has wandered 400 miles since it was first located in 1831. Geophysicists tell us that the North Pole and the South Pole have switched places a number of times. So, too, have cycles of cold moved in and out, redefining the boundaries of ice.

Uncertain in physical nature as it is on maps, the Arctic is largely a place of water in motion and transformation (unlike Antarctica, which is a landmass). Its central ocean—the Arctic—and the nine seas radiating out from it form a constantly moving and changing wilderness of ice.

This is the dark/brilliant, sharp/misty world of the midnight sun and the sunless months; the world of the aurora borealis and the fata morgana. Here icebergs tower and nonexistent mountains appear to block passage. The moon and the sun wear halos and the eyes are quickly blinded by light. Mirage invites and destroys.

Not surprisingly, early accounts are a crazed mirror reflecting the personal and national ambitions of those who came for conquest. From the time of Pytheas (320 B.C.), seafarers came north, lured by tales of wonders and the myth of an open polar sea. The Northwest Passage, the North Pole, the whale fishery, the fur trade, and the salvation of the Native soul were the major targets, while natural resources and national sovereignty are the present concerns. Out of all this endeavor—usually greedy—falls a blizzard of ice journals, logs, and histories, biased and flawed, and in most cases not accessible to the general reader. To make sense of these there are a number of invaluable bibliographic sources that organize, cross-reference, and annotate: *Arctic Bibliography* and the bibliographic works edited by Clive Holland, Alan Cooke, and Alan Day. For the ice journals, Farley Mowat has performed an enormous service by compiling excerpts from works that are long out of print and archived in specialized collections.

The record begins to thicken in the mid-eighteenth century. From Russia, the Great Northern Expedition launched by Peter the Great sent Bering and Chirikov to the north and the east. It was Georg Wilhelm Steller, Bering's naturalist on the voyage of 1741–42, who gave us a record of the first European landfall in what is now Alaska and gave us the only eye witness account and drawing of the Steller's sea cow, soon after exterminated by Russian hunters. (The history and writings of the Russian presence in the Arctic are set aside for this brief overview.)

Late in the eighteenth century, the British were also pushing toward the polar sea from the west. Captain James Cook penetrated as far north as Icy Cape in Alaska in 1778. Overland, Samuel Hearne traveled up the Coppermine River to the arctic coast in 1772, and, in 1789, Alexander Mackenzie up the river that now bears his name.

Meanwhile, whalers were pushing ever northward in their quest for the bowhead. Although this brief account bypasses their enormous exploits and written record, one British whaler deserves note for the influence he exerted: William Scorseby. When he reported, in 1817, that the pack ice was melting, he renewed interest in conquest of the high latitudes. When his book, *Journal of a Voyage to the Northern*

Whale-Fishery, was published in 1820, interest was intensified. Among other information, he brought back the first detailed descriptions of snow crystals in the high latitudes.

In 1818, Sir John Barrow, a former whaler and an official of the English Admiralty, published *A Chronological History of Voyages into the Arctic Regions,* summing up what was then known. The Napoleonic wars were over and England needed new markets and new tasks for its seamen. The Admiralty—and the British government—threw its energy into a renewed campaign for discovery of a Northwest Passage.

That year, 1818, the Admiralty sent a significant expedition of four ships to achieve the goal. Two of the ships were to sail east across the Pole to Siberia and the other two ships to the west; they were to meet in Bering Strait. Among the officers were six men whose names would be indelibly linked with the Arctic: Edward Parry, John Franklin, George Back, Edward Sabine, John Ross, and his nephew James Clark Ross (who determined the location of the North Magnetic Pole in 1831). For decades, these men and their colleagues would dominate the area from Baffin Bay to Bering Strait—the area of the long-sought passage, scattering their names over headlands, bays, and straits.

The disappearance of Sir John Franklin's fourth and final expedition, which left England in 1845, changed everything. During the next dozen years, 50 expeditions went in search of his two missing ships. In the process, the empty spaces of the map filled with relative speed—and at immense cost. The accounts of the search rate among the most gripping of adventure stories and clearly make the point the Admiralty had failed to grasp for many painful years: adaptability in the Arctic means the difference between life and death. Those who learned to dress in fur, eat the resident meat, and sledge instead of walk survived. Those who did not—or would not—failed. To live like the Native inhabitants was essential. Indeed, the Native inhabitants were essential. Their generosity and bravery in helping the often hapless Englishmen (and Americans) goes for the most part unacknowledged. Among the best accounts of the Franklin search are those of Leopold McClintock, the master sledger who found the only written record left by the Franklin expedition; Elisha Kent Kane, the American romantic who really was in quest of the North Pole; and Charles Francis Hall, who brought back Franklin relics from his second journey, 1864–69.

In 1854, the Crimean War turned the interest of Great Britain elsewhere. The sad fate of the Franklin expedition, only partly known to this day, was left to the ice. The search now was for the North Pole. Here, the Americans became major players in what was no longer a commercial venture but more of a sporting event.

In 1860, Kane's former shipboard surgeon, Isaac Israel Hayes, attempted another similar expedition. He was followed by Charles Francis Hall, making his third expedition. When Hall died in 1871—by arsenic poisoning—his *Polaris* expedition continued. Captain George Tyson provides an account of drifting seven months with a party of 19 on an ice floe for 1,800 miles—one of the greatest of all polar stories.

A major American assault on the Pole was launched from the west, through Bering Strait, by the newspaper baron James Gordon Bennett of the *New York Herald.* The *Jeannette* expedition, under the command of Lieutenant George Washington De Long, set out from San Francisco in 1879. Soon into the ice, the ship was fatally caught. De Long's journal, found with his body on the Lena Delta and edited by his widow Emma, provides an astounding account of bravery and of sensitivity to the beauty of a deadly environment.

In 1881, the United States Army launched an attack from the east, following in the path of the British attempt by George Nares. Two years later, Lieutenant Adolphus Washington Greely and six of his original 23 men were found, barely alive. At one point, the party had picked up a pitifully small cache left for them; from newspaper wrappings they learned of De Long's disaster.

The tragedy of De Long provided lessons not lost on Fridtjof Nansen of Norway. Learning from the relics of the *Jeannette,* which turned up three years later in Greenland, he set his little ship *Fram* deliberately into the ice to drift around the Pole, 1893–96. No arctic explorer has written more clearly nor more poetically of the polar regions than Nansen, nor has one added more to knowledge of the Arctic Ocean and the history of its early explorations than this studious and multi-faceted adventurer and diplomat.

It was another Norwegian, Roald Amundsen, who put together all the lessons and won the prize of the Northwest Passage, when he became the first to sail through, with his tiny *Gjoa,* 1903–06. He won the prize of the South Pole, too, and was one of the first to fly—by dirigible—over the North Pole, where he later disappeared in a plane.

The final race for the North Pole came down to two Americans: Robert E. Peary who claimed success on April 6, 1909, and Frederick A. Cook, who asserted he got there first on April 21, 1908. On his return, Cook met only rejection and ultimately imprisonment for a land deal purported to be another hoax. The bitter argument of Peary vs. Cook remains—as unsettled as the pack ice.

During the years of the final race to the Pole, Vilhjalmur Stefansson was just starting out on his explorations of the northern reaches of Canada and Alaska. During his expeditions of 1906–07, 1908–12, and 1913–18, he covered much of the Canadian Archipelago. A prodigious writer, he left a clear trail of books behind, all of which carry his theme of the "friendly Arctic": The Arctic can easily be lived in if one adapts to the lifestyle of its indigenous people.

An important chapter of Stefansson's 1913–18 expedition is the story of the *Karluk*, an ice-locked ship with a fate similar to that of the *Jeannette*. Its story is best told by its captain, Bob Bartlett, a remarkable seaman and chronicler of the Arctic who whaled, sailed with Peary, and sledged through large areas of the far north.

Last of the great arctic explorers was Knud Rasmussen, the ethnographer from Greenland, who walked and sledged the entire distance of the Northwest Passage with two Eskimo companions from Greenland; one of them was a woman, Anarulanguaq, who deserves high honors but whose name is scarcely known. His account of the Fifth Thule Expedition of 1921–24 stands as a major record of the vanishing way of life of the people along his route.

Although less well known, other travelers of the first half of the century provide unusual and important accounts. Hudson Stuck, archdeacon of the Episcopal Church in Alaska, not only led the first party to conquer Mount McKinley in 1913 but also covered thousands of miles in the Arctic by dog sled. Far to the east, the artist Rockwell Kent sailed and walked the wild coast of Greenland in 1929. In 1931, Anne Morrow Lindbergh co-piloted the Great Circle Route. A quiet chronicle of life in Alaska's and Canada's northern reaches from 1911–60 is given by Margaret E. Murie in *Two in the Far North*.

Although most recent explorations have been for oil and gas, some notable expeditions have occurred. In 1988, Helen Thayer skied solo to the Magnetic North Pole accompanied by one dog. Her gripping account proves the Arctic remains as challenging as ever.

Contemporary accounts of note concern themselves not so much with adventure and raw data but with synthesis and reflection. Chief among these are *Arctic Dreams* by Barry Lopez and the works of Richard K. Nelson and Hugh Brody. Indigenous writers deserve attention beyond what can be given here. A. Oscar Kawagley, although writing of an area south of the Arctic Circle, deals with the dominant question of circumpolar life: how to integrate Western and Native worldviews. An unusual and provocative retelling of an Athabaskan legend with modern significance is *Two Old Women* by Velma Wallis. And, although his purview is not strictly the Arctic, no contemporary writer better represents the soul of the far north than poet and essayist John Haines.

Selected Works and Further Reading

Amundsen, Roald, *Roald Amundsen's "The North West Passage": Being the Record of a Voyage of Exploration of the Ship 'Gjoa' 1903–1907,* New York: Dutton, 1908; London: A. Constable, 1908

Arctic Institute of North America, *Arctic Bibliography,* edited by Maret Martna, 16 vols., Montreal: McGill-Queen's University Press, 1953–1975

Barrow, John, Sir, *A Chronological History of Voyages into the Arctic Regions,* London: J. Murray, 1818; reprinted, New York: Barnes & Noble, 1971

Bartlett, Robert Abram, *The Last Voyage of the Karluk,* Boston: Small, Maynard, 1916

———, *The Log of Bob Bartlett: The True Story of Forty Years of Seafaring and Exploration,* New York and London: Putnam's, 1928

Berton, Pierre, *The Arctic Grail: The Quest for the North West Passage and the North Pole, 1818–1909,* New York: Viking, 1988

Blake, Euphemia Vale, ed., *Arctic Experiences, Containing Capt. George E. Tyson's Wonderful Drift on the Ice-Floe . . . ,* New York: Harper & Brothers, 1874; London: S. Low, Marston, Low & Searle, 1874

Brody, Hugh, *Living Arctic: Hunters of the Canadian North,* Vancouver, British Columbia: Douglas & McIntyre, 1987; Seattle: University of Washington Press, 1987; London: Faber and Faber, 1987

Cook, Frederick A., *My Attainment of the Pole,* New York: Mitchell Kennerley, 1911; London: Mitchell Kennerley, 1912

Cook, James, *A Voyage to the Pacific Ocean,* London: G. Nicol and T. Cadell, 1784; New York: Tieboat and O'Brien, 1796

Cooke, Alan, and Clive Holland, *The Exploration of Northern Canada, 500 to 1920: A Chronology,* Toronto, Ontario: Arctic History, 1978

Day, Alan Edwin, *Search for the Northwest Passage: An Annotated Bibliography,* New York: Garland, 1986

De Long, Emma, ed., *The Voyage of the Jeannette,* Boston: Houghton Mifflin, 1883; London: K. Paul, Trench, 1883

Dillard, Annie, *Teaching a Stone to Talk: Expeditions and Encounters,* New York: Harper & Row, 1982; London: Pan, 1984

Franklin, John, Sir, *Narrative of a Journey to the Shores of the Polar Sea, in the Years 1819, 20, 21, and 22,* London: John Murray, 1823; Philadelphia: H. C. Carey, 1824

——, *Narrative of a Second Expedition to the Shores of the Polar Sea in the Years 1825, 26, 27,* Philadelphia: Carey, Lea, and Carey, 1828; London: John Murray, 1828

Greely, A. W., *Three Years of Arctic Service: An Account of the Lady Franklin Bay Expedition of 1881–84, and the Attainment of the Farthest North,* New York: Scribner's, 1885; London: R. Bentley, 1886

Haines, John Meade, *Fables and Distances: New and Selected Essays,* Saint Paul, Minnesota: Graywolf, 1996

——, *The Stars, the Snow, the Fire: Twenty-Five Years in the Northern Wilderness: A Memoir,* Saint Paul, Minnesota: Graywolf, 1989

Hakluyt, Richard, *Hakluyt's Voyages,* edited by Richard David, Boston: Houghton Mifflin, 1981; London: Chatto & Windus, 1981

——, *The Principal Navigations, Voyages, Traffiques and Discoveries of the English Nation . . . ,* reprint of 2nd ed., Glasgow, Scotland: James MacLehose and Sons, 1903

Hall, Charles Francis, *Narrative of the Second Arctic Expedition Made by Charles F. Hall . . . ,* Washington, D.C.: U.S. Government Printing Office, 1879

Hearne, Samuel, *A Journey from Prince of Wales's Fort in Hudson's Bay to the Northern Ocean . . . ,* London: A. Strahan and T. Cadell, 1795; reprinted, New York: Greenwood, 1968

Holland, Clive, *Arctic Exploration and Development, c. 500 B.C. to 1915: An Encyclopedia,* New York: Garland, 1994

Jans, Nick, *The Last Light Breaking: Living Among Alaska's Inupiat Eskimos,* Anchorage: Alaska Northwest, 1993

——, *A Place Beyond: Finding Home in Arctic Alaska,* Anchorage: Alaska Northwest, 1996

Kane, Elisha Kent, *Arctic Explorations: The Second Grinnell Expedition in Search of Sir John Franklin, 1853, 54, 55,* Philadelphia: Childs & Peterson, 1856; London: Trübner, 1857

Kawagley, A. Oscar, *A Yupiaq Worldview,* Prospect Heights, Illinois: Waveland, 1995

Kent, Rockwell, *N by E,* New York: Harcourt, Brace, 1930; London: Cassel, 1930

Lindbergh, Anne Morrow, *North to the Orient,* New York: Harcourt, Brace, 1935; London: Chatto & Windus, 1935

Lopez, Barry Holstun, *Arctic Dreams: Imagination and Desire in a Northern Landscape,* New York: Scribner's, 1986; London: Macmillan, 1986

M'Clintock, Francis Leopold, Sir, *The Voyage of the 'Fox' in the Arctic Seas . . . ,* New York: J. T. Lloyd, 1859; London: J. Murray, 1859

Mackenzie, Alexander, Sir, *Exploring the Northwest Territory: Sir Alexander Mackenzie's Journal of a Voyage by Bark Canoe from Lake Athabasca to the Pacific Ocean in the Summer of 1789,* edited by Ted Hayden McDonald, Norman: University of Oklahoma Press, 1966

Mirsky, Jeannette, *To the North! The Story of Arctic Exploration from Earliest Times to the Present,* New York: Viking, 1934

Mowat, Farley, ed., *The Top of the World Trilogy: Volume I: Ordeal by Ice: The Search for the Northwest Passage; Volume II: The Polar Passion; Volume III: Tundra: Selections from the Great Accounts of Arctic Land Voyages,* Salt Lake City, Utah: Peregrine Smith, 1989

Murie, Margaret E., *Two in the Far North,* New York: Knopf, 1962

Murray, John A., ed., *A Republic of Rivers: Three Centuries of Nature Writing from Alaska and the Yukon,* New York: Oxford University Press, 1990

Nansen, Fridtjof, *In Northern Mists: Arctic Exploration in Early Times,* 2 vols., New York: Frederick A. Stokes, 1911; London: W. Heinemann, 1911

Nares, George S., *Narrative of a Voyage to the Polar Sea During 1875–6 in H.M. Ships*

'Alert' and 'Discovery', London: S. Low, Marston, Searle, and Rivington, 1878

Nelson, Richard K., *Hunters of the Northern Ice,* Chicago: University of Chicago Press, 1969

———, *Make Prayers to the Raven: A Koyukon View of the Northern Forest,* Chicago and London: University of Chicago Press, 1986

———, *Shadow of the Hunter: Stories of Eskimo Life,* Chicago: University of Chicago Press, 1980

Peary, Robert E., *The North Pole: Its Discovery in 1909 Under the Auspices of the Peary Arctic Club,* New York: Frederick A. Stokes, 1910

Rasmussen, Knud, *Across Arctic America: Narrative of the Fifth Thule Expedition,* New York: Putnam's, 1927

Scoresby, William, *Journal of a Voyage to the Northern Whale-Fishery,* London: Hurst, Robinson, 1823

Scott Polar Research Institute, *Manuscripts in the Scott Polar Research Institute, Cambridge, England: A Catalogue,* edited by Clive Holland, New York: Garland, 1982

Stefansson, Vilhjalmur, *The Adventure of Wrangel Island,* New York: Macmillan, 1925; London: J. Cape, 1926

———, *Discovery: The Autobiography of Vilhjalmur Stefansson,* New York: McGraw-Hill, 1964

———, *The Friendly Arctic: The Story of Five Years in Polar Regions,* New York: Macmillan, 1921; London: G. G. Harrap, 1921

———, *Hunters of the Great North,* New York: Harcourt, Brace, 1922; London: G. G. Harrap, 1923

Steller, Georg Wilhelm, *Journal of a Voyage with Bering, 1741–1742,* edited and introduced by O. W. Frost, translated by Margritt A. Engel and O. W. Frost, Stanford, California: Stanford University Press, 1988

Stuck, Hudson, *Ten Thousand Miles with a Dog Sled: A Narrative of Winter Travel in Interior Alaska,* New York: Scribner's, 1914; London: T. Werner Laurie, 1914

———, *A Winter Circuit of Our Arctic Coast: A Narrative of a Journey with Dog-Sleds Around the Entire Arctic Coast of Alaska,* New York: Scribner's, 1920; London: T. Werner Laurie, 1920

Thayer, Helen, *Polar Dream,* New York: Simon & Schuster, 1993; London: Little, Brown, 1993

Wallis, Velma, *Two Old Women: An Alaska Legend of Betrayal, Courage, and Survival,* Fairbanks, Alaska: Epicenter, 1993; London: Women's Press, 1994

The Southern End of the Earth: Antarctic Literature

Elle Tracy

"How was it up there?" is a common response on hearing the news that I spent a year in Antarctica. Almost automatically, we who live north of the Equator hear "arctic" and think "polar, north." Antarctica is the earth's fifth largest continent with an area of about 14 million square kilometers (5.4 million square miles) or 10 percent of its surface; a landscape without sovereignty, unconquered, unoccupied, and never exploited for natural resources. It is the earth's highest, driest, coldest, windiest, darkest continent and remains the world's most natural landscape, because its geography is the most inaccessible and inhospitable to humans. About 30° F colder than corresponding northern latitudes, Antarctica is a continent lapped by oceans, anti-Arctic in the truest sense, given the Arctic ocean is embraced by land. *Oceanus* magazine lists only "sparse vegetation (mostly algae, lichens, and mosses) and microbial life, including bacteria and fungi, and few hardy insects" as indigenous to the 2 percent of the continent not capped by ice.

Unlike the other six continents where thousands of human generations fed children's imaginations with oral stories, unless people go there, they can only learn about Antarctica by reading about it. And unlike the other six continents, Antarctica is the only continent sighted and explored by people after the advent of the printing press.

If the reader agrees that time spent in the natural world affords a venturer self-reflection and that nature writing results from the time a thoughtful writer spends crafting a venturer's response, please understand that Antarctic nature writing must be scarce. Why? Because people who live in Antarctica today—the non-tourist breed—only do so funded by a sovereign nation and focused on science. The 1961 ratification of the Antarctic Treaty, the governing law of the planet south of 60 degrees, reserved these high latitudes for science. Rarely, except through the United States' National Science Foundation and its Artists and Writers Program, can a capable, unfunded writer live in Antarctica to observe and write about it. Pre-Antarctic Treaty, however, articulate venturers in pursuit of whale blubber, conquest, or members of a national navy wrote about how the human spirit becomes electrified living in Antarctica's natural world.

Predominantly, Antarctica is seen through the literary eyes of men. The majority of Antarctica's Heroic Age explorers were English-speaking or European men, who published findings, journals, and armchair-adventure-worthy nonfiction books. Although Russian, Japanese, and South American sailors sighted land, whaled, sealed, and explored the southern oceans, the volume of their writing has been overshadowed by the comparatively prolific English-speaking and European men.

The year I lived in Antarctica is a privilege few ordinary people like me can claim. I lived at 77° 51′S, 166° 40′E, in a four-kilometer-square confine named McMurdo Station, an American scientific enclave about 720 nautical miles north of the South Pole. On my days off during our 26 weeks of austral winter isolation, I explored our New Zealand neighbor's Scott Base library, three kilometers east of us, in search of stories about who had lived there before us. Then I excerpted them in the newspaper I published every other Sunday, so the 257 members of our community, who had no other access, could read them. That is how I discovered the rich literature written by Heroic Age Antarctic explorers (1899–1917) with names like Roald Amundsen, Robert Falcon Scott, Earnest Shackleton, and Douglas Mawson, and by others who accompanied them.

I flew to Christchurch, New Zealand, from Seattle, Washington, on commercial airliners. Then I flew the 3,000 kilometers (2,300 miles) south to McMurdo Station aboard a windowless U.S. Air Force C-141 Star Lifter, wearing 18 pounds of natural-fiber survival clothing, strapped into my seat with cargo straps. Finally, on our third attempt, the eight-hour flight landed 97 of us on the eight-foot-thick sea ice runway at the south end of the Ross Sea, in McMurdo Sound. As exotic as this 13-day beginning was for me (10 days we waited in New Zealand for good landing weather in Antarctica), it paled with comfort and convenience as compared to sailing to the Ross Sea.

Sailing from Littleton, near Christchurch in 1908, Shackleton's *Nimrod* was towed to iceberg territory, to save coal, through what he called "mountainous seas," and 10 degrees of which whalers had named "The Roaring Forties." During his 36-day sail from Littleton to McMurdo Bay in 1910, Scott wrote about his non-complaining companions. These men occupied the "main deck under the forecastle space where the ponies were stabled." The rough seas caused the stable dirt to "leak down into their hammocks and bedding," their belongings to be "thrown about," and water to leak everywhere: "The men have been wetted to the skin repeatedly on deck, and have no chance of drying their clothing. All things considered, their cheerful fortitude is little short of wonderful" (pp. 13–14).

Earlier, after a similar sail to McMurdo Bay in 1902, Dr. Edward Wilson, chief scientist, physician, and artist with Captain Scott on two expeditions, noted "our extreme good fortune in being led to such a winter quarter as this":

[S]afe for the ship, with perfect shelter from all ice pressure . . . sheltered from the S.E. prevailing winds by a range of hills from five to seven and ten hundred feet high and all within sight of not only [Mount] Erebus and its column of smoke . . . but of an immense and splendid range of [Transantarctic] mountains hitherto unknown, which caught and reflected the pink glow of the sun with its wonderful violets night and morning. . . . Nothing was wanting, and our hopes ran very high that night. (*Discovery*, 112)

Imagine a life without a car, with no place or reason to spend money, no access to media, including telephones, living without furnishings, wardrobe, and library. Imagine a community without seniors, children, fresh food, and sun. Imagine being given the responsible freedom to work, eat, sleep, and behave without the influence of family, friends, or familiar laws.

Cold seeps into everything. A person can frostbite their fingers picking up a teaspoon from a drawer in an abandoned hut. A metal banister or doorknob attaches itself to bare skin, only once. Because the air lacks pollutants, distance vision fools people into believing that, for example, the 13,500-foot southernmost active volcano, Mount Erebus, or the 9,000-foot Mount Discovery across the bay, are farther away than they really are, by a magnitude of maybe two or three times.

In this land of ice, breath crystallizes as frost on the hood ruff hairs around the face whenever someone walks outdoors, otherwise, that face would soon sport a mask of ice. To save their skin, people slather skin oil all over after every second day's shower, having only soaped the head, armpits, and groin. Residents drink a minimum of two liters of desalinated sea water every day, or their bodies begin using its blood as its fluid resource. Toss a teacup filled with boiling water into the outside air and watch it precipitate diamond dust as it freezes then floats. When the wind's constant howl subsides, the only sound to be heard when walking alone outside is blood pumping through the veins in one's neck.

The Australian explorer, Douglas Mawson, wrote in 1911 from the base on Commonwealth Bay (66° 54′S 142° 40′E), which he named "The Home of the Blizzard," that when the wind died, a "skin of ice quickly appeared over the whole surface of the water. In the early stages, this formation consisted of loose, blade-like crystals, previously floating freely below the surface and rising by their own buoyancy"—think about how this occurs in salt water. However, should the wind remain calm for a time, these crystals "soon became cemented together. On April 6, within the interval of an hour, an even crust, one inch thick, covered the sea. But the wind returned before the ice was sufficiently strong to resist it, and it all broke up and drifted away to the north" (p. 132).

Everybody works in Antarctica. We scheduled work 53 hours a week. Under 24-hour sun some work doesn't stop: off-loading the annual supply ship, monitoring the weather, or scooping up the benthos in search of yet unclassified underwater creatures. For each scientist in the U.S. Antarctic Program today, seven people work in support completing such tasks as maintaining Scott tents and sleds for field camp use, monitoring inventories of scientific instrumentation and supplies, and populating fire, medical, and food service operations. While all work is paid, funded by tax dollars, participants volunteer for community projects, such as newspaper columnist, shortwave radio disk jockey, or marathon coordinator.

In his 1995 book, scientist Bill Green stepped outside his hut near Lake Fryxell, on the other side of McMurdo Sound, during a lull in his work.

> From where I stood, I could see the stream [of glacial melt water] and the lake and the white cone of Erebus far across McMurdo Sound. For a thousand square miles beyond the hut there was not a single living thing. . . . At this distance the cone of Erebus was smooth and featureless. There was a delicate shade of pink, like tea roses, falling across its slopes. As I looked at it, I saw it differently from before. It stood now in the center of an imagined collage, like something I had seen in the gallery. Around it were objects scattered and indistinct: a crystal of calcite; a map of the world; a bamboo shoot; a night street under deep snow; a weathered crater in the Koolaus; a maple seed; a river bending by the red mill stacks; a cornfield in springtime; a wooden flume; a garden with a table; a molecule of carbon dioxide; a pink shell. Woven among these, in cycles, where the threads of the world, which were carbon and calcium, and these were overlaid by the cycles of yet a larger strand, which was water. And the water appeared to glisten, the way a droplet glistens on a needle of ice. (p. 232)

Apsley Cherry-Garrard describes a typical day in 1911 at the Discovery Hut on McMurdo Sound, that starts about 8 A.M. with "a sizzling on the fire and a smell of porridge and fried seal liver" with "the more hardy ones . . . washing: that is, they rubbed themselves, all shivering, with snow, of a minus temperature, and pretended they liked it. Perhaps they were right, but we told them it was swank." He writes that unlike men who sit in offices to work, "everyone is busy by 9:30. From now until supper at 7 work is done by all. . . . when we go out, each individual quite naturally takes the opportunity to carry out such work as concerns him, whether it deals with ice or rocks, dogs or horses, meteorology or biology, tide-gauges or balloons." He concludes that "the happiest and healthiest members of our party during this first year were those who spent the longest period in the fresh air" (pp. 189–193).

The sun set on April 17, 1992, not to rise again until the 17th of August. Work continued all sunless winter, but at a significantly lower level of sensory input and output. Indoors, we dimmed the lights, lowered the music volume, and spoke more softly to our co-workers. Outdoors, even on the shortest day we could see astronomical twilight—sun 17 degrees below the horizon—for nearly three hours. The moon tracked mostly above the horizon three or four days both before and after its full phase, reflecting off the glacial landscape. Even outside the well-lit station, with the Southern Hemisphere full of stars and pretty persistent Aurora Australis, it was never really too dark to walk about.

Uniformly, every book written about the natural world of Antarctic climes reflects the constant subjugation of the writer to its deadly cold and unforgiving nature. So it's with the consistent urging of the natural Antarctic world that its pristine landscape is revealed in literature.

The watercolorist in Dr. Wilson described two days in May 1903.

> Very low temperatures again, down to –60° F. . . . much colder than . . . last winter. . . . The colour in the north is strikingly beautiful at noon nowadays—a deep band of rich carmine blending upwards with green, hardly any yellow intervening, and above the green comes deep violet or purple. The [ice] floe horizon against this carmine is a deep heliotrope colour. The sky was brilliantly clear and the moon almost full in the west, but on the floe was a mist which gave us three mock moons one above and one on each side of the true moon. There was no halo, but there were horizontal and vertical rays pointing from the moon to the paraselena. There was a trace of prismatic colour in the mock moons, red inside and greenish blue outside.
> (*Discovery*, 258–259)

I agree with Cherry-Garrard when he says, "Exploration is the physical expression of the Intellectual Passion."

> And I tell you, if you have the desire for knowledge and the power to give it physical expression, go out and explore. . . . Some will tell you that you are mad, and nearly all will say, "What is the Use?" For we are a nation of shopkeepers, and no shopkeeper will look at research which does not promise him a financial return within a year. And so you will

sledge nearly alone, but those with whom you sledge will not be shopkeepers: that is worth a good deal. (p. 193)

After returning to the United States, I discovered America's Antarctic post-Heroic Age explorers, U.S. Navy Admiral Richard E. Byrd, who took Paramount Pictures photographers with him on one expedition, and Lincoln Ellsworth who funded his own, and then Jennie Darlington, the first woman to set foot on the continent (and write about Antarctica), and Paul Siple, who helped build the Amundsen-Scott Base at 90° S during the 1957–58 International Geophysical Year. Vivian Fuchs, Sir Edmund Hillary, and Will Steger all walked and wrote about crossing the continent, journaling powerful accounts of survival and hope against the diciest of odds.

So what has all this to do with nature writing? It has to do with transfixing a spirit, infusing a life with possibilities, and with cementing a previously tenuous self-confidence. Today, as I move in our culture, I only need a bird's song, a braille inspection of moss, an urban view of a full moon, a weathered sky, a child's smile, or a senior's wise nod to remind me of how natural I am in the world where I live—Antarctica's gift to me. To overwhelm the mean-spirited events that can occur among petty people with power in isolation situations, I found in the literature of these fellow adventurers a camaraderie of personal peace, a spiritual harkening to community that will motivate me wherever I live—Antarctica's gift to me.

In my omission of fiction, I bow to Fauno Cordes's work, where she set out to discover, read, and list tales about Antarctica, including those set in the subantarctic islands. She excludes historical novels, autobiographical poetry and children's penguin stories, fields she expects to be treated separately, as do I. In her wonderful work, she nods to established classical writers, such as James Fenimore Cooper, Jules Verne, and Rudyard Kipling, who described the far southern natural world from their imaginations. Also worthy of mention is William E. Lenz's thoughtful analysis of two James Croxall Palmer works, *Thulia: A Tale of the Antarctic (1843)* and *Antarctic Mariner's Song (1868)*. For physical locations in costal Antarctica, consult *Sailing Directions (Planning Guide & Enroute) for Antarctica, Second Edition, 1992,* published by the United States Defense Mapping Agency Hydrographic/Topographic Center, DMS Stock No. SDPUB200.

So as sparse as it may be, Antarctic nature writing can be found sprinkled in the journals of explorers, military men, and, lately, a few women who wrote about their lives in Antarctica. The simplicity and purity of the human spirit made available when a human being inserts itself into the most extreme natural world never fails to provoke, inspire, and humble.

Selected Works and Further Reading

Byrd, Richard E., *Alone,* New York: Putnam's, 1938; London: Readers Union, 1938

Cherry-Garrard, Apsley, *The Worst Journey in the World, Antarctic, 1910–1913,* New York: Doran, 1922; London: Chatto & Windus, 1922

Cordes, Fauno, "For Geography 896, San Francisco State University, *The Emerging Face of a Continent,* a Bibliography of Antarctic Fiction, May 1, 1988," unpublished

Darlington, Jennie, as told to Jane McIlvaine McClary, *My Antarctic Honeymoon: A Year at the Bottom of the World,* Garden City, New York: Doubleday, 1956; London: F. Muller, 1957

Green, Bill, *Water, Ice & Stone: Science and Memory on the Antarctic Lakes,* New York: Harmony, 1995

Hain, James H. W., "A Reader's Guide to the Antarctic," *Oceanus,* The International Magazine of Marine Science and Policy 31:2 (Summer 1988), p. 3

Lenz, William E., *The Poetics of the Antarctic, a Study in Nineteenth-Century American Cultural Perceptions,* New York: Garland, 1995

Mawson, Douglas, Sir, *The Home of the Blizzard: Being the Story of the Australian Antarctic Expedition, 1911–1914,* Philadelphia: Lippincott, 1914; London: Heinemann, 1914

Scientific American 207:3 (September 1962)

Scott, Robert Falcon, *Scott's Last Expedition, Volume One Being the Journals of Captain R. F. Scott, R.N., C.V.O.,* New York: Dodd, Mead, 1913; London: Smith, Elder, 1913

Shackleton, Ernest Henry, Sir, *Aurora Australis,* Cape Royd, Antarctica, 1908; reprinted, Shrewsbury, England: Airlife, 1988

——, *The Heart of the Antarctic, Being the Story of the British Antarctic Expedition 1907–1909,* Philadelphia: Lippincott, 1909; London: Heinemann, 1909

——, *The South Polar Times,* 3 vols., London: Smith, Elder, 1907–1914

Spence, Sydney A., *Antarctic Miscellany:*

Books, Periodicals & Maps Relating to the Discovery and Exploration of Antarctica, edited by J. J. H. and J. I. Simper, Mitcham, England: J. J. H. and J. I. Simper, 1980

Steger, Will, and Jon Bowermaster, *Crossing Antarctica,* New York: Knopf, 1992; London: Bantam, 1992

Wilson, Edward Adrian, *Diary of the 'Discovery' Expedition to the Antarctic Regions 1901–1904,* edited by Ann Savours, London: Blandford, 1966; New York: Humanities, 1967

———, *Diary of the 'Terra Nova' Expedition to the Antarctic, 1910–1912,* New York: Humanities, 1972; London: Blandford, 1972

Section 6:

Topics, Genres, Theory,
and Other Arts

Voices from the Western Borderlands:
A Cross-Cultural Study of Chicana,
Native American, and Women Writers
of the American West

Benay Blend

"We need new stories, new terms and conditions that are relevant to the love of land," says the Chickasaw poet Linda Hogan, "a new narrative that would imagine another way to learn the infinite movement at work in the world" (p. 83). In the area west of the 98th meridian, women of many cultures have redefined American attitudes toward nature as they themselves form questions about how to define their places in and responsibility to the landscape. To extend the dialogue to include women writers is to expand the genre of nature writing. As Patrick D. Murphy claims, it is women writers who have come forward to counter the Enlightenment ideal of alienation from the natural world with writing centered on interaction with others and the environment (p. 154).

When an environment is this open, yet diverse, it often produces borders especially fertile for women writers. Where cultures overlap, definitions become fluid, creating a space where bicultural flexibility opens a new range of female possibilities. "For me," says the Creek poet Joy Harjo, "poetry is a bridge over the sea of paradox, the sea is the blood, and it becomes a way to join . . . being Indian and white" (pp. 94, 134). This chapter will examine how women's cultures in the West have reacted to and interacted with the borderland in different, though compatible, ways.

A central theme of this literature is exploration of cultural hybridity, or in Gloria Anzaldúa's terms, "the borderlands"—a literal and figurative terrain that both encourages the integration of ancient with modern cultural beliefs and challenges internalized icons that have historically oppressed women. In *Borderlands/La Frontera*, Anzaldúa's woman-centered narrative agenda contrasts with mainstream feminist theory. Grounding her own identity in *la tierra* (the land), specifically the Texas/Mexico border, with its legacy of political struggle, Anzaldúa reinterprets indigenous discourse in order to develop alternative myths that celebrate the experiences and influences of women. In her experimental autobiography, Anzaldúa equates the earth with woman in that both serve as an imaginative source for stories. Anzaldúa's text is itself a *mestiza*, meaning a hybrid—in this case, a hybrid of autobiography, historical document, and poetry. In her role as "a new *mestiza*," she also crosses gender borders, creating a "new gender, both woman and man, [but] neither" (p. 194).

A borderland—between countries, between cultures, between past and present, and between genders as well as genres—offers, then, a creative place for transformative identity. If, however, as Anzaldúa says, thinking back and forth between two divergent cultures often engenders a more creative, *mestiza* way of looking at the world, there is also a downside to border living. As the writer Alicia Gaspar de Alba puts it, inhabiting a border zone can also lead to the "cultural schizophrenia" that she experienced growing up (p. 291). A self-described "literary wetback," born in El Paso,Texas, just a few miles from the Texas/Mexico border, Gaspar de Alba explores the bewilderment that can result from feeling like an alien in the dominant culture while knowing that she is alienated from her own. But she also dramatizes the positive aspects of border living by comparing the Chicana writer to the *curandera* (medicine woman) or *bruja* (witch); both are keepers of their culture who also have the alchemical power to change raw materials into precious jewels. In her role as writer/*curandera*, Gaspar de Alba transforms cultural myths into "a new language . . . new images . . . [and] new dreams" in which her characters can defy and celebrate their boundaries (p. 291).

This new space is often an internal one with roots in spiritual rather than actual belonging. "I've had to learn my home is within me," says Harjo (p. 76). Similarly, Wendy Rose, in "For My People," celebrates the fact that she is finding a new tradition through her poetry, although, as a mixed-blood Hopi, she often feels "blown/two leaves apart" (p. 3). Anzaldúa's new *mestiza*, more generally, survives because she can transform "home" into a concept she can carry, along with her political commitments, to a place where she can live "*sin fronteras* (without borders) by a crossroads" (p. 195).

In the borderland, landscape is defined as encompassing both the interior and exterior world. In her introduction to *Walking the Twilight: Women Writers of the Southwest*, editor Kathryn Wilder suggests that twilight implies not only a transitional time of day but also a more ephemeral passing from "one realm to another" (I: xvii); this sense of spiritual renewing is reflected in Wilder's choice of writers for this collection. For example, Cathryn Alpert, who writes mostly of the desert despite her short residency there, says that "the desert Southwest is a landscape of interior—of our country and of the heart" (I:166). Similarly, Gladys Swan, who grew up in New Mexico, where she situates many of the characters in her three collections of short stories and two novels, sees the desert as a "territory of the mind," a refuge in an age of moral and physical displacement (II: 65).

One's psychological space—usually influenced by such variables as smells, foods, colors, and personal memories—is connected to one's physical location. For example, although she no longer lives on the reservation, the Tohono O'odham poet Ofelia Zepeda looks back to her culture for inspiration, using memories of how the

women in her family adapted to the rhythms of the desert to write poetry which honors their daily life (p. 1). More explicitly, Diane Glancy, a Cherokee poet, claims that "my poems and writing were the land I cultivated . . . an internal land . . . a homestead within myself" (p. 86). "More than land but of the land—a tradition of mythologies, of ongoing history," Harjo's "inner landscape is a much larger and more visible present" (Harjo, 112, 132). All attest to the Western woman writer's unity in creativity, an ability to juggle cultures and reach deep into an invented inner landscape to create art.

While crossing borders, bridging borders, or simply recognizing the limits of borders is more integral to Chicana and Native American women's literature, the concept of limits or margins is equally important to those Anglo women who found their voices in the West. The term "borderlands" calls attention to the ways in which westward-moving women crossed cultures and moved along borders between cultures in order to negotiate a new sense of home, place, and voice. In contrast to Hispanic,[1] Mexican and Native American women, who established artistic forms of response to the land long before Anglos arrived in the west, European-American women based their worldview on the idea of personal freedom inherent in the male pioneer tradition and on ecological concerns of such male naturalists as Emerson, Thoreau, and John Muir. By incorporating into this environmental ethic the community interests of the female tradition, Anglo women eventually helped to create a new, gender-based literature of the American west.

In *The Land Before Her: Fantasy and Experience of the American Frontiers, 1630–1860*, Annette Kolodny confirms that the prairie served as a sanctuary in which women could lead lives of familiar domesticity, an ideology most often cited in guidebooks and popular novels of the mid-to-late nineteenth century about life on the frontier. European-American women in the latter part of the nineteenth century envisioned the prairie as a potential garden similar to those they left behind. Some, like Nannie Alderston, an upper-class Southerner, lamented that she never stayed in one place long enough to break the "vast monotony" of Montana with planted trees (p. 297).

Before the end of the nineteenth century, however, some women writers, such as Mary Austin, questioned the traditional European-American aggressive stance toward the land and found value in the untouched landscape and lifestyles of those who had for centuries adapted to its ways. A Midwesterner transplanted to the Southwest desert of southern California and later to Santa Fe, New Mexico, Austin served as a key figure in the region's conservation movement, and her nature writing affected environmental values of the arid West.

One thread runs through the work of Austin and her literary daughters: that of honing in on one place and living there until animate and inanimate landscape are home. For example, in *Beyond the Aspen Grove*, Ann Zwinger recounts an enlarged sense of household found in her Colorado home; poet Kathleen Norris returns to the house built by her grandparents in *Dakota: A Spiritual Geography;* and in Wyoming, Gretel Ehrlich, in *The Solace of Open Spaces*, finds the strength to survive her partner's death. Instead of feeling alienated from the natural world, as nature writers often do, Western women replace the male metaphor of returning to the mother (earth) in order to possess her with a model of more reciprocal interaction. In the short story "Holy Dirt," Lisa Chewning, who lives in Pittsburgh, Pennsylvania, but plans to relocate to the Southwest, writes, "I possess the land and am possessed by it" (Wilder, I: 143). Commenting on this new generation of Southwest women writers, Wilder finds that "our words are who we are, and when we find ourselves in alignment with Earth and universe, the words flow" (Wilder, II: x).

Despite the environmental stance of many European-American women naturalists, the land for Hispanic and Native American women writers often exemplifies a heritage that is in conflict with dominant Anglo values. In *The Frontiers of Women's Writing: Women's Narratives and the Rhetoric of Westward Expansion*, the German scholar Brigitte Georgi-Findlay found a region where most literate women were white and middle class, advantages they used to impose their cultural values on the environment and its indigenous people (p. x). Moreover, many popular Anglo writers of the late nineteenth and twentieth century see the land as unstoried, as illustrated in the words of naturalist Florence Krall, who describes relatively unpopulated areas of the West as "undefiled land . . . where nature is untouched by the effects of civilization" (p. 6).

Unlike writers such as Krall, Hispanic writers did not see the land as a place of primal freedom to be imagined in their own words. Fabiola Cabeza de Baca, Cleofus Jaramillo, and Nina Otero Warren, all anthologized in *Infinite Divisions,* edited by Tey Diana Rebolledo and Eliana Rivero, were early-twentieth-century Nuevo Mexicana writers who felt the need to document what they believed was a vanishing cultural heritage. They saw their surroundings as a fertile, pastoral garden of Eden that was a symbol for describing the loss of land. In "Asking for the Bride," Otero Warren describes certain customs which were intended to "perpetuate the ruling class in the New Possessions" (p. 47). Jaramillo, in "Shadows of the Past," presents a similar view of "old-time customs and ways of living" (p. 57). According to Rebolledo, this feeling of change and loss extended also to longing for integration once more with nature (p. 98).

Nuevo Mexicanas of this period were writing in what Genaro Padilla terms "a language and idiom of cultural otherness [English as opposed to their native Spanish] that marks its boundaries of permissible autobiographic utterances" (p. 60). Although Padilla concludes that writing in an alien tongue resulted at times in an effort to placate the dominant audience, he also finds that these early Hispanas have "provided us the opening for clearly revisionary and resistive utterance" (p. 60). Many of the themes of early writers are represented in contemporary writing; references to folkloric elements of healing are made by contemporary women who, following the advice of Cabeza de Baca's "Herb Woman," write their memories into history. "You who can write need not rely upon memory only," this *curandera* tells her client, as she instructs her to "put down the prescriptions I give you each year" (p. 52). The "Herb Woman," combining the qualities of medicine woman, herbalist, and shaman, was portrayed by Cabeza de Baca as not only possessing more freedom of movement but, because she had never married, living outside the confines of society (p. 52).

Like the "Herb Woman," Pat Mora's "Curandera" translates into poetry the relationship between landscape, the mediator who "listens/to the desert" as she gathers herbs for healing, and the power of her resulting magic (p. 144). The *curandera*'s strength springs from knowing nature well: "She closes her eyes/and breathes with the mice and snakes/and wind" (p. 144). Her ability to transform herbs into healing ointments is an alchemical one, and this is a talent shared by the writer, as shown in another poem, "Clever Twist," in which she devises her formula for pulling out of a "tall, black hat" a completed verse (p. 278). Here magic has passed into the pen of the narrator/poet, but like ancient Nahuatl dualities, this modern *curandera*/writer has the capacity for destruction as well as ensuring health. She chooses to exorcise and control evil, for the "best revenge" (against the hold old traditions have on contemporary women's lives?) is "waving a sharp No. 2 pencil" . . . then "gently/ pulling out" a "bloomin' poem" (pp. 278–79).

Early nontribal women—Hispanic and European-American—had one point in common: they often viewed the land as object, as something to be controlled, reshaped, or feared. Native American women, on the other hand, saw it not as an object to be confronted, but rather as a set of entities possessing intelligence and personality and thus engaged in a ritual dialogue with people to ensure balance and harmony among all things. This worldview is well illustrated in the work of Leslie Marmon Silko, a writer steeped in the folklore of her Laguna Pueblo people. For Silko, the term "landscape" as commonly used is misleading because it "assumes the view is somehow outside or separate from the territory he or she surveys." Viewers, according to Silko, "are as much a part of the landscape as the boulders they stand on" (p. 267). Because this sense of reciprocity comes from tribal origin, it appears in the works of numerous other Native American women.

European-American women, as Vera Norwood shows, are also looking for reconnection with a wild terrain from which they have historically been excluded (*Made from This Earth*, 202). In *The Death of Nature*, Carolyn Merchant traces this exclusion to the early modern period, when women were first linked to chaotic nature and both were thought of as forces to be subdued (p. 127). The return to the wild zone of women's writing is apparent in Gretel Ehrlich's memoir, *Islands, the Universe, Home,* when she says that she has "come here [to Wyoming], to seek the wildness in myself and, in so doing, come on the wildness everywhere," because, she says, "I'm part of nature too" (p. 27). For Utah poet Nancy Takacs, there is a sense of recovering the wild in her strong desert women. The protagonist of "Painted Ladies," for example, chooses canyonland over city dwelling as her home. There she experiences a "one-in-a-lifetime / storm of those butterflies," Painted Ladies, in clouds so thick they settle everywhere around her home. Enchanted, and identifying with their wildness, she laments their inappropriate nomenclature, wishing for a different name, or better yet, "nothing, as wild as they / really are."

What if immersion into wilderness brings about its end? Glen Love, in his essay "Revaluing Nature: Toward an Ecological Criticism," calls for a new Western version of the pastoral, one that reverses the common pattern of entry into a green world in order to return (p. 235). However, fiction writers like Liza Besmehn are raising the question of what to do when "folks love [Edward] Abbey's country. Love it to death" ("When Redrocks Talk," 147). In Besmehn's "Desert Rhapsody," her protagonist retreats for several days of "quiet desolation" that end in an unexpected revelation. After noticing her newly made footpath to a nearby creek, she acknowledges that "my presence in the desert is changing it," so on the eighth day, "the desert sends me home" (p. 141).

In order to write at all, some women have had to live not only at the borders of urban and rural areas but also at the margins of their own cultures, where a multicultural perspective sometimes allows them to find a common ground, a space where cultures can be shared and sometimes a new one created. As the Cherokee anthropologist Rayna Green asserts, "identity" is no longer a "matter of genetic make-up or natural birthright," but rather, for people out on the edge, out on the road, "identity is a matter of will, a ceremonial act" (p. 7). Migration to the city has in some sense broken down regional and even ethnic ties, so that responses to this new urban landscape are the same whether the writers live in Albuquerque, New Mexico, or in Los Angeles.

As seen by the contemporary Chicana writer, the city is not the land of hope and opportunity. Yet it does challenge poets like Lorna Dee Cervantes to seek a new connection with the landscape. In "Beneath the Shadow of the Freeway," Cervantes creates a bridge between two landscapes—that of her grandmother's potted plants and her mother's association with the freeway— forging her own identity, "built/with my own hands" (Rebolledo and Rivero, 116). Native American people, particularly urban dwellers, have had to make similar adaptations in order to continue to live in the context of the land. Harjo's poems are often set in cities, especially from the point of view of an Indian woman traveling between them. She has claimed that "my overall sense of home means something larger than any place nameable in this land" (p. 76), and for Harjo, this often means turning to nature and the spirits that dwell there.

This sense of life and intelligence in the land is very different from human emotions that an

Anglo poet might project upon landscape. Harjo takes this knowledge with her as her work traces modern pan-Indian trails crisscrossing the country, recreating in the powwow circuit, the academic lecture circuit, and the poetry reading circuit the often involuntary wandering of her ancestral tribal people. Whether the road is Harjo's path to find herself in Creek country again or the freeway that often symbolizes destruction and progress in the literature of Chicanas writing from the Spanish-speaking barrios, these Western women writers have learned to stand in the middle and interpret for others the psychological space of living between two or more languages, cultures, and histories of their region.

Among recent writers who have looked to the rich and varied heritage of the Western past to find a regenerative and transforming sense of identity in the present is Gloria Anzaldúa, whose *Borderlands* perhaps sums up best themes covered in this chapter. The reconstruction of an ethnic past, the undertaking of metaphorical and literal journeys through the present-day United States, the negotiation of boundary areas inhabited by women of mixed heritages—such are the major issues of Anzaldúa's border feminism, an ideology that deconstructs geopolitical boundaries. "Here every Mexican grows flowers," Anzaldúa says of her birthplace, the valley of south Texas, located along borders with Mexico and the cultural borders of the Southwest. "If they don't have a piece of dirt, they use car tires, jars, cans, shoe boxes. Roses are the Mexican's favorite flower." And so, she thinks, "how symbolic—thorns and all" (p. 91).

As a *mestiza,* a lesbian and a feminist, Anzaldúa feels in a sense that she has no race or ethnic culture. She thus sees herself as a mediator, who can reinterpret history—thorns and all—in a new environment. Faced with conflicting models within her community, Anzaldúa used her ability at self-fashioning to break old and new forms apart. She need not accept mainstream feminist agendas or Chicano ideology; she is free to restructure the contradictory ideals of Anglo and Mexican cultures into a "continual creative motion that keeps breaking down the unitary aspect of each paradigm" (p. 80).

Note

1. When talking about the colonial Southwestern experience, the women are referred to as Spanish/Mexicans or Hispanas. After the Mexican National Period, they are known as Mexicana, and after 1848 as Mexicana or Mexican American or are identified by the regions in which they lived: Californias, Tejanas, Nuevo Mexicanas. I refer to these women writers after 1960 as Chicanas. This nomenclature is an attempt to be historically accurate as well as to define identity as the women would have defined themselves (*see* Rebolledo and Rivero, p. 7–14).

Selected Works and Further Reading

Alderson, Nannie, "A Pretty Hoorah Place," in *The Best of the West: An Anthology of Classic Writing from the American West,* edited by Tony Hillerman, New York: HarperCollins, 1991

Allen, Paula Gunn, ed., *Spider Woman's Granddaughters: Traditional Tales and Contemporary Writing by Native American Women,* Boston: Beacon, 1989; London: Women's Press, 1990

Anderson, Lorraine, ed., *Sisters of the Earth: Women's Prose and Poetry about Nature,* New York: Vintage, 1991

Anzaldúa, Gloria, *Borderlands/La Frontera,* San Francisco: Spinsters/Aunt Lute, 1987

Austin, Mary, *Land of Little Rain,* Boston: Houghton Mifflin, 1903; London: Constable, 1996

Ehrlich, Gretel, *Islands, the Universe, Home,* New York: Viking, 1991; London: Penguin, 1992

——, *The Solace of Open Spaces,* New York: Viking, 1985

Harjo, Joy, *The Spiral of Memory: Interviews,* edited by Laura Coltelli, Ann Arbor: University of Michigan Press, 1996

Hogan, Linda, *Dwellings: A Spiritual History of the Living World,* New York and London: Norton, 1995

Gould, Janice, *Earthquake Weather: Poems,* Tucson: University of Arizona Press, 1996

Green, Rayna, ed., *That's What She Said: Contemporary Poetry and Fiction by Native American Women,* Bloomington: Indiana University Press, 1984

Jeffrey, Julie, *Frontier Women: The Trans-Mississippi West, 1840–1880,* New York: Hill and Wang, 1979

Kolodny, Annette, *The Land Before Her: Fantasy and Experience of the American Frontiers, 1630–1860,* Chapel Hill: University of North Carolina Press, 1984

Krall, Florence, *Ecotone: Wayfaring on the Margins,* Albany: State University of New York Press, 1994

Love, Glen, "Revaluing Nature: Toward an Ecological Criticism," in *The Ecocriticism Reader: Landmarks in Literary Ecology,* edited by Cheryll Glotfelty and Harold Fromm, Athens: University of Georgia Press, 1996

Mora, Pat, "Clever Twist," in *Infinite Divisions: An Anthology of Chicana Literature,* edited by Tey Diana Rebolledo and Eliana S. Rivero, Tucson: University of Arizona Press, 1993

——, *Communion,* Houston, Texas: Arte Público, 1991

——, "Curandera," in *In Other Words: Literature by Latinas of the United States,* edited by Roberta Fernandez, Houston, Texas: Arte Público, 1994

Murphy, Patrick D., *Literature, Nature, and Other: Ecofeminist Critiques,* Albany: State University of New York Press, 1995

Norwood, Vera, *Made from This Earth: American Women and Nature,* Chapel Hill: University of North Carolina Press, 1993

——, "Women's Place: Continuity and Change in Response to Western Landscapes," in *Western Women, Their Land, Their Lives,* edited by Lillian Schlissel, Vicki Ruíz, and Janice Monk, Albuquerque: University of New Mexico Press, 1988

Padilla, Genaro, "Imprisoned Narrative? Or Lies, Secrets, and Silence in New Mexico Women's Autobiography," in *Criticism in the Borderlands: Studies in Chicano Literature, Culture, and Ideology,* edited by Hectór Calderón and José David Saldívar, Durham, North Carolina: Duke University Press, 1991

Rebolledo, Tey Diana, and Eliana S. Rivero, eds., *Infinite Divisions: An Anthology of Chicana Literature,* Tucson: University of Arizona Press, 1993

Rose, Wendy, *Bone Dance: New and Selected Poems, 1965–1993,* Tucson: University of Arizona Press, 1994

Silko, Leslie Marmon, "Landscape, History, and the Pueblo Imagination," in *The Ecocriticism Reader: Landmarks in Literary Ecology,* edited by Cheryll Glotfelty and Harold Fromm, Athens: University of Georgia Press, 1996

Takacs, Nancy, "Painted Ladies," *Petroglyph Magazine* (Fall 1996)

Wilder, Kathryn, ed., *Walking the Twilight: Women Writers of the Southwest,* Flagstaff, Arizona: Northland, 1994

——, *Walking the Twilight II: Women Writers of the Southwest,* Flagstaff, Arizona: Northland, 1996

Zepeda, Ofelia, *Ocean Power: Poems from the Desert,* Tucson: University of Arizona Press, 1995

Zwinger, Ann, *Beyond the Aspen Grove,* New York: Random House, 1970

Playing with Wor(l)ds: Science Fiction as Environmental Literature

Noel Gough

As an academic educator with unabashed ecopolitical commitments (*see* Gough, "Playing"), the standpoint from which I appraise science fiction (SF) and other environmental texts might best be described as "ecocritical." In an essay exploring principles of ecocriticism, William Howarth describes an ecocritic as "a person who judges the merits and faults of writings that depict the effects of culture upon nature, with a view toward celebrating nature, berating its despoilers, and reversing their harm through political action" (p. 69). This definition is, of course, a point of departure for Howarth's speculations, and I share his own reservations about its adequacy. Nevertheless, it serves the present purpose, which is to outline some of the qualities of SF that deserve ecocritical attention. If more attention is focused here on SF's merits than its faults, this is because of the belief that SF may have been relatively undervalued in many disciplines that subject environmental literature to critical scrutiny (*see* Gough, "Environmental," and Gough, "Neuromancing").

This article will also focus on the distinctive features of SF as environmental literature rather than on what it shares with more conventional forms of nature writing. For example, homages to solitude and wilderness, accounts of rambles in remote areas, and other reflections on experience in nature can be found in specific works of SF, such as Ursula K. Le Guin's meditation on scrub oaks in *Always Coming Home* (pp. 239–41)—an exemplary exercise in heightened attentiveness to nature. Furthermore, SF usually responds to the same cultural imperatives that motivate other nature writers, as Brian Aldiss and David Wingrove demonstrate by devoting a whole chapter of their comprehensive history of SF to "the flight from urban culture" that characterized many of the genre's most typical works

between the 1890s and the 1920s. Similarly, Frank Herbert's novel *Dune*, which he dedicated to "dry-land ecologists, wherever they may be," can be seen to reproduce what R. J. Ellis calls the "discourse of apocalyptic ecologism" generated in North America during the 1960s by books like Rachel Carson's *Silent Spring* (p. 104).

As a response to an environmental problem (in this case, massive desertification on the planet Dune), Herbert's story also displays some of SF's least admirable stereotypes, such as the assumption that virtually all problems are amenable to technical solutions (although *Dune* tends to emphasize appropriate and environmentally sensitive technology rather than high-tech gadgetry for its own sake). Less defensibly, given the novel's rhetoric of holistic approaches to environmental problems, Herbert does not explore collective and cooperative approaches to their resolution; the political power to intervene in *Dune's* ecology is invested in an individual—and another SF stereotype—an extraordinary and increasingly autocratic frontier hero. The hero is (of course) male, and *Dune* explicitly reproduces many of the patriarchal discourses that are so disabling in attempts to resolve social and environmental problems alike. However, the subordination of women in *Dune* is less obviously paralleled by the subordination of nature than it is in much SF, where, as Scott Sanders observes, "women and nature bear the same features: both are mysterious, irrational, instinctive; both are fertile and mindless; both inspire wonder and dread in the hero; both are objects of male conquest" (p. 42).

Herbert hoped that *Dune* would be "an environmental awareness handbook" and admitted that the title was chosen "with the deliberate intent that it echo the sound of 'doom'" (quoted in Ellis, 120). But the awareness Herbert sought might have been realized more effectively if he had focused on representing Dune's doom rather than having it "saved" by a macho demagogue, since one of the most significant and distinctive contributions that SF has made to environmental literature has been to represent the endless variety of ways in which life on earth can be destroyed. Stories of natural cataclysm and doom (supplemented by alien invasion, nuclear holocaust, and collisions or near-collisions with other planetary bodies) comprise one of SF's most enduring themes. Rehearsing the limitless possibilities for extinguishing life on earth might seem to be a rather strange way of celebrating nature, since the plethora of plagues, deluges, droughts, glaciations, and other global catastrophes imagined by SF writers can readily be interpreted as extended metaphors of our failed relationship with the earth—of our anxieties about, and alienation from, a threatening, hostile, and even vengeful nature. However, J. G. Ballard, author of *The Drowned World, The Drought*, and other stories of the earth in ecological ruin, is much nearer the mark when he asserts that stories of natural cataclysm are positive and constructive—that the authors of such stories use their imaginations to describe "the infinite alternatives to reality which nature itself has proved incapable of inventing. This celebration of the possibilities of life is at the heart of science fiction" (Ballard, "Cataclysms," 209).

While visions of nature gone awry are now firmly associated with SF, the type of literary imagination they represent is also exemplified in premodern stories, including the deluges in the Babylonian epic of Gilgamesh and the biblical tale of Noah's ark (*see also* Ruddick for an explanation of the significance of the deluge in twentieth-century SF). That natural catastrophe stories have become a species of SF reflects the cultural dominance of modern science in providing our basic understanding of nature. A contemporary story about the devastation wrought by a plague of locusts is more likely to offer a scientific (or plausibly pseudoscientific) explanation for its occurrence than to suggest that it is a manifestation of the wrath of Yahweh or some other supernatural force. But, rather than scientific explanations in themselves, it is the questions raised by science that tend to provide SF writers with their foci of speculation. From its earliest archetypes, such as Mary Shelley's *Frankenstein*—which, in its depiction of the creation of monstrous life, both invented and critiqued one of the first great myths of modern

industrial society—SF has exhibited a deeply ambivalent attitude toward science both as a cultural practice and as a body of knowledge. This ambivalence has become increasingly evident in postmodern culture and the fiction it produces, to the extent that the term "science fiction" has itself become problematic. Many writers and critics now take advantage of the inherent ambiguity of the acronym SF and, like Donna Haraway, use SF to signify "an increasingly heterodox array of writing, reading, and marketing practices indicated by a proliferation of 'sf' phrases: speculative fiction, science fiction, science fantasy, speculative futures, speculative fabulation" (p. 5).

Despite this ambivalence, SF as a form of environmental literature often displays explicit continuities with scientific discourses, especially among those authors who place in the foreground the current truth claims of the natural sciences in their depictions of the earth and other worlds. Some writers represent these claims faithfully and work within their limitations, whereas others question their narrative authority and adequacy. For example, in such stories as Arthur C. Clarke's "The Shining Ones" (which speculates on the life that might be found at extreme depths in the world's oceans) and "A Meeting with Medusa" (which speculates on the life that might be found in Jupiter's atmosphere), both of which appear in Clarke's collection, *The Wind from the Sun*, the author appears to accept without question that the discourse of Western biological science provides an appropriate language for representing both terrestrial and extraterrestrial organisms. Authors like Ursula K. Le Guin are more suspicious of such assumptions. Thus, for example, in "The Author of the Acacia Seeds and Other Extracts from the *Journal of the Association of Therolinguistics*," in *The Compass Rose*, Le Guin satirizes reductionist ethological constructions of animal behavior, and in "She Unnames Them," from *Buffalo Gals and Other Animal Presences*, she draws attention to the ways in which our cultural practices of naming might erode our sense of community with other organisms. Nevertheless, few SF stories ignore, flout, or deny the evidence of science. If they do, then as Le Guin asserts, "the writer must know it, and defend the liberty taken, either with a genuine hypothesis or with a sound, convincing fake" ("Escape," 203).

SF writers often seize on emerging scientific theories and explore the interpretive possibilities of their conceptual languages in new contexts.

For example, in Lewis Shiner's novel *Deserted Cities of the Heart*, the central character, Thomas, is an anthropologist investigating "the application of Ilya Prigogine's dissipative structures to the Mayan collapse, circa 900 A.D." (p. 24). Prigogine's theories provide Shiner with numerous images and metaphors, as in the following passage in which Thomas throws pebbles into a pond beneath a waterfall:

> The turbulence made them dance, two steps to the right, up for a second, then spinning off sideways and down. Waterfalls were very big in Chaos Theory, of which Prigogine's and Thomas' own work were just a part. According to classical physics the patterns should be predictable, because everything that went into them was quantifiable. Volume of water, depth of streambed, angle of gradient, everything. But the patterns were like living organisms, influenced by their own history and their reactions to each other, and they could never be nailed down.
>
> What does this tell us, he thought? (pp. 146–47)

In addition to its explicit reference to science, this passage gestures toward a deeper continuity between SF and scientific texts, which Damien Broderick describes as "attention to the object in preference to the subject" (p. 155). This object orientation is often manifested as a preoccupation with externalities and a corresponding de-emphasis of fine-grained characterization. Indeed, this attention to externalities may mark SF as an environmental literature par excellence, since the narrative development of SF stories tends to privilege the effects of environments on the actions of characters, in contrast to the character-driven action of more conventional realist fiction. Most SF stories speculate on possible human responses to alternative conditions—such as an overpopulated earth or the strange environs of another planet—and it is thus the alternative environment that takes priority in the writer's imagination rather than the characters who serve to demonstrate how the hypothetical conditions might affect humanity in general. This is not to say that the actors in SF stories are invariably featureless puppets, although this was undoubtedly true of much of the pulp magazine SF that dominated the field prior to World War II.

The need to explicate the salient features of an alternative environment as an integral aspect of a developing narrative structure provides a distinctive technical problem for authors of SF and may indeed be, as George Turner asserts, "the one innovatory technique that science fiction has added to the normal repertoire of the fiction writer" (p. 259). Certainly, this problem was not always resolved satisfactorily by some of the pioneer writers of the genre. For example, in *Twenty Thousand Leagues Under the Sea*, Jules Verne situates his speculations about how humans might live for extended periods of time under the world's oceans in the episodic account of the voyage of the submarine *Nautilus,* a nineteenth-century precursor of the starship *Enterprise,* boldly going where no one had gone before. But the story is frequently—and awkwardly—interrupted by Professor Aronnax's encyclopedic catalogues of the sea creatures and other "wonders" he encounters on the voyage, and by Captain Nemo's proto-environmentalist harangues against the irresponsible exploitation of marine resources. By way of contrast, in *The Island of Dr. Moreau*, H. G. Wells relies on allusion and inference, skillfully weaving evolutionary concepts into dialogue and action so as to interrogate the hitherto uncontested boundary between animals and humans that Charles Darwin made problematic.

Turner's own novel, *The Sea and Summer*, also demonstrates convincingly that attention to both object and subject are not irreconcilable. Turner imagines the rise and eventual collapse of a "greenhouse culture" in Australia during the twenty-first century. The effects of global warming on weather and food production are the background to a story of gritty social realism set in a drowning Melbourne. In one particularly insightful chapter, an old woman recalls "the annual glories of the sea and summer" that she enjoyed as a child and describes the gradual changes in the seasons and neighborhood gardens as the effects of rising carbon dioxide concentrations and sea levels became increasingly evident. As the chapter builds toward its moving conclusion ("the ageing woman has what the child desired—the sea and eternal summer") it evokes a palpable sense of loss as childhood memories are retrospectively soured by the consequences of the greenhouse effect.

SF's attention to alternative environments is particularly explicit in stories of other worlds—be they other planets or this world as it might have been or may yet be. Le Guin has produced a rich and extensive body of work in this vein—as author, critic, and teacher—that consistently demonstrates Aldiss and Wingrove's assertion that "good SF does not necessarily traffic in reality; but it makes reality clearer to us" (p. 14). For example, Le Guin's short story "The Eye Altering," begins with a woman, Miriam, standing at the window of an infirmary ward morosely contemplating the view she has looked at for 25 years. She contrasts the "sunlight, the orchards, the white cities" of her homeland with the dull and colorless vistas of New Zion, the perpetually haze-smothered planet on which she now resides: "through the haze the sun, no, not the sun, but NSC641 (Class G) burned swollen and vaporous . . . NSC641 stared, like a bleary eye. You could stare back at it. No glory of gold to blind you" (p. 166).

This story clearly demonstrates how the invention of alternative worlds enables SF to be (as Le Guin writes in "Prophets and Mirrors") "a way of seeing" our own world. At first Miriam's judgments about the qualities in nature that delight or displease the human eye seem eminently reasonable, such as her preference for the golden glory of Old Earth's blinding sun over the swollen and bleary eye of NSC641—indeed, they seem a *natural* choice. But as the story unfolds, we become aware of other ways of seeing. Genya, a "sickly" young man born on New Zion (and Miriam's patient since birth), paints the view from the ward window. To Miriam his painting is "all too realistic," a "hideously recognizable" depiction of "the mud-colored trees and fields, the hazy sky," but she also overhears another young patient ask Genya, "how do you make it so pretty?" (p. 176). It is only when Miriam sees Genya's painting quite literally in a different light that she realizes that to his "altered eye" New Zion is truly beautiful. This realization is metaphorically tied to the resolution of the central human problem that provides the story's narrative tension, which in broad terms concerns the fate of the "sicklies"; Miriam's "correct" diagnosis is enabled by a crucial perceptual shift—by "seeing" the medical problem differently. Thus Le Guin's story not only embellishes the maxim that "beauty is in the eye of the beholder" but also suggests that Miriam's aesthetic and scientific judgments are based on similar presuppositions—that in the epistemology of Old Earth, isomorphic assumptions guide both aesthetic responses to nature and the production of knowledge about its workings.

Le Guin is adept at weaving complex threads of ecology, ethics, language, and criticism into deceptively simple narratives. For example, her short story, "Sur: A Summary Report of the *Yelcho* Expedition to the Antarctic, 1909–1910,"

in *The Compass Rose*, is an apparently straightforward recollection by one member of a group of South American women who explore the Antarctic and reach the South Pole several years before Amundsen's and Scott's all-male expeditions. But as Marlene Barr demonstrates in her reading of "Sur" as an exemplary humanist and antihumanist text, the story also offers readers the opportunity to explore new articulations of the contradictory positions to be found within and between liberal (modernist) and postmodernist discourses of identity, gender, science, nature, and narrative. Through an accretion of small incidents, rather than the heroic gestures of androcentric adventure stories, Le Guin imagines women of color attending to nature in very different ways from European men—whether this be in terms of their treatment of penguins, their approaches to driving sleds and making camps, or the naming of topographical features.

Alternative world stories destabilize many modernist assumptions about the relationships between nature and culture, including the tendency for modern industrial societies to define nature as "other" to culture. In this respect, Brian McHale's thesis that SF is the characteristic genre of postmodernist fiction is pertinent:

> while epistemologically-oriented fiction (modernism, detective fiction) is preoccupied with questions such as: what is there to know about the world? and who knows, and how reliably? How is knowledge transmitted, to whom, and how reliably?, etc., ontologically-oriented fiction (postmodernism, SF) is preoccupied with questions such as: what is a world? How is a world constituted? Are there alternative worlds, and if so, how are they constituted? How do different worlds, and different kinds of world, differ, and what happens when one passes from one world to another, etc.? (p. 247)

Much SF addresses the question "How is a world constituted?" by drawing attention to the ways in which nature is constructed by textual and technological practices. For example, a number of SF stories attest to changes in the meanings of nature that are also apparent in our experience of weather. We may still be sensitive and attentive to the ways in which we engage physically with the weather, but we have also naturalized the technologies through which weather is presented to us as an abstraction. An allusion to this can be found in the first sentence of *Neuromancer*,

William Gibson's prototypical cyberpunk SF novel: "The sky above the port was the color of television, tuned to a dead channel" (p. 3); to interpret or forecast the weather we are more likely to look at television rather than the sky.

Many other SF stories depict ways in which our cultural activities—industrial pollution, urbanization, agribusiness—have literally constructed the greenhouse effect and other atmospheric changes. Bruce Sterling's novel *Heavy Weather* goes further by dramatizing the ways in which our knowledge of climate change is constructed by the global networks of satellites, weather stations, supercomputers, meteorologists, and broadcasters that produce the images, models, and simulations that materially represent such knowledge. *Heavy Weather* follows the exploits of "Storm Troupers"—a mobile commune of scientists, techno-freaks, and media artists—who chase storms in a fleet of secondhand buses housing customized computer labs and portable weather stations, and use robot "birds" linked to virtual reality rigs to "surf" into the eyes of hurricanes and other freakish phenomena that have emerged in the earth's "wrecked atmosphere" by the year 2031. In Sterling's novel it is clear that much of what counts as nature is the measurement and projection of human interactions with the biosphere in and on a virtual ecology of global information flows. In this sense, *Heavy Weather* imaginatively captures Berland's point that "the weather can no longer be considered 'natural' . . . but (like gender and other previously 'natural' concepts) must be understood as [a] socially constructed artifact" (p. 106).

As the technologies of virtual reality, simulation, and bioengineering compel us to renegotiate the boundaries between nature and culture, SF dramatizes our new ontological insecurities and rehearses possible responses to them. Unlike many other nature writers, authors of SF stories are under no obligation to represent either nature or people as they find them and are thus free to play with the people and environments they imagine. By playing with words and imagined worlds, SF writers can invite us to envision different and potentially less disabling relationships between people and environments. So long as they do this, SF writers will continue to receive ecocritical attention.

Selected Works and Further Reading

Aldiss, Brian W., and David Wingrove, *Trillion Year Spree: The History of Science Fiction,* New York: Atheneum, 1986; London: Victor Gollancz, 1986

Ballard, J. G., "Cataclysms and Dooms," in *A User's Guide to the Millennium: Essays and Reviews,* New York: Picador, 1996; London: HarperCollins, 1996

——, *The Drought,* London: Jonathan Cape, 1965; Boston: Gregg, 1976

——, *The Drowned World,* New York: Penguin, 1962; London: Victor Gollancz, 1962

Barr, Marleen S., "Ursula Le Guin's 'Sur' as Exemplary Humanist and Antihumanist Text," in *Lost in Space: Probing Feminist Science Fiction and Beyond,* Chapel Hill, North Carolina, and London: University of North Carolina Press, 1993

Berland, Jody, "On Reading 'The Weather'," *Cultural Studies* 8:1 (1994), pp. 99–114

Broderick, Damien, *Reading by Starlight: Postmodern Science Fiction,* New York and London: Routledge, 1995

Carson, Rachel, *Silent Spring,* Boston: Houghton Mifflin, 1962; London: Hamilton, 1963

Clarke, Arthur C., *The Wind from the Sun: Stories of the Space Age,* New York: Harcourt Brace Jovanovich, 1972; London: Victor Gollancz, 1972

Ellis, R. J., "Frank Herbert's *Dune* and the Discourse of Apocalyptic Ecologism in the United States," in *Science Fiction Roots and Branches: Contemporary Critical Approaches,* edited by Rhys Garnett and R. J. Ellis, New York: St. Martin's, 1990; London: Macmillan, 1990

Gibson, William, *Neuromancer,* New York: Ace, 1984; London: Victor Gollancz, 1984

Gough, Noel, "Environmental Education, Narrative Complexity and Postmodern Science/Fiction," *International Journal of Science Education* 15:5 (September 1993), pp. 607–625

——, "Neuromancing the Stones: Experience, Intertextuality, and Cyberpunk Science Fiction," *Journal of Experiential Education* 16:3 (1993), pp. 9–17

——, "Playing at Catastrophe: Ecopolitical Education After Poststructuralism," *Educational Theory* 44:2 (Spring 1994), pp. 189–210

Haraway, Donna J., *Primate Visions: Gender, Race, and Nature in the World of Modern Science,* New York: Routledge, 1989; London: Verso, 1992

Harding, Lee, ed., *The Altered I: Ursula K.*

Le Guin's Science Fiction Writing Workshop, New York: Berkley, 1978

Herbert, Frank, *Dune,* New York: Ace, 1965; London: New English Library, 1973

Howarth, William, "Some Principles of Ecocriticism," in *The Ecocriticism Reader: Landmarks in Literary Ecology,* edited by Cheryll Glotfelty and Harold Fromm, Athens: University of Georgia Press, 1996

Le Guin, Ursula K., *Always Coming Home,* New York: Harper & Row, 1985; London: Victor Gollancz, 1986

——, *Buffalo Gals and Other Animal Presences,* Santa Barbara, California: Capra, 1987; London: Victor Gollancz, 1990

——, *The Compass Rose,* New York: Harper & Row, 1982; London: Victor Gollancz, 1983

——, *Dancing at the Edge of the World: Thoughts on Words, Women, Places,* New York: Grove, 1989; London: Victor Gollancz, 1989

——, "Escape Routes," in *The Language of the Night: Essays on Fantasy and Science Fiction,* New York: Berkley, 1979

——, "Prophets and Mirrors: Science Fiction as a Way of Seeing," *The Living Light* 7:3 (1970), pp. 111–121

——, *The Word for World is Forest,* New York: Berkley, 1972; London: Victor Gollancz, 1977

McHale, Brian, *Constructing Postmodernism,* New York and London: Routledge, 1992

Ruddick, Nicholas, "Deep Waters: The Significance of the Deluge in Science Fiction," *Foundation* 42 (1988), pp. 49–59

Sanders, Scott, "Woman as Nature in Science Fiction," in *Future Females: A Critical Anthology,* edited by Marleen S. Barr, Bowling Green, Ohio: Bowling Green State University Popular Press, 1981

Shelley, Mary, *Frankenstein; or, The Modern Prometheus,* New York: Doubleday, 1817; London: Routledge, 1817

Shiner, Lewis, *Deserted Cities of the Heart,* New York: Doubleday, 1988

Sterling, Bruce, *Heavy Weather,* New York: Bantam, 1994; London: Millennium, 1994

Turner, George, "Science Fiction as Literature," in *The Visual Encyclopedia of Science Fiction,* edited by Brian Ash, New York: Harmony, 1977; London: Pan, 1977

——, *The Sea and Summer,* London: Faber and Faber, 1987; also published as *The Drowning Towers,* New York: Arbor House, 1987

Verne, Jules, *Twenty Thousand Leagues Under the Sea,* translated by Henry Frith, New York: Dutton, 1965; London: J. M. Dent, 1965

Wells, H. G., *The Island of Dr. Moreau,* New York: Stone & Kimball, 1896; London: Heinemann, 1896

Visual Symbolism and Aesthetic Constructions: National Landscapes in the Making of Finland

Maunu Häyrynen

Landscape has been a crucial element in the creation of the Finnish national self-image. In particular the lake-and-forest landscape is a well-established national icon, but other types of symbolic landscapes exist as well. These have gradually formed a representative system of landscapes, in which geographic and ethnic peripheries have played a prominent role. The concept of "national landscape" has only recently been introduced in Finland, nostalgically evoking the national set of landscapes and associating it with the history of nation-building and the agrarian past.

The international image of Finland is largely based on such nonverbal aspects of its culture as music, design, architecture, or the representation of landscape, a situation for which the language barrier may be held accountable. Foreign visitors have, on the one hand, traditionally assessed the Finnish landscape by the formal standards of the Sublime or the Picturesque and have accordingly been most attracted by rapids, fells, and other sights generally held as spectacular and exotic. On the other hand, the Finns have, after their national awakening in the early nineteenth century, striven intently for the international recognition of "typically Finnish" landscapes, such as the geographically specific lake-and-forest scenery. Inland lake landscape has been systematically utilized as a symbolic image in Finnish national propaganda both at home and abroad, overshadowing other regions or types of landscape.

There seem to be two kinds of implicit criteria for a national landscape. On the one hand, the landscapes have to be typical—that is, to exemplify every principal element of the Finnish landscape and that of the particular area in question. This feature gives the set a systematic and hierarchical structure, mimicking scientific discourse. On the other hand, they have to be unique: there has to be an individual aura that separates a site from the shapeless everyday landscape, deriving from extraordinary physical features, associations with the past, or the magic touch of art, and usually from more than one of these. It is usually experienced in the form of the Romantic gaze, commanding a panoramic view from above.

Not only the landscapes but also the national landscape imagery is divided into two categories—average and marginal landscapes: the stereotypical heartlands and the solitary boundary marks of the national space. In the various stages different dimensions of this duality are stressed: the old Sublime/Picturesque contradiction; the primeval wilderness versus the historic countryside; natural versus urban. These reflect the multifarious functions of the national set of landscapes: to measure up to the international conventions of landscape taste and to identify with the cultural centers, as well as to distinguish Finland from other nation-states.

The Early Image of Finland and Lapland

Before the eighteenth century, Finland was largely a European terra incognita. There had been vague literary remarks about Finns as an ethnic group starting from Tacitus (*Germania*), and the geography of Finland had been more or less reliably presented in maps since the sixteenth century. During the next century more accurate geographic maps, the first topographic maps as well as the first pictorial representations of Finnish landscapes, were produced. This initial interest, reflected, for example, in Eric Dahlberg's illustrated *Suecia antiqua et hodierna* (1667–1715), was a part of Swedish propaganda, with an emphasis on praising the magnificence of the absolutist state. According-ly, it focused on the few cities and castles of Finland, which as a whole was meagerly repre-sented. Although an ancient part of the king-dom, Finland was then considered a peripheral province of the multinational realm, and its specific features had no interest for the ruling elite.

In the early eighteenth century, Lapland start-ed to attract scientists and foreign travelers. (Lapland and Finland were then regarded as two separate areas, but a part of Lapland was later to be joined with Finland, as the country was ceded from Sweden to Russia in 1809.) During his travels in the north in 1732, Carl von Linné (Carolus Linnaeus) had still despised Lapland's barren scenery and ignorant population, betray-ing his classicist and rationalist inclination toward cultivated and prosperous landscapes (*see* von Linné 1889).

Only four years later, however, Lapland was made internationally known by the visit of the expedition sent by the French Academy to meas-ure the shape of the earth. The expedition's leader, Marquis Pierre-Louis Moreau de Mau-pertuis, used the new vocabulary of the Sublime in describing the harsh landscape in an other-wise arid scientific report (de Maupertuis, 118–119). Maupertuis's account became widely known and cited in Europe. One of the best-known references to it was in the revised edition of James Thomson's 1746 poem *The Seasons*, in which he had inserted new verses with toponyms referring to the places Maupertuis had visited ("Winter," *The Seasons*).

As a newly discovered and exotic end of the earth, Lapland received more attention than did Finland proper, causing constant confu-sion between the geographic areas and the eth-nic groups and, subsequently, resentment among the Finns for being equated with the allegedly primitive and Mongoloid Sámi (Hirn). At the same time, a number of foreign visitors were attracted to the area that Maupertuis had described, both before and after 1809. One of the principal interests was the midnight sun, which could be seen around the summer solstice even from heights below the polar circle, the Aavasaksa fell being the most renowned of them (and also within an easy reach from the coast). For the more adventurous there was the route to the North Cape, abounding with fresh material for travel books and *voyages pittoresques*, that

could be published afterwards for the Sublime-thirsty European public.

Finnish Landscape Takes Shape

After Sweden had lost its Baltic provinces and most of Karelia to Russia in 1721, Sweden's strategic interest gravitated to South Finland, which during the rest of the century turned into one of the best-mapped and best-fortified parts of northern Europe. Apart from the military reconnaissance, the general parceling out of land produced accurate large-scale maps from the most inhabited part of the country. The carto-graphic activity made common knowledge of the topographic characteristics of inner Finland, an area which had largely been avoided by trav-elers because of bad rail connections. The first published representation of an inland lake land-scape was, appropriately, on the title page of the volume covering Finland in S. G. Hermelin's 1799 atlas of Sweden. The purpose of the pic-ture was merely to present a sample of the Finnish topography rather than introduce it as a new subject for landscape art. The *voyages pit-toresques* published at the same time still con-centrated on the townscapes, monuments, and estates of the coastal areas and on the wild scenes of fells and rapids.

Consciousness of Finland as a country of its own and of the Finns as a nation became more acute after its union with Russia in 1809. Finland had become an autonomous part of the empire with its own administration, preserving its legis-lation and Swedish as its official language. Finnish scholars, who under Swedish rule had already striven for the establishment of the idea of a distinct Finnish culture, continued to collect information about folk poetry and art, local habits, vernacular-building forms, and other tokens of nationhood. A parallel was even drawn between Finland, Switzerland, and Greece as countries with a well-preserved mythology and an austere nature (Klinge).

Tourism gradually became more organized. Special efforts were made to inform the Russian aristocracy about the true character of their last conquest: a persistent view of Finland in St. Petersburg was that of a cold, wild, sterile, and boring country inhabited by "sad stepsons of Nature," using Alexander Pushkin's words. The polite remarks of Tsar Alexander I during his visits to Finland about the "Italian" beauty of landscape were a meager consolation to his new subjects.

The "Picturesque moment" of Finland, using Christopher Hussey's term, dawned with Carl von Kügelgen, an artist of German origin employed by the Emperor to create a collection of views from the Grand Duchy, *Vues pittoresques de Finlande*. These were systematically acquired from the southern part of the country, including some lake and seacoast landscapes beside towns, ironworks, and historic monuments. The aim of the work was to present Finland as a country that was civilized and industrious but also well endowed with natural beauty. Accordingly, nature was represented as of a central European type, lush and deciduous. Von Kügelgen was the first to depict Finnish landscape systematically employing the techniques and conceptual framework of the Picturesque. According to him, the small-scale variation of land and water provided endless artistic opportunities (von Kügelgen, Pl. 5 and 6).

The Beginning of Nation-Building

The discovery of the picturesqueness of the Finnish landscape was met with anxiety by the rising nationalist movement in the mid–nineteenth century. (At that time, Finland was also made internationally known in the context of the Crimean War, which also was fought in the Baltic.) New individual landscapes were discovered from the inland regions, the most important among them the Punkaharju esker and the Imatra rapids (or "waterfall," as they were called). They were located in an area that had belonged to Russia since 1743 and had been reunited with the Grand Duchy of Finland in 1812. Both landscapes had been honored by imperial visits before the reunion. For the next 100 years they formed the principal attractions for tourists coming from St. Petersburg. Both were exceptional sights: the Imatra rapids were the greatest of the continent by their water volume, whereas Punkaharju was Finland's longest single stretch of esker traversing a watercourse. Imatra became the most important attraction for foreign tourists, whereas Punkaharju became a hallowed site for Finns themselves.

The two principal advocates of the Finnish landscape during the nineteenth century were the national poet Johan Ludvig Runeberg and Zachris Topelius, who has been characterized by W. R. Mead as "the Walter Scott, Alfred Tennyson and H. C. Andersen of Finland" (p. 12). Runeberg wrote the words of the national anthem, "Vårt Land" ("Our Country"), which

was first published in Swedish in 1848 (*Fänrik*, 1: 3). In it he presents the lake landscape as a Finnish *locus amoenus*, inviting the citizens to "... gladly point to sea and strand/And say: "Behold it, far and near/Our native land so dear! (*Tales*, 5). In another well-known poem, "Dån 5 Juli," he made a seasoned warrior point at a sunny lake landscape for a youthful student, asking him whether he could die defending it as others had done before (*Fänrik* 2: 47) (these poems have been discussed by Matti Klinge).

Topelius published in 1845 *Finland framstäldt i teckningar* ("Finland Represented in Pictures"), which included every significant monument, town, and factory as well as a number of natural and farming landscapes. The latter either were associated with historic events or persons or, again, were typical representatives of a region, carefully chosen from a large quantity of material. The intention of the book was to "unite into a whole pictures from the various parts of the country, its most beautiful and remarkable areas, as well as to thus give an as visible picture as possible of the country's Nature" (my translation). Another influential book by him was *Boken om Vårt Land* ("The Book about Our Country") in 1875, originally intended as a school reader in geography and history, which eventually found its way into almost every home in numerous reprints. It represented the people and landscape of the various regions as a family of equal members, the place of honor nevertheless given to the panoramic lake landscape.

The initial promoter of Punkaharju was Runeberg, who found it to be closer to his ideal of a beautiful and harmonic natural landscape than the tumultuous Imatra. Punkaharju was closer to a pastoral landscape, natural and yet idealized. In addition, it could be regarded as more Finnish: rapids and waterfalls existed nearly everywhere, but glacifluvial ridges surrounded by a lake landscape were something not many countries could boast. Punkaharju was picturesque in the sense of William Gilpin and Uvedale Price. A visitor moving along the ridge saw an ever-changing play of light and shadow forming a series of views over the lakes on either side, seen through the trunks of the pine forest and thus combining the two principal elements of the Finnish landscape in an unusual way. In this respect Punkaharju was not unique, but none of the comparable sites had better connections—a main road, later accompanied with a railway.

The central part of the esker became protected in 1840, with the protection taking effect in

1842. In praising its landscape, Topelius was followed by other authors such as the landscape photographer Into Konrad Inha. The latter praised the site in sacred terms, comparing its pine trunks to the pillars of a church. In spite of the numerous literary descriptions, Punkaharju inspired relatively few painters, perhaps due to its excessive popularity as a tourist spot. It was later rediscovered with the arrival of aerial photography, which for the first time enabled an overall view of the site.

Landscape could be used as a seemingly innocent political allegory under pressure from the Russian administration, when more explicit symbols were attacked by censorship. Thus Topelius drew a daring parallel between the Imatra rapids and oppressed nations fighting their way to freedom. Imatra was more commonly represented as an awesome force of nature, irresistibly attracting people to lunge into the stream (much like Niagara Falls in North America).

Unlike the harmonic scenery of Punkaharju, overwhelming natural sights such as Imatra were not admired unreservedly by the Finnish patriots. According to Topelius, it was a patriotic duty for the Finns to settle and cultivate the country, thus promoting civilization and Christianity in the north. This reveals the persistence of the Enlightenment in Finland: while the foreigners came to Finland to see nature untamed—as in the violent surge of Imatra—the Finns wanted to see the utilization and conquest of nature. This goal, however, was hampered by the scant economic and human resources manifested in the destitute poverty of the peasantry and posing a problem for the creators of the national image. As much as Finland was striving for a place among nations, it could not compete with their economic or cultural resources, including landscape.

Runeberg's solution was to render as heroic the Finnish inland as a harsh but beautiful landscape, the inhabitants of which struggled bravely for their sheer subsistence. The divine presence of nature elevated the thoughts in spite of the poverty that regularly forced people to eat bread made of pine bark. Runeberg's heroes were toiling and God-fearing peasants who did not grumble over their lot, neither did they aspire for a grand future.

While Runeberg aesthetically rendered the misery of the countryside into a picture of Georgic honesty and innocence, Topelius advocated economic and social improvements: for him, the morality of the landscape was in exploiting it rather than in dying or starving for it. The forests were there to be reclaimed and harvested; the lakes were important waterways.

It should be borne in mind that the idealized lake-and-forest landscape was a creation of the Swedish-speaking educated class, for whom the discovery of the inland Finns was a revelation. The allegedly uncorrupted Finnish-speaking peasant or soldier was the first "other" to be utilized in the national self-definition, together with the inland landscape.

The Landscapes of National Romanticism

Toward the end of the nineteenth century, Finnish society underwent major changes: industrialization began, cities expanded, the Finnish language was given an official status, and national cultural institutions were founded. A Finnish educated class emerged, becoming interested in the roots of its own language as well as the culture of the more remote and exotic parts of Finland. They were pioneered by the Fennoman students rambling about their fatherland during the mid-nineteenth century. Traveling was aided by improved maps and roads as well as waterway connections. Particular attention was given to the eastern border, from both sides of which Finnish folk poetry had been collected and published by Elias Lönnrot in the form of the national epic *Kalevala* (first edition 1835).

Unlike other Scandinavian nationalist movements, the Fennomans largely turned their backs on history as a basis for national identity, dominated by foreign nations as it had been. In its stead came folklore, which was regarded as an unambiguous testimony of a primeval and heroic past. The deep forests of the east, which had preserved this tradition, became the Finnish mythical Urwald and the alleged origin of the national culture. At the same time, the Orthodox Karelians living in the area were regarded as exotic and original much as the Bardic Welsh or the Ossianic Scots had been in eighteenth-century Britain. Karelia could also be seen as a Finnish frontier, the stage of the nation's Manifest Destiny. The continuation of the landscape across the border was also used as an argument for national expansionism.

The new landscapes were much more rugged in character than the picturesque lake landscape had been. Deserted wilderness became an acceptable subject for the paintings of Akseli Gallen-Kallela, Eero Järnefelt, and Albert Edelfelt.

Gallen-Kallela even built his atelier in its midst, to be followed by other artists of the National Romanticist movement. As in North America, "sublime geology," such as peculiar rock formations, precipices, and fault valleys, was sought after, and the awakening tourism followed closely on the artists' heels. The Swedish-speaking minority found the austere maritime landscape to be their particular variant of primeval landscape, corresponding to their Viking origin myth.

Finnish national romanticism had an escapist character. Students, scholars, and artists traveled in practically uninhabited wildernesses, trying to avoid meeting each other, and the latter erected castle-like timber residences in the middle of nowhere. The Karelianists systematically collected ornaments, tunes, and other folk traditions from both sides of the border. The foremost of the Karelianist national landscapes were the heights of Koli in North Karelia, a white quartzite ridge overlooking a wide lake and surrounding forests by the Russian border. The site was discovered in 1893 and quickly attracted the cream of Finnish artists to capture its outline in paintings, photographs, and literary descriptions, it having also been romantically associated with Sibelius' music. A local attraction was the still ongoing archaic slash-and-burn cultivation, contributing to the bright autumn colors of the heights by maintaining the deciduous pioneer forests. The artists were almost immediately followed by the development of tourism of the site.

Political symbolism was added to the dramatic character of the landscape during the attempted Russification of Finland at the turn of the century. Koli epitomized the beautiful country in distress—nature sharing the people's ordeal. The protection of Koli's central parts was carried out as an experimental area of the Finnish forest research institute in 1923; this did not prevent the later establishment of a ski resort. Koli was visited almost exclusively by Finns, being located slightly off the beaten path for foreigners.

Tourism and the Rediscovery of Lapland

The arctic Upper Lapland was avoided by the National Romantic movement, although it became the object of increasing research activity. It had to wait until the independence of 1917 and the nation's recovery from its devastating civil war before its landscapes became recognized. The fell of Aavasaksa had retained its old fame, and the Kuusamo area by the Russian border had been connected by the painter Akseli Gallen-Kallela with the Karelianist movement, but there had been no interest in the upper north until the railway reached central Lapland in the 1930s. After that, Aavasaksa was all but forgotten, as higher and more spectacular fells emerged nearer and above the polar circle.

Lapland was a landscape for consumption to start with; it was marketed for the tourists as a wild and exotic country with reindeers and picturesque natives (the Lapps, or Sámi), far from the cities' madding crowd. This was especially the case with Petsamo, Finland's new corridor to the Polar Sea and also called its first colony. The state started to establish national parks in Lapland in order to preserve the beauty of nature and to encourage the rapidly evolving winter sports. There was no significant artistic movement to discover the Lapland landscapes, but they became stock items in numerous popular photographic books.

After independence, tourism achieved mass proportions and more remote areas became generally accessible, first of all northern Lapland. It was originally pictured as an exotic, not quite Finnish part of the country and a landscape of touristic consumption. An important step for the Lapland landscape in becoming a national symbol was the founding of Finland's first national parks in 1938, most of which were located there. Another regional type of landscape that was promoted after independence was the cultivated plain of Ostrobothnia. Despite being an atypical Finnish landscape, it became a symbol for land reclamation, free peasantry and extreme right-wing patriotism. This view had been enhanced by the particular role of the area in the civil war. Even the maritime landscapes were assumed as common national symbols, advertising the unity of the nation in spite of its linguistic division.

World War II upset the national set of landscapes, since many important sites were left behind the new border and subsequently were only remembered nostalgically or else forgotten. This bitter loss contradicted the claim of the country's organic integrity. In a certain way Lapland had to replace the ceded Karelia as the new Finnish frontier, the virgin land of reclamation and new opportunities. On the one hand, Lapland became more ruthlessly exploited than any other part of the country—by clear-cutting, mining, and damming the rivers—and, on the other, it became for the remaining part the ultimate landscape of consumption: the celebrated land of skiing, trekking, salmon, and Santa Claus. Once again the images of Lapland were assumed to be symbols of the entire country, above all in travel advertisements.

In the south, postwar urbanization changed the outlook of the countryside and sharpened the antagonism between the city and the country, as new generations learned to know the latter increasingly as a nostalgic place of memories or an environment for recreation. Despite the key role of landscape in the construction of the Finnish national identity, the expression "national landscape" was only introduced in Finland 10 to 15 years ago. Initially, the term was exclusively connected with the Koli heights, which were referred to as *the* national landscape of Finland. In the middle of the debate on European integration, however, an official listing of the Finnish national landscapes was commissioned by the Ministry of the Environment. The definition was simple enough: a landscape that the average Finn could not picture in his or her mind could not be a national landscape. To qualify, a landscape had to be easily conceivable and commonly known and have a "generally recognized significance for [the Finnish] national culture, history or the image of [the] country's Nature." It also had to represent some topographically distinct part of the country. As a result, all together 27 well-known landscapes were listed from around Finland and presented in a report (*National Landscape*).

In this and other instances, Finnish national landscapes have been turned into objects of nostalgia, symbols of an alleged national golden age associated with the nation-building process and the agrarian past. Development projects or encroachments threatening national landscapes have during recent years been met with fierce nationwide protests. The revival of landscape as a national symbol evidently represents to the Finns an element of continuity and security in a world of turbulent changes. Presenting and conserving national landscapes as public amenities may help the current political power to absorb the "future shock" by assuring the public of official commitment to traditional national values and to the welfare state.

To conclude, landscape has been used in the process of Finnish national self-definition in several successive stages: first in the form of the inland lake landscape, discovered by the Swedish-speaking elite of the coastal towns, then in the form of the Urwald/frontier in Karelia, and most recently in the form of Lapland as the last wilderness. In the course of history, the landscape seems to have lost little of its symbolic power. On the contrary, the national set of landscapes has repeatedly been reactivated during turning-point situations, such as wars and other national crises, but also under the ongoing structural change and the integration process. For the urbanized Finns, the countryside remains a symbolic frame of reference. It is also becoming a new basis of national identity, either as a network of institutionally protected sites and areas or as an idealized past.

Selected Works and Further Reading

Anderson, Benedict, *Imagined Communities: Reflections on the Origin and Spread of Nationalism,* London: Verso, 1983; New York: Verso, 1991

Andrews, Malcolm, *The Search for the Picturesque: Landscape Aesthetics and Tourism in Britain, 1760–1800,* Stanford, California: Stanford University Press, 1989; Aldershot, England: Scolar, 1989

Bermingham, Ann, *Landscape and Ideology: The English Rustic Tradition, 1740–1860,* Berkeley: University of California Press, 1986; London: Thames & Hudson, 1987

Daniels, Stephen, *Fields of Vision: Landscape Imagery and National Identity in England and the United States,* Cambridge: Polity, 1992; Princeton, New Jersey: Princeton University Press, 1993

Gilpin, William, *Three Essays: On Picturesque Beauty; On Picturesque Travel; and On Sketching Landscape,* London: R. Blamire, 1792

Hewison, Robert, *The Heritage Industry: Britain in a Climate of Decline,* London: Methuen London, 1987

Hipple, Walter, *The Beautiful, the Sublime, and the Picturesque in Eighteenth-Century British Aesthetic Theory,* Carbondale: Southern Illinois University Press, 1957

Hirn, Yrjö, "Suomi ja Lappi: Muuan vanha väärinkäsitys ulkolaisessa matkakirjallisuudessa" [Finland and Lapland: An Old Misunderstanding in Foreign Travel Literature], in *Matkamiehiä ja tietäjiä: Tutkielmia suomalaisesta sivistyksetä ja Kalevala–romantiikasta* [Travelers and Seers: Treatises on Finnish Culture and the Kalevala Romanticism], Helsinki, Finland: Otava, 1939

Hussey, Christopher, *The Picturesque: Studies in a Point of View,* New York and London: Putnam's, 1927

Inha, Into Konrad, *Suomen maisemia* [Landscapes of Finland], Porvoo, Finland: Söderström, 1909

Jones, Michael, "The Elusive Reality of Landscape: Concepts and Approaches in Landscape Research," *Norsk Geografisk tidsskrift* [Norwegian Geological Journal] 45 (1991), pp. 229–244

Klinge, Matti, *The Finnish Tradition: Essays on Structures and Identities in the North of Europe,* Helsinki, Finland: Societas Historica Finlandiae [Finnish Historical Society], 1993

——, "Die neuen Griechen der Berge" [The New Greeks of the Mountains], in *Bausteine: Die Schweiz und Finnland im Spiegel ihrer Begegnungen* [Building Stones: Switzerland and Finland in the Light of Their Countries], Jahrbuch für finnisch-deutsche Literaturbeziehungen [Yearbook of Finnish-German Literary Relations] 23, edited by Ingrid Schellbach-Kopra and Marianne Grünigen, Zurich, Switzerland: Verlag Neue Zürcher Zeitung, 1991

Kügelgen, Carl von, *Vues pittoresques de Finlande* [Picturesque Views of Finland], St. Pétersbourg, 1823–1824

Linné, Carl von, *Lapplandsresa* [Tour in Lapland], 1889

Lowenthal, David, *The Past Is a Foreign Country,* New York and Cambridge: Cambridge University Press, 1985

Maupertuis, Pierre-Louis Moreau de, *La figure de la terre, déterminée par les observations,* Amsterdam, The Netherlands: Jean Catuffe, 1738; as *The Figure of the Earth Determined from Observations Made by Order of the French King, at the Polar Circle,* London: T. Cox, C. Davis, J. and P. Knapton, and A. Millam, 1738

Mead, W. R., *The Geographical Tradition in Finland,* London: H. K. Lewis, 1963

National Landscape, Helsinki, Finland: Ministry of the Environment, 1994

Runeberg, Johan Ludvig, *Fänrik Ståls sägner: en samling sånger,* Chicago: Hawkinson and Engberg, 1865; as *The Tales of Ensign Stål,* translated by Charles Wharton Stork, Princeton, New Jersey: Princeton University Press, 1938

Topelius, Zacharias, *Boken om vårt land: Läsebok för de lägsta läroverken i Finland: andra kursen* [The Book About Our Country], Helsingfors, Finland: G. W. Edlund, 1905

——, *Finland framstäldt i teckningar* [Finland Represented in Pictures], Helsingfors, Finland: A. W. Groendahl and A. Oehman, 1845–1852

Turner, James, *The Politics of Landscape: Rural Scenery and Society in English Poetry, 1630–1660,* Cambridge, Massachusetts: Harvard University Press, 1979; Oxford: B. Blackwell, 1979

Green Cultural Studies

Jhan Hochman

Green cultural studies is the study of nature once removed, a metastudy trained on nature study or, better, representations of nature. Within cultural studies, green or otherwise, representation presently falls overwhelmingly under the general categories of discipline and cultural formation, word and image. Under discipline, green cultural study of science's representations of and behavior toward nature are primary. In the United States, Donna Haraway and Andrew Ross are the best-known theorists in science studies. Cultural formation can include everything from "Disney to the Exxon Valdez," as Alexander Wilson puts it in the subtitle to his paradigmatic green cultural studies text, *The Culture of Nature*. Andrew Ross, in *Strange Weather,* examines the relations of nature to New Age culture, science fiction, and futurology. The categories of word and image encompass mass media, comics, and advertising. Separately, word could include the study of nature appearing in virtually any form of writing or speech, but falls overwhelmingly within the debated category of literature. Under image, one would find studies of represented nature in the fine arts and photography.

There is, however, one notable bug in this taxonomic machine: writing, specifically literature, has already been colonized and named by literary studies, or English, this discipline having a longer history of addressing writing's relationship to nature. One notable example is Leo Marx's *The Machine in the Garden*. For the last few years, the label "ecocriticism" has been attached increasingly to literary criticism focused on representations of nature. While disciplinary territoriality might lead to literary study's hostility toward or suspicion of the young and ambitious upstart of green cultural studies, a time might eventually come when ecocriticism is understood as a subset of the more expansive category (even as green cultural stud-

ies pays homage to ecocriticism for a portion of its inspiration and methodology).

There is one final area suitable to include within green cultural studies: history. Several indispensable volumes deal with the history of human ideas about nature, or behaviors toward what may be called worldnature (plants, nonhuman animals, elements[1]). The most important of these include R. G. Collingwood's *The Idea of Nature,* Clarence J. Glacken's *Traces on the Rhodian Shore,* and Keith Thomas's *Man and the Natural World*. Such texts aid the green cultural studies theorist in understanding what Raymond Williams meant when he said, "Nature is perhaps the most complex word in the [English] language" (p. 219).[2]

Andrew Ross seems to have been first to demarcate green cultural studies (hereafter abbreviated GCS) as a subdiscipline, calling for a "green cultural criticism" in 1991. Still, Donna Haraway has been on the trail of cultural nature by way of an examination of science since 1978. While Ross and Haraway both critique technology and science, their difference lies primarily in Ross's greater interest in culture and Haraway's more consistent and forceful focus on culture and nature. Although GCS need not be part of a clear agenda for nature, the environmentalist implications of the term "green" are clear. As a result, texts targeting nature and environmentalism for the purpose of nature's exploitation at the hands of cultural expansion are not included as part of GCS.

Culture's double utilization of nature—its flesh as the basis of, or obstruction to, material construction; and its presence or being as ground of representation—necessitates a "green cultural criticism," or better, "green cultural studies." While green cultural criticism is apt, green cultural studies more effectively links green concerns with the many-headed politico-ethical family of cultural studies. At present, cultural studies' prevailing interests are with texts and practices having impact upon people affected, especially adversely, by categories of ethnicity or color, gender, sexuality, economic class, and age (particularly youth subcultures). The inclusion of nature, or what I have already called here "worldnature," is consistent with the aims of race, class, etc., in that worldnature is also adversely affected, not just by a segment of culture but by culture as a whole. While some cultural impact on worldnature is, of course, unavoidable, it is the greater part of exorbitant cultural activity that gives special importance to GCS, the cultural arm of a politics of nature. GCS, then, positions itself as a comprehensive critique of both cultural praxis (theoretical action) and practice (action less theoretical than traditional or habitual), taking little for granted about culture: the "good life" promised by increased knowledge, wealth, and civility is an especial foil for its critique.

History

Cultural studies began in green. Stuart Hall paid tribute to the field's "Ur-texts"—the works not only of Gramsci, but those of the Frankfurt school translated into English in the 1970s (p. 16). In 1944, Horkheimer and Adorno had already theorized alienation from and (Baconian) "blind domination" of nature as the central problem of Enlightenment reason (p. 42). If, for Horkheimer and Adorno, such reason could be turned against itself, or if culture's grounding in nature could be recalled, the subject might come to understand the "truth" of culture: "By virtue of this remembrance of nature in the subject, in whose fulfillment the unacknowledged truth of all culture lies hidden, enlightenment is universally opposed to domination" (p. 40). Horkheimer and Adorno's assertion is crucial for cultural studies—first, because culture can be inferred to grow out of—without being determined by—nature. Therefore, culture neither generates nor wholly perpetuates itself but is everywhere embedded in, and dependent upon, nature. Second (following from the first), "remembrance" of nature propels one toward grounding and critiquing culture—and, especially pertinent for cultural studies, toward theorizing ways out of domination. Third and most important, Horkheimer and Adorno notice and object to increased cultural blurring—even reversal—of traditional roles of nature and culture; they stand opposed to reified, given, naturalized

culture and to nature as an unnatural realm for humans, a situation arising from, and leading to, culture substituting itself for nature. Horkheimer and Adorno's critique of blurring and reversing the roles of nature and culture later becomes a positive trait in a post-structuralist/postmodernist cultural studies.

Consistent with the Frankfurt school's culture critique, Slack and Whitt find that "the project of cultural studies is grounded on a moral and political critique of late capitalism, and more generally of oppressive cultural and social formations" (p. 572). Following Slack and Whitt's first point, nothing is so routinely subjugated and destroyed by late capitalism (and by Marxist/ communist industrialization) as are plants, animals, and elements. As to their second point—this being the crucial rationale for green cultural studies—the capitalist/communist flattening of nontextual nature contributes to and is influenced by a "flattened" textual nature produced by "oppressive cultural and social formations." Material and representational impact is reciprocal and double, easily reifying nature as a realm in which to apply multiple manipulations and annihilations euphemistically labeled as "research," "improvement," and "development."

More recent patriarchs of cultural studies proper—Raymond Williams, Richard Hoggart and E. P. Thompson—make the case for a genuine working-class culture and history against royal or bourgeois histories, and against working-class culture's displacement by "mass" or "popular culture." In general terms, the three theorists, informed by Marxism, conceive of workers as the locus of instrumentalism and deculturation not only by repressive (police and military) and ideological (schools, churches, families) state apparatuses (Althusser, 143), but additionally, or more specifically, by the spread of popular or mass culture. Thus, workers and working-class culture become the first branches of nascent culture study, with roots in Marx. While Marx saw nature as matter, raw material, and "tool house" (*Capital*, 283–285), nature was for him the foundation of culture, of cultural labor. Despite the deadness of Marxian nature, it remains, even if backgrounded and underfoot, the foundation of cultural work and study.

Leaving aside cultural studies arguments about the degree to which individuals are entirely and inescapably dominated from above (interpellation), or accept, consent to, or struggle within a dominating framework (hegemony), cultural studies recognizes, at bottom, political and social power directed at a vast group of raced, classed, gendered, sexualized, and aged people(s) by a small, traditionally unmarked group, increasingly recognized as wealthy, Western, white, heterosexual, adult males. But what cultural studies has recognized only recently is the overclass's characterization of subalterns in terms used to anathematize nature. Poverty, femaleness, color, or youth are labeled as problems in part through their traditional linkage to culture's reified notions of negative nature: unrestrained sexuality, reproduction, passivity, violence, eating, speech, and incivility, not to mention insufficient hygiene and education. Nature's inclusion in cultural studies is thus reciprocally important: first, since nature is made abject in similar terms and by similar practices to people, attention to nature's treatment (actual or representational) provides insights into general theories of power and domination, into numerous connections between repressions and dominations; second, green cultural studies can overturn the inessential definition of nature as mere matter—dead or not fully alive—and to reconfigure it as essential, a nature that matters. Such a nature stands to gain increased theoretical and geographic space within, and despite, cultural expansionism.

Problems/Obstacles

Within the larger centrist political backlash of the 1990s against "environmentalist extremists" and the leftist castigation of environmentalism as too white and too concerned with "lesser" or "soft" issues, nature faces more specific representational hazards when included in cultural studies. First, the terms "natural," "naturalness," and "naturalized" have become cultural studies synonyms of older Marxist terms, "reified" and "essentialized," these latter words referring especially to unquestioned acceptance of Western civilization, an artificial edifice become too natural (Lukács 83). The negative connotation of natural or naturalize as "unquestioned" then becomes attached to culture's unquestioned ideas about nature, finally reaching an apogee with cultural studies' avoidance of the very word, nature, unless rendered conditionally or negated by usurping quotation marks ("nature").

Contrary to the marketplace use of nature and natural to confer positive values on products, cultural studies understands the linguistic derivatives of nature as redolent of the incorrigible constrictions of "natural determinism":

Cultural studies defines itself in part . . . through its ability to explode the category of "the natural"—revealing the history behind those social relations we see as the products of a neutral evolutionary process. It is understandably worried at the prospect of becoming a "natural" discipline itself. (Turner, 6)

By cultural studies' disparagement of natural, by its replacing of "nature" or "natural" with the more humanly alterable "history," nature also risks vilification as an external straitjacket or internal tether, the kind of dictatorial nature opposed to a culture self-congratulatingly referred to as "nurture." Important for what follows is that the boundary between nature and culture is affirmed by Turner's definition: culture and cultural studies are not natural, culture being changeable (positive), nature being adamant (negative).

There is a second related hazard for the entrance of nature into green cultural studies, but this time one intersecting with the post-structuralist–deconstructionist blurring of the nature/culture boundary. Above, nature was demonized as a realm of unfreedom and restriction different from culture, a site of freedom and change. Such a role reversal could stem from Jacques Derrida's blurring of the nature/culture boundary in *Of Grammatology*. With Derrida, the idea of nature becomes dubious not only because it is a cultural "product" or "construction," but because nature is cast in the role of culture (and culture in the role of nature; Derrida, 141). Deconstruction, however, did not stay within the domain of cultural production, but, as a result of over-reading, seeped out into worldnature: not just the idea of nature, but nature itself (worldnature) became culturally constructed. The cultural determination of worldnature is nature in the looking glass: sensorially abstract, cogitatively or significantly concrete. In such a universe, all entities become instantiations of culture. Such neo-idealism or culturism, however, is largely the product of misunderstanding ideas put in stylistically dramatic but questionable terms: for example, when the "construction" in "cultural construction" is understood in not only conceptual terms, but in a physical or material sense; and when ideas about nature are conflated with worldnature.

The disappearance of nature into culture sometimes has a strange result: the naturalization of culture—that is, culture, not cultural studies—calling itself or its products "second nature," "natural," or simply, "nature." With all nature having become culturally constructed and culture become the only game in town, perhaps it is understandable. A specific instance of culture calling itself natural is the idea that technology is part of nature. I have in mind the influential work of Donna Haraway. Haraway's suggestion that technology is a "particular production of nature" ("Promises," 297) is a subset of the argument that humans are part of nature. This scientific categorization of humans as a species of animal counteracts earlier conceptions of humanity as separate and above nature, that humanity lies somewhere between divinity and animality along a great chain of being. But the success of this strategy has also been strained by Haraway's post-structuralist cultural studies in which human culture, not just humanity, is naturalized. This is controversial because if cultural production is part of nature, is natural, then everything from virtual reality to Astroturf is also part of nature, is simply another variety of worldnature. But now recall Turner's claim that cultural studies and culture are not natural. If culture and civilization are exclusive products of human history, if they are unnatural (Turner), how then is technology a "production of nature," even if "particular" (Haraway)?

In *The Culture of Nature,* Alexander Wilson, like Haraway, also argues against border reification but does so without sanctioning as natural such cultural manifestations as technology, and without viewing nature as a mere construction or extension of culture. And, although Wilson cites separation of nature and culture as the primary cause of the degradation of nature and the demise of culture, his plans to break down the radical distance between culture and nature include an explicit call for an expansion of undomesticated nature and limits to urban, suburban, and exurban culture.

Perhaps Deleuze and Guattari in *A Thousand Plateaus*—although they are far more concerned to break down than reassert the culture/nature and animal/human boundaries—offer a more comprehensive scenario than either Haraway or Wilson, one dialectically careful not to abandon advantages accruing to borders and boundaries, to separations in terms of "molar individuals" and "subjects" on "planes of organization." Their view of "becoming-in-the-world" (against being-in-the-world) merges structuralism (boundaries, limits, identities) with poststructuralism (transgressions, joyous confusions, protean fluctuations) into a shape-shifting multi-

plicitous postmodernism (*passim*). Such a view of nature is progressive for several reasons: it allows worldnature independence from culture; encourages dialogue on the meaning of nature; and includes worldnature as another form of being for ethical consideration, for subjectivity. Borders are mussed and meanings are challenged, but carefully, with an eye toward how word and image, institutional discipline and cultural formation, can serve as cultural weapons against worldnature.

With the conflations arising from a necessary questioning of the border between nature and culture, insisting on the correctness of this or that claim may count for less than the materialized agendas to which these claims are, or can be, attached. Therein lies the crucial connection between culture and politics characterizing (green) cultural studies.

Notes

1. "Elements" encompasses minerals, weather, and earth, air, fire, and water.

2. For example: nature (the word); Nature (divine, metaphysical, or scientific entity as in the "Laws of Nature"); "nature" (socially constructed conceptions); nature (the strange mix of metaphysics and physics seen in observed patterns and often referred to as [eco]systems or laws); and material nature (creatures and conditions which I call worldnature). Worldnature freely indicates the nonhuman world and displays caution when including humans and fear when including human culture or artifacts.

Selected Works and Further Reading

Adams, Carol J., *The Sexual Politics of Meat: A Feminist-Vegetarian Critical Theory,* New York: Continuum, 1990

Althusser, Louis, "Ideology and Ideological State Apparatuses," in *Lenin and Philosophy, and Other Essays,* translated by Ben Brewster, London: NLB, 1971; New York: Monthly Review, 1972

Altman, Nathaniel, *Sacred Trees,* San Francisco: Sierra Club, 1994

Anderson, William, *Green Man: The Archetype of Our Oneness with the Earth,* San Francisco and London: HarperCollins, 1990

Baker, Steve, *Picturing the Beast: Animals, Identity, and Representation,* New York and Manchester, England: Manchester University Press, 1993

Berger, John, "Seker Ahmet and the Forest," in *About Looking,* New York: Pantheon, 1980; London: Writers and Readers, 1980

———, "Why Look at Animals," in *About Looking,* New York: Pantheon, 1980; London: Writers and Readers, 1980

Bermingham, Ann, *Landscape and Ideology: The English Rustic Tradition, 1740–1860,* Berkeley: University of California Press, 1986; London: Thames and Hudson, 1987

Collingwood, R. G., *The Idea of Nature,* Oxford: Clarendon, 1945; New York: Oxford University Press, 1960

Dekkers, Midas, *Dearest Pet: On Bestiality,* translated by Paul Vincent, New York and London: Verso, 1994

Deleuze, Gilles, and Félix Guattari, *A Thousand Plateaus: Capitalism and Schizophrenia,* Minneapolis: University of Minnesota Press, 1987; London: Athlone, 1988

Derrida, Jacques, *Of Grammatology,* translated by Gayatri Chakravorty Spivak, Baltimore, Maryland: Johns Hopkins University Press, 1976

Fiddes, Nick, *Meat: A Natural Symbol,* New York and London: Routledge, 1991

Fjellman, Stephen M., *Vinyl Leaves: Walt Disney World and America,* Boulder, Colorado: Westview, 1992

Gelbspan, Ross, "The Heat Is On," *Harper's* 291:1747 (December 1995), pp. 31–37

Glacken, Clarence J., *Traces on the Rhodian Shore: Nature and Culture in Western Thought from Ancient Times to the End of the Eighteenth Century,* Berkeley: University of California Press, 1967

Grant, Barry Keith, *Voyages of Discovery: The Cinema of Frederick Wiseman,* Urbana: University of Illinois Press, 1992

Green, Nicholas, *The Spectacle of Nature: Landscape and Bourgeois Culture in Nineteenth Century France,* New York and Manchester, England: Manchester University Press, 1990

Griffin, Susan, *Woman and Nature: The Roaring Inside Her,* New York: Harper & Row, 1978; London: Women's Press, 1984

Hall, Stuart, "The Emergence of Cultural Studies and the Crisis of the Humanities," *October* 53 (Summer 1990), pp. 11–23

Haraway, Donna, "The Actors Are Cyborg, Nature Is Coyote, and the Geography Is Elsewhere: Postscript to 'Cyborgs at Large'," in *Technoculture,* edited by Constance Penley and Andrew Ross, Minneapolis: University of Minnesota Press, 1991

———, *Primate Visions: Gender, Race, and Nature in the World of Modern Science,* New York: Routledge, 1989; London: Verso, 1992

———, "The Promises of Monsters: A Regenerative Politics for Inappropriate/d Others," in *Cultural Studies,* edited by Lawrence Grossberg, Cary Nelson, and Paula Treichler, New York: Routledge, 1992

———, *Simians, Cyborgs, and Women: The Reinvention of Nature,* New York: Routledge, 1991; London: Free Association, 1991

Hayles, N. Katherine, "Simulated Nature & Natural Simulations: Rethinking the Relation Between the Beholder and the World," in *Uncommon Ground: Toward Reinventing Nature,* edited by William Cronon, New York: Norton, 1995

Hochman, Jhan, "Donna J. Haraway and Technology," *Democracy and Nature* 10 (forthcoming)

———, "Green Cultural Studies: An Introductory Critique of an Emerging Discipline," *Mosaic* 30:1 (March 1997), pp. 81–96

———, *Signs of Nature,* Moscow: University of Idaho Press, 1997

———, "*The Silence of the Lambs*: A Quiet Bestiary," *ISLE* 1:2 (Fall 1993), pp. 57–79

Hochman, Jhan, and Chris Semansky, "Ecotastrophes, Photography, and Millennial Doom: Snapshots of the End," *Genre* 29:1–2 (1996), pp. 1–18

Horkheimer, Max, *The Eclipse of Reason,* New York: Oxford University Press, 1947

Horkheimer, Max, and Theodor W. Adorno, *Dialectic of Enlightenment,* New York: Seabury, 1972; London: Allen Lane, 1973

Irwin, Mark, "Toward a Wilderness of the Artificial," *Ohio Review* 49 (1993), pp. 105–119

Lukács, György, *History and Class Consciousness: Studies in Marxist Dialects,* translated by Rodney Livingstone, Cambridge, Massachusetts: MIT Press, 1971; London: Merlin, 1971

Marx, Karl, *Capital: A Critical Analysis of Capitalist Production,* New York: Humboldt, 1886; London: William Glaisher, 1886

Merchant, Carolyn, *The Death of Nature: Women, Ecology, and the Scientific Revolution,* San Francisco: Harper & Row, 1980; London: Wildwood House, 1982

Mitchell, W. J. Thomas, ed., *Landscape and Power,* Chicago: University of Chicago Press, 1994

Oelschlaeger, Max, *The Idea of Wilderness,* New Haven, Connecticut: Yale University Press, 1991

Penley, Constance, and Andrew Ross, "Cyborgs at Large: Interview with Donna Haraway," in *Technoculture,* Minneapolis: University of Minnesota Press, 1991

Perlman, Michael, *The Power of Trees: The Reforesting of the Soul,* Dallas, Texas: Spring, 1994

Peterson, Dale, and Jane Goodall, *Visions of Caliban: On Chimpanzees and People,* Boston: Houghton Mifflin, 1993

Price, Jennifer, "Looking for Nature at the Mall: A Field Guide to the Nature Company," in *Uncommon Ground: Toward Reinventing Nature,* edited by William Cronon, New York: Norton, 1995

Regan, Tom, and Peter Singer, eds., *Animal Rights and Human Obligations,* Englewood Cliffs, New Jersey: Prentice-Hall, 1976

Ritvo, Harriet, *The Animal Estate: The English and Other Creatures in the Victorian Age,* Cambridge, Massachusetts: Harvard University Press, 1987

Ross, Andrew, *The Chicago Gangster Theory of Life: Nature's Debt to Society,* New York and London: Verso, 1994

——, interview, "Green Ideas Sleep Furiously," *Lingua Franca* (December 1994), pp. 57–65

——, *Strange Weather: Culture, Science, and Technology in the Age of Limits,* New York and London: Verso, 1991

Schiebinger, Londa, *Nature's Body: Gender in the Making of Modern Science,* Boston: Beacon, 1993

Serres, Michel, *The Natural Contract,* translated by Elizabeth MacArthur and William Paulson, Ann Arbor: University of Michigan Press, 1995

Shepard, Paul, *Man in the Landscape: A Historic View of the Esthetics of Nature,* New York: Knopf, 1967

Siebert, Charles, "The Artifice of the Natural," *Harper's* 286:1713 (February 1993), pp. 43–51

Simmons, I. G., *Interpreting Nature: Cultural Constructions of the Environment,* New York and London: Routledge, 1993

Slack, Jennifer Daryl, and Laurie Anne Whitt, "Ethics and Cultural Studies," in *Cultural Studies,* edited by Lawrence Grossberg, Cary Nelson, and Paula Treichler, New York: Routledge, 1992

Smith, Jonathan, "The Lie That Blinds: Destabilizing the Text of Landscape," in *Place/Culture/Representation,* edited by James Duncan and David Ley, New York and London: Routledge, 1993

Thomas, Keith, *Man and the Natural World: A History of the Modern Sensibility,* New York: Pantheon, 1983

Tobias, Michael, *A Vision of Nature: Traces of the Original World,* Kent, Ohio: Kent State University Press, 1995

Tompkins, Jane, *West of Everything: The Inner Life of Westerns,* New York: Oxford University Press, 1992

Thompson, George F., ed., *Landscape in America,* Austin: University of Texas Press, 1995

Tuan, Yi-Fu, *Passing Strange and Wonderful: Aesthetics, Nature, and Culture,* Washington, D.C.: Island/Shearwater, 1993

Turner, Graeme, *British Cultural Studies: An Introduction,* Boston: Unwin Hyman, 1990; 2nd ed., New York and London: Routledge, 1996

Virilio, Paul, *Popular Defense and Ecological Struggles,* New York: Semiotext(e), 1990

Wall, Derek, ed., *Green History: A Reader in Environmental Literature, Philosophy, and Politics,* New York and London: Routledge, 1994

Williams, Raymond, *The Country and the City,* New York: Oxford University Press, 1973; London: Chatto and Windus, 1973

——, *Keywords: A Vocabulary of Culture and Society,* New York: Oxford University Press, 1976; London: Fontana, 1976

Wilson, Alexander, *The Culture of Nature: North American Landscape from Disney to the Exxon Valdez,* Toronto, Ontario: Between the Lines, 1991; Cambridge, Massachusetts: Blackwell, 1992

Wright, Will, *Wild Knowledge: Science, Language, and Social Life in a Fragile Environment,* Minneapolis: University of Minnesota Press, 1992

Zukin, Sharon, *Landscapes of Power: From Detroit to Disney World,* Berkeley: University of California Press, 1991

Speaking for Nature

Karla Armbruster

Henry David Thoreau began his 1862 essay "Walking" by proclaiming,

> I wish to speak a word for Nature, for absolute freedom and wildness, as contrasted with a freedom and culture merely civil, to regard man as an inhabitant, or a part and parcel of Nature, rather than as a member of Society. I wish to make an extreme statement, if so I may make an emphatic one, for there are enough champions of civilization: the minister, and the school-committee, and every one of you will take care of that. (p. 194)

In this passage, Thoreau characterizes himself as an advocate for the nonhuman, a role that involves challenging his culture's prevailing views of nature and of proper human relations to nature. By adopting such a role, Thoreau took a prominent place within an Anglo-American tradition of "speaking for nature" that has worked to oppose the dominant ideologies within Western culture that perceive humans as radically separate from and superior to nonhuman nature. Since Thoreau's time, this tradition of environmental advocacy has gradually taken root and grown to include such diverse voices as John Muir, Robinson Jeffers, Rachel Carson, Alice Walker, and activist groups such as Earth First! and People for the Ethical Treatment of Animals (PETA).

Of course, Thoreau was not the first writer to demonstrate a respect for the natural world that went against prevailing cultural norms. One example cited by Thomas Lyon in *This Incomperable Lande* is the seventeenth-century British clergyman and naturalist John Ray. In his 1691 *The Wisdom of God Manifested in the Works of the Creation*, Ray explicitly argued against the dominant belief that the things of the world were created solely for the use of humankind, and he stressed that the study of nature should widen humans' sense of ethical responsibility to include the nonhuman. Before the nineteenth century, however, conceptions of nature that diverged from dominant attitudes most often took the form of stewardship ethics or arcadian visions that sanctioned and even idealized limited, careful uses of nature. It was not until the nineteenth century that the beginnings of a sustained critique of Western assumptions of human superiority and dominion over nature emerged in the United States, perhaps in response to the dramatic transformation of wilderness that occurred because of the rapid expansion, industrialization, and settlement of the country by the dominant U.S. culture during this period.

The transcendental movement of the nineteenth-century United States is widely associated with this growing respect for and interest in nature; Emerson emphasized the role of the poet as the voice of nature, and Melville created an epic tale of humanity's self-destructive obsession with the domination of nature in *Moby-Dick*. However, as Lawrence Buell has argued, it is Thoreau who spoke most explicitly for nature by arguing for the interconnectedness and equality of all living things. While Buell acknowledges that aspects of Thoreau's works simply reinforced dominant nineteenth-century norms that idealized wild nature while simultaneously sanctioning its destruction, he argues that Thoreau's writings and life were also genuinely radical in that they proposed a "return to nature" as a lived experience, both through his self-conscious attempt to do so as chronicled in *Walden* and through the sense of intimacy with his natural environment that is evident in almost all his works. Even more radical was his holistic view of nature as a vast network of relationships and his sense of the equality among all living things—including humans—implied by such relationships. Significantly, over time Thoreau's attitude evolved into a proto-environmentalist defense of nature in the face of the disappearance of the wild places he loved. This political aspect of Thoreau's relationship to nature is most evident in his later writings, such as the essay "Walking."

While Thoreau's sense that speaking "a word for nature" flies in the face of prevailing cultural norms still holds true in the United States today, the number of writers and activists who have felt compelled to take stances similar to his has steadily grown since his time along with a cultural sense of urgency about the degradation of our natural environment. Among these environmental advocates, the consciousness of speaking for the natural world is manifested in titles such as Gerald Haslam's "Who Speaks for the Earth: A Course on Literature of the Environment" and Edward Abbey's *The Journey Home: A Few Words in Defense of the American West.* The increasing prevalence and cultural impact of this type of environmental advocacy has been documented in Paul Brooks' *Speaking for Nature: How Literary Naturalists from Henry Thoreau to Rachel Carson Have Shaped America* and in Roderick Nash's *The Rights of Nature: A History of Environmental Ethics.*

Forms of Environmental Advocacy

Despite the widespread use of the trope of speaking for nature, different opinions exist as to the exact meaning of the phrase. Perhaps the most all-encompassing definition is the one Brooks embraces in *Speaking for Nature.* In this study of United States "literary naturalists," he includes both writers who have played the "tactical" role of creating "an informed public to confront a clear and present danger" (p. 274) and those whose function is more "strategic": nature writers who by "expressing their profound joy in nature . . . have sharpened our perception of what is at stake and strengthened our resolve to fight for its survival" (Brooks, 274). While all nature writing, by turning "our attention outward to the activity of nature" (Lyon, 7), works toward improving the standing of the nonhuman within human culture, there is an important difference between the broad category of nature writing and the more specific, though sometimes overlapping, category of environmental advocacy—the writing Brooks calls tactical. Nature writing has been characterized by critics such as Peter Fritzell, Lyon, and John Murray as a type of literary nonfiction that reflects some combination of the traditions of science, natural history, and personal narrative and interpretation. In their focus on relationships between humans and the rest of nature, writers who explicitly adopt the stance of speaking for nature often draw on these same traditions, but they are further distinguished by their emphasis on the ethical implications of the relationships they see between humans and the rest of nature. In other words, they take overtly political stances that humans are interconnected with the rest of nature, that they are no more inherently valuable to the whole than any other part of nature, and that Western culture should adapt its values and practices to reflect such beliefs.

Like Thoreau, many of these writers have expressed their advocacy primarily through nonfiction prose. John Muir, who moved as a boy from Scotland to the United States in 1849, became one of the country's foremost wilderness explorers and advocates in the late nineteenth and early twentieth century. In both his writings, such as *My First Summer in the Sierra* and *The Yosemite,* and his activism, such as his efforts to establish Yosemite as a national park and to found the Sierra Club, he drew on a pantheistic vision of the divinity in nature to argue for the inherent value of wilderness. Aldo Leopold, a professional forest and wildlife manager in the first half of the twentieth century, has become renowned not only for his efforts to preserve wilderness and wildlife, but also for *A Sand County Almanac,* his primary philosophical statement published in 1949 (the year after his death); in this work, he expressed his sense of the complexity and interconnectedness of what he called the "land organism": animals, plants, water, air, soil, and the pathways of food and energy that connect them. However, his principal point was even more radical than this sense of interconnectedness; he argued that human beings should understand that they, too, are part of this "organism" and that they should acknowledge this by extending ethical consideration from human beings to "the land." Later in the twentieth century, Rachel Carson followed in the tradition of Muir and Leopold by further challenging dominant anthropocentric and utilitarian attitudes toward nature. After writing several natural history books about the sea during the 1940s and 1950s, Carson took on the role of full-fledged environmental advocate with her controversial 1962 call to arms, *Silent Spring.* In this book, Carson focused on the ways in which humans were interconnected with the rest of nature in order to inform the public that the pesticides designed to kill insects could eventually enter and damage human bodies. However, she also more subtly challenged the dominant cultural attitude that nature existed only to be subjugated and used by humans, suggesting that a more humble attitude of cooperation and respect would be better for all concerned.

The nonfiction form adopted by Muir, Leopold, and Carson flourished as a mode of environmental advocacy in the second half of the twentieth century. This period witnessed Joseph Wood Krutch's *The Voice of the Desert,* an assertion of the fundamental connectedness of humans and nature; Josephine Johnson's *Inland Island,* an unflinching examination of the forces responsible for the Vietnam War and environmental degradation that links and condemns them both; Edward Abbey's *Desert Solitaire* and other works celebrating the desert wildernesses of the U.S. Southwest and critiquing the forces threatening them; John Hay's *In Defense of Nature,* a critique of modern Western culture that proposes a renewed connection with nature as a solution; Barry Lopez's thoughtful, observant treatment of topics ranging from the Arctic and the wolf to the legacy of Christopher Columbus; Terry Tempest Williams' *Refuge,* a deeply moving "genealogy" of the loss of her mother to cancer and her beloved Bear River Migratory Bird Refuge to the rising Salt Lake, as well as of her resulting resolve to fight the forces threatening the health of women and of nature; Wendell Berry's celebrations of the agrarian life as a form of cooperation between humans and nature; Alice Walker's essays, such as "Am I Blue?", that explore and expose human oppression of animals as well as her own complicity in that oppression; Gary Snyder's lyrical, complex exploration of the essential interconnectedness between nature and culture and recommendations for realizing the potential of this kind of relationship in such works as *The Practice of the Wild* and *A Place in Space.*

Despite the prevalence of nonfiction as a form for environmental advocacy, humans speaking for nature have also made excellent use of fiction. For example, Sarah Orne Jewett's 1886 short story "A White Heron" approvingly describes a little girl's choice to value nature over society by protecting the white heron of the title rather than revealing its whereabouts to the hunter who wants to add it to his bird collection. More contemporary authors of fiction that

speak for nature include Abbey, whose work *The Monkey Wrench Gang* celebrates acts of "eco-defense," such as blowing up dams and incapacitating bulldozers, and Ursula Le Guin, who draws on the coyote stories of Native American cultures of the U.S. Southwest in "Buffalo Gals Won't You Come Out Tonight?" in order to propose a new, more holistic and egalitarian way of viewing the natural world for Western culture (Armbruster, pp. 17–46).

We can also find the stance of environmental advocacy in American poetry: witness Robinson Jeffers' impassioned declarations that human beings are no more important that any other part of nature or the universe, Snyder's varied celebrations of human participation in nature and critiques of human attempts to distance themselves from and dominate the natural, and Mary Oliver's gentle, observant testimonials to the complexity, beauty, and spiritual importance of natural entities and phenomena.

Many contemporary writers who take a stance of environmental advocacy also consider themselves environmental activists. However, certain advocates have chosen to identify themselves explicitly with larger programs of environmental activism. Some, like David Brower, have been strongly associated with fairly mainstream environmental and wilderness preservation organizations such as the Sierra Club and the Earth Island Institute. Others speak from more radical positions, such as the movement of ecofeminism. While encompassing a variety of perspectives expressed in works such as Mary Daly's *Gyn/Ecology,* Susan Griffin's *Woman and Nature: The Roaring Inside Her,* and the essays of Ynestra King, ecofeminism is based on a general conviction that there are important connections between the oppression of women and the destruction and misuse of nonhuman nature within male-dominated cultures, and that it is politically essential to explore and emphasize these connections if the domination of women and of nature is to be substantively challenged.

Another radical environmental movement, deep ecology, has been promoted by writers such as Arne Naess, Neil Evernden, and Bill Devall and George Sessions; it is based on the biocentric philosophy that every living thing has an intrinsic worth and right to existence, that all living things and their environments are interconnected, and that no one species is inherently more important than any other. Deep ecology encourages the individual to identify with his or her natural environment so that he or she will realize that hurting that environment hurts the self. This philosophy has served as the basis for a variety of direct-action movements such as Earth First!, founded by Dave Foreman and others in order to actively defend wilderness in the United States. Animal rights groups such as the American Animal Liberation Front and PETA also see themselves as speaking and acting directly in the interest of nature through their commitment to the welfare of nonhuman animals; the philosophical justification for such movements is expressed in the works of authors such as Peter Singer and Tom Regan.

The Problems of Speaking for Nature

Among people concerned with environmental issues, the growing discourse of environmental advocacy is often uncritically accepted as admirable and effective. It is true that this type of advocacy is sorely needed in an age of environmental crisis and that its growth has paralleled an expanding cultural sense of the need to confront environmental problems. However, at the same time, human overuse of natural resources and abuse of other species seem to have continued almost unabated. Of course, the continuing degradation of the environment can be attributed to the strength and persistence of the cultural ideologies and practices that have consistently opposed environmental advocacy's message that humans and nature are interconnected and equally valuable. Nevertheless, it is crucial to ask how even the most well-intended work of advocacy may inadvertently reinforce the very attitudes and behaviors it sets out to challenge. For example, some ecofeminist writers focus so completely on the connections between women and nature that they effectively erase the differences between the two, valorizing women/nature over men/culture in what is merely an inversion of the oppressive opposition that Western culture has long constructed between the two groups. One result of this conflation of women with nature is that women may be encouraged to ignore their own complicity in environmental problems. Other advocates, such as some contemporary wilderness activists, take their responsibility to protect nature from degradation by human culture so seriously that they reinvoke the culture/nature dualism at the heart of that degradation by constructing themselves as the acting, speaking defenders of a passive, silent nature, denying nature a voice or role in its own defense.

One of the factors that has obscured the need for a more critical perspective on environmental advocacy has been the Western cultural assumption that nature cannot speak for itself; because there has seemed to be no alternative to humans speaking for nature, it has seemed unnecessary to examine how we speak for it. However, it is precisely because nature cannot challenge the ways we represent it using human language that we must resist the temptation to objectify and construct nature in any way we choose. And it is important to search for ways to conceive of nature that allow us to "listen" to it, to learn from it and to see it as subject rather than object; as Christopher Manes points out in "Nature and Silence," Western culture may be unable to extend moral consideration to the nonhuman without recognizing its potential for speech or signification.

Significantly, some texts that participate in environmental advocacy work to create an awareness of the many voices of nature by directly adopting the point of view of an animal (such as John Rodman's "The Dolphin Papers") or another natural entity (such as the tree in Le Guin's "The Direction of the Road"). As Patrick D. Murphy has explained in "Ground, Pivot, Motion," works like these "render the signification presented us by nature into a verbal depiction by means of speaking subjects" (p. 152) and thus recognize the potential of the nonhuman to speak and act. Donna Haraway, too, emphasizes the importance of being able to perceive nonhuman "actors" as powerful, active speakers, concluding, "Accounts of a 'real' world do not, then, depend on a logic of 'discovery' but on a power-charged social relation of 'conversation'" (p. 198).

While the idea that nature can speak to us might seem improbable at first, writers like Snyder have argued that nature is already communicating with us in ways that we can learn to understand, and that we disregard at our peril; as he explains in "Wilderness," incorporating the nonhuman into our "councils of government. . . . isn't as difficult as you might think. If we don't do it, they will revolt against us. They will submit non-negotiable demands about our stay on the earth. We are beginning to get non-negotiable demands right now from the air, the water, the soil" (*Turtle Island*, 108). As Snyder suggests, we can learn from nature how better to exist within its limits; however, looking only at such extreme instances risks reinforcing a sense that humans and nature must always be at odds with each other. It is crucial to remind ourselves that such a perspective is deeply ingrained within Western culture, and that there are other cultural traditions from which those of us shaped by the Western tradition can learn. For example, Leslie Marmon Silko, a Laguna Pueblo writer, shares an insight in "Landscape, History, and the Pueblo Imagination" that her culture developed through generations of living in what is now the U.S. Southwest, a harsh, dry environment where "any life at all is precious": "One look and you know that simply to survive is a great triumph, that every possible resource is needed, every possible ally—even the most humble insect or reptile. You realize you will be speaking with all of them if you intend to last out the year" (p. 94). This concept of speaking with nature can remind us that we need to listen as well as speak, that we have something to learn from nature and that it has something to contribute to its own defense. By adopting such a perspective, those of us who wish to speak for nature can even more thoroughly challenge the forces and attitudes working against the survival of us all.

Selected Works and Further Reading

Armbruster, Karla, "Blurring the Boundaries in Ursula Le Guin's *Buffalo Gals Won't You Come Out Tonight*: A Poststructuralist Approach to Ecofeminist Criticism," *Interdisciplinary Studies in Literature and Environment* 3:1 (Summer 1996), pp. 17–46

Brooks, Paul, *Speaking for Nature: How Literary Naturalists from Henry Thoreau to Rachel Carson Have Shaped America,* San Francisco: Sierra Club, 1980

Buell, Lawrence, *The Environmental Imagination: Thoreau, Nature Writing, and the Formation of American Culture,* Cambridge, Massachusetts: Belknap Press of Harvard University Press, 1995

Fritzell, Peter, *Nature Writing and America: Essays upon a Cultural Type,* Ames: Iowa State University Press, 1990

Haraway, Donna, "Situated Knowledges: The Science Question in Feminism and the Privilege of Partial Perspective," in *Simians, Cyborgs, and Women: The Reinvention of Nature,* New York: Routledge, 1991; London: Free Association, 1991

Lyon, Thomas J., ed., *This Incomperable Lande: A Book of American Nature Writing,* Boston: Houghton Mifflin, 1989

Manes, Christopher, "Nature and Silence," *Environmental Ethics* 14:4 (Winter 1992), pp. 339–350

Murphy, Patrick D., "Ground, Pivot, Motion: Ecofeminist Theory, Dialogics, and Literary Practice," *Hypatia* 6:1 (Spring 1991), pp. 146–161

Murray, John, *The Sierra Club Nature Writing Handbook: A Creative Guide,* San Francisco: Sierra Club, 1995

Nash, Roderick, *The Rights of Nature: A History of Environmental Ethics,* Madison: University of Wisconsin Press, 1989

Silko, Leslie Marmon, "Landscape, History, and the Pueblo Imagination," in *On Nature: Nature, Landscape, and Natural History,* edited by Daniel Halpern, San Francisco: North Point, 1986

Snyder, Gary, "The Wilderness," in *Turtle Island,* New York: New Directions, 1974

Thoreau, Henry David, "Walking," in *This Incomperable Lande: A Book of American Nature Writing,* edited by Thomas J. Lyon, Boston: Houghton Mifflin, 1989

Aesthetics and Ecology: A Nonfictional View

Peter Harries-Jones

A customary definition of aesthetics emphasizes the sensuous interpretation of the beautiful in relation to the good—although aesthetics is not exhausted by imaginative interpretation of this reference. Aesthetics expands the field of contemplative attention, and where such attention touches reflectively upon established patterns of learning, aesthetic feeling becomes an important aspect of meaning. Thus aesthetics is a sensuous register of judgments, an interplay between the new and the learned, the moral and the sublime, immediate perception and creative imagination.

Yet for a long period of time in Western countries, the primary realm of aesthetic reference was art history. As Eugene Hargrove points out, aesthetic appreciation of natural beauty developed slowly among the elite of the Western world. The enjoyment of natural beauty coincided with, and was influenced by, the emergence of landscape painting in the seventeenth century and, subsequently, landscape gardening. Both tended to frame nature as picturesque vistas. Whether these elite notions of landscape added to or detracted from a more appropriate appreciation of natural beauty in the Western world is controversial. Hargrove makes the case that appreciation of natural beauty is ontological and, although art historians continued to regard natural beauty as being inferior to artistic beauty, ordinary people considered natural beauty as evidently superior because of its intrinsic value (p. 185).

Pioneers of the modern environmental movement in the United States, such as Aldo Leopold (who died in 1948), still drew upon analogies of art appreciation and to the German philosopher Immanuel Kant for commentaries on how to develop a taste for nature (*Callicott*, 239–247). Aesthetic theory, which derived continuously, if not exclusively, from Kant, encouraged art historians to distance themselves from the object contemplated. In Kant's well-known view, assuming a disinterested attitude freed observers from distractions of practical purposes and enabled them to dwell upon the art object in isolation from its surround. Leopold questioned the appropriateness of an aesthetics arising from disinterested observation. Nature was still a surround, in Leopold's aesthetic, but a surround to be incorporated both perceptually and conceptually. Leopold, in his scattered writing on a "land aesthetic," noted that the less immediately visible aspects of natural history, such as diversity, complexity, species interactions, and phylogenetic antiquity, penetrated the surface of direct sensory experience and gave "hidden riches" to the notion of nature as mere scenery (Leopold, quoted in Callicott, 240–241).

Today ecological aesthetics has moved beyond these sentiments towards the idea that the beauty of living lies in active participation. The new existential unit is that of self plus nature as a single field of relations and processes. Arnold Berleant, in particular, develops a participatory ecological aesthetics. We not only see our living world, he says, but we move with it and we act upon it. Our bodies respond and reestablish us as we move through space and time in active engagement with changing conditions. Vision is an important sense, but the eye is part of the body and its modality is bound in experience with the touch of surfaces and textures. In turn, the paradigms and categories of space, time, and movement which are necessary for any active perception of environment are embedded in cultural practices. Thus we encounter environment not only with the eye but with the body and, surrounding the body, the modalities of our cultural practices (pp. 19–20, 107, 130).

There are evident difficulties in working out how we may gain a sufficiently holistic view of nature in order to construct an aesthetic that is both personal and ecological. Arne Naess, the founder of the deep ecology movement, considers how we may overcome these difficulties. A total view of nature cannot be articulated completely by any single person or group, he says, but it is possible to try to articulate fragments. Naess combines insights drawn from natural science about relations in an electromagnetic or quantum field (*see* below), from psychology of perceptual gestalts, and extends these to ethical and spiritual perspectives about unity in nature.

People are able to experience aspects of nature spontaneously. The spontaneous experience Naess calls the identification process and, since identification is of a gestalt character, the process engenders percepts of wholeness and unity. Naess invites us to consider a relational field, together with many junctions, that represents a totality of our own interrelated experience of nature. Convergence of relations in the field creates a binding effect in the gestalt so that interdependent and non-isolatable fragments of this relational field become self-determining and self-reliant. Gestalts of this sort bind the I and the not-I together, into some *thing* that is recognized as being both different from and similar to ourselves. This can be found, for example, in mythic thought, which is why understanding gestalts in mythic thought enables communication between dissimilar cultures. The same argument holds for self and nature in ecological perception.

Naess's key concept is "Self-realization!", which, in its moral or normative form, guarantees "beautiful action." "Self-realization!" is an arrow, a direction, or a vector that moves along a path from one personal intuition to another, beginning with the isolated self, but ending with a realization that we, ourselves, become part of the increase of others through nature. Beautiful action can be described as an individual acting more consistently and more inclusively from himself or herself toward a whole. Beautiful acts flow naturally from increasing maturity in individuals. The egoistic self grows towards the self-realizing "Self!" In other words, the natural process of maturation activates more of the human personality in relation to more of the milieu in which individuals find themselves. Thus natural maturation achieves an increased ability to perceive holistically, and to generate "beautiful action," as the individual begins to act more consistently from himself or herself towards that whole. Although the experience may sometimes be painful, it is most meaningful and desirable (p. 86).

The problem with gestalts of a very complex character is that they can scarcely be learned in an ordinary fashion, and they are easily destroyed by attempts to analyze the fragments of them in a conscious manner. Perhaps for this reason, when Naess himself tries to bring together his themes of gestalt perception with oneness and wholeness, and "Self-realization!", he admits that he can give only a mere sketch of their possible interrelation. His may seem a very mystical ecological philosophy, Naess states, but the concept of "Self-realization!" makes the individual the center of integration and also focuses on integration as a concrete process. As the self grows toward the self-realizing "Self!", there is a perceptual and normative response to ecological order that enables individuals to clarify challenges to life in our ecosphere (p. 173). The force of Naess' analysis has had a positive impact on the development of transpersonal psychology, a psychology that links humanism with modern environmental issues.

Eco-Theology

A participatory perspective, such as that of Berleant and Naess, rejects dualism of subject cut off from the surround of environment; it also rejects the dualism of body partitioned from mind, and of nature partitioned from culture. This alteration of perspective is far-reaching, not only for a personal aesthetic but also for the way in which such a personal aesthetic may link to institutional religion and the natural sciences. The current lack of concern for an ecological aesthetic in natural sciences is evident, yet, as reported by Roderick Nash, there has been a similar lack of intimacy between the doctrines of Christianity and aesthetic appreciation of nature.

Endorsement of environmentalism by the mainstream churches occurred only after resolution of some burning theological arguments in the 1970s and 1980s. The most prominent issue was whether support for radical environmental positions would encourage nature worship and resurrect animistic beliefs about nature that had been banished in the Christian church since its early foundation (Nash, 87–120). If, on the other hand, the sacred texts had said that humanity had dominion over nature, and the rest of creation existed only for human benefit, then this did indeed provided a rationale for Jews and Christians to exploit nature at will. Recognizing this danger, a number of theologians and practicing Christians began to render alternative interpretations of the sacred texts. One reinterpretation was that dualism between humanity and nature can be more easily resolved if the relation between the human body and material provisioning by nature is envisaged as the relation between ourselves and our bodies, at once part of nature—and its epitome. Another argument was that human dominion over nature did not indicate absolute dominance, but rather indicated a position of trusteeship. As God's most favored beings, humans were charged with overseeing the welfare of all the rest of creation. We were trustees or stewards of nature engaged in the task of completing creation. Both arguments construe a deeper sense of communion with all beings and, through this deeper sense, relate perceptions of natural beauty to our intuitions of the spiritual.

Henryk Skolimowski, a Polish ecophilosopher, builds the rudiments of an eco-theology out of the first of these reinterpretations. For Skolimowski, spirituality is a sublime subject that is essential to the human condition and is one of its defining characteristics. So, too, is the aesthetic dimension. A common theme running all through the sacred texts is how the worship of natural beauty engenders a sense of the integrity of the planet. Beauty is a collective term associated with the coherence of life, its intricate rhythms and symmetries, and the articulation of living structure. The driving force of evolution has chosen symmetry as its basic modus operandi. Primordial symmetry is woven into life-enhancing rhythms that form the basis of life-enhancing structures. We do not need the heavens to explain the presence or absence of beauty, for the evolutionary process is itself sufficient to show that for every element there exists a contrasting element that holds the original element in balance.

The beauty we appreciate in nature is but a collective term for all those processes through which life-enhancing structures have gradually acquired coherence, endurance, and capability. In Skolimowski's interpretation, beauty is both a vehicle of the sacred and an inherent aspect of it. It is also undergoing an evolutionary ascent; its evolutionary radiance is such that a more beautiful object exists more intensively than a less beautiful one because it contains more life in it: "God makes coherence through the structures of beauty. Life makes the journey of transcendence through structures of increasing coherence and performance, and thus of beauty. Such has been the evolutionary story of life" (p. 139).

The crisis of natural beauty that we are experiencing in the second half of the twentieth century is therefore a crisis of humanity. The pathologies of utilitarianism, relativism, and nihilism have already pushed the idea of the intrinsic value of nature to the sidelines; this, in turn, is leading to the devastation of aesthetic values. When beauty loses potency, then the ugly becomes acceptable, and so, in a series of steps, come spiritual squalor and meaninglessness in our lives. The loss of beauty is tantamount to a loss of meaning and, coming on the heels of a loss of coherence, portends a death-ridden culture.

Skolimowski's writing has influenced those in the environmental movement who wish, literally, to back out of industrial society and return to a much less destructive environmental and social order. They agree with Skolimowski that the premise of a deeper understanding of ecology is that of "the world as sanctuary." By assuming the world as sanctuary we may return imaginatively to times when people felt that the world was a sacred place in which to dwell. Then we may recognize that the divine, the beautiful and the sacred are all aspects of one another.

Novelist, poet, and essayist Wendell Berry's aesthetics stem from the second reinterpretation of the Christian position. Unlike Skolimowski's highly abstract writing, Berry favors a simple but strong visual style and a poet's understanding of evocative metaphor. The potency of his argument gains from his own work as a Kentucky smallholding farmer and his experience of the daily and yearly rhythms of agricultural work. His aesthetic merges the spiritual with the practical, each, in his view, requiring the other in order to achieve a unified attack against the unbridled industrialism of our time. The churches may wish to save souls, but they have not been earthly enough. Continuing the conceptual divisions between the natural and the supernatural has been a weakness of the churches' tradition.

Berry regards the farmer's task of the fashioning of living matter, although an external and material set of events, as a process that inwardly forms a spiritual being. Nowhere is this better registered than Berry's repeated references to topsoil, either in its biological aspects or as spiritual metaphor. Living topsoil—"living" in both the biological sense and the cultural sense—is the basic element in the technology of farming. It is also the great connector of our lives, the healer and restorer by which disease passes into health, age into youth, death into life. Without proper care for it we can have no life, for we will have no living energy. We cannot make topsoil, he says, and we cannot make any substitute for it. We can care for it only by assenting to, preserving, and even collaborating in its own processes: "If the soil is regarded as machine, then its life, its involvement in living systems and cycles, must perforce be ignored. It must be treated as a dead, inert chemical mass" (*Standing on Earth*, 13, 169).

Scale is another important aspect of Berry's aesthetic and the cyclical rhythms to which patterns of scale are tied. Small-scale farming occurs within a complex of mutually influential relationships of soil, plants, animals, and people, and a farmer must have a concern for balance and symmetry and recognize a reciprocating connection between them. Good solutions in farming always improve these balances, and, since it is the nature of any organic pattern to be contained within a larger one, so any good solution in farming is one whose pattern preserves the integrity of the pattern that contains it. A bad solution to these problems is bad because it acts destructively upon the larger patterns in which the smaller symmetries are contained (*The Gift of Good Land*, 140–144).

Another important concept in Berry's aesthetic is that of "margins." Good solutions always have wide margins, so that the failure of one solution does not imply the impossibility of another. Industrial agriculture always ignores margins and "goes for broke" by putting all its eggs into the single basket of monoculture. In some contexts Berry uses the notion of margin as a metaphor for flexibility in ecological organization; in other contexts he uses the notion of margin to denote the phenomenon of "edge," the boundary where wildlife and domesticity meet—the margin as a place of interaction (*Home Economics*, 13). The notion of margin takes up a whole chapter in *The Unsettling of America*, perhaps his best-known book of essays. Here Berry relates marginal land to cultures that might be called marginal, such as the Amish of Indiana, Iowa, Pennsylvania, and Ohio, and the Uchucmarca of the Peruvian Andes. He finds their agricultural practices all surprisingly robust.

Both cultures know how diversity contributes to a healthy farm and that a healthy farm will most likely be independent and self-sustaining: "The healthy farm sustains itself in the same way a healthy tree does: by belonging where it is, by maintaining a proper relation to the ground" (*The Unsettling of America*, 183) and, by extension, toward the ground of their own cultures.

Berry celebrates the fact that marginal cultures in marginal places reinforced by a marginal way of thinking are unbroken and still alive. Against these themes of marginality, of kindness to the ground, and of nurture can be placed the rampant expansion of agribusiness with its technology of machines and chemicals. Agribusiness has led to the abandonment of smallholdings and the movement of peoples to towns across the United States and elsewhere. Large-scale agribusiness with its exploitation of land is totally destructive of human responsibility in agriculture, of a sense community, and also of the earth itself (*The Unsettling of America*, 35). Berry's writing has had remarkable impact on the conservationist wing of environmentalism in the United States. It is corroborated in non-Christian countries where there are similar reports of the destruction of the biodiversity of life forms by agribusiness, together with impoverishment of culture, and spirituality (*see* Shiva).

Can Science Include Aesthetics?

Agricultural science, when combined with agribusiness, is incapable of an aesthetic, according to Berry, for agricultural science supports only the inert, the dead, and the destructive. Both Fritjof Capra and Gregory Bateson write of a different science, one not obsessed with the conduct of experimental observation nor with its propensity to subtract all personal feeling from, or relationship to, that which it enumerates and classifies. They write prospectively of a science transformed, one that has time for the sort of exceptionalism that is typical of natural variety, and that begins to associate local contexts with a vision of holism and unity—one that William Blake imagined when he wrote, "To see a World in a Grain of Sand, / And a Heaven in a Wild Flower. . . ."

In Capra's view, aesthetic appreciation of the unity in the cosmos has already begun in quantum physics. The discovery of the quantum principle in the first half of the twentieth century destroyed the concept of an independent world "sitting out there" (*The Turning Point*, 47–49). From then on, scientists in quantum physics had to cross out the old word "observer" and put in its place the new word "participator." The field theories of modern physics today express how the whole universe is engaged in endless motion and activity, a continual dance of cosmic energy in which particles are created and destroyed in continual variation of energy patterns yet give rise to the stable structures of the material world. Capra evokes the Eastern worldview and the mystical traditions of Hinduism, Buddhism, and Taoism to demonstrate parallels between their views about the interconnectedness and interdependence of natural phenomena and the views of modern physics. Both describe a universe where all things and events are ultimately related. Like the dance of Shiva, a flow of energy goes through an endless variety of patterns that melt into one another, the patterns themselves being an essential aspect of each particle's nature which determine many of its properties.

The exploration of the subatomic world repeatedly seems to presuppose unification of concepts hitherto regarded as being opposites and therefore irreconcilable. Here, the properties of any one pattern are determined by the properties of other patterns, so that one is not more fundamental than the other, and each is mutually embodied. In this cosmic dance, movement and change of each pattern "bootstraps" the others. The observer, therefore, participates in a pattern of interconnection in a network of events, which yields a structure of interrelated events, but a structure composed not only of fundamental constituents of matter. In its most extreme form, the "bootstrap" conjecture suggests that structure, the phenomenon that physicists observe in nature, is a creation of our measuring and categorizing mind; "structure" implies the existence of consciousness as necessary for the self-consistency of the whole (Capra, *The Tao of Physics*, 351). Among those contemplating such a direct relation between consciousness and matter, Capra cites David Bohm as going further than anybody else; Bohm explores an order he believes to be inherent at a deeper non-manifest level, one he calls the "implicate order" in *Wholeness and the Implicate Order*. The writings of both Capra and Bohm have had an important influence on the way New Age thinking associates with environmentalism, although the propensity of New Agers to market a highly simplified version of spirituality in conjunction with ideas from quantum physics has drawn adverse comments from ecofeminists (Spretnak, 2, 28).

Gregory Bateson, a biologist and anthropologist, rejects any direct correlation of human consciousness with physical aspects of matter and energy. Bateson believes that whatever ultimate order exists in the material universe can never be grasped. That there is such order Bateson is prepared to grant; but the only holistic order that we human beings can know and comprehend is the organic order of which humanity itself is a part. Borrowing the terms of Carl Jung, Bateson distinguishes between pleroma, the unliving world described by physics (the "void" or "fullness" which can be known only in a limited manner, its appearances explained only through quantitative measurement of its mass or its time or its length), and creatura, a world that continually "speaks of itself," a world in which the very phenomenon described is determined by patterns of information, their differences and their distinctions.

Bateson concentrates on a rigorous understanding of the immanence of order in nature and its systemic capacity to undertake adjustment to change through evolution. Bateson maintains a correlation between systemic natural activity of this sort and the sort of activity that human beings would describe as "learning" (*Mind and Nature*, 91–128). From a systemic point of view, "mind" and "learning" are as much a predominant feature of all biological organization as are its material elements and energy. This is the key notion in his phrase "ecology of mind." Nature has intelligence, it requires intelligence for its own organization, a point that modern biology ought to recognize as fundamental. Individual mammals are certainly able to communicate about relationships with their own young, and even plants are able to communicate about change in their own ecosystem, although the communication of plant adaptation obviously does not involve self-description of circumstances; its form of communication is injunctive, in the context of their cybernetic capacity to adjust (Bateson, quoted in Harries-Jones, 204–206). In Bateson's usage, "mind" designates the way in which all organic orders, or levels of order, learn and respond to each other as a necessary part of their own self-organization; or, in different phrasing, they are part of a common cybernetic order. Here, there is an evident link with the Gaia hypothesis put forward by James Lovelock, namely that the whole biosphere acts cybernetically in order to support life.

The unique aspect of Bateson is that he approaches issues of ecological unity and integrity, together with holism, from the prospect of possible pathologies in human thinking. Rather than portraying an ecological aesthetic as humanity merging with nature, divinity, or cosmos, he argues for increased awareness of evident uncertainties in our knowledge about ecology—that is to say, the paradoxes and double binds in which our own pattern of communicative relations with nature places us. To say anything about creatura is at once to create distinctions and so recursively point to the criteria for making such a distinction. We are always implicated in our own distinctions about creatura, and unlike the material universe, these distinctions that we make will always catch us in the back. It is therefore possible to have an aesthetic that is pathological. In his younger days Bateson analyzed pathologies in Nazi propaganda films about Fatherland and love of nature, and in his later writing he worried over the propensity of natural scientists to love the elegance of abstractions in their theories rather than the natural patterns from which they were initially abstracted.

Nevertheless, his posthumous publication pursues an alternative epistemology for science, and with it a proposal for an alternative methodology—that of abduction instead of induction—so that when the split between mind and problems of matter ceases to be "a central determinant of what is impossible to think about," aesthetics, the beautiful and the ugly, will become accessible to formal scientific thought (*Angels Fear*, 63).

Selected Works and Further Reading

Bateson, Gregory, *Angels Fear: Towards an Epistemology of the Sacred,* New York: Macmillan, 1987

———, *Mind and Nature: A Necessary Unity,* New York: Dutton, 1979; London: Wildwood House, 1979

Berleant, Arnold, *The Aesthetics of Environment,* Philadelphia: Temple University Press, 1992

Berry, Wendell, *The Gift of Good Land: Further Essays, Cultural and Agricultural,* San Francisco: North Point, 1981

———, *Home Economics: Fourteen Essays,* San Francisco: North Point, 1987

———, *Standing on Earth: Selected Essays,* Ipswich, England: Golgonooza, 1991

———, *The Unsettling of America: Culture and Agriculture,* San Francisco: Sierra Club, 1977

Bohm, David, *Wholeness and the Implicate Order,* Boston and London: Routledge and Kegan Paul, 1980

Callicott, J. Baird, *In Defense of the Land Ethic: Essays in Environmental Philosophy,* Albany: State University of New York Press, 1989

Capra, Fritjof, *The Tao of Physics: An Exploration of the Parallels Between Modern Physics and Eastern Mysticism,* Berkeley, California: Shambhala, 1975; London: Wildwood House, 1975

———, *The Turning Point: Science, Society, and the Rising Culture,* New York: Simon & Schuster, 1982; London: Wildwood House, 1982

Hargrove, Eugene C., *Foundations of Environmental Ethics,* Englewood Cliffs, New Jersey: Prentice-Hall, 1989

Harries-Jones, Peter, *A Recursive Vision: Ecological Understanding and Gregory Bateson,* Toronto, Ontario: University of Toronto Press, 1995

Lovelock, J. E., *Gaia: A New Look at Life on Earth,* New York and Oxford: Oxford University Press, 1979

Næss, Arne, *Ecology, Community, and Lifestyle: Outline of an Ecosophy,* New York and Cambridge: Cambridge University Press, 1989

Nash, Roderick F., *The Rights of Nature: A History of Environmental Ethics,* Madison: University of Wisconsin Press, 1989

Shiva, Vandana, *Monocultures of the Mind: Perspectives on Biodiversity and Biotechnology,* Atlantic Highlands, New Jersey, and London: Zed, 1993

Skolimowski, Henryk, *A Sacred Place to Dwell: Living with Reverence upon the Earth,* Rockport, Massachusetts: Element, 1993

Spretnak, Charlene, *States of Grace: The Recovery of Meaning in the Postmodern Age,* San Francisco: Harper SanFrancisco, 1991

Women "Writing" Nature: Exploring Contemporary Travelers and the Idea of Home

Arlene Plevin

"Is it lack of imagination that makes us come to imagined
places, not just stay at home?"
—(Bishop, "Questions of Travel")

Gazing out over a "foreign" landscape, Elizabeth Bishop's fictitious traveler wonders about motivation and location. Bishop's poem creates the idea of a perceived lack prompting exploration: that home in itself, wherever or whatever it may be, is not sufficient. "Questions of Travel" sets up the traveler as one who questions the very idea of travel. As such, it helpfully begins a discussion about the complexities of women traveling and how they write about and shape their journeys. Examining such disparate travel writers as Robyn Davidson, Sorrel Wilby, Mary Morris, and Pam Houston and their varying experiences with nature—ranging initially from Davidson's desire to connect with the Aborigines in Australia to Wilby's seemingly erotic infatuation with the Tibetan landscape—show a multitude of responses to the idea of travel and immersion in nature. Although to find out more about oneself is, in some respects, the classic expectation of travel, what these travel writers often inadvertently court and discover is a complete dissolving of self, a transformative melding from which they emerge with a new sense of center, of "home." Jamaica Kincaid, not usually considered a travel writer, introduces into this mix an anti-travel narrative—an aggressive, in-your-face denial of foreign lands as complacent other and fodder for male or female reconstruction. The question of what travel can engender is paramount for Kincaid, whose narrative *A Small Place* explores the kind of violence it can do.

While some of the writers above might initially have been stirred by what Vera Norwood notes is British traveler Isabella Bird's desire "to experience nature alone," their experiences suggest not only different expectations but also differing concepts of nature (p. 327). While nature can stand for that which is not culture, what it represents is usually deeply personal. As Donna Haraway, writing of what "postmodern strategies" can do, notes: "the certainty of what counts as nature—a source of insight and promise of innocence—is undermined, probably fatally" (p. 152–153). While what constitutes nature is explored differently by Davidson, Wilby, Morris, and Houston, it has historically been viewed as transformative in a particular way for men. Overtly reflecting this, George Evans exclaimed, "The wilderness will take hold of you. It . . . will turn you from a weakling into a man" (quoted in Nash, 141). This view of the metamorphosing power of wilderness was embraced by such public figures as Theodore Roosevelt, whose turn to nature as a domestic producer of masculinity evolved from the cultural logic of the times (Bederman, 174). In part, Roosevelt's use of nature, as a platform upon which men can stage their masculinity, is a form of engagement criticized by ecofeminists. As Patrick D. Murphy notes of Susan Griffin's *Woman and Nature: The Roaring Inside Her,* it "reveals the close connection between women's subjugation and the ways in which men have defined nature, to render all that is defined as nonhuman as discrete objects also only for attention, domination, and conquest" (p. 47).

What it means to travel becomes inextricably intertwined with the journey to nature. For Davidson, Wilby, Morris, and Houston, traveling means being vulnerable—an overall permeability to others' culture and to nature around them. In part, nature becomes a medium for personal change, for some kind of origin perceived as more immediate, more trustworthy than culture, where they can reclaim the tale of self.

Questions of Travel, Questions of Nature

What travel produces, or, indeed, who is able to travel, is historically complicated by other questions as well—power and gender. For James Clifford, "The traveler, by definition, is someone who has the security and privilege to move about in relatively unconstrained ways" (p. 107). Importantly, not everyone has had unlimited access to such freedom, which Clifford acknowledges: "travel's value is complicated by the fact that, historically, women [were] impeded from serious travel" (p. 105). Generally, women who traveled were of independent means, free from domestic ties. While their travel diaries or other accounts might be published during their lifetimes, typically their writing has been overlooked. Overall, the prevailing image of the nineteenth-century female travel writer was of an interestingly peculiar woman who left home, a location that Elizabeth A. Bohls has noted "was literally and symbolically women's place" (p. 17). While male explorers could receive generous financial backing and publicity, women were typically denied this support because they did not fit the image (Bohls, 17). Norwood comments that women were "thought to be more comfortable in rural, cultivated nature—in civilized gardens," a perception that women themselves often did not dispute (p. 324). Understanding where society thought they should or should not be and how they should or should not arrive there has continuously influenced women writing about their travels beyond home, beyond the garden.

Quarrels with travel writing are worth considering, addressing just what or who is the subject. On the topic of the traveling persona, Sallie Tisdale writes in "Never Let the Locals See Your Map" that "the writers themselves are the subject now, not the places they go, and in this particular form of navel-gazing, that means the subject is their own discontent" (p. 67). Certainly for several of the writers examined, discontent motivates part of the journey, but it is shed by the side of the track—in part dissolving by journey's end. Instead, the authors seek a different form of mobility, one which by its bent engages with the local population. There is, of course,

the romance of movement, the displacement that travel of any sort promises with the potential engagement with a place other than home. It is here that Jamaica Kincaid's work is particularly useful in suggesting the complicity of travel and of all kinds of representation—including the idea of nature. *A Small Place* is about Kincaid's homeland, Antigua, and it is so disruptive of the expected invitation to enjoy location, so devoid of the seductive phrases that typically characterize travel writing, that its unexpected dissonance forces contemplation. Just what does travel construct, and who is doing what to whom? From the beginning, Kincaid addresses the reader, the potential visitor: "Let me just show you how you looked to us. You came. You took things that were not yours, and you did not, even, for appearances' sake, ask first. There must have been some good people among you, but they stayed home. And that is the point. That is why they are good. They stayed home" (p. 35).

Instead of the readers/visitors constructing the subjects of the visit—the landscape, the cities, the crafts and creations of the people, or even creating some archetypal travel trope of arrival, there is the narrator denying cooperation: this land will not reflect back the constructed innocence of the visitor. Instead, the visitor will be shown how he or she appeared. While many women travel writers, Mary Kingsley in particular, have overturned and complicated the traditional heroic trope of arrival—the white man unquestionably standing on top of some kind of promontory, surveying the landscape and beginning to name all from his perspective, in what Mary Louise Pratt appropriately calls the "monarch-of-all-I-survey"—Kincaid's narrative refuses the traveler the very right to arrive (p. 201).

Kincaid begins her assault on the visitor's presumption of presence early in the book, writing of the visitor as someone "marveling at the harmony" of Antigua, although she parenthetically notes their real feelings: "(ordinarily, what you would say is the backwardness)" (p. 16). The visitor also marvels at "the union these other people (and they are other people) have with nature" (p. 16). Here Kincaid suggests others label nature as insufficient. A union or connection with it, ironically with the very landscape that draws the tourist, is really "backwards," showing a lack of sophistication. As a source of connection for the tourist, nature is set up as inferior to culture. Nature becomes a kind of "surplus value" for the so-called tourist, commodified as backdrop and consumed in service of an amazingly resistant preconception of what it is supposed to be like.

In the Desert

Kincaid's critique of a dilettante-like involvement with land and people—the tourist as flotsam—helps contrast Robyn Davidson. When asked about her world, Davidson replies, "A couple of years before, someone had asked me a question: 'What is the substance of the world in which you live?' . . . It took me an hour to answer it, and when I did, my answer seemed to come almost directly from the subconscious. 'Desert, purity, fire, air, hot wind, space, sun, desert desert desert'" (p. 50).

For Davidson, whose book *Tracks* chronicles how she came to cross Australia's outback, her response suggests what prompted her across 1,700 miles with four camels and a dog. In part, it is the desert and the promise of unmediated immersion—the long miles far from her past life and the process of preparation, plus the chance of moving among the indigenous people—which motivates her (p. 50). Having "read a good deal about Aborigines," she wanted "a way of getting to know them directly and simply" (p. 50). Writing *Tracks* in the early 1980s, Davidson was conscious of her Australian culture's overall dismissal of native people, and so such a statement at the book's beginning dramatically establishes this desire and its exception to the cultural mores. Davidson emphasizes her perception of that and the gender difference by reproducing one man's telling comment that "' . . . you're not goin' to the Alice alone are ya? Listen 'ere, lady, you're fuckin' done for. . . . Fuckin' niggers run wild up there ya know'" (p. 20). For Davidson, however, the aboriginal people she meets—and those whites who do not share the mainstream perception of them—offer another connection to the land she travels through, in addition to her mode of transport.

Four camels and their sometimes petulant, sometimes affectionate but always camelish personalities encompass Davidson's world. For Davidson, these animals do more than carry her supplies: they are her companions and her occasionally cranky nemeses. Davidson's immersion in her camels is necessary to survival, but her deepening connection to them is part of her process of dissolving some of her own boundaries. How Davidson arrives, the self-conscious aspect of that process, underscores her changing relationship to the natural world around her.

Instead of claiming the role of the conquering white hero, the trope of the arriving male, she twists it by virtue of her means of transport and her motivation. Her camels immediately link her with the desert and some of its people. "The camels were like a key in relating to Pitjantjara people," Davidson observes. "They had a special relationship with these animals" (p. 129).

Davidson's desire to know more about the miles of desert, to be self-sufficient and connected, includes studying it with locals and other experts. "I had learnt about wild foods from Aboriginal friends in Alice Springs, and from Peter Latz, an ethnobotanist whose passion was desert plant-foods. At first, I had not found it easy to remember and recognize plants after they had been pointed out to me, but eventually the scales fell from my eyes" (p. 121). It is hard to miss the Biblical reference to Davidson's improving gaze. As the scales fall, she can see what the desert has to offer—its life-sustaining possibilities and a link made possible by her solo journey and her eroding sense of self-boundaries. Davidson writes enthusiastically about being embraced, unmediated, by the desert, and, once again, her eyes are the site of revelation as she surrenders to all the forces around her. She has unlimited agency: she can dance and call out; mountains have a force from within. She can follow eagles and wish to fly, but her gaze, from eyes "peeled" and open, show the rejuvenating power of her trip, her immersion under her own power in nature (p. 111). What is beyond her becomes her. Limits disappear and even her gaze changes, becoming less proprietary: "The land was not wild but tame, bountiful, benign, giving, as long as you *knew how to see it*, how to be a part of it" (p. 179, emphasis mine). For Davidson, it is one of many scenes of joyousness and generosity. A stripping of self-veneer, made possible through being in the nonhuman created world around her, enables her to become more rooted in her surroundings without co-opting what is about her. This dissolving seems to enable a strength and, in an ironic reversal, a stronger belief in self-sufficiency. Traveling this way, Davidson strips down literally and figuratively. It is an important unsheathing which involves removing barriers and the weight of ownership. Davidson offers: "I had pared my possessions down to almost nothing—a survival kit, that's all. I had a filthy old sarong for hot weather, and a jumper and woolly socks for cold weather . . . I felt free and untrammeled and light and I wanted to stay that way" (p. 252).

Davidson's transformation, however, becomes more than permeability to her surroundings. As she walks further into the outback, struggling with wild camels, her own camels, and the difficult daily tasks of survival, she becomes more at one with her surroundings. Her access and knowledge begins unconsciously as her "environment began to teach me about itself without my full awareness of the process. It became an animate being of which I was a part" (p. 195). In the Western world, usually so dependent on the defended ego, a strong sense of self defined by work, family, and other categories, Davidson's boundaries of self are now infinite, chaotic, but ultimately embracing of another reality. It is not unlike what Murphy writes of when he wonders: "What if instead of alienation we posited *relation* as the primary mode of human-human and human-nature interaction without conflating difference, particularity and other specificities? What if we worked from a concept of relational difference and *anotherness* rather than Otherness?" (p. 35).

This sense of "anotherness" can be seen in how the desert plant foods, the trees, and even the desert itself are Davidson. While the temptation is present to conflate the Aborigines with nature—having one stand in for the other and damaging their differences in a kind of tourist-like romanticizing of the Aborigines as "carriers" of all that is natural—Davidson tempers that possibility by including portraits of the native peoples with whom she spends time. And, by giving them a presence and a voice in her work she welcomes their significance. Eddie, an elder Aborigine, Davidson writes: "was sheer pleasure to be with, exuding all those qualities typical of old Aboriginal people. . . . And I wondered as we walked along, how the word 'primitive' with all its subtle and nasty connotations ever got to be associated with people like this . . . he was healthy, integrated, whole" (p. 165).

Here Kincaid's critique of the tourist echoes; the so-called primitive is whole. It is through her evaluation of a kind of use of the Aborigines that Davidson suggests a definition for tourism, which follows from Kincaid's perspective. Lack of knowledge and superficiality brand the tourist. Davidson is depressed by a photographer whose "photos [were] using the magnificent earth as a backdrop" (p. 143). This trivialization of nature prevents connection and eventually nature as cure. Again and again, nature as cure is felt and seen by Davidson, who leaves the world she knew to enter "a new time, space, dimension," to find another self (p. 157).

Across the World's Roof: Sorrel Wilby

Like Davidson, Sorrel Wilby views travel as a transformative agent, reflecting the romance of losing one's cultural frame of reference along the way to forging a new self. Wilby's *Journey Across Tibet* details the difficulties of walking 2,000 miles across what is revealingly called the roof of the world, sometimes solo, sometimes with the help of a guide or the brief aid of Budget, the recalcitrant donkey who unexpectedly departs after a mere two days on the trail. Wilby's work also chronicles a young woman anticipating the transfiguring aspect of traveling: "I was growing, adapting, learning so much—about myself, the world, and most importantly, about the beauty of its cultural and physical diversity" (p. 7). Similar to her fellow Australian, Davidson, Wilby finds that "buckets of cold water" and the "paradise" around her help throw off the stultifying aspects of civilization, the "last, clinging cobwebs of jet and video bus lag" (38–9). For Wilby, nature is initially inspiration and beauty.

From the beginning, Wilby plunges into Tibetan food, culture, and the land beyond the isolated villages she encounters, often demonstrating a complete lack of proprietary perspective. She doesn't perch on a mountain and "own" it, despite her often bloody travails to get there. From the first, she is aware of her smallness in the landscape, confessing, "I seemed to be floating; small and insignificant" (p. 1). Using the land to explain and understand, not condemn, the practices of the people, Wilby puts, for example, "the Tibetan meat-eating habit down to necessity," contemplating "how barren Tibet had seemed so far—the lack of vegetation, save for the occasional poplar tree, and the rocky, freezing landscape" (p. 14). And in the tradition of complaining about an aspect of travel, Wilby has problems first with her donkey, who quickly mutinies and escapes, to her shoes, which cause her constant torment. Humorously, Wilby projects part of that problem outside herself, and her connection with nature takes on another dimension. For her, an eagle is not only soaring in exalted freedom but mercifully removed from her human and very earthly obstacle of painful feet.

Initially, however, Wilby makes nature her foe. As she struggles in Tibet's cold, with "unexpected adversity" and "poor physical condition," she recognizes that she "had made this land my enemy" (p. 68). It is a recognition she quickly corrects, understanding the need to become part of it. Echoing Davidson's experience, Wilby's immersion in nature is intimate, in part because of the difficult journey and also because of her overt desire to experience as much of the country as she can. It is an enthusiasm for everything encountered that often borders on infatuation. Once Wilby embraces the pain, loneliness, and difficulty that she will experience, accepting and actually welcoming the stretching—indeed changing—of her personal borders, her language reveals an exuberance with everything around her, as well as a new kind of seeing. After months on the barren plains, Wilby's embrace of a tree practically leaps from the page: the tree "was the first I had seen in months, the first I had ever really *seen* in my life. I wanted to . . . hug it, dance around it" (p. 208).

Like Davidson, Wilby finds that stripping down—in this case walking without her pack—enables her to become more self-sufficient and permeable to what is around her. In faith, Wilby now must seek from the people she meets and the land. Because Wilby walks through their countryside, traveling in a way akin to many Tibetans' notion of pilgrimage, she seems to be met with courtesy, warmth, and welcome. Simple food and a sheltered place for sleep enable her to go on. The nomads and other people with whom she stays help her link even more with the mountains, rivers, and long plains. Enabled by their kindness, which she recognizes again and again, her journey allows her to understand herself. When too much exposure causes temporary but painful snow blindness, Wilby moves to another tier of understanding. In part, her affliction indicates a certain youthful naïveté, but, on another level, it signifies a total immersion and surrendering to the environment. Blind, she must now be led by those she wishes to watch through the Tibetan landscape whose stark beauty has filled her heart. In "surrendering," she allows herself to relearn an essential lesson, the generous nature of Tibetans and her own dependence, the limits of her knowledge, and the balm of the natural landscape.

Declaring Travel: Morris

In *Nothing to Declare: Memoirs of a Woman Traveling Alone,* Mary Morris sounds as if tedium and ennui prompts her travels. Acknowledging she "had grown weary of life in New York," she is "ready for a change" and goes "in search of a place where the land and the people and the time in which they lived were somehow connected." It will be San Miguel, Mexico, Morris chooses, where "life would begin to make sense to me again" (p. 4). Unlike Davidson or Wilby, the American Morris orients herself from a kind of "room of her own," a safe place represented by her small apartment, from which she ventures into the newness of Mexico. From this physical and psychological refuge, she finds the desire and strength to open herself up to wonder and to the often brutalized environment around her. While nature for Wilby and Davidson is as far away as one can get from urban culture, for Morris it is more connecting with people, noticing the so-called smaller, less wilderness-like beauty of her neighborhood (p. 5). In her apartment, in the "dustiest, dirtiest place" in the town (p. 9), Morris seeks flowers, "living things" (p. 14). Nature also becomes a means of connecting with people, such as Lupe, the woman who becomes her closest friend, and through whom she learns simply to be in the moment (p. 138).

Morris's description of meditating on a green hummingbird suggests a metaphor for herself as well as a balance that must be struck between humans and nature. For Morris, the tiny bird, "its color that of emeralds as it hung, suspended in midflight, over the heart of a yellow cactus flower in the sun," must be left alone (p. 39). It is a delicate suspension, yet sturdy. From these moments of observation, Morris moves into more intimate links. Nature becomes rebirth and salvation, the means to comfort. In a central scene, Morris enters the ocean "as if into a baptismal" and the water holds her, offering solace and succor (p. 101). At the end of *Nothing to Declare,* Morris creates a powerful reverie symbolizing her integration and escape. In the voice of a woman who has "stood in the jungles of Tikal, surprised at how easy it is to be with myself," Morris envisions herself as a sacrifice in the pyramids of Teotihuacán (p. 243). After the "knife slices . . . birds fly out" and "her heart throbs, resilient" as "suddenly," she writes, "I am rid of my body" (244). Embracing the possibilities travel offers, she declares: "I am the first woman to be granted this privilege, to be sacrificed to the sun, to be free of my body and free to fly" (p. 244).

Through powerful imaginings of herself as an eagle, Morris notes "her sight is excellent" as she reconnects to a bald eagle that, when she was a young girl, had made her "thirsty to take a trip" (p. 224). As this vital bird, Morris returns for "a small girl standing by the side of the road...[who] wants to come with me . . . is asking for the way" (p. 246). It is Morris as she once was, and by her journey's end, having swum in the ocean and flown high in the sky, she is able to enfold that person while becoming someone new.

A Cold "Cure"

It is not only in the comfort of warm weather, however, that connection and change occur. As the subhead under Pam Houston's essay, "A Blizzard under Blue Sky," trenchantly notes: "Winter camping proves to be better than Prozac" (p. 33). Indeed, for the "clinically depressed" Houston, a few days in Utah's cold and quiet with the comfort of her "two best friends, my yin and yang of dogs," affords a quick remedy (p. 34). Outfitted with adequate winter gear from a pal for her first attempt at winter camping, Houston finds that the icy beauty is appealing, challenging, and transforming.

In this setting, with a vision able to see for miles, Houston will venture, expressing, on a more pedestrian level, what the others have worked out. Alienated from her life and unhappy, Houston's time in the backcountry is simply an extension of other experiences. She explains: "There had never been anything wrong in my life that a few good days in the wilderness wouldn't cure" (p. 35). It is the isolation, the comfort of her warm dogs, and the "alternating pain and numbness" of cold which begins to convince her, " I must still be alive." To be alive, in this case, is to let loose fears and doubts, to reconnect with who she was. Houston is able to cut to her center, letting go of depression: "What really happened, of course, is that I remembered about joy" (p. 37).

Going Home

When Sallie Tisdale comments that a person "could almost define modern travel literature as writing that is specifically about disconnection; it is a genre of isolation, marked by hindsight and cool self-possession in the face of disasters, natural and otherwise. Fear—real fear—never bleeds through," she is not commenting on Davidson, Wilby, Morris, Houston, or many other women travel writers (p. 67). For them, the old image of the mostly male explorer no longer confines, although questions of autonomy and

fear do remain. Many of the writers do note their apprehension and uncertainty, especially on the edge of sites, both literal and metaphorical, that they could not have anticipated. While they might have started "disconnected" from their world, the people and places around them, their travels in nature are ultimately about reconnection. It is an intimate reconceptualizing of who they are in the world, which inherently shows a bond that blossoms within, that both is from and is their core. It is a center of self refashioned in nature, which is comfortable with fear and uncertainty, a home in every sense of the word. And it is from this nucleus, simultaneously centered and permeable, that they connect with others, recognizing few boundaries. For many, it is a time and space where, as Davidson puts it succinctly, "I don't think I have ever felt so good in my life" (p. 178).

Selected Works and Further Reading

Bederman, Gail, *Manliness and Civilization: A Cultural History of Gender and Race in the United States, 1880–1917,* Chicago: University of Chicago Press, 1995

Bishop, Elizabeth, *Questions of Travel,* New York: Farrar, Straus and Giroux, 1965

Bohls, Elizabeth A., *Women Travel Writers and the Language of Aesthetics, 1716–1818,* New York and Cambridge: Cambridge University Press, 1995

Clifford, James, "Traveling Cultures," in *Cultural Studies,* edited by Lawrence Grossberg, Cary Nelson, and Paula Treichler, New York: Routledge, 1992

Davidson, Robyn, *Tracks,* New York: Pantheon, 1980; London: Jonathan Cape, 1980

Haraway, Donna J., *Simians, Cyborgs, and Women: The Reinvention of Nature,* New York: Routledge, 1991; London: Free Association, 1991

Houston, Pam, "A Blizzard under Blue Sky," in *Travelers' Tales: A Woman's World,* edited by Marybeth Bond, San Francisco: Travelers' Tales, 1995

Kincaid, Jamaica, *A Small Place,* New York: Farrar, Straus and Giroux, 1988; London: Virago, 1988

Morris, Mary, *Nothing to Declare: Memoirs of a Woman Traveling Alone,* Boston: Houghton Mifflin, 1988; London: Hamilton, 1988

Murphy, Patrick D., *Literature, Nature, and*

Other: Ecofeminist Critiques, Albany: State
University of New York Press, 1995

Nash, Roderick, *Wilderness and the American
Mind,* 3rd ed., New Haven, Connecticut:
Yale University Press, 1982

Norwood, Vera K., "Heroines of Nature: Four
Women Respond to the American
Landscape," in *The Ecocriticism Reader:
Landmarks in Literary Ecology,* edited by
Cheryll Glotfelty and Harold Fromm,

Athens: University of Georgia Press,
1996

Pratt, Mary Louise, *Imperial Eyes: Travel
Writing and Transculturation,* New York
and London: Routledge, 1992

Tisdale, Sallie, "Never Let the Locals See
Your Map," *Harper's* 291:1744
(September 1995), pp. 66–74

Wilby, Sorrel, *Journey Across Tibet,* Chicago:
Contemporary, 1988

Literature as Community: The Essential Utility of the Literature of Earth First!

Steven C. Steel

The broad and currently ill-defined category of "literature and the environment" can include work from a variety of perspectives. For example, an essayist might seek to position nature writing as a coherent genre by critiquing the works of writers such as Henry David Thoreau, John Muir, or Barry Lopez. Alternatively, works that do not specifically focus on nature could be interrogated from a naturalist perspective by exposing how the natural setting reflects on a novel, how a poem's espoused values compare to ecological wisdom, or how resources affect the plot of a play (Glotfelty and Fromm). Overall, ecology and sense of place can serve to inform literary criticism, and this can help define a new and informative synthetic body of work, serving as a new perspective for illumination of literature in much the same way that perspectives of race, class, and gender have in the past (Glotfelty, xix).

This essay exposes a further boundary of ecological literary studies, however. In addition to critiquing mainstream literature from the vantage point of ecological understanding, it is imperative that scholars work to understand the literature of the grass roots of the ecological movement itself, as that literature is a vibrant part of the vitality of that movement. As an example, the radical ecological group Earth First! has generated a significant body of internal group literature, and it is this production of literature that allows the group to continue to function in modes of oppositional criticism of modern mainstream Western industrial culture. Indeed, the literature of the Earth First! movement provides such vital procedure for the group that it can be said that Earth First! would have difficulty surviving as a viable part of the environmental movement without its literary heritage. Understanding Earth First! demands interrogating and understanding the literature of Earth First!, because its symbols, cartoons, poems, songs, and stories provide a significant number of functions for the group's continuation.

Indeed, as Earth First! works to defy the conventional limits of social perspective and thereby serves to challenge the status quo, the group must erect a symbolic frame which unites movement members under a coherent mythos. Once erected, the symbolic mythos must be continually maintained and reiterated both for group members and for those outside the group. For the group to continue as a viable entity, it must have some means whereby its tactics and beliefs are not only reinforced for movement members, but also made to seem influential and irrefutably resilient. It is thus essential to group solidarity and cohesion that a credible symbolic envelope be constructed around the group community; proper explication of Earth First! thus demands an explication of that symbolic envelope.

This task demands a cultural interpretation of the symbolic literature of Earth First! As formulated by Pierre Bourdieu, the critique of a cultural formulation like Earth First! involves a recreation of the symbolic construction of individual, subjective reality, that is, a mastery of the social symbols and how they are interpreted by social agents. The cultural milieu of a group such as Earth First! is thus not a set of rules but reified, socially constructed strategies that allow for social action (Bourdieu, 15). These strategies are symbolic in nature. The word "symbol" is used here as in Anthony Cohen's derivation: not as a mere representation but as a partial and unfulfilled meaning accompanied by the exhortation to be filled by those who employ or are exposed to the symbol. This capacity of symbols is extremely significant in constituting the boundaries that determine a community, including the "community" that is the Earth First! movement. Although awareness of community is held in common by community (e.g. Earth First!) members, the meaning of that community "varies with its members' unique orientations to it" (Cohen, 15). Because of this variability, the "consciousness of community" must be maintained through symbolic construction and manipulation (p. 15). The life of a community thus resides in the reading of its symbolism as it is incorporated into the preexisting discourse of its cultural inhabitants. That symbolism provides a cohesive referential boundary, or "frame," for what would otherwise be an incoherent amalgam of erratic interpretations.

These parameters can be used to focus on the literature of Earth First! by deciphering the symbolic construction and subsequent decoding of that literature. First, however, a brief discussion of the nature of the Earth First! movement and the environmental movement from which it sprang will be useful. Earth First! was founded as an alternative to what several founding members have termed "reform environmentalism." These activists from groups such as the Wilderness Society and the Sierra Club saw such mainstream, "professionalized" environmental groups as seeking constant compromise in a "stampede for influence and credibility" (Manes, 59), and this compromising attitude usually had the effect of slowly but inexorably destroying more and more of the last remaining wilderness areas within the jurisdiction of the United States. The philosophical perspective of the founding members can be described as "deep ecology," which has been defined by Dave Foreman, recognized as the leading organizing force behind Earth First!, as a deep ethical respect for the inherent right of nature to exist unencumbered by the desires of mankind (*Confessions*, 3, 19).

The initial organizing event which proclaimed the founding of Earth First! was the symbolic "cracking" of Glen Canyon Dam, a dam that had been built through compromises agreed to by reformist groups like the Sierra Club and had flooded what was arguably some of the most striking scenery along the Colorado River (*Confessions*, 21–22). This event was followed by a variety of other direct actions termed "ecotage" (sabotage in the name of the environment) by the group, including pouring sand into bulldozer crankcases to debilitate them and the notorious practice of "tree spiking." All these activities derived expediency from the motto of Earth First!, "No Compromise in Defense of

Mother Earth!" From the symbolic green fist as the group's trademark symbol to the obligatory exclamation points at the end of its name and motto, symbolism infuses Earth First! with a unique visibility and power.

The notion of frame analysis as explicated by David Snow and Robert Benford is particularly useful as a theoretical model for deciphering and decoding the essential nature of the symbolic literature of the Earth First! movement. Snow and Benford describe frames as "interpretive schemata" utilized by a social movement to simplify and encode an otherwise complex reality, including objects, situations, and events, so that reality can be more easily naturalized and diffused throughout movement members' consciousness (p. 137). Since frames use symbolic encoding in order to "frame" the collective ideals of the group, the definition and delimitation of those symbols is essential in the process of demarcating the boundaries of that group. The frame has a threefold utility for the movement: it serves to identify problematic conditions, assigns a diagnosis and prescriptive prognosis to those conditions, and allows, through symbolism, for events and experiences to be brought together in a cohesive, meaningful fashion (pp. 137–138). The power of the frame is a function of its legitimacy in the eyes of movement members and its internal cohesion in fashioning a credible and usable mythos for the group.

Earth First! utilizes its extensive literature in order to instill just such a frame for its movement. To reiterate, Earth First! sprang from a rejection of so-called "reform environmentalism" which was seen as giving too much to competing non-environmental interests. The continued destruction of wilderness and infringement on ecosystem integrity thus provides the problematic condition that draws individuals into the Earth First! movement, but, more importantly, specific timber, mining, and cattle corporations and the reform-oriented environmentalist movement are assigned as the "diagnosis" for that condition. The "prognosis" is the formulation of Earth First!: a more radical agenda of intervention into environmental degradation, including passive resistance techniques, the destruction of machinery, and the pounding of 60-penny nails into trees to discourage their use as lumber. Earth First!'s origination thus defined their frame.

Frame definition requires more than simply defining goals; it also requires symbols and myths to serve as frame maintenance devices. Once the frame has been defined, it must be constantly reiterated and reinterpreted to movement members to ensure its survival and continued validity. For Earth First!, the production and dissemination of literature is an essential tool useful in this regard. Earth First! publications include the *Earth First! (EF!) Journal* (the sole movement-wide periodical, used to convey information regarding direct action activities, news, philosophical ruminations, etc.), the *Earth First! (EF!) Songbook* (containing the "folk songs" of the movement with guitar chords so songs can be used at gatherings, as well as pictures, drawings, and other symbols), smaller newsletters such as the *Warrior Poet* published by a group of poets within the movement, and other various slogans, symbols, and images common at gatherings and on T-shirts, bumper stickers, and other paraphernalia.

Much of the symbolism entailed in this literature works as devices for frame maintenance, or "amplification" (Tarrow, 188). One example is the prominent use of the green fist accompanied by the name EARTH FIRST! and the motto "No Compromise in Defense of Mother Earth!" The fist denotes activism, an aggressive seizing of initiative, and internal movement empowerment (Scarce, 61), while the color green differentiates Earth First! as a radical group demanding empowered change within the environmental perspective. The name of the group reiterates that "in any decision consideration for the Earth must come first" (Foreman, "EARTH FIRST!," 188). The use of capital letters and constant use of exclamation points serve as reminders of the urgency of the group's mission and that the time for the "considerate behavior" of reform environmentalism has passed (Scarce, 13). The motto further defines and substantiates the radicalism of Earth First! as it reiterates the group's frame of refusing to compromise with non-environmental interests.

Ecotage is another effective symbolic tool for frame maintenance. Ecotage is alternatively termed "monkeywrenching," from the Edward Abbey novel *The Monkey Wrench Gang*, and the notion of the monkey wrench as a "low-tech instrument" of environmental defense connotes that providing that defense is merely obstructed by a lack of the "will to use the tools at hand" (Morris, 108). The fact that directly intervening in the activities of those who would destroy wilderness demands personal involvement and therefore ownership of the movement cannot be overstated. Ecotage thus further defines Earth First! as a fully activist radical organization.

The emphasis on ecotage is present throughout the literature of Earth First!, including using the monkey wrench as an icon, celebrating ecotage episodes in poetry and song, and publishing abundant "war stories." Indeed, large portions of each edition of the *EF! Journal* are used to publish detailed descriptions of ongoing battles waged against such corporate activities as mining, clear-cutting, and waste dumping. Stories, drawings, and poetry romanticize direct actions taken against corporate destruction of the environment, fully iterating Earth First!'s frame, such as the poem "Sink It!" by Dwight Worker published in the *Journal*:

Bash it and Bend it and Bust it and Break it
Scuttle it and Sink it most any way you can
Maybe we're just grains of sand/in their
    gears of destruction.
But do it do it do it—if you can . . .

More significantly, the literature of direct action and ecotage serves to inscribe the movement's stories, heroes, and martyrs into a lasting mythos of critical engagement for the community group. This allows Earth First! to incorporate the attacks of the mainstream by using them as tools for erecting a culturally coherent strength of solidarity. The development of this cohesive solidarity is formed "in conflict, creating and sustaining solidarity in opposition to the dominant structure" (Fantasia, 27). It is paramount, then, that conflict be symbolized, glorified, and incorporated into a framework that strengthens opposition to the normalized social control forces. This structure is essential for Earth First! as it seeks to operate outside socially approved channels of grievance and instead utilize direct action. This forces Earth First!ers to rely on and trust each other implicitly such that they "rely on their mutual solidarity as the basis of their power" (p. 19). The tactical activities of ecotage are celebrated in Earth First! folk songs and literature, such as the book *Ecodefense*, a "how-to" guide for monkeywrenching. The resulting "war stories" (as stories of direct actions are called by Earth First!ers), cartoons, songs, and poems glorifying battles with timber interests, National Forest Service employees, the mainstream environmental movement, and others serve to congeal a sense of *fraternité*. This enacts a culture of conflict, and a resultant "culture of solidarity" (p. 20).

This war-society implication of Earth First! is thus a priority in Earth First! sensibilities, and much of Earth First!'s literary imagery proclaims a confrontational formulation. One example is the invocation of the Earth First! martyr Judi Bari, an Earth First! organizer and activist well known within the movement who was seriously injured by a pipe bomb that exploded while she was driving through Oakland, California, with fellow activist Darryl Cherney during May 1990 while organizing for the direct action-oriented "Redwood Summer" (Taylor, 261). The Federal Bureau of Investigation (FBI) proclaimed that the pair were the victims of their own terrorist plans gone awry (Helvarg 396). Earth First! folklore holds that the bomb was planted by an informant in order to discredit the movement. Whatever the validity of either story, Judi Bari's plight has been valorized in poem and song, including Cherney's own "Who Bombed Judi Bari?" in the *EF! Songbook:*

. . . Now Judi Bari is an Earth First!
      organizer
The California Redwoods are her home
She called for Redwood Summer/Where the
      Owl and the Black Bear roam
Charlie Hurwitz he runs [timber company]
      MAXXAM out of Houston
Harry Merlo runs L[ouisiana]-P[acific] from
      Portland town
They're the men they call king timber/They
      know how to cut you down . . .
Was no secret what they planned (So I ask
      you now)
Who bombed Judi Bari?/I know you're out
      there still
Have you seen her broken body/Or the spirit
      you can't kill?
Now Judi Bari is the mother of two children
A pipe bomb went rippin' through her womb
She cries at night time/In her Mendocino
      (jail) room
FBI is back again . . . seeking justice is our
      plan
And we'll avenge our wounded comrade/As
      we defend this ravaged land . . .

The martyrdom of Judi Bari is thus canonized into Earth First! legend and used as a call to action for avenging spirits, bringing together Earth First!ers in solidarity against the timber company owners, the FBI, and their violent assaults on environmental activists. Another song by Darryl Cherney and Mike Roselle, "He Looked a Whole Lot Like Jesus," inscribes into legend the infiltra-

tion of Earth First! by an informant and agent provocateur named Fain which led to the arrests of prominent Earth First! activists. The song acts as a cautionary tale, a tale of further martyrdom, and a warning regarding the importance of united vigilance in the face of decided FBI onslaughts. The construction of a culture of conflict is thus a considerable role of Earth First! literature, solidifying the oppositional nature of the movement and reiterating the importance of group cohesion in the face of attack. This facilitates the formation of a culture of solidarity in order to maintain the movement by incorporating mainstream attacks so they become an agent of strength rather than weakness.

A further role of Earth First! literature is to act as devices for symbolic reversal. These symbols serve to build community by juxtaposing Earth First!'s frame with those ideas to which that frame is opposed. As stated above, Earth First!'s organizing principle was opposition to not only the anti-environmental activities of mainstream culture but also to the mainstream reformist environmental movement. Literary efforts serve to reiterate that emphasis. One example is the poem by Matthew Haun entitled "Reduce, Reuse, Recycle" which ridicules those shallow environmentalists who prefer simple, nonthreatening change to the deep lifestyle alteration called for by the Earth First! movement:

. . . Reduce, Reuse, Recycle, Rah!
I feel so good just saying that, let's go out
      and pick some flowers
As we reduce our forest to fiberboard and
      pulp
And recycle the patterns of Political Power
. . . And now I'm driving my bicycle through
      Uptown Traffic
It takes moves never dreamed of by any
      ballet dancer
When I'm nearly run off the road by some
      car
With a bumpersticker that says 'Trees are the
      answer'
I think I've got a better answer for you
Reduce, Recycle, I've never seen it fail
I'm gonna remove your gas cap, Recycle
      some newspaper
And reduce that petro beast to a molotov
      cocktail
. . . And hey, there's money to be made from
      environmental conflict
It's a growth industry and we all play our
      part

The Earth-raper plunders what's left of the
  planet
And the Sierra Club rips off the bleeding
hearts

This poem, chanted in derisive singsong fashion by its author to the delight of the supportive audiences at gatherings, allows for the construction of symbolic reversal. Such symbolic reversal constitutes the community's boundaries by juxtaposing the community (Earth First!) with those outside the community (mainstream society and the reformist environmental movement). By ridiculing and revealing the evils of those outside the community, the community itself is strengthened (Cohen, 63). As the Sierra Club is exposed as charlatan and part of the environmental problem the desirability of Earth First! as viable alternative is asserted. This causes community members to pull more fully into the frame of the community. A large amount of the movement's literature serves a similar purpose, whether by ridiculing the mentality of ranchers (Fritzinger, 26–27), calling those who poach wildlife "manly men" (Keeler, 40–41), or taking the role of the driver of a recreational vehicle (Lyons, 50–51) or a person mesmerized by television (Lyons, 58–59). Symbolic reversal is thus an important component of the movement's symbolic repertoire and forms an essential segment of its literature.

Earth First! literature also serves to liberate the expressiveness of language by expanding its boundaries. For example, the meaning of "forest" is so broad that it applies equally in typical construction to any "collection of trees in close proximity." Old-growth forests, forests which have returned after human disturbance, and human-planted groupings of trees may all be rendered as "forests" with no distinction made between them. The literature of Earth First! derives novel, direct, and subversive expression in order to correct this perceived misrepresentation with a clearer representation (Brantlinger, 104; Ricoeur, 66). For example, calling a human-planted forest a "tree farm" more accurately depicts its true nature and intent: one species, often nonnative, planted in straight rows with chemical and irrigation inputs, harvested in unnatural time spans solely for human use. "Tree farm" not only liberates expression but does so in opposition to the mainstream conception of "reforestation" after removal of old-growth forests.

Photographs can also be used to correct the misrepresentation of environmental reality. As the Sierra Club publishes pictures of pristine nature, the contention that they are adequately protecting the environment is bolstered. Earth First! exposes this fallacy by radically opposing it through publishing photographs and drawings of clear-cuts, bear slaughter, and other violent images that radically contradict mainstream assumptions regarding environmental protection.

Other examples of the use of literature to subvert expression abound. The meaning of "compromise," so cherished in mainstream circles, has been subverted by Earth First! literature to mean the ultimate evil, consigning more and more wilderness to the buzz saw or bulldozer. The meaning of "radical" has likewise been subverted, becoming a badge of honor rather than a term of derision. "Mainstream," "moderation," and a host of other words have been subversively redefined by Earth First!, altering mainstream messages so that they fit into the oppositional message of the movement. One cartoon, for example, represents the direct action of monkey-wrenching a bulldozer, but with a subversive element. The ironic title of the cartoon states, "We're working within the system"—referring to those who decry Earth First! for not doing so. The cartoon, however, reassures that Earth First! does indeed work "within the system"—namely, working within the vital operating systems of bulldozers and other environmentally destructive machinery while disabling them! Earth First! thereby use literature as a "radical creative space" for liberating imagination and expression (hooks, 149).

One last role of Earth First! literature may be the most vital of all. From its original inception in 1980, Earth First! has remained committed to resisting bureaucracy, disdaining hierarchy and leadership to focus instead on local grassroots environmental efforts. Earth First! is carried in the head as an ideal, where it can retain energy and resist co-optation by the larger mainstream system, as opposed to the loss of energy and co-optation suffered by other mainstream environmental groups as perceived by the founders of Earth First! The only true expression of Earth First! congeals around specific environmental threats or direct action activities. When such a need for mobilization occurs, a small group of trusted compatriots plans, executes, and finishes the desired activities in order to block the threat and then disband. This obstructs co-optation, infiltration, and other insidious tactics which could destroy the movement. However, with no meetings, membership, or other centralized structural capabilities, some mechanism for centralizing ideals is essential. Earth First! literature serves to maintain movement coherence as the major set of tools for disseminating movement-wide symbols, writings, and mottoes. This generates a relatively stable mythos for the group, which has no centralized vehicle for imposing one externally.

The literature of Earth First! thus has many substantial cultural characteristics. This literature serves as a set of tools for iterating and reiterating the movement's frame. It allows a culture of conflict to be erected in order to protect the group from mainstream attack. Symbolic reversal helps build cohesion into the movement, an essential task since the community is designed to be structureless. Further, the literature acts to liberate misrepresentation so that a more complete representation of environmental destruction can be allowed. All in all, an investigation of the utility of Earth First! literature—which is largely ignored by academia—is essential in order to understand the continued existence and efficacy of this oppositional grassroots component of the modern environmental movement. Interrogation of the literature of that movement is thus a significant task for the developing conjunction of work on literature and the environment.

Selected Works and Further Reading

Abbey, Edward, *The Monkey Wrench Gang,* Philadelphia: Lippincott, 1975; London: Picador, 1982

Bourdieu, Pierre, *Outline of a Theory of Practice,* New York and Cambridge: Cambridge University Press, 1977

Brantlinger, Patrick, *Crusoe's Footprints: Cultural Studies in Britain and America,* New York: Routledge, 1990

Cherney, Darryl, "Who Bombed Judi Bari?," in *Earth First! Songbook,* Missoula, Montana: Earth First!, 1993

Cherney, Darryl, and Mike Roselle, "He Looked a Whole Lot Like Jesus," in *Earth First! Songbook,* Missoula, Montana: Earth First!, 1993

Cohen, Anthony P., *The Symbolic Construction of Community,* New York: Tavistock, 1985; London: Routledge, 1985

Earth First! Journal

Earth First! Songbook, Missoula, Montana: Earth First!, 1993

Fantasia, Rick, *Cultures of Solidarity: Consciousness, Action, and Contemporary American Workers,* Berkeley: University of California Press, 1988

Foreman, Dave, *Confessions of an Eco-Warrior,* New York: Crown, 1991

———, "EARTH FIRST!," in *Radical Environmentalism: Philosophy and Tactics,* edited by Peter List, Belmont, California: Wadsworth, 1993

Foreman, Dave, and Bill Haywood, eds., *Ecodefense: A Fieldguide to Monkeywrenching,* 2nd ed., Tucson, Arizona: Ned Ludd, 1987

Fritzinger, Dennis, "Song of a Sagebrush Rebel," in *Earth First! Songbook,* Missoula, Montana: Earth First!, 1993

Glotfelty, Cheryll, and Harold Fromm, eds., *The Ecocriticism Reader: Landmarks in Literary Ecology,* Athens: University of Georgia Press, 1996

Haun, Matthew, "Reduce, Reuse, Recycle," *The Warrior Poet* 4:1 (Spring 1995), p. 3

Helvarg, David, *The War Against the Greens: The "Wise-Use" Movement, the New Right and Anti-Environmental Violence,* San Francisco: Sierra Club, 1994

hooks, bell, *Yearning: Race, Gender, and Cultural Politics,* Boston: South End, 1990

Keeler, Greg, "Manly Men," in *Earth First! Songbook,* Missoula, Montana: Earth First!, 1993

Lyons, Dana, "RV," in *Earth First! Songbook,* Missoula, Montana: Earth First!, 1993

———, "TV God," in *Earth First! Songbook,* Missoula, Montana: Earth First!, 1993

Manes, Christopher, *Green Rage: Radical Environmentalism and the Unmaking of Civilization,* Boston: Little, Brown, 1990

Morris, David B., *Earth Warrior: Overboard with Paul Watson and the Sea Shepherd Conservation Society,* Golden, Colorado: Fulcrum, 1995

Ricoeur, Paul, "Althusser's Ideology," in *Althusser: A Critical Reader,* edited by Gregory Elliott, Cambridge, Massachusetts, and Oxford: Blackwell, 1994

Scarce, Rik, *Eco-Warriors: Understanding the Radical Environmental Movement,* Chicago: Noble, 1990

Snow, David A., and Robert D. Benford, "Master Frames and Cycles of Protest," in *Frontiers in Social Movement Theory,* edited by Aldon D. Morris and Carol McClurg

Mueller, New Haven, Connecticut: Yale University Press, 1992

Tarrow, Sidney, "Mentalities, Political Cultures, and Collective Action Frames," in *Frontiers in Social Movement Theory,* edited by Aldon D. Morris and Carol McClurg Mueller, New Haven, Connecticut: Yale University Press, 1992

Taylor, Bron, "The Religion and Politics of Earth First!," *Ecologist* 21:6 (November 1991), pp. 258–266

Worker, Dwight, "Sink It!," *Earth First! Journal* (1996), p. 29

Zakin, Susan, *Coyotes and Town Dogs: Earth First! and the Environmental Movement,* New York: Viking, 1993

Notes on Contributors

Maysa Abou-Youssef has been an instructor in the English department of Indiana University of Pennsylvania and Cairo University, Fayoum, Egypt. She received her doctoral degree from Indiana University of Pennsylvania in 1997 with a dissertation on translation theory and representations of Egyptian culture.

Reiko Akamine holds M.A. degrees from the University of the Ryukyus and the University of Nevada at Reno and specializes in English and Japanese environmental and women's literatures. She has published such essays as "A Voice from the Wilderness: Gary Snyder's Poetry on Wild Nature," "Ghost, Madness, Battle: A Female Identity in *The Woman Warrior*," and "Place and Mythopoesis: A Cross-Cultural Study of Gary Snyder and Michiko Ishimure." She also translates literary works, including Michiko Ishimure's novel *Lake Of Heaven.*

Ken Akiyama is professor of American studies at Poole Gakuin University in Osaka, Japan. He has written extensively about New England Puritanism and transcendentalism.

Bruce Allen is an associate professor of English at Juntendo University, Japan. His primary research interests are nature writing and comparative literature. A graduate of Amherst College and Sophia University, he has lived in Japan for more than 15 years. His most recent book is *Voices of the Earth: Stories of People, Place and Nature.* He is a member of the editorial board of ASLE-Japan.

Karla Armbruster lives outside of Boulder, Colorado, and teaches literature and American studies in a residential program at the University of Colorado. She received her Ph.D. from Ohio State University in 1996 with a dissertation on environmental advocacy in American literature and culture, which she is revising into a book. She is also pursuing research and teaching interests in environmental literary criticism, bioregionalism, and women's perspectives on environmental issues.

Pamela Banting is an award-winning poet, fiction and nonfiction writer, critic, and editor who lives in Calgary, Alberta. In 1995 she published *Body Inc.: A Theory of Translation Poetics,* and her edited anthology of Western Canadian nature writing and writing about place, *Writing the Land*, is scheduled for publication in 1998.

Benay Blend received her doctorate in American Studies from the University of New Mexico. Her major areas of interest are Western women writers, environmental issues, and history of the American West. She is an instructor in the English and history departments of the Louisiana School for Math, Science and the Arts, a state-supported boarding school for gifted students.

Susanne Bounds has worked in both teaching and geology in the desert Southwest, the landscape of which she loves. She currently teaches writing and literature at Morehead State University in Eastern Kentucky, incorporating women's, multicultural, and environmental issues into her courses.

Michael P. Branch is associate professor of literature and environment at the University of Nevada, Reno, where he serves as coordinator of graduate studies in Literature and Environment. He is book review editor of *ISLE* and past president of the Association for the Study of Literature and Environment (ASLE). He has published more than 40 books, articles, chapters, and reviews on nature writing and environmental literature and is co-editor of *The Height of Our Mountains: Nature Writing from Virginia's Blue Ridge Mountains and Shenandoah Valley* and *Critical Essays on Literature and Environment* and is currently editing a scholarly collection of early American nature writing.

Claude Brew is professor of English and department chair at Gustavus Adolphus College in St. Peter, Minnesota. He has camped, fished, and roamed Minnesota's Arrowhead and northwestern Wisconsin for more than 25 years.

G. A. Cevasco teaches English at St. John's University in New York.

Lucia Cherciu was born in Tulnici, Romania. She earned her B.A. and M.A. in English at the University of Bucharest and is completing a Ph.D. in American Literature at Indiana University of Pennsylvania. She has presented conference papers on Arthur Miller and postmodernist fiction.

Karen Cole is associate professor of literature at the Louisiana Scholars' College at Northwestern State University, where she teaches women's studies, Southern literature, and interdisciplinary seminars. She has published on nineteenth-century female humorists and on Kate Chopin. She is currently editing the correspondence of Southern garden writers Caroline Dormon and Elizabeth Lawrence.

John Cooley is a professor of English and environmental studies at Western Michigan University. He has written extensively on environmental and nature writing, including the work of Adirondack writer Anne LaBastille. His most recent book is the edited collection *Earthly Words: Essays on Contemporary Nature and Environmental Writers.*

Seodial Deena is a graduate of the University of Guyana, Chicago State University, and Indiana University of Pennsylvania, where he received his Ph.D. in literature and criticism. He is an assistant professor at East Carolina University, where he coordinates the multicultural literature program and teaches multicultural, world, postcolonial, African American, and Caribbean literatures. He has published in several scholarly journals, including *College Language Association Journal, Commonwealth Review, The Literary Griot,* and *The Journal of Caribbean Literature.* His book *Colonization, Canonization* is forthcoming.

Nick Drayson is a naturalist and writer, living in Canberra, Australia. After arriving from England in 1982, he fell in love with Australia's unique plants and animals and began writing about them in popular magazines. He also earned an M.A. in zoology at the Australian National University before beginning his present study into the literature of Australian natural history, concentrating on pre–twentieth-century perceptions of flora and fauna. In addition to his own writing for popular and scientific publications in Australia, he is compiling a popular anthology of Australian natural history writing.

Cecilia Konchar Farr, associate professor of English at the College of St. Catherine in St. Paul, Minnesota, earned her Ph.D. at Michigan State University in 1990. She specializes in autobiographical theory and has published essays on Melville, Thoreau, and other American writers as well as on various feminist issues. She currently serves as chair of the Women's Caucus of the Modern Language Association and as an executive director of the Society for Studies in American Autobiography.

Roberto Forns-Broggi is an assistant professor of Spanish in Colorado. He has taught at Peruvian high schools and universities and has published a book and articles about reading and creative writing. In 1995 he obtained a Ph.D. in Spanish at the University of Arizona. He is currently working on an anthology of Latin American ecological poetry in translation as well as a bilingual undergraduate textbook of nature poems.

Oliver Friggieri, born in Malta, is head of the department of Maltese and professor at the University of Malta. For his M.A. and Ph.D. theses he did research on the influence of Italian literature on Maltese poetry. He writes poetry, novels, and literary criticism and is the author of the fundamental critical works on Maltese literature. Most of his works have been translated into various languages. He is a member of the Association Internationale des Critiques Littéraires (Paris) and has addressed about 50 international congresses. The list of his works includes: *Storia della Letteratura Maltese, Le rituel du crepuscule, A Distraught Pilgrim, Storie per una sera,* and *Dizzjunarju ta' Termini Letterarji.*

Timothy Gaynor is a part-time lecturer in the School of Humanities at Oxford Brookes University and taught in Nicaragua in 1997. His 1996 dissertation focused on the Chilean writer Isabel Allende. He is also interested in travel writing about South America.

Terry Gifford, a poet and critic, is senior lecturer at Bretton Hall College of Leeds University. With Neil Roberts he co-authored *Ted Hughes: A Critical Study.* His most recent book is *Green Voices: Understanding Contemporary Nature Poetry.* In addition to four collections of poetry, he has recently collaborated with three other poets on the collection *The Blue Bang Theory: New Nature Poetry.* He is director of the annual International Festival of Mountaineering Literature at Bretton Hall College.

Barbara Gordon is a doctoral candidate at the University of Virginia studying contemporary Spanish literature. She has written on doubles and identity in Juan José Millás and Naturalism à la Emilio Pardo Bazán. In conjunction with her doctoral research, she has interviewed numerous well-known contemporary Spanish writers.

Noel Gough is associate professor in the Faculty of Education, Deakin University, Australia, and is also editor (Australasia) of the *Journal of Curriculum Studies* and an executive editor of the *Australian Educational Researcher.* Many of his publications are concerned with the heuristic potential of science fiction in curriculum, pedagogy, and educational inquiry.

Richard Harmond is an associate professor of history at St. John's University in New York. He is the editor of the *Long Island Archives Conference Newsletter* and the associate editor of the *Long Island Historical Journal.*

Peter Harries-Jones is a member of the Department of Anthropology, York University, Ontario. His earlier work was in the field of African society and politics. More recently he has turned to the study of social movements and environmentalism, with particular reference to the interplay between the environmental movement and ecological philosophy. Recent publications include *Making Knowledge Count: Advocacy and Social Science* and *A Recursive Vision: Ecological Understanding and Gregory Bateson.*

Maunu Häyrynen, junior fellow at the Academy of Finland, Research Council for the Environment and Natural Resources, Helsinki, has an M.A. in conservation studies from the University of York Institute of Advanced Architectural Studies and a Ph.D. in art history from the University of Helsinki. Dr. Häyrynen's dissertation treated the movement from scenic parks to reform parks in Finland from the 1880s to the 1930s.

Roslynn D. Haynes is associate professor of English at the University of New South Wales in Sydney, Australia. Having trained in both biochemistry and the humanities, she is particularly interested in interdisciplinary areas of study. Her published books include *H.G. Wells: Discoverer of the Future, From Faust to Strangelove: Representations of the Scientist in Western Literature,* and *Explorers of the Southern Sky: A History of Australian Astronomy,* which she co-authored with her astronomer husband. She has just completed *Seeking the Centre: The Australian Desert in Literature, Art, and Film.* Haynes teaches courses in Australian studies, nineteenth- and twentieth-century English literature, and science and literature.

Andrea W. Herrmann is professor of rhetoric and writing at the University of Arkansas at Little Rock and holds degrees in TESOL and applied linguistics. She is currently working on an ethnography titled *At Desert's Edge: Life in an Arizona Ghost Town.* While many of her publications focus on computers and writing, her ethnographic interests have led her more deeply in recent years into studies of literary nonfiction and the environmental dimensions of Western American life.

Jhan Hochman has a Ph.D. in English from SUNY-Stony Brook and an M.A. in cinema studies from New York University. His work in green cultural studies has appeared in *Genre, Democracy and Nature, ISLE,* and *Mosaic.* His *Signs of Nature* concerns the theory and practice of green cultural studies by way of film, novel, and theory.

Jeremy Hooker is a poet, critic, teacher, and broadcaster. He has published nine collections of poetry, including *A View from the Source: Selected Poems, Their Silence a Language,* and *Our Lady of Europe.* His critical books include monographs on David Jones and John Cowper

Powys and edited books on Alun Lewis and Frances Bellerby. He is currently Professor in the School of English and Creative Studies at Bath Spa University College, Bath, England.

Shogo Ikuta is professor of English at Kanazawa University, Japan. His research mainly focuses on seventeenth- and eighteenth-century English natural history. Among his writings are "Sir Thomas Browne's Natural History: A Note on Pseudododoxia Epidemica" and "White's Selborne: Natural History and the 'Sense of Place'." He is currently speculating on the border crossing of natural history and nature writing.

Deborah Janson is an associate professor of German at West Virginia University, where she teaches courses on language and on literature from the eighteenth to the twentieth centuries. Her research interests include literature of the German Democratic Republic, parallels between Christa Wolf and ecofeminism, ecocritical readings of texts from various periods, and German bourgeois tragedies.

Rochelle Johnson is completing her Ph.D. in American literature at the Claremont Graduate School. Her research focuses on discerning the cultural work of nature writing in nineteenth-century United States. With co-editor Daniel Patterson, she has edited Susan Fenimore Cooper's *Rural Hour* (forthcoming).

Alexander V. Kamenets is an expert in pedagogy, the sociology of culture, and history of the Russian theater. He is a department head at the Institute for Heritage and author of more than 100 publications in Russian, including a student manual on the history of Russian theater, *Theater and Music Art in Russia*, and a two-volume glossary *The Theatres of Russia*.

Yong-ki Kang received his Ph.D. in American literature from Indiana University of Pennsylvania, where he wrote a dissertation on nonfoundationalist environmental ethics in Barbara Kingsolver, N. Scott Momaday, and Gary Snyder. He teaches English at a university in South Korea.

Sadamichi Kato is professor of American literature at Nagoya University, Japan. His recent interests are exemplified by the presentation he made in 1996 on the conservation movement

titled "John Muir and Kumagusu Minakata" at the ASLE Symposium on Japanese and American Environmental Literature.

Richard Kerridge is senior lecturer in English and course director for the M.A. in creative writing at Bath Spa University College. He teaches undergraduate and graduate courses in writing and environmentalism. Co-author of *Nearly Too Much: The Poetry of J. H. Prynne* and co-editor of *Writing the Environment*, he has published widely on contemporary writing and on writing and environmentalism. He received the BBC Wildlife Award for Nature Writing in 1990 and 1991.

Takashi Kinoshita is a professor of English literature and English cultural studies at Ehime University, Japan. He is co-editor of *Book Guide to English Literature* and *Book Guide to English and American Poetry* and co-author of *Images of 'Body' in English Literature* and *Images of 'Family' in English and American Literature*. He is also collaborating on a translation of Terry Tempest Williams's *Desert Quartet: An Erotic Landscape*.

Olga Lavrenova is a research fellow at the Institute for Heritage, where cultural geography is her main academic field. She has published various essays in Russian, including "The Geographic Space in Works of American Writers," "The Artistic Space of Eighteenth-Century Russian Poetry," and "The Geographic Space of Nineteenth and Early Twentieth Century Russian Poetry."

Paul Lindholdt earned his Ph.D. in early American literature and culture with a dissertation that was published in 1988 by the University Press of New England as *John Josselyn, Colonial Traveler*. More recently he has come to specialize in nature writing and environmental literature by writing for lay and academic audiences and by teaching in the English Department at Eastern Washington University, which is located on the Upper Columbia Plateau.

Brad Lookingbill is assistant professor of history at Columbia College, Missouri, and a Ph.D. in history from the University of Toledo. His publications include essays in *Great Plains Quarterly* and *Chronicles of Oklahoma*.

Ralph H. Lutts is a member of the faculty at Goddard College, a research associate with the Virginia Museum of Natural History, and president of the American Nature Study Society. His book *The Nature Fakers: Wildlife, Science & Sentiment* was published in 1990.

Tom Lynch received his Ph.D. in 1989 from the University of Oregon for a dissertation on American haiku poets and is a widely published haiku poet himself. His principle academic interests revolve around ethno-criticism and eco-criticism, and he has numerous publications and presentations comparing Native America and Euro-American perspectives on the landscape.

Christopher MacLachlan is a lecturer in the School of English of the University of St. Andrews. He has published several essays on Scottish authors and is general editor of the Association for Scottish Literary Studies and editor of the journal *Scotlands*. He is preparing an edition of Matthew Lewis's Gothic novel *The Monk*.

Julia Martin lives in Cape Town, South Africa, where she teaches English at the University of the Western Cape. Her research involves developing a theory/practice of environmental literacy that is situated in this region. She has published several essays that attempt to bring into conversation issues in Buddhism, ecology, and feminist postmodernism and has a special interest in the work of Gary Snyder in this regard. She also writes poetry and story-essays and makes ceramic sculptures.

Yuri L. Mazourov combines his activity at the Institute for Heritage with teaching at the Moscow State Lomonosov University. For several years he was a department head at the Moscow publishing house Mysl. An expert on issues of natural heritage and ecological culture, he is the author of nearly 100 publications on these subjects.

James Mc Elroy teaches at the University of California, Davis. He has published articles and reviews on Irish literature in *The New York Times*, *The Los Angeles Times*, and *World Literature Today*.

Patrick D. Murphy is a professor of English and teaches in the Graduate Program in Literature

and Criticism at Indiana University of Pennsylvania. Founding editor of *ISLE: Interdisciplinary Studies in Literature and Environment*, he is currently the Art and the Natural Environment section editor for the journal *Organization and Environment*. Author of *Understanding Gary Snyder* and *Literature, Nature, and Other: Ecofeminist Critiques*, he has edited and co-edited several other books, including, with Greta Gaard, *Ecofeminist Literary Theory, Criticism, and Pedagogy*. He has recently completed a monograph tentatively titled *Farther Afield in Literary Ecology* (forthcoming 1999) and is co-editing, with Roberto Forns-Broggi, a special issue of the *Hispanic Journal* on ecology in Latin American literature.

Juliana Makuchi Nfah-Abbenyi is assistant professor of English and postcolonial literature at the University of Southern Mississippi and author of *Gender in African Women's Writing: (Re)Constructing Identity, Sexuality, and Difference*. She has contributed chapters to several books and published in such scholarly journals as *Canadian Woman Studies*, *Comparative Literature in Canada*, and *Notre Librairie*, and her fiction has appeared in *Callaloo*.

Sheila Nickerson lives in Juneau, Alaska, where she has worked as editor of *Alaska's Wildlife* for the state and as an instructor of creative writing at the University of Alaska. A poet and prose writer, her most recent title is *Disappearance: A Map—A Meditation on Death and Loss in the High Latitudes*.

C. Christopher Norden is a professor of English at Lewis-Clark State College in Idaho. In addition to Shakespeare, modernism, and minority literatures, he teaches interdisciplinary courses in environmental studies, including Wilderness and Ethics & Ecology. He is writing a comparative study focusing on Aboriginal Australian, Inuit, and North American Indian novelistic traditions.

Christine Ombaka is a lecturer at Maseno University College, Kenya, where she teaches English and communication. She obtained her B.Ed. degree from Nairobi University and an M.A. degree in English at Lancaster University, England. Her current interests are in African culture, gender, and environment in African literature, including poetry and folklore.

Masataka Ota teaches English literature at Daito-bunka University. His research interests focus on British poetry, and he has published such works as *A Student's Guide to British and American Poetry, The Poetics of Reality and Illusion: The Romantics and Modern Poetry,* and *A Japanese Translated Version of Paul Muldoon's Selected Poems 1968–1983.*

Daniel Patterson studies early American literature and teaches in the English Department of California State University, San Bernardino. He has written about Edward Taylor and now focuses on early American nature writing. He often collaborates with Rochelle Johnson.

Linden Peach is reader in English at the University of Loughborough. His publications include *Ancestral Lines: Culture and Identity in the Work of Six Contemporary Poets* (1993), *Toni Morrison* (1995) and *Angela Carter* (1997). He is the editor of *Critical Casebooks: Toni Morrison* (1997) and co-author (with Angela Burton) of *English as a Creative Art: Literary Concepts Linked to Creative Writing* (1995).

Daniel J. Philippon is a Ph.D. candidate in English at the University of Virginia, where he is completing a dissertation on the role of five American nature writers in the formation of environmental organizations. He is co-editor of *The Height of Our Mountains: Nature Writing from Virginia's Blue Ridge Mountains and Shenandoah Valley* and has contributed chapters, articles, and reviews on environmental literature in such journals as *ISLE, North Dakota Quarterly,* and *Western American Literature.* He is public relations coordinator for the Association for the Study of Literature and Environment and co-editor of the *ASLE Handbook on Graduate Studies in Literature and Environment.*

Kamala Platt is an assistant professor at the University of the Incarnate Word in San Antonio, Texas, and a doctoral student in comparative literature at the University of Texas, Austin. Her dissertation and a book manuscript, "Cultural Poetics in the Environmental Justice Movements: Organization, Theories, and Resistance in India and Greater Mexico," study the practice, theory, and aesthetics of women generating cultural poetics that promote environmental justice. In order to better understand the practice and theory of political struggle, she creates her own visual, performance, and written works, and supports grassroots activism toward environmental, gender, and racial justice.

Arlene Plevin is a doctoral student in English at the University of Washington. As a former writer and editor for the National Wildlife Federation and the author of *Cycling: A Celebration of the Sport and the World's Best Places to Enjoy It,* she has traveled extensively.

Dale Pratt is an assistant professor of Spanish literature at Brigham Young University. His interests include nineteenth-century narrative and relationships between literary and scientific discourses. He has written on metafiction, metatheater, and on images of science in Spanish literature.

Rebecca Raglon teaches courses on environmental thought and fiction at Simon Fraser University, Burnaby, British Columbia. Her work has appeared most recently in *Environmental Ethics, The Environmental History Review,* and *Women's Studies.* A book of her short stories entitled *The Gridlock Mechanism* was published in 1992.

Marcos Reigota graduated in biology then completed a master's degree in the philosophy of education, a doctorate in the pedagogy of biology at the Catholic University in Louvain, and a postdoctorate at the University of Geneva. He has been a visiting researcher at the London School of Economics and the Central Library in Zurich. He is the author of books and articles published in Argentina, Mexico, Brazil, Nicaragua, Canada, Belgium, France, Greece, Italy, Portugal, Switzerland, and Sweden. He has also been employed as a consultant for the WWF, IUCN, BIRD, and PNUD.

Neil Roberts is reader in English literature at the University of Sheffield. As well as studies of George Eliot and George Meredith, he was written *The Lover, The Dreamer and The World: The Poetry of Peter Redgrove* and, with Terry Gifford, *Ted Hughes: A Critical Study.* He is currently completing a study entitled *Narrative and Voice in Postwar Poetry.*

Lex Runciman has published six books, including most recently *A Forest of Voices: Reading and Writing the Environment* (with Chris

Anderson) and *The Admirations*, which won the Oregon Book Award for poetry in 1989. His essay "Fun?" was reprinted in *Landmark Essays on the Writing Process*, edited by Sondra Perl. He lives in Oregon's Willamette Valley and teaches at Linfield College.

Glenn Sandiford is an award-winning Adirondack journalist. His first book, *Deepe in the Adirondacks* is a biography of an Adirondack guide.

F. Marina Schauffler, an environmental writer from Maine, is completing her dissertation on ecological metanoia through the interdisciplinary Natural Resources Program at the University of New Hampshire. She teaches courses in Environmental Humanities at Bates College.

Don Scheese is associate professor of English and chair of Environmental Studies at Gustavus Adolphus College in St. Peter, Minnesota, where he teaches courses on American literature, nature writing, and environmental history. He has lectured and published extensively on various topics related to literature and the environment and is author of *Nature Writing: The Pastoral Impulse in America*.

Marian Scholtmeijer lives and teaches English in northern British Columbia. She is the author of *Animal Victims in Modern Fiction: From Sanctity to Sacrifice* and of several articles on culture and animals.

Judith Schwartz is a Ph.D. candidate in English at Temple University. She is at work on a dissertation exploring pastoral elements in the poetry of George Oppen.

Barry Silesky is the author of the biography *Ferlinghetti: The Artist in His Time* as well as a collection of poems, *The New Tenants*, and of "short-short fictions." Since 1987 he has also been editor of the literary journal *ACM* and a professor of liberal arts at the School of the Art Institute of Chicago.

Steven C. Steel is an assistant professor for the Center for Environmental Programs at Bowling Green State University. He also teaches biology and chemistry at Waite High School in Toledo, Ohio, where he coaches football and advises

quiz bowl, drama, and newspaper. He is researching radical social and ecological theory and how they inform construction of communality.

Patti Capel Swartz discovered the desert and Southwestern women's writing while living in California. She currently lives and teaches writing and literature classes at Morehead State University in Eastern Kentucky, where women's and multicultural issues inform her teaching.

Tsutomu Takahashi is an associate professor of English at Kyushu University, Japan. He received his Ph.D. in comparative literature from Pennsylvania State University and has taught American literature as well as the English language. His many publications include articles on Herman Melville and Nathaniel Hawthorne. He is currently working on a book-length project on environmental literature in Japan.

Elle Tracy lived and worked in Antarctica from September 1991 to October 1992. A graduate of the Will Steger-founded Antarctic studies program at Hamline University, she often lectures to schools about Antarctica. "Cold Type," about publishing in Antarctica, appeared in *Aldus Magazine* (March 1993). In 1997 she made materials from her Antarctic library and ephemera collection available in Ohio for the centennial exhibition of the Adrien de Gerlache de Gomery expedition artifacts.

JoAnn Myer Valenti, professor of communications at Brigham Young University, received a doctorate in natural resources and bachelor's and master's degrees in journalism and mass communications. She serves on the board of the Society of Environmental Journalists and is a fellow in the American Association for the Advancement of Science.

Yuri Vedenin is director of the Russian Research Institute for Cultural and Natural Heritage of the Russian Academy of Sciences and the Ministry of Culture in Moscow. His main academic fields are social geography and cultural heritage preservation. Author of more than 180 publications, his most recent is *Geography of Arts*, published in 1997.

Laura Dassow Walls received her Ph.D. in 1992 from Indiana University and is an assistant professor of English at Lafayette College in Easton, Pennsylvania. Her book, *Seeing New Worlds: Henry David Thoreau and Nineteenth-Century Natural Science*, further explores the intersections of science and literature. She has published articles in *American Quarterly, ISLE,* and *Nineteenth-Century Contexts,* and she is currently writing a book on Emerson and science.

Tamara L. Whited is an assistant professor of history at Indiana University of Pennsylvania. Her 1994 dissertation treated the politics of reforestation as played out between rural communities and the state in the Alps and Pyrenees from 1860 to 1940. She teaches French history, modern European history, and environmental history.

Wu Dingbo teaches at Shangha International Studies University and is one of the foremost experts on Chinese science fiction. He has published widely in China on American literature and has translated literary works from Chinese to English and English to Chinese. He is the co-editor with Patrick D. Murphy of *Science Fiction from China: Eight Stories* and the *Handbook of Chinese Popular Culture.*

Katsunori Yamazato is a professor of American studies at the University of the Ryukyus, Okinawa, Japan. He has written articles on Gary Snyder and other aspects of American nature literature and is involved in several projects translating Snyder's poetry and prose into Japanese. He is also contributing articles to and co-editing various ASLE–Japan reference works on nature literature.

Yang Ming-tu is an associate professor in the English department at Tamkang University, Taipei. Former editor of *Tamkang Review,* he has written *Shui Tui Tzu Fables,* translated plays by Jean Anouilh and William Butler Yeats into Chinese, and compiled 11 books for English language study.

Title Index

General Index

German Romanticism, 207
Japanese conservation movement, 290
Minnesota
North Woods writing, 98, 102–105
Mississippi River valley (U.S.), 6
Mitford, Mary Russell, 160
Miyazaki Koshoshi, 284
Miyazawa Kenji, 287
Miyoshi Tatsuji, 287
Mkhize, Piwe, 342
Mkhwane, Bheki, 342
Molver, Eileen, 338
Momaday, N. Scott, 99
Monbiot, George, 387
Montague, John, 180
Monterey (California), 89–90
Monticello (Virginia), 65
Moodie, Susanna, 101, 132
Moon, Soon-tae, 295, 296
Mora, Pat, 79, 405
Moraga, Cherríe, 79
Morales, Aurora Levins, 79
Moritz, Yunna, 233
Morris, Mary, 444–445
Morris, William, 153
Morton, Thomas, 4
Morton, W. L., 133
Moscow (Russia), 225, 231, 232
mosquito, 42
Mount Marcy (N.Y.)
Adirondack wilderness, 52
mountain
French literature, 200–205
Japanese literature, 278–279
German Romanticism, 208
Welsh literature, 192
Mowat, Farley, 135
Mozambique, 331
Mudrooroo (Colin Johnson), 270–272, 275
Mueller, Marnie, 387
Mugo, Micere, 333
Muir, Edwin, 187
Muir, John
nineteenth century nature literature, 21, 22, 23
speaking for nature, 430
spiritual transformation in nature, 84–85
Muir, Willa, 187
Mukherji, S. B., 321
Murie, Margaret E., 127, 392
Murillo, Rosario, 376
Muroo Saisei, 287
Murphy, Grace, 127
Murphy, Patrick, 403, 432, 440, 459
Murzayev, Eduard, 246
Muzaffar, May, 355
Mwangi, Meja, 331

Naes, Arne, 434, 435
Nagara River (Japan), 292
Naima, Michael, 351

Naipaul, V. S., 371
Nakagami Kenji, 285
Nakano, Koji, 292
Nansen, Fridtjof
Nares, George, 391
Nash, Roderick
Adirondack writings, 53
aesthetics and nature, 435
Nasrallah, Emily, 355
Natal (South Africa), 342
National Science Foundation (U.S.), 395
Native Americans
African literature, 342
Canadian environmental writing, 135, 136, 142
cross cultural writing of the American West, 403–408
early American natural histories, 14
North Woods writing, 99
women in the wilderness, 126
natural history
Amazon, 387
Australian literature, 264–269
early American nature writing, 6, 7, 9, 13–17
English prose, 150, 161
nineteenth century nature literature, 18–25
realistic wild animal stories, 109–115
Virginia, 60
natural theology, 21
Navajo, 72, 79
Nehru, Jawaharlal, 319
Nekrasov, Nikolai, 230
Neruda, Pablo, 374
Neto, Agostinoh, 335
Neva River (Russia), 229, 231
New Brunswick, 132
New England
early exploration, 4, 5, 14
Frost's religious meanings in poems, 89
New France
North Woods writing, 100–101, 132
New Jersey
haiku writing, 120
New Mexico
cross cultural writing of the American West, 404
women's desert writing, 78, 79
New World
American desert writing, 70
early American natural histories, 13–17
exploration literature, 3–12
garden writing, 64, 65
North Woods writing, 99–101
New York, 52
New York (N.Y.), 45
New Zealand
Maori novel, 270–276
Nfah-Abbenyi, Juliana Makuchi, 459
ecology, postcolonialism and African women, 344–349
Ngobese, Gugu, 341